The Bulgarian State in 927–969
The Epoch of Tsar Peter I

Edited by

Mirosław J. Leszka, Kirił Marinow

BYZANTINA LODZIENSIA

Series of the Department of Byzantine History of the University of Łódź

Founded by

Professor Waldemar Ceran

in

1997

№ XXXIV

BYZANTINA LODZIENSIA

XXXIV

The Bulgarian State in 927–969
The Epoch of Tsar Peter I

Edited by

Mirosław J. Leszka, Kirił Marinow

Translated by

Lyubomira Genova

Marek Majer

Artur Mękarski

Michał Zytka

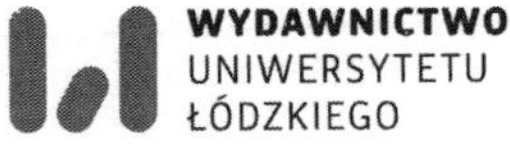

Mirosław J. Leszka, Kirił Marinow – University of Łódź
Faculty of Philosophy and History
Institute of History, Department of Byzantine History
27a Kamińskiego St., 90-219 Łódź (Poland)
bizancjum@uni.lodz.pl

Published by Łódź University Press & Jagiellonian University Press

First edition, Łódź–Kraków 2018
W.088620.18.0.K

ISBN978-83-8142-115-7 – paperback Łódź University Press
ISBN 978-83-233-4545-9 – paperback Jagiellonian University Press
ISBN 978-83-8142-116-4 – electronic version Łódź University Press
ISBN 978-83-233-9933-9 – electronic version Jagiellonian University Press

Łódź University Press
8 Lindleya St., 90-131 Łódź
www.wydawnictwo.uni.lodz.pl
e-mail: ksiegarnia@uni.lodz.pl
phone: +48 (42) 665 58 63

Distribution outside Poland

Jagiellonian University Press
9/2 Michałowskiego St., 31-126 Kraków
phone: +48 (12) 631 01 97, +48 (12) 663 23 81, fax +48 (12) 663 23 83
cell phone: +48 506 006 674, e-mail: sprzedaz@wuj.pl, www.wuj.pl

Contents

Chapter IV

Chapter V

Chapter VI

Chapter IV

Chapter V

Chapter VI

Chapter VII

Chapter VIII

Part Three: The Interpretations

A. Medieval Visions

Chapter I

Chapter II

Chapter III

B. Modern views

Chapter IV

Foreword

Tsar Peter I (927–969) had not previously been the subject of a monograph. This is despite the fact that he was the longest reigning monarch in the history of mediaeval Bulgaria, and being counted among the saints by the Bulgarian Church. There had been, however, works discussing the reigns of his two predecessors – Boris I and Symeon I – his grandfather and father, and also the life of the most popular anchorite living in his times, St. John of Rila.

On the one hand it appears to be understandable, since the scarcity of the sources relating to his reign does not allow constructing a full image of either Peter himself, nor of his reign. Despite the appearances, however, the silence of the sources from his era did not shield this ruler from numerous negative judgements about him, formulated by generations of scholars. They spoke of his lack of character, torpid governance and his focus on religious over political matters. He was accused of being a protégé of Constantinople and serving the Byzantine cause, and leading the state into a social breakdown, which manifested itself through, i.a., the Byzantinisation of the court and the development of the Bogomilist heresy. Finally, counted amongst his failures was the political disintegration which resulted in the state's downfall – under Rus' and Byzantine pressure – near the end of his reign and during the reign of his son and successor, Boris II.

These evaluations suffered from a one major methodological fault – assessing Peter primarily from the perspective of the accomplishments of the aforementioned two great predecessors. Boris-Michael led to Bulgaria's Christianisation and an instilling among his subjects a new literary and liturgical language with which they could express their faith and through which they adapted the grand cultural achievements of the Christian Byzantium for their own use. These two elements had a powerful influence on the final consolidation of the state and the subjects of the Bulgarian rulers. Symeon, who not only contributed to the great cultural growth of Bulgaria, but was primarily remembered on the pages of history as an able and ambitious ruler who led Bulgaria to the apex of military might, establishing the country as a power at the international arena and in the political sphere. In comparison with them, the reign of their descendant appeared indistinct at best, or outright decadent – devoid of any great territorial gains or major cultural developments.

On the other hand, from the mid-twentieth century, there had been burgeoning attempts at re-interpreting the reign of this ruler, rightly questioning the portrayal of Peter's reign fixed by the classic Bulgarian mediaevists (and others), while the research into (widely understood) material culture is providing increasingly more information about Bulgaria of his time. For these reasons it seems to be fully justified to finally undertake larger scale research into Peter's portraiture and the country he ruled. In other words, to fill the existing gap in historiography regarding this matter, and at the same time restore Peter to his rightful place in history.

This task, realised within the framework of the National Science Centre (NCN), Poland, research grant was undertaken on the following pages by an international team of scholars: employees of the Department of Byzantine History and the Ceraneum Centre of the Łódź University (Poland) and of the Department of History of Bulgaria of the St. Clement of Ohrid University of Sofia (Bulgaria), with the minor participation of the Department of Old and Medieval History of the St. Cyril and St. Methodius University of Veliko Tarnovo (Bulgaria). In our reseach we made two fundamental assumptions – that the original sources required a new reading taking into account the most recent achievements of the worldwide Byzantine and mediaeval Bulgarian studies, and that the portrayal of Peter and his reign would be presented in fullest against the backdrop of the Bulgarian state between 930s and the 960s.

We hope that this monograph is going to contribute to the preservation of a more balanced and generally positive evaluation of Peter I's role in the history of mediaeval Bulgaria.

* * *

We would like to thank our Colleagues from *Ceraneum* and from the Department of Byzantine History and the Department of Slavic Studies, all of University of Łódź (Poland), for the supportive attitude towards our work: Prof. Maciej Kokoszko, Prof. Georgi Minczew, Prof. Teresa Wolińska, Prof. Sławomir Bralewski, Prof. Ivan Petrov, Dr. Paweł Filipczak, Dr. Agata Kawecka, Dr. Andrzej Kompa and Dr. Małgorzata Skowronek. We thank Professor Jarosław Dudek from the University of Zielona Góra for the meticulous and positive editorial review. We thank Dr. Michał Zytka for editing and proofreading the English text. We would also like to give thanks to Elżbieta Myślińska-Brzozowska for providing the illustrations (drawings) for this volume.

* * *

This book was written as part of a research project financed by the National Science Centre (Poland). Decision number: DEC-2014/14/M/HS3/00758 (*The Bulgarian State in 927–969. The Epoch of Tsar Peter I the Pious*).

The Editors

Zofia A. Brzozowska
Mirosław J. Leszka, Kirił Marinow

Sources and Modern Scholarship

1. Sources

1.1. Foreign Sources

The sources that constitute the basis for the considerations presented in this volume have predominantly been penned by the Byzantine authors[1]. Crucially, many of the accounts which we are going to examine here were

---

[1] The Reader will find a thorough overview of the Byzantine sources that include information about Peter and Maria in the following work: Т. Тодоров, *България през втората и третата четвърт на X век: политическа история*, София 2006 [unpublished PhD thesis], pp. 19–17, 150–152. See also, i.a.: В. Гюзелев, *Значението на брака на цар Петър (927–969) с ромейката Мария-Ирина Лакапина (911–962)*, [in:] *Културните текстове на миналото – носители, символи, идеи*, vol. I, *Текстовете на историята, история на текстовете. Материали от Юбилейната международна конференция в чест на 60-годишнината на проф. д.и.н. Казимир Попконстантинов, Велико Търново, 29–31 октомври 2003 г.*, София 2005, p. 32; А. Николов, *Политическа мисъл в ранносредновековна България (средата на IX – края на X в.)*, София 2006, pp. 233–236; Т. Тодоров, *Владетелският статут и титла на цар Петър I след октомври 927 г.: писмени сведения и сфрагистични данни (сравнителен анализ)*, [in:] *Юбилеен сборник. Сто години от рождението на д-р Васил Хараланов (1907–2007)*, Шумен 2008, pp. 94–95.

written during tsar Peter's life, or soon after his death. The most detailed description of the developments of 927, i.e. the negotiations leading to the conclusion of peace between the Empire and Bulgaria (the guarantee of which was to have been the marriage between Peter and a granddaughter of Romanos I Lekapenos), we find in a narrative written down in the 10th century in Constantinople. It was created by authors from the so-called 'circle of Symeon Logothete': Continuator of George the Monk (Hamartolos), Symeon Logothete, Leo Grammatikos and Pseudo-Symeon Magistros[2].

The output of the anonymous Continuator of George the Monk includes the description of events from 842 onwards – from the point at which George's narrative ended. The fragments devoted to Peter and Maria are practically identical with the relevant passages in the *Chronicle of Symeon Logothete*. The text is known in two variants. Redaction A, older, written down prior to 963, describes the events prior to 948, i.e. the death of Romanos I Lekapenos. The later redaction B includes the history of Byzantium up to 963 (enhanced with certain additional details). The older version of the *Chronicle of Symeon Logothete* is highly similar to redaction A of the *Continuation of George the Monk*, while the newer version closely resembles redaction B. In this monograph, we are not going to differentiate between the redactions A and B, as the passages relating to Maria Lekapene and Peter in both variants are identical. They include first and foremost an unusually extensive and detailed narrative of the events of 927, the beginning of Peter's reign, the description of his brothers'

[2] On the subject of Symeon Logothete and the works associated with his name, see: В.Н. Златарски, *Известията за българите в хрониката на Симеон Метафраст и Логотет*, [in:] idem, *Избрани произведения в четири тома*, vol. I, ed. П. Петров, София 1972, pp. 359–573; А.П. Каждан, *Хроника Симеона Логофета*, ВВ 15, 1959, pp.125–143; W. Swoboda, *Kontynuacja Georgiosa*, [in:] *SSS*, vol. II, p. 468; М. Каймакамова, *Българска средновековна историопис*, София 1990, pp. 170–171; J. Howard-Johnston, *Byzantium, Bulgaria and the Peoples of Ukraine in the 890s*, [in:] *Материалы по археологии, истории и этнографии Таврии*, vol. VII, ed. А.И. Айбабин, Симферополь 2000, pp. 343–345; S. Wahlgren, *Autor und Werk*, [in:] Symeon Logothete, pp. 3–8; A. Brzóstkowska, *Kroniki z kręgu Symeona Logotety*, [in:] *Testimonia*, vol. V, pp. 64–67; W. Treadgold, *The Middle Byzantine Historians*, New York–Basingstoke 2013, pp. 197–224.

actions against him[3] as well as a mention of the Bulgarian tsaritsa's visits to Constantinople in the later period[4].

Textologically separate, but related in content, are the *Chronicle of Pseudo-Symeon Magistros* and the *Chronicle of Leo Grammatikos*. Their descriptions of the developments of 927 are similar to the ones discussed above, but presented more concisely[5].

The second, later redaction of the *Chronicle of Symeon Logothete*, completed ca. 963, most likely served as the basis for the anonymous author of the first part of book VI of the *Continuation of Theophanes*, written at roughly the same time[6]. It is hardly surprising, therefore, that this work's

---

[3] Continuator of George the Monk, pp. 904–907; Symeon Logothete, 136. 45–51.

[4] Continuator of George the Monk, p. 913; Symeon Logothete, 136.67.

[5] Leo Grammatikos, pp. 315–317; Pseudo-Symeon Magistros, 33–34, pp. 740–741.

[6] *Continuation of Theophanes* encompasses the period between 813 and 961. Books I–IV have been written by an anonymous author on Constantine VII Porphyrogennetos' orders. Book V (*Life of Basil*) is often attributed to the emperor himself, while book VI most likely had two authors. Its first part, covering the period after 886 until the death of Romanos I Lekapenos (948) was written by an anonymous author, most likely during Nikephoros II Phokas' reign (963–969). As some scholars think, it is dependent on one of the editions of Symeon Logothete's work, in the version of Continuator of George the Monk (edition B). The second, describing years 948–961, is associated with the person of Theodore Daphnopates and was created – it is thought – prior to 963. On the subject of authorship, source basis and the message of *Continuation of Theophanes*: А.П. Каждан, *Из истории византийской хронографии X в.*, I, *О составе так называемой "Хроники Продолжателя Феофана"*, ВВ 19, 1961, pp. 76–96; A. Markopoulos, *Théodore Daphnopatès et la Continuation de Théophane*, JÖB 35, 1985, pp. 171–182 (he considers the association of Daphnopates with *Continuation of Theophanes* as exceedingly problematic); J. Signes Codoñer, *Algunas consideraciones sobre la autoría del Theophanes Continuatus*, Ery 10, 1989, pp. 17–28 (he ascribes the authorship of books I–V to Constantine VII himself); J. Ljubarskij, *Theophanes Continuatus und Genesios. Das Problem einer gemeinsamen Quelle*, Bsl 48, 1987, pp. 45–55; idem, *Сочинение Продолжателя Феофана. Хроника, история, жизнеописания?*, [in:] Продолжатель Феофана, *Жизнеописания византийских царей*, ed. idem, Санкт-Петербург 1992, pp. 293–368; J.M. Featherstone, *Theophanes Continuatus VI and De Cerimoniis I, 96*, BZ 104, 2011, pp. 115–123 (he supposes that the source's compilation was done by *parakoimomenos* Basil, son of Romanos I Lekapenos, during the reign of Nikephoros II Phokas); I. Ševčenko,

account of the circumstances in which the Bulgarian-Byzantine peace treaty of 927 was concluded is also highly similar to the descriptions mentioned above. It also includes a strikingly close depiction of the marriage between Maria and Peter, as well as a record of the tsaritsa's several journeys to Constantinople, where, accompanied by her children, she paid visits to her relatives[7].

Some information on Peter's times was also included in the works of later Byzantine chroniclers: John Skylitzes[8] and John Zonaras[9]. Both of these authors included a description of the facts of 927, based on the above-mentioned earlier accounts but presented in a more condensed form[10]. Moreover, they also noted an event that, for obvious reasons, could not have been mentioned by the authors of the earlier historiographical works (concluded in the early 960s) – i.e. the death of Maria[11] and the

Introduction, [in:] *Chronographiae quae Theophanis Continuati nomine fertur Liber que Vita Basilii Imperatoris amplectitur*, ed. idem, Berlin 2011, pp. 3–13; J.M. Featherstone, *Theophanes Continuatus: a History for the Palace*, [in:] *La face cachée de la littérature byzantine. Le texte en tant que message immédiat*, ed. P. Odorico, Paris 2012, pp. 123–135.

[7] Continuator of Theophanes, VI, 22–23, 35, pp. 412–415, 422.

[8] *Sýnopsis historión* encompasses the period between 811 and 1057. It was most likely written during the 1070s. For more information about John Skylitzes and his work, see i.a.: H. Thurn, *Ioannes Skylitzes, Autor und Werk*, [in:] John Skylitzes, pp. VII–LVI; W. Seibt, *Johannes Skylitzes: Zur Person des Chronisten*, JÖB 25, 1976, pp. 81–85; J. Bonarek, *Romajowie i obcy w Kronice Jana Skylitzesa. Identyfikacja etniczna Bizantyńczyków i ich stosunek do obcych w świetle Kroniki Jana Skylitzesa*, Toruń 2003, pp. 15–24; C. Holmes, *The rhetorical structure of Skylitzes' Synopsis Historion*, [in:] *Rhetoric in Byzantium*, ed. E. Jeffreys, Aldershot 2003, pp. 187–199; J.-C. Cheynet, *John Skylitzes, the author and his family*, [in:] John Skylitzes, *A Synopsis of Byzantine History, 811–1057*, transl. J. Wortley, Cambridge 2010, pp. IX–XI; B. Flusin, *Re-writing history: John Skylitzes' Synopsis historion*, [in:] John Skylitzes, *A Synopsis...*, pp. XII–XXXIII.

[9] This work encompasses the history from the creation of the world until 1118, and was written soon after that year. On John Zonaras and his chronicle: K. Ziegler, *Zonaras*, [in:] *RE*, vol. X.A.1, 1972, col. 718–732; I. Grigoriadis, *Linguistic and literary studies in the Epitome Historion of John Zonaras*, Thessaloniki 1998; T.M. Banchich, *Introduction*, [in:] *The History of Zonaras from Alexander Severus to the Death of Theodosius the Great*, transl. idem, E.N. Lane, New York 2009, pp. 1–19; W. Treadgold, *The Middle...*, p. 388sqq.

[10] John Skylitzes, pp. 222–224; John Zonaras, pp. 473–475.

[11] John Skylitzes, p. 255; John Zonaras, p. 495.

final years of Peter's reign[12]. Another, particularly significant, source for the final years of Peter's reign is the *History* of Leo the Deacon[13].

The works of Constantine VII Porphyrogennetos[14] deserve particular attention. He was of a similar age to Peter and his spouse and was married to her aunt – Helena Lekapene; he also participated in the events of 927 and most likely knew Maria personally. However, the 'purple-born' author is not objective: he is unsympathetic to our heroine's family and does not conceal his outrage that she, a granddaughter of emperor Romanos I Lekapenos, married a foreign, Slavic ruler. Constantine included an evaluation of this marriage in chapter 13 of the treatise *On the Governance of the Empire*[15].

---

[12] John Skylitzes, p. 255sqq; John Zonaras, p. 495sqq.

[13] Leo the Deacon was born ca. 950, and received a thorough education. As a clergyman, he was associated with the patriarchate of Constantinople and the imperial court. He participated in the disastrous expedition of Basil II against the Bulgarians in 986. His work was written after that event. On the subject of life and works of Leo the Deacon, see i.a.: С.А. Иванов, *Полемическая направленность Истории Льва Диакона*, ВВ 43, 1982, pp. 74–80; O. Jurewicz, *Historia literatury bizantyńskiej*, Wrocław 1982, pp. 181–182; М.Я. Сюзюмов, *Лев Диакон и его время*, [in:] Лев Диакон, *История*, transl. М.М. Копыленко, ed. Г.Г. Литаврин, Москва 1988, pp. 137–165; *The History of Leo the Deacon. Byzantine Military Expansion in the Tenth Century*, ed. A.-M. Talbot, D.F. Sulivan, with assistance G.T. Dennis, S. McGrath, Washington 2006, pp. 9–52; A. Kazhdan, *History of Byzantine Literature (850–1000)*, ed. Ch. Angelidi, Athens 2006, pp. 278–286.

[14] On the subject of Constantine VII Porphyrogennetos: P. Lemerle, *Byzantine Humanism: the First Phase. Notes and Remarks on Education and Culture in Byzantium from the Origins to the 10th Century*, transl. H. Lindsay, A. Moffatt, Canberra 1986, p. 310sqq; A. Toynbee, *Constantine Porphyrogenitus and His World*, London 1973; T.E. Gregory, *The Political Program of Constantine Porphyrogenitus*, [in:] *Actes du XVe Congrès International des Études Byzantines*, vol. IV, Athènes 1985, pp. 122–133; G. Tanner, *The Historical Method of Constantine Porphyrogenitus*, BF 24, 1997, pp. 125–140.

[15] Constantine VII Porphyrogennetos, *On the Governance of the Empire*, 13, pp. 72–74. This work was created between 944 and 952, although some of its parts may have been written earlier. Љ. Максимовић, *Структура 32. поглавља списа De admistrando imperio*, ЗРВИ 21, 1982, p. 31 – believes that chapter 32 was written between 927/928 and 944). A detailed analysis of the work: Константин Багрянородный, *Об управлении империей*, ed. Г.Г. Литаврин, А.П. Новосольцев, Москва 1989, pp. 276–457 (a list of academic literature – pp. 460–468). Cf. also: T. Živković, *De conversione Croatorum et Serborum. A Lost Source*, Belgrade 2012. For the opinion of Constantine Porphyrogennetos

Another of his works, the *Book of Ceremonies*[16], may also prove a valuable source. While it would be futile to search the pages of this text for direct remarks on Maria, it does provide us with some important information about the official status and titulature of the mid-10th century Bulgarian ruler[17].

Peter and Maria Lekapene are also mentioned, although very rarely, by the western European sources. A particular role in this is played by the contemporary to the tsar couple Liutprand of Cremona, who came to Constantinople on a diplomatic mission twice (in 949 and in 968)[18]. The person of Maria and the circumstances of her marriage with the Bulgarian ruler drew Liudprand's attention during both of his stays in the Byzantine capital. In 968, the reasons were obvious – the goal of his visit to Constantinople was, after all, to negotiate Nikephoros II Phokas's agreement to marry a 'purple-born' Byzantine woman to the son of Otto I. The Byzantine-Bulgarian marriage of 927 may have been an important argument during these negotiations, in that the rule according to which a woman from the imperial family could not marry a foreign ruler was

---

on the Bulgarians, as well as on the causes of this ruler's negative attitude towards the Lekapenos family and their dynastic marriage of 927, see: Г. Литаврин, *Константин Багрянородный о Болгарии и Болгарах*, [in:] *Сборник в чест на акад. Димитър Ангелов*, ed. В. Велков, София 1994, pp. 30–37; F. Tinnefeld, *Byzantinische auswärtige Heiratspolitik vom 9. zum 12 Jahrhundert*, Bsl 54.1, 1993, pp. 21–22; Т. Тодоров, *Константин Багренородни и династичният брак между владетелските домове на Преслав и Константинопол от 927 г.*, ПКШ 7, 2003, pp. 391–398; В. Гюзелев, *Значението*..., pp. 30–31; A. Paroń, "*Trzeba, abyś tymi oto słowami odparł i to niedorzeczne żądanie*" – *wokół De administrando imperio Konstantyna VII*, [in:] *Causa creandi. O pragmatyce źródła historycznego*, ed. S. Rosik, P. Wiszewski, Wrocław 2005, pp. 345–361; А. Николов, *Политическа*..., pp. 269–279.

[16] It was created near the end of Constantine VII – likely during the years 957–959. On the subject of this source – J.B. Bury, *The Ceremonial Book of Constantine Porphyrogenitus*, EHR 22, 1907, pp. 209–227; 417–439; A. Moffatt, *The Master of Ceremonies' Bottom Drawer. The Unfinished State of the De cerimoniis of Constantine Porphyrogennetos*, Bsl 56, 1995, pp. 377–388; M. Manini, *Liber de Caerimoniis Aulae Byzantinae: prosopografia e sepolture imperiali*, Spoleto 2009.

[17] Constantine VII Porphyrogennetos, *The Book of Ceremonies*, II, 47, pp. 681–682.

[18] Liudprand of Cremona, *Retribution*, III, 38, p. 86; Liudprand of Cremona, *Embassy*, 16, 19, pp. 194–195.

not strictly adhered to at the Constantinopolitan court[19]. Curiously, Liudprand is also the only author to mention that, upon entering into marriage, Maria adopted a new name (Irene, i.e. 'Peace'), symbolically underscoring the role she was to play in the Byzantine-Bulgarian relations after 927[20].

1.2. Native Sources

Regarding times of Peter and Maria, the native sources primarily serve a complementary role. These are largely works that have been translated from Greek, with minor authorial additions. Entirely original works are less common. It is worth noting that tsaritsa Maria, aside from sphragistic material, does not appear at all in sources of Bulgarian origin. Among the Old Bulgarian texts that include mentions of tsar Peter, of particular interest are: *Sermon against the Heretics* of Cosmas the Priest and *Tale of the Prophet Isaiah*.

The *Sermon against the Heretics* may be considered as the first Slavic heresiological treatise. It was written by Cosmas the Priest. This work was most likely created either directly after tsar Peter's death, or during the 1040s. It is the fundamental source for learning about the Bogomilist heresy and – from a broader perspective – about the religious life in the contemporary Bulgaria[21]. *Tale of the Prophet Isaiah* (previously referred to as *Bulgarian Apocryphal Chronicle*) is in turn an excellent testimony of the mediaeval Bulgarian historical and 'national' identity, which in recent times became the basis for the study of the political ideology in Bulgaria during the period being examined here. This semi-legendary

[19] T. Wolińska, *Konstantynopolitańska misja Liudpranda z Kremony (968)*, [in:] *Cesarstwo bizantyńskie. Dzieje. Religia. Kultura. Studia ofiarowane Profesorowi Waldemarowi Ceranowi przez uczniów na 70-lecie Jego urodzin*, ed. P. Krupczyński, M.J. Leszka, Łask–Łódź 2006, pp. 208–212.

[20] J. Shepard, *A marriage too far? Maria Lekapena and Peter of Bulgaria*, [in:] *The Empress Theophano. Byzantium and the West at the turn of the first millennium*, ed. A. Davids, Cambridge 1995, pp. 126–127; В. Гюзелев, *Значението...*, p. 30.

[21] *Średniowieczne herezje dualistyczne na Bałkanach. Źródła słowiańskie*, ed. G. Minczew, M. Skowronek, J.M. Wolski, Łódź 2015, pp. 19–20, 67–70 (see there for further literature).

vision of history was created either during the latter half of the eleventh century or – what is more likely – during the twelfth century[22].

In a study that requires the analysis of native sources (such as, e.g., research into the titulature of the Bulgarian rulers), the historian needs to seek additional information by examining the Slavic translations of Byzantine chronicles. From among the above-mentioned Greek historiographical texts, both versions of the *Continuation of George the Monk* as well as the work of John Zonaras were certainly translated into the language of the Orthodox Slavs[23].

The Slavic translation of the *Continuation of George the Monk* was completed in Bulgaria in the late 10th early 11th century, and it was based on the newer, expanded redaction of the text (B), written after 963. Therefore, the Slavic translation dates back to merely several decades later than the original Greek version (i.e., incidentally, soon after Maria's death). According to numerous scholars, the Slavic translation is unusually faithful to the original, preserving a version of the text that is closer to the protograph than some of the extant Byzantine copies[24].

---

[22] On the subject of this work, see: K. Marinow, *Kilka uwag na temat ideologiczno-eschatologicznej wymowy "Bułgarskiej kroniki apokryficznej"*, FE 4.6/7, 2007, pp. 61–75; D. Češmedžiev, *Bułgarska tradycja państwowa w apokryfach: car Piotr w "Bułgarskiej kronice apokryficznej"*, transl. Ł. Mysielski, [in:] *Biblia Slavorum Apocryphorum. Novum Testamentum*, ed. G. Minczew, M. Skowronek, I. Petrov, Łódź 2009, pp. 139–147; М. Каймакамова, *Значението на български апокрифен летопис (XI в.) като извор за ранносредновековната българска култура*, [in:] *Stephanos Archaeologicos in honorem Professoris Stephcae Angelova*, ed. К. Рабаджиев, София 2010, pp. 593–612; И. Билярски, *Сказание на Исая пророка и формирането на политическата идеология на ранносредновековна България*, София 2011 [= I. Biliarsky, *The Tale of the Prophet Isaiah. The Destiny and Meanings of an Apocryphal Text*, Leiden–Boston 2013]; М. Каймакамова, *Власт и история в средновековна България (VII–XIV в.)*, София 2011, pp. 183–216; V. Tapkova-Zaimova, A. Miltenova, *Historical and Apocalyptic Literature in Byzantium and Medieval Bulgaria*, Sofia 2011, pp. 274–300.

[23] Д.И. Полывянный, *Царь Петр в исторической памяти болгарского средневековья*, [in:] *Средновековният българин и "другите". Сборник в чест на 60-годишнината на проф. дин Петър Ангелов*, ed. А. Николов, Г.Н. Николов, София 2013, p. 139.

[24] А.П. Каждан, *Хроника Симеона...*, p. 126; W. Swoboda, *Kontynuacja Georgiosa...*, p. 468; М. Каймакамова, *Българска...*, pp. 170–171; A. Brzóstkowska, *Kroniki...*, pp. 64–66.

Interestingly enough, another translation of the *Chronicle of Symeon Logothete* (vel *Continuation of George the Monk*), entirely independent from the translation discussed above, was produced in the 14th century in the South Slavic area. It was based on the older redaction of the Byzantine chronicle (A), covering events until 948. In the manuscripts of this translation, the work is unequivocally ascribed to Symeon Logothete[25]. Again, the fragments of the source referring to Peter and Maria Lekapene were rendered particularly faithfully, free from abbreviations or editorial interpolations[26].

The Bulgarian translation of the *Chronicle of John Zonaras* (from the second half of the 12th century) and especially the 14th century Serbian redaction can hardly be considered complete. In the manuscripts containing the most extensive version of the Slavic text, we encounter a lacuna between the reign of Leo VI (886–912) and that of Basil II (976–1025)[27]. Looking for direct references to Peter's times, therefore, we would be searching them in vain. Interestingly, some information about Peter and Maria was included into the synopsis of John Zonaras' work by the anonymous author of the manuscript РНБ, F.IV.307, containing a fourteenth-century Slavic translation of the chronicle of Symeon Logothetes[28].

Remarks about Maria Lekapene and Peter can also be found in several Old Russian historiographical sources which were dependent content-wise, and sometimes even textologically, on Slavic translations of Byzantine chronicles. Thus, the highly detailed description of the events of 927 as well as the passage on Maria's later visits to Constantinople – *de facto* re-edited fragments of the *Continuation of George the Monk*

---

25 Г. Острогорский, *Славянский перевод хроники Симеона Логофета*, SK 5, 1932, pp. 17–37; А.П. Каждан, *Хроника...*, p. 130; W. Swoboda, *Symeon Logotheta*, [in:] *SSS*, vol. V, pp. 506–507; М. Каймакамова, *Българска...*, pp. 187–188; Т. Тодоров, *България...*, pp. 155–156; idem, *Владетелският...*, p. 98; A. Brzóstkowska, *Kroniki...*, p. 66.

26 Symeon Logothete (Slavic), pp. 136–137, 140.

27 О.В. Творогов, *Паралипомен Зонары: текст и комментарий*, [in:] *Летописи и хроники. Новые исследования. 2009–2010*, ed. О.Л. Новикова, Москва–Санкт-Петербург 2010, pp. 3–101.

28 John Zonaras (Slavic), pp. 146, 156, 159.

– were weaved into the text of the *Hellenic and Roman Chronicle* of the second redaction[29]. The latter is a monumental relic of Rus' historiography of the late Middle Ages, compiled prior to 1453 on the basis of native accounts as well as Byzantine sources acquired in the East Slavic area (e.g. the *Chronicle of George the Monk* and the *Chronicle of John Malalas*)[30]. Three short notes about Lekapene and her husband, based i.a. on the Bulgarian glosses to the Slavic translation of the *Chronicle of Constantine Manasses* (14th century)[31], can also be found in two (interrelated) 16th-century Russian compilations which contain an extensive history of the world: the *Russian Chronograph* of 1512 and the *Nikon Chronicle*[32].

In the context of examining the titulature of Peter and Maria, as well as of the position of the tsaritsa at the Preslavian court, the sphragistic material may provide us with important information. It is beyond any doubt that, during the period 927–945, tsar Peter was depicted on official seals accompanied by his spouse. A relatively high number of artifacts of this kind have survived to our times. Ivan Yordanov, a specialist in medieval Bulgarian and Byzantine sigillography, divided them into three types[33]:

I. *Peter and Maria – basileis/emperors of the Bulgarians* (after 927) – a depiction of Peter and Maria is found on the reverse. The tsar is shown on the left-hand side of the composition, the tsaritsa

[29] *Hellenic and Roman Chronicle*, pp. 497–498, 501; Z.A. Brzozowska, *The Image of Maria Lekapene, Peter and the Byzantine-Bulgarian Relations Between 927 and 969 in the Light of Old Russian Sources*, Pbg 41.1, 2017, pp. 50–51.

[30] Т.В. Анисимова, *Хроника Георгия Амартола в древнерусских списках XIV–XVII вв.*, Москва 2009, pp. 9–10, 235–253; Т. Вилкул, *Літопис і хронограф. Студії з домонгольського київського літописання*, Київ 2015, pp. 372–387.

[31] *Среднеболгарский перевод Хроники Константина Манассии в славянских литературах*, ed. Д.С. Лихачев, И.С. Дуйчев, София 1988, pp. 232, 237.

[32] М.А. Салмина, *Хроника Константина Манассии как источник Русского хронографа*, ТОДРЛ 32, 1978, pp. 279–287; А.А. Турилов, *К вопросу о болгарских источниках Русского хронографа*, [in:] *Летописи и хроники. Сборник статей*, Москва 1984, pp. 20–24 [= *Межславянские культурные связи эпохи Средневековья и источниковедение истории и культуры славян. Этюды и характеристики*, Москва 2012, pp. 704–708].

[33] There are also some atypical artefacts. Cf. И. Йорданов, *Корпус на средновековните български печати*, София 2016, pp. 269–271.

on the right (from the viewer's perspective). Both are portrayed in the official court dress of Byzantine emperors: Peter wearing stemma and divitision, Maria wearing stemma of female type, divitision and loros. The Bulgarian rulers are holding between them a double-crossed patriarchal cross, which ends with a small globe at the lower end. They are grasping it at the same height. The inscription presents them as the *basileis* of the Bulgarians: Πέτρος καὶ Μαρίας βασιλεῖς τῶν Βουλγάρων[34].

II. *Peter and Maria – autocrators/augusti and basileis of the Bulgarians* (940s) – the depiction of the tsar and his spouse on the reverse does not differ fundamentally from the one described above. Peter's crown has clearly visible plates on the front hoop and pendants; the divitisions are different; the hands of two rulers are represented below the globe at the end of the patriarchal cross. Because of the poor state of preservation of all specimens of this type, the accompanying writing can be reconstructed in several ways: Πέτρος καὶ Μαρίας ἐν Χριστῷ αὐτοκράτορες Βουλγάρων (*Peter and Maria in Christ Autocrators of the Bulgarians*); Πέτρος καὶ Μαρίας ἐν Χριστῷ αὔγουστοι βασιλεῖς (*Peter and Maria in Christ augusti and basileis*); Πέτρος καὶ Μαρίας ἐν Χριστῷ αὐτοκράτορες βασιλεῖς Βουλγάρων (*Peter and Maria in Christ autocrators and basileis of the Bulgarians*). According to numerous scholars, the second interpretation should be considered correct; on the other hand, in his most recent publications, Ivan Yordanov is inclined to accept the third reading[35].

[34] И. Йорданов, *Корпус на печатите на Средновековна България*, София 2001, pp. 58–59; В. Гюзелев, *Значението...*, p. 27; И. Божилов, В. Гюзелев, *История на средновековна България. VII–XIV в.*, София 2006, p. 275; И. Йорданов, *Корпус на средновековните...*, pp. 86–89. All seal inscriptions in this book quoted as reconstructed by Ivan Yordanov.

[35] J. Shepard, *A marriage...*, pp. 141–143; Г. Атанасов, *Инсигниите на средновековните български владетели. Корони, скиптри, сфери, оръжия, костюми, накити*, Плевен 1999, pp. 98–99; И. Йорданов, *Корпус на печатите...*, pp. 59–60; В. Гюзелев, *Значението...*, p. 27; И. Божилов, В. Гюзелев, *История...*, pp. 275–276; Т. Тодоров, *България...*, pp. 156–159; idem, *Владетелският*

III. *Peter and Maria, pious basileis/emperors* (940–50s) – on the reverse of the *sigillum*, we find a depiction of Peter and Maria, portrayed similarly as in the previous types. There are also certain differences: in Peter's crown, which has pendants again; in the details of the divitisions. The couple is holding a cross – the tsar from the left, the tsaritsa from the right side. However, contrary to the seal images of type I and II, the hands of the monarchs are placed at different heights. In the majority of cases, the tsar's hand is higher; however, there are also examples in which it is Maria who is holding the cross above her husband's hand. This is the largest group of seals of a Bulgarian ruler. Over eighty-eight specimens struck with unknown number of boulloteria, but in any case more than a dozen, are documented. One of specimens (No 142) in the blank is silver and therefore the seal is an argyrobulla. The most characteristic feature of this group is that Peter and Maria are represented, but the inscription refers only to Peter, calling him a pious emperor: Πέτρος βασι[λεὺς] εὐσ[εβ]ής[36].

Three other types of seals exist (IV–VI); these depict and mention in the inscription the tsar alone. According to some scholars, the sphragistic material of this type was created already after Maria Lekapene's death, i.e. during the 963–969 period:

IV. *Peter, emperor of the Bulgarians* (Πέτρος βασιλεὺς Βουλγάρων) – bust of the ruler facing. On his head, a low crown (stemma) surmounted with a cross and pendants hanging from it ending with three large pearls. He wears divitision and loros and holds (r. hand) a globus cruciger.

статут..., pp. 99–101; С. Георгиева, *Жената в българското средновековие*, Пловдив 2011, pp. 313–315; M.J. Leszka, K. Marinow, *Carstwo bułgarskie. Polityka – społeczeństwo – gospodarka – kultura, 866–971*, Warszawa 2015, pp. 159–160; И. Йорданов, *Корпус на средновековните*..., pp. 90–95.

[36] J. Shepard, *A marriage*..., pp. 143–146; И. Йорданов, *Корпус на печатите*..., pp. 60–63; В. Гюзелев, *Значението*..., p. 27; И. Йорданов, *Корпус на средновековните*..., pp. 95–110.

V. *Peter, despotes* (Πέτρος δεσπότης) – facing bust of the ruler. On his head, a low crown surmounted with a cross and pendants hanging at either side. All facial features are visible. The ruler has a rounded beard and wears divitision and loros. The new unusual elements in this type of seals are the mirror-reversed inscription, the incomplete (abbreviated) name of the ruler and his title despotes. This type fails into two groups.

VI. *Peter, tsesar* [*i.e. emperor*] *of the Bulgarians* (**Петръ цѣсаръ Блъгаромъ**) – facing bust of the ruler. On his head, stemma surmounted with cross and pendants hanging at either side of his face. He wears divitision and loros and holds (r. hand) globus surmounted with double-crossed patriarchal cross. The seals fall in two groups: an original bronze die and lead seals[37].

The relics characterised above do not exhaust the source material in which we may find information about our protagonists. Other, not yet mentioned here accounts and artefacts will be presented later in this volume.

2. Literature on the Subject

Due to lack of space, we will omit the overview of the academic literature, and only draw attention to several works that have been particularly useful in writing of this monograph. Among these, the works of Todor R. Todorov[38] occupy a special place, as the newest and the most original take on the political history of Bulgaria in Peter's times. Of considerable

[37] И. Йорданов, *Корпус на средновековните...*, pp. 110–119.

[38] Т. Тодоров, *България...* (regrettably, this work is not available in print); idem, *Владетелският...*, *passim*; idem, *Вътрешнодинастичният проблем в България от края на 20-те–началото на 30-те години на X в.*, Истор 3, 2008, pp. 263–279.

interest are the works of Vassil N. Zlatarski[39], Vassil Gyuzelev and Ivan Bozhilov[40], Plamen Pavlov[41], Angel Nikolov[42], Ivan Yordanov[43] or John V.A. Fine[44]. The texts of Jonathan Shepard[45] and Vassil Gyuzelev[46] in particular are of fundamental importance for the study of the history and role of Maria Lekapene. Regarding the religious matters, including ecclesiastical organisation, the most crucial were the works of Bistra Nikolova[47]. Regarding matters of culture, one should point at the very least to the works of Riccardo Picchio[48], Dimitri Obolensky[49], Miliana Kaymakamova[50], and the monumental works *Кирило-Методиевска енциклопедия*[51] and the *История на българската средновековна литература*[52], which include papers by the most outstanding scholars;

[39] В.И. Златарски, *История на българската държава през средните векове*, vol. I/2, *Първо българско Царство. От славянизацията на държавата до падането на Първото царство (852–1018)*, София 1927.

[40] И. Божилов, В. Гюзелев, *История...*, *passim*.

[41] П. Павлов, *Векът на цар Самуил*, София 2014; idem, *Години на мир и "ратни беди" (927–1018)*, [in:] Г. Атанасов, В. Вачкова, П. Павлов, *Българска национална история*, vol. III, *Първо българско царство (680–1018)*, Велико Търново 2015, pp. 403–479.

[42] А. Николов, *Политическа...*, *passim*.

[43] И. Йорданов, *Корпус на средновековните...*, *passim*.

[44] J.V.A. Fine, *A Fresh Look at Bulgaria under Tsar Peter I (927–69)*, ByzS 5, 1978, pp. 88–95; idem, *The Early Medieval Balkans: a Critical Survey from the Sixth to the Late Twelfth Century*, Ann Arbor 1983.

[45] J. Shepard, *A marriage...*, *passim*.

[46] В. Гюзелев, *Значението...*, *passim*.

[47] Б. Николова, *Православните църкви през българското средновековие (IX–XIV)*, София 2002; eadem, *Монашество, манастири и манастирски живот в средновековна България*, vol. I, *Манастирите*, vol. II, *Монасите*, София 2010; eadem, *Устройство и управление на българската православна църква (IX–XIV в.)*, ²София 2017.

[48] See the collected papers of this author in a Bulgarian translation: *Православното Славянство и старобългарската културна традиция*, transl. А. Джамбелука-Коссова, София 1993.

[49] D. Obolensky, *Byzantine Commonwealth: Eastern Europe, 500–1453*, New York 1971.

[50] М. Каймакамова, *Българска...*

[51] *Кирило-методиевска енциклопедия*, vol. I–IV, София 1985–2003.

[52] *История на българската средновековна литература*, ed. А. Милтенова, София 2009.

for military matters, the books of Dimitar Angelov, Stephan Kashev and Boris Cholpanov are of the greatest interest[53]. Regarding the characterisation of the geographic location and the resulting conditions for the development of the historical Bulgarian state during the discussed period, we relied on the two largest monographs devoted to the physical geography of Bulgaria: the work edited by Kiril Mishev[54], and the newest encyclopaedia by Svetlin Kiradzhiev[55]. Where the matters of economy and relics of material culture are concerned, we have made use of the numerous studies presenting the results of archaeological research[56]. We will limit ourselves to mentioning only the general works – multi-author monograph edited by Dimitar Angelov[57] and Lyuben Berov[58], and the works by Nikola Mavrodinov[59], Krastyu Miyatev[60], Stancho Vaklinov[61], Totyu Totev[62],

---

[53] Д. Ангелов, С. Кашев, Б. Чолпанов, *Българска военна история от античността до втората четвърт на X в.*, София 1983; Д. Ангелов, Б. Чолпанов, *Българска военна история през средновековието (X–XV в.)*, ²София 1994.

[54] *География на България в три тома*, vol. III, *Физико-географско и социално-икономическо*, ed. К. Мишев, София 1989.

[55] С. Кираджиев, *Енциклопедичен географски речник на България*, София 2013.

[56] See also some of the general works – Т. Тотев, *Тридесет години археологически разкопки в Преслав*, Архе 16.3, 1974, pp. 48–60; С. Ваклинов, *Плиска за тридесет години*, Архе 16.3, 1974, pp. 28–38; Г. Джингов, *Археологически проучвания на поселищния живот в средновековна България*, Век 8.3, 1979, pp. 48–56; Р. Василев, *Проучванията на славянските археологически паметници от Северна България от края на VI до края на X в.*, Архе 21.3, 1979, pp. 12–22; Д. Овчаров, *Българската средновековна археология през последните десет години (1974–1984)*, Архе 26.4, 1984, pp. 46–61; A. Popov, *La ville médiévale bulgare d'après les recherches archéologiques*, BHR 12.1, 1984, pp. 63–73, specifically pp. 63–66.

[57] *История на България в четиринадесет тома*, t. II: *Първа българска държава*, ed. Д. Ангелов, София 1981.

[58] *Стопанска история на България 681–1981*, ed. Л. Беров et al., София 1981.

[59] Н. Мавродинов, *Старобългарското изкуство. Изкуството на Първото българско царство*, София 2013 (a new edition of the 1959 book).

[60] К. Миятев, *Архитектурата в средновековна България*, София 1965.

[61] S. Waklinow, *Kultura starobułgarska (VI–XI w.)*, transl. K. Wierzbicka, Warszawa 1984.

[62] Т. Тотев, *Преславската култура и изкуство през IX–X век. Студии и статии*, София 2000; idem, *Great Preslav*, Sofia 2001.

Liliana Simeonova[63], Rasho Rashev[64], and Deyan Rabovyanov[65], or the newest take on the development of the Bulgarian economy in the early mediaeval period by Ivan Biliarsky and Plamen Pavlov[66]. The research series *Pliska–Preslav*, *Corpus Preslav* and *Preslavian Literary School*[67] are also of great importance.

[63] Л. Симеонова, *Пътуване към Константинопол. Търговия и комуникации в Средиземноморския свят (края на IX – 70-те години на XI с.)*, София 2006.

[64] Р. Рашев, *Българската езическа култура VII–IX в.*, София 2009.

[65] Д. Рабовянов, *Извънстоличните каменни крепости на Първото българско царство (IX – началото на XI век)*, София 2011.

[66] И. Билярски, *Фискална система на средновековна България*, Пловдив 2010; П. Павлов, *Стопанско развитие на Първото българско царство*, [in:] И. Тютюнджиев, М. Палангурски, А, Костов, И. Лазаров, П. Павлов, И. Русев, *Стопанска история на България*, Велико Търново 2011, pp. 14–21.

[67] ППре 1–12; Пр.Сб 1–7; ПКШ 1–17.

PART ONE
THE EVENTS

I

Mirosław J. Leszka

Peter's Way to the Bulgarian Throne

Peter, the protagonist of our book, came from the family that ruled Bulgaria from the early ninth century, and whose progenitor was khan Krum (?802–814)[1], a great commander and lawgiver, and a conqueror of the Byzantines. His line also gave rise to several other exceptional, broad-minded rulers who gave impetus to the dynamic development of the state they governed. Boris I (852–889)[2], Peter's grandfather, may certainly be counted among them: accepting baptism in 866, he introduced Bulgaria into the sphere of Christian civilisation. Similarly Symeon I the Great (893–927)[3], our protagonist's father, a political visionary, an excellent commander, and an educated man with understanding of cultural matters.

---

[1] On the subject of this ruler's reign, see i.a.: P.E. Niavis, *The Reign of the Byzantine Emperor Nicephorus I (AD 802–811)*, Athens 1987; P. Sophoulis, *Byzantium and Bulgaria, 775–831*, Leiden 2012.

[2] Vassil Gyuzelev's work about this Bulgarian ruler remains the classic on the subject (В. Гюзелев, *Княз Борис Първи. България през втората половина на век*, София 1969).

[3] Symeon was the subject of the works of i.a. И. Божилов, *Цар Симеон Велики (893–927). Златният век на Средновековна България*, София 1983; M.J. Leszka, *Symeon I Wielki a Bizancjum. Z dziejów stosunków bułgarsko-bizantyńskich w latach 893–927*, Łódź 2013; *Българският златен век. Сборник в чест на цар Симеон Велики*

Symeon took the reins of power in 893, in rather particular circumstances. His predecessor and elder brother, Vladimir-Rasate, had been removed from power by his father, Boris-Michael, who only in 889 gave up the throne in Vladimir's favour. Vladimir-Rasate's four-year reign (889–893)[4] had not been appreciated by Boris I, most likely because of the former's abandonment of his father's foreign policy, and personal incompetence of the young ruler. Boris-Michael deprived Vladimir of the throne, had him blinded[5] and imprisoned, which ended in the former ruler's death[6]. The effectiveness of Boris I's actions attests that his position, despite the four-year 'retirement', had still been strong, which might suggest that he retained, despite residing in a monastery, certain attributes of power. A symbolic expression of the exceptional position

---

(893–927), ed. В. Гюзелев, И.Г. Илиев, К. Ненов, Пловдив 2015. See also: Х. Трендафилов, *Цар и век. Времето на Симеона. Четири инсталации*, Шумен 2017.

[4] See the recent work on the subject of the reign of Vladimir-Rasate: M.J. Leszka, *Symeon*..., pp. 44–58 (further bibliography within).

[5] On the blinding as a penalty towards dethroned rulers or usurpers, see: Г. Владимиров, *Византийско-българският културен диалог в светлината на едно наказание*, Мин 5.3, 1998, pp. 15–19. The scholar noted that blinding had not been used as a punishment in Bulgaria during the pagan period. The sole case thereof, and a rather peculiar one, that we can find in the sources relates to khan Krum. *Menologion of Basil II* (col. 276) states that he became blind by the will of God, which was supposed to have been the punishment for the cruel treatment of Manuel, the Archbishop of Adrianople. According to this relation, the Bulgarian ruler was subsequently strangled. Georgi Vladimirov, collowing in Yurdan Trifonov's footsteps (Ю. Трифонов, *Достоверен ли е разказът за ослепяване на Борисовия син Владимир*, УП 26, 1927, pp. 864–890), thinks that there can be no certainty on the matter of Vladimir-Rasate's blinding. Even if it did take place, then this type of penalty, likely borrowed from Byzantium, did not gain popularity in Bulgaria. On blinding as a punishment in Byzantium: J. Herrin, *Blinding in Byzantium*, [in:] *Polypleuros nous. Miscellanea für Peter Schreiner zu seinem 60 Geburtstag*, ed. C. Scholtz, G. Makris, München–Leipzig 2000, pp. 56–68.

[6] Such information can be found in Theophylaktos, the Archbishop of Ohrid, in the *Life of Clement* (XIX, 60). We read there: *after him* [*Boris-Michael*] *the power went to his son Vladimir, who died after four years* – that is, in 893. Nikolay Kochev (Н. Кочев, *Народният събор в Преслав през 893/4*, [in:] *1100 години Велики Преслав*, ed. Т. Тотев, vol. I, Шумен 1995 pp. 50–51) thinks that in this passage Theophylaktos did not speak of Vladimir's physical demise, but rather of his death to the community of the faithful. This interpretation however seems a too far-fetched one.

of Boris-Michael within the state post–889 was the title he was using: *monk and a ruler of Bulgaria* (μοναχός; ἐκ Θεοῶ ἄρχων Βουλγαρίας)[7]. His role would have therefore fit in the strongly established in Bulgarian tradition (as some would have it) institution of diarchy[8].

Nearly all of the sources at our disposal see Boris-Michael as the sole cause of Vladimir-Rasate's downfall, and elevating Symeon to the throne. There is however a single, most laconic at that, relation which presents the matter in a different light. In the *Miracle of St. George with the Bulgarian* we find this information: *yet the blessing of God and of Michael was upon Symeon, who having deprived his brother of power had taken his throne*[9]. We are not however able to determine whether this is an expression of a true causal role of Symeon in his brother's dethronement. It seems certain that Symeon knew both Vladimir's policies, and Boris-Michael's attitude towards it rather well, and was not merely a tool in his father's hands. It is doubtful that Boris would not have discussed with Symeon that he would become the ruler of Bulgaria after Vladimir's removal. Such a move, after all, was quite exceptional. Firstly, Symeon had been a monk, and to take the throne he needed to break his vows[10]. The situation was made complicated and awkward by the fact that accepting a monastic schema made seeking any lay dignities (not to mention ruling a state) impossible. Both Boris and Symeon must have been aware of this. In Byzantine literature, we can find a condemnation of the abandonment of monastic

[7] И. Йорданов, *България при Борис I (852–889, †907). Приносът на сфрагистиката*, [in:] *Християнската култура в средновековна България. Материали от национална научна конференция, Шумен 2–4 май 2007 г. по случай 1100 години от смъртта на Св. Княз Борис-Михаил (ок. 835–907 г.)*, ed. П. Георгиев, Велико Търново 2008, pp. 43–44.

[8] On the functioning of this institution: В. Бешевлиев, *Първобългарите. Бит и култура*, София 1981, pp. 45–50.

[9] *Miracle of St. George with the Bulgarian*, p. 143: **бы бл҇веније б҇жїе и михаиле на сумеѡнѣ. и прѣје столь сьгнавь бра.** Cf. В. Гюзелев, *Княз Борис...*, pp. 466–467; Е. Александров, *Интронизирането на княз Симеон – 893 г. (Дипломатическоправни проблеми)*, Pbg 15.3, 1991, p. 13.

[10] A monastic schema was accepted until the end of one's life. There was no law or regulation that determined the procedure of abandoning it (М. Спасова, *На коя дата и през кой месец се е провел преславският събор от 893 година*, ПКШ 8, 2005, p. 89, fn. 25).

life in favour of gaining power in such works as, e.g., *Spiritual meadow* by John Moschos, translated into Old Bulgarian near the end of the ninth or during the early tenth century. Bulgarian readers would have found in it the following words:

> And the Elder had said: Believe me children, when I say that a great glory and fame [await] those, who forsake the empire and become monks, for that which is knowable with mind is more worthy of respect than that what is sensual. It is therefore a great shame and disgrace when a monk abandons his condition and becomes an emperor.[11]

It cannot be ruled out that some would have read this as a commentary on the recent event, and that they would have shared this opinion.

The seizing of power by Symeon caused controversy also because he was not the eldest, nor even the second eldest of Boris' sons. It is thought that the inheritance law regarding the Bulgarian throne involved the two eldest male offspring of the ruler[12]. The firstborn son was titled *kanartikin* (καναρτικείνος), the second – *bulias-tarkan* (βουλίας ταρκάνος)[13]. In the light of this rule, the power should have gone to Gabriel, Boris' second son. Our knowledge of him is very scarce[14], therefore finding the reasons for

---

[11] John Moschos (Slavic text), p. 250.9–14: **Рече пакы старьць вѣроу имѣте ми чада глаголющоу ꙗко велика хвала и велика слава ц҃рꙋ отъмещоущѧ сѧ и бывающоу мьнихоу поне же чьстнѣиша сѫть разоумьнаꙗ чювьствьныхъ** (ἐπειδὴ τιμιώτερά ἐστι τὰ νοητὰ τῶν αἰσθητῶν). **тако и великъ срамъ ѥсть и бечьстиѥ мнихоу. оставлѧющю мьнишьскыи чинь. и бывающю ц҃рю.** Greek text: John Moschos, col. 3020B–C. On this source testimony: А. Николов, *Политическа мисъл в ранносредновековна България (средата на IX–края на X в.)*, София 2006, p. 121.

[12] Й. Андреев, *Йоан Екзарх и някои въпроси във връзка с наследиаването на царската власт в средновековна България*, ПКШ 1, 1995, pp. 309–310. On the titulature and the rights of the heirs to the throne: П. Георгиев, *Титлата и функциите на българския престолонаследник и въпросът за престолонаследието при цар Симеон (893–927)*, ИП 48.8/9, 1992, pp. 3–12.

[13] I. Biliarsky, *Word and Power in Mediaeval Bulgaria*, Leiden–Boston 2011, pp. 218–219.

[14] Of Gabriel, we know only that he was the second son of Boris and Maria. There have been attempts to identify him with known figures of the time, but these have not been met with a common agreement. Cf. Й. Андреев, *Гаврил*, [in:] idem,

which he did not succeed the eldest of the brothers cannot move beyond the realm of conjecture. The simplest explanation of the matter would be that by 893 he was simply no longer alive. Otherwise, potential factors that could have come to the fore were Symeon's abilities, appreciated by Boris, or perhaps a particularly strong bond between the two.

The fact that Symeon had taken power after his brother caused doubts among his contemporaries. These are attested by a fragment of John the Exarch's *Hexameron*, in which we read that *among the Bulgarians the power passes not only from father to son, but from brother to brother. We know that this was the case also among the Khazars*[15]. The author from Symeon's circle clearly formulated the view about the legality of such transmission of power. A reference to the Khazars, and also showing in the preceding passage that this tradition had ancient roots was intended to provide a stronger basis for this statement. John reached for such reasoning because he clearly could not find examples of such practice in Bulgaria's history. Stressing that one could inherit from his brother perhaps resulted not only from the fact that Vladimir was deprived of power, but also because he lacked a male heir who could have inherited the throne from his father.

To conclude these brief considerations regarding the seizing of power by Symeon (the father of the present monograph's protagonist), one might say that he became a Bulgarian monarch on the initiative and with active participation of Boris-Michael, that he acquiesced to it, and maybe even in part brought it about thanks to his own actions. It does not seem that the new ruler of Bulgaria was a mere tool in his father's hands. It must be remembered that Symeon was at the time nearing thirty years of age, he

---

И. Лазаров, П. Павлов, *Кой кой е в средновековна България*, [3]София 2012, p. 129. From the formal point of view, Vladimir's son should have become his successor. While we do not know if he even had one, one might suspect that Rasate, who in 893 was around forty, already had children of an age appropriate for taking the reins of power.

[15] John the Exarch, pp. 241.14–245.1 (140a.21–28, 140c.1), 243.21–28. On this passage: Й. Андреев, *Йоан Екзарх*..., pp. 313–315; Г.Н. Николов, *Прабългарската традиция в християнския двор на средновековна България (IX–XI в.). Владетел и престолонаследие*, [in:] *Бог и цар в българската история*, ed. К. Вачкова, Пловдив 1996, pp. 125–126; А. Николов, *Политическа мисъл*..., pp. 121–123. On the subject of succession of power among the Khazars, see: J. Dudek, *Chazarowie. Polityka – kultura – religia, VII–XI w.*, Warszawa 2016, pp. 278–282.

knew the situation within the country, and although he was not being prepared for taking the throne, he must have possessed intellectual qualities that gave hope he would soon gain the appropriate experience and sophistication that would allow him to master the difficult art of ruling a country[16]. It is not entirely out of the question that Boris-Michael's decision to remove Vladimir and elevate Symeon was subsequently confirmed by an assembly of church and state dignitaries[17].

* * *

I hope that the somewhat wider presentations of the circumstances in which Symeon I the Great took power will allow the reader to visualise the fact that Peter's complicated path to regal power, and the fight to maintain it – which are going to be discuss below – was not something unprecedented in the history of contemporary Bulgaria. A reflection that Symeon's personal experiences affected his decision regarding the setting of the matter of succession would also have not been without basis. The man who in taking the reins of power broke a number of rules would certainly have found it easier to, e.g., bypass his eldest son when contemplating succession. Furthermore, Boris-Michael made it clear that the ruler's will on the matter was the deciding factor.

It would seem that soon after abandoning the monastic robes and taking the throne Symeon got married. We do not know the name of his first wife; we only know that she gave him at least one child – Michael[18]. After her death, Symeon re-married. His chosen was a sister of George Sursuvul, his close collaborator[19]. We do not know her name, either. The

[16] M.J. Leszka, *Symeon*..., pp. 58–63.

[17] This did not, however, happen during the so-called Council of Preslav, dated to 893/894, which most likely is only an invention. Cf. *Ibidem*, s. 64–65.

[18] Continuator of Theophanes, p. 412; Symeon Logothete, 136.45; cf. John Skylitzes, p. 225.

[19] On the subject of George Sursuvul, see: П. Павлов, *Георги Сурсувул*, [in:] Й. Андреев, И. Лазаров, П. Павлов, *Кой кой*..., pp. 139–143. This author supposes that George may have been a son of the *kavkhan* Theodore, and his successor. *Kavkhan* was the second person in the state after the ruler, his closes adviser, and as some scholars think – even his co-ruler. This dignity was for life, and may

high position of her brother indicates that she came from a powerful family. It was from this union that Peter was born[20]. There is no source information that would allow us to determine when it happened. Considering that in 927 Peter was still unmarried, and that in the same year he was able to marry and take power (formally, he needed to be 16), one should accept that he was born no later than in the early 910s.[21]

We know practically nothing about Peter's history until the point in which he took power after his father in 927. It can be assumed that Symeon, who was thoroughly educated and displayed wide intellectual interests[22], had taken care to ensure that his son was a well-educated man and had an understanding of (widely understood) cultural matters.

Peter had three brothers: Michael, John and Benjamin (Bayan), but the question of seniority among them is not entirely clear. Only a single

---

have been hereditary. More about the role of a *kavkhan* in the Bulgarian state, i.a.: И. Венедиков, *Военното и административното устройство на България през IX и X в.*, София 1979, pp. 28–41; Ц. Степанов, *Власт и авторитет в ранно-средновековна България (VII – ср. IX в.)*, София 1999, pp. 85–86; В. Бешевлиев, *Първобългарски надписи*, София 1992, pp. 67–69; В. Гюзелев, *Кавханите и ичиргу боилите на българското ханство-царство*, Пловдив 2007, pp. 51–121; Т. Славова, *Владетел и администрация в ранносредновековна България. Филологически аспекти*, София 2010, pp. 10–15.

[20] Continuator of Theophanes, p. 412; Symeon Logothete, 136.45; cf. John Skylitzes, p. 225.

[21] Thus e.g. Pavel Georgiev (П. Георгиев, *Превратът през 927 г.*, ПКШ 10, 2008, p. 429). He thinks this may have occurred in 911. Plamen Pavlov maintains that this happened ca. 907, since according to him, at the time when Peter was taking the power he may have been ca. twenty (П. Павлов, *Георги...*, p. 140). It would not seem that the information that in 913 Symeon was accompanied in his expedition to Constantinople by his sons (υἱοί – Continuator of Theophanes, p. 385) or children (παῖδες – John Skylitzes, p. 200) was of any help in determining even a hypothetical date of Peter's birth. None of the accounts mention the names of Symeon's progeny, nor their number. We are also aware that, beside the fact that Michael was Symeon's eldest son, the seniority of the others is uncertain. We also do not know whether there was some age boundary beyond which a child could have participated in such an undertaking. In a situation where we cannot even be sure whether Peter was accompanying his father, the accounts of *Continuation of Theophanes* and of John Skylitzes should be considered of no value where determining Peter's age is concerned.

[22] On the subject of Symeon's education, see: M.J. Leszka, *Symeon...*, pp. 29–34. Cf. Х. Трендафилов, *Цар и век...*, p. 157sqq.

tradition provides us with a source regarding this matter; it is of Byzantine provenance. In the *Continuation of Theophanes*, we read:

> Symeon died in Bulgaria; overcome by dementia and ravaged by a heart attack, he lost his mind and unjustifiably violated the law, putting forward his son Peter, born from his second wife, the sister of George Sursuvul, as the archont; he also made him the guardian of his sons. Michael, his son from his first wife, he ordered to become a monk. John and Benjamin, in turn, the brothers of Peter, still wore Bulgarian dress (στολῇ Βουλγαρικῇ).[23]

Although apparently well-versed in these events, the anonymous author of this account (found in the sixth book of the *Continuation of Theophanes*) followed the trend visible in Byzantine literature and limited themselves to the basic information only[24]. From the Byzantine author's perspective, the key point was that there had been a conflict over the matter of succession after Symeon. For some reason, the latter decided to remove Michael – his eldest son (by his first wife) and the original heir[25]

[23] Continuator of Theophanes, p. 412. Cf. Symeon Logothete, 136.45; John Skylitzes, p. 225.

[24] On the subject of the authorship and source base of the sixth book of the *Continuation of Theophanes* see: chapter *Sources and Modern Scholarship*.

[25] Apart from narrative sources (Continuator of Theophanes, p. 412; Symeon Logothete, 136.45; John Skylitzes, p. 225), the sigillographic material also confirms that Michael had been designated as heir by Symeon – И. Йорданов, *Корпус...*, pp. 140–143. There are seven seals associated with Michael. Unfortunately, they are not well preserved, so that it is not easy to decipher and interpret their inscriptions, as well as to determine their definitive association with Michael. This matter was recently analyzed e.g. by Т. Тодоров, *България през втората и третата четвърт на X век: политическа история*, София 2006 [unpublished PhD thesis], pp. 86–88; Б. Николова, *Печатите на Михаил багатур канеиртхтин и Йоан багатур канеиртхтин (?). Проблеми на разчитането и атрибуцията*, [in:] *Средновековният българин и "другите". Сборник в чест на 60-годишнината на проф. Дин Петър Ангелов*, ed. А. Николов, Г.Н. Николов, София 2013, p. 127–135; И. Йорданов, *Корпус...*, pp. 140–143. The latter author, despite the stated reservations, concluded (p. 143) that they most likely belonged to the *baghatur* and heir to the throne – *kanartikin* (βαγατουρ κανε ηρτχι θυινος) – and not to the *baghatur* of the heir to the throne, nor to the *baghatur* of *khan* 'Irtchithuin'.

– from the line of succession[26]. To prevent Michael from making potential claims to the throne, Symeon had him become a monk, following the Byzantine custom in this matter[27]. He also designated Peter, his son by his second wife, as the heir. Since at the moment of his father's death Peter was very young[28] and relatively inexperienced, he was entrusted to the care of George Sursuvul, Symeon's brother-in-law and collaborator. From the Byzantine perspective, John and Benjamin (Bayan) – the other two sons of Symeon – took no part in this contest for their father's power.

As regards the order in which Symeon's sons entered the world, the account only provides us with a sufficient basis to state that Michael was the firstborn son of the Bulgarian ruler. It does not offer any indication as to the order of seniority among the remaining three sons. One might only speculate that John – since he was mentioned first – was older than Benjamin. Whether Peter was older or younger than his brothers, or whether he was born between them, is impossible to determine. The account in question does not rule out the possibility that the other three sons were full brothers rather than half-brothers. The Byzantine author, as I emphasized above, only stated that Michael's mother was the first wife of Symeon, and Peter's – the second. Unlike Michael, John and Benjamin

---

[26] We do not know the name of his mother or the date of his birth. He must have been born after 893, and perhaps prior to 907 (П. Георгиев, *Превратът*..., p. 429).

[27] We do not know when this happened. It has been suggested that this event was associated with the supposed disagreement between Symeon and his eldest son, caused by another escalation of the conflict with Byzantium in 924–925 (or rather in 923–924). The available source material does not, however, allow the verification of this conjecture. On this subject see e.g.: П. Георгиев, *Титлата*..., pp. 10–11; П. Павлов, *Братята на цар Петър и техните загавори*, Ист 7.4/5, 1999, p. 2; Т. Тодоров, *България*..., pp. 88–100. As regards the monastery in which he lived, it may have been the monastery in Ravna, which had strong ties to the ruling dynasty. It was located relatively close to Pliska (specifically, 25 km to the south-east). On this monastery see: Б. Николова, *Монашество, манастири и манастирски живот в средновековна България*, vol. I, *Манастирите*, София 2010, pp. 188–255.

[28] There are no sources to answer the question of when Peter was born. Given the fact that in 927 he was still unmarried, but on the other hand old enough to get married and seize power (formally he was allowed to do this at the age of 16), he must have been born in the early 910s at the latest. Georgiev (П. Георгиев, *Превратът*..., p. 429) believes that he was born in 911.

are unambiguously described as Peter's brothers, which might suggest that Michael's relation to Peter differed from that of the other two. Nonetheless, one should probably not ascribe particular significance to this. Besides, it should be borne in mind that, having eliminated Michael, Symeon could designate any of his sons as his successor, regardless of his age.

The passage under examination closes with the surprising statement that John and Benjamin continued to wear Bulgarian dress. It is commonly thought that it was an expression of their attachment to the proto-Bulgar tradition[29]. If we accept this information at face value we could consider it – as was recently suggested – as the reason for which the two sons got stripped of their power by their father: by cultivating the Old Bulgarian tradition, they would have opposed Symeon's efforts to shape Bulgaria after the Byzantine model, even if they shared their father's vision of fighting the southern neighbor. The younger Peter may have been more enamored with Byzantine culture, so dear to his father. However such an assumption is highly hypothetical – whereas, in fact, it seems that a far more prosaic explanation for the passage is at hand. It may be that the Byzantine authors, who favored Peter, intended to discredit his brothers by pointing out their barbarity. In this manner, they could justify the fact that he came to power instead of his brothers[30]. Moreover, it cannot be ruled out that we simply do not understand the nature of this passage, which may be of idiomatic or proverbial nature.

It follows from the above considerations that John was most likely the second or third son of Symeon. After Michael was removed from the line of succession, he was not designated as his father's heir any longer. While the opinion that Symeon did appoint him as his successor (*kanartikin*) is present in the scholarship on the subject, it should be stated outright that the basis for such a hypothesis is fairly shaky[31]. Another view, advanced

---

[29] It is also associated with the account of Liudprand of Cremona (*Retribution*, III, 29), which mentions that Bayan was supposedly a user of magic and could turn himself into a wolf.

[30] M.J. Leszka, K. Marinow, *Carstwo bułgarskie. Polityka – społeczeństwo – gospodarka – kultura. 866–969*, Warszawa 2015, p. 152, fn. 13.

[31] К. Попконстантинов, *Епиграфски бележки за Иван, Цар Симеоновият син*, БСП 3, 1994, pp. 72–73. This is to be seen from the sphragistic material, i.e. the

by Todor Todorov, holds that John may have been appointed heir to Peter. Based on the same sphragistic material as the aforementioned hypothesis, the claim is likewise rather doubtful.

Peter had taken power after his father's death[32], at the turn of May and June of 927. As can be seen from the earlier considerations, it happened after Michael, Symeon's firstborn, was deprived of his right to the throne, which constituted a departure from the practice that was the most common in Bulgaria[33]. The available source material is not sufficient to answer the question as to the reasons for Symeon's decision. Logical reasoning, rather than source analysis, leads researchers to the judgement that it was a consequence of the influence of Peter's mother, the second wife of the Bulgarian ruler, and of her brother, George Sursuvul[34]. This view can

---

seals associated with John (И. Й о р д а н о в, *Корпус*..., pp. 135–139; П. Г е о р г и е в, *Титлата*..., p. 9sqq). See also: П. Г е о р г и е в, *Превратът*..., pp. 432–433. He may have held the dignity of *kanartikin* as early as 926, and was previously titled *boilatarkan*, as was usually the case with the ruler's second son. The question of the reliability of the sigillographic sources related to John has been analyzed by Bistra Nikolova (Б. Н и к о л о в а, *Печатите*..., pp. 127–135). The author points out the uncertainty of their readings as well as their very association with John. She concludes, as does the present author, that the *sigilla* associated with John should instead be linked with some dignitary by the same name from the 9th or 10th century.

[32] It is commonly accepted that Symeon died on the 27th of May 927. E.g.: В.Н. З л а т а р с к и, *История на българската държава през средните векове*, vol. I/2, *Първо българско Царство. От славянизацията на държавата до падането на Първото царство (852–1018)*, София 1927, p. 513; S. R u n c i m a n, *The History of the First Bulgarian Empire*, London 1930, p. 177; И. Б о ж и л о в, *Цар Симеон*..., p. 146; А. Н и к о л о в, *Политическа мисъл*..., p. 151. Nonetheless, it is also possible that it occurred several days later, at the beginning of June. On this subject, see: M.J. L e s z k a, *Symeon*..., p. 227.

[33] On the subject of the takeover of power in Bulgaria, see: Г.Г. Л и т а в р и н, *Принцип наследственности власти в Византии и в Болгарии в VII–XI вв.*, [in:] *Славяне и их соседи*, vol. I, Москва 1988, pp. 31–33; Г.Н. Н и к о л о в, *Прабългарската*..., pp. 124–130; Т. Т о д о р о в, *Към въпроса за престолонаследието в Първото българско царство*, ППр 8, 2000, pp. 202–207; П. Г е о р г и е в, *Титлата*..., pp. 10–11; П. П а в л о в, *Братята*..., p. 2.

[34] E.g. Г. Б а к а л о в, *Царската промулгация на Петър и неговите приемници в светлината на българо-византийските дипломатически отношения след договора от 927 г.*, ИП 39.6, 1983, p. 35; J.V.A. F i n e, *The Early Medieval Balkans: a Critical Survey from the Sixth to the Late Twelfth Century*, Ann Arbor 1983, p. 160.

be modified to state that Sursuvul, taking advantage of Symeon's illness, convinced him to transfer power over to Peter, who then became declared his father's co-ruler. Pavel Georgiev, the creator of this hypothesis, thinks that this constituted a form of a *coup d'etat*[35]. Another view present in the scholarship would have it that Symeon declared Peter his co-ruler several years before his death, adopting a traditional Byzantine practice. In this case, our protagonist would have served in this role since 924[36].

Regardless of the particular circumstances in which Peter had taken power, the available source material only allows us to state that his elevation to the throne was done on Symeon's initiative, or with his permission, and with depriving at least the eldest of his sons of his right to succession. This situation constituted a potential threat to the new ruler.

Peter began his reign in Bulgaria at a difficult time, facing the failure of the campaign in Croatia and an unresolved conflict with Byzantium.

[35] П. Георгиев, *Превратът...*, p. 433; П. Павлов, *Векът на цар Самуил*, София 2014, pp. 15–16.

[36] Т. Тодоров, *България...*, p. 100; idem, *За едно отражение на съвладетелската практика в Първото българско царство през втората половина на IX – първите десетилетия на X в.*, [in:] *България, българите и Европа – мит, история, съвремие*, vol. IV, *Доклади от Международна конференция в памет на проф. д.и.н. Йордан Андреев "България, земя на блажени...", В. Търново, 29–31 октомври 2009 г.*, ed. И. Лазаров, Велико Търново 2011, pp. 173–181. According to this author, Peter became his father's co-ruler after Michael was removed from power.

II

Mirosław J. Leszka

Bulgarian-Byzantine Relations during the Reign of Symeon I the Great (893–927)

In order to understand Peter's situation regarding his relations with the empire after his father's death, it seems advisable to begin with a general overview of his father's policy towards Byzantium.

Following Bulgaria's conversion to Christianity in 866, the Bulgarian-Byzantine relations, which had previously been far from harmonious, took on a peaceful, religion-based character. Nevertheless, this state of affairs did not last longer than until the beginning of the 890s: the mutual relations deteriorated under Vladimir-Rasate (889–893) and escalated into an open confrontation under Symeon I (893–927), Peter's father. Having assumed power in 893, Symeon found himself in conflict with emperor Leo VI because of changes in the regulations concerning Bulgarian trade in the Empire; the animosity would ultimately result in the outbreak of war between the two countries[1]. Thus, Symeon had to elaborate a way

---

[1] On the causes and course of the war see: Г. Ц а н к о в а-П е т к о в а, *Първата война между България и Византия при цар Симеон и възстановяването на българската търговия с Цариград*, ИИИ 20, 1968, pp. 167–200; T. W a s i l e w s k i, *Bizancjum i Słowianie w IX w. Studia z dziejów stosunków politycznych i kulturalnych*, Warszawa 1972, pp. 221–223; И. Б о ж и л о в, *Цар Симеон Велики (893–927): Златният век на Средновековна България*, София 1983, pp. 87–89; i d e m, *Византийският свят*, София 2008, pp. 379–381; i d e m, В. Г ю з е л е в, *История на средновековна България*.

of handling the Byzantines in the early days of his reign. It was no longer possible to pursue the strategy chosen by Boris-Michael after his conversion to Christianity in 866, aimed at preserving peace with Byzantium.

The events of 893–896 show that during the initial stage of his rule, Symeon would deal with the Empire so as to defend the position to which the Bulgarian state (in terms of both territory and prestige) and its ruler had been elevated during his father's reign. The policy he pursued was informed by the belief that the Empire had no right to use the common religion as a justification for its claims to sovereignty over Bulgaria. The title of ἐκ Θεοῦ ἄρχων Βουλγαρίας, for which Symeon finally settled, can be regarded as an indication of the compromise he decided to accept[2]. In the years that followed, the ruler, taking advantage of the good relations with the Empire, focused on internal affairs. The development of the city of Preslav – the state's new political center – was among his main endeavors, as was his promotion of literature. The latter shows that his efforts were designed to build a sense of national pride and to provide an adequate ideological framework for a country functioning in the Christian ecumene[3].

VII–XIV в., София 2006, pp. 246–247, 266–267; N. O i k o n o m i d e s, *Le kommerkion d'Abydos, Thessalonique et la commerce bulgare au IXe siècle*, [in:] *Hommes et richesses dans l'Empire byzantin*, vol. II, *VIIe–XVe siècle*, ed. V. K r a v a r i, J. L e f o r t, C. M o r r i s s o n, Paris 1991, pp. 241–248; J. K a r a y a n n o p o u l o s, *Les causes des luttes entre Syméon et Byzance: un réexamin*, [in:] *Сборник в чест на акад. Димитър Ангелов*, ed. В. В е л к о в, София 1994, pp. 52–64; В. В а ч к о в а, *Симеон Велики. Пътят към короната на Запада*, София 2005, pp. 53–54; И. Б и л я р с к и, *Фискална система на средновековна България*, Пловдив 2010, pp. 139–140; M.J. L e s z k a, *The Monk versus the Philosopher. From the History of the Bulgarian-Byzantine War 894–896*, SCer 1, 2011, pp. 55–70; i d e m, *Symeon I Wielki a Bizancjum. Z dziejów stosunków bułgarsko-bizantyńskich w latach 893–927*, Łódź 2013, pp. 67–98.

[2] И. Й о р д а н о в, *Корпус на средновековните български печати*, София 2016, pp. 60–68. The author indicates that, in his seal iconography, Symeon followed the path paved by his father (p. 68). Cf. also Т. С л а в о в а, *Владетел и администрация в ранносредновековна България. Филологически аспекти*, София 2010, pp. 236–239.

[3] The search for the past – necessarily pagan – coupled with the efforts to integrate it into the new Christian historical consciousness is reflected both in the small number of extant original works and in the translations. It is no coincidence that the *List of Bulgarian Khans*, containing a mythical vision of the origins of the Bulgarian state, was referred to during Symeon's reign. See e.g.: А. Н и к о л о в, *Политическа мисъл*

Boris-Michael's death in 907, as some scholars believe, changed Symeon's situation[4]. He regained the complete freedom to rule his country the way he wanted and was given a chance to take his relations with the Empire to a new level, as he apparently became convinced of his right to claim the title of *basileus*. It was apparently in mid-913, as Bulgaria's relations with Byzantium under emperor Alexander deteriorated, that he decided to put this idea into action[5] and proclaimed himself *basileus*, abandoning the previous title of ἐκ Θεοῦ ἄρχων – the one approved by Byzantium[6]. In all likelihood, he realized that the Byzantines would not be willing to accept the step he took and that it would inevitably require a demonstration of military power, or even war. Thus, he attempted to take advantage of the opportunity to kill two birds with one stone. First, he utilized the fact that Alexander, by refusing to pay him tribute, had broken the terms of the existing peace treaty. The breach of the agreement by the emperor made it possible for Symeon to shift the blame for the outbreak of the war onto Byzantium. Second, he integrated the issue of the recognition of his new title into the broader demand concerning the tribute in question. In this way, he was able to avoid giving some of the members of the Bulgarian elite a reason to accuse him of taking up arms only in order to satisfy his personal ambitions. The Bulgarians' march on Constantinople in the summer of 913, which turned

в ранносредновековна България (средата на IX – края на X в.), София 2006, pp. 151–230; ИБСЛ, p. 37sqq; М. Каймакамова, *Власт и история в средновековна България VIII–XIV в.*, София 2011, pp. 115–156. These works contain references to various further studies on the issue.

[4] М. Войнов, *Промяната в българо-византийските отношения при цар Симеон*, ИИИ 18, 1967, p. 168sqq.

[5] For more on Alexander's policy towards Bulgaria see: Н. Овчаров, *Една хипотеза за българо-византийските отношения през 912–913 г.*, Архе 31.3, 1989, pp. 50–57; Р. Рашев, *Княз Симеон и император Александър*, [in:] idem, *Цар Симеон Велики. Щрихи към личността и делото му*, София 2007, pp. 32–41; M.J. Leszka, *Symeon…*, pp. 118–124.

[6] А. Николов, *Политическа…*, pp. 129–139; idem, *"Великият между царете". Изграждане и утвърждаване на българската царска институция през управлението на Симеон I*, [in:] *Българският златен век. Сборник в чест на цар Симеон Велики (893–927)*, ed. В. Гюзелев, И.Г. Илиев, К. Ненов, Пловдив 2015, p. 165sqq; M.J. Leszka, *Symeon…*, pp. 129–133.

out to be an effective manifestation of power, was Symeon's success[7]. Not only did the Byzantines resume paying the tribute, but they also recognized Symeon's imperial proclamation, although the latter was illegal from Constantinople's perspective[8]. Having accomplished all his plans, Symeon could feel satisfied, the more so because he had achieved his goals without shedding a drop of Christian blood. It may have been directly after August 913 that he began using the title εἰρηνοποιὸς βασιλεύς (peace-making *basileus*) on his seals[9], an appellation that is still the subject of an ongoing debate. According to Ivan Duychev, the title manifested Symeon's political program, an important element of which was to establish peace both with the Empire and within his own country[10]. Ivan Bozhilov maintains that the phrase should be understood as pointing to Symeon's plan to establish a new order (τάξις). The latter, referred to by the scholar as the *Pax Symeonica*, was in his opinion conceived as an attempt to replace or at least balance the existing *Pax Byzantina* in the Christian ecumene. In this plan, Symeon envisaged himself to become the same kind of *pater familias* among the family of rulers and nations that the Byzantine emperor had been; furthermore, the Bulgarians were to assume the role of the new chosen people, who – just like the Byzantines – enjoyed God's protection and were capable of defending Christianity and preserving the cultural heritage of Rome and Greece[11].

[7] On the Bulgarian expedition against Constantinople see: Д. Ангелов, С. Кашев, Б. Чолпанов, *Българска военна история от античността до втората четвърт на X в.*, София 1983, pp. 266–268; M.J. Leszka, *Symeon...*, pp. 134–137.

[8] On the conditions of the agreement in question see: А. Николов, *Политическа...*, pp. 130–139; M.J. Leszka, *Symeon...*, pp. 138–158.

[9] И. Йорданов, *Корпус на средновековните български печати...*, pp. 68–73. The inscription is an acclamation. The same inscription can be found in the *Book of Ceremonies* by Constantine VII Porphyrogennetos (I, 77, p. 373). Bozhilov (*L'ideologie politique du tsar Syméon: pax Symeonica*, BBg 8, 1986, pp. 82–83) provides other examples of the term being used in Byzantine texts.

[10] I. Dujčev, *Relations entre Slaves méridionaux et Byzance aux Xe–XIIe siècles*, [in:] idem, *Medioevo bizantino-slavo*, vol. III, *Altrisaggi di storia, politica eletteraria*, Roma 1971, p. 188.

[11] И. Божилов, *Цар...*, pp. 114–115; idem, *L'ideologie...*, pp. 81–85. Symeon must have carried out the program in several stages. First, the ruler was to obtain Byzantium's

Bozhilov, however, appears to be taking his idea of the *Pax Symeonica* too far: one is inclined to doubt the validity of ascribing such a deep meaning to a formula originating in imperial Byzantine acclamations, the more so because the Bulgarian scholar associates it more with Charlemagne than with Byzantium[12]. The interpretation offered by Duychev, and shared by other scholars such as Jonathan Shepard[13] and Rasho Rashev[14], is considerably more compelling. By using the term εἰρηνοποιός to refer to himself in 913, Symeon sent a clear message: he wished to be perceived as a ruler who established peace with Byzantium. It should be borne in mind that his contemporaries considered peace to be a supreme value – as Nicholas Mystikos put it, *it brought with it nothing but good and was pleasing to God*[15]. Symeon was perfectly aware of this, which led him to use the motive in his propaganda.

---

consent to use the imperial title. His next steps involved marrying his daughter off to Constantine VII, being granted the status of his guardian (*basileopator*) and, consequently, acquiring influence over the empire's government. My criticism of the view that Symeon strove to obtain the title of *basileopator* can be found in: M.J. Leszka, *Symeon*..., pp. 144–146. See also: Н. Кънев, *Стремял ли се е българският владетел Симеон I Велики (893–927 г.) към ранг на византийски василеопатор?*, [in:] idem, *Византинобългарски студии*, Велико Търново 2013, pp. 111–119.

[12] И. Божилов, *Цар*..., pp. 113–114; idem, *L'ideologie*..., pp. 83–84. Bozhilov refers to the title used by Charlemagne, which included the adjective *pacificus* ('the one who brings peace'). The Bulgarian scholar claims that the title was used with reference to the Frankish Empire, which the ruler created by conquering the lands of Bavaria, Saxony and the kingdom of the Lombards, as well as by subjugating the Slavs, the Avars and the Muslims in Spain. Even if this was the case, the fact remains that Bozhilov is silent about the route by which this element of Carolingian political ideology would have reached the court in Preslav and become an inspiration to Symeon. On Carolingian political ideology see: W. Falkowski, *Wielki król. Ideologiczne podstawy władzy Karola Wielkiego*, Warszawa 2011, *passim*.

[13] J. Shepard, *Symeon of Bulgaria-Peacemaker*, [in:] idem, *Emergent elites and Byzantium in the Balkans and East-Central Europe*, Farnham–Burlington 2011, pp. 52–53.

[14] Р. Рашев, *"Втората война" на Симеон срещу Византия (913–927) като литературен и политически факт*, [in:] idem, *Цар Симеон*..., p. 94.

[15] Nicholas Mystikos, 16, pp. 108, 110; 17, p. 110; 23, p. 160. The way in which the issue of peace was treated in Byzantium has been covered by: С.Н. Малахов, *Концепция мира в политической идеологии Византии первой половины X в.: Николай Мистик и Феодор Дафнопат*, АДСВ 27, 1995, pp. 19–31; J. Haldon, *Warfare, State and Society in the Byzantine World*, London 1999, pp. 13–33; J. Chrysostomides,

In 913, it seems, Symeon hoped to build a lasting peace with Byzantium; however, it was not long before he realized that his plans were difficult to carry out. The changes in the composition of the regency council, to be presided over by widowed empress Zoe Karbonopsina, forced him to search for new ways of securing stable, peaceful relations with Byzantium (the council ruled the Empire on behalf of Constantine VII, and the changes in question were introduced at the beginning of 914). It may have been at that time that Symeon, or one of his advisors, came up with the idea of a marriage between the members of the ruling dynasties of Bulgaria and Byzantium[16]. The Byzantines did not accept the offer; nor, it seems, did they confirm the terms of the 913 agreement (although they probably did not terminate it either)[17]. Be that as it may, Symeon found himself confronted with the necessity of reorienting his plans. It appears that, until 917, he still believed that maintaining peace was possible. However, the aggressive policies of Byzantium, which resulted in the outbreak of the war[18], finally made him change his attitude towards the Empire and redefine the parameters of Bulgaria's participation in the Christian community.

Thus, Symeon took up the gauntlet thrown by the Byzantines. For more than six years, he waged war against Byzantium – in Byzantine territory[19]. His first significant victories (especially the battle of Anchialos) left him convinced that he was in the position to demand that Byzantium

---

Byzantine Concepts of War and Peace, [in:] *War, Peace and World Orders in European History*, ed. A.V. Hartmann, B. Heuser, London–New York 2001, pp. 91–101; P.M. Strässle, *Krieg und Frieden in Byzanz*, B 74, 2004, pp. 110–129; K. Marinow, *Peace in the House of Jacob. A Few Remarks on the Ideology of Two Biblical Themes in the Oration 'On the Treaty with the Bulgarians'*, BMd 3, 2012, pp. 85–93.

[16] M.J. Leszka, *Symeon…*, pp. 142–144.

[17] *Ibidem*, pp. 160–163.

[18] On the causes and course of the 917 war see: В.Н. Златарски, *История на българската държава през средните векове*, vol. I/2, *Първо българско Царство. От славянизацията на държавата до падането на Първото царство (852–1018)*, София 1927, pp. 380–388; Д. Ангелов, С. Кашев, Б. Чолпанов, *Българска военна…*, pp. 268–272; И. Божилов, *Цар…*, pp. 121–126; idem, В. Гюзелев, *История…*, pp. 255–256; J. Shepard, *Symeon…*, pp. 34–45; M.J. Leszka, *Symeon…*, pp. 167–185.

[19] On this period in the Byzantine-Bulgarian relations see: Д. Ангелов, С. Кашев, Б. Чолпанов, *Българска военна…*, pp. 272–277; И. Божилов, *Цар…*, pp. 126–144; idem, В. Гюзелев, *История…*, pp. 256–260; M.J. Leszka, *Symeon…*, pp. 187–217.

Seal depicting Symeon I the Great with the inscription:
Συμεὼν ἐν Χρισ[τῷ] βασιλε[ὺς] Ῥομέων, Bulgaria, ca. 921.
Drawing (after R. Rashev): E. Myślińska-Brzozowska

recognize Bulgaria's unique status in the Christian world. A symbolic representation of the way in which his approach had changed was his assumption of a new title – *basileus Romeon* (βασιλε[ὺς] Ῥομέων), i.e. *basileus of the Rhomaioi* – the same as the one borne by Byzantine rulers[20].

---

[20] И. Йорданов, *Печати на Симеон, василевс на Ромеите (?–927)*, BMe 2, 2011, pp. 87–97; idem, *Корпус...*, pp. 73–81. We have a significant number of this type of *sigilla* (27). They bear the following inscription: Συμεὼν ἐν Χρισ[τῷ] βασιλε[ὺς] Ῥομέων (*Symeon in Christ basileus of the Rhomaioi*). Particularly noteworthy is the fact that they also contain the formula Νικοπυου λεονιπυο πολὰ τὰ ἔ[τη] (*to the Victory-maker the Lion-like many years*). Contrary to the phrase 'creator of peace,' probably introduced in 913, the new type of seals emphasizes Symeon's military victories – or, to put it more broadly, the military aspect of his imperial power. See also: К. Тотев, *За една група печати на цар Симеон*, [in:] *Общото и специфичното в Балканските народи до края на XIX в. Сборник в чест на 70-годишнината на проф. Василика Тъпкова-Заимова*, ed. Г. Бакалов, София 1999, pp. 107–112.

By proclaiming himself *basileus* of the *Rhomaioi*, which must have taken place between the beginning of 921 and October–November 923, he indicated that he would neither recognize Romanos Lekapenos (whom he considered a usurper) as the leader of the Christian ecumene nor accept the role of his 'spiritual son'.

What was the meaning of Symeon's assuming the title of *basileus*? Scholars are divided on this issue. Some have claimed that Symeon strove to capture Constantinople and, by taking the place of Byzantine emperors, to build a form of universal Bulgarian-Byzantine statehood[21]. According to others, he wanted to be recognized as the ruler of the Byzantine West (the lands owned by Byzantium in Europe)[22] or even as the successor of the Roman emperors who had ruled the western part of the Roman Empire[23].

It does not seem likely that Symeon's goal was to capture Constantinople and to turn it into a capital city to be used as a base from which his Slav-Greek state would be governed. Even in the period of his greatest victories, he did not undertake any serious operation that could lead to the seizure of Byzantium's capital (his plan to threaten it by forging an alliance with the Arabs went awry[24]). He considered Preslav the center of his state. He put a lot of effort into developing and beautifying the city; collecting relics was one of the ways in which he tried to raise it to the position of a religious center[25]. Would he have acted in this way if he had been blinded by the idea of taking over the Byzantine capital?

---

[21] F. Dölger, *Bulgarisches Cartum und byzantinisches Kaisertum*, ИБАИ 9, 1935, p. 57; G. Ostrogorski, *Avtokrator i samodržac*, [in:] idem, *Vizantija i Sloveni*, Beograd 1970, pp. 303–318.

[22] Р. Рашев, *Втората...*, p. 93.

[23] В. Вачкова, *Симеон...*, *passim*.

[24] К.С. Кръстев, *България, Византия и Арабският свят при царуването на Симеон I Велики*, BMd 3, 2012, pp. 371–378; M.J. Leszka, *Symeon...*, pp. 200–201.

[25] This aspect of Symeon's policy is stressed by: A. Nikolov, *Making a New Basileus. The Case of Symeon of Bulgaria (893–927). Reconsidered*, [in:] *Rome, Constantinople and Newly-Converted Europe. Archaeological and Historical Evidence*, vol. I, ed. M. Salamon et al., Kraków–Leipzig–Rzeszów–Warszawa 2012, pp. 101–108. Preslav became the center of the cult of Boris-Michael, Bulgaria's first Christian ruler, canonized soon after his death. His grave, it is believed, was located in the chapel of the so-called Royal Church (М. Ваклинова, И. Щерева, *Княз Борис I и владетелската църква на Велики Преслав*, [in:] *Християнската култура в средновековна България. Материали от*

Or should Symeon's use of the title in question be interpreted in terms of an appeal to the tradition of an emperor independent of Constantinople, conventionally referred to as the emperor of the West[26]? Unfortunately, it is impossible to give a positive answer to the question either – there is no evidence indicating that the Bulgarian ruler attempted to invoke the tradition of a western center of imperial power. The lack of such evidence has even been noted by Vesselina Vachkova[27], who recently advanced the notion of Symeon as a ruler of the West (in the sense of the western part of the Roman Empire).

On the other hand, a view that can be justified is that Symeon strove to weaken Byzantium's position in the Balkans and aimed to capture space in which Bulgaria could play a dominant role. It is in this context that the term 'West' (*dysis*) appears[28], found in the correspondence of Nicholas Mystikos[29] and in the letters of Romanos I Lekapenos. In the fifth letter, the latter accuses the Bulgarian ruler of plundering the 'whole West' and taking its people into captivity; Romanos adds that, because of his misconduct, Symeon cannot be called emperor of the *Rhomaioi*[30]. The issue of the 'West' appears in the sources once more in the account of the circumstances of Symeon' death. His statue, which is believed to have

---

национална научна конференция, Шумен, 2–4 май 2007 г., по случай 1100 години от смъртта на св. Княз Борис-Михаил (ок. 835–907 г.), ed. П. Георгиев, Велико Търново 2008, pp. 185–194).

[26] It is quite remarkable that the sphragistic material at our disposal offers no hint that Symeon used the title of *basileus* of the *Rhomaioi* and the Bulgarians; still, it needs to be stated that this title did reflect the reality, as the Bulgarian ruler's subjects included both *Rhomaioi* and Bulgarians.

[27] В. Вачкова, *Симеон...*, p. 84. Cf. П. Павлов, *Християнското и имперското минало на българските земи в ойкуменичната доктрина на цар Симеон Велики (893–927)*, [in:] *Източното православие в европейската култура. Международна конференция. Варна, 2–3 юли 1993 г.*, ed. Д. Овчаров, София 1999, pp. 112–114.

[28] On the meaning of the terms *dysis* ('West') and *hesperia* ('western lands') see: В. Вачкова, *Симеон...*, p. 76; eadem, *Понятието "Запад" в историческата аргументация на средновековна България*, SB 25, 2006, pp. 295–303.

[29] Nicholas Mystikos, 27, p. 190. In the letter, the patriarch suggests that Symeon wanted to rule over the whole West – which, in the patriarch's opinion, was not possible because *the sovereignty of all the West belongs to the Roman Empire* (transl. p. 191).

[30] Theodore Daphnopates, *Letters*, 5, p. 59.

stood on the hill of Xerolophos, had its face turned westwards[31]. By the 'West,' the three sources in question seem to mean Byzantium's European territories or, more broadly, Byzantium's sphere of influence in the Balkans. Only the first two accounts (not without certain reservations)[32], coupled with the analysis of certain steps taken by the ruler towards the Serbs and the Croats, can be used to support another view: that Symeon sought the Byzantines' approval of his rule over the territories they had lost to him, as well as their abandoning the competition for influence over the areas inhabited by the Serbs and Croats[33].

I do not consider it likely that Symeon planned to take over the whole Byzantine west. Rather, in my opinion, he merely wanted to be recognized as a ruler equal to Byzantine emperors in the Balkan sphere; his assumption of the title in question should be regarded as a manifestation of this intention. On November 19th (most probably 923[34]), he met with

[31] Continuator of Theophanes, pp. 411–412; John Skylitzes, p. 221; John Zonaras, p. 473; Pseudo-Symeon Magistros, p. 740.

[32] One is advised to exercise great caution in using the letters of Nicholas Mystikos and Romanos I Lekapenos to determine Symeon's actual demands, as the letters reflect Symeon's diplomatic war with Byzantium. In diplomatic wars, one puts forward far-reaching demands in order to achieve specific goals. Besides, the letters written by Byzantine authors do not necessarily reflect the thoughts expressed in the Bulgarian ruler's original writings. It is worth noting that Nicholas Mystikos is the only author who explicitly addresses Symeon's attempts to establish his rule over the West. All that Romanos I Lekapenos says in his letter, on the other hand, is that he who ravages the lands of the *Rhomaioi* cannot be called their emperor: hence, the letter concerns not so much the attempt to rule the West as the use of the title. If Symeon had actually wanted to take over the *all the West*, why would he have demanded that the Byzantines concede to him lands (known as the *mandria*) which formed a part of this West?

[33] Cf. J. Shepard, *Bulgaria. The Other Balkan "Empire"*, [in:] *New Cambridge Medieval History*, vol. III, ed. T. Reuter, Cambridge 2000, pp. 567–585.

[34] Although Byzantine sources appear to be very precise in specifying the year, the month, the day of the week and even the hour of the event, the date is open to debate (cf. S. Runciman, *The Emperor Romanus Lecapenus and his Reign. A Study of Tenth-Century Byzantium*, Cambridge 1969, pp. 246–248). J. Howard-Johnson (*A short piece of narrative history: war and diplomacy in the Balkans, winter 921/2 – spring 924*, [in:] *Byzantine Style, Religion and Civilization. In Honour of Sir Steven Runciman*, ed. E. Jeffreys, Cambridge 2006, p. 348) recently expressed his view on this matter, making a strong case for dating Symeon's meeting with Romanos to Wednesday, November 19th, 923.

Romanos I Lekapenos to make peace. Although it seems that the rulers failed to come to a final agreement, they managed to resolve some of the contentious issues, which sufficed for Symeon to cease his hostilities against Byzantium[35]. No source mentions Symeon's aggressive steps against the southern neighbor. Quite on the contrary, there is evidence to suggest that the ruler made active attempts to reach a final settlement with the Empire. According to Todor Todorov[36], this is indicated by a passage in the oration *On the Treaty with the Bulgarians*, in which Symeon is compared to the Old Testament king David, while the peace with Byzantium is likened to the Temple in Jerusalem[37]. The idea of the erection of the temple was put forth by David/Symeon, but it was implemented by Salomon/Peter. According to the Bulgarian scholar, the author of the oration hinted that it was Symeon who had entered into negotiations with the Byzantines and laid foundations for the prospective peace, while Peter/Salomon simply concluded what his father had started[38]. The marriage between Peter

---

[35] According to J. Howard-Johnston (*A short piece...*, p. 352), Symeon reached agreement with Romanos on several issues: 1. the war was ended; 2. Lekapenos was recognized by Symeon as Byzantium's legal ruler; 3. Symeon was granted the status of brother of the Byzantine emperor and was given the right to bear the title of *basileus* (of the Bulgarians); still, Symeon's claims to the title of *basileus* of the *Rhomaioi* were not accepted. Certain other matters, especially those regarding Byzantium's territorial concessions, were left for further negotiations. The Bulgarians laid claim to the areas referred to in one of Romanos's letters as the *mandria*. Most likely, the disputed territories included cities on the Black Sea coast, along with their surrounding areas, which – were they to remain in Byzantine hands – would pose a threat to the very core of the Bulgarian state.

[36] Т. Тодоров, *"Слово за мир с българите" и българо-византийските отношения през последните години от управлението на цар Симеон*, [in:] *България, българите и техните съседи през векове. Изследвания и материали од научна конференция в памет на д-р Христо Коларов, 30–31 октомври 1998 г., Велико Търново*, ed. Й. Андреев, Велико Търново 2001, pp. 141–150.

[37] *On the Treaty with the Bulgarians*, 16, 278.371–378. Cf. K. Marinow, *In the Shackles of the Evil One. The Portrayal of Tsar Symeon I the Great (893–927) in the Oration On the Treaty with the Bulgarians*, SCer 1, 2011, pp. 187–188. In some sources, Symeon is compared with king David due to his fondness for books (on this issue see: P. Рашев, *Цар Симеон – "нов Мойсей" или "нов Давид"*, [in:] idem, *Цар Симеон...*, pp. 60–72). What Symeon and David were to have in common was the fact that neither of them transferred their power to the eldest son.

[38] Cf. the discussion on the topic in: K. Marinow, *In the Shackles...*, pp. 187–188.

and Maria, a Byzantine princess, was one of the key elements of the peace treaty under discussion. Symeon had once rejected the idea of becoming related to the Lekapenoi[39]; nonetheless, after 923, seeing no prospect of forging bonds with the Macedonian dynasty, he changed his stance and was ready to establish kinship with the Lekapenoi. Thus, Peter not only did not betray his father's wishes, but he in fact brought his plans to successful completion. However, that did not happen until a later stage of his rule. Right after his father's death and his rise to power, he took certain steps to show that he was ready to resume hostilities against Byzantium – a move designed to make Romanos I Lekapenos agree to what Peter considered the most favorable peace settlement[40].

[39] Nicholas Mystikos, 16, p. 10.

[40] It is worth noting that, in the light of recent research, it is no longer possible to claim that Symeon was preparing another expedition against Constantinople shortly before his death. Cf. M.J. Leszka, *Symeon...*, pp. 225–227.

III

Mirosław J. Leszka
Kirił Marinow

Peace

1. Negotiations

The first and most important task faced by Peter after his rise to power was to establish peace with Byzantium. However, he and George Sursuvul, his guardian and advisor, did not decide to enter (continue?) the peace talks right away. Quite on the contrary, they renewed hostilities against Byzantium, with the purpose of strengthening their negotiating position during the future peace talks[1]. Both sides of the conflict soon realized that the cost of continuing the war would be too high. Peter, taking advantage of his first victories, sent monk Kalokir[2] to present Romanos I Lekapenos

---

[1] In the summer, perhaps at the beginning of August, Bulgarian forces entered eastern Thrace. Cf. Continuator of Theophanes, p. 412; Т. Тодоров, *България през втората и третата четвърт на X век: политическа история*, София 2006 [unpublished PhD thesis], p. 123.

[2] Continuator of Theophanes, p. 412; John Skylitzes, p. 228. It is quite remarkable that his mission was to be carried out in secret; this may suggest that Peter and George were wary of how their troops might react to their plan. Kalokir carried a chrysobull, which must have contained the conditions upon which Bulgaria was prepared to conclude peace. On Kalokir's mission see: Т. Тодоров, *България...*, p. 123; П. Ангелов, *Духовници-дипломати в средновековна България*, SB 27, 2009, p. 145.

with the proposal of opening peace negotiations[3]; the emperor accepted the offer[4]. There is no reason to doubt that the peace talks were initiated by the Bulgarian ruler. Nor should we call into question that his move was well-prepared and carefully thought out[5]. The Bulgarian society was exhausted by the long period of wars waged by his father – sources record a severe famine suffered by the people and the threat posed by the country's neighbors[6].

[3] According to Byzantine chroniclers, one of the reasons which led the Bulgarian authorities to embrace a conciliatory approach towards Byzantium in 927 was the danger of invasion from Bulgaria's neighbors – the Croats, Turks (Hungarians) and others (Symeon Logothete, 136.46–47; Continuator of Theophanes, p. 412; John Skylitzes, p. 222). However these opinions do not bear scrutiny. The essential argument against them lies in the anti-Byzantine military operation itself: it could not have taken place if Bulgaria's other borders had not been secure. More to the point, the information about the simultaneous invasion by Bulgaria's neighbors would suggest the existence of a coalition created, in all probability, by the Byzantines, from whom the Bulgarians should also fear hostile actions. The existence of any agreement with the empire seems to be at odds with the Hungarians' rejection of the Byzantine proposal to form an alliance with the Pechenegs, which happened in the same year (G. Moravcsik, *Byzantium and the Magyars*, Budapest 1970, p. 54). Perhaps the only real move which the Byzantines did make was to spread rumors inside the Bulgarian court regarding Byzantium's military action against Bulgaria. Based on this interpretation, the Bulgarian operation against Byzantium could be interpreted in terms of a reaction to the news of the formation of an anti-Bulgarian coalition, that is, in terms of a demonstration of force and a proof that Symeon's ancestor was not afraid of Byzantium's intrigues. However, the Byzantine authorities' swift assent to the peace proposal, coupled with the absence of any anti-Bulgarian action by Bulgaria's neighbors both in that year and in the years that followed, prove that Bulgaria was not facing any external threat (И. Божилов, В. Гюзелев, *История на средновековна България VII–XIV в.*, София 2006, pp. 272–273; Х. Димитров, *Българо-унгарски отношения през средновековието*, София 1998, pp. 71–72; Т. Тодоров, *България...*, p. 119; M.J. Leszka, K. Marinow, *Carstwo bułgarskie. Polityka – społeczeństwo – gospodarka – kultura, 866–971*, Warszawa 2015, pp. 155–156, 167).

[4] Continuator of Theophanes, p. 412.

[5] However, it should be noted that this view is not universally accepted. Plamen Pavlov (П. Павлов, *Векът на цар Самуил*, София 2014, pp. 16–17), for example, claims that the relevant sources are tendentious, blowing things out of proportion. Thus, the theory holds that it was the Bulgarians who positively responded to the peace proposals put forward by the Byzantines. However, Pavlov seems to be going too far in his interpretation of the events.

[6] Assuming that the sources do not draw on the topos referring to the circumstances of the peace concluded by khan Boris in the 860s, connected with his baptism

Peter knew he was left with no other option but to make peace – his father, who had not escalated the conflict with Byzantium for a few years, must have made him understand the need to end the war – but wanted its terms to be the most favorable for Bulgaria. As a way of suggesting his readiness to renew the war on a large scale, he decided to launch an attack upon Byzantine territory. The action he took was intended to force the Byzantines into concessions; besides, Peter may have wanted to strengthen his position within his own country, especially in view of the possible opposition from his brothers, whom he had removed from power. The conclusion of peace with Byzantium would have given him more freedom of action in Bulgaria, in addition to enabling him to secure Byzantine military support[7]. Romanos I Lekapenos, too, neither wanted to nor was able to continue this long war and was prepared to make the concessions that he had refused when dealing with Peter's father. It was certainly easier for the Byzantines to make peace with Peter than with his father, from whom they had suffered numerous defeats: Peter was a blank slate for them. It is hardly surprising that the author of the oration *On the Treaty with the Bulgarians* claimed that God had removed Symeon and replaced him with Peter to enable the latter to establish peace. In this way, Peter became a tool in God's hands[8].

In response to Peter's peace proposal, Romanos I Lekapenos sent two envoys, the monk Theodosios Abukes and the court priest Constantine of Rhodes, to Mesembria, where peace talks were to be held. It was agreed that the final settlement would be negotiated in Constantinople. The Bulgarian delegation headed by George Sursuvul arrived in the Byzantine capital[9];

(M.J. Leszka, K. Marinow, *Carstwo*..., p. 155, fn. 26). Cf. the reservations of И. Божилов, В. Гюзелев, *История*..., pp. 272–273; П. Павлов, *Векът*..., pp. 16–17.

[7] M.J. Leszka, K. Marinow, *Carstwo*..., p. 155.

[8] *On the Treaty with the Bulgarians*, 7, p. 264.159–177; 16–17, pp. 276.362–278.390; R.J.H. Jenkins, *The Peace with Bulgaria (927) Celebrated by Theodore Daphnopates*, [in:] *Polychronion. Festschrift F. Dölger*, ed. P. Wirth, Heidelberg 1966, pp. 293, 297; K. Marinow, *Not David but Salomon: Tsar Peter I (927–969) according to the Oration 'On the Treaty with the Bulgarians'* (in press).

[9] Symeon Logothete, 136.46–47; Continuator of Theophanes, p. 412; John Skylitzes, p. 222. The Bulgarian delegation also included Symeon, *kalutarkan* and *sampsis* (κουλοὺ τερκανός, καλοὺ τερκάνος), who may have been husband

the envoys negotiated the preliminary terms of the prospective peace and informed Peter of the decisions taken during their negotiations.

2. Peace Treaty

Once it was given its final form, the peace treaty was signed. What were its provisions? Unfortunately, the text of the agreement itself is not extant; for this reason, we must rely on its approximate reconstruction[10]. The only thing we know for certain is that it provided for the marriage between the Bulgarian monarch and Maria, daughter of Christopher, Romanos I Lekapenos's son and co-ruler[11]. It is also likely that the Byzantines would have recognized Peter's right to bear the title

of Symeon I the Great's sister, Anna; Stephen the Bulgarian (probably *kavkhan*), perhaps a nephew of the late tsar; as well as three dignitaries whose names remain unknown, namely the *kron* (κρόνος), *magotin* (μαγοτῖνος) and *minik* (μηνικός). On the Bulgarian delegation see: В.Н. Златарски, *История*..., pp. 523–524. It should be stressed that the delegation consisted of men who were Peter's close collaborators, comprising the ruler's council (known as the *great bolyars*). On the course of the peace negotiations see: J. Shepard, *A marriage too far? Maria Lekapena and Peter of Bulgaria*, [in:] *The Empress Theophano. Byzantium and the West at the turn of the first millennium*, ed. A. Davids, Cambridge 1995, p. 122sqq; И. Божилов, В. Гюзелев, *История*..., pp. 273–274; Т. Тодоров, *България*..., pp. 123–134.

[10] The terms of the Bulgarian-Byzantine agreement of 927 are analyzed by: S. Penkov, *Bulgaro-Byzantine Treaties during the Early Middle Ages*, Pbg 5.3, 1981, pp. 48–49; В.Д. Николаев, *Значение договора 927 г. в истории болгаро-византийских отношений*, [in:] *Проблемы истории античности и средних веков*, ed. Ю.М. Сапрыкин, Москва 1982, pp. 89–105; J.V.A. Fine, *The Early Medieval Balkans: a Critical Survey from the Sixth to the Late Twelfth Century*, Ann Arbor 1983, pp. 160–162, 214–216; E. Aleksandrov, *The International Treaties of Medieval Bulgaria (Legal Aspects)*, BHR 17.4, 1989, pp. 41, 42, 44, 48; Т. Тодоров, *България*..., pp. 127–133; S. Pirivatrić, *Some Notes on the Byzantine-Bulgarian Peace Treaty of 927*, Bslov 2, 2008, pp. 40–49; С. Звездов, *Договорът от 927 година между България и Византия*, H.BJHE 23.3, 2015, pp. 264–277.

[11] More on this event see in Part One, chapter IV, point 2 of the book.

of *basileus* (emperor of the Bulgarians)[12]. Both sides agreed on the exchange of war prisoners – in particular, the Byzantine captives were to be allowed to return home[13]. The treaty must have addressed the issue of the border between the two states, although scholars are not in agreement as to how this issue was resolved. Most subscribe to the view that the border was redrawn along the same line that had separated the two states before 913, which means that the empire regained the lands it had lost as a result of the defeats following the battle of Anchialos in 917[14]. It can also be assumed that the agreement contained provisions regarding the tribute to be paid to the Bulgarians (a point traditionally addressed in Bulgarian-Byzantine treaties)[15],

[12] βασιλεὺς Βουλγάρων/Βουλγαρίας – cf. Г. Б а к а л о в, *Средновековният български владетел. Титулатура и инсигнии*, ²София 1995, pp. 169–172; Г. А т а н а с о в, *Инсигниите на средновековните български владетели. Корони, скиптри, сфери, оръжия, костюми, накити*, Плевен 1999, pp. 96–99; А. Н и к о л о в, *Политическа мисъл в ранносредновековна България (средата на IX–края на X в.)*, София 2006, p. 234; Т. Т о д о р о в, *Владетелският статут и титла на цар Петър I след октомври 927 г.: писмени сведения и сфрагистични данни (сравнителен анализ)*, [in:] *Юбилеен сборник. Сто години от рождението на д-р Васил Хараланов (1907–2007)*, Шумен 2008, pp. 93–108.

[13] C o n s t a n t i n e VII P o r p h y r o g e n n e t o s, *On the Governance of the Empire*, 13, p. 74 (159–160): *so many Christian prisoners were ransomed* (transl. p. 75). Such a provision is alluded to in the oration *On the Treaty with the Bulgarians*, 5, p. 260.105–110. See also: Т. Т о д о р о в, *България...*, pp. 128, 139; M.J. L e s z k a, K. M a r i n o w, *Carstwo...*, p. 155; K. M a r i n o w, *Византийската имперска идея и претенциите на цар Симеон според словото "За мира с българите"* КМС 25, 2016, p. 347, fn. 25.

[14] The issue is discussed in detail by Petar Koledarov (П. К о л е д а р о в, *Политическа география на средновековната българска държава*, vol. I, *От 681 до 1018 г.*, София 1979, pp. 50–51). A different opinion is expressed by Plamen Pavlov (П. П а в л о в, *Векът...*, p. 20), according to whom the Bulgarians returned to the Byzantines only those territories that formed something of a temporary military zone (for example, the fortress of Vize), while the empire preserved the areas extending from the Strandzha mountains in the east to Ras (today's Novi Pazar in Serbia) in the west, including such centers as Vodena, Moglena, Kastoria and others; Byzantium also retained parts of the so-called Thessalonike Plain, northern Epiros, as well as today's Albania and Kosovo. See also: Т. Т о д о р о в, *България...*, pp. 127–128; M.J. L e s z k a, K. M a r i n o w, *Carstwo...*, p. 155, fn. 33.

[15] A hint of such an obligation is to be found in a passage from the work by Leo the Deacon, where the author mentions that the Bulgarians called for Nikephoros II Phokas to pay *the customary tribute* (IV, 5; transl. p. 109). Some scholars (S. R u n c i m a n,

principles regulating trade relations between the two countries[16] as well as Bulgaria's (and perhaps also Byzantium's) obligation to provide the ally with military assistance[17].

In addition, the 927 treaty is believed to have covered a number of religious issues. The Bulgarian church was granted full autonomy and the archbishop who stood at its head was given the right to bear the title of patriarch[18].

Furthermore, Todor Todorov recently formulated an interesting view concerning the Byzantine-Bulgarian negotiations held in Constantinople in October 927. The scholar is of the opinion that two distinct documents were signed during that time: the peace treaty, resolving the political conflicts between the Empire and Bulgaria, as well as a distinct marriage arrangement. What issues were addressed in the latter? Todorov is inclined to believe that the provisions regarding the marriage introduced a fundamental change in the status of the Bulgarian ruler in relation to

The Emperor..., p. 99; J.A.V. Fine, *The Early*..., p. 181) claimed that under the 927 treaty, Byzantium, instead of paying an annual tribute, agreed to transfer a certain amount of money for Maria, Peter's wife, each year. It seems that Todor Todorov (Т. Тодоров, *България*..., pp. 129–130) is right in claiming that until Maria's death, the Byzantines' commitment to pay her a certain amount of money existed side by side with their obligation regarding the annual tribute.

[16] There is no overt evidence to confirm that trade issues were dealt with in the agreement in question, but bearing in mind the fact that these issues were under dispute at the beginning of Symeon's reign, and that they were also responsible for the outbreak of the war in 894–896 to some extent, their omission from the treaty would be unexpected. Cf. Т. Тодоров, *България*..., pp. 130–131.

[17] Д. Стоименов, *Към договора между България и Византия от 927 г.*, Век 17.6, 1988, pp. 19–22. According to this author, the existence of the military alliance is attested to by the Bulgarians' participation in the campaigns carried out by the Byzantines against the Arabs in the years 954–955 and 958. Doubts as to the Bulgarians' participation in these campaigns have been raised by Todorov (Т. Тодоров, *България*..., pp. 131–132). The fact mentioned in support of the existence of the alliance is that Nikephoros II Phokas called for the Bulgarians to stop the Hungarian invasions of the lands of the empire (John Zonaras, XVI, 27, 14–15, p. 513) This argument, too, is open to debate, cf. Т. Тодоров, *България*..., p. 132. Although the arguments in favor of the view that the 927 treaty involved provisions regarding military assistance are insecure, the inclusion of this issue in the treaty cannot be entirely excluded.

[18] More about this aspect of the peace treaty see in Part Two, chapter VII, point 1 of the book.

the emperors in Constantinople and determined the rank of the envoys sent to the Bosphoros from Preslav. In addition, the document may have resolved the issue of Maria Lekapene's dowry, which was given the form of an annual financial subsidy to be paid by Constantinople to the Bulgarian tsaritsa throughout her life[19].

* * *

Concluding considerations regarding the terms of the treaty of 927, one may say that the resolutions agreed at the time must have been satisfactory to both sides, as evidenced by the fact that they became the foundation of a lasting peace.

[19] T. Тодоров, *България*..., p. 133.

IV

Zofia A. Brzozowska

The Byzantine Consort of the Bulgarian Ruler: Maria Lekapene

According to some of the scholars attempting to recreate the biographies of Bulgarian tsaritsas, the character of the relevant medieval sources can be most fully summarized with the principle: *do not mention them, or speak of them poorly*[1]. This also applies to Maria Lekapene, wife of tsar Peter. While the former part of the statement seems to pertain primarily to contemporary authors, the latter is common among modern historians, constructing their narratives based on exceedingly small source material and accusing the tsaritsa of an unambiguously negative impact on the events taking place in the Bulgarian state during the 10th century[2].

---

[1] *В данните от изворите и от специализираната литература по отношение на повечето от българските владетелки важи принципът "Или нищо, или лошо". Поемайки тежестта на короната, те сякаш се дематериализират до степента на безплътни сенки на своите съпрузи или пък се митологизират като разюздани юди самовили, обсебени от сатанински егоцентризъм, алчност, коварство и всякакви низки щения* [*In source texts and specialist literature alike, most Bulgarian female royals are subject to the principle: "Do not mention them, or speak of them poorly". Accepting the burden of the crown, these women seem to dematerialize into disembodied shadows of their husbands; alternatively, they are mythologized as unbridled witches and demons, obsessed with diabolical egocentrism, greed, treachery, and all sorts of base desires.*], (В. Игнатов, *Българските царици. Владетелките на България от VII до XIV в.*, София 2008, p. 6).

[2] В.Н. Златарски, *История на българската държава през средните векове*, vol. I/2, *Първо българско Царство. От славянизацията на държавата до падането на*

1. Origins and Early Years

We do not know when Maria Lekapene was born. Considering that in 927 she was considered to be of suitable age to enter into marriage, as well as to be betrothed to Peter, her birth can be tentatively dated between 907 and 915[3]. She was the daughter of Christopher Lekapenos, the eldest son of emperor Romanos I and his wife Theodora (Christopher was elevated to the position of co-emperor and third co-ruler of the empire in May 921[4]). As a descendant of the Lekapenoi family, Maria had Armenian blood in her veins. However, curiously enough, her background also includes a Slavic ancestor: according to Constantine VII Porphyrogennetos, her mother Sophia was the daughter of Niketas Magistros, a Slav from the Peloponnesos[5]. The latter is also mentioned in the *Continuation of George the Monk*, the *Chronicle*

Първото царство (852–1018), София 1927, pp. 535–536; П. Мутафчиев, *История на българския народ (681–1323)*, София 1986, p. 201.

[3] Jonathan Shepard suspects that Maria was about twelve years old in 927 (J. Shepard, *A marriage too far? Maria Lekapena and Peter of Bulgaria*, [in:] *The Empress Theophano. Byzantium and the West at the turn of the first millennium*, ed. A. Davids, Cambridge 1995, p. 136), while Vassil Gyuzelev dates her birth to 911, which would make her sixteen years old at the time of her marriage to Peter (В. Гюзелев, *Значението на брака на цар Петър (927–969) с ромейката Мария-Ирина Лакапина (911–962)*, [in:] *Културните текстове на миналото – носители, символи, идеи*, vol. I, *Текстовете на историята, история на текстовете. Материали от Юбилейната международна конференция в чест на 60-годишнината на проф. д.и.н. Казимир Попконстантинов, Велико Търново, 29–31 октомври 2003 г.*, София 2005, p. 28). Cf. also M.J. Leszka, K. Marinow, *Carstwo bułgarskie. Polityka – społeczeństwo – gospodarka – kultura. 866–971*, Warszawa 2015, p. 156, where our protagonist's birth is dated to ca. 912.

[4] Continuator of Theophanes, VI, 1, p. 398. Cf. S. Runciman, *The Emperor Romanus Lecapenus and His Reign. A Study of Tenth-Century Byzantium*, Cambridge 1969, pp. 65–66; A.R. Bellinger, Ph. Grierson, *Catalogue of the Byzantine Coins in the Dumbarton Oaks Collection and in the Whittemore Collection*, vol. III, *Leo III to Nicephorus III. 717–1081*, Washington 1993, p. 528.

[5] Constantine VII Porphyrogennetos, *On the Themes*, p. 91. Cf. В. Гюзелев, *Значението…*, s. 28; А. Николов, *Политическа мисъл в ранносредновековна България (средата на IX-края на X в.)*, София 2006, pp. 273–274; *PMZ II*, vol. V, pp. 20–22, *s.v. Niketas* (#25740).

of Symeon Logothete, the *Chronicle of Pseudo-Symeon Magistros* and the *Continuation of Theophanes*[6].

The future Bulgarian tsaritsa was most likely the eldest child of Christopher and Sophia, who married prior to Romanos I Lekapenos's ascension to power[7]. Since Maria's father was crowned in 921, and her mother was only elevated to the rank of *augusta* in February 922 (after empress Theodora's death)[8], our heroine did not enjoy the prestigious title of *porphyrogennete*, i.e. imperial daughter 'born in the purple[9].'

Maria had two younger brothers, neither of whom was to play any significant political role: Romanos, who died in childhood, and Michael. The latter had two daughters – Sophia and Helena (who married an Armenian, Gregory Taronites)[10]. Particularly notable among Maria's influential relatives was her aunt, Helena Lekapene, who in 919 married Constantine VII Porphyrogennetos, remaining by his side until 959. Two of Maria's uncles, Stephen and Constantine, also donned the imperial purple when they were elevated by Romanos I to the position of co-rulers in 923, whereas the third uncle, Theophylaktos, became the patriarch of Constantinople (933–956)[11].

---

[6] Continuator of George the Monk, pp. 905, 908; Symeon Logothete, 135.30; 136.16.48.54; Pseudo-Symeon Magistros, 36, p. 742; Continuator of Theophanes, VI, 22, 25, pp. 413, 417.

[7] S. Runciman, *The Emperor...*, p. 64.

[8] Continuator of George the Monk, p. 894; Pseudo-Symeon Magistros, 24, p. 733; Continuator of Theophanes, VI, 9, s. 402; John Zonaras, XVI, 18, p. 471. Cf. S. Runciman, *The Emperor...*, p. 67; J. Shepard, *A marriage...*, p. 136; В. Гюзелев, *Значението...*, p. 28; А. Николов, *Политическа...*, p. 274.

[9] S. Georgieva, *The Byzantine Princesses in Bulgaria*, BBg 9, 1995, p. 167.

[10] S. Runciman, *The Emperor...*, pp. 78, 234; J. Shepard, *A marriage...*, p. 136.

[11] S. Runciman, *The Emperor...*, pp. 64–67; G. Minczew, *Remarks on the Letter of the Patriarch Theophylact to Tsar Peter in the Context of Certain Byzantine and Slavic Anti-heretic Texts*, SCer 3, 2013, p. 115. Among Maria's relatives who held high state offices one might also take note of the *protovestiarios* and *parakoimomenos* Basil Lekapenos – illegitimate son of Romanos I from his relationship with an unnamed woman of Slavic or Bulgarian origin (И. Йорданов, *Печати на Василий Лакапин от България*, [in:] *Средновековният българин и "другите". Сборник в чест на 60-годишнината на проф. дин Петър Ангелов*, ed. А. Николов, Г.Н. Николов, София 2013, pp. 159–166).

There are several key questions to be asked regarding Maria's origins, position and connections: How many years did she spend in the palace in Constantinople? What kind of education did she receive there? To what extent did she have an opportunity to familiarize herself with court ceremonies and the Byzantine ideology of power? Consequently, how justified is it to view her as consciously transplanting certain elements of Byzantine political culture onto Bulgarian soil?

Constantine VII Porphyrogennetos had told Maria's grandfather that he, born and raised outside of the imperial court, lacked a sufficient understanding of its rules and thus also the basic competencies required for being a ruler[12]. The same judgement could also be applied to Christopher Lekapenos, who crossed the threshold of the palace in Constantinople as a fully mature man, by then both a husband and a father[13]. This leads to the next question: when did Maria herself enter the palace? The latest possible date seems to be February 922, when our protagonist's mother, Sophia, was elevated to the rank of *augusta*. The ceremonial court duties associated with this promotion[14] necessitated permanent residence in the capital city and the palace. The Bulgarian tsaritsa-to-be, then, spent at least five years at the imperial court. It is worth adding that she was a teenager at the time – the period in life in which one's personality, habits and preferences are shaped most deeply.

It is difficult to determine how thorough Maria's education was. Analyzing several anonymous commemorative poetic texts written after Christopher's death, Jonathan Shepard concluded that he valued knowledge and considered it important to ensure that his children obtain an education worthy of their standing. Thus, Maria's curriculum during her

[12] Constantine VII Porphyrogennetos, *On the Governance of the Empire*, 13, p. 72. Cf. S. Georgieva, *The Byzantine Princesses…*, p. 167; T. Тодоров, *Константин Багренородни и династичният брак между владетелските домове на Преслав и Константинопол от 927 г.*, ПКШ 7, 2003, p. 393.

[13] S. Runciman, *The Emperor…*, p. 64; A.R. Bellinger, Ph. Grierson, *Catalogue…*, p. 528.

[14] J. Herrin, *Theophano. Considerations on the Education of a Byzantine Princess*, [in:] *The Empress Theophano. Byzantium and the West at the turn of the first millennium*, ed. A. Davids, Cambridge 1995, pp. 72–73 [= J. Herrin, *Unrivalled Influence. Women and Empire in Byzantium*, Princeton 2013, p. 245].

stay at the palace may have been extensive, covering both religious and lay matters (fundamentals of law and general familiarity with the imperial Byzantine court ceremonial, as well as rules of diplomacy)[15]. Judith Herrin goes even further, assuming that Maria's relatives hoped that her marriage would render her a *sui generis* representative of Byzantine interests at the Bulgarian court[16]. Thus, she may have been actively prepared for this role. The British scholar attempts to compensate for the lack of source material concerning Maria by comparing her biography with that of another Byzantine woman married to a foreign ruler – Theophano, wife of emperor Otto II. According to Herrin, Theophano's later political activity attests to the education she received before her marriage, one which was intended to prepare her comprehensively for the role of an imperial wife and mother. No less interesting (from the perspective of our subject) seems to be the case of Agatha, one of the daughters of Helena Lekapene and Constantine VII Porphyrogennetos: she was sufficiently competent and knowledgeable in matters of state to assist her father in chancery work, helping him not only as a secretary, but also as a trusted adviser and confidant[17].

Even if Maria Lekapene was not as profoundly erudite as her cousin, her stay at the imperial court in Constantinople must have resulted in her gaining experience that would help her adapt to the role of the Bulgarian tsaritsa. Spending time in the chambers of the Great Palace, Christopher's daughter likely had numerous opportunities to familiarize herself with both the official court ceremonial and with the unwritten rules observed by those in the highest echelons of power. Our protagonist had no dearth of positive examples to follow: we must not forget that her aunt Helena, her grandmother Theodora as well as her mother Sophia all wore the imperial purple. Spending time in their company and observing them, Maria had favorable circumstances to develop an understanding of what it meant to be a Byzantine empress.

---

[15] J. Shepard, *A marriage...*, pp. 137–138. Cf. M.J. Leszka, K. Marinow, *Carstwo...*, p. 156.

[16] *She represents the out-going Byzantine princess, who had to perform an ambassadorial role in the country of her new husband* (J. Herrin, *The Many Empresses of the Byzantine Court (and All Their Attendants)*, [in:] eadem, *Unrivalled Influence...*, p. 229).

[17] Eadem, *Theophano...*, pp. 248–253.

2. The Year 927 – a Wedding among Peace Negotiations

The sequence of events from Maria Lekapene's life best illuminated by the sources comes from the period during which she became married (October 8th, 927). The matrimonial knot was to guarantee the peace concluded several days earlier between the empire and Bulgaria. Interestingly, as correctly observed by Jonathan Shepard, Maria was the only 10th-century Byzantine woman of high status who married a foreign ruler, and whose marriage was not only noted by the native historiographers, but also described by them in detail[18]. In comparison, the marriage of Anna Porphyrogennete (*nota bene*, the daughter of Maria's cousin – Romanos II) to Kievan prince Vladimir I is only mentioned by John Skylitzes in his chronicle in passing, where the author states that emperor Basil II turned the ruler of Rus' into his brother-in-law in order to secure his military support[19].

Therefore, we get to know Maria at a time when she is being presented to the Bulgarian envoys as a potential wife for their ruler. The anonymous Continuator of George the Monk – as well as other Byzantine writers following in his footsteps – noted that Christopher's daughter filled George Sursuvul and his companions with delight[20]. This statement, however, should not be used to draw far-reaching conclusions concerning her appearance or other qualities. Quite simply, it seems, it would have been inappropriate for foreign guests to display any other emotions during a meeting with an imperial descendant and relative, who was soon to become their own ruler. We could hardly expect the Byzantine authors to have characterized Maria in a negative manner.

---

[18] J. Shepard, *A marriage...*, p. 127.

[19] John Skylitzes, p. 336. Cf. John Zonaras, XVII, 7, p. 553. The chronicler also mentions the marriage of Anna and Vladimir I as well as the death of the Porphyrogennete in another part of his narrative: John Skylitzes, p. 367.

[20] Continuator of George the Monk, p. 905; Symeon Logothete, 136.48; Leo Grammatikos, p. 316; Continuator of Theophanes, VI, 22, p. 413. John Skylitzes (p. 223), contrary to the earlier chroniclers, directly stated that Maria was indeed exceptionally beautiful.

Interestingly, the mission of bringing Peter to Constantinople was entrusted to Maria's maternal grandfather – the aforementioned Niketas Magistros[21]. Our heroine was not present for her fiancé's ceremonious welcome in the Byzantine capital (which took place in the northern part of the city, Blachernai); neither did she take part in the peace negotiations.

On the day of her marriage – October 8th, 927 – Maria Lekapene proceeded to the Church in the Monastery of the Holy Mother of the Life-Giving Spring, located beyond the Theodosian walls, accompanied by *protovestiarios* Theophanes, patriarch of Constantinople Stephen II as well as numerous state dignitaries and courtiers[22]. Interestingly, the church chosen may have reminded the Byzantines and the Bulgarians of their earlier, troubled relations: after all, the temple had been set on fire on Symeon's orders, and it was in its vicinity that the peace negotiations between this ruler and Romanos I had taken place in 923[23]. Furthermore, it was Maria's grandfather who ordered the rebuilding of the ravaged church[24]. The marriage ceremony between the church's restorer and Symeon's son, then, may have had a clear propaganda significance. It suggested that Romanos I Lekapenos was the one who managed to neutralize the Bulgarian threat and perhaps – to some extent – repair the damage the Bulgarians had inflicted on the empire's lands in the past[25].

---

[21] Continuator of George the Monk, p. 905; Symeon Logothete, 136.48; Continuator of Theophanes, VI, 22, p. 413.

[22] Continuator of George the Monk, p. 905; Symeon Logothete, 136.49; Leo Grammatikos, p. 317; Pseudo-Symeon Magistros, 34, p. 741; Continuator of Theophanes, VI, 23, p. 414; John Skylitzes, p. 223.

[23] Continuator of George the Monk, pp. 893–894; Symeon Logothete, 136.31; Pseudo-Symeon Magistros, 29, p. 736; Leo Grammatikos, p. 311; Continuator of Theophanes, VI, 15, p. 406; John Skylitzes, p. 219; John Zonaras, XVI, 18, pp. 470–471. Cf. M.J. Leszka, *Wizerunek władców pierwszego państwa bułgarskiego w bizantyńskich źródłach pisanych (VIII – pierwsza połowa XII w.)*, Łódź 2003, p. 118; idem, *Symeon I Wielki a Bizancjum. Z dziejów stosunków bułgarsko-bizantyńskich w latach 893–927*, Łódź 2013, p. 207; idem, K. Marinow, *Carstwo...*, p. 157.

[24] A. Kompa, *Konstantynopolitańskie zabytki w Stambule*, [in:] *Z badań nad wczesnobizantyńskim Konstantynopolem*, ed. M.J. Leszka, K. Marinow, A. Kompa, Łódź 2011 [= AUL.FH 87], p. 167.

[25] J. Shepard, *A marriage...*, p. 129.

Byzantine chroniclers agree that the rite of the sacrament of marriage was personally performed by patriarch Stephen II. He blessed Maria and Peter and put the marriage crowns on their heads (this is sometimes interpreted in historiography as the crowning ceremony of the newlywed couple)[26]. The ceremony was witnessed by George Sursuvul and *protovestiarios* Theophanes. A wedding feast followed, after which Maria returned to the palace accompanied by Theophanes[27].

On the third day after the wedding, Romanos I Lekapenos organized another reception, which took place on a magnificently decorated ship anchored off the Pege coast. The anonymous Continuator of George the Monk stresses that the emperor feasted at the same table as Peter, his son-in-law Constantine VII Porphyrogennetos and his own son, Christopher. The participating Bulgarians are reported to have asked Romanos I for a favor: if we are to believe the chronicler, they wanted the father of their new tsaritsa proclaimed second co-ruler of the Empire. The emperor readily agreed to elevate the status of his eldest son (likely having suggested the request to his guests himself, during the earlier talks), thus reducing Constantine VII Porphyrogennetos to the third position among the empire's rulers[28]. We do not know whether Maria was present at this reception. Considering the requirements of the Byzantine court etiquette, we may assume that she was elsewhere at the time, in the quarters reserved

---

[26] В. Гюзелев, *Значението…*, p. 29; Т. Тодоров, *България през втората и третата четвърт на X век: политическа история*. София 2006 [unpublished PhD thesis], pp. 169–173.

[27] Continuator of George the Monk, pp. 905–906; Symeon Logothete, 136.49; Leo Grammatikos, p. 317; Pseudo-Symeon Magistros, 34, p. 741; Continuator of Theophanes, VI, 23, p. 414; John Skylitzes, p. 223.

[28] Continuator of George the Monk, p. 906; Symeon Logothete, 136.49–50; Leo Grammatikos, p. 317; Pseudo-Symeon Magistros, 34, p. 741; Continuator of Theophanes, VI, 23, p. 414; John Skylitzes, pp. 223–224; John Zonaras, XVI, 19, pp. 474–475. Cf. J. Shepard, *A marriage…*, p. 132; Т. Тодоров, *Константин Багренородни…*, p. 396; П. Павлов, *Години на мир и "ратни беди" (927–1018)*, [in:] Г. Атанасов, В. Вачкова, П. Павлов, *Българска национална история*, vol. III, *Първо българско царство (680–1018)*, Велико Търново 2015, p. 412.

exclusively for ladies – celebrating her marriage in the company of her mother Sophia, aunt Helena and other female relatives and high-ranking women.

Once all the wedding-related events were over, the newlyweds departed for Bulgaria. Christopher, Sophia and *protovestiarios* Theophanes accompanied them to the Hebdomon, where the imperial couple ate their final meal with their daughter and son-in-law. Afterwards came the time for the sorrowful parting: Maria's tearful parents hugged her, bade farewell to Peter, and returned to the city. The newlyweds, in turn, made their way to Preslav. As mentioned by the Continuator of George the Monk, Maria brought with her innumerable riches[29]; besides, she was likely accompanied by several trusted people who would advise and assist her in the new environment[30].

Curiously, in the account of the authors contemporary to the events of 927, there is a unique passage related to Maria's farewells with her parents. The Byzantine chroniclers attempt to describe Maria's internal experiences and present her personal views on her marriage with the Bulgarian ruler, discussing her mixed feelings during the journey to her new country. Maria was sad to be separated from her mother, father, relatives and the palace in Constantinople, which she by then considered her family home. At the same time, however, she was filled with joy – not only because she had married a man of imperial status, but also because she had been proclaimed a Bulgarian ruler herself[31].

The titulature and status of Peter's wife at the Preslav court will be discussed in detail in a later part of this chapter. At this point, however, it is interesting to point out a different circumstance. According to the Byzantine sources, Maria was far from perceiving her marriage with the Bulgarian monarch as a misalliance unacceptable for a woman of

---

[29] Continuator of George the Monk, pp. 906–907; Symeon Logothete, 136.51; Leo Grammatikos, p. 317; Continuator of Theophanes, VI, 23, pp. 414–415; John Skylitzes, p. 224.

[30] M.J. Leszka, *Wizerunek...*, p. 125; В. Гюзелев, *Значението...*, p. 29.

[31] Continuator of George the Monk, pp. 906–907; Symeon Logothete, 136.51; Continuator of Theophanes, VI, 23, p. 415.

her standing, nor did she see it as dictated by the need of reaching a compromise. Moreover, she did not consider Symeon's son a barbarian, and departing for Bulgaria by no means filled her with dread. It is useful to compare the passage under discussion with the narrative about another 'female experience,' associated with an analogous situation from the 10th century – Anna Porphyrogennete's attitude towards her prospective marriage with Vladimir I, as portrayed in the Old Rus' historiographical text known as the *Russian Primary Chronicle*. The text as we know it today was redacted in the 1110s, i.e. at a time when, in Rus', Svyatoslav's son was considered worthy of comparison with Constantine I the Great – a thoroughly Christian ruler. Thus, the source informs us that the sister of Basil II and Constantine VIII was most reluctant to wed the Kievan ruler, arguing that such marriage meant a fate little better than captivity, or perhaps even death. According to the anonymous author, Anna's two brothers pleaded with her to act according to their will, and even had to force her to board the ship that was to take her to Cherson. Much like our protagonist, the Porphyrogennete parted with her close ones in tears, but her emotions were quite different from Maria's conflicting feelings[32].

Interestingly, none of the extant sources mention Peter's view of Maria and the marriage arranged by George Sursuvul. In other words: how prestigious, honorable and politically advantageous was it for the young Bulgarian tsar to tie the knot with a woman from the Lekapenos family, who did not carry the title of *porphyrogennete* and was not even a daughter of the emperor (who, incidentally, was neither 'born in the purple' nor the sole ruler)?

The chroniclers from the so-called circle of Symeon Logothete, who had personal ties to the court of Romanos I, and other writers well-disposed towards this ruler (e.g. Arethas of Caesarea or Theodore Daphnopates, considered the author of *On the Treaty with the Bulgarians*) present the agreement of 927 – whose stability was, after all, guaranteed by the marriage of Maria and Peter – as a substantial diplomatic achievement of the Lekapenos emperor, ensuring the long-desired peace on the northern border of Byzantium and neutralizing the Bulgarian threat for a long

---

[32] *Russian Primary Chronicle*, AM 6496, pp. 111–112.

time[33]. Traces of this approach – no doubt propagandist to some extent – are also visible in the account of Constantine VII, although he was fully open about his aversion towards the Lekapenoi and their policies[34]. Even in the Bulgarian *Tale of the Prophet Isaiah*, we find the statement that Peter lived in cordial friendship with the Byzantine emperor, ensuring prosperity for his subjects for many years[35].

Liudprand of Cremona's remark on Maria's adopting her new name upon entering marriage should most likely be considered in the context of this 'pacifist' propaganda of the Byzantine court. After all, what we find in the *Antapodosis* is an exaggeration of the idea expressed in all of the above-mentioned texts: that Romanos I achieved the neutralization of Symeon's expansionist, anti-Byzantine plans, as well as the creation of a firm association between the Bulgarians and the Empire through signing a peace treaty advantageous for Constantinople. The originality of Liudprand's approach lies in his particular underscoring of Maria's role in this process: her marriage, according to the bishop of Cremona, became the foundation of a long-lasting friendship between Byzantium and Bulgaria. Therefore, according to the western diplomat, naming

---

[33] J. Shepard, *A marriage...*, pp. 130–131; А. Николов, *Политическа...*, pp. 237–238; A. Brzóstkowska, *Kroniki z kręgu Symeona Logotety*, [in:] *Testimonia*, vol. V, p. 64; K. Marinow, *In the Shackles of the Evil One. The Portrayal of Tsar Symeon I the Great (893–927) in the Oration On the treaty with the Bulgarians*, SCer 1, 2011, pp. 157–190; idem, *Peace in the House of Jacob. A Few Remarks on the Ideology of Two Biblical Themes in the Oration On the Treaty with the Bulgarians*, BMd 3, 2012, pp. 85–93; M.J. Leszka, K. Marinow, *Carstwo...*, pp. 160–162.

[34] Constantine VII Porphyrogennetos, *On the Governance of the Empire*, 13, p. 74. Cf. T. Тодоров, *Константин Багренородни...*, p. 395.

[35] *Tale of the Prophet Isaiah*, p. 17: тогⷣа ѹбо вь д҃ни и лѣтⷣ с҃тго Пеⷮра ц҃ря бльгарьскагⷪ быⷭ изьѡбылїа ѿ всего. сирѣчь пшеница и масло и меда жⷷ и млѣка и вина, и ѿ всего дарованїа б҃жїа врѣше и кипѣше. и не бѣ ѡскѫдѣнїе ни ѡ щоⷨь. Нь бѣ ситость изьѡбильсⷮво ѿ всего до изволенїа б҃жїа (*In the days and years of St. Peter, the tsar of the Bulgarians, there was plenty of everything, that is to say, of wheat and butter, honey, milk and wine, the land was overflowing with every gift of God, there was no dearth of anything but by the will of God everything was in abundance and to satiety).* Cf. K. Marinow, *Kilka uwag na temat ideologiczno-eschatologicznej wymowy "Bułgarskiej kroniki apokryficznej"*, FE 4. 6/7, 2007, pp. 70–72; M.J. Leszka, K. Marinow, *Carstwo...*, p. 162.

young Maria with an appellation meaning 'peace' was dictated by the desire to underline her special status as a *custodes pacis*[36].

It is worth noting that the ideological meaning of names of empresses was occasionally used by them for propaganda purposes. Irene, for instance, masterfully used this aspect of her name by establishing an iconographic program of coins bearing her image, or by changing the name of Beroe (a border town located in a previously troubled area) to Eirenoupolis ('City of Irene' / 'City of Peace') in 784[37]. On the other hand, it should be borne in mind that no source except for Liudprand's account contains the information about Maria Lekapene changing her name to Irene. If such an act indeed took place, it ought to be treated as strictly symbolic. Had Peter's wife decided to formally change her name, the official *sigilla* used in Bulgaria in the years 927–945 would have borne the name of Irene, whereas, on surviving artifacts of this kind, we invariably find the name Maria[38].

However, let us return to the issue of what political benefits and prestige Peter may have gained through marrying a representative of the Lekapenos family. The consequences of the peace treaty of 927, including the unquestionable elevation of the Slavic ruler's status in the international

---

[36] Liudprand of Cremona, *Retribution*, III, 38, p. 86. Cf. S. Georgieva, *The Byzantine Princesses...*, p. 166; J. Shepard, *A marriage...*, p. 126; В. Гюзелев, *Значението...*, p. 30; А. Николов, *Политическа...*, p. 234.

[37] J. Herrin, *Women in Purple. Rulers of Medieval Byzantium*, London 2002, p. 81; K. Kotsis, *Defining Female Authority in Eighth-Century Byzantium: the Numismatic Images of the Empress Irene (797–802)*, JLA 5.1, 2012, pp. 199–200.

[38] J. Shepard, *A marriage...*, pp. 141–143; Г. Атанасов, *Инсигниите на средновековните български владетели. Корони, скиптри, сфери, оръжия, костюми, накити*, Плевен 1999, pp. 98–99; И. Йорданов, *Корпус на печатите на Средновековна България*, София 2001, pp. 58–60; В. Гюзелев, *Значението...*, p. 27; И. Божилов, В. Гюзелев, *История на средновековна България. VII–XIV в.*, София 2006, pp. 275–276; Т. Тодоров, *България...*, pp. 156–159; idem, *Владетелският статут и титла на цар Петър I след октомври 927 г.: писмени сведения и сфрагистични данни (сравнителен анализ)*, [in:] *Юбилеен сборник. Сто години от рождението на д-р Васил Хараланов (1907–2007)*, Шумен 2008, pp. 99–101; С. Георгиева, *Жената в българското средновековие*, Пловдив 2011, pp. 313–315; M.J. Leszka, K. Marinow, *Carstwo...*, pp. 159–160.

arena (associated with Byzantium's recognition of his right to the title of emperor/tsar of the Bulgarians), are discussed elsewhere in this monograph. Here, on the other hand, we shall deal with a few questions of another kind, such as: Did Peter consider the opportunity to marry Maria an honor? Was this view shared by those around him, as well as by other contemporary European rulers?

Both of the above questions should, in fact, be answered in the positive. There can be no doubt that Maria and Peter's marriage was an unprecedented event – never before had such a high-ranking Byzantine woman, daughter and granddaughter of emperors, been married to a foreign monarch, ruling a people that had only become Christian some sixty years earlier. The momentousness of this act was hardly diminished by the fact that the young tsar's fiancée was not 'born in the purple[39].' The Byzantine-Bulgarian marriage was likely the talk of European courts, becoming a source of inspiration for rulers of other countries to aim for similar arrangements.

This assertion is confirmed by two sources: chapter 13 of the treatise *On the Governance of the Empire* by Constantine VII and the account by Liudprand of Cremona. The former work, written before 952, includes a series of specific arguments with which a *basileus* – Romanos II, to whom the work is dedicated, and his successors – should reject claims of foreign rulers who, referring to what happened in 927, should wish to arrange a marriage with a woman from the imperial family (either for themselves or for one of their sons). The Porphyrogennetos advised that, during such negotiations, Romanos I should be presented as a simpleton, who not only lacked the knowledge about the most basic customs of the Empire, but in fact knowingly disregarded them. Moreover, he ignored the law of the Church and the prohibition of Constantine I the Great, who supposedly strictly forbade his sons to enter into marriage with representatives of any of the foreign peoples, to the exception of the Franks. Constantine VII also advised emphasizing the low position of Christopher Lekapenos,

[39] S. G e o r g i e v a, *The Byzantine Princesses*..., p. 167; В. Г ю з е л е в, *Значението*..., p. 30; M.J. L e s z k a, K. M a r i n o w, *Carstwo*..., p. 158.

who was – according to him – merely the third in the hierarchy of the rulers, thus lacking any actual power[40].

In this part of the narrative, Porphyrogennetos undoubtedly vented his personal antipathy and resentment[41]. On the other hand, it is also clear from his reasoning that, during his reign, the tendency among foreign rulers to seek dynastic marriages with Constantinople had indeed increased; the 927 arrangement served as a pivotal precedent here. Reading chapter 13 of the treatise *On the Governance of the Empire*, one might even conclude that the rulers of the northern peoples, among them the Rus' and the Khazars, sought concessions on three specific points from the emperors: they wished to be sent imperial regalia, have the Byzantines disclose the secret formula for 'Greek fire,' and have them agree to a marriage between a Byzantine woman of high status with a representative of their own house[42].

Having died in 959, Constantine VII Porphyrogennetos did not live to see further such marriages, which he considered so abominable: Theophano only married Otto II in 972[43], while Constantine's own

---

[40] Constantine VII Porphyrogennetos, *On the Governance of the Empire*, 13, pp. 70–74. Cf. Г. Литаврин, *Константин Багрянородный о Болгарии и Болгарах*, [in:] *Сборник в чест на акад. Димитър Ангелов*, ed. В. Велков, София 1994, pp. 30–37; J. Herrin, *Theophano...*, p. 242; S. Georgieva, *The Byzantine Princesses...*, p. 167; Т. Тодоров, *Константин Багренородни...*, pp. 391–397; В. Гюзелев, *Значението...*, pp. 30–31; A. Paroń, "*Trzeba, abyś tymi oto słowami odparł i to niedorzeczne żądanie" – wokół De administrando imperio Konstantyna VII*, [in:] *Causa creandi. O pragmatyce źródła historycznego*, ed. S. Rosik, P. Wiszewski, Wrocław 2005, pp. 345–361; M.J. Leszka, K. Marinow, *Carstwo...*, p. 158; П. Павлов, *Години на мир...*, p. 411; С. Звездов, *Договорът от 927 година между България и Византия*, H.BJHE 23.3, 2015, p. 268; idem, *Българо-византийските отношения при цар Петър I*, София 2016, pp. 17–18.

[41] Д.И. Полывянный, *Царь Петр в исторической памяти болгарского средневековья*, [in:] *Средновековният българин и "другите". Сборник в чест на 60-годишнината на проф. дин Петър Ангелов*, ed. А. Николов, Г.Н. Николов, София 2013, p. 139.

[42] Constantine VII Porphyrogennetos, *On the Governance of the Empire*, 13, pp. 68–74.

[43] On the political and cultural consequences of this marriage see: I. Ševčenko, *Byzanz und der Westen im 10. Jahrhundert*, [in:] *Kunst im Zeitalter der Kaiserin Theophanu. Akten des Internationalen Colloquiums veranstaltet vom Schnütgen-Museum*,

granddaughter Anna married Vladimir I in 988/989. Some scholars are of the opinion that, in his last years, the 'purple-born' emperor had to counter the ambitions of another Rus' ruler – princess Olga, who sought to marry her son Svyatoslav to one of the emperor's descendants (either daughter or granddaughter). Seeking consent for such a marriage may have been one of the goals of her visit to Constantinople (most likely in 957). The Kievan ruler's plan was not well received by Constantine VII, however. The fiasco of the marriage negotiations likely deepened Olga's dissatisfaction with the results of her diplomatic mission, stressed by the author of the *Russian Primary Chronicle*. The memory of her far-reaching intentions did, however, survive in the Old Rus' historiographical tradition. According to experts on the matter, it may be reflected in the above-mentioned oldest Kievan chronicle, whose extant form dates back to the early years of the 12th century: it includes a seemingly completely improbable story of Constantine VII Porphyrogennetos proposing to marry Olga[44].

Neither Romanos II nor his successors heeded the advice laid out in the treatise *On the Governance of the Empire*, as can be seen from Liudprand of Cremona's account of his diplomatic mission to Constantinople in 968: his objective was to win Nikephoros II Phokas's approval for the marriage between the son of emperor Otto I with a member of the Byzantine

---

ed. A. von Euw, P. Schreiner, Köln 1993, pp. 5–30; H.K. Schulze, *Die Heiratsurkunde der Kaiserin Theophanu. Die griechische Kaiserin und das römisch-deutsche Reich 972–991*, Hannover 2007; M. Smorąg Różycka, *Cesarzowa Teofano i królowa Gertruda. Uwagi o wizerunkach władczyń w sztuce średniowiecznej na marginesie rozważań o miniaturach w Kodeksie Gertrudy*, [in:] *Gertruda Mieszkówna i jej rękopis*, ed. A. Andrzejuk, Radzymin 2013, pp. 129–133.

[44] *Russian Primary Chronicle*, AM 6463, pp. 61–64. Cf. J.P. Arrignon, *Les relations internationales de la Russie Kiévienne au milieu du Xe siècle et le baptême de la princesse Olga*, [in:] *Actes des congrès de la Société des historiens médiévistes de l'enseignement supérieur public. 9e congrès*, Dijon 1978, pp. 172–173; Г. Литаврин, *Византия, Болгария, Древняя Русь (IX–начало XII в.)*, Санкт-Петербург 2000, pp. 198, 211; А.В. Назаренко, *Древняя Русь на международных путях. Междисциплинарные очерки культурных, торговых, политических связей IX–XII вв.*, Москва 2001, p. 302; F. Tinnefeld, *Zum Stand der Olga – Diskussion*, [in:] *Zwischen Polis, Provinz und Peripherie. Beiträge zur byzantinischen Geschichte und Kultur*, ed. L.M. Hoffmann, A. Monchizadeh, Wiesbaden 2005, p. 557.

imperial family. The diplomat admitted that, during the negotiations, he brought up the marriage between the daughter of Christopher Lekapenos and Bulgarian tsar Peter. The argument, however, was rejected by the Greek side, as Liudprand was told that Maria's father was not a *porphyrogennetos* – a remark that could almost have been taken directly from Constantine VII's work[45].

To sum up, Peter could be confident that he was obtaining an honor that many other monarchs had sought in vain. It was most likely the desire to boast of his Byzantine wife that led him to consistently include her image (and in some cases – also her name) on official Bulgarian seals during the period 927–945. Notably, this was a wholly new practice in the self-presentation of the Preslav court – none of the female Bulgarian rulers before Maria (and none after her) were honored in this manner[46].

What is more, the marriage was not only a source of splendor for Peter, but also brought tangible political benefits with it. By marrying Maria in 927, Symeon's son entered the family that produced four of the five Roman emperors ruling at the time: Romanos I and his sons Christopher, Stephen and Constantine. Through his marriage to Maria, Peter also became closely tied to Constantine VII Porphyrogennetos. In 933, the list of his politically influential connections was further extended by Theophylaktos, the new patriarch of Constantinople. Thus, the alliance with the ambitious 'Lekapenos clan' may have appeared to the young Bulgarian ruler as having a considerable political potential.

Consequently, we should probably agree with those scholars who view the previously mentioned seals (depicting Peter and Maria) as artifacts

[45] Liudprand of Cremona, *Embassy*, 16, p. 194. Cf. J. Shepard, *A marriage*..., p. 122; В. Гюзелев, *Значението*..., p. 31.

[46] S. Georgieva, *The Byzantine Princesses*..., pp. 167, 201; В. Гюзелев, *Значението*..., p. 27. Only a few of the later Bulgarian royal women could boast such a distinction. Irene Palaiologina, wife of John Assen III (1279–1280) used her own seal. Among women depicted on coins were, e.g., Irene Komnene, regent for her son Michael I Assen (1246–1256); Theodora Palaiologina, wife of two consecutive tsars – Theodore Svetoslav (1300–1321) and Michael III Shishman (1323–1330); Theodora, second wife of John Alexander (1331–1371) and Anna, married to John Stratsimir (1356–1396). Г. Атанасов, *Инсигниите*..., pp. 190–192; В. Игнатов, *Българските*..., pp. 85–87, 89–90; С. Георгиева, *Жената*..., pp. 320–323, 348, 352–354.

of a commemorative and propagandist nature. The *sigilla* were created to commemorate the peace treaty of 927 as well as to highlight the significance of this event for the Bulgarian state and its ruler[47]. It is also possible that Symeon's son wanted to use them to show how much he valued the family connection with Romanos I. One more thing is worth noting in this connection – the name and depiction of Maria disappear from Peter's seals after 945 (at the time when the Lekapenos family was removed from power and when Constantine VII Porphyrogennetos began his sole rule)[48]. One may, therefore, get the impression that both Maria's inclusion into the self-presentation scheme of the Bulgarian ruler in 927, as well as her removal in 945, were dictated by diplomacy and foreign policy: in both cases, it was a bow to the reigning *basileus*[49].

3. Maria Lekapene as a Mother

There is no doubt that Maria fulfilled what medieval people considered the basic duty of a wife and empress consort – she gave Peter male offspring, providing him with an heir. Relating the events that occurred at the close of the 10th century, Byzantine chroniclers (among them John Skylitzes and John Zonaras) mention two of Maria and her husband's sons, who reigned in Bulgaria in succession: first Boris II, then

[47] И. Божилов, В. Гюзелев, *История*..., p. 276; M.J. Leszka, K. Marinow, *Carstwo*..., p. 159; И. Йорданов, *Корпус на средновековните български печати*, София 2016, p. 89.

[48] S. Runciman, *The Emperor*..., pp. 229–237; Г. Атанасов, *Инсигниите*..., p. 100; Т. Тодоров, *Константин Багренородни*..., pp. 396–397; А. Николов, *Политическа*..., pp. 269–278; Т. Тодоров, *България*..., p. 159; Г. Атанасов, *Печатите на българските владетели от IX–X в. в Дръстър (Силистра)*, [in:] *От тука започва България. Материали от втората национална конференция по история, археология и културен туризъм "Пътуване към България", Шумен 14–16.05. 2010 година*, ed. И. Йорданов, Шумен 2011, p. 289.

[49] И. Йорданов, *Корпус на печатите*..., p. 63; M.J. Leszka, K. Marinow, *Carstwo*..., p. 160.

Roman[50]. The couple had at least one more child, however. This is clear from the information included in the *Continuation of George the Monk*, as well as in the *Chronicle of Symeon Logothete*, and repeated in the *Continuation of Theophanes*: after the death of her father, Maria embarked on her final journey to Constantinople, taking her three children with her. Interestingly, while the phrasing in the original Greek version of these works does not specify the sex of the tsaritsa's children (μετὰ παίδων τριῶν)[51], the 14th century author of the Slavic translation of the *Chronicle of Symeon Logothete* altered the source's information, stating that she arrived in the city on the Bosporos with her three sons (**съ тримы сн҃овы**)[52].

Thus, in the literature on the subject we occasionally encounter the view that Maria and Peter had a third son aside from the male offspring noted by the Byzantine sources. He would have been Plenimir, whose name appears in the laudatory part of the *Synodikon of tsar Boril*, directly after the mention of Peter and before that of Boris and Romanos[53]. It cannot be ruled out that Plenimir was the first child of the imperial couple, who – because of a premature death or poor health – did not play any significant role in the history of the Bulgarian state. Consequently, he would not have been noted by the Byzantine chroniclers[54].

Ivan Duychev, in an article devoted to this character, drew attention to another interesting question: while both of Peter and Maria's sons present in the Byzantine chronicles bore the names of their great-grandfathers

---

[50] John Skylitzes, pp. 255, 288, 297, 310, 328, 329, 346; John Zonaras, XVI, 23, p. 495; XVII, 1, p. 522; XVII, 2, p. 529; XVII, 4, p. 536; XVII, 6, p. 547; XVII, 8, p. 560.

[51] Continuator of George the Monk, p. 913; Symeon Logothete, 136.67; Continuator of Theophanes, VI, 35, p. 422. A similar wording is found in the oldest translation of the *Continuation of George the Monk* into Slavic (as well as in the Old Rus' *Hellenic and Roman Chronicle* of the second redaction, based on the latter): **с троимъ дѣтеи**. Continuator of George the Monk (Slavic), 10, p. 566; *Hellenic and Roman Chronicle*, p. 501.

[52] Symeon Logothete (Slavic), p. 140.

[53] *Synodikon of Tsar Boril*, pp. 149–150; В. Игнатов, *Българските царици*..., p. 14; M.J. Leszka, K. Marinow, *Carstwo*..., p. 187.

[54] И. Дуйчев, *Българският княз Пленимир*, МПр 13.1, 1942, pp. 19–20; S. Georgieva, *The Byzantine Princesses*..., pp. 168–169.

(Bulgarian prince Boris-Michael and emperor Romanos I Lekapenos), the couple's hypothetical firstborn child would have been given the exceedingly rare Slavic name Plenimir[55]. It may be useful to examine the etymology of this anthroponym here. Excluding the possibility of an error on the part of the scribe who completed the late, 16th-century copy of the *Synodikon of Tsar Boril* in which we find the laudation, we could assume that the name had the shape **Плѣнимиръ**[56]. This is a compound consisting of two Old Church Slavic nouns: **плѣнъ** ('captivity, prize of war') and **миръ** ('peace'). As we saw earlier, Constantine VII Porphyrogennetos and the author of *On the Treaty with the Bulgarians* claim that one of the consequences of the peace of 927 was the exchange of prisoners, owing to which many Byzantine soldiers held in Bulgarian captivity could return to their homeland[57]. Perhaps this took place at the time (928) during which the Bulgarian imperial couple's firstborn entered the world? Maria Lekapene, aware of the propaganda significance of rulers' names (according to Liudprand of Cremona, she became known as Irene in 927), may have arranged for her eldest child to receive a symbolic name – one referring to the peace treaty concluded a few months earlier, and to the accompanying exchange of prisoners of war.

Maria and Peter may also have had one or several daughters. In the historiography, the two girls from the Bulgarian 'royal family' (βασιλικὸν γένος) who – according to Leo the Deacon – were sent to Constantinople in 969 as the spouses-to-be of Basil II and Constantine VIII have occasionally been considered to have been Maria and her husband's children[58].

---

[55] И. Дуйчев, *Българският княз...*, p. 20. John Skylitzes (p. 346) adds that Romanos was also called Symeon, in honor of his grandfather.

[56] *Synodikon of Tsar Boril*, pp. 149–150.

[57] Constantine VII Porphyrogennetos, *On the Governance of the Empire*, 13, p. 74; *On the Treaty with the Bulgarians*, 5, p. 260.105–110. Cf. Т. Тодоров, *Константин Багренородни...*, pp. 395–396; K. Marinow, *In the Shackles...*, p. 178; idem, *Peace...*, p. 85; M.J. Leszka, K. Marinow, *Carstwo...*, p. 156; С. Звездов, *Договорът...*, p. 267; K. Marinow, *Византийската имперска идея и претенциите на цар Симеон според словото "За мира с българите"*, *КМС* 25, 2016, p. 347, fn. 25; С. Звездов, *Българо-византийските отношения при цар Петър I...*, pp. 13–14.

[58] Leo the Deacon, V, 3, p. 79; И. Дуйчев, *Българският княз...*, p. 18; В. Игнатов, *Българските...*, p. 14.

Similar views have been expressed concerning the anonymous Bulgarian woman who became one of the wives of Vladimir I, prince of Rus', and who bore him two sons (the elder received the rather telling name of Boris-Romanos[59]). Both of these hypotheses, however, have to be rejected for chronological reasons. Rather, the princesses mentioned above may have been Maria's granddaughters and Boris II's daughters: born ca. 960, they may have been considered of appropriate age to become the fiancées of the sons of Romanos II and Theophano[60]. Similarly, even if we were to assume that Vladimir's Bulgarian wife was a very late child of Maria, it would be difficult to accept that she was the mother of prince Gleb-David, most likely still a teenager in the year of his death (1015). The woman in question – if we were to acknowledge the hypothesis of her Preslav origin in the first place – may have been a granddaughter of the Bulgarian tsaritsa (e.g. a child of Boris II, or of one of her daughters)[61].

---

[59] *Russian Primary Chronicle*, AM 6488, p. 81. А.А. Молчанов, *Владимир Мономах и его имена. К изучению княжеского именника Рюриковичей X–XII вв.*, Слав 2004.2, pp. 81–83; А.Ф. Литвина, Ф.Б. Успенский, *Выбор имени у русских князей в X–XVI вв. Династическая история сквозь призму антропонимики*, Москва 2006, pp. 477–478.

[60] S. Georgieva, *The Byzantine Princesses...*, p. 169; G. Atanasov, *On the Origin, Function and the Owner of the Adornments of the Preslav Treasure from the 10th century*, ABu 3.3, 1999, p. 91; idem, *Инсигниите...*, pp. 234–235; M.J. Leszka, K. Marinow, *Carstwo...*, p. 190.

[61] Based on anthroponomical material, certain contemporary Russian historians are inclined to consider the mother of Boris-Romanos and Gleb-David to have been a descendant of the Bulgarian royal family, albeit without specifying their exact relation to Maria Lekapene and Peter (А.А. Молчанов, *Владимир Мономах...*, pp. 81–83; А.Ф. Литвина, Ф.Б. Успенский, *Выбор...*, pp. 477–488). The literature on the subject, however, features several other views on her origins. Among other things, it has been assumed that she came from Volga Bulgaria (Е.В. Пчелов, *Генеалогия древнерусских князей IX–начала XI в.*, Москва 2001, pp. 202–204; В. Игнатов, *Българските царици...*, p. 109). An interesting point of view has also been put forth by Polish scholar Andrzej Poppe. He argues that the Bulgarian woman mentioned in the *Russian Primary Chronicle* is in fact the Byzantine Anna, and that the term used there should be considered not so much an ethnonym as a sobriquet. It would have been given to the 'purple-born' imperial daughter in Constantinople or in Rus' due to her connections to the court in Preslav – after all, tsaritsa Maria Lekapene was her aunt (A. Poppe, *La naissance du culte de Boris et Gleb*, CCM 24, 1981, p. 29; idem, *Walka o spuściznę po Włodzimierzu Wielkim 1015–1019*, KH 102.3–4, 1995, pp. 6–10). This view is shared by

Georgi Atanassov theorizes that the small diadem found in the so-called 'Preslav treasure' (which contained the imperial family's jewelry, hidden during the war of 969–971) may have belonged to one of the daughters of Maria Lekapene. The Bulgarian scholar is of the opinion that the girl accompanied her mother on one of her journeys to Constantinople, and that the diadem was an exquisite gift from her Byzantine relatives[62] – one of the many treasures that the tsaritsa, according to the aforementioned chroniclers, received from Romanos I Lekapenos[63].

In the literature on the subject, there have been occasional attempts to establish the time at which Maria's two sons (as well as the third, unnamed child) were born, based on the above-mentioned accounts in the Byzantine sources. After all, the anonymous Continuator of George the Monk and the authors dependent on him state that when the Bulgarian tsaritsa arrived in Constantinople for the final time, her father was no longer among the living[64]. Considering that Christopher Lekapenos died in August 931, one should assume that Maria's visit took place in the autumn of that year at the earliest. Numerous scholars tend to use this date to argue that the relations between the Empire and Bulgaria became cooler in the later period, so that Maria stopped visiting her relatives[65]. It should be pointed out, however, that the relevant sources do not suggest

---

Ukrainian researcher Nadezhda Nikitenko (Н.Н. Никитенко, *София Киевская и ее создатели. Тайны истории*, Каменец-Подольский 2014, pp. 106–107). A different opinion is presented e.g. by Alexandr Nazarenko (А.В. Назаренко, *Древняя Русь...*, p. 449). Finally, one should mention the rather controversial suppositions of certain Bulgarian historians that Boris-Romanos and Gleb-David were Vladimir and Anna's children, but that Anna, contrary to the testimony of Byzantine and Old Rus' chroniclers, was the daughter or perhaps granddaughter of Maria Lekapene and Peter (in the latter case, she would have been Boris II's daughter); И. Добрев, *Българите за руския народ, държава и култура*, София 2011, pp. 562–576.

[62] G. Atanasov, *On the Origin...*, pp. 91–92; idem, *Инсигниите...*, p. 235.

[63] Continuator of George the Monk, p. 913; Symeon Logothete, 136.67; Continuator of Theophanes, VI, 35, p. 422.

[64] Continuator of George the Monk, p. 913; Symeon Logothete, 136.67; Continuator of Theophanes, VI, 35, p. 422.

[65] И. Дуйчев, *Българският княз...*, p. 19; Г. Атанасов, *Инсигниите...*, p. 99; А. Николов, *Политическа мисъл...*, p. 244; Т. Тодоров, *България...*, p. 159; idem, *Владетелският...*, p. 101; Г. Атанасов, *Печатите...*, p. 289.

that Maria's final visit to the Byzantine capital took place immediately after her father's death. According to the chroniclers, the official reason for the Bulgarian tsaritsa's journey was the wish to visit her grandfather – therefore, all that we can conclude is that it took place prior to 944, when Romanos I Lekapenos was deposed[66]. Accordingly, the imperial couple's three children could have been born at any time between 928 and 944.

Maria, like many other medieval royal consorts, most likely wanted to fulfil her duty as soon as possible. At the time of Christopher's death, therefore, she could easily have been a mother of three already. It is difficult to say, however, whether she would have decided to take them on the rather long and exhausting journey as early as 931. They would have been between one and three years old at the time; it is doubtful that a responsible mother would have exposed an infant to hardships that could result in serious health issues. Rather, we should assume that Maria's final visit to Constantinople took place in 933/934, when her children were at the ages of three to six[67].

On the other hand, it cannot be completely ruled out that Boris and Roman were born considerably later than is commonly thought[68]. It should be borne in mind that Leo the Deacon, relating the events of 971, clearly mentions that Boris was a father of two infant children at the time[69]. Had he been born soon after his parents' wedding in 927, one would expect that in the 970s his children would have been fully grown.

---

[66] И. Дуйчев, *Българският княз...*, p. 19; S. Georgieva, *The Byzantine Princesses...*, p. 168.

[67] The remark about Maria's visits to Constantinople was placed by the Continuator of George the Monk (and, following him, by Symeon Logothete and the Continuator of Theophanes) between the information on Theophylaktos Lekapenos's elevation to the patriarchal see of Constantinople (February 933) and the note on the marriage of his brother Stephen as well as on the first raid by the Hungarians (April 934). Continuator of George the Monk, p. 913; Symeon Logothete, 136.67; Continuator of Theophanes, VI, 35, p. 422.

[68] It is possible that they were not among the children taken by Maria to Constantinople in 933/934 at all. Conversely, she may have been accompanied by her daughters, the prematurely deceased Plenimir, or another son who died before reaching adulthood.

[69] Leo the Deacon, VIII, 6, p. 136.

In summary, the existing source material does not unequivocally settle the question of how many children Peter and Maria had; the exact time of their birth likewise remains uncertain. In all likelihood, the imperial couple had three sons (Plenimir, Boris and Roman) and several daughters, whose names we do not know.

4. On the Bulgarian Throne at Peter's Side

Maria Lekapene was Bulgarian tsaritsa from October 927 until her death, most likely in the early 960s. Thus, she would have been on the Preslav throne for about thirty-five years. It is worth asking what role Maria Lekapene came to play in her new homeland, and what position she occupied as the wife of tsar Peter in the contemporary power structures.

Significantly, none of the surviving written sources mention Maria's activity in public affairs. We find no traces of the tsaritsa's independent actions even in the sphere traditionally assigned to a Christian empress consort: there are no accounts of her charitable or foundation activities, or of propagating and strengthening Christianity (such evidence exists in relation to the Rus' princesses of the same period, Olga and Anna Porphyrogennete).

Thus, the common view in older Bulgarian historiography according to which the tsaritsa enjoyed an exceptionally high position at the Preslav court – including real political power and the ensuing possibility of influencing Peter's decisions[70] – could only find confirmation in the sphragistic material. The latter includes, for example, the aforementioned lead *sigilla* from 927–945, on the reverse of which we find the depiction of the royal couple (based on the Byzantine model). The creation of

[70] В.Н. Златарски, *История*..., pp. 535–536; П. Мутафчиев, *История*..., p. 201. Cf. Г. Бакалов, *Средновековният български владетел. Титулатура и инсигнии*, ²София 1995, p. 183; В. Гюзелев, *Значението*..., p. 27; В. Игнатов, *Българските царици*..., p. 14.

such artifacts can hardly be considered the result of Maria's personal ambition and independent efforts, not consulted with her husband and his advisers. The seal images in question were certainly not a reflection of the status of Peter's spouse as an actual co-ruler, as some researchers think[71]. As previously mentioned, such items served primarily to commemorate the events of 927. They were also a convenient means of propaganda, through which the Bulgarian ruler was able to express his attachment to the Lekapenoi family; finally, they served to legitimize Peter's title. In this context, Maria – granddaughter of the Byzantine emperor – was merely a rather passive vehicle of imperial status; it was thanks marrying her that the Bulgarian monarch gained the formal right to use the title of tsar/emperor[72].

It is worth noting that in the social realities of the 10th century, the expression of appreciation for the spouse's lineage – and the desire to flaunt it to one's subjects, as well as other courts – was by no means equivalent to granting her even the slightest degree of tangible political power. In fact, it did not even guarantee fulfilling elementary obligations and being respectful towards her. Let us refer once again to the relationship between the prince of Rus' and Anna Porphyrogennete, described in the sources in much more detail than that of the Bulgarian royal couple. Much like Peter, Vladimir I put his wife in the limelight of public

---

[71] S. Georgieva, *The Byzantine Princesses…*, p. 168; И. Йорданов, *Корпус на печатите…*, p. 59; С. Георгиева, *Жената…*, pp. 313–314; Д.И. Полывянный, *Царь Петр…*, p. 138; П. Павлов, *Години…*, p. 413; И. Йорданов, *Корпус на средновековните…*, p. 89.

[72] Г. Бакалов, *Царската промулгация на Петър и неговите приемници в светлината на българо-византийските дипломатически отношения след договора от 927 г.*, ИП 39.6, 1983, p. 36; F. Tinnefeld, *Byzantinische auswärtige Heiratspolitik vom 9. zum 12 Jahrhundert*, Bsl 54.1, 1993, p. 23; Г. Бакалов, *Средновековният български владетел…*, p. 170; Г. Атанасов, *Инсигниите…*, pp. 96–98; И. Йорданов, *Корпус на печатите…*, p. 59; И. Божилов, В. Гюзелев, *История…*, p. 276; А. Николов, *Политическа…*, p. 239; Т. Тодоров, *България…*, p. 163; P. Boroń, *Kniaziowie, królowie, carowie… Tytuły i nazwy władców słowiańskich we wczesnym średniowieczu*, Katowice 2010, p. 40; С. Георгиева, *Жената…*, p. 314; M.J. Leszka, K. Marinow, *Carstwo…*, pp. 159–160; С. Звездов, *Договорът…*, pp. 267–268; idem, *Българо-византийските отношения при цар Петър I…*, p. 14; Z.A. Brzozowska, *Rola carycy Marii-Ireny Lekapeny w recepcji elementów bizantyńskiego modelu władzy w pierwszym państwie bułgarskim*, VP 66, 2016, p. 452.

life, making it clear that she was 'born in the purple' – daughter and sister of Constantinopolitan emperors. While no seals of this ruler survive, while the golden and silver coins minted by this him only show the enthroned prince himself[73], it is nonetheless known that princess Anna's name was mentioned in official documents (e.g. in the short redaction of the so-called *Church Statute of prince Vladimir*)[74]; besides, her painted image adorned the Church of Divine Wisdom in Kiev[75], and the memory of her imperial origins survived in later Rus' historiography.

On the other hand, the ambiguous chronology of the birth of Vladimir's sons has allowed certain researchers to speculate that the Rus' prince may have moved away from Anna due to her infertility. Such opinions might be considered exaggerated, although one other issue is clear – even if the Porphyrogennete remained the sole official spouse of Vladimir I until her death in 1011/1012, it did not hinder her husband from pursuing erotic relationships with (numerous) other women[76].

There is also no evidence in the source material to support the claim, advanced by certain Bulgarian scholars, that Maria served as a 'Byzantine spy' at the Preslav court[77]. Such views are based wholly on the aforementioned enigmatic remark by the Continuator of George the Monk (further repeated by Symeon Logothete and the author of the *Continuation of Theophanes*) on how the tsaritsa traveled to Constantinople several times, accompanied by her children, to visit her father and grandfather – the latter being emperor Romanos I Lekapenos[78]. It goes without saying

---

[73] М.П. Сотникова, И.Г. Спасский, *Тысячелетие древнейших монет России. Сводный каталог русских монет X–XI вв.*, Ленинград 1983, pp. 60–81, 115–180.

[74] Я.Н. Щапов, *Княжеские уставы и церковь в Древней Руси XI–XIV вв.*, Москва 1972, pp. 115–127; idem, *Древнерусские княжеские уставы XI–XV вв.*, Москва 1976, p. 66. For a summary of the discussion on the authenticity of the *Church Statute of Prince Vladimir* and selected works on the subject cf.: G. Podskalsky, *Chrześcijaństwo i literatura teologiczna na Rusi Kijowskiej (988–1237)*, transl. J. Zychowicz, Kraków 2000, pp. 270–272.

[75] Н.Н. Никитенко, *София Киевская...*, pp. 75–117.

[76] А.Ю. Карпов, *Владимир Святой*, Москва 2004, pp. 287–288.

[77] В.Н. Златарски, *История...*, pp. 535–536; П. Мутафчиев, *История...*, p. 201; В. Игнатов, *Българските царици...*, p. 14.

[78] Continuator of George the Monk, p. 913; Symeon Logothete, 136.67; Continuator of Theophanes, VI, 35, p. 422.

that, during such visits, Maria might have provided her Byzantine relatives with information about the plans and doings of her husband; however, we do not have sufficient source material to determine what was discussed during her sojourns in the Byzantine capital. It should be emphasized that Maria and her children's journeys to Constantinople could not have taken place without Peter's knowledge and consent. It would have been unlikely for the tsar to be amenable to such undertakings – and to allow them – had they been detrimental to the Bulgarian reason of state.

Unfortunately, the paucity of source material renders it impossible to prove another hypothesis. As I have mentioned before, the Byzantine historians agree that Maria, both in 927 and during her later visits to the empire's capital, received innumerable riches from her relatives[79]. One is led to wonder whether these goods were not offered for a specific purpose: after all, with their aid, coupled with a modicum of diplomatic skills, Maria could have won over many of the people surrounding Peter, thus gaining some influence over his policies.

A view that needs to be debunked as a historiographical myth concerns the alleged far-reaching Byzantinisation of Old Bulgarian culture during Maria Lekapene's presence at the court. As correctly pointed out by Jonathan Shepard, Bulgaria had been drawn into the sphere of Byzantine civilization much earlier, while the reception of the elements of Byzantine traditions was a long-lasting process. Thus, in 927, our heroine arrived in a country whose political and intellectual elites were already quite familiar with the culture of Eastern Christianity, as well as with the views on monarchy prevalent in Constantinople[80]. Suffice it to say that during the reign of Peter's father Symeon I the Great – a ruler educated in Constantinople and undoubtedly fascinated with the Eastern Roman ideals of imperial power[81] – several Greek legal compilations had already been adapted in Bulgaria. These included fragments of the

---

[79] Continuator of George the Monk, p. 907, 913; Symeon Logothete, 136.51; 136.67; Continuator of Theophanes, VI, 23, 35, pp. 415, 422.

[80] J. Shepard, *A marriage...*, p. 140.

[81] M.J. Leszka, *The Monk versus the Philosopher. From the History of the Bulgarian-Byzantine War 894–896*, SCer 1, 2011, pp. 55–57; idem, *Symeon...*, pp. 29–34.

Ekloga, *Nomokanon of Fifty Titles* and *Nomokanon of Fourteen Titles*[82], as well as deacon Agapetos's *Ekthesis*, 72 chapters of advice to emperor Justinian I the Great (a brief treatise providing a synthetic exposition of Byzantine 'imperial theology'), translated into Slavic[83].

The fact that, by the year 927, the Preslav court was well-acquainted with the accomplishments of Byzantine civilization does not, however, exclude the possibility of Maria's personal impact on her new milieu. The tsaritsa most likely attempted to embed in the Bulgarian capital the customs and elements of court ceremonial that she knew from the Constantinople palace[84]; nevertheless, due to insufficient source material, we are unable to determine the scope of her influence. Most likely, it did not extend beyond the walls of the tsar's seat and the narrow circle of people directly surrounding her[85]. The archaeological material (e.g. the aforementioned 'Preslav treasure' as well as the most recent discoveries of Bulgarian researchers) allows us to conclude that during Maria's time, Byzantine models of female fashion became commonplace in Preslav; in that period, jewelry produced in the workshops of Constantinople came to be greatly desired by ladies from the highest social circles[86].

Maria and Peter's reign did see, however, a fundamental shift in the manner in which medieval Bulgarians perceived their tsaritsa and her role within the state. Until 927, women occupying the throne in Preslav – unlike contemporary Byzantine empresses – had been almost invisible

[82] Г. Бакалов, *Средновековният...*, p. 136; K. Maksimovich, *Byzantine Law in Old Slavonic Translations and the Nomocanon of Methodius*, Bsl 65, 2007, p. 10; Т. Славова, *Юридическа литература*, [in:] *История на българската средновековна литература*, ed. А. Милтенова, София 2008, pp. 195–197.

[83] А. Николов, *Старобългарският превод на "Изложение на поучителни глави към император Юстиниан" от дякон Агапит и развитието на идеята за достойнството на българския владетел в края на IX – началото на X в.*, Pbg 24.3, 2000, pp. 77–85; idem, *Политическа...*, pp. 214–230, 250–268.

[84] J. Shepard, *A marriage...*, pp. 140–141; M.J. Leszka, *Wizerunek...*, pp. 124–125; idem, *Образът на българския цар Борис II във византийските извори*, SB 25, 2006, p. 146.

[85] П. Павлов, *Години...*, p. 416.

[86] G. Atanasov, *On the Origin...*, pp. 85–92; idem, *Инсигниите...*, pp. 193, 230–235; С. Тодорова-Чанева, *Женският накит от епохата на Първото българско царство. VII–XI в.*, София 2009, pp. 26–28.

in the public sphere: they were not mentioned in official diplomatic correspondence, nor were their images included on coins or seals. The sole predecessor of our protagonist whose name survived in historical texts is another Maria, wife of Boris-Michael; meanwhile, both of Symeon I the Great's spouses (including Peter's mother) will forever remain anonymous[87]. As Magda Hristodulova and Sashka Georgieva rightly observe, Maria Lekapene should be considered the first medieval Bulgarian female royal to enter the public sphere[88]. This elevation in the status of the Preslav tsaritsa during this era can be associated with the introduction of the Byzantine view regarding the role of the empress within the state to Old Bulgarian culture[89].

There can be no doubt that Maria's titulature was modeled on the appellations used by Constantinopolitan empresses. On the official seals of the Bulgarian royal couple, produced soon after 927, we find a Greek inscription in which Maria and Peter are titled emperors of the Bulgarians: Πέτρος καὶ Μαρίας βασιλεῖς τῶν Βουλγάρων[90]. During the 940s, the writing accompanying the images of the couple was modified somewhat; the most likely reconstruction is Πέτρος καὶ Μαρίας ἐν Χριστῷ αὔγουστοι βασιλεῖς or Πέτρος καὶ Μαρίας ἐν Χριστῷ αὐτοκράτορες βασιλεῖς Βουλγάρων[91]. Thus, the analysis of the sigillographic evidence allows us to state that

---

[87] Г. Атанасов, *Инсигниите...*, pp. 182, 184; В. Игнатов, *Българските царици...*, pp. 9–12.

[88] М. Христодулова, *Титул и регалии болгарской владетельницы в эпоху средневековья (VII–XIV вв.)*, EB 1978.3, p. 142; С. Георгиева, *Жената...*, pp. 312, 352.

[89] J. Herrin, *The Imperial Feminine in Byzantium*, PP 169, 2000, pp. 5–35 [= J. Herrin, *Unrivalled Influence: Women and Empire in Byzantium*, Princeton 2013, pp. 161–193].

[90] It should not be considered surprising that Maria and Peter are described here with the term βασιλεῖς. In Byzantine sphragistics and numismatics, this was the accepted form of describing two co-rulers, regardless of their sex. For example, on the coins minted in the years 914–919, Zoe Karbonopsina and her minor son Constantine VII Porphyrogennetos were titled βασιλεῖς Ῥωμαίων (A.R. Bellinger, Ph. Grierson, *Catalogue...*, p. 12).

[91] J. Shepard, *A marriage...*, p. 142; Г. Атанасов, *Инсигниите...*, pp. 98–99; И. Йорданов, *Корпус на печатите...*, pp. 58–60; В. Гюзелев, *Значението...*, p. 27; И. Божилов, В. Гюзелев, *История...*, pp. 275–276; Т. Тодоров, *България...*, pp. 156–159; idem, *Владетелският...*, pp. 99–101; С. Георгиева, *Жената...*, p. 313; M.J. Leszka, K. Marinow, *Carstwo...*, pp. 159–160; И. Йорданов, *Корпус на средновековните...*, pp. 90–95.

Maria used the titles conventionally worn by women reigning in the Byzantine capital: *basilissa* and *augusta*[92].

We also find some interesting information in the works of Byzantine chroniclers. The anonymous Continuator of George the Monk, Symeon Logothete and – dependent on both of them – the Continuator of Theophanes noted a particularly significant detail: Maria Lekapene, just after her marriage with Peter, was proclaimed 'ruler of Bulgarians' (δέσποινα Βουλγάρων) in Constantinople[93]. It is worth nothing that the term found here – *despoina* – was, according to numerous researches, an appellation used by Byzantine empresses interchangeably with the titles of *augusta* and *basilissa*[94].

The sources mentioned above do not, however, allow us to provide a definitive answer to the question of how Maria's Slavic subjects addressed her. Given that the tsaritsa does not appear in a single original medieval Bulgarian text, a scholar studying the titulature of Peter's wife is forced to rely on the analysis of Slavic translations of Byzantine chronicles. The author of the oldest translation of the *Continuation of George the Monk*, writing – as mentioned before – at the close of the 10th century or during the first decades of the 11th century, translated the passage about the title granted to Maria in 927 with extreme fidelity. The Greek term *despoina* is – in accordance with its etymology – rendered as *vladyčica*, i.e. 'female ruler' (причетася моужю црю и владычица блъгаром нарена)[95].

---

[92] Z.A. Brzozowska, *Cesarzowa Bułgarów, Augusta i Bazylisa – Maria-Irena Lekapena i transfer bizantyńskiej idei kobiety–władczyni (imperial feminine) w średniowiecznej Bułgarii*, SMer 17, 2017, p. 18.

[93] Continuator of George the Monk, p. 907; Symeon Logothete, 136.51; Continuator of Theophanes, VI, 23, p. 415.

[94] S. Maslev, *Die staatsrechtliche Stellung der byzantinischen Kaiserinnen*, Bsl 27, 1966, p. 310; E. Bensammar, *La titulature de l'impératrice et sa signification. Recherches sur les sources byzantines de la fin du VIIIe siècle à la fin du XIIe siècle*, B 46, 1976, pp. 270, 286–287; L. Garland, *Byzantine Empresses. Women and Power in Byzantium AD 527–1204*, London–New York 1999, p. 2; B. Hill, *Imperial Women in Byzantium 1025–1204. Power, Patronage and Ideology*, New York 1999, pp. 102–117; L. James, *Empresses and Power in Early Byzantium*, Leicester 2001, pp. 118–127; Z.A. Brzozowska, *Cesarzowa...*, p. 5.

[95] Continuator of George the Monk (Slavic), 7, p. 562; А. Николов, *Политическа...*, pp. 134, 236.

In another Slavic translation of this chronicle, completed in the Balkans in the 14th century, we find a notable semantic shift: the text states outright that Maria was called *carica* (tsaritsa, empress) of the Bulgarians (**ц҃рю припрѧжесѧ мѫжꙋ и царица Блъгаромь наречесѧ**)[96]. One can suspect that the latter term was the most popular appellation used in Preslav when referring to Peter's wife. At that time, it most likely took the form *cěsarica*. In the subsequent centuries, it went through several phonetic changes (*cěsarica* ≥ *cesarica* ≥ *cьsarica* ≥ *carica*), acquiring its final form known from later works: *carica*[97].

The *Book of Ceremonies* by Constantine VII Porphyrogennetos confirms that during the 10th century, the Bulgarian tsaritsa was listed in the official diplomatic protocol. The imperial author, who was one of the eyewitnesses of the ceremonies that accompanied the signing of the 927 peace treaty, admitted that the status of the Preslav monarch had changed during his reign: he had become a 'spiritual son' of the *basileus*. Notably, however, the 'purple-born' author does not mention any alteration in the Bulgarian tsaritsa's titulature that would have accompanied this – according to him, both before and after 927 she was to be addressed *by God archontissa of Bulgaria* (ἐκ Θεοῦ ἀρχόντισσα Βουλγαρίας)[98].

The placing of Maria's image on the lead seals from the years 927–945 should also be considered a result of transplanting Byzantine traditions onto Bulgarian soil. Scholars who claim that portraying the ruler's wife

---

[96] Symeon Logothete (Slavic), p. 137; А. Николов, *Политическа...*, pp. 134, 236.

[97] G. Moravcsik, *Zur Geschichte des Herrschertitels "caesar>царь"*, ЗРВИ 8, 1963, p. 234; L. Moszyński, *Staro-cerkiewno-słowiańskie apelatywy określające osoby będące u władzy*, BP 2, 1985, p. 44; Г. Бакалов, *Средновековният...*, pp. 155–158; Z.A. Brzozowska, *Geneza tytułu "car" w świetle zabytków średniowiecznego piśmiennictwa słowiańskiego*, WS 46, 2012, pp. 36–38; eadem, *Car i caryca czy cesarz i cesarzowa Bułgarów? Tytulatura Piotra i Marii-Ireny Lekapeny w średniowiecznych tekstach słowiańskich (Jak powinniśmy nazywać władców bułgarskich z X stulecia)*, WS 62, 2017, pp. 17–26.

[98] Constantine VII Porphyrogennetos, *The Book of Ceremonies*, II, 47, pp. 681–682; М. Христодулова, *Титул...*, p. 142; Г. Бакалов, *Царската...*, p. 37; idem, *Средновековният...*, pp. 171–172; Т. Тодоров, *България...*, p. 152; idem, *Владетелският...*, p. 95; P. Boroń, *Kniaziowie...*, pp. 40–41; M.J. Leszka, K. Marinow, *Carstwo...*, pp. 206–207.

on an official *sigillum* was a phenomenon characteristic only of 10th-century Bulgaria, with no analogue in Byzantine sigillography or numismatics, are mistaken[99]. The tradition of portraying empresses (mothers, sisters, wives and daughters of the *basileis*) on coinage and seals was cultivated in Byzantium – albeit with interruptions – since the 4th century. It is worth noting that the depiction of the empress had only disappeared from the coins and sigillographic material created within the Empire a few years before the signing of the 927 peace treaty, due to the 919 deposition (termination of regency) of Zoe Karbonopsina, mother of Constantine VII[100]. Still, the practice was not discontinued in the later period: towards the end of his life, Peter could see Byzantine coins and seals with the image of empress Theophano, as regent for her minor sons[101].

The similarity between the seal images of the Bulgarian royal couple and the analogous depictions of Zoe and Constantine VII Porphyrogennetos from 914–919 is striking. Nearly all of the gold coins and lead *sigilla* produced on Zoe orders were made according to one and the same design, with the obverse portraying Christ or the Mother of God, and the reverse – a likeness of the rulers. Constantine is on the left side of the composition, with Zoe to the right; they are holding the patriarchal cross between them, and on some of the artifacts, the mother's hand is above that of her son. The images are accompanied by an inscription identifying them as βασιλεῖς Ῥωμαίων. One is, therefore, led to conclude that the creators of the Bulgarian *sigillum* modeled it on the Byzantine artifacts from 914–919[102].

---

[99] Г. Атанасов, *Инсигниите...*, pp. 98, 184; Т. Тодоров, *България...*, pp. 162–163; idem, *Владетелският...*, p. 104.

[100] S. Maslev, *Die staatsrechtliche...*, p. 325; Ph. Grierson, *Byzantine Coins*, London–Berkeley–Los Angeles 1982, pp. 179–184; A.R. Bellinger, Ph. Grierson, *Catalogue...*, pp. 12, 530–569; L. Garland, *Byzantine Empresses...*, pp. 120–121; Z.A. Brzozowska, *Cesarzowa...*, p. 16.

[101] S. Maslev, *Die staatsrechtliche...*, p. 326; Ph. Grierson, *Byzantine Coins...*, p. 184; A.R. Bellinger, Ph. Grierson, *Catalogue...*, p. 12; L. Garland, *Byzantine Empresses...*, p. 271; Z.A. Brzozowska, *Cesarzowa...*, p. 16.

[102] J. Shepard, *A marriage...*, pp. 143–144; Z.A. Brzozowska, *Cesarzowa Bułgarów...*, pp. 16–17.

Curiously, a dig in Preslav uncovered a lead *sigillum* from the 10th–11th century layer, almost entirely devoid of figural elements, belonging – according to the inscription – to *basilissa* Maria (Μαρήᾳ βασήλησᾳ). Some scholars are of the opinion that the artifact could be Maria's personal seal, manufactured after 945[103]. The use of a dedicated *sigillum privatum* by the Bulgarian tsaritsa would provide another piece of evidence suggesting that Byzantine ideas concerning the role of the imperial spouse became widespread in 10th-century Preslav. Suffice it to say that there are extant 10th–11th century seals of Byzantine empresses (e.g. Theodora), of eminent Constantinople ladies (usually titled *zoste patrikia*)[104], and of Rus' princesses (e.g. of Maria, daughter of Constantine IX Monomachos), the latter far from ignorant of the status of women at the palace in Constantinople[105].

Seal depictions are also the sole type of sources based on which one might attempt to reconstruct the official court dress of the Bulgarian tsaritsa in the 10th century, along with her insignia. No such data is available from archaeological digs, even from the aforementioned 'Preslav treasure.' As Georgi Atanassov's research shows, the diadem found in the collection could not have belonged to Maria, as it was intended for a very young woman – one of the daughters or granddaughters of the tsaritsa[106].

Since Maria and Peter were depicted on all of the *sigilla* holding the patriarchal cross, we are unable to conclude whether the Bulgarian

[103] Т. Михайлова, *Печат на "Мария Василиса" от Преслав*, НСЕ 3.2, 2007, pp. 39–41; Т. Тодоров, *Владетелският...*, pp. 101–102; И. Йорданов, *Корпус на средновековните...*, pp. 119–121.

[104] S. Maslev, *Die staatsrechtliche...*, p. 324; Ph. Grierson, *Byzantine Coins...*, pp. 175, 178; A.R. Bellinger, Ph. Grierson, *Catalogue...*, pp. 12, 428, 457–465; L. Garland, *Byzantine Empresses...*, pp. 102–103; В.С. Шандровская, *Печати титулованных женщин Византии*, АДСВ 33, 2002, pp. 89–101; J. Herrin, *Women in Purple...*, p. 191; Н. Кънев, *Византийската титла патрикия-зости (IX–XI в.). Приносът на сфрагистиката за попълване на листата на носителките на титлата*, Истор 4, 2011, pp. 191–198.

[105] В.Л. Янин, *Актовые печати Древней Руси X–XV вв.*, vol. I, *Печати X – начала XIII в.*, Москва 1970, pp. 17–19, 33, 130, 173, 183–184, 210–211.

[106] G. Atanasov, *On the Origin...*, pp. 81–94; idem, *Инсигниите...*, pp. 224–243.

tsaritsa used a scepter and a sphere, i.e. the insignia we find in depictions of Byzantine empresses of the 8th–9th centuries. The diadem and robes worn by Maria as portrayed on the artifact under examination do bear a marked resemblance to the elements of clothing depicted on seals and coins of Zoe Karbonopsina (914–919), as well as on a mid-10th century ivory tablet showing a full-figure Byzantine imperial couple: Romanos II and Bertha-Eudokia[107].

The diadem on Maria's head is a middle Byzantine *stemma* of the female type, differing from the male variant in its ornamentation. On many of the seals of Maria and Peter from 927– 945, we see long, shoulder-length *prependoulia* (triple pearl pendants), as well as a richly decorated headband with a cross on top and two conical pinnacles on each side[108]. Due to the poor state of preservation of the seals' outer parts, it is significantly more challenging for scholars to ascertain what type of robe the tsaritsa is wearing: according to some researchers, it is a *loros*, according to others – a chlamys[109]. Both of these, we may note, were a part of the official court attire of Byzantine empresses[110].

---

[107] Г. Атанасов, *Инсигниите...*, pp. 99, 186, 256; M.G. Parani, *The Romanos Ivory and the New Tokali Kilise: Imperial Costume as a Tool for Dating Byzantine Art*, CAr 49, 2001, pp. 15–28; Т. Тодоров, *България...*, p. 163; idem, *Владетелският...*, p. 104.

[108] J. Shepard, *A marriage...*, p. 144; Г. Атанасов, *Инсигниите...*, pp. 185–186; И. Йорданов, *Корпус на печатите...*, pp. 58–59; Т. Тодоров, *България...*, pp. 162, 255–256; idem, *Владетелският...*, p. 103; Г. Атанасов, *Печатите...*, p. 287; Н. Кънев, *Четири непубликувани оловни печата от района на Шумен*, Истор 5, 2012, p. 63.

[109] J. Shepard, *A marriage...*, p. 144; Г. Атанасов, *Инсигниите...*, p. 186; И. Йорданов, *Корпус на печатите...*, pp. 58–59; Т. Тодоров, *България...*, pp. 162, 255–256; idem, *Владетелският...*, p. 103; Г. Атанасов, *Печатите...*, p. 287; Н. Кънев, *Четири...*, p. 63; П. Павлов, *Години...*, p. 432.

[110] A.R. Bellinger, Ph. Grierson, *Catalogue...*, pp. 122–123; J. Herrin, *The Imperial Feminine...*, p. 16; M.G. Parani, *The Romanos Ivory...*, p. 18; Z.A. Brzozowska, *Cesarzowa...*, p. 18.

5. Maria's Death

Two Byzantine authors mention Maria's death in their chronicles: John Skylitzes and John Zonaras (relying on the former). The account of interest to us is located in the part of the narrative devoted to the final stage of emperor Romanos II's life[111]. Thus, several scholars are inclined to assume that Peter's wife died at the same time as Constantine VII Porphyrogennetos's son, i.e. in 963[112].

Nonetheless, the particulars of the two chroniclers' narrative need to be taken into account. They mention Maria's demise in a somewhat incidental manner, focusing their attention on something rather different: Peter's efforts to renew the peace treaty of 927. The necessity to reconfirm the provisions of the treaty – by then decades old – was the result of the accession of a new emperor in Constantinople, not of the Bulgarian tsaritsa's death[113]. Hence, the year 963 should be considered a *terminus ante quem* of Maria's death, rather than its specific date. Perhaps, then, those scholars who argue that Maria departed this life in the early 960s are correct[114].

An interesting aspect of the issue of dating Maria's death has been illuminated by Todor Todorov. The scholar draws attention to the following fact: Liudprand of Cremona, who mentioned Symeon I the Great, Romanos I Lekapenos, Christopher, Maria and Peter in his *Antapodosis* (written in the years 958–962), pointed out that the Bulgarian tsar was the only one still of among the living. Perhaps, then, the tsaritsa – like her father-in-law, grandfather and father – died somewhat earlier than

[111] John Skylitzes, p. 255; John Zonaras, XVI, 23, p. 495; John Zonaras (Slavic), p. 146.

[112] S. Georgieva, *The Byzantine Princesses*..., pp. 169–170; Т. Тодоров, *България*..., p. 160; idem, *Владетелският*..., p. 102; С. Звездов, *Българо-византийските отношения при цар Петър*, Мин 2016.3, p. 15.

[113] M.J. Leszka, K. Marinow, *Carstwo*..., p. 174.

[114] J. Shepard, *A marriage*..., p. 147; С. Звездов, *Българо-византийските отношения при цар Петър*..., p. 15; idem, *Българо-византийските отношения при цар Петър I*..., pp. 44–45.

is commonly assumed, i.e. sometime before the bishop of Cremona started writing his account[115].

At this point, it is also worth noting that the literature on the subject features occasional attempts to link Maria's death with the removal of her name and images from the official seals of the Bulgarian monarch. If one were to accept this assumption, one would have to date Maria's demise significantly earlier, around 945[116]. However, it would be rather difficult to reconcile such dating with John Skylitzes' account.

We do not know anything about the circumstances of Maria's death. We can only guess that she ended her life as a lay person, without donning monastic robes in her later years. It seems that if the tsaritsa had decided to undertake such transition, it would have been noted by Bulgarian writers, who devoted their attention primarily to those female royals who ended their earthly existence in a monastery[117].

The fact that Maria showed no interest in living in a monastic community may have been one of the reasons why she was almost entirely absent from the historical memory of medieval Bulgarians. It is worth asking what other factors determined why Maria, a woman who hailed from an imperial family and whose marriage to Peter was a point of pride for him and his subjects, was forgotten during subsequent centuries.

Among the causes of this phenomenon, one should indicate primarily the lack of a native, Old Bulgarian historiographical tradition. After all, there is not a single extant chronicle from tsar Peter's times that would include a description and evaluation of his rule. It should be pointed out that the memory of the role of princess Anna Porphyrogennete, wife of Vladimir I, in the process of Christianization of East Slavs survived in medieval Rus' writings mainly owing to the account in the *Russian Primary Chronicle* (the work that inspired the creators of the subsequent annals). The Old Bulgarian authors, on the other hand, did not create

---

[115] Т. Тодоров, *България...*, p. 161; idem, *Владетелският...*, p. 103.

[116] J. Shepard, *A marriage...*, p. 147; В. Гюзелев, *Значението...*, p. 27; Т. Тодоров, *България...*, pp. 160–161; idem, *Владетелският...*, pp. 102–103.

[117] Г. Николов, *Български царици от Средновековието в "ангелски образ"*, ГСУ. НЦСВПИД 93(12), 2003, pp. 299–303.

their own vision of Peter and Maria's reign, one that would have been independent of Byzantine chronicles translated into Slavic.

The fact that the sources dedicated to tsar Peter as a saint of the Bulgarian Church are silent on the subject of Maria may be explained by the specific character of this ruler's cult. It has been noted repeatedly in the literature on the subject that, contrary to many other monarchs from the sphere of *Slavia Orthodoxa*, he was worshipped not as the one responsible for Christianizing his country, but as the saint who deepened the Christian piety of Bulgarians. For this reason, works devoted to Peter focus on monastic themes in particular. They highlight the spiritual connection between the ruler and St. John of Rila, as well as his personal predilection for monastic life and the fact that he accepted the Little Schema near the end of his life[118]. There were even frequent efforts, for example in the *Tale of the Prophet Isaiah* or in the 13th century *Service of St. Tsar Peter*, to paint the picture of Symeon's son as a man who lived a semi-ascetic life and remained unmarried[119]. In this model, there was simply no room for a woman or wife, even one of such high birth as Peter's Byzantine consort – a daughter and granddaughter of Constantinopolitan emperors.

[118] I. Biliarsky, *Saint Jean de Rila et saint tsar Pierre. Les destins des deux cultes du Xe siecle*, [in:] *Byzantium and the Bulgarians (1018–1185)*, ed. K. Nikolaou, K. Tsiknakis, Athens 2008, pp. 172–174; idem, *St. Peter (927–969), Tsar of the Bulgarians*, [in:] *State and Church. Studies in Medieval Bulgaria and Byzantium*, ed. V. Gjuzelev, K. Petkov, Sofia 2011, pp. 187–186; M.J. Leszka, *Rola cara Piotra (927–969) w życiu bułgarskiego Kościoła. Kilka uwag*, VP 66, 2016, pp. 435–437.

[119] *Tale of the Prophet Isaiah*, p. 17; *Service of St. Tsar Peter*, p. 392. Cf. Д.И. Полывянный, *Царь Петр...*, pp. 143–145.

V

Mirosław J. Leszka
Kirił Marinow

The Internal Situation

1. Fighting Internal Opposition

1.1. John's Plot

Peter, soon after concluding peace with Byzantium and arriving with Maria in Preslav, found himself faced with a plot headed by his brother John. This event likely happened in 928[1]. John's goal was to remove Peter from the Bulgarian throne, and its takeover.

The fundamental source of information about this endeavour is the Byzantine text discussed herein. It states the following:

[1] Based on the sources at our disposal, it is not possible to precisely date this event. The Byzantine authors placed it in their narratives between the conclusion of peace with Byzantium (October 927) and Michael's rebellion. The latter is traditionally dated to 928, on the assumption that it was a rapid reaction to the conclusion of peace with Byzantium. It cannot be ruled out, however, that the plot happened later, in 929 or even in 930. It had to have happened before Michael's rebellion, but this is dated only vaguely to 930 (without indicating even the time of year). Assuming that the rebellion started as a consequence of the discovery of John's plot, it is possible that it happened shortly after that event.

> An attack on Peter the Bulgarian was attempted by John, along with other dignitaries of Symeon (μεγιστάνων Συμεών). When this was revealed, John was flogged and locked in prison, and the others were subjected to unprecedented tortures.[2]

This relation is used to describe John's actions as an expression of disagreement with Peter's peaceful policy towards Byzantium. This is supposedly seen from the statement that John was supported by Symeon's notables, seen as the anti-Byzantine 'war party.' Such nature of John's actions would have also been indicated by the fact that both he and Benjamin (Bayan), as is mentioned, *still wore Bulgarian dress*[3].

In our view, the Byzantine relation should be approached with considerable caution. The anonymous author, as well as other Byzantine sources, does not after all mention any reasons for the attempted coup, and only state that such an event took place. Who were these Bulgarian notables described as 'Symeon's dignitaries?' Does this appellation alone really allow seeing them as the representatives of the 'war party?' We cannot have certainty here.

On the one hand, one might somewhat mischievously say that at the time when the rebellion was stirring, all of the Bulgarian notables could have been described as 'Symeon's.' Peter had not been ruling for long enough to build support that would have been his own. Whatever backing he had was inherited from his father, and thus Peter's environment necessarily included 'dignitaries of Symeon,' with George Sursuvul in the lead. It is also worth noting, as I mentioned, that in the final years of Symeon's reign his policy was not aimed at direct military confrontation with Byzantium, and undoubtedly at least some of his collaborators did not share the anti-Byzantine sentiment[4]. On the other hand, it

---

[2] Continuator of Theophanes, p. 419; cf. Symeon Magister, 136.60; John Skylitzes, p. 225.

[3] Continuator of Theophanes, p. 412; Symeon Magister, 136.45; John Skylitzes, p. 225.

[4] M.J. Leszka, *Symeon I Wielki a Bizancjum. Z dziejów stosunków bułgarsko-bizantyńskich w latach 893–927*, Łódź 2013, p. 208–214.

seems likely that for the Byzantine author, writing with a hindsight that unambiguously presented Symeon as an enemy of Byzantium, the phrase 'dignitaries of Symeon' referred to those who were hostile towards the Empire. Furthermore, from the Byzantine author's perspective the fact that 'dignitaries of Symeon' were active meant that there have been, after all, some 'dignitaries of Peter,' in whose favour the former have lost their previous positions, which they did not want to accept. The line dividing the two groups was not necessarily dictated by their attitudes towards Byzantium, but also by Symeon's decision regarding succession, as a result of which George Sursuvul and his associates became more significant.

We also have no basis for quantifying the size of this group. The term 'dignitaries of Symeon' may have equally well meant a narrow group of Symeon's close collaborators, for some reason set aside by Peter, as well as a more numerous group of magnates who, for various reasons, did not support the new ruler[5].

---

[5] On the subject of this agreement see also: Т. Тодоров, *Вътрешнодинастичният проблем в България от края на 20-те–началото на 30-те години на X в.*, Истор 3, 2008, p. 271. For more information on the subject of John's possible supporters see: В.Н. Златарски, *История на българската държава през средните векове*, vol. I/2, *Първо българско Царство. От славянизацията на държавата до падането на Първото царство (852–1018)*, София 1927, p. 536–537; И. Божилов, *Българите във Византийската империя*, София 1995, p. 308; К. Попконстантинов, *Епиграфски бележки за Иван, Царсимеоновият син*, БСП 3, 1994, p. 73; П. Павлов, *Братята на цар Петър и техните заговори*, Ист 7.4/5, 1999, p. 2–3. Ichirgu-boila Mostich, one of the most influential collaborators of Symeon, was to be found among them. On the subject of Mostich, see С. Станчев, В. Иванова, М. Балан, П. Боев, *Надписът на чъргубиля Мостич*, София 1955; Й.А. Йорданов, В. Гюзелев, *Чъргубиля Мостич (костни останки, образ, гроб)*, [in:] *Проф. Д.и.н. Станчо Ваклинов и средновековната българска култура*, ed. К. Попконстантинов, Б. Борисов, Р. Костова, Велико Търново 2005, p. 211–215; В. Гюзелев, *Кавханите и ичиргу боилите на българското ханство-царство*, Пловдив 2007, according to index; И. Лазаров, *Мостич*, [in:] Й. Андреев, И. Лазаров, П. Павлов, *Кой кой е в средновековна България*, ^{3}София 2012, p. 503–504. The hypothesis about Mostich's participation was put forward by, e.g. К. Попконстантинов, *Епиграфски...*., p. 73. This hypothesis has no basis in the sources. It is also worth noting that according to Gyuzelev Mostich and George Sursuvul are one and the same person.

Based on the analysed text, the actions taken by John appear to have been a court plot that was defused through its discovery[6]. From time to time, however, attempts are made to paint a different picture of John's plot as a more serious undertaking that reached beyond the capital city of Preslav. Four inscriptions, or rather their fragments, of which one was found in Preslav, one in Ravna and two in Murfatlar, constitute the source base for this view. These inscriptions, according to i.a. Kazimir Popkonstantinov, ought to be associated with John's coup. The most critical for the re-interpretation of John's coup is the inscription found in an old rock church of a monastery by Murfatlar. It is written, like the other three, in Slavic script and is read as: **ИВАН ЦѦР**. This is taken as indicating that John was proclaimed ruler of Bulgaria, and that he had supporters in, i.a., northern Dobrudzha[7]. It is not certain, however, that this inscription refers to John the son of Symeon. Other people who may have been meant here include John Tzymiskes, the Byzantine emperor. As such, both the question of John being proclaimed tsar and attempts to view his coup as something more than a local Preslavian undertaking have to be shelved unless other sources can be found.

John's plot was discovered, and both he himself and its other participants were punished. Peter treated his brother mercifully (John was flogged, imprisoned and probably forced to become a monk), and dealt more harshly with his supporters[8].

---

[6] One might conclude that the plot had no repercussions beyond the capital. Byzantine authors would likely have mentioned it, had that been the case, as they did regarding Michael's rebellion against Peter in 930, which happened outside of the capital (Continuator of Theophanes, p. 420; John Skylitzes, p. 226).

[7] К. Попконстантинов, *Епиграфски...*, p. 73–74; П. Павлов, *Векът на цар Самуил*, София 2014, p. 20–21; idem, *Години на мир и "ратни беди" (927–1018)*, [in:] Г. Атанасов, В. Вачкова, П. Павлов, *Българска национална история*, vol. III, *Първо българско царство (680–1018)*, Велико Търново 2015, p. 418. Cf. Т. Тодоров, *Вътрешнодинастичният...*, p. 269–270.

[8] Continuator of Theophanes, p. 419; cf. Symeon Logothete, 136.60; John Skylitzes, p. 225.

1.1.1. John's Fate after the Plot

Sometime after the plot had been dealt with, John[9] left Bulgaria for Constantinople. According to Byzantine sources, he was supposedly transported by the Byzantine envoy John the rector without Peter's knowledge[10]. In the empire's capital, John broke monastic vows, marrying a certain Armenian, and receiving wealth from the emperor. Romanos Lekapenos imparted exceptional significance to the wedding of Symeon's son, as it was witnessed by Christopher, the son and co-emperor of Romanos as well as Peter's father-in-law, and by the aforementioned John the rector[11].

It is difficult to believe that John, until recently a pretender to the throne, travelled to Constantinople without Peter's approval[12]. The latter perhaps did not want him in Bulgaria, where he would have been a potential threat to his rule. A possible execution, blinding or long-term imprisonment of the plotter in Bulgaria, created the potential threat of a new rebellion by John's supporters. Abroad, without the support of Bulgarian dignitaries, John was far less dangerous. Besides, his inclusion into the Byzantine aristocracy may have compromised the erstwhile pretender to Bulgarian crown in the eyes of his supporters, if he really had been championing anti-Byzantine policies. Romanos Lekapenos' attitude towards John may be explained by the fact that John was, after all, the brother of Christopher's son-in-law, which would likely explain

---

[9] It is possible that until that time he was imprisoned in Preslav in one of the towers located by the eastern part of the inner walls (К. Попконстантинов, *Епиграфски...*., p. 75).

[10] Symeon Magister, 136.60; Continuator of Theophanes, p. 419; John Skylitzes, p. 225.

[11] Symeon Magister, 136.60; Continuator of Theophanes, p. 419; John Skylitzes, p. 225.

[12] Similarly – П. Павлов, *Братята...*, p. 4; Л. Симеонова, *Щрихи към историята на тайната дипломация, разузнаването и контраразузнаването в средновековния свят*, [in:] *Тангра. Сборник в чест на 70. Годишната на Акад. Васил Гюзелев*, ed. М. Каймакамова et al., София 2006, p. 504–506; П. Павлов, *Векът...*, p. 21.

the co-emperor's presence at John's wedding. Additionally, the emperor was thusly securing the stability of the freshly concluded peace with his northern neighbour. Some scholars, however, accept the Byzantine authors' story at its face value; accordingly, John would become a kind of a spectre, a threat hovering over the Bulgarian ruler[13]. Even if this were so, John was never actively used in this role. We know nothing about his later fate. One could say that sending John to Byzantium removed him from the picture.

Sending John to Constantinople appears to indicate that the Byzantines were not involved in his plot. Following a lengthy war, Byzantium needed a lasting peace with Bulgaria, and from Constantinopolitan perspective, it was Peter, related by marriage with the Lekapenos dynasty, who guaranteed it. Undermining his position would have threatened the peace, concluded with difficulty, and thus the Byzantine interests.

1.2. Michael's Rebellion

It is possible that the failure of John's plot had spurred Michael, Symeon I the Great's firstborn son (who remained in a monastery at the beginning of Peter's reign), into action. It was most likely in 930[14] that

[13] E.g. J.V.A. Fine, *The Early Medieval Balkans: a Critical Survey from the Sixth to the Late Twelfth Century*, Ann Arbor 1983, p. 162; И. Божилов, В. Гюзелев, *История на средновековна България. VII–XIV в.*, София 2006, p. 278; cf. M.J. Leszka, K. Marinow, *Carstwo...*, p. 153; П. Павлов, *Братята...*, p. 5; idem, *Години...*, p. 419–421. This hypothesis, however, cannot be positively verified. It is often forgotten in this context that Peter's wife was Christopher's daughter, and it is difficult to imagine that her father, potentially Romanos' heir, would have wanted to move against her husband – although of course one cannot rule out the possibility.

[14] The date is approximate: none of the sources inform us when it happened. Since both in Continuator of Theophanes and in John Skylitzes it precedes an event from March 931 (misfortunes that befell Constantinople Continuator of Theophanes, p. 420; Symeon Magister, 136.61; cf. John Skylitzes, p. 226, which presents the same events, but without dates), it is accepted it happened in 930 (В.Н. Златарски, *История...*, p. 840). Regarding the *terminus post quem*, the problem is more serious, since we only have the information that Michael's rebellion happened after John's plot which, as previously mentioned, is dated only approximately, most commonly to 928.

Michael moved against Peter. The information at our disposal about this event comes from two Byzantine sources: *Continuation of Theophanes* and from John Skylitzes[15]. Because of their importance for this topic, we quote them in full:

Continuator of Theophanes (p. 420):

> However also the monk Michael, brother of Peter, attempting with all strength to gain power over the Bulgarians, started a rebellion in a certain Bulgarian fortress. To him flocked Scythians, who refused to obey Peter's rule. After his [Michael's] death, they attacked Roman territories, that is they went from Maketidos through Strymon to Hellas, entered Nikopolis and there plundered everything.

John Skylitzes (p. 226; transl., p. 218, with minor changes – M.J.L., K.M.):

> Now Michael, Peter's other brother, aspired to become ruler of the Bulgarians. He occupied a powerful fortress and greatly agitated the Bulgarians lands. Many flocked to his banner but, when he died shortly after, these people, for fear of Peter's wrath, entered Roman territory. They reached Nikopolis by way of Macedonia, Strymon and Helladikon theme, laying waste everything that came to hand, and there, finally, settled (καὶ τέλος ἐν αὐτῇ σαββατίσαντες). In due course and after a number of reverses, they became Roman subjects.[16]

[15] Continuator of Theophanes, p. 420; John Skylitzes, p. 226.

[16] John Skylitzes, p. 226 (transl. J. Wortley, p. 248 with a change in translation of the word σαββατίσαντες). John Wortley, the author of the translation, proposed the reading σαββατίσαντες, derived from σαββατίζω – *took a Sabbath rest*. It seems however that John Skylitzes used the word σαββατίζω in the meaning 'to settle', 'to find rest'; *Lexikon zur byzantinischen Gräzität, besonders des 9.–12. Jahrhunderts*, vol. VII, ed. E. Trapp, Wien 2011, p. 1518 ('zur ruhe kommen'; 'sich niederlassen'). Cf. В.Н. Златарски, *История...*, p. 837 (*се настанили*); John Skylitzes (Bulg.), p. 257 (*се установили*). See also *Testimonia*, vol. VI, p. 157 (*obchodzili szabat*); John Skylitzes (French) (*ils observèrent le repos comme pour un sabat*). The remark of Anna Kotłowska that it referred to celebrating Holy Saturday does not appear to be correct in this context (*Testimonia*, vol. VI, p. 156, fn. 79).

The quoted sources present the rebellion's progress in a fundamentally similar manner. They only differ in specifics. The most important differences are in the names used to described Michael's supporters, and the territory which they crossed first during their flight after Michael's death. In *Continuation of Theophanes* his supporters were called 'Scythians' (Σκύθαι), while in John Skylitzes' work – Bulgarians. In *Continuation* the first Byzantine territory through which the refugees passed was called Μακέτιδος, while in Skylitzes – Μακηδονίας. We will discuss these differences below.

As can be seen from the quoted sources, our knowledge about Michael's rebellion is very modest. We do not know where the uprising began. The only hint that can be drawn in this regard is from information about his supporters' initial flight from Bulgaria; however, here we encounter a problem. As we mentioned, *Continuation of Theophanes* informs that they went through Maketidos, while John Skylitzes, that through Macedonia. It is not entirely clear which territories the anonymous author meant using the name Maketidos[17], and on what basis John Skylitzes used the term Macedonia instead. Vassil N. Zlatarski thought that Maketidos referred to the territories of historical Macedonia (most likely between Struma and Mesta), and Michael's rebellion took place in *Струмската область* [*Struma region*][18]. This idea found a relatively common acceptance in later academic literature and nowadays it is thought, albeit sometimes with a degree of caution, that the areas where Michael's rising was happening were in contemporary south-western Bulgaria[19]. Supporters of this idea think that the fortress which became Michael's temporary headquarters may have been the central point of one of the local comitates, e.g. Devol[20]. Those scholars who take as

[17] It needs to be clearly emphasised that this name was used in book VI of *Continuation of Theophanes* only once, and in a context that does not allow clarification as to which area it referred.

[18] В.Н. Златарски, *История...*, p. 838.

[19] П. Мутафчиев, *История на българския народ (681–1323)*, София 1986, p. 201; J.V.A. Fine, *The Early Medieval Balkans. A Critical Survey from the Sixth to the Late Twelfth Century*, Ann Arbor 1983, p. 162; П. Павлов, *Братята...*, p. 5.

[20] See e.g. J.V.A. Fine, *The Early...*, p. 162–163; П. Георгиев, *Титлата и функциите на българския престолонаследник и въпросът за престолонаследието при цар*

the basis for their considerations about the place of Michael's rebellion the account of John Skylitzes (who claimed that the refugees first entered Macedonia) are in a clear minority. This is mainly due to the fact that book VI of *Continuation of Theophanes* was created far earlier than Skylitzes' account, as well as due to Zlatarski's authority. We have to keep in mind that Skylitzes meant Macedonia as it was understood by the Byzantines, which indicates that one ought to seek the location of the rebellion's beginnings either in the Bulgarian part of Thrace, or perhaps even somewhere in the vicinity of Bulgarian main centres – Preslav and Pliska[21]. The reliability of the *Continuation of Theophanes* and John Skylitzes' accounts has relatively recently been thoroughly examined by Todor Todorov, who pointed out that while John's account appears to be the more logical in terms of the route of the flight of Michael's supporters (they would have consistently travelled in the south-westerly direction), one should nonetheless give primacy to *Continuation of Theophanes*. According to Todorov, Skylitzes did not understand the meaning of the name Maketidos – which does not appear in his work – as used by the author of the book VI of *Continuation*, identifying it instead with Macedonia (in its Byzantine form), since this fitted with his view of the progression of Michael's supporters. In turn, the use of the archaic name Maketidos in *Continuation of Theophanes* is explained by Todorov as a tendency – common throughout the entire work, and also seen in book VI – for employing archaic names. In the passage about Michael we find not only Maketidos, but also the Scythians making an appearance, and we find an explanation, reaching into the distant past, of how the city of Nikopolis got its name[22]. Although Todorov's arguments cannot be disregarded,

---

Симеон, ИП 48. 8/91992, p. 11; И. Божилов, В. Гюзелев, *История*..., p. 278–279; П. Павлов, *Братята*..., p. 5–6.

[21] Т. Тодоров, *Вътрешнодинастичният*..., p. 275; cf. П. Коледаров, *Цар Петър I*, ВС 51, 1979, p. 199; Х. Димитров, *История на Македония*, София 2004, p. 60. On the extent of the territory of Macedonia as understood by the Byzantines, see П. Коледаров, *Македония*, [in:] *KME*, vol. II, p. 592–593; T.E. Gregory, *Macedonia*, [in:] *ODB*, vol. II, p. 1261–1262.

[22] Continuator of Theophanes, p. 420. Nikopolis was to have received its name to commemorate the victory of Octavian Augustus over Antony and Cleopatra, the result of which was, as the author of book VI of the *Continuation of Theophanes* writes,

they do not, however, allow one to definitively reject Skylitzes' account. Simply because the name of Maketidos did not make an appearance in his work, it does not necessarily follow that he did not understand its meaning. The use of the term Macedonia may have been a conscious move stemming from knowledge that the author of *Continuation of Theophanes* used the appellation Maketidos either incorrectly, incomprehensibly or, which cannot be ruled out, in an entirely correct manner[23]. This awareness may have been a consequence of the fact that John Skylitzes had a wider relation about this event, the trace of which is inclusion of information that was not given by the anonymous author of book VI of the *Continuation*. The fragment in question states that after Nikopolis was captured, the refugees: *finally, settled. In due course and after a number of reverses, they became Roman subjects*[24].

It is noteworthy that the monastery in which Michael resided after being removed from the line of succession may have possibly been the one in Ravna. One might expect that he had links with it even at the time when he was Symeon's official heir. After all, it is here that six of the seven known seals that are linked with his name have been found[25]. It cannot be ruled out that his father allowed Michael, after replacing him with another heir and forcing monasticism upon him, to spend his life there. Considering the geographical location of this monastery, it seems more logical that he would have sought – and found – support for his rebellion against Peter in its vicinity, and therefore near Pliska and Preslav and the lands of Thrace, rather than in south-western Bulgaria.

---

subjugation of Egypt to Rome. This is an obvious reference to the battle of Actium in 31 BCE, however this is not mentioned *expressis verbis* in the Byzantine source.

[23] Let us repeat once more that the Byzantine author used the name Maketidos only once. Therefore, there can be no certainty as to how he understood it. One should be reminded that the suggestion of V.N. Zlatarski is only a hypothesis.

[24] John Skylitzes, p. 221; transl. p. 248.

[25] Б. Николова, *Печатите на Мицхаил багатур канеиртхтин и Йоан багатур канеиртхтин (?). Проблеми на разчитането и атрибуцията*, [in:] *Средновековният българин и "другите". Сборник в чест на 60-годишнината на проф. Дин Петър Ангелов*, ed. А. Николов, Г.Н. Николов, София 2013, p. 127; И. Йорданов, *Корпус на средновековните български печати*, ed. П. Георгиев, София 2016, p. 140–143.

The above considerations force us to treat the question as to which territories Michael's rebellion spread as impossible to definitely answer at this time.

The question of the support of Michael's rebellion is also far from resolved. It is thought, for example, that Michael was backed by some part of the Bulgarian magnates, as well as by members of other social groups[26]. This statement, however, lacks a basis in sources. John Skylitzes writes very generally that Michael was supported by many, without specifying who they were. Even greater confusion into this matter is introduced by *Continuation of Theophanes*, in which we read: *To him flocked Scythians, who refused to obey Peter's rule*[27]. Not only does it not clarify in any way which social groups supported Michael, but also introduces the ethnonym Σκύθαι to describe them. This caused a long debate on the subject of who these Scythians could have been. Assuming that the name was used to differentiate Michael's supporters from Bulgarians, and assuming that his rebellion was happening on Macedonian territories (in the sense proposed by V.N. Zlatarski), one would see them as the Bulgarians from the Kouber group[28], or even Serbs, who were relocated to Bulgaria after 924[29]. It would seem that neither the first, nor the second view is correct. It does seem appropriate to agree with Todorov that the use of the ethnonym Scythians' was due to a preference for archaic language, visible in this passage of *Continuation of Theophanes*, and that in this case one ought to give precedence to John Skylitzes' narrative, where Michael's supporters are seen simply as Bulgarians[30]. It is worth noting that attempts to see these Scythians as ethnically different from Bulgarians would be at odds with the logic of the argument of the *Continuation of Theophanes*' anonymous author. He writes, after all, that Michael wanted to gain power over Bulgarians and that he took control

[26] И. Божилов, В. Гюзелев, *История*..., p. 279.

[27] Continuator of Theophanes, p. 420.

[28] В.Н. Златарски, *История*..., p. 838–839; П. Павлов, *Братята*..., p. 5.

[29] О.В. Иванова, *Восстание в 930 г. в Болгарии и болгаро-византийские отношения*, [in:] *Славяне и их соседи. Международные отношения в епоху феодализма*, ed. Г.Г. Литаврин, Москва 1989, p. 34–44.

[30] Т. Тодоров, *Вътрешнодинастичният*..., p. 277.

of a particular Bulgarian fortress. In this context it would appear obvious that those who joined him must have been Bulgarians who renounced their allegiance to Peter. Had the Byzantine author meant anyone else than Bulgarians when referring to the Scythians, we could have expected to find some words of explanation. Let us remember that in book VI of *Continuation of Theophanes* this name appears only once, which means it had not been used in any context other than Bulgarian. One should note that throughout the entire work known as *Continuation of Theophanes* the ethnonym 'Scythians' appears only six times[31]. That for Byzantine authors of the tenth century it was possible to interchangeably use the ethnonyms Bulgarians and Scythians can be attested by a passage from book V of *Continuation of Theophanes* (*Life of Basil*), which was written, it is thought, by Constantine Porphyrogennetos[32].

The view that the Byzantine author meant Bulgarians when using the name Scythians was strengthened by Todorov by referring to Romanos II's chrysobull related to the Kolovou monastery. In it, we find some Σκλάβοι Βούλγαροι, who settled on the lands belonging to said monastery[33]. Further evidence is found in the document of the patriarch Nicholas Chrysoberg from April 989, in which we read about another monastery (τοῦ Ὀρφανοῦ), the lands of which suffered looting during the raids of τῶν ἐκ γειτόνων οἰκούντων Βουλγάρων[34]. Because the monasteries, both located on the Chalkidike Peninsula, are merely 10 km apart, one may assume the same Bulgarians were involved. Ivan Bozhilov considered these Bulgarians to have been Michael's supporters, who after leaving Bulgaria first settled in Epirus, and subsequently may have been relocated – or moved of their own volition – to the Chalkidike Peninsula[35]. This hypothesis of Bozhilov is accepted by Todorov, which allows him to strengthen the view (in our opinion correct) that the Scythians

[31] Continuator of Theophanes, p. 11, 13, 217, 284, 288, 420.

[32] Continuator of Theophanes, p. 216–217.

[33] F. Dölger, *Ein Fall slavischer Einsiedlung im Hinterland von Thessalonike im 10. Jahrhundert*, SBAW.PHK 1, 1952, p. 7; G. Soulis, *On the Slavic settlement in Hierissos in the tenth century*, B 23, 1953, p. 67–72; *Acts of Iviron*, I, p. 11; II, 32, 1, 12–13.

[34] *Acts of Lavra*, I, 8, p. 117.11.

[35] И. Божилов, *Българите...*, p. 17.

in *Continuation of Theophanes* are simply Bulgarians. It needs to be strongly emphasised, however, that Bozhilov's view is only a hypothesis, although a plausible one. One might note that the two sources are separated by over a quarter of a century, and in the case of patriarch Nicholas Chrysoberg, the text may have been referring to not so much the direct participants of the rebellion, but to their descendants. Either way, it cannot be ruled out that the long journey of Michael's supporters came to a close when they settled at the end of 950s and beginning of 960s on the Chalkidike Peninsula, in the vicinity of Hierissos.

It would seem that, based on the current source base, one may formulate a general hypothesis that Michael's rebellion had a local character, and that its supporters included the inhabitants of the taken fortress and the nearby populace. Contrary to what some scholars say[36], no large scale (if any at all) military activity took place during the rebellion. It cannot be ruled out that the only fortress captured by Michael fell into his hands not as a result of fighting, but as a result of a betrayal arranged through some earlier agreements. Furthermore, Michael's supporters left Bulgarian territory not as a result of action on the part of Peter's army but, as the sources inform[37], out of fear of them.

One might wonder whether Michael's rising really did constitute a more serious threat to Peter's reign than John's plot, as some scholars think[38]. Considering specific actions (taking of a fortress) this was indeed the case, however it would seem that if John's plot, involving Bulgarian elites and active in the very heart of the country, entered its active phase, then it would have had a better chance of success than Michael's local uprising, which likely would have been crushed without much difficulty by forces loyal to Peter.

It does not appear that Michael's rising was inspired by the Byzantines, who in this way would have been destabilising situation in Bulgaria, and thus weakened its position relative to their own. The clearest indication that this was not the case lies in the fact that while

---

[36] Т. Тодоров, *Вътрешнодинастичният*..., p. 274,

[37] Continuator of Theophanes, p. 420; John Skylitzes, p. 226.

[38] Т. Тодоров, *Вътрешнодинастичният*..., p. 274.

Michael's supporters sought refuge within the Empire, they were not welcomed there with open arms, and their march towards Nikopolis resembled a looting raid. The Byzantines were only able to enforce their dominion over them with the use of military might. Had the rebels been in prior communication with the Empire, one might have expected that they would have been supported by the Byzantines during their flight, and would have been peacefully settled on the indicated territory.

* * *

Michael's rebellion failed. His sudden death[39] made any further action of his supporters against Peter pointless. This is a clear indication that the rising of Symeon's eldest son was solely an expression of the fight for power within the ruling family. Michael's death ended the several-year period of struggles for the Bulgarian throne after Symeon's death. Peter emerged victorious, and from that point onward his position in the Bulgarian state was secured.

2. Characterisation of Domestic Policy

It is quite remarkable that once Michael's attempt failed, Peter virtually disappeared from the Byzantine sources for a period of over thirty years. As a consequence, our knowledge of his rule at the time when Maria was by his side is very limited (which, in fact, also holds true for the later period); what we do know mainly concerns religious issues, the Bogomilist heresy being regarded as the most important among them[40]. Although

---

[39] That this happened at an advantageous moment, from Peter's perspective, and to a man still relatively young, might, and does, raise suspicion. However, the fact that Byzantine authors, to whom it also must have been obvious that Michael's death was a boon for Peter, made no such aspersions makes one refrain from any speculations on this subject.

[40] On Bogomilism see e.g.: D. Obolensky, *The Bogomils*, Cambridge 1948; Д. Ангелов, *Богомилството в България*, София 1961; S. Runciman, *The Medieval*

the heresy unquestionably deserves attention, its significance has been blown out of proportion by scholars. Its emergence is usually linked with Peter's reign, although in fact it can be traced back to Symeon's times. We are able to determine neither its social base nor the measures which were taken against it, inspired by both lay and church authorities. The fact that Peter turned to Theophylaktos Lekapenos, patriarch of Constantinople and Maria's uncle[41], for help and counsel, indicates that he took note of it and considered it a threat. Nevertheless, it must be noted that this deeply religious ruler, driven by the commitment to the idea of the purity of the religion adhered to by his subjects, may have dealt with the movement in a manner incommensurate with its actual strength and size[42]. It should also be kept in mind that Bogomil views – those regarding theology as

---

Manichee. A Study of the Dualist Heresy, Cambridge 1982; S. B y l i n a, *Bogomilizm w średniowiecznej Bułgarii. Uwarunkowania społeczne, polityczne i kulturalne*, BP 2, 1985, p. 133–145; Д. А н г е л о в, *Богомилство*, София 1993; Y. S t o y a n o v, *The Other God. Dualist Religions from Antiquity to the Cathar Heresy*, New Haven 2000, p. 125–166; G. M i n c z e w, *Remarks on the Letter of the Patriarch Theophylact to Tsar Peter in the Context of Certain Byzantine and Slavic Anti-heretic Texts*, SCer 3, 2013, p. 113–130; i d e m, *Słowiańskie teksty antyheretyckie jako źródło do poznania herezji dualistycznych na Bałkanach*, [in:] *Średniowieczne herezje dualistyczne na Bałkanach. Źródła słowiańskie*, ed. G. M i n c z e w, M. S k o w r o n e k, J.M. W o l s k i, Łódź 2015, p. 13–57.

[41] *Letter of the Patriarch Theophylact to Tsar Peter*. The letter was recently analyzed by: G. M i n c z e w, *Remarks on the Letter*... (the work includes the bibliography devoted to this issue).

[42] It must not be forgotten that according to the Byzantine doctrine of power, the ruler was obliged to ensure the purity of his subjects' faith as fundamental to their salvation. This principle became instilled in Bulgaria right after its conversion to Christianity. Interestingly, Peter was reminded of it in a letter that he received from the patriarch of Constantinople: *A faithful and God-loving soul is such a great treasure – our spiritual son, the best and the most notable of our relatives – especially if it is the soul of the ruler and leader which, as Yours, can love and worship what is good and beneficial. By leading a prudent life and by behaving well, it not only secures good for itself but, surrounding everyone under its authority with great care, gives them everything that is important and that concerns their salvation. Can there be anything more important and more beneficial than the uncorrupted and sincere faith and the healthy concept of divinity thanks to which we worship one God, the purest and holiest God, with clear consciousness? And that is the most important element of our salvation* (*Letter of the Patriarch Theophylact to Tsar Peter*, p. 311). See also: А. Н и к о л о в, *Политическа мисъл в ранносредновековна България (средата на IX – края на X в.)*, София 2006, p. 245–269.

well as those expressing criticism of the existing social order – must have been an issue of concern for the ruler even if they were not shared and perpetrated by a significant number of people.

The need to return to the ideals of the first Christians and to establish an intimate relationship with God was reflected in the development of the monastic movement, especially in its eremitic version[43]. Although one could hardly claim any detailed knowledge of the issue, Peter's ties to monasticism were clearly very strong. Bearing witness to this is his acceptance of the Little Schema shortly before his death, as well as the fact that his cult as a saint flourished mainly in connection with his monastic activity[44]. Peter is known to have held monks in high regard, especially John of Rila, Bulgaria's most famous saint, an anchorite and the founder of the monastic community that gave rise to the celebrated Rila Monastery[45].

---

[43] For more on Bulgarian monasticism in the century in question see: Б. Николова, *Монашество, манастири и манастирски живот в средновековна България*, vol. I, *Манастирите*, София 2010, p. 41–270.

[44] On this issue see: И. Билярски, *Покровители на Царство. Св. Цар Петър и св. Параскева-Петка*, София 2004, p. 21–24; idem, М. Йовчева, *За датата на успението на цар Петър и за култа към него*, [in:] *Тангра. Сборник в чест на 70-годишнината на акад. Васил Гюзелев*, ed. М. Каймакавова et al., София 2006, p. 543–557; Д. Чешмеджиев, *Култът към българския цар Петър I (927–969): монашески или държавен?*, [in:] *Љубав према образовању и вера у Бога у православним манастирама*, *5. Међународна Хиландарска конференција. Зборник изабраних радова 1*, Beograd–Columbus 2006, p. 245–257; Б. Николова, *Цар Петър и характерът на неговия култ*, Pbg 33.2, 2009, p. 63–77; eadem, *Монашество...*, vol. II, *Монасите*, София 2010, p. 826–843; М. Каймакамова, *Култът към цар Петър (927–969) и движещите идеи на българските освободителни въстания срещу византийската власт през XI–XII в.*, BMd 4/5, 2013/2014, p. 417–438; Д. Чешмеджиев, *Култовете на българските светци през IX–XII в. Автореферат*, Пловдив 2016, p. 13–15.

[45] John was born around 876. We have no certain information about his origin and the reasons for which he decided to settle in the Rila Mountains to live the life of a hermit – one that gave him the fame and reputation which he did not seek. In any case, he founded the community of which he became the first hegumen. He died as a hermit; in all probability, his life came to an end in 946. For more on John of Rila's life see: И. Дуйчев, *Рилският светец и неговата обител*, София 1947; I. Dobrev, *Sv. Ivan Rilski*, vol. I, Linz 2007; Б. Николова, *Монашество...*, p. 790–815; Й. Андреев, *Иван Рилски*, [in:] idem, И. Лазаров, П. Павлов, *Кой кой...*, p. 270–275.

Thoroughly impressed by John's holiness[46], the ruler – according to his hagiographers – went to a lot of trouble trying, unsuccessfully, to secure a meeting with the holy hermit; after the latter's death, he saw to it that his remains were transferred from his hermitage in Rila to Sofia[47].

There is no doubt that Peter took care of the Church and provided material support to it. However, we are not able to adduce any details regarding this aspect of his activity. It cannot be ruled out that scholars such as Plamen Pavlov[48] are right in claiming that Peter was not easily influenced by the clergy, as well as that his policy towards the Church was rational and consistent with the interests of his state. He sought, for example, to hinder the Church from excessively increasing its holdings – an approach modeled on the policy used by Byzantine emperors.

Peter's reign is often described as a period of a deteriorating economy and a resulting impoverishment of the masses of the Bulgarian society, especially the peasants. However, the picture is based not on reliable sources but on arbitrary assumptions, arising from the interpretation of the growth of the Bogomil movement as a reaction to the material deprivation of the Bulgarian society. Without engaging in a detailed polemic with this view, it is worth noting that there is historical evidence to suggest that Bulgaria's economic situation was not as poor as usually described. This is borne out by the fact that the Bulgarian lands became a tasty morsel for Svyatoslav I, prince of Kievan Rus', who not only displayed much zeal in plundering them but, as some scholars believe, was even going to settle there. We may point to the well-known description of Pereyaslavets on the Danube, reportedly uttered by the prince – a picture quite at odds with the notion of Bulgaria's economic decline:

---

[46] И. Дуйчев, *Рилският…*, p. 123sqq; *Ziemscy aniołowie, niebiańscy ludzie. Anachoreci w bułgarskiej literaturze i kulturze*, ed. G. Minczew, Białystok 2002, p. 19. Cf. Б. Николова, *Монашество…*, p. 274–285; 626–628, 790–815.

[47] Naturally, detailed information to be found in hagiographic accounts must be treated with caution. Then again, there seems to be nothing surprising about the notion of a pious ruler willing to meet a hermit. Doubts have been raised as to whether Peter had a hand in transferring John's remains to Sredets (nowadays Sofia); the problem has been analyzed by: И. Дуйчев, *Рилският…*, *passim*. Cf. Д. Чешмеджиев, *За времето на пренасяне на мощите на св. Иоан Рилски от Рила в Средец*, BMd 6, 2015, p. 79–89.

[48] П. Павлов, *Векът…*, p. 55–57.

> не любо ми есть в Киевѣ быти. хочю жити с Переяславци в Дунаи. яко то есть середа в земли моеи. яко ту вся благая сходятся. ѿ Грекъ злато паволоки. вина [и] овощеве розноличныя. и-Щехъ же из Угоръ сребро и комони. из Руси же скора и воскъ медъ. и челяд.
>
> I do not care to remain in Kiev, but should prefer to live in Pereyaslavets on the Danube, since that is the centre of my realm, where all riches are concentrated; gold, silks, wine, and various fruits from Greece, silver and horses from Hungary and Bohemia, and from Rus' furs, wax, honey, and slaves.[49]

This description, not to move too far away from the letter of the source, can be treated at least as evidence proving that trade in the Bulgarian territories was not in decline. The problem is, however, that scholars analyzing the source recently raised doubts as to the account's reliability. In their opinion, as far as Svyatoslav's expeditions are concerned, the account confuses Pereyaslavets with Veliki Preslav. In reality, the source needs to be regarded as reflecting the role of the first city as a trading center in the eleventh and twelfth centuries; the description of the emporium's central location and the goods that flowed into it from all directions is based on biblical accounts regarding the significance and wealth of Tyre and Jerusalem[50].

The account found in the *Tale of the Prophet Isaiah* testifies to the fact that, despite the skeptical remarks regarding the previous passage, Peter's

---

[49] *Russian Primary Chronicle*, AM 6477, p. 68 (transl., p.86). Cf. A. K i j a s, *Stosunki rusko-bułgarskie do XV w. ze szczególnym uwzględnieniem stosunków kulturalnych*, BP 2, 1985, p. 115; М. Р а е в, *Преслав или Переяславец на Дунае? (Предварительные замечания об одном из возможных источников ПВЛ и его трансформации)*, НЗУІЗНС 20, 2008, p. 37–40. See also: J. B a n a s z k i e w i c z, *Jedność porządku przestrzennego, społecznego i tradycji początków ludu. (Uwagi o urządzeniu wspólnoty plemienno-państwowej u Słowian)*, PH 77, 1986, p. 448–449.

[50] И. Д а н и л е в с к и й, *Повесть временных лет: герменевтические основы изучения летописных тестов*, Москва 2004, p. 163–167; В. Р ы ч к а, *Чью славу перея́л Переяслав?*, НЗУІЗНС 16, 2005, p. 129–134; М. Р а е в, *Переяславец на Дунав – мит и действителност в речта на княз Святослав в Повесть временных лет*, ГСУ. НЦСВПИД 95.14, 2006, p. 193–203; M.J. L e s z k a, K. M a r i n o w, *Carstwo…*, p. 166.

reign was indeed remembered as a period of prosperity – or at least that people chose to remember it that way. In the *Tale*, we read:

> **тогⷣа ѹбо вь д҃ни и лѣтⷣ с҃тго Пеⷮра ц҃ря бльгарьскагⷪ быⷭ изьѡбылїа ѿ всего. сирѣчь пшеница и масло и меда жⷷ и млѣка и вина, и ѿ всего дарованїа б҃жїа врѣше и кипѣше. и не бѣ ѡскѹдѣнїе ни ѡ щомⷨь. Нь бѣ ситость изьѡбилсⷮво ѿ всего до изволенїа б҃жїа**

> In the days and years of St. Peter, the tsar of the Bulgarians, there was plenty of everything, that is to say, of wheat and butter, honey, milk and wine, the land was overflowing with every gift of God, there was no dearth of anything but by the will of God everything was in abundance and to satiety[51].

[51] *Tale of the Prophet Isaiah*, p. 17.

VI

Mirosław J. Leszka
Kirił Marinow

Foreign Policy

Peter's foreign policy, calculated to maintain Bulgarian territories without the need for involvement in armed conflicts, was for the most part successful until the mid-960s, that is, throughout the entirety of Maria Lekapene's presence at the court in Preslav. The Serbian issue is considered to be its only more serious failure. For chronological reasons, it is from this question that we will begin the analysis of the international standing of Bulgaria during the era of Peter's reign.

1. The Serbian Question

During the beginnings of tsar Peter's reign there was a change in the nature of the Bulgarian-Serbian relations. In order to better understand what happened during that time, we will devote some attention to the relations between the two southern Slavic states during the final phase of the reign of Symeon I the Great, who during that time had undertaken certain steps to subjugate the Serbs.

A Bulgarian intervention in Serbia took place in most likely 923. It was a consequence of changing of sides by Pavle of Serbia, son of Bran, who was until then a Bulgarian ally. For reasons unknown, and in unclear circumstances, he has sided with the Byzantines. In this situation, Symeon decided to remove him from the throne and replace him with yet another nominee of his choosing. Zacharias, son of Pribislav, having been held by the Bulgarian ruler for several years, became this candidate. Thanks to Bulgarian support he was able to remove Pavle. Having attained power, however, the new ruler of Serbia rejected his alliance with Bulgarians and approached the Empire instead. A few years earlier Zacharias was Romanos Lekapenos' candidate for the ruler of Rashka[1]. Perhaps this change of loyalties that Symeon had not anticipated was due to personal reasons (Zacharias' long stay in Constantinople could have resulted in strong ties with the imperial court; it was the Bulgarian ruler who previously prevented him from taking the Serbian throne and kept him prisoner in Preslav). Perhaps it was an attempt of gaining independence with Byzantine aid. However, we do not have any sources that would allow us to verify these hypotheses. Regardless of what motives were behind Zacharias' decision, he must have expected Symeon's reaction to his protege's betrayal. The Bulgarian ruler sent against him an army led by Marmais and Theodore Sigritzes. Their expedition ended in complete fiasco, the clearest proof of which was the death of both Marmais and Sigritzes. Their heads, as Constantine Porphyrogennetos informs, were sent along with weapons to Constantinople as proof of victory[2].

---

[1] Constantine VII Porphyrogennetos, *On the Governance of the Empire*, 32, p. 158. On the subject of this event cf. also: Константин VII Порфирогенит, *Спис о народима*, [in:] *FBHPJS*, vol. II, p. 55, fn. 184–185; И. Божилов, *Цар Симеон Велики (893–927). Златният век на Средновековна България*, София 1983, p. 138; J.A.V. Fine, *The Early Medieval Balkans. A Critical Survey from the Sixth to the Late Twelfth Century*, Ann Arbor 1983, p. 152; Т. Живковић, *Јужни Словени под византијском влашћу 600–1025*, Београд 2002, p. 416. On Zacharias – Т. Живковић, *Портрети владара раног средњег века. Од Властимира до Борића*, Београд 2006, pp. 57–63.

[2] Constantine VII Porphyrogennetos, *On the Governance of the Empire*, 32, p. 158.

In response to the events in Serbia Symeon decided to organise another expedition against Zacharias (924?)[3], accompanied by another candidate to the Serbian throne. This time it was Chaslav, son of Klonimir and a Bulgarian woman whose name we do not know[4]. Hearing the news of the approaching Bulgarian army, Zacharias abandoned Rashka and fled to Croatia. Bulgarians took control of Serbia and, what is noteworthy, did not place Chaslav on the throne[5], but subjected it to their own governance. Part of the Serbian populace was relocated into Bulgaria. It is clear, then, that Symeon drew conclusions from his previous policy towards Serbia. Maintaining an alliance by placing his own candidate on its throne did not work; in this situation the only way of maintaining influence in Rashka was to incorporate it into Bulgarian state. Perhaps this move was partially influenced by the tense relations with Croatia[6].

* * *

[3] Also in this case the dating of the Bulgarian expedition can be argued either way. It may have taken place in 924 or 925, perhaps even in 926 (thus e.g. Т. Живковић, *Јужни Словени...*, p. 419, fn. 1423). The Bulgarian troops were led according to Constantine VII Porphyrogennetos by (Constantine VII Porphyrogennetos, *On the Governance of the Empire*, 32, p. 158): Kninos (Κνῆνος), Himnikos (Ἡμνῆκος), Itzboklias (Ἡτζβόκλιας). Constantine's relation suggests that these were the names of Bulgarian commanders. Most likely, however, these were names of positions or dignities – В.Н. Златарски, *История на българската държава през средните векове*, vol. I/2, *Първо българско царство. От славянизацията на държавата до падането на Първото царство*, София 1927, pp. 475–476, fn. 1. On the subject of Ἡμνῆκος cf. also Т. Славова, *Владетел и администрация в ранносредновековна България. Филологически аспекти*, София 2010, pp. 105–109.

[4] About this Serbian ruler – Т. Живковић, *Портрети...*, pp. 49–57.

[5] It seems Chaslav was used in order to neutralise any stronger opposition from the Serbian notables, who may have given up their support for their current ruler Zacharias more easily knowing that he will be replaced with their compatriot. Constantine VII Porphyrogennetos (*On the Governance of the Empire*, 32, p. 158) writes that Serbian *zhupans* were summoned under the pretext of acknowledging a new ruler, only to be subsequently imprisoned by the Bulgarians. Chaslav, meanwhile, was transported to Bulgaria, where he remained until the end of Symeon's reign and throughout the beginning of Peter's.

[6] Т. Тодоров, *България през втората и третата четвърт на X в. Политическа история*, София 2006 [unpublished PhD thesis], p. 196.

In the beginning of tsar Peter's reign Chaslav left Bulgaria and journeyed to the Serbian lands. The only author to mention this was Constantine Porphyrogennetos. Due to its unique nature, we will quote the account in full:

> Seven years afterwards Tzeëslav escaped from Bulgarians with four others, and entered Serbia from Preslav, and found in the country no more than fifty men only, without wives or children, who supported themselves by hunting. With these he took possession of the country and sent message to the emperor of the Romans asking for his support and succour, and promising to serve him and be obedient to his command, as had been the princes before him. And thenceforward the emperor of the Romans continually benefit him, so that the Serbs living in Croatia and Bulgaria and the rest of the countries, whom Symeon had scattered, rallied to him when they heard of it. Moreover many had escaped from Bulgaria and entered Constantinople, and these the emperor of Romans clad and comforted and sent to Tzeëslav.[7]

This passage was examined many times already, however not all the questions it raises have been settled. The first of these is the dating of Chaslav's departure from Preslav. Scholarly works place it between 928 and 933/934[8]. This chronological quandary is a consequence of two uncertainties. Firstly, it is unclear from which point one should count the seven years (even leaving aside the question of how accurate that information is). Secondly, the dating of the events marking the opening point of this situation is ambiguous as well. George Ostrogorsky dated Chaslav's departure from Bulgaria to 928, thinking that Constantine Porphyrogennetos counted the seven years from Zacharias' bid for power

---

[7] Constantine VII Porphyrogennetos, *On the Governance of the Empire*, 32, pp. 158, 160 (transl. – pp. 159, 161).

[8] Cf. Г. Острогорски, *Порфирогенитова хроника српских владара и њени хронолошки подаци*, [in:] idem, *Сабране дела Георгија Острогорског*, vol. IV, *Византија и словени*, Београд 1970, pp. 84–86; И. Божилов, В. Гюзелев, *История на средновековна България. VII–XIV в.*, София 2006, p. 279; Т. Тодоров, *България*..., p. 194.

in Serbia (920/921)[9]. Other scholars saw the beginning of the seven year period in the transferring of the Serbian lands under direct Bulgarian rule and imprisonment of Chaslav in Preslav. Due to differences in dating of this event (between 924 and 926) scholars pointed to years between 931 and 933[10] as the moment during which Chaslav left Bulgaria. This question cannot be resolved, although we are leaning towards the dating which takes as its starting point the imposition of direct control over Serbia by Symeon (most likely in 924), because of the logic of Constantine Porphyrogennetos's argument[11]. It needs to be pointed out, however, that from the perspective of Chaslav's actions and their results, the significance of when exactly he left Preslav is secondary. It will suffice to say that it happened during the first years of tsar Peter's reign.

Constantine Porphyrogennetos presented Chaslav's actions, which ultimately resulted in regaining of independence by Serbs, albeit with the acknowledgement of Byzantium's authority. According to the learned emperor, the Serbian prince acted against the will and interests of the Bulgarian ruler, whose oversight he managed to evade, and achieved success thanks to the Byzantine emperor's support. Modern scholars fairly universally accept this version of events as true, stressing that the loss of Serbian lands during the early years of Peter's reign was a major

---

[9] Г. Острогорски, *Порфирогенитова…*, pp. 84–86. G. Ostrogorsky's supposition was accepted by, i.a.: И. Дуйчев, *Отношенията между южните славяни и Византия през X–XII в.*, [in:] idem, *Избрани произведения*, vol. I, *Византия и славянския свят*, София 1998, pp. 64–65; P. Stephenson, *Byzantium's Balkan Frontier. A Political Study of the Northern Balkans, 900–1204*, Cambridge 2000, p. 27; Т. Тодоров, *България…*, p. 194. Criticism of this view – Т. Живковић, *Јужни…*, p. 421, fn. 1428.

[10] И. Божилов, В. Гюзелев, *История…*, p. 279; Т. Живковић, *Јужни…*, p. 421. A compromise solution was recently proposed by Plamen Pavlov (П. Павлов, *Години на мир и "ратни беди" (927–1018)*, [in:] Г. Атанасов, В. Вачкова, П. Павлов, *Българска национална история*, vol. III, *Първо българско царство (680–1018)*, Велико Търново 2015, p. 422) according to whom Chaslav's flight took place in 928, and the Byzantines extended help to him in 931.

[11] It would seem the learned emperor is writing about the seven years in the context of Chaslav. The latter most recently appeared in Constantine Porphyrogennetos's narrative in a passage devoted to occupation of Serbian lands by Bulgarians.

setback for the tsar[12]. It would seem, however, that one may have certain doubts as to the veracity of this account. Caution is advised due to the clear hostility of Constantine Porphyrogennetos towards Bulgarians. The issue was discussed some time ago by Gennadiy G. Litavrin[13]. The emperor, it would seem, negatively evaluated the 927 peace treaty between Bulgaria and Byzantium. He expressed it through criticism of the marriage, arranged as a result of the conclusion of peace, between tsar Peter and Maria, daughter of Christopher and granddaughter of Romanos Lekapenos[14].

Constantine Porphyrogennetos formulated a view, *nota bene* contrary to some of the facts he presented, that the Serbian ruler was never subject to the prince of Bulgaria, and always accepted the authority of the Byzantine emperor[15]. With such attitude of the emperor one might

[12] M.J. Leszka, K. Marinow, *Carstwo bułgarskie. Polityka – społeczeństwo – gospodarka – kultura. 866–971*, Warszawa 2015, p. 154.

[13] Г. Литаврин, *Константин Багрянородный о Болгарии и Болгарах*, [in:] *Сборник в чест на акад. Димитър Ангелов*, ed. В. Велков, София 1994, pp. 30–37; cf. Т. Тодоров, *България...*, p. 195.

[14] Constantine VII Porphyrogennetos, *On the Governance of the Empire*, 13, p. 72. Cf. J. Shepard, *A Marriage too Far? Maria Lekapena and Peter of Bulgaria*, [in:] *The Empress Theophano. Byzantium and the West at the Turn of the First Millennium*, ed. A. Davids, Cambridge 1995, pp. 121–149; Т. Тодоров, *Константин Багренородни и династичният брак между владетелските домове на Преслав и Константинопол от 927 г.*, ПКШ 7, 2003, pp. 391–398; A. Paroń, *"Trzeba, abyś tymi oto słowami odparł i to niedorzeczne żądanie" – wokół De administrando imperio Konstantyna VII*, [in:] *Causa creandi. O pragmatyce źródła historycznego*, ed. S. Rosik, P. Wiszewski, Wrocław 2005, pp. 345–361; В. Гюзелев, *Значението на брака на цар Петър (927–969) с ромейката Мария-Ирина Лакапина (911–962)*, [in:] *Културните текстове на миналото – носители, символи, идеи*, vol. I, *Текстовете на историята, история на текстовете. Материали от Юбилейната международна конференция в чест на 60-годишнината на проф. д.и.н. Казимир Попконстантинов, Велико Търново, 29–31 октомври 2003 г.*, София 2005, pp. 27–33; Z.A. Brzozowska, *Rola carycy Marii-Ireny Lekapeny w recepcji elementów bizantyńskiego modelu władzy w pierwszym państwie bułgarskim*, VP 66, 2016, pp. 443–458; eadem, *Cesarzowa Bułgarów, Augusta i Bazylisa – Maria-Irena Lekapena i transfer bizantyńskiej idei kobiety-władczyni (imperial feminine) w średniowiecznej Bułgarii*, SMer 17, 2017, pp. 1–28.

[15] T. Živković (*De conversion...*, p. 178) thinks that this passage *had originally belonged to the Constantine's primary source on the Serbs*. Even if this was so, the learned emperor fully shared the view about the Serbs being subject to Byzantium. The topic

expect that he presented the story of Chaslav's departure from Preslav and his return to Serbian lands in a manner unfavourable to Bulgarians and highlighting the prince's subordination to Byzantium, thanks to which he was able to take over Serbia.

Todor Todorov[16] also pointed out that the learned emperor's narrative about the Serbs ended with this event. It is doubtful indeed that no further information concerning the Serbian ruler in the following two decades would have reached the emperor, particularly when the ruler in question acknowledged the emperor's authority. This may indicate (a thought that the Bulgarian scholar did not state clearly) that the subsequent fate of the Serbs (until the time when *On the Governance of the Empire* was written) was omitted by the emperor as it would have starkly clashed with the statement about Serbs' subordination to Byzantium. Nonetheless, it cannot be ruled out that the reason for the narrative's sudden end was not intentional, and that chapter 32 was simply not finished, like the vast majority of chapters in the work of Constantine Porphyrogennetos[17].

Aside from the story's timbre, our doubts may be raised by some of its particular details. It is difficult, in our opinion, to imagine that Bulgarians would have allowed Chaslav, with a group of his companions, to flee Preslav. The story is strikingly similar to an implausible account according to which Byzantines have taken John, Peter's brother, away from Preslav, without the latter's agreement[18]. The Serbian prince was, one might presume, too important and potentially dangerous to Bulgarian interests in Serbia to have been left without adequate guard.

It would also be difficult to accept as truth that the Byzantines, soon after concluding peace that put an end to a lengthy armed struggle with Bulgaria, would have taken the risk of entering a new conflict with tsar Peter – which, after all, could have led to renewed military operations. The

---

appeared several times in the earlier parts of chapter 32, although without the Bulgarian context (Constantine VII Porphyrogennetos, *On the Governance of the Empire*, 32, pp. 152, 154, 158).

[16] T. Тодоров, *България...*, p. 195.

[17] T. Živković, *De conversione...*, pp. 23–24.

[18] Symeon Magister, 136.60; Continuator of Theophanes, p. 419; John Skylitzes, p. 225.

description of taking control of Serbian lands by Chaslav likewise appears far from truth and heavily manipulated in order to highlight Byzantium's role. The text states that after arriving on Serbian lands Chaslav encountered no more than *fifty men only, without wives or children, who supported themselves by hunting*[19], and it was only thanks to the Byzantine emperor's support that he managed to encourage Serbs to return to their country.

The doubts presented above allow, one might think, to view Chaslav's departure from the Bulgarian capital in a different light. It cannot be ruled out that he returned to Serbian lands with an agreement, or perhaps even at the behest of tsar Peter, with Byzantine aid. At the time when a permanent Bulgarian-Byzantine alliance was in effect, Serbian lands ceased to be an area of rivalry between the two states. One might add that the Croatian threat has been neutralised[20], that threat having been one of the reasons why in the past Symeon decided to introduce direct

---

[19] Constantine VII Porphyrogennetos, *On the Governance of the Empire*, 32, p. 158 (transl. p. 159). This fragment is in accord with an earlier passage of *On the Governance of the Empire*, stating that after the Bulgarian expedition of 924 *the country was left deserted* (trans. p. 159). One has to agree with Evgeniy P. Naumov (Е.П. Наумов, *Становление и развитие сербской раннефеодальной государственности*, [in:] *Раннефеодальные государства на Балканах. VI–XII вв.*, ed. Г.Г. Литаврин, Москва 1985, pp. 201–208; cf. Константин Багрянородный, *Об управлении империей*, ed. Г.Г. Литаврин, А.П. Новосельцев, Москва 1991, p. 382, fn. 48), that this is most certainly an exaggeration. Constantine Porphyrogennetos thus deprecated the subjugation of Serbia to Bulgaria. On the Serbian prisoners of war in Bulgaria – Y.M. Hristov, *Prisoners of War in Early Medieval Bulgaria (Preliminary reports)*, SCer. 5, 2015, pp. 90–91; idem, *Военнопленниците в българо-сръбските отношения през ранно средновековие*, Епо 23.1, 2015, pp. 86–98. Cf. also remarks about the lack of Bulgarian garrisons in Serbia – П. Коматина, *О српско-бугарској граници у IX и X в.*, ЗРВИ 52, 2015, p. 36.

[20] The sources lack information about Bulgarian-Croatian fighting at the beginning of Peter's reign, there is only information about anti-Bulgarian coalition which also included Croatia, which, as is known, did not take any action (Continuator of Theophanes, p. 412; John Skylitzes, p. 221; John Zonaras, p. 473). It is thought that a peace treaty was concluded between Bulgaria and Croatia, as a result of activity of the papal legates Madalbert and John. Cf. И. Дуйчев, *Отношенията...*, p. 63; D. Mandić, *Croatian King Tomislav defeated Bulgarian Emperor Symeon the Great on May 27, 927*, JCrS 1, 1960, pp. 32–43; Т. Живковић, *Јужни...*, p. 419, fn. 1423; M.J. Leszka, *Symeon I Wielki a Bizancjum. Z dziejów stosunków bułgarsko-bizantyńskich w latach 893–927*, Łódź 2013, pp. 223–224; Т. Тодоров, *България...*, pp. 116, 196.

Bulgarian rule over Serbian lands. It could be said that tsar Peter returned to the policy of enthroning rulers friendly to Bulgaria in Serbia. Chaslav, a half-Bulgarian, may have given hope that he would act according to Bulgarian interests which were not contrary to those of the Byzantines[21].

Our knowledge of Chaslav's reign is practically non-existent, aside perhaps for its finale. In the work of the so-called Priest of Duklja we find a Serbian ruler named Chaslav[22] who is identified with Chaslav from *On the Governance of the Empire*. It is known that he fought with Hungarians and, after initial successes, he was defeated and imprisoned in Srem[23]. He was then to have been drowned by them in the river Sava. The Serbian-Hungarian conflict is considered by some scholars to be a consequence of the Serbian alliance with Byzantium against a Bulgarian-Hungarian coalition[24]. The very existence of the latter, however, is far from obvious. On the contrary, it seems that at least until the early 940s Bulgaria and Byzantium had a common policy towards the Hungarians, who threatened both of the states[25]. In fighting Hungarians, the Serbs were promoting not only Byzantine, but also Bulgarian interests[26]. Chaslav's death occurred ca. 943/944[27] and one might think that at least until that time (and possibly until the end of tsar Peter's reign) Serbia maintained ties with both Bulgaria and Byzantium[28].

---

[21] Т. Тодоров, *България...*, p. 196.

[22] Priest of Duklja. Analysis of the Priest of Duklja's relation about Chaslav – vol. II, pp. 204–209.

[23] It is not certain whether the cited author had in mind the Srem settlement, or the region. Cf. *Historia Królestwa Słowian czyli Latopis Popa Duklanina*, transl., ed. J. Leśny, Warszawa 1988, p. 152, fn. 135.

[24] Х. Димитров, *Българо-унгарски отношения (927–1019)*, ИПр 50/51.2, 1994/1995, pp. 6–7; idem, *Българо-унгарски отношения през средновековието*, София 1998, pp. 73–74.

[25] This view is presented by Todorov (Т. Тодоров, *България...*, pp. 197–201), supporting it with strong arguments.

[26] Е.П. Наумов, [in:] Константин Багрянородный, *Об управлении империей...*, p. 382, fn. 53; Т. Живковић, *Јужни...*, p. 422; Т. Тодоров, *България...*, p. 199; П. Павлов, *Години на мир...*, p. 428.

[27] Т. Живковић, *Јужни...*, pp. 422; 423; idem, *Портрети...*, p. 72. Other dates of Chaslav's death are also present in the scholarly works – e.g. Х. Димитров, *Българо-унгарски отношения през средновековието*, София 1998, p. 74 (between 950 and 960).

[28] Cf. remarks of T. Živković (*On the Northern Borders of Serbia in Early Middle Ages*, [in:] idem, *The South Slavs between East and West. 550–1150*, Belgrade

2. Hungarians

According to the Byzantine chroniclers, one of the reasons which caused the Bulgarian government to adopt an amicable policy towards Byzantium was to have been the threat of an invasion by the neighbouring peoples. The sources mention by name primarily the Croatians, the Turks (Hungarians), and the Serbs[29]. However, the claims of these authors (who were dependent on one another) do not stand up to scrutiny. The main argument against them is the anti-Byzantine military action undertaken by Peter and George Sursuvul, which would not have happened if the borders of the Bulgarian states had not been secure. This is particularly the case when one considers that the information of a concerted military action by Bulgaria's neighbours would have indicated the existence of some form of a coalition that would have likely been organised by the Byzantines – as it was also their actions that the Bulgarians supposedly feared. The idea of any kind of such an agreement with the Empire seems to be countered by the Hungarians' rejection, in the same year, of the Byzantine proposal to enter into an agreement with the Pechenegs[30]. Perhaps, then, the only real move on the part of Constantinople was the spreading of some rumours at the Bulgarian court about a possible anti-Bulgarian military action that was, supposedly, being planned. In such case, the Bulgarian ruler's armed expedition could be seen as a reaction to the information about this alleged coalition. A show of force on the

---

2008, p. 255) on the subject of Belo, the legendary successor to Chaslav (Priest of Duklja, LXXII).

[29] Symeon Magister, 136.46–47 (Croatians); Continuator of Theophanes, p. 412 (Croatians, Turks); John Skylitzes, p. 228 (Croatians, Turks, Serbs). As can be seen from the above, the Serbs only appear in Skylitzes, a source that is much later than the other two. In the context of the considerations presented above regarding Chaslav, one should cast doubt on Skylitzes' relation regarding the possible participation of Serbs in this coalition. It is worth remembering that at the time of Symeon's death they were subordinated to Bulgarians. It would seem that this is another argument in favour of the view that the anti-Bulgarian coalition from 927 is merely an invention of Byzantine sources.

[30] G. Moravcsik, *Byzantium and the Magyars*, Budapest 1970, p. 54.

part of Symeon's descendant would have indicated that he did not fear the Roman scheming. However, a quick and decisive agreement of the Byzantine government to the proposed peace treaty, combined with the lack of information about any kind of raid of foreign peoples on Bulgaria during that year, and the next few to follow, clearly attests to the lack of any real external threat[31].

The matter of relations between Bulgaria and Hungary during Peter's reign is far from being settled for good, the main difficulty stemming from the problem of establishing the relations of the latter with Byzantium. It is known that the Hungarians from time to time organised looting expeditions into the Byzantine Empire's territories. The earliest such undertakings recorded in the sources date to April of 934, when the raiders were said to have plundered eastern Thrace and reached Constantinople[32], and taken numerous hostages. Romanos Lekapenos did not undertake a military action against the raiders, and instead decided to negotiate the release of the Byzantine captives from the Hungarians. The negotiations were handled by the *protovestiarios* and *patrician* Theophanes, who arranged for an exchange of captives, while supposedly gaining the Hungarians' respect in the process[33]. The next raid took place in 943. At that time the Hungarians most likely also reached Attica and the Corinthian Isthmus. As previously, the matter of their withdrawal from the Byzantine lands was not resolved on a battlefield, but through negotiation, once again conducted by patrician Theophanes[34]. This period of somewhat arbitral resolution of the Hungarian raids came to an end during the late 950s, just prior to Constantine VII Porphyrogennetos's

---

[31] И. Божилов, В. Гюзелев, *История...*, pp. 272–273; Х. Димитров, *Българо-унгарски отношения...*, pp. 71–72.

[32] G. Moravcsik, *Byzantium...*, pp. 55–56; В. Тъпкова-Заимова, *Цар Петър. Вътрешно- и външнополитичееска дейност*, [in:] *История на България в четиринадесет тома*, vol. II, *Първо българска държава*, ed. Д. Ангелов, София 1981, p. 372; И. Божилов, В. Гюзелев, *История...*, p. 290; Х. Димитров, *Българо-унгарски отношения...*, pp. 72–73.

[33] Continuator of Theophanes, pp. 422–423.

[34] Continuator of Theophanes, pp. 430–431. G. Moravcsik, *Byzantium...*, p. 56; T. Antonopoulos, *Byzantium, the Magyar Raids and Their Consequences*, Bsl 54, 1993, p. 260.

death. The 959 expedition of the Hungarians ended in their defeat at the hands of the Byzantine army commanded by Pothos Argyros[35]. The following Hungarian raid, in 960, ended in a similar fashion. This time the Hungarians were stopped by the *domestikos of the West*, Leo Phokas (the Younger)[36]. The year 961 brought another Hungarian raid on Thrace. *Continuation of Theophanes* states that the Hungarians were defeated by patrician Marianos Argyros[37]. It would seem that the Hungarians became active once more only near the end of Nikephoros Phokas's reign. While we do not have information about specific expeditions, even if one were to ignore Nikephoros's accusations laid at Peter's door – that he allowed the Hungarian troops to pass through his lands on the way to Byzantium[38], the same is attested in a relation by Liudprand of Cremona, who was staying in Constantinople in 968. The bishop mentioned that during Nikephoros's reign, Hungarians have taken captive 500 Byzantines from the area of Thessalonike, and carried them away into their lands. He also mentioned the activity of a 200 strong Hungarian troop in the vicinity of Constantinople. Forty of the warriors from this unit were taken into captivity by the Byzantines; they were subsequently incorporated into the emperor's guard[39]. Liudprand also related that the Byzantines did not allow him to leave Constantinople, claiming that Arabs held dominion over the sea, while Hungarians – over the land. While the author of the *Legatio* claimed that this was not true[40], the fact that such a pretext was used attests that it must have been at least plausible.

[35] Continuator of Theophanes, pp. 462–463; T. Antonopoulos, *Byzantium*..., p. 261; cf. Х. Димитров, *Българо-унгарски отношения*..., pp. 75, 86 (fn. 27).

[36] Leo the Deacon, pp. 18–19; *Life of Athanasios of Athos*, p. 74; cf. П. Мутафчиев, *Маджарите и българо-византийските отношения през третата четвърт на X в.*, [in:] idem, *Избрани произведения*, vol. II, София 1973, pp. 457–458; Х. Димитров, *Българо-унгарски отношения*..., pp. 75, 87 (fn. 29–31). On Leo Phokas – I. Burić, *Porodica Foka*, ЗРВИ 17, 1976, pp. 253–254.

[37] Continuator of Theophanes, p. 480. Cf. В.Н. Златарски, *История*..., p. 568; П. Мутафчиев, *Маджарите*..., p. 458; Х. Димитров, *Българо-унгарски отношения*..., pp. 75, 87 (fn. 33).

[38] John Zonaras, XVI, 27, p. 513.

[39] Liudprand of Cremona, *Embassy*, 45; cf. G. Moravcsik, *Byzantium*..., p. 59.

[40] Liudprand of Cremona, *Embassy*, 46.

How the looting raids mentioned above are linked to Bulgaria? Hungarians, to reach Byzantine lands from their homeland, after crossing the Danube, were most likely to have moved along the *via militaris* (along the Belgrade–Naissos–Sredets–Philippoupolis route), and therefore through Bulgarian territory, over ca. 600 km.

The route taken by the Magyars through the Bulgarian territory was rather specific. First, between Belgrade and Naissos, it cut through a densely forested area, the so-called *Silva Bulgarica*. Soon after passing Naissos, it entered a mountainous region, and run along small ravines, all the way until the Sofia Valley, the central point of which was Sredets (the ancient Serdica). Following from there it entered a mountainous region several tens of kilometres long and, having crossed the Ihtiman Pass, it finally entered the lowland areas of the northern Thrace, with its main centre in Plovdiv. From here, it was not far to the Byzantine border and the more densely populated Aegean areas[41].

It should be noted that the central areas of the Bulgarian state, with the highest population density and the capital Preslav, were located at a considerable distance from this route, and were furthermore protected from the south and south-west by the mountain ranges – Stara Planina and Sredna Gora.

The attitude of the Bulgarian ruler appears to suggest that either along the entirety of the discussed part of the famed military road, with the exception of the larger urban centres, the network of settlements was poorly developed, or the Preslav's ruler, not feeling strong enough to stop the hostile raids, was prepared to sacrifice the small local settlements for the price of not having to engage in military action, which could result in even greater losses. He likely counted on the larger strongholds' ability to withstand the raid, or was aware that the Hungarians were not interested in besieging them.

[41] On the subject of this route, see i.a.: K.J. J i r e č e k, *Die Heerstrasse von Belgrad nach Constantinopel und die Balkanpässe. Eine Historisch-Geographische Studie*, Prag 1877; П. М у т а ф ч и е в, *Старият друм през "Траянови врата"*, СБАН.КИФ 55.27, 1937, pp. 19–148; F. D a l l' A g l i o, "*In ipsa silva longissima Bulgariae*"*: Western chroniclers of the Crusades and the Bulgarian forest*, BMd 1, 2010, pp. 403–416.

The situation along the aforementioned route during the eleventh–twelfth centuries appears to confirm the first of the above hypotheses – while the road was exceptionally convenient, the human habitation along its length was not particularly prominent, and perhaps it was even – because of those using it – purposefully neglected to a degree at some stages[42].

In considering the above question we may be, however, submitting ourselves to the dictate of the Byzantine authors, who after all only noted those of the Hungarian expeditions that reached the empire's territories, while ignoring the raids that only affected Bulgarian lands[43]. Besides, this is also indicated by the Bulgarian reply to the accusation that the raiders were let through the Tsardom's territory, which resulted in them reaching the Byzantine areas – the Bulgarians, on many occasions, unsuccessfully asked the Byzantines for military aid to fight the Magyars. This may be an indication that Bulgaria was raided more frequently than Byzantium.

Hungarians were a factor that Peter needed to somehow account for throughout the entirety of his reign. What was Peter's attitude towards them? The answer to this question, for the lack of sufficient light that would be shed on this issue by the sources, is formulated in a variety of ways. One may distinguish three main positions[44]. According to some of the scholars, the movements of the Hungarians, who entered Bulgarian lands as invaders, were possible because of the weakness of Peter's rule[45]. Others think that the Magyars crossed Bulgaria maintaining 'armed

[42] Cf. for the period of Byzantine rule over this area – K.J. Jireček, *Die Heerstrasse...*, pp. 86, 116; К. Гагова, *Кръстоносните походи и средновековна България*, София 2004, p. 39; Е. Койчева, *Първите кръстоносни походи и Балканите*, София 2004, pp. 140, 143–144.

[43] Cf. S. Runciman, *The History of the First Bulgarian Empire*, London 1930, p. 186.

[44] Т. Тодоров, *България през втората и третата четвърт на X век: политическа история*, София 2006 [unpublished PhD thesis], p. 197; Х. Димитров, *Българо-унгарски отношения...*, pp. 72–73.

[45] П. Мутафчиев, *Маджарите...*, p. 460; В. Тъпкова-Заимова, *Цар Петър...*, p. 372; Д. Ангелов, Б. Чолпанов, *Българска военна история през средновековието (X–XV в.)*, София 1994, p. 14; T. Antonopoulos, *Byzantium...*, p. 258.

neutrality', with the silent (forced) consent of the tsar[46]. The third view assumes that the Hungarians appeared in Bulgaria as allies, after both sides came to an appropriate agreement. How this could have been reconciled with the peace treaty with Byzantium? Simply enough: the Bulgarian-Hungarian alliance would have been made in secrecy. Those supporting the latter view think that the potential Bulgarian-Hungarian co-operation would have been a consequence of the Byzantium's support for the Serbs, who became independent from Bulgaria at the beginning of Peter's reign[47].

On the basis of the existing sources it would be very difficult to take an unequivocal position regarding tsar Peter's attitude towards the Hungarians, however it does not mean that one cannot formulate some remarks and indicate one's own position on the matter.

Hungarian expeditions were organised, with some pauses, over the course of over thirty years, and involved varying forces. In this situation it would appear logical to conclude that the Bulgarian attitude towards the particular raids would have differed[48]. The sources' lack of information about the behaviour of the Hungarians while they were marching through Bulgarian lands may mean that they did not pose a particular threat to the Bulgarians, and their outcomes had no significant impact, therefore it cannot be ruled out that tsar Peter, being aware that Hungarians wanted to reach Byzantine lands, did not see a reason to engage in a military action to stop them[49]. The silence of the Byzantine sources could however be deceptive, especially as we lack native Bulgarian sources on

---

[46] В.Н. Златарски, *История...*, pp. 541–542; И. Божилов, В. Гюзелев, *История...*, p. 291.

[47] В. Гюзелев, *Добруджанският надпис и събитията в България през 943 г.*, ИП 25.6, 1969, pp. 43–45; П. Коледаров, *Цар Петър I*, ВС 51, 1982, p. 200; J.A.V. Fine, *The Early...*, s. 162–163; P. Stephenson, *Byzantium's...*, p. 39; Х. Димитров, *Българо-унгарски отношения...*, p. 73sqq.

[48] Cf. П. Павлов, *Векът на цар Самуил*, София 2014, pp. 24–25.

[49] It cannot be ruled out, however, that the Bulgarians informed the Byzantines about the Hungarians moving through their lands – much like they did in case of the Rus' expeditions (*Russian Primary Chronicle*, AM 6449, 6452, pp. 45, 46). On the latter subject, see: А.Н. Сахаров, *Дипломацията на древна Русия, IX – първата половина на X в.*, София 1984, p. 204sqq.

this matter. In this context it might be worth reminding Peter's reply to Nikephoros Phokas's demand regarding stopping of the Hungarian raids venturing towards Byzantine lands by Bulgarians. The Bulgarian tsar supposedly accused the Byzantines that, despite their demands that Bulgarians stop the Hungarian raids, they themselves did not provide any assistance in this regard[50].

It cannot be therefore ruled out that the Bulgarians were only observing, monitoring as we would say nowadays, the behaviour of the Hungarians moving through their lands, with the awareness that it was the Byzantines who were being targeted. It is also worth noting here that, in the light of the preserved sources, the first two raids (in 934 and 943) were evidently incidental in nature, and therefore likely came as a surprise to the Bulgarian ruler. It is notable that they were not met with a vigorous resistance on the part of Byzantium, either. It cannot be ruled out that Todorov was right when he claimed that at the time Bulgaria and Byzantium had a common policy towards the Hungarians, aimed at neutralising the threat by buying the peace[51]. The Bulgarian scholar pointed out that the main figure representing the Byzantine side in solving the problems that arose from the Hungarian raids in 934 and 943 was *protovestiarios* Theophanes, the man who also participated in the negotiations that led to the conclusion of the Bulgarian-Byzantine treaty in 927. Of particular significance here are the two seals of Theophanes (from the time when he was a *protovestiarios* and a *patrician*) found in Preslav, and therefore from the period between 934 and 941[52]. This indicates at the very least that during the time of Hungarian raids an important person from the imperial court remained in touch with the Preslav court, which may have created a chance for developing a common policy towards the Hungarian threat. That Byzantium and Bulgaria were implementing such a policy towards the Hungarians at that time can be attested, according to Todorov, by the relation of Liudprand of Cremona, who stayed in Constantinople for the first time relatively soon after the second Hungarian raid and who

[50] John Zonaras, XVI, 27, 14–15, p. 513.

[51] Т. Тодоров, *България...*, pp. 197–201.

[52] On Theophanes' career, Т. Тодоров, *България...*, pp. 200, 222. Cf. И. Йорданов, *Печатите от стратегията в Преслав*, София 1993, pp. 37–38.

wrote that the Hungarians: *had made the nations of the Bulgarians and the Greeks tributary*[53].

The subsequent raids of the Magyars, those from the second half of the 950s and from the 960s, were a result of the change of direction of their expansion, which occurred after their defeat in battle against Otto I at the Lechfeld in 955[54]. The German victory freed Western Europe from the Hungarians looting raids, redirecting them towards the Balkan Peninsula. Only when faced with these tsar Peter had to specify his attitude towards the intruders.

As was mentioned above, from the late 950s the Byzantines abandoned the previous practice of neutralising Hungarian threat through diplomatic means in favour of military solutions, taking decisive steps to defend their territory. The change in the Byzantine attitude towards the Hungarian looting expeditions are associated on the one hand with the Hungarian defeat at the Lechfeld, which undermined the myth of their invincibility, and on the other with the changes on the imperial throne. The first military reaction to the Hungarian incursion into Byzantine lands is recorded to have happened during the final months of Constantine VII Porphyrogennetos's reign[55]. His successors, Romanos II and Nikephoros Phokas, followed the same path.

---

[53] L i u d p r a n d o f C r e m o n a, *Retribution*, II, [7], p. 39: *Bulgariorum gentem atque Graecorum tributariam fecerant*; transl. p. 79; Liudprand stayed in Constantinople in 949. The remark mentioned above appeared in the context of the events from the close of the ninth century, however it did not match the realities of the period at all, and it should be associated with the times preceding Liudprand's first visit to Constantinople (П. М у т а ф ч и е в, *Маджарите*..., p. 455, fn. 31; *contra*, although without providing arguments, Х. Д и м и т р о в, *Българо-унгарски отношения*..., p. 74). It would seem that – if one were to accept Petar Mutafchiev's conclusion – Liudprand's relation could indicate no more than the fact that Bulgarians and Byzantines decided against organising a joint resistance against the Hungarians, and for some reasons preferred to pay them tribute.

[54] On the subject of the battle of Lechfeld, see i.a.: J.K. K u n d e r t, *Der Kaser auf dem Lechfeld*, CMAe 1, 1998, pp. 77–97; R.Ch. B o w l u s, *Die Schlacht auf dem Lechfeld*, Ostfildern 2012.

[55] Practically throughout nearly the entirety of the autonomous reign of Constantine Porphryrogennetos Hungarians abstained from taking hostile actions against Byzantium, which has led some scholars to the conclusion that he concluded with

Perhaps the Byzantines attempted to convince the Bulgarians to undertake similar actions, which potentially could have made it impossible for the Hungarians to reach Byzantine lands, or at least would have made the journey more difficult. Tsar Peter, as we may surmise, either could not or did not want to take such course of action, and maintained his policy of concessions towards the Hungarians. Perhaps in some cases Hungarian troops entered Bulgarians lands with the tsar's silent permission, in others – without it. It would however be unlikely that this was happening as a result of an active and lasting Bulgarian-Hungarian alliance[56]. It would be difficult to imagine that the existence of such an agreement could be kept hidden from the Byzantines. Had that been

---

them a peace agreement (eg.: Х. Димитров, *Българо-унгарски отношения...*, p. 75; G. Moravcsik, *Byzantium...* p. 56). This view is based on the relation from *Continuation of Theophanes*, in which it is said that following the raid of 943 there was a five-year period of peace in the Hungarian-Byzantine relations. The source does not however state that this peace was a result of a concluded peace treaty. It is also notable that the next recorded Hungarian action is as late as 959.

[56] The chief proponent of this view is Hristo Dimitrov (Х. Димитров, *Българо-унгарски отношения...*, pp. 73–80). The arguments he raised, however, do not seem convincing. They are based on a loose interpretation of the remarks found in the sources of unclear chronology and undertones (the third Greek edition of the *Apocalypse of Pseudo-Methodius*, pp. 98–99; a poem of an anonymous author *For the Strategos Katakalon – FGHB*, vol. V, p. 306; *De re militari liber* (18, 24–28, pp. 292–293), associating of tsar Peter's attitude towards Hungarians with the question of Byzantine policy towards Serbia – which we have put into doubt while discussing Bulgarian-Serbian relations – or drawing conclusions purely on the basis of coincidence of events (e.g. activity of Hungarians on Byzantine lands in 968, mentioned by Liudprand of Cremona, *Embassy*, 45 (he speaks here of the activity near Thessalonike and Constantinople, involving units of 300 and 200 men, and therefore small in number, which was already mentioned earlier) as fulfilling commitments of the alliance with Bulgaria, threatened at the time by Byzantium, p. 78). The views of Dimitrov regarding the functioning of a Bulgarian-Hungarian alliance since the time when Constantine VII started ruling on his own are accepted by Todorov (Т. Тодоров, *България...*, pp. 202–203). Cf. remarks by И. Божилов, В. Гюзелев, *История...*, pp. 290–291; V. Gjuzelev, *Bułgaria a państwa i narody Europy Środkowej w X w.*, transl. K. Marinow, [in:] *Byzantina Europaea. Księga jubileuszowa ofiarowana Profesorowi Waldemarowi Ceranowi*, ed. M. Kokoszko, M.J. Leszka, Łódź 2007, pp. 134–135 (the author clearly articulated the view that the Hungarian expeditions would not have been possible without Peter's favourable attitude); П. Павлов, *Векът...*, p. 25.

the case, then they certainly would have had to react to such an attitude of the Bulgarians, which would after all have been contrary to the letter of the treaty of 927. We find no trace of such a course of action in the sources, which is all the more telling because of the distance that the Byzantine authors maintained towards the Bulgarians, and as such they would have likely commented on the Bulgarian disloyalty, and Byzantines' own reaction to it. It seems clear that the Bulgarian-Hungarian relations were characterised by a considerable dynamism, resulting from both the Byzantine reluctance to provide military support for Bulgarians to counter the possible lightning-fast Magyar incursions, as well as from the autonomy of the individual Hungarian chiefs[57].

There is a view in scholarship that after 963 the Hungarians started to take action against the Bulgarians, which in some way was associated with the renewed Bulgarian-Byzantine treaty, supposedly of a clearly anti-Hungarian nature[58]. It should be noted however that this view lacks a strong basis in the source material. Not only do we not have a certainty that such a treaty existed, we even more so do not know on what conditions it would then have been renewed. It is difficult to say whether the Hungarian raids described by John Zonaras[59] – the ones that supposedly forced Bulgarians to reach an agreement with Hungarians – really referred to this period, rather than being a reference to the aforementioned Hungarian expeditions into Byzantine lands.

3. Relations with Otto I

Peter's policy towards the Hungarians is associated in modern scholarship with the issue of the relations between Bulgaria and the German state ruled by Otto I. Our knowledge about the attitude of tsar Peter

[57] П. Павлов, *Векът*..., pp. 24–25.
[58] V. Gjuzelev, *Bulgaria*..., p. 135.
[59] John Zonaras, XVI, 27, 13, pp. 512–513.

towards the increasingly more powerful state of Otto I – who in 955 defeated the Hungarians at Lechfeld, successfully discouraging them from further raids, and in 962 accepted an imperial crown, which was a visible reflection of his exceptional role in Europe[60] – is, to put it mildly, sparse. It is practically limited to a single episode, captured by Ibrahim ibn Yaqub. This traveller, merchant and diplomat writes that during his stay in Magdeburg (965/966)[61] he encountered representatives of the tsar of Bulgarians, who acted as envoys to Otto I (called Hōtto here). To our disappointment, Ibrahim ibn Yaqub did not write a single word on the reason for their arrival to the imperial court[62]. In this situation the scholars may only guess that either Peter wanted to gain German assistance against the Hungarians, when he was not able to obtain it from Byzantium, or the potential agreement with Otto was intended to strengthen Bulgaria's position *vis a vis* Constantinople[63]. Perhaps the Bulgarian ruler wanted to secure the position of his state, in the context of both the growing German power and the intensifying German-Byzantine conflict; in particular since the political situation in which the Bulgarians have found themselves has changed considerably. Firstly, as was already mentioned, Otto was elevated to an imperial dignity in 962 and undertook efforts to have his title recognised at the Constantinopolitan court. This may have troubled Peter, whose own imperial title had been, after all, received

---

[60] On the imperial coronation of Otto I – G. Althoff, *Ottonowie. Władza królewska bez państwa*, transl. M. Tycner-Wolicka, Warszawa 2009, pp. 84–91.

[61] J. Widajewicz, *Studia nad relacją Ibrahima ibn Jakuba*, Kraków 1946, p. 11; Ibrahim ibn Jakub, p. XLI (Otto I remained in Magdeburg prior to 26 of May 965; and subsequently during the March–August period of 966); cf. P. Engels, *Der Reisebericht des Ibrahim ibn Ya'qub (961/966)*, [in:] *Kaiserin Theophanu. Begegnung des Ostens und Westens um die Wende des ersten Jahrtausends. Gedenkschrift des Kölner Schnütgen – Museums zum 1000 Todesjahr der Kaiserin*, ed. A. von Euw, P. Schreiner, vol. I, Köln 1991, p. 417.

[62] Ibrahim ibn Jakub, p. 148.

[63] С.А. Иванов, *Византийско-болгарские отношения в 966–969 гг.*, ВВ 42, 1981, p. 98; В. Гюзелев, *Българските пратеничества при германския император Отон И в Магдебург (965 г.) и в Кведлинбург (973 г.)*, [in:] *Civitas Divino-Humana. In honorem Annorum LX Georgii Bakalov*, ed. Ц. Степанов, В. Вачкова, София 2004, pp. 386–387; idem, *Bułgaria a państwa...*, pp. 135–136.

from the Byzantines and who, being aware of the increased significance of the German ruler, may have feared his own position being negated by Otto. It was therefore advisable for Peter to establish peaceful relations with Otto and obtain the confirmation of the status (title) also from him. Let us add that in the context of the German-Bulgarian relations, the attitude of Liudprand, the envoy of Otto I, was rather telling. During his stay at the Byzantine court in 968, he was clearly surprised and outraged by the fact that the representative of the Bulgarian ruler was shown greater respect than he – a bishop, and an imperial envoy[64]. In 963, the power in Byzantium was seized by Nikephoros II Phokas, an outstanding military commander, who was realising an expansionist external policy, aimed at retaking the lands formerly belonging to the empire. In this situation it was good to find a strong ally in case of a confrontation with the southern neighbour, or at least ensure their own neutrality in a Byzantine-German conflict. It cannot be also ruled out that the arrival of the Bulgarian envoys to Magdeburg had the character of an ordinary diplomatic visit, with the usual goal of maintaining mutual relations. It would seem that their presence at the imperial court did not bear any specific fruit, and was not important for either of the sides (certainly not for the Germans, which may be seen from the scornful towards Bulgarians narration by Liudprand of Cremona, who was after all an imperial envoy), for beside Ibrahim ibn Yaqub it has not been recorded by any other source (neither Latin, nor Bulgarian). It would appear in turn that the visit may have unsettled Nikephoros Phokas in the context of the conflict that was developing

[64] Liudprand of Cremona, *Embassy*, 19. The Byzantines supposedly had to explain to him that the special position of the Bulgarian envoy has been reserved for him in the 927 peace treaty. From the above it can be surmised that the bishop of Cremona was not well versed in the Byzantine-Bulgarian relations. It would seem however, that this may be put in doubt. Firstly, because Liudprand, in his earlier work *Antapodosis*, written after a visit in Constantinople in 949, showed good knowledge of the Bulgarian-Byzantine treaty of 927 (III, 29, III, 38), and he also referred to this even in in *Embassy* (16, 19) and calls Peter by the Greek title *vasileus* (19). Secondly, what is perhaps even more important, in 968, by pretending he knows nothing about the status of the Bulgarian envoy who was after all representing a ruler bearing an imperial title, Liudprand indicated that beside the Byzantine ruler only his own master could be referred to as an emperor.

between him and Otto I[65]. It needs to be emphasised however that we will not find a confirmation of this hypothesis in any of the Byzantine sources.

4. The Rus' and the Pechenegs

On their north-western border, Bulgarians interacted with Rus' and Pechenegs. Little is known on the subject of the relations between Bulgaria and Kievan Rus' until the military expeditions of Svyatoslav in the late 960s. The sources took note of the attitude of the Bulgarians towards the expeditions of prince Igor to Constantinople in 941 and 943[66]. In both cases Bulgarians were said to have given an advance warning to the Byzantines about the Rus' movements[67]. This clearly attests that they maintained a loyal attitude towards the Empire. Igor's second expedition is associated with the question of the Bulgarian-Pecheneg relations. It would seem that these have generally been peaceful during Peter's reign[68].

---

[65] On the Byzantine-German relations during Nikephoros II Phokas's reign – J. Shepard, *Western approaches (900–1025)*, [in:] *The Cambridge History of the Byzantine Empire, c. 500–1492*, ed. idem, Cambridge 2008, pp. 542–549.

[66] On the subject of these raids, see i.a.: Н.Я. Половой, *О дате второго похода Игоря на греков и похода русских на Бердаа*, ВВ 14, 1958, pp. 138–147; idem, *К вопросу о первом походе Игоря против Византии. (Сравнительный анализ русских и византийских источников)*, ВВ 18, 1962, pp. 85–104; C. Zuckerman, *On the Date of the Khazars' Conversion to Judaism and the Chronology of the Kings of the Rus Oleg and Igor. A Study of the Anonymous Khazar Letter from the Genizah of Cairo*, REB 53, 1995, p 264–267; J.-P. Arrignon, *Le traite byzantino-russe de 944, acte fondateur de l'Etat de la Kievskaja Rus'?*, BB 100, 2016, pp. 93–105.

[67] The Rus' expedition of 941 ended in failure. After initial successes, the Rus' were crushed on land, in several skirmishes, by John Kourkouas, while their fleet was destroyed by the aforementioned Theophanes who, in recognition of this victory, was given the title of *parakoimomenos*. Continuator of Theophanes, pp. 423–426. Cf. Н.Я. Половой, *К вопросу о первом...*; Т. Тодоров, *България...*, pp. 204–205.

[68] И. Божилов, *Българийа и печензите (896–1018 g.)*, 29.2, 1973, pp. 53–62; Т. Тодоров, *България...*, p.204; Х. Димитров, *България и номадите до*

Bulgarians – aware of the threat that these nomads posed to the north-eastern regions of the Bulgarian state, and in particular taking into account how politically unstable a partner they have been – made effort to maintain peaceful relations with them[69]. At the same time Bulgarians fortified the most threatened territory, open from the north to Pecheneg raids – i.a. by building strongholds in Vetrena (in the Silistra province) and in Dinogentia (near the village of Garvan, in northern Dobrudzha)[70].

The only trace indicating the possible worsening of the Bulgarian-Pecheneg relations is information from the *Russian Primary Chronicle*, regarding the aforementioned expedition of Igor on Constantinople in 943[71]. According to this source, Igor, after reaching an agreement with the Byzantines, supposedly sent Pechenegs that were accompanying him to loot Bulgarian lands[72]. It is difficult to say how credible this relation is, and why Igor would have acted in this manner. The view that he would have repaid the Pechenegs in this way for their participation in the expedition is not particularly convincing. A more plausible explanation for Igor using the Pechenegs against Bulgarians is the desire for revenge on the latter for warning the Byzantines about the Rus' expedition, or perhaps an attempt at neutralising a possible Bulgarian military threat to the Rus'[73].

началото на XI век, Пловдив 2011, pp. 224–232; A. P a r o ń, *Koczownicy w krajobrazie politycznym i kulturowym średniowiecznej Europy*, Wrocław 2015, p. 320.

[69] C o n s t a n t i n e V I I P o r p h y r o g e n n e t o s, *On the Governance of the Empire*, 5, p. 52: *And so the Bulgarians also continually struggle and strive to maintain peace and harmony with the Pechenegs. For from having frequently been crushing defeated and plundered by them, they have learned by experience the value and advantage of being always at peace with them* (transl. p. 53). To some degree this was a continuation of Symeon I the Great's policy.

[70] П. П а в л о в, *Години...*, p. 431.

[71] *Russian Primary Chronicle*, AM 6452, p. 46.

[72] *Russian Primary Chronicle*, AM 6452, p. 46: *Igor' heeded them, and bade the Pechenegs ravage Bulgaria. He himself, after receiving from the Greeks gold and palls sufficient for his whole army, returned again and came to Kiev* (transl. p. 73). The lack of clarity of this relation even led some scholars to indicate that the target of the Pecheneg attack was not the Danubian Bulgaria, but the abodes of the so-called Black Bulgarians in Priazov. Cf. П. П а в л о в, *Години...*, p. 430.

[73] В.Д. Н и к о л а е в, *К истории болгаро-русских отношений в начале 40-ых годов X в.*, ССл 1982, 6, pp. 53–54; cf. Г.Г. Л и т а в р и н, *Древная Русь, Болгария и Византия в IX–X вв.* [in:] *История, култура, этнография и фолклор славянских*

For fulfilling Igor's wish the Pechenegs would have likely received payment that they could supplement with the loot taken from Bulgarians. This interpretation is, of course, purely hypothetical, especially since we cannot be certain that the Pechenegs had, in fact, acted in accordance with Igor's will.

To support the view that this had indeed been the case some of the scholars bring forward an inscription, discovered in 1950 in the village of Mircea Vodă, located in Dobrudzha (in modern-day Romania). The inscription, unfortunately, is very poorly preserved. Only a few words can be deciphered: the date 6451 (943/944), the name of *zhupan* Dimitar, and probably 'Greece', or 'Greeks'[74]. According to Vassil Gyuzelev, the *zhupan* Dimitar mentioned in the inscription halted the Pechenegs, allies of Igor, near the mouth of Danube, after they entered Bulgarian lands encouraged by the Byzantine emperor, who with their aid wanted to take revenge on Bulgarians for allowing the Hungarian expedition to pass through into the lands of the Empire[75]. Even if one were to accept that the inscription from Mircea Vodă was a confirmation of the information from the *Russian Primary Chronicle* about the Pecheneg incursion into Bulgarian lands, then in the context of the above considerations regarding the contemporary attitude of Bulgarians and Byzantines towards Hungarians one has to reject with full conviction the idea that the Pechenegs acted at the instigation of Romanos Lekapenos[76].

народов, IX международный съезд славистов, Киев, сентябрь 1983. Докладъ советской делегации, Москва 1983, p. 72; Х. Димитров, *България...*, p. 225.

[74] Text of the inscription – M. Wójtowicz, *Najstarsze datowane inskrypcje słowiańskie X–XIII wiek*, Poznań 2005, pp. 21–23; cf. Б. Джонов, *Още за Добруджанския надпис от 943 година*, [in:] *Лингвистични и етнолингвистични изследвания в памет на акад. Вл. Георгиев (1908–1986)*, ed. Ж. Бояджиев, И. Дуриданов, София 1993, pp. 159–165.

[75] В. Гюзелев, *Добруджанският...*, pp. 45–47. Cf. I. Božilov, *L'inscription du jupan Dimitre de l'an 943 (théories et faits)*, EHi 1973.6, pp. 11–28; idem, В. Гюзелев, *История на Добруджа*, vol. II, *Средновековие*, Велико Търново 2004, s. 63; S. Mihailov, *Über die Dobrudza-Inschrift von 943*, BHR 33, 2005, pp. 3–5; Х. Димитров, *България...*, pp. 228–230.

[76] Cf. Т. Тодоров, *България...*, p. 206.

It would seem however that the inscription from Mircea Vodă, due to its fragmentary nature, cannot be treated as a source of knowledge for the Bulgarian-Pecheneg relations during Peter's times. On the basis of the temporal coincidence with Igor's expedition, and of the place in which it was found, it is not possible to conclude to what it actually pertained. In this situation, for elucidating this matter we are left with only the laconic and unclear relation from the *Russian Primary Chronicle* and Constantine Porphyrogennetos's unspecific opinion about the Bulgarians' pursuance of peaceful relations with the Pechenegs.

VII

Mirosław J. Leszka
Kirił Marinow

Last Years of Peter's Reign (963–969)

Since the autumn of 927, throughout the 40 years of Peter's reign the Byzantine-Bulgarian relations were peaceful. Unfortunately, beside this general observation little else can be said of them. For the Byzantine historians, who still remain the main source of information on the history of Bulgaria of this period, they were not sufficiently interesting or important to be discussed. The native Bulgarian sources do not contain information on the subject, either.

We do know that the Preslav court maintained contacts with Constantinople. The visits of Maria-Irene to Constantinople, during which she met with her family, are a trace of this[1], much like the correspondence between Peter and Theophylaktos, the patriarch of Constantinople, regarding the Bogomil heresy[2]. However, it was only during the 960s that the Bulgarian-Byzantine political contacts intensified. Perhaps it

[1] Z.A. Brzozowska wrote more on this subject in the chapter devoted to Maria (Part One, chapter IV, points 3–4).

[2] For more information on this subject, see Part Two, chapter VII, point 3 of the book. A seal of this leader of the Byzantine Church, found most likely during an archaeological dig in Preslav, is a trace of the aforementioned correspondence – И. Йорданов, *Печат на византийския патриарх Теофилакт (933–956), намерен в Преслав*, [in:] *Тангра. Сборник в чест на 70. годишнината на Акад. Васил Гюзелев*, ed. М. Каймакавова et al., София 2006, pp. 353–557.

was in 963, during the empress Theophano's regency[3], and after the death of Maria-Irene, the peace of 927 was renewed.[4] Another view present in the academic works is that at that time Peter's sons were sent to Constantinople as hostages[5]. It needs to be noted, however, that this view – based on a passage from John Skylitzes' work – should be treated with considerable caution. It cannot be ruled out that Peter's sons arrived in the Byzantine capital much later – or not at all[6].

---

[3] On Theophano's regency – M.J. Leszka, *Rola cesarzowej Teofano w uzurpacjach Nicefora Fokasa (963) i Jana Tzymiskesa (969)*, [in:] *Zamach stanu w dawnych społecznościach*, ed. A. Sołtysik, Warszawa 2004, pp. 228–231.

[4] Such conclusion can be drawn from the relation of John Skylitzes (p. 255: *When the wife of Peter, the emperor of the Bulgars, died, he made a treaty with emperors ostensibly to renew the peace, surrendering his own sons, Boris and Romanos, as hostages. He himself died shortly afterwards, whereupon the sons were sent to Bulgaria to secure the ancestral throne and to restrain the 'children of the counts' from further encroachments* (transl. p. 246). It needs to be pointed out, however, that the Byzantine historian is far from being precise in this passage, as he combined in practically one sentence events that occurred over the course of six years. The reason for the renewal of the treaty is also doubtful. If anything, it should have been associated with the death of Romanos II, not of Maria-Irene, as the renewal of a peace treaty occurred with the new ruler's ascension to throne. Regarding the credibility of John Skylitzes' relation, see i.a.: И. Божилов, В. Гюзелев, *История на средновековна България VII–XIV в.*, София 2006, pp. 305, fn. 25, and 307, fn. 51. It cannot be ruled out that this fragment is an interpolation.

[5] В.Н. Златарски, *История на българската държава през средните векове*, vol. I/2, *Първо българско Царство. От славянизацията на държавата до падането на Първото царство (852–1018)*, София 1927, pp. 569, 592. Nikola P. Blagoev (Н.П. Благоев, *Българският цар Роман*, МПр 6.3, 1930, pp. 19–22), thought that in 963 Peter's sons remained in Constantinople not as hostages, but in relation to Romanos II's death. Plamen Pavlov, in turn (П. Павлов, *Векът на цар Самуил*, София 2014, pp. 27–28), thought that the young princes travelled to the Byzantine capital to obtain education, much like their grandfather Symeon did a century before. John Skylitzes (p. 328) included intriguing information that Romanos was supposedly castrated on the orders of the *parakoimomenos* Joseph, who is identified with Joseph Bringas, the mainstay of Theophano's regency, which would have indicated that the deed was committed in 963. This information, too, raises doubts. It was included alongside the description of Romanos' flight from Byzantium in the 970s or 980s, therefore some scholars who treat John's relation seriously place this event right after 971, and explain it with a fear that the potential offspring of Romanos (let us remind here that he was a great-grandson of Romanos Lekapenos) could be used in future in fight for the imperial throne. An Armenian author, Asochik, also writes about Romanos as of a eunuch, although without mentioning his name (Asochik, pp. 185–186).

[6] John Skylitzes, p. 255; cf. John Zonaras, p. 495. If one were to take this fragment literally, one would need to state that Peter's sons arrived in Constantinople

1. The Crisis in Bulgarian-Byzantine Relations

In the winter of 965/966 or 966/967 there had been a drastic change in the Bulgarian-Byzantine relations[7]. During that time, Peter sent envoys to Constantinople with the mission of reminding the Byzantines to pay the annual tribute to Bulgaria, which was guaranteed in the peace treaty of 927. As Leo the Deacon relates, Nikephoros Phokas reacted to this demand very sharply. Not only did he call Bulgarians *wretched and abominable Scythian people*, and Peter himself as *thrice a slave and leather-gnawing ruler*

---

soon before their father's death, which would allow linking this event with 968, rather than with 963, since Peter died on 30th of January 969.

[7] The dating of this event is uncertain. There are two main views in the scholarship on this matter: 965/966 or 966/967. It would seem that the latter date is more likely. The arguments for each of the positions (or backing of one of the other) can be found by the Reader in i.a. the following works: M. Дринов, *Началото на Самуиловата държава*, [in:] idem, *Избрани съчинения в два тома*, vol. I, *Трудове по българска и славянска история*, ed. И. Дуйчев, София 1971, pp. 398–399; В.Н. Златарски, *История...*, pp. 570, 572, 577–578, fn. 4; Н.П. Благоев, *Критичен поглед върху известията на Лъв Дякон за българите*, МПр 6.1, 1930, pp. 27–31; S. Rucіman, *The History of the First Bulgarian Empire*, London 1930, pp. 198–201; П. Мутафчиев, *Маджарите и българо-византийските отношения през третата четвърт на X в.*, [in:] idem, *Избрани произведения*, vol. II, София 1973, pp. 463, 468, 471, 474; Р.О. Карышковский, *О хронологии русско-византийской войны при Святославе*, ВВ 5, 1952, p. 138; A.D. Stokes, *The Background and Chronology of the Balkan Campaigns of Svyatoslav Igorevich*, SEER 40/94, 1961, pp. 44–57; R. Browning, *Byzantium and Bulgaria. A comparative studies across the Early Medieval Frontier*, London 1975, pp. 70–71; С.А. Иванов, *Византийско-болгарские отношения в 966–969 гг.*, ВВ 42, 1981, p. 90; В. Тъпкова-Заимова, *Падане на Североизточна България под византийска власт*, [in:] *История на България*, vol. II, *Първа българска държава*, София 1981, p. 389; А.Н. Сахаров, *Дипломатия Святослава*, Москва 1982, pp. 102, 108; J.V.A. Fine, *The Early Medieval Balkans: a Critical Survey from the Sixth to the Late Twelfth Century*, Ann Arbor 1983, pp. 163, 181–182; И. Божилов, В. Гюзелев, *История на средновековна България. VII–XIV в.*, София 2006, pp. 295, 306, fn. 36; J. Bonarek, *Przyczyny i cele bułgarskich wypraw Światosława a polityka Bizancjum w latach sześćdziesiątych X w.*, SH 39, 1996, p. 77, przyp. 183; А. Николов, *Политическа мисъл в ранносредновековна България (средата на IX – края на X в.)*, София 2006, p. 280; Т. Тодоров, *България през втората и третата четвърт на X век: политическа история*, София 2006 [unpublished PhD thesis], p. 228; П. Павлов, *Години на мир и "ратни беди" (927–1018)*, [in:] Г. Атанасов, В. Вачкова, П. Павлов, *Българска национална история*, vol. III, *Първо българско царство (680–1018)*, Велико Търново 2015, p. 432.

clad in a leather jerkin and an archon', what without a doubt was a grave insult, he also ordered the envoys to be slapped in the face[8] and emphatically rejected Bulgarian claims. The emperor was said to have been so irritated by the occurrence that almost immediately after the envoys' departure he organised a military expedition against the Bulgarians.

The above relation of Leo the Deacon and, in general, the reasons for the eruption of hostility between Peter and Nikephoros Phokas, while have been analysed multiple times by scholars, did not find a universally accepted interpretation. For example, Vassil N. Zlatarski considered Peter's move to have been fully conscious. The Bulgarian ruler wanted to shrug off the humiliating position in which he found himself (sending his sons to Constantinople as hostages) after renewing the peace in 963, and did so by using his alliance with the Hungarians[9]. Sir Steven Runciman raised the possibility that Peter was counting on Nikephoros to be fully occupied fighting the Saracens, which would have made it impossible to deny the Bulgarian demands[10]. Plamen Pavlov, however, accepted that it was a provocation on the part of the Bulgarian ruler that was intended to make the Byzantine emperor aware that his successes on the eastern front were possible only thanks to the peaceful relations with Bulgaria[11]. According to another view, the Bulgarian mission arrived at an unfavourable moment – the emperor was celebrating his successes in fighting the Arabs in the East, and found the Bulgarian demands demeaning. In this case, a degree of happenstance is assumed; an unfortunate coincidence that influenced the course of events[12]. Other scholars think that Nikephoros himself sought confrontation, as a reaction to the conclusion of an anti-Byzantine Bulgarian-Hungarian alliance[13]. It also cannot be

[8] Leo the Deacon, IV, 5 (transl. 110).

[9] В.Н. Златарски, *История*..., pp. 569–570.

[10] S. Runciman, *The History*..., pp. 198–199.

[11] П. Павлов, *Векът*..., p. 29; idem, *Години*..., p. 29.

[12] Idem, *Забравени и неразбрани. Събития и личности от Българското средновековие*, София 2010, p. 39.

[13] В. Гюзелев, *Българските пратеничества при германския император Отон I в Магдебург (965 г.) и в Кведлинбург (973 г.)*, [in:] *Civitas Divino-Humana. In honorem Annorum LX Georgii Bakalov*, ed. Ц. Степанов, В. Вачкова, София 2004, p. 387.

ruled out that the emperor's actions were pre-emptory, and were linked to the Bulgarian preparations for a move against Thessalonike and its surroundings, which has been discussed above.

Setting aside the questions that raise justified doubts in the above propositions – the matter of the treaty of 963, the sending of the Bulgarian ruler's sons as hostages to the Byzantine capital, or the conclusion of a Bulgarian-Hungarian alliance – it would seem that there are two elements of the source relations that are indisputable. Firstly, the Bulgarian envoys arrived as every other year (let us remember that such missions must have occurred also during the previous years, and already during the reign of Nikephoros II Phokas) for the tribute that was their due, and guaranteed by the treaty of 927. Secondly, from the perspective of the Empire, the problems with their northern neighbour had already been brewing for some time, and the matter that was the most irritating was the ineffectuality of the Bulgarian authorities in stopping the Hungarian expeditions. Perhaps the emperor decided that the Bulgarians have not been fulfilling the part of the agreement of 927 regarding the military support for the Empire, in this case understood as taking upon themselves the role of a buffer for the Byzantine territories. What would have been the meaning of the peace with the Bulgarians if the Balkan areas of the Empire were harassed by raiders? A no less important question in the context of the emperor's policy of reclaiming lands of the Empire was the matter of re-establishing relations with the Bulgarians in a truly imperial spirit, perfectly illustrated by the words that Leo the Deacon put into the emperor's mouth:

> the most mighty and great emperor of the Romans is coming immediately to your land, to pay you the tribute in full, so that you may learn, O you who are thrice a slave through your ancestry, to proclaim the rulers of the Romans as your masters, and not to demand tribute of them as if they were slaves[14].

[14] Leo the Deacon, IV, 5, (transl. p. 110).

This ruled out any obligations towards the northern neighbour and, because of this, it would seem that Nikephoros's stance should be read as termination of the 'deep peace' of 927.

In the light of the rest of Leo the Deacon's relation, the emperor, outraged by the Bulgarian envoys, led an expedition against Bulgaria. He was said to have conquered a number of border strongholds, however after reaching the mountains of Haimos and familiarizing himself with the local conditions, abandoned further action. He was concerned that the Byzantine army, unprepared for action in the mountainous conditions, could be wiped out by the Bulgarians. This worry stemmed from the emperor realizing that: *on several previous occasions the Romans came to grief in the rough terrain of Mysia, and were completely destroyed*[15].

There is no doubt that Leo the Deacon referred primarily to the defeats suffered by the Byzantines in the *kleisourai* – fortified mountain passes – of Haimos, in particular the incident on July 811, when the emperor's namesake and one of his predecessors on the throne, Nikephoros I, perished[16]. Some scholars cast doubt on the value of the entirety of Leo's relation, as in their opinion it is not likely that such a consummate and experienced commander as Nikephoros, who fought in the mountainous terrain throughout his entire life, would have been reticent to venture into Bulgarian *kleisourai*. They do not accept Leo the Deacon's statement that the emperor learned of the nature of the mountains' formation only during the expedition, once he reached the border with Bulgaria. They also do not believe that the inaccessibility of the territories occupied by the Bulgarians became the chief motive for abandoning the rest of the campaign. When it comes to discussing the described events, these

---

[15] Leo the Deacon, IV, 6 (transl. p. 111). See also: A.-M. Talbot, D.F. Sullivan, *Introduction*, [in:] Leo the Deacon, p. 14.

[16] М.Й. Сюзюмов, С.А. Иванов, *Комментарий*, [in:] Лев Диакон, *История*, transl. М.М. Копыленко, ed. Г.Г. Литаврин, Москва 1988, p. 182, fn. 22; Р. Мутафчиев, *Лекции по история на Византии*, vol. II, ed. Г. Бакалов, София 1995, p. 250. Other propositions (С.А. Иванов, *Византийско-болгарские...*, p. 93; *The History of Leo the Deacon...*, p. 111, fn. 42) associated, i.a., with the past of the Phokas family itself, including the Byzantine defeat at Anchialos in 917. It is worth noting that Leo himself attested to his knowledge of both the defeat of Nikephoros I, and of the battle of Anchialos, in another part of his work – Leo the Deacon, VI, 9; VII, 7.

scholars give primacy to the (later than Leo the Deacon's) account of John Skylitzes, according to whom Nikephoros was merely visiting the border strongholds of the Empire, and his actions against Bulgaria were limited to sending a letter to tsar Peter with the demand: *to prevent the Turks* [that is, the Hungarians] *from crossing the Danube to raid Roman land*[17]. According to them, therefore, there had been no Byzantine expedition into Bulgaria during the late spring and early summer of 967, since at the time the emperor was pursuing a campaign in the West (as far as Macedonia) due to the threat to territories in Italy posed by Otto I's armies[18]. The emperor's impulsive reaction to the Bulgarian envoys' demands, and his supposed expedition into Bulgaria were a result of the official imperial court propaganda, aimed at increasing the largely diminished authority of the Byzantine ruler. There had been riots in Constantinople against the ruler, and a tragic accident in the hippodrome which caused the deaths of many of the capital's inhabitants[19]. The emperor wished to divert attention from the poor situation – if not by achieving some quick and easy success, then by at least spreading rumours of one. Leo, the later author of *History*, became one of the victims of this propaganda, accepting it at face value[20].

---

[17] John Skylitzes, pp. 276–277 (transl. p. 163). The quoted letter was sent by the emperor from the border, and not some time later, after visiting Greece – this view is held by Vassilka Tapkova-Zaimova (В. Тъпкова-Заимова, *Падане*..., p. 389).

[18] On the threat to the Byzantine holdings in Italy, see: R. Jenkins, *Byzantium. The Imperial Centuries AD 610–1071*, Toronto–Buffalo–London 1966, p. 285; T. Wolińska, *Konstantynopolitańska misja Liutpranda z Kremony (968)*, [in:] *Cesarstwo bizantyńskie. Dzieje. Religia. Kultura. Studia ofiarowane Profesorowi Waldemarowi Ceranowi przez uczniów na 70-lecie Jego urodzin*, ed. P. Krupczyński, M.J. Leszka, Łask–Łódź 2006, pp. 207–208; J. Shepard, *Western approaches (900–1025)*, [in:] *The Cambridge History of the Byzantine Empire, c. 500–1492*, ed. idem, Cambridge 2008, p. 542sqq.

[19] Cf. Leo the Deacon, IV, 6; John Skylitzes, pp. 275–276

[20] С.А. Иванов, *Византийско-болгарские*..., pp. 91–93, 94–96, 98–100; М.Й. Сюзюмов, С.А. Иванов, *Комментарий*..., p. 182, fn. 18, 21; cf. Р.О. Карышковский, *О хронологии*..., p. 133. The generally positive opinion of Phokas and Tzymiskes, found also in other sources, indicates the propaganda success of both of these rulers – A.-M. Talbot, D.F. Sullivan, *Introduction*..., p. 32. The credibility of the claim that Nikephoros became afraid of the dangers lurking in Bulgaria is also questioned by Tapkova-Zaimova (В. Тъпкова-Заимова, *Падане*..., p. 389) and Ivan Bozhilov, Vassil Gyuzelev (И. Божилов, В. Гюзелев, *История на*

It would seem that these doubts are not entirely substantiated. First and foremost, Leo the Deacon and John Skylitzes both agree that after sending away the Bulgarian envoys (although one might have doubts as to whether the event really happened in the atmosphere presented by Leo the Deacon[21]), the emperor was indeed present at the Bulgarian border. One may point to several important reasons for which the Byzantine ruler appeared there. It seems logical and natural that the emperor was visiting the areas threatened by the Hungarian raids, especially since he could expect that Peter, in response to having his demands refused, would once again allow the Hungarians venturing towards Byzantium to pass through Bulgarian lands without resistance[22]. Displaying the might of the Byzantine army at the Bulgarian border was certainly intended to make it clear to Peter that the empire's intervention was possible at any time. The goal of this demonstration may have been to exert pressure on the tsar so that he would abandon the possibility of co-operation with Hungarians (even if it consisted only of silent acquiescence to them crossing the borders of the Tsardom), and contacts with emperor Otto I[23]. The expedition to the Bulgarian border was undoubtedly intended to raise the emperor's authority. It was not, however, risky, since the border lay within

---

Добруджа, vol. II, *Средновековие*, Велико Търново 2004, pp. 64–65, in particular fn. 53). It is accepted as true, in turn, by Pavlov (П. П а в л о в, *Залезът на Първото българско царство (1015–1018)*, София 1999, p. 31).

[21] It is interesting that the violent reaction of the Byzantine rulers to Bulgarian demands of tribute can be found in multiple Byzantine sources, for example in the cases of Constantine VI (796) or Alexander in 912. This creates an impression that it might be a topos.

However, some scholars treat the information about Nikephoros Phokas's reaction seriously. Some time ago an interesting, if difficult to accept, proposition for rationalising Nikephoros Phocas' vehemence was presented by Todor R. Todorov (Т. Т о д о р о в, *България*..., pp. 231–236). He indicated that the emperor's outburst was a reaction to claims of tsar Peter (a son-in-law of a Byzantine emperor, and a father to sons born from a Byzantine imperial princess) to the imperial throne.

[22] П. П а в л о в, *Години*..., pp. 434–435. Cf. J. S h e p a r d, *Bulgaria: the Other Balkan "Empire"*, [in:] *The New Cambridge Medieval History*, vol. III: c. 900 – c. 1204, ed. T. R e u t e r, Cambridge 1999, p. 583.

[23] On the contemporary Bulgarian-Hungarian relations and negotiations of tsar Peter with emperor Otto, see above.

the distance of only a few days' march from the capital, and following the execution of the plan, Nikephoros was able to inform the public opinion in Constantinople of the success[24]. At the time the Byzantines were chiefly concerned with opposing German aggression in the west, and the display of military might on the Bulgarian border was undoubtedly an act towards deterrence in that regard. Exerting pressure on the Bulgarians did not have to indicate that actual military action occurred[25]. We do not rule out that during that time Nikephoros strengthened the garrisons of the cities and strongholds he visited, as there is surviving information attesting

[24] Presented differently by Sergiey A. Ivanov (С.А. Иванов, *Византийско-болгарские*..., pp. 98–99). This author's view, accoding to which the news of the supposed victory over Bulgarians was proclaimed while the emperor was locked up in the palace, is not convincing.

[25] We express this opinion despite the source information indicated by Petar Tivchev (П. Тивчев, *За войната между Византия и България през 977 г.*, ИП 25.4, 1969, pp. 80–88; П. Коледаров, *Политическа география на средновековната българска държава*, vol. I, *От 681 до 1018 г.*, София 1979, p. 50; idem, *Цар Петър I*, ВС 51, 1982, pp. 202–203; П. Павлов, *Векът*..., pp. 29–30. The monastic donations pointed out by Tivchev, in which we find a reference to Nikephoros's war with Bulgarians is a forgery, which exaggerates the emperor's actions. Cf. С.А. Иванов, *Византийско-болгарские*..., p. 100, fn. 95. In turn, Yahya of Antioch (7.118, pp. 122–123), while a fairly reliable historian, did occasionally mix up various events related to the Bulgarian-Byzantine relations from the second half of the tenth century – in this particular case he mirrored, it seems, the official position of the imperial court, which was reflected in the Greek sources, which he most likely used to some extent. Cf. comment by В.Н. Златарски, *История*..., p. 572, fn. 2; П. Мутафчиев, *Маджарите*..., p. 471, fn. 51; С.А. Иванов, *Византийско-болгарские*..., p. 99; А. Николов, *Политическа*..., p. 280, fn. 139. As Pavlov (П. Павлов, *Години*..., p. 435) thinks, neither is the 'logic of events' a sufficient argument for the view about a military confrontation Cf. Romilly J.H. Jenkins (*Byzantium*..., p. 280), who does not inform at all about Nikephoros's expedition towards the border, and Mark Whittow (*The Making of Byzantium, 600–1025*, Berkeley–Los Angeles 1996, pp. 294, 326), who in mentioning the events of 967 limited himself to stating that there had been *a military demonstration on the Bulgar frontier in Thrace*, and referred to the events being examined as *the Bulgarian crisis of 967*. Ivan Bozhilov has doubts regarding the nature of the emperor's moves – И. Божилов, В. Гюзелев, *История на Добруджа*..., pp. 64–65, in particular fn. 54. Angel Nikolov (А. Николов, *Политическа*..., p. 280), however, presents a chain of logic similar to ours.

that the emperor was fortifying the borderland areas[26]. Therefore the accusation that the emperor started a war with Bulgaria only to immediately abandon it and move further west, leaving the northern border of Byzantium open to Bulgarian retaliation, does not seem to be well supported[27]. Nikephoros Phokas rightly assumed that tsar Peter did not feel powerful enough (or simply had no reasons) to attack Byzantium for the sole reason that imperial army was briefly stationed by the border[28], especially since the Bulgarian ruler received the letter, mentioned by John Skylitzes, from Nikephoros.

This raises a question, however: why Nikephoros did not attack a weaker opponent if he was not worried about retaliation? It seems we can point to two basic reasons. The first one is that the emperor was focused on anti-German operations, with the present eastern matters being relegated to the background[29]. The second comes down to the fact that facing a weaker opponent in an open field and on one's own territory was rather different from venturing into enemy's mountainous terrain, where the numerical advantage lost a lot of its significance, and the shape of terrain put Bulgarians in a more favourable position. It was the aforementioned experience of the gruelling warfare in the mountains of Cilicia that told Nikephoros not to engage his forces in military operations in the area of Haimos. Why would he throw Byzantine soldiers into an always uncertain mountainous combat, when the Bulgarians could be

---

[26] This can be attested by the epigraphic material from Philippi. This stronghold was said to have been rebuilt during Nikephoros Phokas's reign by one Leo, a *tourmarches*, an underling of a *strategos* of the Strymon theme whose name we do not know. Paul Lemerle (*Philippes et la Macédoine orientale à l'époque chrétienne et byzantine. Recherches d'histoire et d'archéologie*, Paris 1945, pp. 141–144) dates this undertaking to 965–967; cf. П. Коледаров, *Политическа...*, p. 50; С. Пириватрић, *Самуилова држава. Обим и карактер*, Београд 1998, p. 43, fn. 40; see also J. Shepard, *Other...*, p. 583.

[27] С.А. Иванов, *Византийско-болгарские...*, pp. 94–96.

[28] Cf. J. Bonarek, *Przyczyny...*, p. 291. Differently – Х. Димитров, *Българо-унгарски отношения през средновековието*, София 1998, pp. 77–78, who thought that the Hungarian raid on the Aegean Macedonia in 968 was inspired by the Bulgarians.

[29] Cf. i.a. К. Иречек, *История на българите. С поправки и добавки от самия автор*, ed. П.Х. Петров, София 1978, pp. 211–212, fn. 2.

attacked without unnecessary risk? As a consummate strategist he must have known that Bulgaria was more easily entered from the north than through the passes of Stara Planina.

It seems that even if one were to set aside the aforementioned reasons, Nikephoros did not intend to become involved in military action against Bulgaria, and decided to use others for this purpose. He sent the patrician Kalokiros with a diplomatic mission to the prince of Kiev, Svyatoslav, to convince him to raid the Bulgarian Tsardom from his direction[30]. He was therefore driven not by fear of entering Bulgaria, but by reason and pragmatism[31]. After all, he was still waging a war in the East[32], which – despite the newly-reached agreement with the Arabs – was far from over[33]. He was therefore aware that fighting on two fronts, in both cases on difficult terrain was, in the long run, risky[34]. Furthermore, the conflict with

[30] Cf. the comments of i.a.: M. Д р и н о в, *Началото...*, p. 399; W.K. H a n a k, *The Infamous Svjatoslav: Master of Duplicity in War and Peace?*, [in:] *Peace and War in Byzantium. Essays in Honor of George T. Dennis, S. J.*, ed. T.S. M i l l e r, J. N e s b i t t, Washington 1995, pp. 141–142; С. П и р и в а т р и ћ, *Самуилова...*, p. 43; P. S t e p h e n s o n, *Byzantium's Balkan Frontier. A Political Study of the Northern Balkans, 900–1204*, Cambridge 2000, p. 48. More on the other aspects of Kalokiros' mission – A.N. С а х а р о в, *Дипломатия...*, pp. 108–112, 127–130; J.V.A. F i n e, *The Early...*, pp. 181–182.

[31] Even a disciplined army, acting in accordance with all the rules of war, having forced the enemy to retreat was reluctant to follow him through hard-to-reach places, due to the possibility of falling into ambush – cf. the example of Isaac I Comnenos in 1059 – M i c h a e l P s e l l o s, VII, 70. Cf. also the advice in the polemological literature – M.J. L e s z k a, K. M a r i n o w, *Carstwo...*, pp. 181–182, fn. 125.

[32] J. B o n a r e k, *Przyczyny...*, pp. 290, 292–293; M. W h i t t o w, *The Making...*, p. 326; С. П и р и в а т р и ћ, *Самуилова...*, p. 43; W. T r e a d g o l d, *A History of the Byzantine State and Society*, Stanford 1997, p. 502; M. S a l a m o n, *Państwa słowiańskie w kręgu kultury bizantyńskiej*, [in:] *Wielka historia świata*, vol. IV: *Kształtowanie średniowiecza*, ed. i d e m, Kraków 2005, p. 490.

[33] В.Н. З л а т а р с к и, *История...*, p. 573; С.А. И в а н о в, *Византийско-болгарские...*, p. 96.

[34] R.J.H. J e n k i n s, *Byzantium...*, p. 280; В. Т ъ п к о в а-З а и м о в а, *Падане...*, p. 389; J. B o n a r e k, *Przyczyny...*, p. 290; P. S t e p h e n s o n, *Byzantium's Balkan...*, p. 48.

emperor Otto I was becoming further inflamed[35]. It cannot be also ruled out that the fame of Bulgarians as spirited highlanders and vanquishers of the Byzantines, in particular of one of their emperors[36], had played a role. It is therefore possible that they were considered to have been a far more dangerous foe in mountainous terrain than the Arabs, with whom the Byzantines were fighting in the mountains of Asia Minor[37].

Peter, undoubtedly, observed the actions of Nikephoros Phokas. Perhaps he was surprised by the sharp reaction to his policy. There is no doubt that the tsar was not seeking war with the Empire, and that he wanted to preserve peace – however he did want, like many of his predecessors, Constantinople's respect for Bulgarian interests and independence.

1.1. Testimony of the *Life of St. Phantinos the Younger*

In 1993 Enrica Follieri published a previously unknown work about an important personage in the Byzantine monastic life of the tenth century:

[35] On Nikephoros Phokas' policy towards Otto I, see: – С.А. Иванов, *Византийско-болгарские...*, pp. 94–96, and the works cited in the note 18.

[36] Cf. П. Павлов, *Залезът...*, p. 31; idem, *Векът...*, p. 31. The defeat of Nikephoros I reverberated throughout both the Christian *oikoumene* and the Muslim world – W. Swoboda, *Nicefor I*, [in:] *SSS*, vol. III, p. 372; J. Wortley, *Legends of Byzantine Disaster of 811*, B 50, 1980, pp. 533–562; P. Schreiner, *Das Bulgarienbild im Europäischen Mittelalter*, EB 18.2, 1982, p. 67.

[37] On the subject of the contemporary opinion of Bulgarians see i.a.: P. Schreiner, *Das Bulgarienbild...*, pp. 58–68; T. Moriyasu, *Images des Bulgares au Moyen Age*, [in:] *Studia Slavico-Byzantina et Mediaevalia Europensia. In memoriam Ivan Dujčev*, vol. I, ed. П. Динеков et al., София 1988, pp. 41–43; J. Bonarek, *Romajowie i obcy w Kronice Jana Skylitzesa. Identyfikacja etniczna Bizantyńczyków i ich stosunek do obcych w świetle Kroniki Jana Skylitzesa*, Toruń 2003, pp. 128–156, 169–171, 175–176; J. Shepard, *A marriage too far? Maria Lekapena and Peter of Bulgaria*, [in:] *The Empress Theophano. Byzantium and the West at the turn of the first millennium*, ed. A. Davids, Cambridge 1995, pp. 131, 134, 136–137, 138–139.

The above conclusions regarding the borderland expedition of the emperor Nikephoros II Phokas in 967 have been drawn from the work of K. Marinow, *Hémos comme barrière militaire. L'analyse des* écrits *historiques de Léon le Diacre et de Jean Skylitzès au sujet de la campagne de guerre des empereurs byzantins Nicéphore II Phocas en 967 et de Jean I Tzymiscès en 971*, BMd 2, 2011, pp. 443–466, specifically pp. 444–454.

Life of St. Phantinos the Younger[38]. This work, written by an anonymous author, was most likely written between 986–996, soon after its protagonist's death[39]. Phantinos, born in Calabria (most likely in 902), near the end of his life settled near Thessalonike. It is during this period of his life a certain episode took place which, as some scholars think, sheds new light on tsar Peter's policy towards Byzantium around 965. For, as the author of the *Life* stated, Bulgarians wished to pillage the area around the city in which the saint resided, which terrified the then governor of the city, *doux* Pediasimos[40], who, not having sufficient military force to counter the aggression, decided to set everything within the city's walls to torch, so that the invaders would have nothing to plunder, no shelter, and no sustenance. This decision indirectly affected the Saint, who lived in one of the monasteries near Thessalonike. Phantinos, inspired by the Holy Spirit, convinced the dignitary to abandon his idea for, he prophesied, Bulgarians shall be defeated, without the use of mortal weapons. This indeed came to pass, as many of the Bulgarians died by God's will, which thwarted their aggressive plans towards Thessalonike. The fulfilment of the prophecy attested to the Saint's exceptional gift[41].

The discussed relation was treated by the abovementioned scholars seriously. They think that between 965 and 967 the tsar of Bulgaria planned military action into the Byzantine territories located to the southwest of the empire's borders – the ones located near the aforementioned metropolis[42]. Due to the inability of a more precise dating of this episode it is not known whether it was supposed to happen before the Bulgarian

---

[38] *Life of St. Phantinos the Younger*, 49, p. 456. On the subject of this source: E. Follieri, *Introduzione*, [in:] *Life of St. Phantinos the Younger*, p. 3sqq.

[39] The date of Phantinos' death is not certain. It may have occurred in 967, but it cannot be ruled out that it happened in 974 (on the 14th of November). On this subject, see: *PMZ II*, vol. V, pp. 435–436, s.v. *Phantinos* (#26576); В. Гюзелев, *Сведения за българите в Житието на свети Фантино Млади от X в.*, Pbg 36.2, 2012, p. 31.

[40] *PMZ II*, vol. V, pp. 350–351, s.v. *Pediasimos* (#26401).

[41] *Life of St. Phantinos the Younger*, 49, p. 456.

[42] P. Yannopoulos, *La Grece dans la vie de S. Fantin*, B 65, 1995, pp. 484–493; В. Гюзелев, *Сведения...*, pp. 34–36; Г.Н. Николов, *Българският цар Самуил*, София 2014, p. 13. The dating of this event to 965–967 is a consequence of accepting the view that Phantinos settled near Thessalonike in 965, and died in 967.

diplomatic mission to Nikephoros II Phokas, to be discussed below, or after this event. It is therefore impossible to specify whether it was a reaction to the Byzantine ruler's refusal to pay tribute to Bulgarians, which was guaranteed by the peace treaty of 927. Had that been the case, then the expedition of the Byzantine ruler towards the Bulgarian border would have had a preventive character – its goal would have been to pre-empt a possible Bulgarian attack[43]. It cannot be, however, ruled out that the Bulgarian plans were a response to the actions of the Byzantine autocrat, or to the conclusion of an anti-Bulgarian Byzantine-Rus' treaty, and the statement in the text that it was not through the armed force but because of a Divine action that the Bulgarians perished in large numbers is more general in nature and does not refer to some presumed defeat of their armies near Thessalonike, but to the invasion of Rus' on their state (this will be discussed below).

If one were to accept the relation of the *Life* at face value and locate it, as the aforementioned scholars do, near the end of Peter's reign, then on the one hand it would be contrary to the rather commonly held view about tsar Peter's passivity in the military sphere, at the same time shedding new light on his relations with Nikephoros II Phokas (and perhaps also on the causes of the conflict between the two). On the other hand, it would indicate that the contemporary Bulgarian expansion was focused on the south-westerly direction, rather than on that of Constantinople[44].

It should be clearly emphasised, however, that the hagiographic, most non-specific, nature of this account, and the impossibility of precise dating of the event presented in the *Life*, does not allow for making such far-reaching conclusions and attempts at reconstructing contemporary events[45]. This is especially the case considering the source itself mentions

---

[43] P. Yannopoulos, *La Grèce...*, p. 491; cf. Г.Н. Николов, *Българският...*, p. 13.

[44] В. Гюзелев, *Сведения...*, p. 35; Г.Н. Николов, *Българският...*, p. 13.

[45] E.g. Vassil Gyuzelev (В. Гюзелев, *Сведения...*, pp. 35–36) thinks that this relations attests to the Bulgarian looting raids on the area near Thessalonike and an expansionist policy aimed at this Byzantine metropolis, which became one of the reasons for the worsening of relations with Byzantium and undertaking of aggressive policy towards his northern neighbour by Nikephoros Phokas. This is an interesting idea, however due to lack of other sources, impossible to verify.

that these were merely rumours, supposed wishes (plans) of organising the aforementioned expedition by the Bulgarians, and their thwarting was accomplished by a Divine intervention. Furthermore, the intent of the author, who was writing his work *post factum* (during the 986–996), was to indicate the prophetic ability of St. Phantinos, who foretold the Bulgarian defeat[46].

2. The Invasion of Svyatoslav (968)

The incitement of the Kievan prince Svyatoslav against Bulgaria was of particular significance for the country's future fortunes. Some of the scholars asked: why didn't the Byzantines involve Pechenegs in this matter? After all, they already had some experience in this, and the Byzantine-Pecheneg relations were good at the time. It cannot be ruled out that the decision was to some extent influenced by the Byzantines' knowledge of the efficacious overtures of the Bulgarian diplomacy working towards maintaining peaceful relations with these nomads; nonetheless it appears that the crux of this decision lie in something else: the lack of trust towards the Pechenegs, and the desire to turn the Rus' into a permanent ally in the long run[47].

Much has already been written about the reasons for which Nikephoros Phokas turned to the prince of Kiev with the proposal of organising a military expedition against Bulgaria, as well as of the reasons for which it was accepted, and about the goals which Svyatoslav set for himself when he moved against the Bulgarians.

One cannot really doubt that on Nikephoros's part, this was an attempt at neutralising Bulgaria at the time when he was facing a conflict with

[46] M.J. Leszka, K. Marinow, *Carstwo...*, p. 176.

[47] П. Павлов, *Векът...*, p. 31; A. Paroń (*Pieczyngowie. Koczownicy w krajobrazie politycznym i kulturowym średniowiecznej Europy*, Wrocław 2015, pp. 330–331) rightly draws attention to the latter topic. We wrote of the Bulgarian-Pecheneg relations earlier.

Otto I and the permanent conflict with the Arabs. The emperor was worried about Peter's contacts with Otto, and arranging peaceful relations[48] with the Hungarians, without taking into account Byzantine interests. Perhaps Nikephoros Phokas wanted to teach the Bulgarians a lesson, which would have been made all the easier for being accomplished through someone else. It cannot be ruled out that by choosing the Rus', the emperor also wanted to engage the Bulgarians with an enemy that was both powerful and less known to them – at least in direct confrontation. In this manner, he would have accomplished his goal without spilling Bulgarian blood himself, which would have made a later Bulgarian-Byzantine agreement easier. What is even more important, by making use of a previously developed strategy of attacking Bulgaria from the north (e.g. during the years 894–896[49]) with the aid of the peoples inhabiting the steppes surrounding the Black Sea, he was not risking spilling Byzantine blood. Furthermore, if it became necessary to involve his own military forces, he would have been in an advantageous position, as the Bulgarians would have been forced to fight on two fronts; this pincer manoeuvre would have manifestly made the coordination of the military effort more difficult, and weakened Bulgarian resistance[50].

It has been pointed out that Nikephoros Phokas's request for assistance from Svyatoslav is sometimes explained by the desire for having the latter being prevented from acting against Byzantine interests in Crimea and the Azov Sea region[51].

Notably, despite the mutual tensions, the diplomatic relations between Constantinople and Preslav were being maintained. It is known, for

---

[48] П. Павлов, *Векът*..., p. 31.

[49] For more information on this conflict, see i.a. – M.J. Leszka, *Symeon I Wielki a Bizancjum. Z dziejów stosunków bułgarsko-bizantyńskich w latach 893–927*, Łódź 2013, pp. 76–96.

[50] On the tradition of this type of activity see: K. Marinow, *Zadania floty cesarskiej w wojnach bizantyńsko-bułgarskich (VII–XI w.)*, [in:] *Byzantina Europea. Księga jubileuszowa ofiarowana Profesorowi Waldemarowi Ceranowi*, ed. M. Kokoszko, M.J. Leszka, Łódź 2007, pp. 381–392.

[51] В.Н. Златарски, *История*..., p. 545; А.Н. Сахаров, *Дипломатия*..., p. 127; legitimate concerns regarding this question – J. Bonarek, *Przyczyny*..., p. 293.

example, that near the end of June of 968 – at the time when Svyatoslav was either finishing the preparations for his expedition into Bulgaria, or after it has already started – a Bulgarian envoy was present in the Byzantine capital. His presence was noted by Liudprand of Cremona, Otto I's envoy[52]. Unfortunately, we do not know the purpose of the Bulgarian envoy's visit[53].

Svyatoslav, involving himself in the Bulgarian enterprise, was in a fairly comfortable situation. He received a generous payment from the Byzantines (15 *kentenaria* of gold), and in the case of a success against the Bulgarians he would have been able to gain many times more in loot. Should the campaign fail, he could return to Kiev and satisfy himself with the Byzantine reward. The matter of Svyatoslav's resettlement to Dobrudzha and the building of his own state there is a matter of some discussion in the academic works[54]. An interesting proposition, in this context, was presented over twenty years ago by a Polish scholar Jacek Bonarek. According to him, the aim of Nikephoros Phokas's agreement with Svyatoslav was to break Bulgaria apart into two separate states – the northern territories were to become a Rus' state ruled by Svyatoslav, while the southern Bulgaria was to be fully subject to Byzantium, and therefore devoid of any threat to Constantinople. It would have become a buffer against raids from the north, including from the Rus' themselves[55]. Leaving the matter of whether the hypothesis is correct aside, we would like to draw attention to the doubts we have regarding one of the core arguments brought forth by the scholar in its support. Bonarek thought that the reason for which Svyatoslav did not take action in southern Bulgaria while Nikephoros II Phokas was still alive was adherence to an understanding he had with the latter. It would seem that it was not so

[52] Liudprand of Cremona (*Embassy*, 19) saw him during his visit in Constantinople near the end of June 968.

[53] П. Павлов, *Години...*, p. 439. The author suspects that the Bulgarian envoys' goal may have been investigating of the Byzantines' intentions. He explains the good reception of the Bulgarian envoy in Constantinople and creating hope of co-operation with a desire to mislead the Bulgarians.

[54] J. Bonarek, *Przyczyny...*, pp. 294–296.

[55] *Ibidem.*

much the desire to follow the letter of the agreement with the emperor that stopped the Kievan prince from taking this action, but rather the lack of time for such an undertaking while the Byzantine ruler was still alive. It needs to be said that the dating accepted by the Polish scholar for the first expedition of Svyatoslav to year 967 is far from certain. There are weighty arguments for dating it instead to the late summer of 968[56]. If this is correct, then the prince of Rus', who in the same year returned to Kiev, would not have been physically able to take action in southern Bulgaria, since despite the original successes his position was uncertain and unstable. The situation in 969, when Svyatoslav returned to the Danubian regions during the summer, was similar. It is worth pointing out that regardless of whether an agreement regarding the partition of Bulgaria had been made, if Svyatoslav wanted to subordinate to himself the entirety of Bulgaria, he would have to face a Byzantine reaction[57].

Regardless of the aims that the Rus' and Byzantines had – the Bulgarians had to offer resistance to Svyatoslav's invasion. According to Leo the Deacon, the prince of Kiev led sixty thousand men against Bulgaria[58]. This number would undoubtedly have been large if we were to take it literally. Scholars doubt it is correct, and for a good reason, since from the perspective of the mobilisation potential of mediaeval European states

---

[56] There are two views in the scholarship regarding the dating of Svyatoslav's first expedition. The arguments for the year 967 have been presented most fully by Stokes (*The Background…*), and his arguments have been shared by i.a.: J.V.A. F i n e, *The Early…*, p. 182; D. O b o l e n s k y, *Byzantine Commonwealth. Eastern Europe, 500–1453*, New York 1971, pp. 128–129; J. B o n a r e k, *Przyczyny…*, p. 297. The dating of the expedition to year 968 was widely substantiated by Karishkovskiy. His arguments were further developed by С. П и р и в а т р и ћ, *Два хронолошка прилога о крају Првог бугарског царства*, ЗРВИ 34, 1995, pp. 51–55.

[57] For a different argument against Bonarek's hypothesis see: A. P a r o ń, *Pieczyngowie…*, p. 331, fn. 67, according to which *Fokas zapraszając Rusów na stałe na Bałkany złamałby jedną z fundamentalnych zasad polityki Bizancjum, która sprzeciwiała się ruskiemu osadnictwu na wybrzeżach Morza Czarnego* [*In permanently inviting the Rus' to the Balkans, Phokas would have broken one of the fundamental rules of the Byzantine policy, which opposed the Rus' settlement along the Black Sea coast*].

[58] L e o t h e D e a c o n, V, 2. This author talks of sixty thousand 'burly men', and in addition there would also have been some mercenaries present. The *Russian Primary Chronicle* in turn makes a mention of ten thousand (AM 6479, p. 71).

– in particular when organising expeditions into enemy territory – it would have been unrealistic, and should only be understood as a general description of the size of the Rus' army, meaning it was very numerous. Some scholars however think that the number may be treated seriously, but rather in association with Svyatoslav's attempt to settle in Dobrudzha. There would have been sixty thousand of those who went with the prince of Kiev towards the Danube[59], but soldiers would have been only a part of it[60].

Hearing of the Rus' expedition, Peter sent his army against them. The first clash between the invaders and the Bulgarian forces occurred on the banks of Danube, in August 968. It likely happened in the vicinity of Dristra (Dorostolon) soon after the Rus' disembarked from the boats in which they crossed the river[61]. Despite their difficult position, the invaders managed to defeat the Bulgarians, who retreated to Dorostolon. It seems that their success was a result of either surprise, or underestimating of the attacking forces by the Bulgarians[62]. Tsar Peter did not have enough time to move forces sufficient to stop the Rus' making their way across the Danube. This initial defeat influenced the further course of conflict. Bulgarians – as the sources would have it – were pushed to the defensive. John Skylitzes informs that: *They* [the Rus' – M.J.L., K.M.] *laid waste many of the Bulgarians' cities and lands, collected a large amount of booty and then to their own lands*[63].

---

[59] М.Й. Сюзюмов, С.А. Иванов, *Комментарий*..., p. 188, fn. 10; J. Bonarek, *Przyczyny*..., p. 295; W.K. Hanak, *The Infamous*..., p. 141, fn. 10. Aside from the objections raised in the literature of the subject, it is also worth noting the fact that Leo the Deacon, who as the only one provided this number, juxtaposed it with a force of Bulgarian warriors exactly have their size, who attacked the Rus' after the latter made their way to the southern shore of the Danube. It would seem that by using these numbers Leo the Deacon wanted to tell the readers that the Rus' have been numerous, and the Bulgarians were half their strength in number – and nothing more. Cf. Г.Г. Атанасов, *О численности русской армии князя Святослава во время его походов в Болгарию и о битве под Дристрой (Доростолом в 971 г.)*, ВВ 72, 2013, pp. 86–102 (on pp. 86–90 an analysis of the sources and scholars' views); see also: П. Павлов, *Векът*..., p. 33.

[60] J. Bonarek, *Przyczyny*..., pp. 295–296.

[61] Leo the Deacon, V, 2. П. Павлов, *Векът*..., p. 34, indicates the vicinity of Pereyaslavets as the location of the first clash.

[62] It cannot be ruled out that Peter, fearing the Byzantines' attack, left some of his forces to defend the border with the Empire (cf. П. Павлов, *Векът*..., p. 34).

[63] John Skylitzes, p. 277 (transl. 266 – with minor change – M.J.L., K.M.).

Russian Primary Chronicle, in turn, tells that eighty of the Bulgarian cities were captured, and that Svyatoslav made Pereyaslavets (?) into his own command centre and, moreover, was receiving tribute from the Greeks[64].

The Bulgarians' situation was becoming difficult, but certainly not hopeless. Svyatoslav was unable to defeat the main Bulgarian forces, or to capture the capital Preslav, which could have resulted in the Bulgarian forces' offensive. Further clashes, however, did not come to pass, for upon hearing the news of the Pecheneg siege of Kiev, Svyatoslav departed to relieve the city, carrying away, as both the Byzantine and Rus' sources claim, plentiful spoils of war[65].

Some of the scholars think that in 968, just after Svyatoslav's first expedition and still during Peter's reign, there was a rapprochement between Bulgaria and Byzantium[66]. Emperor Nikephoros Phokas, worried about

[64] *Russian Primary Chronicle*, AM 6475, p. 66. In the light of the above doubts regarding the credibility of this fragment of *Russian Primary Chronicle*, the information contained therein should be treated with a dose of scepticism. Georgi Atanassov (Г.Г. Атанасов, *О численности...*, p. 87, fn. 2) thought that there could be a grain of truth in the relation. He indicated that in Dobrudzha and north-eastern Bulgaria, and therefore the lands where the main military activity of the war of 969–971 had been taking place, in the second half of the tenth century there had been more than fifty strongholds, and the Dobrudzha stone wall incorporated thirty fortified points. The Bulgarian scholar's calculations are meant to indicate that, potentially, there had been a sufficient number of strongholds of various sizes and significance that the Rus' could have had captured. It is doubtful whether the anonymous author had information that was this precise regarding the number of captured strongholds, and most likely he merely wanted to convey that they were numerous. Cf. П. Павлов, *Векът...*, p. 34. Information about the payment of tribute by the Byzantines should be treated with reserve, unless it referred to the promised payment for raiding Bulgaria.

[65] John Skylitzes, p. 277; *Russian Primary Chronicle*, AM 6476, pp. 66–68. Some scholars do not rule out that the Pecheneg raid on Rus was a result of the Bulgarian diplomatic activity. This hypothesis, referring not so much to the sources but to the earlier co-operation of the Pechenegs and Bulgarians during Symeon's times, is not possible to verify. Cf. И. Божилов, В. Гюзелев, *История на Добруджа...*, p. 67; P. Stephenson, *Byzantium's Balkan...*, pp. 48–49; A. Paroń, *Pieczyngowie...*, pp. 332–333.

[66] E.g.: B. Stokes, *The Background...*, p. 54; J. Bonarek, *Przyczyny...*, p. 298; Т. Тодоров, *България...*, p. 236. The former two however place Svyatoslav's expedition in 967.

a potential Bulgarian-Rus' alliance, sent envoys to Preslav: patrician Nikephoros Erotikos and Philotheos, the Bishop of Euchaita[67]. As Leo the Deacon wrote, they were welcomed in the Bulgarian capital, as the Bulgarians were counting on Byzantine assistance against Svyatoslav[68]. The Bulgarian-Byzantine alliance was renewed, and it was to be sealed through the marriages of the Bulgarian princesses (?) with Basil and Constantine, the sons of Romanos II and Theophano[69]. It would seem, however, that the scholars who point out that the envoys were sent to Preslav in 969[70], already during the reign of Boris II, are correct. The argument for this view is offered by Leo the Deacon's relation, from which we may surmise that little time has passed between the Byzantine diplomatic mission in Preslav and the arrival of the Bulgarian princesses in Constantinople[71]. The latter occurred shortly before the death of Nikephoros Phokas, who was murdered in the night between 10th and 11th of December. John Tzymiskes, his killer and successor, rejected the planned marriages.

---

[67] John Skylitzes (p. 310) mentions that the Archbishop of Euchaita participated in 371 in the negotiations conducted by the Byzantines with the Pechenegs after the battle of Dristra (Dorostolon). His name, however, was Theophilos. The *Russian Primary Chronicle* (AM 6479, p. 73) noted in this context the name of the Byzantine envoy, Theophilos, who is referred to as *synkellos*. On the subject of how Philotheos of Leo the Deacon became Theophilos of John Skylitzes and of the *Russian Primary Chronicle* – M. Raev, *The Russian-Byzantine Treaty of 971. Theophilos and Sveneld*, REB 64/65, 2006/2007, pp. 329–338. See also: A. Paroń, *Pieczyngowie...*, pp. 335–337.

[68] Leo the Deacon, V, 3.

[69] Leo the Deacon, V, 3. The Byzantine historian mentioned that one of the arguments for renewing the alliance was religious in nature. The Byzantines and Bulgarians were united by the common faith, which the Rus', at the time still pagans, did not share with them. The author also pointed out that the common faith was also brought up during the negotiations as a factor uniting the two sides. We do not know the names, or parents, of the prospective brides-to-be of Basil and Constantine.

[70] М.Й. Сюзюмов, С.А. Иванов, *Комментарий...*, p. 190, fn. 21.

[71] Leo the Deacon, V, 3: *The Mysians accepted the deputation, put the girls of royal blood on the cart... and sent [them] to Emperor Nicephoros*, (transl. p. 111).

3. Death of Peter

Defeats in the war with the Rus' were said to have impacted on tsar Peter's health. Supposedly upon hearing the news of the first defeat he suffered an epileptic seizure[72]. He then decided to become a monk and enter a monastery[73]. Soon afterwards – on the 30th of January 969 – he passed away[74]. The illness and death of the experienced ruler contributed to some extent, one may suppose, to the lack of preparation of the Bulgarians in their subsequent clash with the Rus'. Boris II, Peter's successor, was not able to organise an effective defence, nor gain a measurable assistance from the Byzantines.

---

[72] Leo the Deacon, V, 2. The worsening of Peter's health was to have taken place upon hearing the news of the first setback in the conflict with the Rus'. It is difficult to say how much of this information is true. It cannot be ruled out that at the time of Svyatoslav's expedition Peter was already seriously ill, and the defeat merely contributed to the further development of the disease. It is striking that the circumstances of Peter's death resemble those accompanying Symeon's, his father's, death, or those of Samuel, a West Bulgarian ruler. Symeon was said to have died as a result of receiving news about the Bulgarian defeat in a battle against the Croats (cf. M.J. Leszka, *Symeon*..., pp. 227–230), while Samuel – after the shock he received after the disastrous battle of Belassitsa and seeing the Bulgarian warriors that had been blinded at Basil II's orders (John Skylitzes, p. 349; the question of the blinding of Bulgarian soldiers was recently analysed by Peter Schreiner (*Die vermentliche Blendung. Zu den Ereignissen von Kleidion*, [in:] *Европейският Югоизток през втората половина на X – началото на XI век. История и култура*, ed. В. Гюзелев, Г.Н. Николов, София 2015, pp. 170 –187), who concluded that it did not actually take place (see *ibidem* for further reading).

[73] Peter likely accepted the so-called Small Schema, which allowed him to keep the name given to him during baptism. It is possible that he entered into the monastery traces of which have been discovered near the Golden Church, and which, as was mentioned above, are associated with the ruling dynasty. Some scholars doubt whether Peter has taken monastic vows; this is discussed in the present book.

[74] It is commonly accepted that Peter's death occurred on the 30th of January, for on this day he was venerated in the liturgical calendar of the Bulgarian Church. We know from Leo the Deacon (V, 2) that the death happened soon after Svyatoslav's first expedition. There is a discussion regarding the year of this event – whether it happened in 969 or 970. It would seem that this problem was solved by a Serbian scholar, Srdjan Pirivatrić (С. Пириватрић, *Два хронолошка*..., pp. 55–62), who presented convincing arguments for the year 969.

VIII

Mirosław J. Leszka
Kirił Marinow

The Year 971

After tsar Peter's death (on 30th of January 969), Nikephoros Phokas decided to send the late ruler's sons, Boris and Roman, back to Bulgaria, likely counting on them becoming guarantors of stability in Bulgaria, and of improved relations with Byzantium[1]. Boris took the reins of power after

[1] В. Тъпкова-Заимова, *Падане на Североизточна България*, [in:] *История на България*, vol. II, *Първа българска държава*, ed. Д. Ангелов, София 1981, p. 390; П. Павлов, *Борби за оцеляване. Упадък на българската държавност, 927–1018*, [in:] *История на българите*, vol. I, *От древността до края на XVI век*, ed. Г. Бакалов, София 2003, pp. 283–284 (scholars date Peter's death to January of 970, thus Boris' ascension to the throne would have also taken place during this year); cf. В.Н. Златарски, *История на българската държава през средните векове*, vol. I/2, *Първо българско Царство. От славянизацията на държавата до падането на Първото царство (852–1018)*, София 1927, p. 589; И. Божилов, В. Гюзелев, *История на средновековна България VII–XIV в.*, ²София 2006, p. 297 (these works date Peter's death to 30th of January 969). One needs to remember, however, that we cannot be certain whether the sons of Peter were in the hands of Nikephoros II Phokas. It cannot be ruled out that Boris was in Preslav at the time his father passed away, and may have taken the reins of power even before his death. On Boris II – П. Павлов, *Борис II (опит за ново тълкуване на семейно-династичните проблеми в Преславския двор при цар Петър)*, Пр.Сб 5, София 1993, pp. 46–51; Г.Н. Николов, *Българският цар Самуил*, София 2014, pp. 17–20; П. Павлов, *Векът на цар Самуил*, София 2014, pp. 37–52.

his father. Taking advantage of Svyatoslav's absence from Bulgaria (who departed the previous year to relieve Kiev, besieged by the Pechenegs), the new tsar regained part, or perhaps even all, of the lands lost to the Kievan prince[2]. There was also a clear rapprochement with Byzantium. Nikephoros Phokas sent envoys, as was discussed before, the patrician Nikephoros Erotikos and Philotheos, bishop of Euchaita[3]. They were received well in Preslav. The renewed alliance was to be further strengthened by marriages of the Bulgarian tsarinas (?) with Basil and Constantine, sons of Romanos II and Theophano[4]. The candidates for wives of the young princes arrived in Constantinople in November/December 969[5]. The union, however, was not finalised. On the night of 10th to 11th of December Nikephoros II Phokas was murdered, and his successor, John I Tzymiskes, did not see a need to create ties with the Preslav court.

Boris II was not able to stabilise the situation in Bulgaria, as in the meantime Svyatoslav returned to the scene. He arrived one the shores of Danube during the summer of 969[6]. The first, and it seems decisive, clash with the Bulgarian forces took place by the Pereyaslavets. Svyatoslav

[2] В. Тъпкова-Заимова, *Падане...*, p. 390.

[3] Some of the scholars date this diplomatic mission to 968, and the reign of Peter (e.g.: A.D. Stokes, *The Background and Chronology of the Balkan Campaigns of Svyatoslav Igorevich*, SEER 40/94, 1961, p. 54; J. Bonarek, *Przyczyny i cele bułgarskich wypraw Światosława a polityka Bizancjum w latach sześćdziesiątych X w.*, SH 39, 1996, p. 298). It would seem, however, that those who point to year 969 are correct (М.Я. Сюзюмов, С.А. Иванов, *Комментарий*, [in:] Лев Диакон, *История*, transl. М.М. Копыленко, ed. Г.Г. Литаврин, Москва 1988, p. 190, fn. 21). What is relevant here is the temporal proximity of the mission and the arrival in Constantinople of the prospective Bulgarian brides-to-be of Constantine and Basil. Their arrival closely preceded the death of Nikephoros Phokas (December 969). Euchaita's chief priest also appears during the negotiations with the Pechengs in 971 after the battle Dristra, although in John Skylitzes and in the *Russian Primary Chronicle* his name is given as Theophilos. On this subject, see: M. Raev. *The Russian-Byzantine Treaty of 971. Theophilos and Sveneld*, REB 64/65, 2006/2007, pp. 329–340.

[4] Leo the Deacon, V, 3. We do not know whose daughters they were, nor what names bore the prospective brides of Basil and Constantine.

[5] И. Божилов, В. Гюзелев, *История...*, p. 297.

[6] On the question of the date of Svyatoslav's return – С.А. Иванов. *Византийско-болгарские отношения в 966–969 гг.*, ВВ 42, 1981, p. 98; J. Bonarek, *Przyczyny...*, pp. 298–300; И. Божилов, В. Гюзелев, *История...*, p. 297.

emerged victorious[7]. The sources make no mention of him encountering further resistance from the Bulgarians. Skylitzes only related that *the Russian people occupied Bulgaria* (τὴν Βουλγαρίαν χειρωσαμένῳ), and that Boris and Roman, sons of Peter, were taken captive[8]. Svyatoslav himself, as the Byzantine chronicler recorded, intended to remain in Bulgaria permanently[9]. We do not know exactly which part of the Bulgarian territory has gone under Rus' control, nor how complete it was; one might assume that they held Dobrudzha once again. Their influence reached Preslav[10], and they have certainly held Dristra[11], one of the most important, if not the most important, centre of the contemporary Bulgaria. The way in which Svyatoslav arranged his relations with the Bulgarians isn't clear.

[7] *Russian Primary Chronicle*, AM 6479: *Svyatoslav arrived before Pereyaslavets, and the Bulgarians fortified themselves in the city. They made one sally against Svyatoslav; there was great carnage, and the Bulgarians came off victors. But Svyatoslav cried to his soldiery, "Here is where we fall. Let us fight bravely, brothers and companions!" Toward evening, Svyatoslav finally gained the upper hand, and took the city by storm* (transl. p. 87); cf. John Skylitzes, p. 277. More on this event and Pereyaslavets – И. Божилов, В. Гюзелев, *История на Добруджа*, vol. II, *Средновековие*, Велико Търново 2004, pp. 67–68; М. Раев, *Преслав или Переяславец на Дунае? (Предварительные замечания об одном из возможных источников ПВЛ и его трансформации)*, НЗУІЗНС 20, 2008, pp. 37–40.

[8] John Skylitzes, pp. 287–288 (transl. p. 275).

[9] Certain role in arriving at this decision was played by Kalokiros, who intended, with Rus' support, to proclaim himself emperor and promised to give Bulgarian lands to Svyatoslav, once John Tzymiskes was defeated. Andrzej Poppe (*Sjatoslav The Glorious and the Byzantine Empire*, [in:] *Byzantium, New Peoples, New Powers: the Byzantino-Slav Contact Zone, from the Ninth to the Fifteenth Century*, ed. M. Kaimakamova, M. Salamon, M. Smorąg Różycka, Cracow 2007, pp. 133–137), correctly, considers the thread of imperial ambitions of Kalokiros as Leo the Deacon's (himself a supporter of the Phokas family) invention, and who thus wanted to disguise the co-operation between Bardas Phokas and Svyatoslav.

[10] A Rus' garrison was present here, but it seems it resided in the so-called Outer City. The Rus's access to the Inner City, where the tsar's palace and the treasure were located (this is stressed by Leo the Deacon, which could suggest that it was not touched by Svyatoslav) was in some way limited (Leo the Deacon, VIII, 6; John Skylitzes, p. 297).

[11] On Dristra's significance in the Bulgarian state, see: Г. Атанасов, *Християнският Дуросторум–Дръстър. Доростолската епархия през Късната античност и Средновековието IV–XIV v. История, археология, култура и изкуство*, Варна 2007.

This matter has been debated on many occasions, with no decisive conclusions. Some scholars think that an alliance, aimed against Byzantium, was made between the two peoples; others reject the possibility of such an alliance outright[12]. The latter position seems closer to the truth. While Svyatoslav had to reach some form of an agreement with the Bulgarians, it does not mean that the relations between the two sides were those of allies. Boris II was controlled by Svyatoslav, and maintained his formal position[13], becoming a guarantor of the loyalty of his subjects to the Rus'. The forced arrangement resulted in Bulgarians' presence in Svyatoslav's army, which was mentioned by the sources as early as those for the period of the campaign of 970[14]. During that year Svyatoslav's army, strengthened by Bulgarians, Pechenegs and Hungarians, moved across Thrace, occupied Philippopolis and reached Arkadioupolis. Here, it clashed with the troops from Asia Minor, deployed to the Balkan front by John Tzymiskes. They were led by magister Bardas Skleros. The latter turned out to be an adroit commander and, despite the enemy's numerical advantage, emerged victorious from the struggle[15]. He was not, however, able to deal the enemy

[12] Supporting the idea of an existence of such an alliance is П. Мутафчиев, *Русско-болгарские отношения при Святославе*, [in:] idem, *Избрани произведения*, vol. II, ed. Д. Ангелов, София 1973, pp. 240–254; against it, in turn, is П. Павлов. *Борби...*, pp. 286–287.

[13] This is supported by the fact that at the time of Preslav's conquest by John Tzymiskes, he appeared in front of the emperor dressed in tsar's robes (John Skylitzes, p. 297).

[14] Leo the Deacon, VI, 12; John Skylitzes, p. 289.

[15] On the campaign of 970: Д. Ангелов, Б. Чолпанов, *Българска военна история от втората четвърт на X до втората половина на XV в.*, София 1989, pp. 15–18; И. Божилов, В. Гюзелев, *История...*, p. 298; A. Paroń. *Pieczyngowie. Koczownicy w krajobrazie politycznym i kuturowym średniowiecznej Europy*, Wrocław 2015, p. 335. More on the events that took place in Philippoupolis: А. Данчева-Василиева, *Пловдив през Средновековето IV–XIV в.* София 2009, pp. 40–41. Having captured the city, Svyatoslav supposedly commited mass atrocities (there is a mention of twenty thousand impaled Bulgarians; the number is likely exagerrated), the repressions aimed at breaking the spirit of resistance among the Bulgarians (М.Я. Сюзюмов, С.А. Иванов, *Комментарий...*, p. 199, fn. 62). This indicates, one can assume, also the fact that few Bulgarians marched in Svyatoslav's army, if the prince did not hesitate to thus treat their kinsmen. The memory of deeds commited

a finishing blow, as he was recalled by the emperor and sent back to the East, to quash the usurpation attempt of Bardas Phokas. Meanwhile, Svyatoslav's army, having suffered substantial losses, withdrew. Diplomatic negotiations did not lead to a solution that would have been satisfactory to the Byzantines, that is, withdrawal of the Rus' army from the Bulgarian lands. In this situation, John Tzymiskes decided to prepare a military expedition. It started in the spring of 971.

It is worth noting that Svyatoslav had to be aware that he did not subjugate the entirety of Bulgaria. He was under a constant threat of a hostile action from the Bulgarians inhabiting the lands free of the Rus' rule, and thus of a threat of a war on two fronts. This could, at least to some extent, explain a certain degree of freedom he allowed Boris, given to prevent such situation from arising. What influence Boris II had on the lands free from the Rus' presence is a different question.

From the information presented above it is clear that the position of the Bulgarians on the eve of the Byzantine expedition was complicated. They were certainly burdened by the Rus' occupation, and at least for the time being they were unable to take effective steps to free themselves of Svyatoslav. Perhaps they were counting on Byzantine intervention that would result in his expulsion, however they could not have lost sight of the fact that the latter appeared on their lands on Byzantine instigation. Although the Byzantine policy towards Bulgaria has changed since that time, the mistrust towards the Byzantines must have been nonetheless present among the Bulgarian nobles. This feeling would have been shared by Boris II himself. It may have been further fuelled by his personal experiences and a good awareness of the contemporary political situation in Byzantium. After all, Boris resided for some time in Constantinople as a hostage, his mother was a Byzantine, and he received a classical education. It cannot be ruled out that he knew of the anti-Bulgarian

by Rus' in Philippoupolis may have influenced the behaviour of Bulgarians during John Tzymiskes' expedition, at least until the point when the Byzantines besieged the Rus' in Dristra. It is notable that we do not know whether Philippoupolis was in Byzantine or Bulgarian hands at the time when it was captured by Svyatoslav. It seems likely that it held at the time by the Byzantines (А. Данчева-Василиева, *Пловдив...*, p. 41).

attitudes among the Byzantine Empire's elites, and that he kept in mind that Bulgarian lands used to belong to the Byzantine Empire[16].

Bulgarians appear in the narrative of Leo the Deacon and John Skylitzes only at the point when the Byzantine army breached Preslav's walls. The two authors recorded that Boris II and the Byzantine emperor met at that time. Leo the Deacon wrote:

> And it is said that then Boris, the king of the Mysians, whose face was thickly covered with reddish [hair], was captured with his wife and two infant children, and brought before the emperor. The latter received him and treated him honourably, calling him ruler of the Bulgarians, and saying that he came to avenge the Mysians, who had suffered terribly at the hands of the Scythians.[17]

While John Skylitzes stated:

> Boris the king of the Bulgarians was taken still wearing the royal insignia, together with his wife and children. They were brought to the emperor who received them graciously, calling [Boris] emperor of the Bulgarians. He released all the Bulgarians they had captured – leaving them free to go wherever they would, saying that he was not come to enslave the Bulgarians but rather to free them. It was only the Russians whom he regarded as enemies and intended to treat as adversaries.[18]

The undertone of both of these relations is in essence the same[19]. The victorious emperor of the Byzantines treated Boris graciously,

---

[16] Г.Г. Литаврин, *Константин Багрянородный о Болгарии и Болгарах*, [in:] *Сборник в чест на акад. Димитър Ангелов*, ed. В. Велков, София 1994, pp. 32–36.

[17] Leo the Deacon, VIII, 6 (transl. p. 182).

[18] John Skylitzes, p. 297 (transl. p. 283; with minor change – M.J.L., K.M.).

[19] Cf. Н.П. Благоев, *Критичен поглед върху известията на Лъв Дякон за българите*, МПр 6.2, 1930, pp. 25–26; С.А. Иванов, *Κοίρανος τῶν Βουλγάρων. Иоанн Цимисхий и Борис II в 971 г.*, [in:] *Общество и государство на Балканах в средние века*, Калинин 1982, pp. 47–58; Л. Симеонова, *Образът на българския владетел във византийската книжнина (средата на IX – началото на XI в.)*, [in:] *Представата за*

acknowledged him as the ruler of the Bulgarians and clearly identified himself as an ally of the latter, indicating that his only enemy were the Rus' (Scythians). His assurances were intended, even before the war has ended, to gain Bulgarians' co-operation in the fight against Svyatoslav. It is notable that the Bulgarians of Preslav did not act as Byzantines' allies, and did not take any steps to enable them to enter the city. Perhaps their behaviour was dictated by the fear of the Rus' garrison in Preslav, but it is more likely that they were either hostile towards the Byzantines, or did not know what to expect of them, nor what treatment to expect at their hands. That the Byzantines themselves did not consider Bulgarians their allies can be attested by the fact that the Byzantine chroniclers clearly speak of the capturing of Boris II and the Bulgarians in Preslav[20]. Such behaviour of both sides makes it clear that neither before the expedition, nor while it was underway, no action was taken to reach an accord, and no subsequent joint action against Svyatoslav took place.

Leo the Deacon's relation on the next stage of the fighting for Preslav may attest to the hostility of the Bulgarians towards the Byzantines. The Byzantine historian stated that some of the Bulgarians locked themselves in, along with a small force of the Rus', within the fortifications of the tsar's palace, and fought alongside them until the very end. The reason for this is that they: *were hostile to the Romans, because they were the cause of the Scythians' coming to them*[21]. Although John Skylitzes does not mention this episode, it seems that one may trust the Deacon on this,

---

"Другия" на Балканите, ed. N. Данова, В. Димова, М. Калицин, София 1995, p. 21; J. Bonarek, *Romajowie i obcy w kronice Jana Skylitzesa. Identyfikacja etniczna Bizantyńczyków i ich stosunek do obcych w świetle kroniki Jana Skylitzesa*, Toruń 2003. p. 148; M.J. Leszka, *Wizerunek władców pierwszego państwa bułgarskiego w bizantyńskich źródłach pisanych (VIII – pierwsza połowa XII wieku)*, Łódź 2003, pp. 139–140.

[20] It cannot, however, be ruled out that both Boris II, as well as some of the Bulgarians, have been not so much captured, as willingly submitted themselves to the Byzantines. The fact that despite the opportunity to take shelter in the fortified palace and to offer further resistance (as the Rus' and the other Bulgarians have done) they have decided to refrain from taking such steps attests to this. Leo the Deacon and John Skylitzes wanted to underscore the significance of the victory by claiming that Boris II and some of his supporters and retinue were captured by the Byzantines.

[21] Leo the Deacon, VIII, 7 (transl. p. 183).

not only because he was writing soon after the described events, but also because he had no reasons to portray the Byzantine-Bulgarian relations in a better light which, at the time he was writing, were at the stage of an open military conflict. John Skylitzes, meanwhile, was writing at a time when the Bulgarian lands have already been a part of the Empire for several decades, and highlighting such episodes would not have helped with their integration.

As indicated above, the stance that John Tzymiskes adopted towards the Bulgarians (attitude to Boris II, release of the Bulgarian hostages, making it clear that the Byzantine expedition was directed against the Rus', in aid of the Bulgarians) was clearly aimed at winning them over for the fight against Svyatoslav. This creates a question of whether the Byzantine emperor accomplished his goal. To answer it, one has to go back to the narratives of Leo the Deacon and John Skylitzes on the fate of the campaign of 971.

According to Leo the Deacon, when the Bulgarians heard that Preslav was captured, they started coming over to the Byzantines' side. It is likely that when the Byzantine emperor was moving out towards Dristra (Dorostolon), he took Boris II with him; tsar's presence may have made gaining the support of Bulgarians through whose lands the Byzantine army was marching easier. Leo the Deacon mentioned that on the way to Dorostolon the Byzantines gained assistance from the inhabitants of Pliska, of otherwise unknown Dineia, as well as of others, not mentioned by name, Bulgarian settlements[22]. Voluntary shift of Bulgarians

---

[22] Leo the Deacon, VIII, 8; cf. A. Madgearu, *Byzantine Military Organization on the Danube 10th–12th Century*, Leiden–Boston 2013, p. 31. John Skylitzes (p. 298) presents the matter differently, claiming that the emperor appointed a strategos after capturing each centre, and was also to have: *plundered many fortress and buildings* (transl., p. 285), and left them for the soldiers to plunder. It is difficult to reconcile this relation with Leo's information. It is doubtful that John would have allowed his soldiers to loot Bulgarian cities prior to the confrontation with Svyatoslav, although during the war looting could have occasionally occurred nonetheless. Such treatment may have been given to those settlements that resisted the Byzantines (perhaps because of the presence of Rus' warriors). There is another possible explanation of John Skylitzes' description. The passage may have related to the situation after Svyatoslav was defeated, when Tzymiskes decided to incorporate Bulgarian lands into the empire. In those

to the Byzantine side may attest to associating their presence with the hope of removing the Rus' from their lands, and that they have not perceived the Byzantines as a threat. It seems that at that time John Tzymiskes has not yet taken steps that could have indicated that he intended to subordinate Bulgarian lands to Constantinople. It would also seem that this attitude may be considered a confirmation of the fact that the Bulgarians were not allied with Svyatoslav. If that were to have been the case, then such an alliance was forced, and Bulgarians used the first opportunity they got to break it. It cannot be ruled out that to some extent the decision to join the Byzantine side was a result of realisation that an effective defence was impossible. Svyatoslav's lack of trust towards the Bulgarians can be attested by the fact that before the battle with Tzymiskes he ordered execution of three hundred of them; those executed were influential and of high birth[23]. Leo the Deacon mentioned that this was a reaction to: the Mysians were rebelling against their alliance with him, and going over to the emperor"[24]. It is possible that these were Bulgarian mercenaries, and not an allied contingent[25] or, what is perhaps even more likely, hostages. Their execution would have been a logical step at a time when their presence in Svyatoslav's camp was no longer guaranteeing the loyalty of their kinsmen. John Skylitzes also mentioned twenty thousand Bulgarians, hostages of Svyatoslav, whom the latter ordered shackled or tied up before the battle with the Byzantines, so that they would not support his enemy[26]. Leo the Deacon also made a note of this event; however he did not specify the number of Bulgarians who

---

circumstances both the Bulgarians' resistance, and the Byzantine attitude, would have been logical.

[23] Leo the Deacon, VIII, 9; John Skylitzes, p. 298 (also mentioned the three hundred executed Bulgarians, although without indicating as clearly that their deaths came as a response to Bulgarians coming over to the Byzantine side).

[24] Leo the Deacon, VIII, 9 (transl. 184).

[25] П. Павлов, *Борби...*, p. 287.

[26] John Skylitzes, p. 300. Regarding the credibility of the number given by the Byzantine author, one should, I think, remain sceptical. It is worth noting that the same number is given by him in the context of the events in Philippoupolis in 970 where, as I mentioned before, twenty thousand Bulgarians were to have been impaled on Svyatoslav's orders.

were subject to this treatment[27]. This move also emphatically showed that the latter were considered to be hostile.

The above remarks clearly indicate that the Rus' dominion over Bulgarian lands was rather illusory and based on coercion rather than on a mutually beneficial accord.

Rejecting the perspective of the sources (let us once again stress, of Byzantine provenance), according to which Bulgarians flocked to Byzantine side after the events at Preslav, allows us to form a view that they have not so much abandoned Svyatoslav and joined the Byzantine side, but rather by their own reckoning they were simply retaking freedom and regaining power over their own lands. They have been very quickly disappointed, as the Byzantines, having defeated Svyatoslav, instead of leaving decided to impose their own authority over the Bulgarian territories.

In the description of the clashes by Dristra, which lasted for several months[28] and were described by both of the authors, we do not find any references to Bulgarians' participation therein. While such participation cannot, of course, be ruled out[29], the fighting that took place occurred only between the *Rhomaioi* and the Rus'. As such, the victory over the latter was exclusively due to the emperor and his army. Acknowledging any participation of the Bulgarians in this success would have only diminished it, as after the victory the Byzantines moved in turn against the Bulgarians, occupying most of their country. The *Rhomaioi* – traitors moving against their allies, to whom in some part they owed victory. This would certainly not have been a cause for pride.

It cannot be ruled out that the Byzantines have taken early steps to subordinate Bulgaria even during the siege of Dorostolon. However, if we were to treat Skylitzes' relation about placing garrisons in Bulgarian

---

[27] Leo the Deacon, VIII, 9.

[28] On events by Dristra, see e.g.: S. McGrath, *The Battles of Dorostolon (971). Rhetoric and Reality*, [in:] *Peace and War in Byzantium. Essays in Honor of George T. Dennis, S.J.*, ed. T.S. Miller, J. Nesbitt, Washington 1995, pp. 152–164; D.P. Hupchick, *The Bulgarian-Byzantine Wars for Early Medieval Balkan Hegemony. Silver-Lined Skulls and Blinded Armies*, [s.l.] 2017, pp. 238–240.

[29] For arguments for the Bulgarians' participation on the Byzantine side, see: Д. Ангелов, Б. Чолпанов, *Българска...*, pp. 25–26.

cities with reserve, then aside from garrisoning Preslav, we find no traces of such activities. On the other hand, we can indeed find hints of certain tensions in the Bulgarian-Byzantine relations during this period, visible in pillaging of Bulgarian lands by the Byzantines. Aside from Skylitzes' relation, this can be attested by Leo the Deacon, writing about desecration and looting by Magister John Kourkouas: *for he is said to have plundered many of the* [*churches*] *in Mysia and to have refashioned their furnishings and holy vessels into personal valuables*[30]. He was punished for his deeds, and suffered death at the hands of the Rus'. Leo treats this information with caution, preceding it with 'for he is said', however since he mentioned it at all, he must have considered it at least somewhat credible.

Having defeated Svyatoslav, the *Rhomaioi* took steps to incorporate Bulgarian lands into the Empire[31]. It is notable that both the historians relate this process very briefly. Its description by Leo the Deacon is limited to the statement that John Tzymiskes subordinated (καθυποτάξας) Mysia to the *Rhomaioi*[32], while in John Skylitzes, a remark that the emperor has provided adequate protection for the strongholds and cities on both sides of the river (Danube)[33]. Each of the authors, on the other hand, devoted considerable attention to the triumph that the emperor celebrated after his return to Constantinople. Neither of them said a word about the attitude of Bulgarians towards the Byzantine aggression, creating an impression that it was not met with any resistance. This is difficult to imagine, although it is likely that any resistance would have been weak, a consequence on the one hand of the great losses Bulgarians took in their wars against the Rus', and on the other of being surprised by the Byzantines, who unexpectedly turned from allies to invaders.

John Tzymiskes returned to the Byzantine capital and celebrated his victory over the Rus' and Bulgarians with a triumph. The city's inhabitants welcomed him with gifts of crowns and insignia made of gold

---

[30] Leo the Deacon, IX, 5 (transl. p. 192).

[31] On the subject of the organisation of Bulgarian lands under Byzantine rule, see: M.J. Leszka, K. Marinow, *Carstwo bułgarskie. Polityka – społeczeństwo – gospodarka – kultura, 866–971*, Warszawa 2015, pp. 197–199 (there further bibliography).

[32] Leo the Deacon, IX, 12.

[33] John Skylitzes, p. 310.

and precious stones, and asked him to board a specially prepared wagon, decorated with gold and pulled by white horses. The emperor accepted the crowns and sceptres, and in return bestowed numerous gifts on the capital's inhabitants, but did not want to ride on the wagon. Instead, he placed upon the gilt throne located on the vehicle an icon of the Mother of God holding Christ on her hands, carried away from Preslav, and put before it the imperial robes and crowns of the Bulgarian rulers. Wearing a diadem, he followed the wagon on horseback, holding the received crowns and diadems in his hands. The procession went through the entire city, all the way to the Church of the Holy Wisdom, where after prayers of thanksgiving Tzymiskes offered the finest of the Bulgarian crowns to God, as a token offering of the plunder. He then made his way to the imperial palace, where tsar Boris was officially deprived of the insignia of imperial power, instead being honoured with the dignity of a *magister*[34]. The official triumph of the Byzantine ruler put an end to the existence of an independent Bulgarian Tsardom in a highly symbolic fashion, in accordance with the Byzantine political ideology and a Divine blessing. The emperor's actions perfectly fit with the moves taken previously, such as renaming of the older Bulgarian centres, including the capital Preslav, or placing of his own *strategoi* in the strongholds in north-eastern Bulgaria. The steps taken in the capital were their continuation and complementation, and indeed their climax. Even the presence of the Preslavian icon of the Mother of God in Constantine's capital was intended to attest to the fundamental changes in the Byzantine-Bulgarian relations. The image had likely been the protector of the Bulgarian capital (following the Constantinopolitan model), and was taken as a result of the emperor's successful campaign.

[34] Leo the Deacon, IX, 12. According to John Skylitzes (p. 310) Boris was deprived of the insignia on the Forum of Constantine.

PART TWO
THE STRUCTURES

I

Kirił Marinow

The Environment and Geopolitics of the State

From the seventh to the eleventh centuries, Bulgaria encompassed the areas in the central and north-eastern part of the Balkan Peninsula. Of course, the territories that made up the Bulgarian state during this period underwent significant changes, and expanded in every direction[1]. The tenth century in this respect marked an important turn. At that time, tsar Symeon I managed to move the country's borders southwards and westwards, but lost a significant part of the Bulgarian lands north of the Danube Valley. The most important geopolitical transformation of the Bulgarian state came in the last quarter of the century. Its centre, along with its main cities, shifted from the north-eastern Danube territories to the south-western areas of Macedonia. The purpose of this text, however, is not to offer a detailed discussion of the territorial changes to which the Bulgarian state was subjected in the early Middle Ages. Nor is it to offer an insight into territorial policies carried out by successive Bulgarian rulers.

[1] For the analysis of the border changes of the Bulgarian Tsardom during Peter's reign see e.g. the following works: П. Коледаров, *Политическа география на средновековната българска държава*, vol. I, *От 681 до 1018 г.*, София 1979; K. Gagova, *Bulgarian-Byzantine Border in Thrace from the 7th to the 10th Century (Bulgaria to the South of Haemus)*, BHR 14.1, 1986, pp. 66–77; P. Soustal, *Tabula Imperii Byzatini*, vol. VI, *Thrakien (Thrakē, Rodopē und Haimimontos)*, Wien 1991, pp. 91–93.

Instead, it aims to provide a general description of the territories that remained under Bulgarian rule in the period under consideration, and to highlight their importance to the Bulgarian state from its rise in the second half of the seventh century to its collapse in the early eleventh century, with special regard to tsar Peter's reign.

A significant feature of the Bulgarian Black Sea coast between Cape Emine in the east, that is, the eastern branch of the Balkan Mountain range (ancient and mediaeval Haimos, which predominantly consist of today's ranges of Predbalkan, Stara Planina and Sredna Gora), and the Danube delta in the south is the cliffs. Consequently, this part of the coast is not particularly open towards the sea, which can clearly be seen in the Emine – Varna – Cape Kaliakra line[2]. The mountain slopes of the eastern Balkan and the Mominsko Plateau, which lie between Emine and Varna, drop sharply into the sea, thus making the coast inaccessible, and the cliffs that rise up to 65 metres in height on the Kaliakra peninsula, near today's Kavarna, account for this inaccessibility between Varna and Cape Kaliakra. In this area there are only three points at which the Black Sea coast can be accessed: at the mouth of the River Kamchiya, which flows through the mountains, at the mouth of the River Provadiyska near Varna and at the mouth of the River Batova, near Kranevo, slightly north of the last locality[3]. This was borne out by emperor Constantine VII, who in his description of the route which took the Varangian merchants along the western coast of the Black Sea to Constantinople, mentions the following stopping points that they made during their travels through the Balkans: the Danube delta, Konopas and Constantia, the estuary

---

[2] For more on these capes and mediaeval settlements and fortifications see: Б. Петрунова, *Нови археологически данни за крепостта Калиакра*, [in:] *Каварна. Средище на българския Североизток. Сборник доклади от научна конференция Каварна – 2007 г.*, ed. eadem, Х. Кузов, Д. Мирчева, Каварна 2007, pp. 126–139; K. Marinow, *Twierdza Emona. Na nadmorskich stokach średniowiecznego Hemusu*, VP 28, 2008, pp. 617–633; Г. Джингов, *Тиризис. Акре. Калиакра*, [2]Каварна 2010, pp. 5–9, 28–62; Б. Петрунова, *Реликвите на Калиакра*, Добрич 2014.

[3] See: Z. Czeppe, J. Flis, R. Mochnacki, *Geografia fizyczna świata*, Warszawa 1969, pp. 243, 244; Ц. Михайлов, Х. Тишков, Л. Зяпков, Д. Горунова, *Дунавска равнинно-хълмиста област*, [in:] *География на България в три тома*, vol. II, *Физико-географско и социално-икономическо*, ed. К. Мишев, София 1989, pp. 60–65.

of the River Provadiyska, the same of River Kamchiya and the Mesembria harbour located south of the Balkan Mountains[4]. For this reason too, the Bulgarians fortified this part of the coast with earthen ramparts in order to prevent the imperial fleet from disembarking troops to attack the Khanate's interior. Given the above, it is understandable – although geography was not the only factor here, nor was it the most important one – that the sea, leaving aside the threat of invasion from these points, did not play a significant part in the history of the Bulgarian state in the early Middle Ages, nor economically – for primary sources say nothing of the existence of a Bulgarian merchant fleet at that time[5]. Moreover, there was no harbour in this part of the coastline in the period from the mid-ninth century to the beginning of the 970s. It was not until the establishment of the lasting Byzantine rule over this area, which took place in the eleventh century, that Varna (ancient Odessos) saw its revival as a stronghold and an important harbour city[6]. In addition, ethnographic studies show that traditionally Bulgarian cuisine had mainly freshwater fish on its menu[7]. However, this fact does not mean that sea fishing was completely unimportant, especially, which is quite understandable, for those who lived on the coast (the Greek population from such cities as Mesembria, Anchialos and Sozopolis must have engaged in this activity). In addition,

---

[4] Constantine VII Porphyrogennetos, *On the Governance of the Empire*, 9, p. 62.96–104. For identifications see: П.С. Коледаров, *Историческата география на Северозападното Черноморие по данните на Константин Багренородни*, ИП 33.3, 1977, pp. 50–64.

[5] Р. Рашев, *Първото българско царство и морето*, [in:] *Средновековна България и Черноморието (Сборник доклади от националната конференция Варна – 1980)*, ed. А. Кузев, Т. Йорданов, Варна 1982, pp. 47–56. Views to the contrary, which are based on a specific interpretation of one passage from the *Hexameron* by John the Exarch or on the discovery of pictures representing ships in the old Bulgarian capitals, are in my opinion unconvincing – see: Ц. Чолова, *Данни за българския външнотърговски обмен и мореплаване в Шестоднева на Йоан Езгарх*, Век 8.4, 1979, pp. 62–65; Д. Овчаров, *Български средновековни рисунки-графити*, София 1982, pp. 53–56.

[6] В. Плетньов, *Варна през Средновековието (VII–XIV в.)*, [in:] idem, И. Русев, *История на Варна*, vol. II, *Средновековие и Възраждане (VII в. – 1878 г.)*, Варна 2012, pp. 162, 183–192; idem, *Крепостта Варна според писмените извори от IX–XII в.*, ДобСб 30, 2015, pp. 193–219.

[7] Х. Вакарелски, *Етнография на България*, София 1974, pp. 193–210, 218.

in archaeological findings, clay weights used for fishing nets, the bones and vertebrae of fish species from the sturgeon family, iron hooks and clam shells, provide evidence of a preponderance of inland fishing[8].

In Northern Thrace, south of the Balkan Mountains, between Cape Emine in the north and the Strandzha massif in the south, the topography of the Black Sea coast is slightly different. Opening out onto the sea, the land is more accessible here than in the north. It is also more indented and, as such, provides good mooring. This can be said especially of the deep Burgas bay that wedges its way inland, making it possible to sail down the River Sredetska to Develtos. In the ninth and tenth centuries Develtos played an important economical role as the customs post situated on the border between Bulgaria and Byzantium[9]. North of the bay, there lay the two most important harbours of Northern Thrace – Anchialos and Mesembria[10]. The former was located on the sea promontory, near the salt pans[11], as is indicated by the etymology of the word. The latter lay

[8] Z. Kurnatowska, *Słowiańszczyzna Południowa*, Wrocław 1977, p. 104; В. Гюзелев, *Икономическо развитие, социална структура и форми на социална и политическа организация на прабългарите до образуването на българската държава (IV–VII в.)*, *Архе* 21.4, 1979, p. 14; Й. Чангова, *Перник*, vol. III, *Крепостта Перник VIII–XIV в.*, София 1992, p. 18; Л. Дончева-Петкова, *Одърци. Селище от Първото българско царство*, vol. I, София 1999, p. 59; Х. Матанов, *В търсене на средновековното време. Неравният път на българите (VII–XV в.)*, София 2014, pp. 112–113.

[9] И. Йорданов, *Печатите на комеркиарията Девелт*, ПП 2, 1992, pp. 17–85; idem, *Печатите на комеркиарията Девелт. Addenda et corrigenda*, [in:] *Нумизматични и сфрагистични приноси към историята на Западното Черноморие. Международна конференция Варна, 12–15 септември 2001*, ed. И. Лазаренко, В. Йотов, В. Иванов, В. Славчев, Варна 2004, pp. 230–245. On the center itself see: М. Балболова-Иванова, *Средновековый Девелт в VIII–X вв.*, [in:] *Bulgaria Pontica Medii Aevi*, vol. IV–V/1, ed. В. Гюзелев, София 2003, pp. 79–84.

[10] On these centres see: V. Gjuzelev, *Die mittelalterliche Stadt Mesembria (Nesebăr) im 6.–15. Jh.*, BHR 6.1, 1978, pp. 50–59; idem, *Anchialos zwischen der Spätantike und dem frühen Mittelalter*, [in:] *Die Schwarzmeerküste in der Spätantike und frühen Mittelalter*, ed. R. Pillinger, A. Pülz, H. Vetters, Wien 1992, pp. 23–33.

[11] Б. Розов, *Солниците при гр. Поморие*, ГП 4.4/5, 1950, pp. 20–23; С. Кираджиев, *Енциклопедичен географски речник на България*, София 2013, p. 426. There are actually salt lakes near this town. In etymological terms, the name can also be linked to the coastal location of the town – М. Лазаров, В. Гюзелев,

on a small peninsula connected to the mainland by a narrow dike. Sources of thermal waters known for easing the ailments (such as, gout) of Bulgarian nobles and Byzantine emperors (Constantine IV, for example)[12] were found in the neighbourhood of Mesembria. South of the Burgas bay, there were two harbours – Sozopolis and Agathopolis[13]. Of particular note here is the fact that these centres survived the so-called migration period and Bulgaria's territorial expansion, including the wars waged against Byzantium in the first half of the ninth century. This guaranteed their sustainable development. Both harbours – Anchialos and Mesembria – managed to establish strong relations with Byzantine Constantinople; the strength of these relations could be seen in the unswerving support the cities received from the imperial fleet and in the ethnically dominant position of the Greek and Anatolian population that lived there. While close relations were also established with other cities located at the seaside, those whose hinterland was uninhabited up until the turn of the eighth and ninth centuries, were neglected. In the ninth and tenth centuries Sozopolis and Agathopolis probably served as important trading centres between Byzantium and Bulgaria, having been operated by the Byzantines from the sea. However, it must be stressed that the role of official trade centre between the two countries was assumed by Develtos, after its reconstruction[14].

Увод, [in:] *История на Поморие*, vol. I, *Древност и съвремие*, ed. А. Орачев, В. Василчина, Бургас 2011, pp. 13–14.

[12] Nikephoros, 36, p. 90.11–13; Theophanes, AM 6171, p. 358.27–28.

[13] On Sozopolis – Б. Димитров, *Созопол*, [in:] *Български средновековни градове и крепости*, vol. I, *Градове и крепости по Дунав и Черно Море*, ed. А. Кузев, В. Гюзелев, Варна 1981, pp. 388–407; И. Йорданов, *Средновековният Созопол според данните на сфрагистиката*, AMV 7.2, 2008, pp. 114–162; B. Dimitrov, *Sozopol*, Sofia 2012, pp. 199–220. On Agathopolis – idem, *Агатопол*, [in:] *Български средновековни градове*..., pp. 412–426; Ц. Дражева, *Най-южната българска черноморска крепост Ахтопол*, [in:] *Каварна*..., pp. 211–221.

[14] For more on the significance of the Black Sea in the history of mediaeval Bulgaria see: Б. Димитров, *Средновековна България и морето. Исторически очерк*, Мор 3.2, 1981, pp. 219–231; V. Gjuzelev, *Il Mar Nero ed il suo litorale nella storia del Medieovo Bulgaro*, BBg 7, 1981, pp. 11–24; idem, *Черноморската област в политическата история на Средновековна България*, [in:] *Чиракман – Карвуна – Каварна. Сборник*, ed. В. Василев, М. Велев, София 1982, pp. 76–82; С. Георгиева, *Черно море като географски фактор в историята на Първото българско царство*,

A long strip of grassland could be seen stretching along the north and west coast of the Black Sea. It extended to Dobrudzha (referred to in the Middle Ages as the Karvuna land, according to the *Tale of the prophet Isaiah*[15]), behind the so-called Madara Plateau. The strip played an important part in the history of the Bulgarian state. On the one hand it enabled the establishment of regular contacts – political, economic, cultural and migrational (i.e. it guaranteed the influx of people into the Bulgarian territory) – with nomads from the Black Sea steppes and, possibly, from areas in central Asia. On the other hand it put Bulgaria in constant danger of being attacked by these nomads from the north-east. The Bulgarians themselves arrived in this territory from the Black Sea coast in the latter half of the seventh century. An undulating area in the west of forests and grassy plains, Dobrudzha (the steppes extends mainly over its eastern part) provided a perfect framework for the development of a nomadic economy – one which gave priority to animal husbandry. The role played by this area, in the initial period of the Bulgarian settlement south of the Danube delta, can be in no doubt. However, one can safely assume that animal breeding still played a significant role in the ninth and tenth centuries, along with land cultivation that was already in progress[16]. Scholars maintain that the name Karvuna is derived from the Greek word κάρβων, that is, coal, which concludes that the region's inhabitants must have been involved in the production of charcoal. This observation adds a significant element to our knowledge of the economic development of this area[17].

[in:] *Средновековните Балкани; политика, религия, култура*, ed. Л. Симеонова, София 1999, pp. 28–32; К. Станев, *Морето – неусвоеното пространство на Първото българско царство*, Ист 15.2/3, 2007, pp. 25–34.

[15] *Tale of the Prophet Isaiah*, f. 401a–b, pp. 14.33–34, 15.7.30–31.

[16] Cf. V. Gjuzelev, *Naturrumliche Bedingungen, Grenzen und Namen von Dobruda im Mittelalter (14.–17. Jh.)*, [in:] idem, *Mittelalterliches Bulgarien. Quellen, Geschichte, Haupstdte und Kultur*, Istanbul 2001, pp. 345–366.

[17] В. Бешевлиев, *Из късноантичната и средновековната география на Североизточна България*, ИАИ 25, 1962, pp. 1–18; However, the view has recently been called into doubt. It is indicated that the Karvuna land is referred to in the *Tale* as inhabited by the Bulgarians, also known as the Cumans and it is known that the Danube residence of Cuman leaders was called Karabuna (near today's Tatarbunary). The area

The natural migration corridor, extending to Madara, offered an easy access to the Danubian Plain. Lying west of this corridor, the plain was comprised of territories between the lower Danube Valley in the north and the Balkan Mountains, including their foothills, in the south. This area formed the nucleus of the Bulgarian state from the seventh century, when the state seized control of it, to the fall of the eastern Bulgaria in 971. The Bulgarians ruled over this area also between 986 and 1000, and the western part of it remained in their control even longer, up to the fall of the fortress Bdin (today's Vidin) in 1003 (the fortress seems to have been Bulgaria's most important centre in the north-western part of the plain)[18], by which time the state's political centre had already shifted to Macedonia. According to Bulgarian sources, the territory under discussion formed the so-called interior of the Bulgarian state[19] which was home to most settlements and to the country's political centres, including of course its

---

was thus etymologically linked to the name of the town rather than the kind of economic activity for which the area was known – Г. Атанасов, *Добруджанското деспотство. Към политическата, църковната, стопанската и културната история на Добруджа през XIV век*, Велико Търново 2009, p. 21. However, the opinion is not widely held.

[18] On the fortress see: С. Михайлов, *Археологически проучвания на крепостта Баба Вида във Видин*, Архе 3.3, 1961, pp. 1–8; W. Swoboda, *Widin*, [in:] *SSS*, vol. VI, pp. 421–422; Б. Кузупов, "*Замъкът Баба Вида*", МПК 20.4, 1980, pp. 7–12; А. Кузев, *Бдин*, [in:] *Български средновековни градове...*, pp. 98–115; В. Вълов, *Седалището и териториалният обхват на Бдинската област от средата на IX до началото на XI век*, ИМСБ 13, 1987, pp. 21–45; V. Beševliev, *Die Herkunft des Stadtnamens* **Бъдынь**, LBa 31.1/2, 1988, pp. 43–44; М. Николова, *Към въпроса за името на град Видин*, ИМСБ 14, 1988, pp. 75–97; П. Балабанов, С. Бояджиев, Н. Тулешков, *Крепостно строителство по българските земи*, София 2000, p. 60; Г.Н. Николов, *Централизъм и регионализъм в ранносредновековна България (края на VII – началото на XI в.)*, София 2005, pp. 192–193; Л. Симеонова, *Крепостта Видинис/Бдин и "завръщането на Византия на Дунава": реализация и крах на една имперска мечта*, SB 32, 2017, pp. 61–93.

[19] Г. Владимиров, *Дунавска България и Волжска България. Формиране и промяна на културните модели (VII–XI в.)*, София 2005, pp. 65–66; М. Каймакамова, *Образуването на българската държава в българската средновековна историопис*, [in:] *Тангра. Сборник в чест на 70-годишнината на акад. Васил Гюзелев*, ed. eadem et al., София 2006, pp. 71–72, 76, 86, 87; P. Sophoulis, *Byzantium and Bulgaria, 775–831*, Leiden–Boston 2012, pp. 75–76. The analogical structure of territorial division was preserved during the reign of Cometopouloi dynasty – С. Пириватрић, *Самуилова држава. Обим и карактер*, Београд 1997, pp. 90, 129, 171–172, 192.

capitals – Pliska (towards the end of the ninth century) and Great Preslav (from the end of the ninth century to 971)[20]. In the tenth century, the Byzantines wrote of the Haimos Mountains range (later called Balkan by the Ottoman Turks) and the river Danube as being the most distinctive features of the region's topography, and also considered this territory to be the core of the Bulgarian state[21]. They also began to use the term

[20] On these centres see: Р. Панова, *Столичният град в културата на средновековна България*, София 1995, pp. 90–140; eadem, *The Capital City in the Medieval Bulgarian State*, JÖB 46, 1996, pp. 437–440; П. Георгиев, *Столиците на княз Борис-Михаил – хронология и типологическа характеристика*, [in:] *Християнската култура в средновековна България. Материали от национална научна конференция, Шумен 2–4 май 2007 година по случай 1100 години от смъртта на св. Княз Борис-Михаил (ок. 835–907 г.)*, ed. idem, Велико Търново 2008, pp. 154–163; D. Ziemann, *Pliska and Preslav: Bulgarian Capitals between Relocation and Invention*, [in:] *Българско Средновековие: общество, власт, история. Сборник в чест на проф. д-р Милияна Каймакамова*, ed. Г.Н. Николов, А. Николов, София 2013, pp. 170–185. On Pliska – Д. Овчаров, *Плиска*, [in:] idem, Т. Тотев, А. Попов, *Стари български столици. Плиска. Велики Преслав. Търновград*, София 1980, pp. 9–69; ППре 4, 1985, pp. 5–131; *Материали за картата на Средновековната българска държава (територията на днешна Североизточна България)*, ed. Р. Рашев, ППре 7, 1995, pp. 247–263; С. Бояджиев, *Архитектурата на българите от VII до XIV век в три тома*, vol. I, *Дохристиянска архитектура*, София 2008, pp. 30–143; Р. Рашев, *Българската езическа култура VII–IX в.*, София 2009, pp. 45–104; *Археологическа карта на Плиска*, ed. А. Аладжов, София 2013; Н. Мавродинов, *Старобългарското изкуство. Изкуството на Първото българско царство*, ²София 2013, pp. 51–74; on Preslav – W. Swoboda, *Presław Wielki*, [in:] *SSS*, vol. IV, pp. 335–343; D. Ovčarov, *Emergence et développement de la ville de Preslav. IX*ᵉ*–X*ᵉ *siècles (Quelques problèmes et aspects)*, BHR 7.2, 1979, pp. 51–61; Т. Тотев, *Преслав*, [in:] Д. Овчаров, Т. Тотев, А. Попов, *Стари български столици...*, pp. 71–133; ППре 4, 1985, pp. 132–222; *Материали за картата на Средновековната българска държава...*, pp. 175–190; Т. Тотев, *Археологические данные о Преславе*, ШУЕКП.ТКИБ 2, 1998, pp. 61–68; П. Балабанов, С. Бояджиев, Н. Тулешков, *Крепостно строителство...*, pp. 157–170; Т. Тотев, *Преславската култура и изкуство през IX–X век. Студии и статии*, София 2000; idem, *Great Preslav*, Sofia 2001; I. Jordanov, *Preslav*, [in:] *The Economic History of Byzantium. From the Seventh through the Fifteenth Century*, vol. II, ed. A.E. Laiou, Washington 2002, pp. 667–671; С. Бояджиев, *Архитектурата на българите...*, pp. 149–172; Р. Рашев, *Българската езическа култура...*, pp. 105–115; Н. Мавродинов, *Старобългарското изкуство...*, pp. 182–231.

[21] *On the treaty with the Bulgarians*, 12, p. 274.307–310; K. Marinow, *In the Shackles of the Evil One: The Portrayal of Tsar Symeon I the Great (893–927) in the Oration 'On the Treaty with the Bulgarians'*, SCer 1, 2011, pp. 166–167.

Mysoi/Mysians – a reference to a Thracian tribe that had once inhabited this territory – which was synonymous with 'Bulgarians'. Along with the Karvuna land, this area became one of the most important in the Bulgarian state. In addition to playing a significant economic role, it constituted the country's agricultural centre, known for the cultivation of various crops. Unsurprisingly, Byzantine troops resorted to a scorched earth policy while withdrawing from Pliska in 811. By destroying the harvests and killing farm animals, the Byzantines hoped to strike a serious blow to the Khanate's economy. In fact, the Bulgarians spent eleven months trying to eliminate the negative effects of the devastation inflicted by the enemy[22]. The significance of this food supply base became clear in the mid-ninth century, when poor harvests caused a great famine in the Khanate and led the Bulgarians to turn to their southern neighbours for help. This step resulted in the conclusion of an official peace between the feuding parties and in the acceptance of Christianity by khan Boris I, the Bulgarian ruler[23]. The eastern part of this plain, the so-called Ludogorie, also played an important economic role. Covered with forest between the Danube Valley and the foothills of the Balkan Mountain (the above mentioned Predbalkan), it served as a reservoir of wood and venison[24]. As can be seen from epigraphic sources and osteological findings, it constituted one of the main sources of food for Bulgaria's population. The Danubian Plain – the part located south of the river Danube – which was most important to the Bulgarians was irrigated by a number of rivers, all of which were the Danube's right-bank tributaries: Archar, Lom, Tsibritsa and Ogosta starting from the western part of the Balkan Mountain; the Vit, Osam and Yantra that flow down from the central massif; the Rusenski Lom, originating in the eastern part of the mountains, and the largest of them all – the Iskar that runs through the Sofia Valley and crosses the mountain range. In the east there were two rivers flowing into the Black Sea – the

[22] Cf. Theophanes, AM 6301, pp. 495.22 – 496.6.

[23] T. Wasilewski, *Bizancjum i Słowianie w IX wieku. Studia z dziejów stosunków politycznych i kulturalnych*, Warszawa 1972, pp. 126–127.

[24] Ц. Михайлов, Х. Тишков, Л. Зяпков, Д. Горунова, *Дунавска...*, pp. 50–59; Б. Илиев, *Родно Лудогорие. Алманах*, София 2008, pp. 28, 36–40; С. Кираджиев, *Енциклопедичен...*, pp. 327–328.

River Provadiyska and the River Kamchiya. All these rivers would have had a positive effect on the development of husbandry in the area under discussion. The inhabitants relied on them for fish and drinking water[25].

Stretching between the so-called Iron Gates in the west and the river's delta in the east, the Lower Danube covers a distance of over 500 kilometres. It cuts through the Danubian Plain, forming a natural northern border of the nucleus of the Bulgarian state. The Byzantines described the Danube as a river that, though very deep, is easy to cross because of its weak current[26]. Although the river often marked the state's border, it posed no serious obstacle. It iced over and was thus easy to cross in the winter[27], and the river's islands made its crossing even easier. Some scholars claim that the Danube did not form an important demarcation line, and the people on both of its banks did not much differ from each other in cultural terms. In this part of Europe, the role of such a barrier fell to the Carpathian Mountains and their natural southern extension – the Balkan Mountain range[28]. This may account for Bulgaria's territorial expansion in this direction, especially after the fall of the Avar Khaganate. Regardless of whether this opinion is justified, the river played a very important role in Bulgaria's history. First of all it was navigable down the whole length of the part dealt with here, and – as is not the case of a sea fleet – we have evidence that the Bulgarians had a river fleet as early as the 820s. Although the evidence is incidental and concerns a military expedition to Pannonia, it seems obvious that the river was used for

---

[25] On the role of the plain see: Ц. Михайлов, Х. Тишков, Л. Зяпков, Д. Горунова, *Дунавска...*, pp. 29–65; Д. Митова-Джонова, *Общонародното и регионалното в културно-историческото развитие на Дунавската равнина*, София 1989; С. Кираджиев, *Енциклопедичен...*, pp. 194–196.

[26] *On Strategy*, p. 62.4–7; В.В. Кучма, *"Византийский Аноним VI в.": основные проблемы источников и содержания*, [in:] idem, *Военная организация Византийской Империи*, С.-Петербург 2001, p. 214. Ivan Venedikov (И. Венедиков, *Прабългарите и християнството*, Стара Загора 1998, p. 14), who concedes the difficulty one encountered in trying to cross the river and seize control of the Danubian fortresses that guarded its crossing, adds that barbarians ran over the limes in the south without destroying it.

[27] Cf. Anna Komnene, III, 8, 6, pp. 106.18 – 107.30 (the Pechenegs' example).

[28] *The Natural Regions of the Balkan Paninsula (after Cvijić)*, GRev 9.3, 1920, pp. 200–201; Z. Czeppe, J. Flis, R. Mochnacki, *Geografia...*, p. 240.

both economic and commercial purposes, especially in the latter half of the ninth and in the tenth centuries. This is attested to by the existence of harbours in the Danube Dristra and in Pereyaslavets (Little Pereslav) situated in the Danube delta[29]. However, it is difficult to say whether the last city, referred to in *Russian Primary Chronicle* as the main centre of the Bulgarian lands and the hub of commercial exchange between the south and the north[30], actually played such a role as early as the 960s. Scholars raise some serious doubts about it. Strategically important was the role of the delta of the great river. During the formation of the Danube Khanate, it served as home to Onglos – the khan's main seat (probably until the mid-eighth century, when the role of the capital was assumed

[29] В.Б. Перхавко, *Переяславец "Повести временных лет"*, Век 17.4, 1988, pp. 20–24; N. Oikonomides, *Presthlavitza, the Little Preslav*, [in:] idem, *Byzantium from the Ninth Century to the Fourth Crusade. Studies, Texts, Monuments*, Hampshire 1992 (no XIV), pp. 1–10; O. Damian, C. Andonie, M. Vasile, *Cetatea byzantină de la Nufăru. Despre problemele unui sit suprapus de oasezare contemporană*, Peu 1 (14), 2003, pp. 237–266. On Dorostolon see: П. Мутафчиев, *Съдбините на средновековния Дръстър*, [in:] idem, *Избрани произведения в два тома*, vol. II, ed. Д. Ангелов, София 1973, pp. 19–103; А. Кузев, *Дръстър*, [in:] *Българските средновековни градове...*, pp. 177–185; *Дуросторум–Дръстър–Силистра: сборник с изследвания*, ed. С. Христов, Р. Липчев, Г. Атанасов, Силистра 1988; И. Йорданов, *Дуросторум – Доростол – Дръстър според данните на сфрагистиката (VI–XIV в.)*, ДобСб 30, 2015, pp. 49–103. Different views have been put forward regarding the location of Pereyaslavets. The vicinity of the Romanian Nufăru has recently been indicated – И. Коновалова, В. Перехавко, *Древная Русь и Нижнее Подунавие*, Москва 2000, pp. 55–56; P. Stephenson, *Byzantium's Balkan Frontier. A Political Study of the Northern Balkans, 900–1204*, Cambridge 2000, pp. 56–57 (after Nicolas Oikonomides). On the doubts concerning the role this centre played in the period under consideration see: М. Раев, *Переяславец на Дунав – мит и действителност в речта на кнчз Святослав в "Повесть временных лет"*, ГСУ.НЦСВПИД 95 (14), 2006, pp. 193–203. Although Bulgarian scholars accept the existence of such a harbour on Păcuiul lui Soare (The Island of the Sun) – see for example D. Ovčarov, *La forteresse protobulgare sur l'île danubienne Păcuiul lui Soare*, [in:] *Dobrudža. Études ethno-culturelles*, ed. idem, Sofia 1987, pp. 57–68 – when the Island remained under the rule of Bulgarian rulers, archaeological findings suggest that it was built under Byzantine rule, during the reign of John Tzymiskes at the earliest – P. Diaconu, D. Vilceanu, *Păcuiul lui Soare*, vol. I, Bucurști 1972. Thus, the harbour may have fallen into Bulgarian hands for a while no sooner than towards the end of the tenth century.

[30] *Russian Primary Chronicle*, AM 6477, p. 68.

by Pliska) and where the Bulgarians originally settled[31]. In the latter half of the eight century the delta made it possible for the Byzantine fleet to sail into the rear of the Bulgarians' main territory and forced them to fight on both fronts (in other words, the Bulgarians found themselves in the Byzantines' clutches), thus weakening the defence of the southern demarcation line that blocked access to the Danubian Plain, that is, the Balkan Mountain massif. It also needs to be added that the river Danube was one of Bulgaria's largest reservoirs of drinking water and home to various species of fish to be found on the mediaeval menu[32].

It remained in dispute for as long as Bulgaria maintained control of such areas as the Wallachian Plain, situated north of the lower Danube, the Transylvanian Plateau, the Moldavian Plateau stretching over the central, southern and eastern territory of today's Romania, and Bessarabia that is part of today's Moldavia. It seems that the Bulgarians quickly managed to extend their influence over the Wallachian Plain and the Bessarabian territories that formed part of the migration corridor stretching along the Black Sea coastline. In the west, the grassy steppe extended as far as today's Bucharest. The Transylvanian Plateau, bounded to the east and south by the Carpathian mountain range and guarded by the Avars, formed a natural enclave to which the Bulgarians, in that stage of building their state, could not obtain access. This area is also bounded to the west by the Apuseni Mountains, which along with the Carpathian bend are easier to access along the east-west line, but steeper are in the south. Transylvania was probably ruled by the Bulgarian khans from the fall of the Avar Khaganate to the arrival of Hungarian tribes, that is, for almost the entire ninth and the beginning of the tenth centuries. The region encompasses

[31] On Onglos see e.g.: Р. Рашев, *Българската езическа култура*..., pp. 29–33; D. Ziemann, *Onglos – once again*, BMd 3, 2012, pp. 31–43.

[32] Ц. Михайлов, Х. Тишков, Л. Зяпков, Д. Горунова, *Дунавска*..., pp. 31–36; Л. Симеонова, *Пътуване по Дунава (IX–XI в.)*, [in:] *Пътуванията в средновековна България. Материали от първата национална конференция "Пътуване към България. Пътуванията в средновековна България и съвременният туризъм", Шумен, 8–11.05.2008 г.*, ed. И. Йорданов, Велико Търново 2009, pp. 104–109; С. Кираджиев, *Енциклопедичен*..., p. 194. Cf. В. Тъпкова-Заимова, *Долни Дунав – limes и limen между Византия и славянския свят*, [in:] *Руско-български връзки през вековете*, ed. Д. Ангелов, София 1986, pp. 39–45.

the upland and mountain areas. It is dominated by plateaus, intersected by numerous valleys[33]. Because of its iron, non-ferrous metals (including silver), rich salt deposits, and the abundance of timber and animals, it played a significant role in the economic life of Bulgaria, but probably not in Peter's times. The mountainous and grassland areas were favourable to animal husbandry. The Wallachian Plain, irrigated by a number of rivers from the Danube's left-bank tributaries (e.g. Jiu, Olt, Argeş, Dîmboviţa), was perfectly fit for cultivation, and so was the river's right-bank area. It can be said that the Wallachian Plain played a role similar to that of the Danubian Plain south of the Danube River. Some scholars are of the opinion that low-lying and grassland areas on both banks of the river shared similar cultural characteristics and enjoyed strong mutual relationships. From a strategic viewpoint, the area of the so-called 'Bulgaria north of the river Danube' formed the Bulgarian state's northern border and acted as a buffer zone that blocked access to the country's political centre, which was situated in the southern part of the valley of the great river. This area also brought the Bulgarians into contact with Great Moravia, the Frankish kingdom (in the north-west), Slavic tribes (in the north) and steppe nomads (in the north-east).

Although Bulgaria's topography was quite diverse, there was one feature which distinguished it and which dominated the landscape of both the Balkan Peninsula and the rest of southern Europe. This was the preponderance of mountains, intersected by fertile valleys and lowlands. The mountain ranges kept human enclaves isolated from each other and

[33] M. C o m ş a, *Die bulgarische Herrschaft nördlich der Donau während des 9. und 10. Jh. Im Lichte der archäologischen Forschungen*, D 4, 1960, pp. 395–422; S. B r e z e a n u, *La Bulgarie d'au-delà de l'Ister a la lumière des sourses écrites medievales*, EB 20.4, 1984, pp. 121–135; N.-Ş. T a n a o c s a, T. T e o t e o i, *L'extension de la domination bulgare au nord du Danube aux VIIIe–IXe siécles*, EB 20. 4, 1984, pp. 110–120; J. N o u z i l l e, *Transylwania. Obszar kontaktów i konfliktów*, transl. J. P r a k s a, Bydgoszcz 1997, pp. 21–23; A. M a d g e a r u, *Transylvania and the Bulgarian Expansion in the 9th and 10th Centuries*, AMN 39/40.2, 2002/2003, pp. 41–65. See Ian M l a d j o v (*Trans-Danubian Bulgaria: Reality and Fiction*, ByzS 3, 1998, pp. 85–128), who argues for Bulgaria's presence north of the Danube river also in the tenth century, although the view is not widely held. For more on Transylvania in this period see: I.M. Ţ i p l i c, *Transylvania in the Early Middle Ages (7th–13th c.)*, Alba Iulia 2006.

separated the peninsula's interior from the coastline areas – those that opened out onto the outside world[34].

The southern parts of the Danubian Plain gradually transition into the foothills of the Balkan Mountains, and are made up of a number of acclivities, which stretch over the length of 460 kilometres and encircle the Balkan Mountain range proper from the north. The massif itself runs in a long curve of 550 kilometres, from the Iron Gates in the west to Cape Emine in the east[35]. The width of the mountain range in question varies between 20 and 50 kilometres and that of its foothills between 20 and 45 kilometres. The total area of both is 24 000 square kilometres. Although the mountains are not high – their western range rises to an average height of 849 m (the highest peak reaches a height of 2168 m), most mountain passes in the central part of the range rise to a height of over 1000 m above sea level with peaks of over 2000 m above sea level (the highest of them being 2376 m). In the mountains' eastern ranges, the average altitude does not exceed 385 m above sea level. Together, they form the region's distinct geographical barrier that naturally separates the Danubian Plain in the north from Sub-Balkan valleys in the south and south-west (along with the Sofia Valley, also called Sofia Field) as well from the Northern Thrace in the south-east. The mountains formed the Danube area into a distinct territory in which the centre of the Bulgarian state was situated. They also provided a climatic barrier between the territories characterised by the continental climate to the north, and those lying to the south, which remain within the orbit of both transitional and Mediterranean climates. This mountain range also marks a boundary between different species of fauna and flora: Siberian-European in the north and Mediterranean in the south. Finally it is also the main watershed that divides the Black Sea and the Aegean Sea.

[34] For more on the issue see: F. B r a u d e l, *La Méditerranée et le Monde méditerranéen à l'époque de Philippe II*, Paris 1949 (I am using the Polish edition of the book, see: F. B r a u d e l, *Morze Śródziemne i świat śródziemnomorski w epoce Filipa II*, vol. I, transl. T. M r ó w c z y ń s k i, M. O c h a b, wstęp B. G e r e m e k, W. K u l a, [2]Warszawa 2004, pp. 29–58); Х. М а т а н о в, *Балкански хоризонти. История, общества, личности*, vol. I, София 2004, pp. 8–9, 26, 38, 48, 68, 83, 98–99, 103, 107, 123, 136, 161, 183, 189–190, 197, 199, 203, 267, 297.

[35] In terms of the way the terrain lies and not based on the geological structure of the massif. In line with the latter the proper mountain range starts at the Bielogradchik Pass.

The massif's characteristic feature is its steady descent in the eastward direction, which made the coastal parts of the mountains open to all sorts of influences from the south. It was not accidental that the local mountain passes were crossed mainly by people travelling along the north-south line, especially when the centres of early mediaeval Bulgaria were located north of the eastern part of the Balkan Mountains. The central and eastern part of the mountains was easier to access from the north – here the mountains slowly morph into something of a mountain foreland that joins gently with the Danubian Plain. Unlike its northern counterpart, the southern slopes of the massif drop sharply down into Thracian territories. The only exception here is the western side of the Balkan Mountains[36]. Because of the way the land lay it was the Bulgarians, and not the Byzantines, who maintained control of the interior of the massif for most of the early Middle Ages. Archaeological research shows that the colonisation of the Balkan Mountains did not get fully under way until the final years of the First Bulgarian Empire. In the previous period, especially from the late seventh to the early ninth centuries, the mountains served as a buffer zone which the Bulgarian state deliberately left devoid of any significant settlement, but nevertheless deployed its troops in order to patrol and control it. The Bulgarian settlements were concentrated mainly in the area of the Danubian Plain[37].

From an economic point of view, these mountains, the most densely forested part of the Balkans[38], would have served as a timber repository

---

[36] On the topography of the mountains see: В. Маринов, *Стара-Планина (Природна физономия и културно-стопанска структура)*, Род 2.1, 1939, pp. 121–143; Л. Динев, Л. Мелнишки, *Стара планина*, София 1962; H. Maruszczak, *Bułgaria*, Warszawa 1971, pp. 294–304; П. Пенчев, Х. Тишков, М. Данева, Д. Горунова, *Старопланинска област*, [in:] *География на България*..., pp. 85–113; Х. Тишков, Ц. Михайлов, Л. Зяпков, Д. Горунова, *Предбалканска област*, [in:] *География на България*..., pp. 65–85; В. Николов, М. Йорданова, *Планините в България*, София 2002, pp. 9–44; С. Кираджиев, *Енциклопедичен*..., pp. 431–432, 519–521.

[37] Cf. Л. Динев, Л. Мелнишки, *Стара*..., pp. 53–54.

[38] *Ibidem*, pp. 12, 13, 14, 16, 18, 37–39; Z. Czeppe, J. Flis, R. Mochnacki, *Geografia*..., p. 242; H. Maruszczak, *Bułgaria*..., p. 160; Х. Тишков, Ц. Михайлов, Л. Зяпков, Д. Горунова, *Предбалканска област*..., pp. 67, 69, 72, 74, 75, 77, 79, 80–81, 82, 84, 85; П. Пенчев, Х. Тишков, М. Данева,

from antiquity to the modern era. Mountain pastures were well suited for livestock farming and, along with a gradual increase in the number of settlers, played an increasingly important role in the development of this aspect of the Bulgarian economy. The Bulgarians, such as the Thracians and Romans before, may also have been involved in exploiting ores that existed in the area[39].

On the southern slopes of the Central Balkan Mountains are the Sub-Balkan valleys (Pirdop, Karlovo, Kazanlak), which form something of a furrow that separates the Balkan Mountains from other range, that is, Sredna Gora – sometimes called the Anti-Balkan[40]. Both massifs connect four mountain thresholds. These connections run high in the mountains and this may have been the reason why both massifs, from antiquity to the modern era, were not treated as two distinct mountain ranges – that is, Stara Planina and Sredna Gora – but were instead given a single name of Haimos. Sredna Gora is 250 kilometres long and 50 kilometres wide. It extends from the Iskar river valley in the west to the Tundzha river valley in the east, covering an area of about 5950 square kilometres (with the highest acclivity of 1604 m above sea level). With the assistance of two mountain thresholds the western part of these mountains links up with the Rhodope massif, wedging its way between the Northern Thracian Plain and the Sofia Valley and forming a barrier that, running in the east-west direction, separates the mountainous regions of the Western Balkans from the low-lying terrains of Northern Thrace[41]. It is the western part of Sredna Gora that is intersected by the famous ancient Succi

---

Д. Горунова, *Старопланинска област*..., pp. 89–90, 93–94, 95, 96, 98–99, 101, 103, 105, 107, 109, 110–111, 113; В. Николов, М. Йорданова, *Планините*..., pp. 10, 19–24, 38, 39, 42, 43, 44.

[39] Д. Ангелов, *Стопански живот*, [in:] *История на България в четиринадесет тома*, vol. II, *Първа българска държава*, ed. i d e m, София 1981, p. 341.

[40] Z. Czeppe, J. Flis, R. Mochnacki, *Geografia*..., pp. 239, 240; Г.Д. Данов, *Средна гора. пътеводител*, София 1971, p. 9; H. Maruszczak, *Bułgaria*..., pp. 124, 316–317; С. Кираджиев, *Енциклопедичен*..., p. 421.

[41] Г.Д. Данов, *Средна гора*..., pp. 9, 11; H. Maruszczak, *Bułgaria*..., p. 317; К. Мишев, *Южнобългарска провинция*, [in:] *География на България*..., p. 134; В. Николов, М. Йорданова, *Планините*..., p. 45; С. Кираджиев, *Енциклопедичен*..., pp. 515–516.

Pass (the Ihtiman Pass), known in the Middle Ages as Imperial Kleisoura and towards the end of the tenth century also referred to by some Byzantine authors as Bulgarian Kleisoura[42]. This mountain pass marked a borderline between Thrace and Illyria. The ancient military road (*via militaris*), i.e. the Balkans main artery, ran through the pass. From a strategic point of view, it was the most important mountain pass in this part of the Balkan Peninsula. To control it was to control the flow of goods and people.

South-west of the Balkan Mountains and west of Sredna Gora there is the Sofia Field, a long valley, with Sredets as its most important city (the ancient Serdica, referred to in mediaeval times as Triaditsa, today's Sofia)[43]. This area constituted an important communication hub intersected by the routes running from the north-west to south-east (the so-called military road) and from the north-east to south-west (from the Danubian Plain through the Western Balkan Mountains to Macedonia by the Struma river valley)[44]. The Sofia Field, along with the lands lying north-west of it, opened onto the Central Danube and Pannonia. For this reason, in the tenth century, the route was often taken by Hungarians who either invaded Bulgaria or advanced further afield into Byzantine territories. In the north it enabled the Bulgarians to penetrate into Macedonian areas. It should be added that west of the bend of the Balkan Mountains there

---

[42] И. Велков, *Траяновите врата*, Век 1.3, 1931, pp. 33–35; П. Мутафчиев, *Старият друм през "Траянови врата"*, СБАН.КИФФО 55.27, 1937, pp. 19–148; Д. Митова-Джонова, *Confinium Succi и Mutatio Soneium през античността и ранновизантийската епоха*, Ана 1.2/3, 1994, pp. 77–99; В. Гълъбова, *История на Ихтиман*, vol. I, София 2007, pp. 25–34. Cf. В. Василев, *Ихтиманският край в древността*, Век 18.6, 1989, pp. 47–58.

[43] For more on the issue see: *Сердика*, vol. I, *Археологически материали и проучвания*, ed. Т. Герасимов, София 1964; *Сердика*, vol. II, *Археологически материали и проучвания*, ed. В. Велков, София 1989; Г. Цанкова-Петкова, *Сердика – Средец през ранното средновековие (IX–XII в.)*, [in:] *София през вековете*, vol. I: *Древност, Средновековие, Възраждане*, ed. П. Динеков, София 1989, pp. 42–54; П. Павлов, *Средец (София) в историята на Първото българско царство*, [in:] *1200 години Сердика – Средец – София в България*, ed. Б. Петрунова, М. Ваклинова, София 2009, pp. 4–38; А. Данчева-Василева, *История на средновековна София от IV–XIV век*, София 2017.

[44] А. Данчева-Василева, *Град Сердика (Средец) в политическата история на България (809–1018 г.)*, ИП 60.3/4, 2004, p. 17.

was another natural migration corridor. It ran southwards, through the Morava Valley, in the direction of Macedonia. In the early Middle Ages it was used by the *Sclavenoi*, the western branch of the Slavs, who advanced into Byzantine territories[45].

Lying south and east of the Ihtiman Pass were fertile terrains of Northern Thrace that constituted the fertile hinterland of the western coast of the Black Sea. This area is characteristically bounded by the massif Haimos in the north and north-west, by the Rhodope Mountains in the south and south-west and by the Strandzha Massif (along with the mountains Sakar and Hasekiyata) in the south and south-east. From the east, Northern Thrace opens out onto the sea. This was another area that played an important economic role, notably in terms of the development of commerce, agriculture and fishing. The low-lying areas of this part of Thrace offered good conditions for farming, and two large rivers, Hebros (today's Maritsa) and its left tributary, the river Tundzha, added fresh fish to the people's diet. The mild climate acted as an additional incentive for people to settle there. Philippoupolis (today's Plovdiv)[46] was its most important centre, but there were also other important cities such as Beroe (today's Stara Zagora)[47], Stilvnos (today's Sliven)[48] and those I have already mentioned – Sozopolis, Develtos, Anchialos and Mesembria – along the coast.

In the era of an independent Bulgarian state (i.e. between the seventh and the eleventh centuries, with a break between 971–976/986, and

---

[45] Т. Живковић, *Јужни словени под византијском влашћу (600–1025)*, Београд 2002, pp. 264, 274, 300. Cf. С.А. Иванов, *Оборона Византии и география "варварских" вторжении через Дунай в первой половине VI в.*, ВВ 44, 1983, pp. 27–47; idem, *Оборона балканских провинции Византии и проникновение "варваров" на Балкану в первой половине VI в.*, ВВ 45, 1985, pp. 35–53.

[46] On this centre see: А. Данчева-Василева, *Пловдив през Средновековието IV–XIV в.*, София 2009, pp. 31–54, 214–223, 244–246, 272–274, 289–291, 314–323, 326, 355–356.

[47] For more on the fortress see: Г.Н. Николов, *Военно-политическа история на средновековния град Боруй*, ВС 50.3, 1981, pp. 34–44; П. Балабанов, С. Бояджиев, Н. Тулешков, *Крепостно строителство...*, pp. 105–110, 125–128.

[48] С. Табаков, *Опит за история на град Сливен*, vol. I, *Сливен и Сливенско до началото на XIX в.*, ed. И. Тодоров, com. П. Ангелов, В. Дечев, София 1986; И. Щерева, К. Вачева, Д. Владимирова-Аладжова, Туида–Сливен, София 2001.

between the twelfth and fourteenth centuries; in 1018/1019–1185 the lands of the dissolved Bulgarian state were, at least formally, an integral part of the Empire), Northern Thrace, because of its geopolitical location, became an arena of military rivalry between Bulgaria and Byzantium. For this reason it can be considered to have formed something of a border area between the two states, a natural buffer zone (especially between 681 and 816) providing a direct link between their capitals – Pliska and Preslav on one hand and Constantinople on the other. In addition, it gave the Byzantines a certain amount of freedom in organising military expeditions against Bulgaria and provided them with strong fortresses in which to find shelter in case of failure. From the Bulgarian perspective, the Northern Thrace formed a perfect bulwark that prevented the Byzantines from invading the heart of Bulgaria and that provided the Bulgarians with the possibility of planning attacks against Byzantine capital and Aegean Thrace. What was of crucial importance during the military campaigns conducted in Thrace was to seize control of the Adrianople fortress. On one hand, it served as an outpost for the imperial troops setting out on their expeditions to the north, on the other it formed something of a gate providing access to the road leading to the Byzantine capital. For this reason the Bulgarian armies usually marched in a southerly direction, along the rivers Maritsa and Tundzha and thence to Constantinople. In cultural terms Asia Minor exercised a greater influence on Thrace than did the areas located behind the Stara Planina range. It was due to the accessibility of this area from the Black Sea and the smaller height of the Strandzha mountains that along with the territories lying south of them usually remained part of the Byzantine Empire[49].

---

[49] On Thrace's economic and political significance see: Д. Ангелов, *Тракия и българо-византийските отношения до падането ий под османска власт*, ИТНИ 1, 1965, pp. 61–91; W. Swoboda, *Tracja*, [in:] *SSS*, vol. VI, pp. 120, 122–123; Д.В. Момчилов, *Североизточна Тракия VII–X век*, Епо 3.2, 1995, pp. 62, 64; К. Гагова, *Тракия през българското Средновековие. Историческа география*, [2]София 2002, pp. 29–30; Д. Момчилов, *Култура и политика на Първото българско царство в Североизточна Тракия (по археологически данни)*, Варна 2007, pp. 13, 204, 211, 217, 223. Cf. also H. Maruszczak, *Bułgaria*..., p. 107; К. Мишев, С. Велев, И. Вапцаров, М. Йорданова, Д. Горунова, *Тракийско-Странджанска област*, [in:] *География на България*..., pp. 135–166. On Byzantine cultural exchange

The Rhodope mountains occupy most of the southern section of the north-eastern part of the Balkan Peninsula. The mountains are about 220–240 kilometres long and 100 kilometres wide, occupying about 18 000 square kilometres. The range's average altitude is 785 above sea level (the highest peak rises to over 2190 metres), but their western part is much higher than the eastern one. In the west the mountains border on the Pirin and Rila alpine ranges, forming part of the Rilo-Rhodope massif[50]. In addition to containing mineral deposits, the Strandzha and Rhodope mountains played an important role in the development of pastoral farming economy[51]. It was not until the ninth century that this territory became part of the Bulgarian state. The Bulgarians seemed quite satisfied with the life they lived in the mountains. The Rhodopes not only offered them shelter but also the possibility of mounting a surprising attack on the Aegean coast.

Further to the west, there lay the historical Macedonia, a colourful country of mountains and valleys. Difficult to access, the valleys were filled with settlements developing in isolation from each other. Although there was the second most important Byzantine metropolis in Macedonia, Thessalonike, situated at the Aegean Sea coast, the country, especially in its mountainous parts, remained beyond the reach of Constantinopolitan authorities. In the mid-ninth century, Macedonia, in spite of its remoteness, became an integral part of the Bulgarian state, and so did the territories of Northern Thrace lying significantly closer to Bulgaria's main centres. It was partly due to the fact that the areas west of the Ihtiman Pass lay at that time within the Bulgarian state. The incorporation of Macedonian territories into the Danube Bulgaria appears to have been something

zones see, more generally, D. Obolensky, *Byzantine Frontier Zones and Cultural Exchanges*, [in:] *Actes du XIVe Congrès International des Études Byzantines*, Bucarest, 6–12 Septembre 1971, vol. V, ed. M. Berza, E. Stănescu, Bucareşti 1974, pp. 303–313; R. Theodorescu, *Au sujet des "corridors culturels" de l'Europe sud-orientale, I*, RESEE 21.1, 1983, pp. 7–22; idem, *Au sujet des "corridors culturels" de l'Europe sud-orientale, II*, RESEE 21.3, 1983, pp. 229–240.

50 И. Вапцаров, С. Велев, М. Йорданова, Д. Горунова, *Рило-Родопска област*, [in:] *География на България...*, pp. 166–219; С. Кираджиев, *Енциклопедичен...*, pp. 458–460.

51 Д. Ангелов, *Стопански...*, p. 341.

of a logical consequence of Bulgaria's rule over the Sofia Field. The actions carried out under the protection of mountain ranges and earlier contacts with their compatriots (or the tradition of such contacts) of the so-called khan Kouber's group enabled the Bulgarians to penetrate these areas and annex them to their state in mid-ninth century[52]. It was more difficult for the Byzantine armed forces to get to the mountainous Macedonia. During the rule of the Cometopouloi dynasty the nucleus of the Bulgarian state shifted to the geographical Macedonia with Ohrid and Prespa as its centres, and its mountainous topography was one of the factors that enabled Bulgaria to resist the Byzantine aggression. The Vardar and Struma rivers were among the rivers along which there ran communication corridors. In the western part of the mountains there were the silver deposits. The Macedonian mountains were of course home to animal husbandry[53]. Grapevine and fruit were also grown here. In the tenth and eleventh

[52] On these contacts see: G. Cankova-Petkova, *Bulgarians and Byzantium during the first Decades after the Foundation of the Bulgarian State*, Bsl 24.1, 1963, pp. 51–52; М. Войнов, *Някои въпроси във връзка с образуването на българската държава и покръстването на българите*, ИИИ 10, 1962, pp. 282–283, przyp. 14; В. Гюзелев, *Езическа България*, [in:] И. Божилов, В. Гюзелев, *История на средновековна България VII–XIV век*, София 1999, pp. 96, 121, 127, 161; Г. Атанасов, *Тервел. Хан на България и кесар на Византия*, Силистра 2004, pp. 22–23; Г.Н. Николов, *Централизъм...*, pp. 67, 94. I would like to emphasise that it was the memory and tradition rather than the actual relations with Bulgarian settlement, although it is difficult to determine that in 9th century there was no such settlement at all – cf. W. Swoboda, *Kuber...*, [in:] *SSS*, vol. II, pp. 554–555; V. Beševliev, *Die Protobulgarische Periode der bulgarischen Geschichte*, Amsterdam 1981, pp. 170–172; J.V.A., Fine, *The Early Medieval Balkans. A Critical Survey from the Sixth Century to the Late Twelfth Century*, Ann Arbor 1983, p. 191; В. Поповић, *Кврат, Кубар и Аспарух*, Ста 37, 1986, pp. 125–126 (the author locates those Bulgarians in 9th–10th c. in the area of Albania); З. Пляков, *Населението в областта на Средна Струма през VII–IX век*, [in:] *Четвърти международен Конгрес по славянска археология, София – 1980 (Доклади и съобщения)*, vol. I, ed. Д. Ангелов, София 1992, pp. 386–391; П. Павлов, *Истини и заблуди за светия цар Петър*, [in:] idem, *Забравени и неразбрани. Събития и личности от българското средновековие*, София 2010, pp. 33, 34; idem, *Векът на цар Самуил*, София 2014, pp. 21–22 (according to the last author the mentioned in the sources macedonian *Scythians*, who supported Michael's rebelion against tsar Peter, were descendants of the Kouber's Bulgarians).

[53] A.E. Laiou, C. Morrisson, *The Byzantine Economy*, Cambridge–New York 2007, pp. 63, 93, 171–172.

centuries, during the reign of tsars Symeon and Samuel, the Bulgarian state found itself in control of mountainous territories in Albania and the indigenous Serbian areas of Rashka and Zeta. The control of these territories enabled Bulgaria to engage in the Croatian affairs and to undertake action along the Adriatic coast.

All the territories characterised above were held together by a network of routes. In the ninth and tenth centuries the famous *via militaris*, cutting across the north-east part of the Balkan mountains and linking Belgrad with Constantinople, was the most important of them. In earlier periods the Bulgarians tried to seize control of it as it was often used by their opponents. Crucial for keeping it under control were political centres that lay along it and that played a very important role in the long-distance trade linking Byzantine megalopolis with Central and Western Europe. The centres were: Belgrade, Naissos, Sredets, Philippoupolis – the cities that lay within Bulgaria's borders, and Adrianople which was part of the Empire. It should be stressed that in the period under consideration, that is, in the latter half of the ninth century, the road regained its importance after two hundred years of insignificance[54]. It owed its renaissance to three factors: firstly, the beginning of this century saw the fall of the Avar Khaganate, a political organism that stood in the way of freely using the road; secondly, the official acceptance of Christianity by the Bulgarians, which resulted in a few decades of peaceful relations with Byzantium; thirdly, Byzantine-Frankish and Byzantine-Moravian relations were given a new lease on life following the consolidation of the Carolingian state and the restoration of the imperial power in the west. All of this was followed by the revival of trade exchange. True, the situation along the *via militaris* deteriorated following the final settlement of Magyars in Pannonia, which took place towards the end of this century, and the Byzantine-Bulgarian

[54] Λ. Симеонова, *Пътуване към Константинопол. Търговия и комуникации в Средиземноморския свят (края на IX – 70-те години на XI в.)*, София 2006, pp. 102–103; M. McCormick, *Origins of the European Economy: Communications and Commerce AD 300–900*, Cambridge 2001 (I am using the Polish edition of the book, see: M. McCormick, *Narodziny Europy. Korzenie gospodarki europejskiej, 300–900*, transl. A. Bugaj, Z. Dalewski, J. Lang, I. Skrzypczak, Warszawa 2009, pp. 76–80, 527–531).

wars during the reign of Symeon the Great posed a hindrance to the free transfer of goods between Byzantium and the western world (one needs to add that these difficulties were only temporary because the intensity of these wars varied and, especially in the first decade of the tenth century, there were long periods of relative peace). Following the conclusion of the peace in 927, the relations again returned to normality, although the Hungarian menace cast its shadow on them. The remark appears to be quite important given the fact that the Bulgarians controlled several hundred kilometres of the route between Belgrade and Plovdiv. Thus the state ruled by Borys-Michael, Vladimir-Rasate, Symeon and Peter can be assumed to have derived profits from an important trade route running through its territory (leaving aside its purely military aspects and taking into consideration only trading relations)[55].

However, when one looks at the map of Bulgaria, one is inclined, after taking into account the location of its capitals (above all the Great Preslav), to conclude that their connection with Constantinople, Bulgaria's most important politico-economic partner, was even more important than the military route mentioned above[56]. A more westerly route ran from Constantinople to Adrianople, along the valley of the river Tundzha and further north through Probaton (today's Sinnaköy) and Diampolis (today's Yambol) and the mountain massif – through Varbitsa Pass – to Preslav. By taking the extension of the route, one could get to Pliska, passing through the fortifications in the village of khan Krum. The eastern branch of the road forked off in Constantinople and ran through the mountains Strandzha to the fortress Potamoukastel[57] (in the north it ran almost parallel to the *via militaris*) and along the western coastline of the Black Sea, joining together again in Develtos, that is, at the

---

[55] The following monographs are still the best works on the route: K.J. Jireček, *Die Heerstrasse von Belgrad nach Constantinopel und die Balkanpässe. Eine Historisch-Geographische Studie*, Prag 1877; П. Мутафчиев, *Старият друм…* Cf. also M. Madzharov, *Roman Roads in Bulgaria. Contribution to the Development of Roman Road System in the Provinces of Moesia and Thrace*, Veliko Tarnovo 2009, pp. 70–131.

[56] Similarly – Л. Симеонова, *Пътуване…*, p. 105.

[57] On this fortification see: Ж. Аладжов, *Къде се е намирал Потамукастел от средновековните извори*, ПС 2, 2000, pp. 289–291; К. Гагова, *Тракия…*, p. 281.

official customs point of both states[58]. From Develtos it ran to the fortress Markellai, situated at the southern foot of the Eastern Balkan Mountains and through the Rish Pass (the so-called Verigava in Byzantine sources)[59] in a straight line to Pliska[60]. Further north from Pliska to the Danubian Dristra and, perhaps, Pereyaslavets. Then, after crossing the big river, it ran through Transylvania and the valleys of the river Mureş and the river Someş to the Moravian lands (probably to the so-called Solnograd, today's Szolnok in Hungary), serving as the route used to export the Transilvanian (Bulgarian) salt, but surely in the ninth century, and not during tsar Peter's reign[61]. The communication line I have just briefly described, played the

[58] Г. Аянов, *Стари пътища и селища край тях през Странджа и Сакар*, ИАИ 15, 1946, pp. 94–113.

[59] On this identification see: В. Бешевлиев, *Географията на България у византийските автори*, ИНМВ 23 (38), 1987, pp. 43–44; Д. Момчилов, *Южните части на Ришкия и Върбишкия проходи и "Еркесията" през Първото българско царство*, [in:] ППр 8, 2000, p. 241. A different view has recently been expressed by Pavel Georgiev (П. Георгиев, *Главният път през Веригава през ранното средновековие*, [in:] *История на пътя. Черно море между Изтока и Запада. XII-ти Понтийски четения във ВСУ "Черноризец Храбър"*, ed. С. Табакова-Стоева, Варна 2007, pp. 7–25), who identifies Verigava with either Dyulino or Emine (or Seaside) Passes.

[60] Ж. Добрева, *Пътната мрежа между Плиска и Ришния проход VII–IX век*, [in:] *Пътуванията...*, pp. 151–158; П. Георгиев, *Хинтерландът на Абоба-Плиска: пътни комуникации, селищни и военни средища*, [in:] *Eurika. In honorem Ludmilae Donchevae-Petkovae*, ed. В. Григоров, М. Даскалов, Е. Коматарова-Балинова, София 2009, pp. 333–353. More generally, see: С.Т. Недев, *Пътища в Източна Стара Планина от създаването на българската държава до Освобождението и от Османското владичество*, ИВНД 15.1, 1973, pp. 213–226; Д. Момчилов, *Пътна и селищна система между Източна Стара Планина и "Еркесията" IV–XIV в. (Върбишки, Ришки и Айтоски проход)*, Варна 1999.

[61] V. Chaloupecký, *Dvě studie k dějinám Podkarpatska*, I: *Sůl z Bulharska (892)*, II: *Kdy bylo horní Potisí připojeno k Uhrám*, SFFUKB 3.30 (4), 1925, pp. 1–11; P. Ratkoš, *K otazce hranice Veľkej Moravy a Bulharska*, HČSAV 3, 1955, pp. 212–215; B. Primov, *Certain Aspects of the International Importance of the First Bulgarian Empire*, EHi 5, 1970, p. 201; G. Kovach, *Date cu privire la transportul sări pe Mureș (sec. X–XIII)*, Zir 12, 1980, pp. 193–200; Д. Ангелов, *Вътрешна и външна търговия през VIII–X в.*, [in:] *Стопанска история на България 681–1981*, ed. Л. Беров et al., София 1981, p. 47; idem, *Стопански...*, p. 347; K. Polek, *Podstawy gospodarcze Państwa Wielkomorawskiego*, Kraków 1994, p. 82; A. Madgearu, *Salt Trade and Warfare in Early Medieval Transylvania*, EN 11, 2001, pp. 271–283; idem, *Transylvania and the Bulgarian Expansion in the 9th and 10th Centuries*, AMN 39/40.2, 2002/2003,

most important role in the relations between Bulgaria and Byzantium. Its northern part, crossing the eastern areas of the Danubian Plain, offered Bulgaria's capitals access to the Danube Valley and the lands on the left bank of the river. East of the connection was the route following the coastline (it is sometimes referred to as the *via pontica*)[62], linking the most important harbours of the Black Sea coast. It ran through the Dyulino or Emine Pass in the eastern part of the Balkan Mountains and the area of Lake Varna, reaching the Danube Delta.

The ancient road linking Belgrade in the west and the delta of the Danube in the east ran along the right bank of the Danube Valley, passing through Bdin, Nikopolis and Dristra. The route was opened for trade following the fall of the Avar Khaganate, although scholars suggest there were some impediments in its use because of the Byzantine-Bulgarian wars during the reign of Symeon[63]. Parallel to it was the route running along the northern foothills of the Predbalkan and linking Preslav and Vratitsa (today's Vratsa) in the west, a place through which led the shortest route to Serdica, south of the mountain range[64]. It had its counterpart at the southern slopes of Haimos, linking the coastline Anchialos and Sredets[65]. A branch of the road extended to Beroe at the foot of the east-

pp. 50–51; В. Йотов, *Българският контрол на "Пътя на солта" в Трансилвания през IX в. (по археологически данни)*, [in:] *Великотърновският Университет "Св. св. Кирил и Методий" и българската археология*, vol. I, ed. Б. Борисов, Велико Търново 2010, pp. 487–495; П. Павлов, *Стопанско развитие на Първото българско царство*, [in:] И. Тютюнджиев, М. Палангурски, А, Костов, И. Лазаров, П. Павлов, И. Русев, *Стопанска история на България*, Велико Търново 2011, p. 21.

[62] Л. Симеонова, *Пътуване…*, p. 105; П. Георгиев, *Главният път Византия – България до края на VIII век*, [in:] *Пътуванията…*, pp. 84–103.

[63] Л. Симеонова, *Пътуване…*, pp. 136–138.

[64] П.Х. Петров, *Средновековна Вратица*, [in:] *История на град Враца. От Древността до Освобождението*, ed. Е. Бужашки et al., София 1976, p. 74; К. Дочев, *Стари римски пътища в Централна Долна Мизия (II–IV в. сл. Хр.)*, ИРИМВТ 7.4, 1994, pp. 61–76; V. Tăpkova-Zaimova, *Frontières médiévales et réseau routier au sud du Danube*, BMd 1, 2010, pp. 1–15. See also: Д. Димитрова, *Археологически паметници във Врачански окръг*, София 1985; Б. Николов, *От Искър до Огоста. История на 151 села и градове от бившия Врачански окръг*, София 1996.

[65] P. Soustal, *Tabula…*, pp. 135–136; К. Гагова, *Тракия…*, p. 104.

ern part of the Anti-Balkan, linked Beroe with Philippoupolis[66]. There was also a route that branched off from the *via militaris* at the latitude of Adrianople, linking the latter with Develtos[67]. Some minor tracks, which also branched off from the military road, cut across the Rhodope mountain range and enabled one to get to one of the most important tracks of the Peninsula, known as *via Egnatia*, linking Dyrrachion with Constantinople[68]. *Via Egnatia* also ran through Thessalonike, but only its western part lay within the Bulgarian State and until the last quarter of the tenth century it didn't play a significant role in the history of the state in question. However, its role increased along with the shift of what is known as the inner area of the Bulgarian state towards Macedonia[69]. The route leading from the Danube Valley, along the river Morava and through Naissos and Vranje to Skopje has already been mentioned.

This incomplete description of the mediaeval Bulgaria's communication routes, deliberately focusing on the most important ones of them, clearly indicates that the way the land lay in this part of the Balkans tended to favour the latitudinal arrangement of the main routes[70]. Of course, in the north-eastern and central parts of the Balkans the longitudi-

---

[66] P. Soustal, *Tabula*..., p. 135; К. Гагова, *Тракия*..., pp. 103–104.

[67] P. Soustal, *Tabula*..., pp. 143–145; cf. К. Гагова, *Тракия*..., p. 105.

[68] P. Soustal, *Tabula*..., pp. 139–140, 141, 142–143; К. Гагова, *Тракия*..., p. 105. On *via Egnatia* see e.g.: G.L.F. Tafel, *De via Romanorum militari Egnatia qua Illyricum Macedonia et Thracia iungebantur*, Tübingae 1837; J. Votýpka-Pecha, L. Vidman, *Via Egnatia mezi Elbasanem a Ochridským jezerem*, FPh 82.2, 1959, pp. 187–196; G.S. Xeidakis, E.G. Varagouli, *Design and Construction of Roman Roads: The Case of Via Egnatia in the Aegean Thrace, Northern Greece*, EEG 3.1, 1997, pp. 123–132; M. Fasolo, *La via Egnatia I. Da Apollonia e Dyrrachium ad Herakleia Lynkestidos*, ²Roma 2005; A. Gutsche, *Auf den Spuren der antiken Via Egnatia – vom Weströmischen ins Oströmische Reich: Ein historischer Reiseführer durch den südlichen Balkan: Albanien – Mazedonien – Griechenland – Türkei*, Schweinfurt 2010.

[69] Cf. Т. Филипоски, *Прашањето за проодноста на западниот дел от патот Via Egnatia (Драч–Солун) во втората половина на IX век*, [in:] *Пътуванията*..., pp. 110–119; J. Shepard, *Communications across the Bulgarian lands – Samuel's poisoned chalice for Basil II and his successors?*, [in:] *Европейският Югоизток през втората половина на X – началото на XI век. История и култура*, ed. В. Гюзелев, Г.Н. Николов, София 2015, pp. 217–235; С. Георгиева, *Цар Самуил в съперничество с Византия за контрол над Виа Егнация и Драч*, Епо 25.1, 2017, pp. 188–195.

[70] *The Natural Regions*..., pp. 199–200; H. Maruszczak, *Bulgaria*..., pp. 15, 196.

nal road network was formed too, crossing the Haimos, Strandzha, Rhodope and Dinaric mountain ranges. However, the mountains constituted a natural communication barrier separating particular areas, and the main routes ran either along the rivers or through mountain valleys[71]. One should also keep in mind water routes which also played an important economic role. Sources attest to the fact that the Lower Danube and the river Hebros (Maritsa) were both navigable, the latter up to the city of Adrianople in Thrace[72]. Of course the sea route, along the coast of the Black Sea, Aegean Sea and Adriatic Sea was the most convenient[73]. However, it has already been mentioned that the last route was out of Bulgarian merchants' reach. Among the inland areas of water mentioned above only the Danube Valley lay within Bulgaria's borders while the navigable part of the river Hebros was outside these borders.

The above remarks regarding the geopolitical significance of the territories that made up the Bulgarian state from the second half of the

---

[71] For more details on Bulgaria's communication system see: В. Тъпкова-Заимова, *Към въпроса за военните пътища през Първото българско царство*, ИП 14.1, 1958, pp. 58–73; J.-Ch. Poutiers, *A propos des forteresses antiques et médiévales de la plaine Danubienne (Essai de reconstruction du réseau routier entre Iskăr et Ogosta)*, EB 11.2, 1975, pp. 60–73; P. Soustal, *Tabula...*, pp. 132–146; K. Belke, *Roads and travel in Macedonia and Thrace in the middle and late Byzantine period*, [in:] *Travel in the Byzantine World. Papers from the Thity-forth Spring Symposium of Byzantine Studies, Birmingham, April 2000*, ed. R. Macrides, Aldershot 2001, pp. 73–90; A. Avramea, *Land and Sea Communications, Fourth–Fiftheenth Centuries*, [in:] *The Economic History of Byzantium. From the Seventh through the Fifteenth Century*, vol. I, ed. A.E. Laiou, Washington D.C. 2002, pp. 64–74; К. Гагова, *Тракия...*, pp. 99–110; V. Tăpkova-Zaimova, *Frontières médiévales et réseau routier au sud du Danube*, BMd 1, 2010, pp. 1–15.

[72] E. Todorova, *River Trade in the Balkans during the Middle Ages*, EB 20, 1984, p. 47; P. Soustal, *Tabula...*, p. 135; К. Гагова, *Тракия...*, pp. 103–104.

[73] Cf. K. Marinow, *Zadania floty cesarskiej w wojnach bizantyńsko-bułgarskich (VII–XI w.)*, [in:] *Byzantina Europea. Księga jubileuszowa ofiarowana Profesorowi Waldemarowi Ceranowi*, ed. M. Kokoszko, M.J. Leszka, Łódź 2007, pp. 381–392; R. Kostova, *"Bypassing Anchialos": The West Black Sea coast in naval campaigns 11th to 12th c.*, [in:] *Тангра...*, pp. 579–597; eadem, *The Lower Danube in the Byzantine Naval Campaigns in the 12th c.*, [in:] *Cultură și civilizație la Dunărea de Jos*, vol. XXIV, Călărași 2008, pp. 269–281.

seventh century to the beginning of the eleventh century in general, and during the tsar Peter I reign in particular, can be regarded as an introduction to the issue, providing a general framework within which to discuss it and showing that Bulgarians' arrival in the Lower Danube and their settlement in the territories between the valley of the river and the Balkan Mountain range resulted in making these areas become the heart of the Bulgarian statehood in the early Middle Ages. Favourable to such a development was certainly the existence of natural barriers, both water and mountainous ones, separating the heart of the state from the regions that surrounded it. With such a location of Bulgaria's centre, including the location of its capitals, the country's territorial development was determined for centuries to come, and so were its economic and political partners, as well as cultural influences it fell under.

It seemed quite natural for Bulgaria to extend its rule northwards, especially as its main opponent, Avar Khaganate, ceased to exist. However, after reaching the height of its territorial expansion in the ninth century, the Bulgarians focused on preserving the status quo. The areas south of the Carpathian Mountains were for the longest time part of Bulgaria. Because of the *via militaris* the Bulgarians became open to influences from Central and Western Europe, just as did Transylvania. They were also exposed to constant danger of being invaded by nomadic tribes from the north, the more so as the steppe made it possible to get very near Bulgaria's capitals. From the end of the ninth century the danger faced by Bulgaria was made use of by Byzantium. Because of its proximity, Byzantium rose to the position of Bulgaria's main political Balkan partner. The constant danger, coupled with the nearness of Byzantine harbours, led the Bulgarians to resort to a policy of expansion. The way in which they attempted to remove the danger from their borders was by moving the latter southwards.

No less important was the expansion into the territories of Bulgaria's southern neighbour – more fertile than those in the north. And the same can be said of the territories inhabited by Slavs. Taking control of Sofia's Field enabled the expansion into Macedonian territories. The latter turned out to be no less enduring than that directed toward Thrace territories, which were located much closer to Bulgaria's political core. The control of territories in northern Greece, Albania or Serbia turned out to be more ephemeral.

The fall of the north-eastern Bulgaria, followed by the shift of its political centres to south-western territories, entailed a change in the country's geopolitical situation. The change opened up a new possibility of territorial expansion, especially in Illyria and continental Greece. However, this expansion had to be accompanied by the abandonment of an active policy in Thrace. And soon it was stopped by Basil II's reconquista[74].

[74] On the topic see: P.M. S t r ä s s l e, *Krieg und Kriegführung in Byzanz. Die Kriege Kaiser Basileios' II. gegen die Bulgaren (976–1019)*, Köln–Weimar–Wien 2006.

II

Kirił Marinow

The Economy

1. Agriculture and Animal Husbandry

There seems to be no doubt that land cultivation formed the basis of Bulgaria's economic life in the tenth century. However, there are very few written sources in which this view is confirmed (one can mention here *Pope Nicolas' Response to the Bulgarians*, Cosmas' *Sermon against the Heretics*, the *Long Life of Clement of Ohrid*). The source that has been traditionally cited in this context is the so-called Farmer's Law. Its creation is linked to the Slavs' presence in the Balkans and their becoming part of the ethnic composition of the Bulgarian state in the early Middle Ages. Controversy surrounding this legal monument – the uncertainty regarding the period in which it was created and the part of the Empire to which it referred – prevents us from considering it a fully reliable source of information when it comes to the Balkan territories[1]. However, the traditional view of the crucial role of farming in Bulgaria's economy is supported by archaeological sources which testify to the use of husbandry

[1] M. Svoronos, *Notes sur l'origine et la date du Code rural*, TM 8, 1981, pp. 487–500; И. Божилов, *Добруджа през Ранното Средновековие (VI – нач. XI в.)*, [in:] idem, В. Гюзелев, *История на Добруджа*, vol. II, *Средновековие*, Велико Търново 2004, p. 52.

techniques in early mediaeval Bulgaria – the excavated artifacts include agricultural tools such as ploughshares, sickles, hoes, shovel ferrules[2]. Excavations also uncover the remains of cultivated crops – wheat, rye and millet in the main. Flax, used in the manufacture of clothing, was also exported to Byzantium. Some place names of early mediaeval origin also seem to be indicative of the use of various husbandry techniques in the period before the Bulgarians' arrival at the Danube areas – as an example one can mention here such names as Nivani – derived from niva (lea), Razhenichani – razh (rae) or Zarnentsi – zarno (grain). The lands that made up the Bulgarian state provided a good framework for the development of agriculture – suffice it to mention the fertile and well irrigated plains of Mysia (Moesia), Northern Trace and part of Macedonia. One should add that a large share of agriculture in the economy of the Balkan cities was a specific feature of their development. This also holds true for the Bulgarian capitals – Pliska and Preslav. The cultivation of grapevine, fruit and vegetables underwent rapid development in the ninth and tenth centuries. The three-field system of crop rotation had grown in popularity. Farming was typically extensive and, as such, vulnerable to climatic changes. Attempts were made to remedy this situation by building warehouses for storing food surpluses. Methods of storing food weren't dissimilar to those used in Byzantium. The burden of farming lay on the shoulders of the most numerous social group of the Middle Ages – free peasants, organised in special districts or neighbouring communities[3].

[2] Й. Чангова, *Средновековни оръдия на труда в България*, ИАИ 25, 1962, pp. 19–55; Т. Тотев, *Колективна находка от средновековни оръдия на труда от с. Златар*, Архе 8.4, 1966, pp. 33–35; В. Антонова, *Новооткрита находка от земеделски сечива при Плиска*, Пр.Сб. 3, 1983, pp. 263–268; Й. Чангова, *Перник*, vol. III, *Крепостта Перник VIII–XIV в.*, София 1992, pp. 7–17; В. Йотов, Г. Атанасов, *Скала. Крепост от X–XI век до с. Кладенци, Тервелско*, София 1998, pp. 83–87; Л. Дончева-Петкова, *Одърци. Селище от Първото българско царство*, vol. I, София 1999, pp. 55–59; И.Х. Джамбов, *Средновековното селище над античния град при Хисар*, Асеновград 2002, pp. 58–60. More generally, see: Л. Беров, *Икономическото развитие на България през вековете*, София 1974, pp. 25–26.

[3] Л. Беров, *Икономическото развитие на България...*, pp. 24–25; Д. Ангелов, *Развитие на селското стопанство през VIII–X в.*, [in:] *Стопанска история на България 681–1981*, ed. Л. Беров et al., София 1981, pp. 37–38; idem, *Стопански живот*, [in:] *История на България в четиринадесет тома*, vol. II, *Първа българска*

Animal husbandry formed a traditional part of the Bulgarian economy. It was also certainly known to the Slavs[4]. I have already mentioned that the central part of the Dobrudzha region provided a perfect framework for this type of farming[5], and so did the so-called 'Pliska Field', in which the Bulgarians founded their capital[6], the foothills of the Balkan Mountains and the Balkan Mountains proper, the mountain areas of Macedonia and, in part, the Rhodope Mountains. In the latter half of the ninth century, these were joined by the upland areas of Transylvania (the Carpathian Mountains). Among the animals reared in the sub-mountain areas were cows, oxen, buffalos, sheep, pigs, horses and domesticated birds[7], of which

---

държава, ed. i d e m, София 1981, pp. 339–340; Ж. А л а д ж о в, *Бележки за винопроизводството в ранното българско средновековие*, ППре 5, 1992, pp. 216–221; И. Б о ж и л о в, *Добруджа...*, pp. 51–52; П. П а в л о в, *Стопанско развитие на Първото българско царство*, [in:] И. Т ю т ю н д ж и е в, М. П а л а н г у р с к и, А. К о с т о в, И. Л а з а р о в, П. П а в л о в, И. Р у с е в, *Стопанска история на България*, Велико Търново 2011, p. 17. On the existance of one-crop system on some territories of the Bulgarian state, especially in the mountains, see: Г. Ц а н к о в а-П е т к о в а, *Към въпроса за селскостопанската техника в средновековна България и някои съседни балкански области*, ИИИ 13, 1963, pp. 123–137.

[4] Z. K u r n a t o w s k a, *Słowiańszczyzna Południowa*, Wrocław 1977, pp. 93, 100–104; В. Г ю з е л е в, *Икономическо развитие, социална структура и форми на социална и политическа организация на прабългарите до образуването на българската държава (IV–VII в.)*, Архе 21.4, 1979, pp. 13–14; П. Д о б р е в, *Стопанска култура на прабългарите*, София 1986, pp. 34–40.

[5] For this see Part Two, Chapter I, of the present monograph.

[6] In spite of the doubts that have recently been expressed (cf. D. Z i e m a n n, *Pliska and Preslav: Bulgarian Capitals between Relocation and Invention*, [in:] *Българско Средновековие: общество, власт, история. Сборник в чест на проф. д-р Милияна Каймакамова*, ed. Г.Н. Н и к о л о в, А. Н и к о л о в, София 2013, pp. 179–183) I find that Pliska was, if not the first and the only one, then the most important centre of power in Bulgaria in the early Middle Ages and, until the establishment of Preslav, Bulgaria's only capital.

[7] Г.К. Р и б а р о в, *Бозайниците в бита на жителите от ранновизантийското и средновековно селище на Хисарлъка (Сливен)*, Архе 32.4, 1990, pp. 50–58; З. Б о е в, Н. И л и е в, *Птиците и тяхното значение за жителите на Велики Преслав (IX–X в.)*, Архе 33.3, 1991, pp. 44–53; Й. Ч а н г о в а, *Перник...*, pp. 18–21; Н. И л и е в, *Говедовъдството във Велики Преслав (IX–X в.)*, Архе 36.3/4, 1994, pp. 66–70; Л. Н и н о в, *Животновъдна и ловна дейност на обитателите на крепостта*, [in:] В. Й о т о в, Г. А т а н а с о в, *Скала...*, pp. 329–343; Л. Д о н ч е в а-П е т к о в а, *Одърци...*, p. 59; Л. Н и н о в, *Животновъдна и ловна дейност в средновековнот*

use was made both in farming and warfare (combat mounts were given special care), and in the production of shoes (articles made of wool and skin were quite widespread), clothing and food (meat, dairy products, fats). *Pope Nicholas' response to the Bulgarians* provides strong evidence of the significant role of meat (especially lamb and pork) in the Bulgarians' diet in the latter half of the ninth century. Hunting for animals in the country's mountains and forests was a natural way of securing the meat supply[8]. Some Arab sources testify to the use of animals as means of payment. A pair of oxen, used as the main labour and transport force in agriculture, served as the basic measurement unit and the basis on which taxes imposed on individual households were calculated[9]. Animal husbandry began to be dominated by the small horned cattle, the large one being used mainly as animal draft force. Horses were imported from Central Europe and Byzantium and it didn't take long before they replaced the native steppe breeds. Breeders and shepherds inhabited city centres, although animals were raised mainly in rural areas. Written sources testify to the existence (although their testimony refers to the eleventh century, it is highly likely to be true also of earlier periods) of the groups of specialied mountain shepherds who, after spring and summer spent in the Carpathians and Macedonia's mountain pastures (in the tenth century they hadn't yet began to migrate in the direction of the Haimos mountain range), would come down from the mountains to live for the rest of the year in the valleys and lowlands. I am referring here to the people known as the Vlachs (as the Byzantines called them), that is, probably, the descendants of the

---

селище край село Одърци, [in:] Л. Дончева-Петкова, *Одърци...*, pp. 171–173; Н. Хрисимов, *Храната в Първото българско царство*, [in:] *Стандарти на всекидневието през Средновековието и Новото време*, ed. К. Мутафова et al., Велико Търново 2012, pp. 201–232. For more on the topic see Part Two, Chapter III of this book.

[8] Й. Чангова, *Перник...*, pp. 17–18; Л. Нинов, *Животновъдна и ловна дейност...*, pp. 329–330 (tab. 1), 337, 339–340 (tab. 9), 343.

[9] G. Cankova-Petkova, *Byzance et le developpement social et économique des états balkaniques*, [in:] *Actes du premier Congres International des Études Balkaniques et Sud-Est Européennes, Sofia, 26 âout – 1 septembre 1966*, vol. III, *Histoire (V^{e}–XVe ss.; XVe–XVIIe ss.)*, ed. V. Tăpkova-Zaimova, S. Dimitrov, E. Sarafova, Sofia 1969, pp. 345–346.

Romanised Thracian tribes[10]. An interesting thesis regarding the significance of the Bulgarian economy, especially the livestock farming, was put forward by Mihail Voynov. According to the scholar, access to Bulgaria's economic potential was one of the reasons why the Byzantines, in the 970s, decided to invade the territories of their northern neighbour. The main concern here was to ensure food supply for Constantinople, and the Bulgarian lands were known for a great number of farmed animals with which one could hope to meet the nutritional needs of the inhabitants of the Byzantine capital[11].

2. Crafts and City Development

Sources from the ninth and tenth centuries (*Hexameron* by John the Exarch, *The Miracle of Saint George with the Bulgarian*, *Law for Judging the People*) indicate a significant development and an advanced level of craftsmanship in Bulgaria. They also testify to the existence of the division of labour and the specialisation of production. Qualified artisans, working in regular workshops, especially in the cities, were commissioned to manufacture particular articles. The craft production fulfilled state orders and met the needs of those whom we can describe as private customers. Bulgaria's territorial expansion, the development of new buildings, both sacral and secular (fortresses, palaces, monasteries, bathhouses, churches etc.), and the construction of new roads and bridges, all of them

[10] M. G y ó n i, *La transhumance des Vlaques balkaniques au Moyen Âge*, Bsl 12, 1951, pp. 29–42; Д. А н г е л о в, *Развитие на селското...*, pp. 38–40; i d e m, *Стопански...*, pp. 340–341; И. Б о ж и л о в, *Добруджа...*, p. 52. On the Vlachs see: E. S c ă r l ă t o i u, *The Balkan Vlachs in the Light of Linguistic Studuies (Highlights and Contributions)*, RESEE 17.1, 1979, pp. 17–37; T.J. W i n n i f r i t h, *The Vlachs: The History of a Balkan People*, London 1987; I. C z a m a ń s k a, *Problem pochodzenia Wołochów*, [in:] *Wędrówka i etnogeneza w starożytności i średniowieczu*, ed. M. S a l a m o n, J. S t r z e l c z y k, Kraków 2004, pp. 327–335.

[11] M. V o j n o v, *Byzance et le potentiel economique de la Bulgarie*, EB 13.2, 1977, pp. 129–131.

created demand for artisans, their skills and products. Excellent Byzantine workshops weren't able to fulfil all the orders, and there was no such need. Trade and the spoils of war didn't suffice to satisfy the demand for weapon (both offensive and defensive) and the horse-riding gear. The country needed to develop its own workshops. Mining activity was probably already in progress (the ore extraction), as evidenced by old Slav toponyms such as Rudishte or Rudnik – both derived from the word 'ruda' ('ore'). The discovery of iron lumps testifies to the exploitation of bog iron ore and the use of bloomeries for its processing. In addition to the processing of metals[12], the country was also involved in the production

[12] See: С. Витлянов, *Данни за обработката на желязо в центровете на Първото българско царство*, [in:] *Средновековният български град*, ed. П. Петров, София 1980, pp. 137–143; Й. Чангова, *Към проучването на старобългарската металопластика през IX–X век*, Пр.Сб 3, 1983, pp. 198–202; В. Плетньов, В. Павлова, *Ранносредновековни ремъчни накрайници във Варненския археологически музей*, ИНМВ 28 (43), 1992, pp. 158–223; Й. Чангова, *Перник...*, pp. 22–38, 127–145, 149–163, 166–198 (however part of the finds are imports); М. Долмова, *За добива на злато и сребро в средновековна България*, ГНАМ 9, 1993, pp. 141–150; С. Станилов, *Старобългарски ремъчни украси с правоъгълна форма*, [in:] *Сборник в чест на акад. Димитър Ангелов*, ed. В. Велков, София 1994, pp. 177–189; Л. Дончева-Петкова, *Пещи за добиване на желязо край западната крепостна стена на Плиска*, ППр 7, 1995, pp. 34–41; С. Витлянов, *За някои моменти в развитието на българското средновековно железообработване*, [in:] *Медиевистични изследвания в памет на Пейо Димитров*, ed. Т. Тотев, Шумен 1995, pp. 306–314, specifically pp. 307–309; В. Йотов, Г. Атанасов, *Скала...*, pp. 93–124; Л. Дончева-Петкова, *Одърци...*, pp. 61–62, 99–114, 120–130; И.Х. Джамбов, *Средновековното селище...*, pp. 63–64, 66–67; С. Бонев, *Творби на металопластиката със светци от Преслав*, ПКШ 7, 2004, pp. 404–411; В. Плетньов, *Производството на коланни гарнитури в ранносредновековна България*, Пр.Сб 6, 2004, pp. 228–240; Д. Станчев, *Ранносредновековни пръстени от фонда на Историческия музей – Русе*, [in:] *Проф. д.и.н. Станчо Ваклинов и средновековната българска култура*, ed. К. Попконстантинов, Б. Борисов, Р. Костова, Велико Търново 2005, pp. 220–229 (it is important to underline some of the findings are Byzantine imports); В. Григоров, *Метални накити от средновековна България (VII–XI в.)*, София 2007; С. Дончева, *Медалиони от средновековна България*, Велико Търново 2007; Д. Момчилов, *Материалната култура от времето на Първото българско царство в Североизточна Тракия през IX–X в.*, [in:] *Проблеми на прабългарската история и култура*, vol. IV.2, *Сборник в памет на ст.н.с. I ст. д.и.н. Димитър Ил. Димитров*, ed. Р. Рашев, София

of glass[13], various tools (including of course lumberjack, blacksmith and quarrying tools, as well as those used in construction works) and weapons. Wood, stone and bone working were also well-developed[14]. Workshops were established for the manufacture of construction ceramics[15],

2007, pp. 291–294; Е. Евтимова, *Занаятчийски изделия от Велики Преслав*, [in:] *Иванка Акрабова-Жандова. In memoriam*, ed. М. Ваклинова et al., София 2009, pp. 199–211; Д. Момчилов, *Старобългарски апликации от фонда на историческия музей – Карнобат*, [in:] *Laurea. In honorem Margaritae Vaklinova*, vol. II, ed. Б. Петрунова, А. Аладжов, Е. Василева, София 2009, pp. 167–178; С. Станилов, *Художественият метал на Златния век (IX–XI в.). Продължение на темата*, [in:] *Великотърновският Университет "Св. св. Кирил и Методий" и българската археология*, vol. I, ed. Б. Борисов, Велико Търново 2010, pp. 423–436; С. Бонев, С. Дончева, *Старобългарски производствен център за художествен метал при с. Новосел, Шуменско*, Велико Търново 2011; Д. Момчилов, *Паметници на металопластиката от Маркели*, ИНАИ 40, 2012, pp. 141–149. Widely on the topic, see: Г. Коняров, *Принос към историята на рударството и металургията в България*, София 1953; H. Mamzer, *Studia nad metalurgią żelaza na terenie północno-wschodniej Bułgarii we wczesnym średniowieczu*, Wrocław 1988. On earliest period see: С. Станилов, *Художественият метал на българското ханство на Дунава 7–9 век*, София 2006.

[13] See: Л. Дончева-Петкова, Ж. Златинова, *Стъкларска работилница край западната стена в Плиска*, Архе 20.4, 1978, pp. 37–48; Т. Балабанов, *За началото на стъклообработването и стъклопроизводството в Средновековна България*, [in:] Пр.Сб 3, 1983, pp. 228–240; Й. Чангова, *Перник...*, pp. 145–147; Й. Штапова, *О производстве стекла в епоху Первого болгарского царства*, Пр.Сб 4, 1993, pp. 151–165; Л. Дончева-Петкова, *Одърци...*, p. 64; Ц. Комитова, *Стъклени гривни от Мелник*, [in:] *Приноси към българската археология*, vol. III–IV, ed. С. Станилов et al., София 2006, pp. 99–107.

[14] See: Т. Тотев, *За обработка на кост в средновековна България*, Архе 4.3, 1963, pp. 83–92; С. Бонев, *Художествената резба върху кост – връзки и влияния с другите приложни техники през X век*, Пр.Сб 3, 1983, pp. 149–159; Й. Чангова, *Перник...*, pp. 38–55, 145–149, 163–166; Т. Тотев, *Към въпроса за творчеството на преславските майстори на рязана кост през IX–X в.*, ППр, 6, 1993, pp. 109–115; С. Бонев, *За преславската костена пластика*, ПКШ 1, 1995, pp. 344–347; Л. Дончева-Петкова, *Одърци...*, pp. 62, 62–64, 82–88; Л. Нинов, *Остеологична характеристика на костените и роговите изделия*, [in:] Л. Дончева-Петкова, *Одърци...*, pp. 174–177; И.Х. Джамбов, *Средновековното селище...*, pp. 64–66; С. Бонев, *Преславската резба върху кост – стари творби и нови находки*, [in:] *Иванка Акрабова-Жандова...*, pp. 143–153.

[15] See: С. Ангелова, *За производството на строителна керамика в Североизточна България през ранното средновековие*, Архе 13.3, 1971, pp. 3–21;

kitchenware, tableware and the so-called ceramic icons produced for worship purposes[16]. Of importance was also the role of artistic and decorative handicraft (articles made of clay, metal and bones). The

Т. Т о т е в, *Керамични пещи в чашата на язовир "Виница" край Преслав*, Архе 15.4, 1973, pp. 58–68; В. В ъ л о в, *Водоснабдяването на средновековните български градове и крепости (VII–XIV в.)*, Архе 19.1, 1977, pp. 14–15, 19–21, 24–26, 27; Й. А л е к с и е в, *Грънчарски пещи и жилища-полуземянки от IX–X в. край с. Хотница, Великотърновски окръг*, Архе 19.4, 1977, pp. 55–60; М. В а к л и н о в а, *Материали и производство на преславската каменна пластика*, Пр.Сб 5, 1993, pp. 68–101; Д. М о м ч и л о в, *Материалната култура*..., pp. 294–295.

[16] See: А. М и л ч е в, *Разкопки в Плиска западно от Вътрешния град през 1959 г.*, Архе 2.3, 1960, pp. 30–43; Л. Д о н ч е в а-П е т к о в а, *Технология на раннославянската и старобългарската битова керамика (края на VI–X в.)*, Архе 11.2, 1969, pp. 10–24; Б. С у л т о в, *Новооткрит керамичен център при с. Хотница от римската и старобългарската епоха*, Архе 11.4, 1969, pp. 12–24, specifically pp. 22–24; Л. Д о н ч е в а-П е т к о в а, *Трапезната керамика в България през VIII–XI в.*, Архе 12.1, 1970, pp. 12–25; e a d e m, *Средновековни глинени съдове с вътрешни уши*, Архе 13.4, 1971, pp. 32–38; E.C. S c h w a r t z, *Medieval Ceramic Decoration in Bulgaria*, Bsl 43.1, 1982, pp. 45–50; Т. Т о т е в, *Манастирът "Тузлалъка" – център на рисувана керамика в Преслав през IX–X в.*, София 1982; Й. Ч а н г о в а, *Перник*..., pp. 57–77; Т. Т о т е в, *Преславските ателиета за рисувана керамика*, ППре 7, 1995, pp. 101–109; В. Й о т о в, Г. А т а н а с о в, *Скала*..., pp. 64–82; Л. Д о н ч е в а-П е т к о в а, *Одърци*..., pp. 64–82; И.Х. Д ж а м б о в, *Средновековното селище*..., pp. 47–57; Т. Т о т е в, *Observations sur la cèramique peinte du monastère aux alentours de l'église ronde (l'église d'Or) a Preslav*, [in:] *Bulgaria Pontica Medii Aevi*, vol. IV–V/1, ed. В. Г ю з е л е в, София 2003, pp. 255–276; Р. В а с и л е в, *Колекция от ранносредновековна керамика и съдове уникати от манастира до спирка Равна, Провадийско*, [in:] *Тангра. Сборник в чест на 70-годишнината на акад. Васил Гюзелев*, ed. М. К а й м а к а м о в а et al., София 2006, pp. 367–382; Д. М о м ч и л о в, *Материалната култура*..., pp. 287–291; К. С т о е в а, *Битовата керамика от манастира в местността Манастирчето край Велики Преслав (предварително съобщение)*, [in:] *Великотърновският Университет*..., pp. 525–538; Т. Т о т е в, *Нови материали и наблюдения за трапезната рисувана керамика от два манастира във Велики Преслав*, ПКШ 10, 2008, pp. 404–417; С. С т а н и л о в, *Наблюдения по формирането на орнаменталната система в българската художествена керамика от IX–X век*, [in:] *Иванка Акрабова-Жандова*..., pp. 129–142; Т. Т о т е в, *Две рисувани белоглинени трапезни блюда с литургическо предназначение и употреба от селище във Велики Преслав*, ПКШ 11, 2010, pp. 254–259; i d e m, *Святая Богородица в искусстве Великого Преслава (IX–X вв.)*, ПКШ 13, 2013, pp. 350–360. For more on the topic, see: Л. Д о н ч е в а-П е т к о в а, *Българска битова керамика през ранното средновековие*, София 1977; Т. Т о т е в, *Керамичната икона в средновековна България*, София 2001.

manufacture of such articles established its presence especially in Preslav[17]. Spinning, weaving and needle-craft were also represented[18].

In spite of the significant development and progressing specialisation of craft production, rural households satisfied their craftwork needs, at least in part, out of their own production, although commissioned work wasn't entirely absent from the Bulgarian countryside either. The links between rural areas and city markets were still very poor (although not non-existent). As in Byzantium, the more important sectors of the craft production remained under the control of the state, which means

[17] See: С. Станилов, *Метални гарнитури за ремъци и облекло от двореца във Велики Преслав*, ППре 7, 1995, pp. 110–135; С. Витлянов, *Новооткрити накитни предмети и елемнти на облеклото от Велики Преслав*, ПКШ 7, 2004, pp. 412–423; idem, *Характер и локализация на производствените структури в първите столични центрове на българската държава Плиска и Велики Преслав*, [in:] *Пътуванията в средновековна България. Материали от първата национална конференция "Пътуване към България. Пътуванията в средновековна България и съвременният туризъм", Шумен, 8–11.05.2008 г.*, ed. И. Йорданов, Велико Търново 2009, pp. 373–381; Т. Тотев, Р. Рашев, *Нови данни за старобългарското изкуство (VIII–X в.)*, ПКШ 12, 2012, pp. 387–394, specifically pp. 390–394 (Christian period). Relying on the name of one of the tsarist residences in today's Albania, namely Koprinishta (here in plural, derived from the word *koprina* – 'silk'), where, during the fighting against Basil II in 1018, bolyar Ivats, one of the commanders of the Bulgarian army took shelter, some scholars claim the Bulgarians may have been familiar with the techniques of the production of silk (П. Павлов, *Стопанско...*, p. 19). However, this view runs counter to what we learn from *Russian Primary Chronicle* (AM 6477, p. 68), in which precious fabrics (certainly silk ones), brought to Bulgaria from Byzantium from at least the end of the 960s, are mentioned. Of course, if we take seriously the account of the *Chronicle* into consideration (for that see below), however even if we doubt it there are also other evidences for such an imports from the Empire. The name of the residence can also be understood as referring to a place in which a large amount of silk goods was gathered, a kind of a synonym of the seat of a ruler who enjoyed the exclusive right to wear robes made of this material. The name would be an excellent match for one of the residences of the Bulgarian tsar. However, we can't confidently dismiss the view that under the rulers of the Cometopouloi dynasty the Bulgarians obtained access to one of the most strictly guarded Byzantine secrets, that is, the production of silk. This toponym is simply the only evidence of the fact we have. At this stage of the research process it must be treated only as weakly documented hypothesis.

[18] Cf. Й. Чангова, *Перник...*, pp. 55–57; Л. Дончева-Петкова, *Одърци...*, pp. 89–91.

that only some artisans manufactured goods for the domestic market[19]. It was no different with monastic communities which, while striving to satisfy mainly their own needs, were probably also involved in producing goods for worship purposes and completed orders placed by outsiders – for example, by representatives of the Church hierarchy[20]. This view is of course based on the assumption that the remains of some of the buildings discovered by archaeologists can be legitimately identified with former monasteries.

Although, as is indicated by archaeological excavations (mostly of a surface type), there was a great number of settlement sites in Bulgaria (30 masonry fortresses and 280 unfortified settlements are known to have existed in Dobrudzha alone)[21] in the second phase of the early Middle

[19] Д. Ангелов, *Развитие на занаятите и рударството през VIII–X в.*, [in:] *Стопанска история…*, pp. 40–42; idem, *Стопански живот…*, pp. 341–342; Г.Г. Литаврин, *Внутренный кризис, новый подьем и борьба за независимость*, [in:] *Краткая история Болгарии. С древниейших времен до наших дней*, ed. idem, Москва 1987, p. 83; И. Божилов, *Добруджа…*, pp. 52, 56; П. Павлов, *Стопанско…*, p. 19.

[20] С. Витлянов, *За стопанския облик на манастира при Голямата базилика в Плиска*, Архе 26.2/3, 1984, pp. 95–102; idem, *Стопанският облик на столичните манастири през IX–X век*, ППре 7, 1995, pp. 92–100; idem, *Die bulgarischen Klöster (im Mittelalter) – universale Produktionszentren*, ШУЕКП.ТКИБ 6, 2004, pp. 145–149.

[21] For Dobrudzha see: И. Божилов, *Добруджа…*, pp. 30–31; Г. Атанасов, *Добруджанското деспотство. Към политическата, църковната, стопанската и културната история на Добруджа през XIV век*, Велико Търново 2009, p. 13. For the whole country territory see e.g.: В. Тъпкова-Заимова, *Крепости и укрепени градове през Първото българско царство. Според сведения от византийските автори*, ВС 25.3, 1956, pp. 40–61; Ж. Въжарова, *Средновековни обекти по долините на реките Цибрица и Огоста (по материали от разузнаването през 1962–1963 г.)*, ИАИ 28, 1965, pp. 231–245; П.С. Коледаров, *Към въпроса за развитието на селищната мрежа и нейните елементи в средищната и източната част на Балканите от VII до XVIII в.*, ИИИ 18, 1967, pp. 89–146; С. Ваклинов, *За характера на ранно-българската селищна мрежа в Североизточна България*, Архе 14.1, 1972, pp. 9–13; Ж. Въжарова, *Селища и некрополи (края на VI–XI в.)*, Архе 16.3, 1974, pp. 9–27; М. Деведжиев, *Кратка история на селищното развитие по българските земи*, София 1979, pp. 68–118; Р. Василев, *Проучванията на славянските археологически паметници от Северна България от края на VI до края на X в.*, Архе 21.3, 1979, pp. 12–22; Б. Борисов, *Средновековното село през IX–XII в. на територията на днешна Югоизточна България*, [in:] *Проф. д.и.н. Станчо Ваклинов…*, pp. 310–317;

Ages, the municipal centres proper were far and few between[22]. Their rise and development was twofold. Some were Byzantine cities captured by the Bulgarians and some grew around the centres of Bulgarian power brought into existence *in crudo radice*[23]. The former can be divided into two groups: those which existed until the invasion of the Bulgarians at the end of the seventh century (for example, Dorostolon/Dristra) or were seized through conquest in the ninth and tenth centuries (e.g. Serdica, Beroe, Philippoupolis, Mesembria, Anchialos, Develtos, Sozopolis); and those which had had been destroyed in the period before the arrival of khan Asparuh, and, having been abandoned by the subjects of Byzantine emperors, were reconstructed in the ninth century (for example, Bdin, Belgrade, Skopje, Sirmium)[24] by Bulgarian rulers who, in rebuilding them, drew

Т. Овчаров, *Селища от Първото българско царство във Великотърновска област*, [in:] *Оттука започва България. Материали от втората национална конференция по история, археология и културен туризъм "Пътуване към България" – Шумен, 14–16.05.2010 година*, ed. И. Йорданов, Шумен 2011, pp. 430–434.

[22] Cf. Л. Беров, *Икономическото развитие на България...*, pp. 28–29.

[23] See: Г.Г. Литаврин, *Внутренный кризис...*, p. 83. More widely on the topic: А. Аладжов, *Византийският град и българите VII–IX век (по археологически данни)*, София 2009.

[24] On these centres see: Dorostolon/Dristra – А. Кузев, *Дръстър*, [in:] *Български средновековни градове и крепости, vol. I, Градове и крепости по Дунав и Черно Море*, ed. А. Кузев, В. Гюзелев, Варна 1981, pp. 177–185; Г. Атанасов, *Християнският Дуросторум–Дръстър. Доростолската епархия през късната античност и Средновековието IV–XIV в. История, археология, култура и изкуство*, Варна 2007, pp. 79–231; Serdica/Sredets/Triaditsa – А. Данчева-Василева, *История на средновековна София от IV–XIV век*, София 2017, pp. 21–125; Beroe – Г.Н. Николов, *Военно-политическа история на средновековния град Боруй*, ВС 50.3, 1981, pp. 34–44; D. Янков, *Средновековни гробове от Стара Загора*, [in:] *Историко-археологически изследвания. В памет на проф. д-р Станчо Ваклинов*, ed. К. Попконстантинов, Велико Търново 1994, pp. 121–127; K. Kaltschev, *Das Befestigungssystem von Augusta Traiana – Beroe (Heute Stara Zagora) im 2.–6. Jh.U.Z.*, ABu 3.2, 1998, pp. 88–107; Philippoupolis/Plovdiv – А. Данчева-Василева, *Пловдив през Средновековието IV–XIV в.*, София 2009, pp. 31–54, 214–223, 244–246, 272–274, 289–291, 314–323, 326, 355–356; Mesembria – Ж. Чимбулева, *Месемврия–Несебър*, [in:] В. Велков, Л. Огненова-Маринова, Ж. Чимбулева, *Месембрия–Месемврия–Несебър*, София 1991, pp. 72–91; V. Gjuzelev, *Die mittelalterliche Stadt Mesembria (Nesebăr) im 6.–15. Jh.*, BHR 6.1, 1978, pp. 50–59; Anchialos – В. Гюзелев, *Анхиало*, [in:] *Български средновековни градове...*, pp. 356–382; В. Гюзелев,

inspiration from Byzantium, relying on the assistance of the captive craftsmen from the Empire. In the last case the Slav settlers usually took over the ruins of the former city.

Among the cities which grew around the centres of Bulgarian power, one should mention Pliska and Great Preslav. The Byzantines referred to them using words πόλις and ἄστυ, which were usually used to refer to towns. Among them were also some of the centres along the Danube and Black Sea shores and some larger cities inland. The Bulgarian province in turn was predominantly home to small fortresses (performing mainly military function) and administrative and church centres, referred to in the sources as κάστρον, φρούριον, ἔρυμα, πόλισμα, κομόπολις and πολίχνιον[25].

Средновековният Анхиало (VI–XV в.), [in:] *История на Поморие*, vol. I, *Древност и съвреме*, ed. А. Орачев, В. Василчина, Бургас 2011, pp. 45–65; Develtos – Ch. Dimitrov, *Die frühmittelalterliche Stadt Debeltos zwischen Byzanz und Bulgarien vom achten bis zehnte Jahrhundert*, [in:] *Die Schwarzmeerküste in der Spatantike und frühen Mittelalter*, ed. R. Pillinger, A. Pülz, H. Vetters, Wien 1992, pp. 35–45; М. Балболова-Иванова, *Средновековый Девелт в VIII–X вв.*, [in:] *Bulgaria Pontica Medii Aevi*, vol. IV/V.1, ed. В. Гюзелев, София 2003, pp. 79–84; Sozopolis – Б. Димитров, *Созопол*, [in:] *Български средновековни градове...*, pp. 388–407; idem, *Sozopol*, Sofia 2012, pp. 199–220; Bdin – С. Михайлов, *Археологически проучвания на крепостта Баба Вида във Видин*, Архе 3.3, 1961, pp. 1–8; W. Swoboda, *Widin*, [in:] SSS, vol. VI, pp. 421–422; Б. Кузупов, *Замъкът "Баба Вида"*, МПК 20.4, 1980, pp. 7–12; А. Кузев, *Бдин*, [in:] *Български средновековни градове...*, pp. 98–115; В. Вълов, *Седалището и териториалният обхват на Бдинската област от средата на IX до началото на XI век*, ИМСБ 13, 1987, pp. 21–45; V. Beševliev, *Die Herkunft des Stadtnamens* БъдФнь, LBa 31.1/2, 1988, pp. 43–44; П. Балабанов, С. Бояджиев, Н. Тулешков, *Крепостно строителство по българските земи*, София 2000, p. 60; Г.Н. Николов, *Централизъм и регионализъм в ранносредновековна България (края на VII – началото на XI в.)*, София 2005, pp. 192–193; Belgrad – J. Калић-Мијушковић, *Београд у средњем веку*, Београд 1967; Skopje – А. Дероко, *Средновековни град Скопје*, САН.С 120, 1971, pp. 1–16; И. Микулчић, *Старо Скопје со околните тврдини*, Скопје 1982; Srem – В. Поповић, *Сирмиум, град царева и мученика*, Сремска Митровица 2003; S. Turlej, *Sirmium w późnym antyku*, [in:] *Florilegium. Studia ofiarowane Profesorowi Aleksandrowi Krawczukowi z okazji dziewięćdziesiątej piątej rocznicy urodzin*, ed. E. Dąbrowa, T. Grabowski, M. Piedgoń, Kraków 2017, pp. 445–460.

[25] See: В. Тъпкова-Заимова, *Крепости и укрепени градове...*, p. 40; P.S. Koledarov, *On the Initial Type Differentiation of Inhabited Localities in the Central Balkan Peninsula in Ancient Times*, EH 3, 1966, pp. 31–52; idem, *Place-Names*

The layout of all these centres was typically based on the division into the internal and external town. The former was where the authorities (both religious and secular) were based while the latter, inhabited by the majority of the population, was where the economic life was concentrated[26]. Throughout the Middle Ages, the economic activity of the inhabitants of Bulgarian cities, and of many other cities in the Balkans, was marked by the combination of land cultivation with craftwork[27].

classification in the central part of the Balkan Peninsula in the Middle ages, [in:] *Actes du premier Congres International des Études Balkaniques et Sud-Est Européennes, Sofia, 26 âout – 1 septembre 1966*, vol. III, *Histoire (V^e–XVe ss.; XVe–XVIIe ss.)*, ed. V. Tăpkova-Zaimova, S. Dimitrov, E. Sarafova, Sofia 1969, pp. 277–286.

[26] See: Д. Ангелов, *Към въпроса за средновековния български град*, Архе 2.3, 1960, pp. 9–22; С. Лишев, *Още веднъж за възникването на българския средновековен град*, ИП 30.6, 1974, pp. 70–77; Й. Чангова, *Към въпроса за устройството на средновековния български град (IX–XIV в.)*, [in:] *Архитектурата на Първата и Втората българска държава. Материали*, ed. Г. Кожухаров, София 1975, pp. 79–101, specifically pp. 80–93, 98–99; Д.И. Димитров, *Възникването на градски центрове в Североизточна България*, [in:] *Средновековният български град...*, pp. 35–45; Д. Овчаров, *Възникване и оформяне на Преслав като средновековен град (IX–X в.)*, [in:] *Средновековният български град...*, pp. 107–116; П. Петров, *Някои проблеми на средновековния български град*, [in:] *Средновековният български град...*, pp. 8–10, 12–13, 17–19; Д. Ангелов, *Възникване и устройство на градовете*, [in:] *Стопанска история...*, pp. 49–52; idem, *Стопански живот...*, pp. 350–352; С. Михайлов, *За някои характерни черти на българския средновековен град*, Пр.Сб 3, 1983, pp. 188–195; Р. Рашев, *Аул и град в България през VIII–IX в.*, [in:] *Сборник в чест на акад. Димитър Ангелов...*, pp. 170–177; М. Ваклинова, *Градът на българското средновековие*, [in:] *Bulgarian medieval town. Technologies*, ed. И. Щерева, К. Маламед, София 1995, pp. 2–6; И. Божилов, *Добруджа...*, pp. 29–35; П. Павлов, *Стопанско...*, pp. 18–19. See also: С. Михайлов, *За някои характерни черти на българския средновековен град*, Пр.Сб. 3, 1983, pp. 188–195; Р. Панова, *Морфология на средновековния български град*, ИП 56.1/2, 2000, pp. 3–21; eadem, *Аспекти на морфологията на средновековния български град*, Мин 9.1, 2002, pp. 19–30.

[27] Г.Г. Литаврин, *Внутренный кризис...*, p. 84; for a later period see: Д.И. Полывянный, *Балканский город XIII–XV вв. – типология и специфика развития*, EB 20.1, 1984, p. 47.

3. Trade

Trade exchange between different Bulgarian urban centres, and especially the economic relations between the cities and the rural areas, aren't well documented. The primary sources contain very few references regarding the functioning of the fairs in which different commodities were traded. It is sometimes argued that the self-sufficiency of the majority of farms and the extensive system of obligations (the so-called angaria)[28] imposed on the subjects by the state didn't encourage the expansion of the domestic market[29]. Although these opinions are fully justified, the domestic trade is logical and it would be a mistake to deny it. Even the highly self-sufficient farms weren't able to meet all the agriculture-based needs. It was especially with regard to the use of high quality metal articles that one had to rely on the services of a qualified blacksmith. In addition, one shouldn't lose sight of the specialised artisans who weren't engaged either in land cultivation or in animal husbandry and had to acquire food through trade, even if many of them were employed in the state workshops. The Bulgarian state consisted, in the main, of free people, and the various obligations they were required to fulfil didn't prevent them from (after all, in fulfilling these obligations they were supposed to work for a specific amount of time or produce a specific number of articles) performing some paid work. That this was the case is indicated by the development of city centres and the progressing diversification of their craft production. Excavations carried out in Bulgaria's capital cities have revealed a number of rooms interpreted as commercial *loca*[30]. All of this is evidence of the economic activity that involved the production, if only vestigial, of articles for sale

[28] For more on taxes and the obligations imposed on the subjects by the state see: G. Cankova-Petkova, *Byzance*..., pp. 345–347; И. Билярски, *Фискална система на средновековна България*, Пловдив 2010.

[29] Л. Беров, *Икономическото развитие на България*..., pp. 27–29. Cf. С. Лишев, *За проникването и ролята на парите във феодална България*, София 1958, pp. 59–80.

[30] Й. Чангова, *Търговски помещения край южната крепостна стена в Преслав*, ИАИ 21, 1956, pp. 232–290; А. Милчев, *Проучвания на раннославянската култура в България и на Плиска през последните двадесет години*, Архе 6.3, 1964, p. 30; idem, *Занаятчийски и търговски помещения северно от южната порта на вътрешния*

and wasn't bound up only with the disposal of the surplus of one's own products. Based on both the written and archaeological sources, it can be argued that the Bulgarians were engaged mainly in barter trade (goods traded for goods), since Bulgaria didn't mint its own coins in the period under consideration, and the Byzantines ones were hoarded. As can be inferred from al-Masudi's account, the Bulgarians paid for purchased goods with farmed animals[31]. However, it can't be ruled out that the Byzantine coin was also used as a means of payment (probably in larger cities). It is recently argued that there were mints near Great Preslav (in, among others, Nadarevo, Novosel, Smyadovo) minting imitations of silver and gold Byzantine coins. Their existence dates from the end of the ninth to the third quarter of the tenth centuries[32]. This view, which may be true, supports the belief in the partial introduction of coin into the Bulgarian state.

The growth, both quantitative and qualitative, of the agricultural and craft output, coupled with some specialisation of the Bulgarian economy (articles traditionally manufactured by the Bulgarians and valued by foreign merchants) made it possible for the subjects of the Bulgarian rulers to enter a wider international market.

It must be stressed that the baptism of the Bulgarians and the establishment of the lasting peace between Bulgaria and Byzantium in the 860s resulted in the strengthening of the economic ties between the two countries. This is indicated by the increased number of Byzantine emperors'

град на Плиска, [in:] *Архитектурата на Първата и Втората българска държава…*, pp. 246–271.

[31] С. Лишев, *За проникването и ролята на парите…*, pp. 59–117; Д. Ангелов, *Вътрешна и външна търговия през VIII–X в.*, [in:] *Стопанска история…*, pp. 42–43; idem, *Стопански живот…*, pp. 342–346; И. Божилов, *Добруджа…*, p. 56; Л. Симеонова, *Пътуване към Константинопол. Търговия и комуникации в Средиземноморския свят (края на IX – 70-те години на XI с.)*, София 2006, p. 140; П. Павлов, *Стопанско…*, pp. 19–20. Cf. И. Йорданов, *Характер на монетната циркулация в средновековните български столици Преслав и Търново*, [in:] *Средновековният български град…*, pp. 229–239.

[32] Cf. Т. Тихов, *Някои аспекти на външната търговия на България и Византия през периода VII–X век*, [in:] *Пътуванията в средновековна България…*, pp. 330, 332–333.

bronze and gold coins found in Dobrudzha and in the Danube Delta[33]. It was necessary to provide new church buildings with proper decorations and to equip them with all kinds of objects used in Christian ceremonies. Bulgarian aristocracy was becoming increasingly interested in acquiring luxury goods: jewellery and Syrian and Byzantine clothes[34]. The higher clergy also tried to emulate way of life of their Byzantine confreres. Glazed ceramic vessels, Syro-Mesopotamian faience, Syrian glassware containing relief representations were imported to Preslav[35] from the Empire while slaves[36], metal ores (including iron), flax products, flax itself (from the valley of the river Struma and the Black Sea area), skins, honey, wax and cattle husbandry products were exported by Bulgarian merchants to Constantinople. The latter even had their own marketplace in the Byzantine capital. It was located probably near the seat of Rus' merchants, in a district surrounding the St. Mamas Monastery (?)[37]. It is worth noting

[33] See: E. Oberländer-Târnoveanu, *La monnaie dans l'espace rural byzantin des Balkans orientaux – un essai de synthèse au commencement du XXIe siècle*, Peu 1 (14), 2003, pp. 335–406, specifically pp. 344–347, 376–377; Gh. Mănucu-Adameşteanu, *La diffusion de la monnaie byzantine en Dobroudja aux IXe–Xe siècles*, RESEE 34.4, 1996, pp. 275–287. For the last scholar this is evidence of Byzantium's presence in particular centres of Dobrudzha.

[34] See: И. Кючукова, И. Йорданов, *Византийските тъкани и българският владетелски двор (X в.) (Печат на епарха, химатин и екзопрат Филотей, намерен в Преслав)*, [in:] *Laurea*..., pp. 155–165. Authors analyse Philotheos' seal from the beginning of the tenth century found in Preslav. Philotheos was a Byzantine dignitary responsible for overseeing the export of silk robes. Identifying him with, known from the sources of the period, a bishop by the same name who tried adherents of the usurper Constantine Doukas, they advance the thesis that he was sent to Bulgarian Symeon to give him imperial robe. The Byzantine authorities had just granted the Bulgarian ruler the right to use the title *basileus*. For more on the restrictions and permissions regarding the export of partticular Byzantine goods see: Л. Беров, *Икономическото развитие на България*..., p. 30; Л. Симеонова, *Пътуване*..., pp. 245–251.

[35] Cf. i.a.: М. Манолова, *Към въпроса за разпостранението на белоглинената византийска трапезна керамика в българските земи от края на VIII до края на XII век*, Архе 41.1/2, 2000, pp. 1–15.

[36] Bulgaria's transit role and Bulgarian merchants' participation in this trade is more likely, see: Л. Симеонова, *Пътуване*..., pp. 137–140.

[37] The idea is of S. Runciman (*A History of the First Bulgarian Empire*, London 1930, p. 144). On the Rus' quarter see e.g. Т. Томов, *Константинопол и руската колония (до 1204 г.)*, София [s.a.], pp. 54, 67.

that trade with the Empire was based on monetary payments. Bulgarian merchants bought luxury goods, sought after in their own country, with the money they had obtained for their own products[38]. An important trading point, in addition to Constantinople, was Thessalonike, especially at the beginning of the tenth century, when the Bulgarian border ran at a distance of 22 kilometres to the north of this metropolis. Testament to the city's extensive trade is the sigillographical material from the customs post located there. Byzantine sources also refer to the commercial activity of the Slavs (the Drougovitai and the Sagudates) from southern Macedonia who, remaining in part under Bulgarian rule, traded with merchants from Thessalonike[39].

Scholars have identified a few trading points between Byzantium and Bulgaria, including Adrianople, Constantinople and Thessalonike[40]. In order to get to these cities, Bulgarian merchants took land routes, relying on draught animals for transporting their commodities[41]. The main point handling Bulgaro-Byzantine trade in Thrace, Develtos was certainly among the most important trade centres in question. The goods which Bulgarian merchants took to Byzantine capital were, in all probability, loaded onto ships in this town[42]. It isn't certain whether Pereyaslavets' role in the north was similar to the role Develtos played in the south. There is sigillographical evidence indicating Bulgarians' contacts with Byzantine officials responsible for overseeing trade with foreigners,

[38] See: B. P r i m o v, *Certain Aspects of the International Importance of the First Bulgarian Empire*, EHi 5, 1970, pp. 195–197; Л. Б е р о в, *Икономическото развитие на България...*, pp. 29–30; Д. А н г е л о в, *Вътрешна и външна търговия...*, pp. 44–45; i d e m, *Стопански живот...*, pp. 346–347; Л. С и м е о н о в а, *Пътуване...*, pp. 144–146; Т. Т и х о в, *Някои аспекти...*, pp. 329–331, 332; С. С о р о ч а н, *Об эволюции торгово-економической политики Византии на Нижнем Подунавье в VII–X вв.*, Пр.Сб 7, 2013, pp. 249–251.

[39] B. P r i m o v, *Certain Aspects...*, p. 207; Й. Ч а н г о в а, *Перник...*, pp. 199, 202; Т. Т и х о в, *Някои аспекти...*, p. 331. Cf. П. Г е о р г и е в, *Дипломатически и търговски знаци-печати във Византия и славянските страни*, ГСУ.НЦСВПИД 82 (2), 1988, pp. 21–32.

[40] Й. И в а н о в, *Византийски комеркиарии за България (681–971)*, [in:] *Договори, хора, съдби*, ed. В. М и х н е в а, С. П е т к о в а, В. П а в л о в, Варна 2000, pp. 17–24.

[41] Л. С и м е о н о в а, *Пътуване...*, pp. 133, 141–142.

[42] *Ibidem*, pp. 133, 134–135.

but some scholars link it with the activity, which took place not in the latter half of the tenth century but in the 1030s, of Byzantines themselves[43]. The famous passage from *Russian Primary Chronicle* put into Svyatoslav's mouth might be regarded as evidence that Bulgaria maintained trade relations with many countries and was visited by merchants from many parts of Europe. Gold and, most likely, silk robes, wines and fruit were brought in from Byzantium, silver and horses from Czech and Hungary and skin, wax, honey and slaves from Ruthenia[44]. Although the present state of research doesn't allow us to deny emphatically the importance of this city for Bulgaria's economy during Peter's reign, the source's famous account seems to reflect Byzantium's trade with Ruthenia and other territories in the eleventh and at the beginning of the twelfth centuries[45].

Located along the river Danube and the western coast of the Black Sea, such harbour centres as Bdin, Dristra, Develtos, Mesembria, Anchialos, Sozopolis, and, perhaps, Pereyaslavets (the list could be extended to include other less known places), played a significant role in Bulgaria's long-distance trade. This goes especially for contacts with Ruthenian and Byzantine merchants who used water route along the Sea. The former stopped at convenient places along the Bulgarian coast, supplying themselves with food they needed on the way to Constantinople and offering in exchange some of the goods they transported[46]. There is linguistic evidence to suggest the existence of direct or indirect economic contacts between Bulgarians and the inhabitants of the Italian Peninsula already

[43] И. Коновалова, В. Перехавко, *Древная Русь и Нижнее Подунавие*, Москва 2000, pp. 54, 63; М. Раев, *Переяславец на Дунав – мит и действителност в речта на кнчз Святослав в "Повесть временных лет"*, ГСУ.НЦСВПИД 95 (14), 2006, p. 195.

[44] *Russian Primary Chronicle*, AM 6477, p. 68.

[45] М. Раев, *Переяславец...*, pp. 193–203.

[46] See: B. Primov, *Certain Aspects...*, pp. 201–206; Л. Беров, *Икономическото развитие на България...*, pp. 30–31; Д. Ангелов, *Вътрешна и външна търговия...*, pp. 44–49; idem, *Стопански живот...*, pp. 346–350; И. Божилов, *Добруджа...*, p. 56; Л. Симеонова, *Пътуване...*, pp. 134, 152–156; П. Павлов, *Стопанско...*, pp. 20–21.

during the tenth century[47]. Bulgarian merchants are likely to have acted as intermediaries between East and West and between Byzantium and Central Europe[48].

Conclusion. The first issue that needs to be stressed are the strong ties linking the Bulgarian and Byzantine economies, both in terms of trade and in terms of the lessons the Bulgarians drew from these contacts. Some Bulgarian areas – Thracian, Macedonian and the Black Sea regions – were agriculturally linked with the main urban centres of the Empire, including in particular Constantinople and Thessalonike. These regions served as the supply base of these metropolises, providing them with food and gaining a significant financial and technological support, including the possibility of growing new crops, raising new animals and, generally, knowing the achievements of Byzantine agriculture.

The state control of some sectors of the craft production, the possibility of bringing goods from Byzantium and the dominance of barter trade – all of this appears to indicate that Bulgaria's urban economy in the ninth and tenth centuries still remained underdeveloped. The agricultural and livestock economy was dominant in the state of the Bulgarian tsars and a great number of the inhabitants of Bulgarian cities were involved in it. Following its territorial expansion, the state became increasingly involved in the international trade, although of course it wasn't until the era of Crusades that the economic relations between East and West underwent a rapid development[49]. There is no doubt that the long periods of peace and the use of Byzantine economic achievements (mainly through trade) contributed to the development of the Bulgarian economy which made significant progress in the period under consideration[50].

---

47 B. Primov, *Certain Aspects*..., p. 207.

48 Л. Симеонова, *Пътуване*..., pp. 137, 140–141.

49 П. Павлов, *Стопанско*..., pp. 18, 19, 20–21.

50 Л. Беров, *Икономическото развитие на България*..., p. 31; G. Cankova-Petkova, *Byzance*..., pp. 341–348.

The above outline doesn't of course address all the aspects of the development of the Bulgarian economy in the period of the First (here Christian) Bulgarian Empire. Its focus is limited only to some of its elements. I have also avoided going into too many details, trying to present a general picture of the Bulgarian economy in the period in consideration[51].

[51] For more on the topic see: Б. Примов, *За икономическата и политическата роля на Първата българска държава в международните отношения на средновековна Европа*, ИП 17.2, 1961, pp. 33–62; Г.Г. Литаврин, *Темпове и специфика на социално-икономическото развитие на средновековна България в сравнение с Византия (от края на VII до края на XII в.)*, ИП 26.6, 1970, pp. 23–40; С. Лишев, *Българският средновековен град. Обществено-икономически облик*, София 1970; Р. Комсалова, *Социално-икономическите проблеми на средновековна България в българската медиевистика след Втората световна война*, Пловдив 2000; P. Pranke, M. Zečević, *Handel interregionalny od X do XII wieku. Europa Środkowa, Środkowo-Wschodnia, Półwysep Skandynawski i Półwysep Bałkański. Studium porównawcze*, Toruń 2016, pp. 123–148.

III

Nikolay Hrissimov

Everyday Life

To judge by the evidence at our disposal, the day-to-day existence during the long reign of tsar Peter can hardly be considered as a separate entity, independent from the overall reality of the First Bulgarian Empire. Accordingly, the present text provides a generalised picture of the life of mediaeval Bulgarians in the period following Christianisation; the circumstances pertaining specifically to the time of tsar Peter were, of course, taken into account whenever possible. The analysis covers the basic components that determined all of the remaining aspects: the climate and the environmental characteristics; the status of men, women and children; the issues of housing, food, holidays, and celebration.

1. Climate and Environment

Depending on which part of the world a human being inhabits, he or she is surrounded by particular kinds of flora and fauna, atypical for other latitudes. This, in turn, determines his or her dietary habits and clothing. The territory of early mediaeval Bulgaria was situated primarily in a region characterised by a moderate continental climate; the extreme south and south-west territories are characterised by a Mediterranean climate, while the north-east parts of the erstwhile First Bulgarian Empire display to a certain extent a continental climate. However, as regards the climate during early Middle Ages, it has been believed in recent decades – following the study by H. Lamb[1] – that it was warmer than in the 20th century; this phenomenon is known as the Second Climate Optimum, the Viking Interval[2], or the Mediaeval Warm Period[3]. The chronological extent of the Mediaeval Warm Period is defined variously by different groups of scholars. According to one school of thought, the period began around 750/800 CE and ended around 1200/1250 CE[4]; other researchers situate it between ca. 900/950 CE and 1200/1250 CE[5]. Irrespective of which of the two estimates is closer to the truth, the onset of the warmer period would coincide with a time at which the First Bulgarian Empire visibly flourished. In the former case, that would be the Bulgarian expansion in the Balkans, beginning with the victorious campaigns of conquest led by khan Krum and his successors; in the latter case, it would overlap with the apogee of the Bulgarian state in the entire mediaeval period – the *Pax Symeonica*. The same chronological stage of early mediaeval Bulgaria corresponds to the settlement of territories situated in the foothills and ranges of the Balkan Mountains[6]; the occupation of the higher-situated territories began already in the 9th century[7]. This is an indirect indication

[1] H. Lamb, *Climate, History, and the Modern World*, [2]London–New York 1995.

[2] Г. Балтаков, Р. Кендерова, *Кватернерна палеогеография*, Варна 2003, p. 198.

[3] H. Lamb, *Climate*...

[4] W.S. Broecker, *Was the Medieval Warm Period Global?*, Scie 291 (5508), Feb. 23, 2001, pp. 1497–1499; M.K. Hughes, H.F. Diaz, *Was there a "Medieval Warm Period", and if so, where and when?*, CliC 26.2/3, p. 109–142; P.D. Nunn, *Climate Environment and Society in the Pacific during the last Millenium*, Amsterdam 2007, pp. 12, 59–86; Г. Балтаков, Р. Кендерова, *Кватернерна*..., p. 198.

[5] P.D. Jones, M.E. Mann, *Climate* Over *Past Millenia*, RG 42, 2002/2004, pp. 19–20.

[6] Р. Рашев, *Появата на средновековни селища във високите части на Стара планина*, ШУЕКП.ТКИБ 1, 1997, pp. 108–113.

[7] Н. Хрисимов, *За времето на усвояване на предпланинските и планинските райони в Първото българско царство*, ИРИМГ 2, 2015, pp. 55–69.

that the population of the country had grown, so that new lands were being sought for cultivation to ensure subsistence.

During the early Middle Ages, Europe was significantly less populous than in the Classical Period and late Antiquity. The factors responsible for this population decrease are numerous and diverse. In any case, in the early mediaeval period – in view of the substantial depopulation – inhabited areas were largely limited to plains situated roughly 300 m above sea level. This fact is evident from the mapping of settlements and necropolises from the time of the First Bulgarian Empire as presented in the work by Uwe Fiedler: it clearly shows that plains were compactly occupied on both sides of the lower course of the Danube, with isolated points outside of the clearly defined areas here and there[8]. Regardless of the mode of existence – sedentary or mobile (nomadic) – these territories remained the most desirable for habitation. Typically, these areas contained the most fertile soils, yielding ample crops and thus ensuring a relatively secure subsistence. It should be borne in mind that the basic livelihoods of the two main components of the Bulgarian nation – agriculture in the case of the Slavs and livestock-breeding in the case of the Proto-Bulgarians – were likewise principally connected with plains. Even the earthen ramparts barring the mountain roads leading to Byzantium were not positioned on the ridges of the Balkan Mountains, but rather in their foothills[9], which once again confirms the association of the population of the First Bulgarian Empire primarily with the plains it inhabited.

The early mediaeval Bulgarian was perfectly familiar with – and able to distinguish – the characteristics of each time of year. In the *Sermon on the Fourth Day* from John the Exarch's *Hexameron*, we find spot-on descriptions of the four seasons as they appear in moderate latitudes, along with an attempt at an explanation of each of them. Even the subtleties of calculating the difference between the solar and the lunar year are described, as well as the five basic climates of the earth[10].

---

[8] U. Fiedler, *Studien zu Gräberfeldern des 6.–9. Jahrhunderts an der unteren Donau*, I, Bonn 1992, p. 335, tab. 115.

[9] Cf. P. Рашев, *Старобългарски укрепления на Долния Дунав VI–XI в.* Варна 1982.

[10] John the Exarch (transl. Н.Ц. Кочев), pp. 172–191.

2. Society

The Middle Ages were a time dominated by men in politics as much as in everyday life. In fact, this holds true for all Eurasian societies whose life was governed by monotheistic religions. In the case of Christianity, this 'right' of men was derived from the 'fundamental law' of the time, i.e. the Holy Scripture: it is the Bible that determines the Middle Ages as a time fully monopolised by men in Christian-populated territories. Thus, the man was the 'protagonist' of the period: all political and religious power was concentrated in his hands, with rare exceptions (for this very reason, he will remain slightly off the main narrative). However, along with the above-mentioned 'powers', conferred on the man by the religion, his life was burdened by all the basic responsibilities on the level of both society and family. He was the one who held authority. He was the one who fought (a warrior); he was traditionally described as the producer of goods in a mediaeval society (a craftsman and merchant); he was expected to supply food for his family (a farmer and livestock-breeder). During the Christian period of the First Bulgarian Empire, he was the intermediary between the people and God (a priest). All these activities and duties of the man made him a 'public figure' of the Middle Ages. Accordingly, the man is either directly or indirectly present in all chapters of the present work.

Unlike in the classical western societies of the period, the early mediaeval Bulgarian society – or rather its male part – cannot be conveniently divided into three sharply defined groups (cult officials, warriors and workers), all of them subordinate to the ruler. According to Ivan Bozhilov, these only developed in Bulgaria in the 14th century[11]. On the other hand, in the early mediaeval Bulgarian society (even in the 9th century), only two of the aforementioned three groups were clearly identifiable: the warriors (aristocracy) and the common people. Cult officials – to the extent they can be distinguished from the remainder of the aristocracy in the first place – initially did not constitute a separate social class. They

[11] И. Божилов, *Българското общество през 14. век. Структура и просопография*, Пловдив 2014, pp. 64–141.

only transformed into one in the centuries following Christianisation, fulfilling the developing need for a class of cult officials organised into an effective, hierarchically arranged system. They can be further divided into those directly associated with the cult and those who – as related by Cosmas the Priest – found an easier way of living in the monasteries. In order to achieve a fuller picture of the role and functions of the man in the period under discussion, we need to revisit the structure of the contemporary society. This largely amounts to restating what has already been said above, as the picture of the society presented so far is based entirely on data pertaining to the men of the period. This is caused by the nature of the sources at our disposal: the Byzantine and Latin traditions also derive from the Christian perspective of the world, where, as has already been said, the basic roles were assigned to men. Women and children were only mentioned when their presence somehow enhanced the narrative concerning the primary subject. Needless to say, an exception to this general rule is found in the lives of female saints.

2.1. Women

In early mediaeval Bulgaria, the woman was excluded from the context of the primary course of events; this was a regular situation in the entire mediaeval world, dominated by religion. Responsible for the original sin according to the Scripture, and a symbol of sinfulness herself, the woman was bound to remain in the shadow of the man. Furthermore, while the life of the early mediaeval western European woman may be reconstructed with considerable precision based on the surviving sources (especially laws[12]), for her Bulgarian counterpart the extant information is most scanty. The reconstructions proposed by Sashka Georgieva[13] and Donka Petkanova[14] represent more of an idealised image of the woman, as considered appropriate by ecclesiastical authors and particularly in the extant

[12] Н. Христова, *Жените в Западна Европа, V–IX век*, Велико Търново 2004.

[13] С. Георгиева, *Жената в българското Средновековие*, Пловдив 2011.

[14] Д. Петканова, *Разноликото Средновековие*, Велико Търново 2006, pp. 131–159.

legal texts; as a matter of fact, however, this picture is rather far removed from that of an actual mediaeval woman. In the Bulgarian tradition, just like in Byzantium, the presence of women in source texts is a rarity; to the extent that they were mentioned at all, the women in question were almost invariably members of the aristocracy[15].

The crucial rituals and practices connected with marriage in the period under discussion were prescribed by ecclesiastical laws; nonetheless, certain specifically Bulgarian traits are visible too, aptly described in the *Response of Pope Nicholas I to the Bulgarians* (some of the relevant phenomena also echo in late 19th – early 20th century folk culture). This pertains e.g. to the dowry, described in responses III and XLIX[16], the premarital relations between the families and reaching marriage-related settlements (III)[17], the regulations concerning who can(not) marry whom (II, XXXIX)[18], the relations among the 'spiritual' fathers and sons (II)[19], the performance of the wedding ritual (III)[20], and second marriage due to widowhood or another reason (III)[21]. The concept of a second marriage did exist in the life of mediaeval Bulgarians, although it was only possible for men – following the death of the first wife (III)[22] or her act of adultery (XCVII)[23]. As regards widows, they were expected to join a monastery (LXXXVII) – a custom to which the pope firmly objected, explaining that it was a form of violence against women[24].

[15] I. Kalavrezou, *Images of Women in Byzantium*, [in:] *Everyday Life in Byzantium*, ed. D. Papanikola-Bakirdzi, Athens 2002, p. 241.

[16] Nicholas I (ed. Д. Дечев), pp. 10–15, 58–60.

[17] Nicholas I (ed. Д. Дечев), pp. 10–15; cf. Л. Старева, *Български обичаи и ритуали*, София 2005, pp. 139–141.

[18] Nicholas I (ed. Д. Дечев), pp. 8–11, 46–47; Д. Маринов, *Българско обичайно право*, София 1995, pp. 150–153; Л. Старева, *Български...*, p. 132.

[19] Nicholas I (ed. Д. Дечев), pp. 8–11; Д. Маринов, *Българско...*, p. 153.

[20] Nicholas I (ed. Д. Дечев), pp. 10–15; Д. Маринов, *Българско...*, pp. 157–158.

[21] Nicholas I (ed. Д. Дечев), pp. 12–15; Д. Маринов, *Българско...*, pp. 165–167.

[22] Nicholas I (ed. Д. Дечев), pp. 12–13.

[23] Nicholas I (ed. Д. Дечев), pp. 94–95.

[24] Nicholas I (ed. Д. Дечев), pp. 90–91.

According to one survey of the legal situation of women and children in the newly Christian Bulgarian state, based on the extant legal texts of the period in question, the Bulgarian society underwent a 'revolution of sorts' encompassing institutions, administration of justice, social order, marriage, and proprietary relations: it was the time when written regulations replaced customary laws[25]. This 'revolution' is also said to have engendered far-reaching changes in the life and status of the woman in the early mediaeval Bulgarian society, as manifested in the fact that *the new laws (the* **Законъ соудный людьмъ** *[Law for Judging the People] as well as the Slavic Ekloga) provided women and children with extensive legal protection, as a result of which the husband, his father or other male relatives were no longer able to deal with them as they wished*[26].

No Eurasian society (be it classical or barbarian, sedentary or nomadic) known from historical sources from Antiquity or the Middle Ages fails to display some kind of protection of private property and marriage (either to one or to multiple wives). This can be conveniently illustrated by the fact that each and every offense connected with family life and relations between the sexes known from mediaeval Bulgaria had a counterpart in the Byzantine society; the relevant transgressions had, in fact, been incriminated already in the pagan Roman laws, long before the Roman Empire became a Christian state[27]. This latter fact plainly demonstrates that this regulatory force was hardly introduced by Christianity; rather, it is embedded in every society, independent of its religious beliefs.

In view of the facts described above, it can scarcely be claimed that an actual 'revolution' swept the Bulgarian society due to its accepting Christianity as the official religion. No phenomenon like this can be observed in the institutions, which generally retained their customary Proto-Bulgarian names; in the rare cases when these were changed

---

[25] Л. Симеонова, *Правна защита на жените и децата в новопокръстеното българско общество (Закон за съдене на хората, Еклога)*, SB 27, 2009, p. 117.

[26] *Ibidem*, p. 124.

[27] Cf. Г. Петрова, *Престъпленията в средновековна България*, София 1992, pp. 81–130.

(the introduction of the imperial title would serve as the prime example here), this can be ascribed to certain quite specific circumstances. Similarly, no substantial change is discernible in the sphere of administration of justice.

The non-revolutionary character of the period in question is conspicuous in the cycle of miracles of St. George known as the *Tale of the Iron Cross*, where it can be observed that a Bulgarian woman enjoyed significantly more rights than her Byzantine sister. In two successive instances in the *Tale* – to wit, in the 6th miracle (i.e. the *Miracle of the Possessed Youth*) as well as in the transition to the following, 7th miracle – the narrative mentions the division of property within the family; in both cases, women participate in the process actively. In the first example, the woman in question is a widowed mother dealing with her son, and in the second – a wife dealing with her husband[28]. In the former case, the division is described thus:

> Some days later, the youth came to an agreement with his mother and, having bid farewell to her, he left. And taking half of the possessions, he gave it away, freeing four people who had been his subjects, and became a monk.[29]

The second split – between a married couple – had the following form: *The two of us have divided our possessions and freed our subjects – about 15 people, giving them the necessary means of subsistence…*[30] Thus, in the first of the divisions under discussion, we may note the fully equal status of both of the surviving members of the family – the widowed mother and the son; no discrimination based on gender or age is applied. Although not described as explicitly as the first case, even the second one is arguably likely to represent an instance of equal division of the property in half, given the way the splitting is described (as a common act, administered together). Based on these two accounts, then, it could be asserted that – as far as possession is concerned – women in the early mediaeval Bulgarian society were on equal terms with men.

---

[28] *Tale of the Iron Cross*, pp. 201–202.
[29] *Tale of the Iron Cross*, p. 201.
[30] *Tale of the Iron Cross*, p. 202.

In the times following the adoption of Christianity in Bulgaria, the geographical proximity of Byzantium as well as the common religion resulted in numerous similarities in the sphere of daily life in the two states. Accordingly, the existing information concerning Byzantine women is potentially of use for analysing the situation in Bulgaria. In the Byzantine Empire, as in the Christian world in general, women were strictly barred from public (let alone political) life. There was no place for them in either state or church hierarchy. They were allotted a more active role in the private sphere, however – particularly within the family. A 'good' woman was expected to proceed through four roles: virgin, wife, mother and widow; the 'bad' ones were those who did not fit into the above model in any way, especially prostitutes[31]. The most vital social role of the woman was motherhood[32]. It is by no means coincidental that the most revered figure in Christianity aside from Christ himself is his mother – the Theotokos, with the focus precisely on her maternal role. The second most important function of the woman, subordinate only to motherhood, was that of caring for the home[33]. This role entailed providing food for the family (preparing the basic products) as well as the production of clothes, etc.

In medieval literature, as in the contemporary society in general, there existed two parallel stereotypes to which women were compared: Eve (symbolising sin) and the Theotokos (symbolising motherhood, mercy and the hope for salvation). There were also numerous aphorisms concerning the two types of women – 'good' and 'bad'; depending on the point of view of a given compiler, the former or the latter type dominated[34]. These two entirely opposed perspectives of the woman can also be observed at the level of everyday life, as evidenced by epigraphy and graffiti. Among the many mundane objects unearthed during the excavations in Preslav, we find a seemingly ordinary spindle whorl; it would hardly attract any attention were it not for the fact that it bears an inscription. Carefully engraved by someone's hand, it reads: **ЛОЛИНЪ ПРѦСЛЕНЪ**

[31] L. J a m e s, *Men, Women, Eunuchs: Gender, Sex, and Power*, [in:] *The Social History of Byzantium*, ed. J. H a l d o n, Oxford 2009, p. 35.

[32] *Ibidem*.

[33] *Ibidem*.

[34] Д. П е т к а н о в а, *Разноликото*..., pp. 11, 132.

(*Lola's whorl*)[35]. On the other hand, even more interestingly, a graffito reading **МАРИНА СОУКА СОУКА ЧРИВАВА** (*Marina, bitch, pregnant bitch*) has been found in what is perhaps the least expected place – among the ruins of a monastery, namely the one near Ravna[36].

When discussing the Bulgarian women of the period, it is interesting to note a remark by Byzantine historian Leo the Deacon – a contemporary 'onlooker from the side-lines' – concerning female members of the aristocracy. Recounting the wedding of two minor Bulgarian princesses to Byzantine emperors Basil II and Constantine VIII, he mentions that the two girls were put on carts, adding that: *it is customary for Mysian* [i.e. Bulgarian] *women to ride on wagons*[37].

In the social life of early cultures, one of the principal aspects distinguishing women according to position and status was dress. An ethnographic analysis of the clothing of a Bulgarian woman from the previous century enables us to produce her 'portrait' – that is, to determine her region of origin, her financial status, whether she is a 'maiden', wife or widow, etc.[38] It should be assumed that women's clothing in the First Bulgarian Empire conveyed all of this information as well; however, the scarcity of the pertinent pictorial and archaeological data makes it challenging to reconstruct early mediaeval women's attire and image with any greater precision.

In a man's world such as the Middle Ages, where women only rarely found their way to written sources, their social status connected them first and foremost with motherhood and home life. Apart from these unalienable duties, however, the life of a Bulgarian woman during the pagan period would sometimes involve certain typically masculine actions and behaviours such as participation in the defence of the country. Bigamy was not uncommon among the population. On the other hand, as opposed to the women of the Byzantine Empire, Bulgarian women enjoyed

[35] K. Popkonstantinov, O. Kronstainer, *Старобългарски надписи*, vol. I, Salzburg 1994, p. 189.

[36] *Ibidem*, pp. 220–221.

[37] Leo the Deacon, V, 3, p. 80 (transl. p. 131).

[38] Р. Ганева, *Знаците на българското традиционно облекло*, София 2003, pp. 7–161.

considerable property rights; they paralleled those of men, as testified to by both legal and narrative sources. The imposition of Christianity by the Bulgarian state and the accompanying introduction of new church laws did not bring about immediate changes in day-to-day existence, whose pivotal aspects continued to be regulated by customary law until as late as the beginning of the 20th century. As regards the everyday life of women, it was – save for a handful of privileges – mostly regulated by a great number of prohibitions of both utilitarian and superstitious/religious character. Women's dress of the period was characterised by comfort and practicality in the case of the ordinary population and by exquisiteness in that of the aristocracy.

2.2. Children

Children during the Middle Ages remained deep in the shadow of their parents; it may, in fact, be more correct to call them their shadows. They were instructed to behave like adults from their early years. All of their activities, their play, and even their dress mimicked that of their parents.

Christianity teaches that the conception of each human being occurs in sin; but on the other hand, the Church clearly trusted that the growth of 'God's children' turned them into living symbols of the Lord's glory[39]. Giving birth – due to the lack of proper knowledge in this sphere among the population, and in view of the level of popular medicine – was tremendously perilous both for the mother and the new-born child. Not infrequently, the outcome would be fatal for both. The first few hours were crucial for the new-born's adaptation and survival. This was presumably the reason behind arranging an 'incubation period' of sorts for the mother and her baby. In this connection, we may mention answer LXVIII from the *Response of Pope Nicholas I to the Bulgarians*, where the question concerns the number of days following birth after which the mother may

[39] Р. Ф о с и е, *Обикновеният човек през Средновековието*, transl. В. Б о я д ж и е в а, София 2009, p. 40.

enter the church[40]. In the popular tradition, the period between giving birth and the reintegration with the remainder of the community was limited to 40 days.

The subsequent key moment in the life of a child in mediaeval Bulgaria was baptism. After it was carried out, the child became part of the Christian community. Even if it managed to survive the first forty days, the child was bound to confront a whole array of deadly diseases, quite often leading to a premature death. The data from early mediaeval necropolises show a stunningly high rate of child mortality, reaching 63% at some burial sites[41]. Thus, due to their fragility, children were viewed as particularly precious in the Bulgarian society; they were carefully raised and scrupulously protected. This is evident from the abundant number of apotropaic objects discovered with children's burials in cemeteries[42].

Having survived all the potential complications of infancy – which, due to natural selection, was exclusively the privilege of the most viable individuals – young people of both sexes faced the transition to the category of adults[43]. They had to demonstrate that they were fit to occupy the appropriate place among the adults of the society to which they belonged, with full rights. This was done in accordance with special initiation rituals, which were simultaneously a form of trial for the youngsters, designed to show to what extent they were ready to be accepted to the group of adults. However, the existence of initiation rituals among Bulgarians of the period under discussion is only attested to by indirect data[44].

[40] Nicholas I (ed. Д. Дечев), pp. 76–77.

[41] С. Ангелова, Л. Дончева-Петкова, М. Даскалов, *Двуобредният ранносредновековен некропол край село Топола, Каварненска община*, [in:] *Проблеми на прабългарската история и култура*, vol. III, ed. Р. Рашев, Шумен 1997, p. 143; Е. Коматарова-Балинова, *Децата в обществото на средновековните българи (по данни от езическите некрополи)*, [in:] *Eurika. In honorem Ludmilae Donchevae-Petkovae*, ed. В. Григоров, М. Даскалов, София 2009, pp. 185–186.

[42] Е. Коматарова-Балинова, *Децата...*, p. 195.

[43] Initiations in various contexts, in diverse geographical settings and in different variants have been studied, the most fully by Mircea Eliade. Cf.: М. Элиаде, *Тайные общества. Обряды, инициации и посвящения*, Москва–Санкт-Петербург 1999, pp. 23–253.

[44] Н. Хрисимов, *За прехода от детство към зрелост в българското Ранно средновековие*, BalkF 19.1/2, 2016, pp. 92–100.

The life of each child was filled with various sorts of games and play, as it mostly still is nowadays. Bulgarian children would play both all the games known from the adult world – such as draughts (Bulg. *dama*), knucklebones (or jacks; Bulg. *ashitsi*), or backgammon and chess in the case of aristocracy – and a whole range of typical children's games, largely consisting in imitating the activities of adults. Toys – the 'trademark' of childhood – were manufactured from various materials; in view of the exceptionally poor level of preservation to our times, it may be surmised that they were generally not durable. Although no toys made of organic materials are extant in Bulgaria, we may illustrate this point with similar objects that have survived in related contemporary cultures, such as Rus' or the Alans (in the Caucasus)[45]. They show that, irrespective of the geographic location, toys replicated the form of objects used by adults, while children's play imitated the behaviour of their parents and was aimed at developing habits that would become useful in their later lives.

In the Proto-Bulgarian tradition, the firstborn heirs to the throne as well as their younger brothers (who might potentially inherit the throne too) bore special titles. These were ὁ κανάρ τικείνος and βουλίας ταρκάνος – i.e., respectively, *kanartikin* and *boila tarkan* (*vulia tarkan*). In Constantine VII Porphyrogennetos' *Book of Ceremonies*, they are mentioned next to one another immediately following the ruler and his consort[46]. Royal children would – just as their 'regular' counterparts – generally spend their time playing. Next to that, however, they were educated so that they could, one day, fulfil their prospective duties. We have reliable information on these matters from the time following Christianisation.

---

[45] Cf. Н.А. Морозова, *Игрушки Древнего Новгорода*, [in:] *Новгород и Новгородская земля. История и археология. (Тезисы научной конференции)*, vol. III, ed. И.Ю. Акундинов, Новгород 1990, pp. 69–71; А.А. Йерусалимская, *Кавказ на Шелковом пути*, Санкт-Петербург 1992 (№ 23, 24); eadem, *Мощевая Балка: необычный археологический памятник на Северокавказском Шелковом пути*, Санкт-Петербург 2012, p. 205, ill. 122/а–г. It is also worth noting that, like clothes worn by children, even clothes of dolls are not assigned to a separate category, but rather included in the general gender-based classification introduced by the author.

[46] Constantine VII Porphyrogennetos, *The Book of Ceremonies*, II, 47, p. 681.

A special compilation of texts – dubbed the **Кънѧжии изборьникъ**[47] (*Knyazhii Izbornik*, i.e. 'Prince's Miscellany') by William R. Veder – was created in order to serve as a handbook for the heirs to the throne. This was a gnomology miscellany, i.e. an anthology comprising aphorisms and wisdoms. Its conception as well as the use of a question-and-answer format unmistakably show that the *Izbornik* had pedagogical purposes and was envisaged as personal instruction from father to son. This is also evident from the fact that the most common verbal form used in the *Izbornik* is the second-person imperative. Emphasis in these texts is laid on Christian dogma and ethics[48].

As indicated above, the text also makes it possible to determine the addressee of the miscellany more exactly. It is clear that he belonged to the young generation of an affluent family; but the fact that the final part of the work is modelled on the *Mirror for Justinian* (a 'mirror of princes' written for emperor Justinian I) directly indicates that it was meant for the heir to the throne. Another clue pointing in this direction is the exchange **цѣсарь – кънѧзь** ('emperor' -- 'prince') in the forms of address used in the text[49].

Through the analysis of certain textologically related works, Veder traces the stages of the development of the *Prince's Miscellany* and hypothetically reconstructs the following three redactions:

1) the so-called *Menaion Izbornik*, compiled ca. 900 for *kanartikins* Michael and Peter;

2) the *Knyazhii Izbornik*, compiled ca. 930 for *kanartikin* Boris (II);

3) the *Izbornik of John the Sinner* compiled ca. 960 for the heir of tsar Boris II[50].

---

[47] У. Федер, ***Кънѧжии изборьникъ** за възпитание на канартикина*, vol. I, *Увод и показалци*, vol. II, *Текст*, Велико Търново 2008.

[48] *Ibidem*, vol. I, p. 10. Further details on the *Prince's Miscellany* and *Izbornik 1076* can be found here, in the chapter 7.1.

[49] *Ibidem*, p. 11.

[50] *Ibidem*, p. 12; W.R. Veder, *A Certain Father's Edifying Words to His Son*, [in:] У.Р. Федер, *Хиляда години като един ден*, София 2005, p. 139–144; idem, *За една*

The reconstructed date of the completion of the *Menaion Izbornik* makes it plain that its author must have been none other than tsar Symeon himself.

The latest of the three – the *Izbornik of John the Sinner* – was stolen from the royal library in Preslav in 971 and served as the protograph of the *Izbornik of 1076*, also known as the *Second Izbornik of Symeon* or as the *Izbornik of Svyatoslav*[51].

In view of the concrete addressee of the miscellany, its circulation was apparently limited to one exemplar per generation; this type of dynasty-internal imperial pedagogy is a quite exceptional phenomenon, without parallel in other mediaeval European cultures[52]. In Byzantium, for example, the so-called 'mirrors of princes' would enter the court from outside (to the exception of the *Counsels on Imperial Conduct*, written ca. 1406–1413 by emperor Manuel II Palaiologos[53]), whereas here the author of the earliest *Izbornik* may be identified as tsar Symeon himself.

If the children of the Bulgarian imperial family spent their time on activities and play useful for their future, the childhood of ordinary Bulgarians was hardly as pre-planned. Their life abounded in adversities and hardships both in its earliest stages and later on.

The existence of such moments of serious trouble is testified to by the practice of *izgoystvo*, i.e. selling one's own children, known from pagan Bulgaria. The existence of the custom is attested e.g. in the so-called *Foreword to Repentance*, a recently identified text dating back to the period shortly after Christianisation[54]. One of the later redactions of the *Foreword*, preserved in the *Miscellany of Paisiy* of the 14th century, differs from the original primarily by certain stylistic corrections; but there are also three essential modifications, showing the mitigation of the harsh

тълкувателна творба, преведена от Методиевите ученици, [in:] i d e m, *Хиляда...*, pp. 145–150; i d e m, *The Izbornik of John the Sinner: A Compilation from Compilations*, [in:] i d e m, *Хиляда...*, p. 185–199.

[51] I d e m, *За една тълкувателна...*, p. 145.

[52] I d e m, **Кънажии изборьникъ**..., vol. I, p. 12.

[53] *Ibidem*, p. 12, fn. 7.

[54] А. К а л о я н о в, *Славянската православна цивилизация. Началото: 28 март 894 г.*, Плиска–Велико Търново 2007, pp. 32, 299.

requirements of the time immediately following Christianisation. The passage concerning the practice of *izgoystvo* is shortened and fitted out with a new ending, based on the *Sermon on Spiritual Benefit* by Peter the Monk. This addition of a part of Peter the Monk's work indicates that the redaction under discussion arose later than the middle of the 10th century; this is confirmed by the softened tone. The above-mentioned alterations show which of the two variants represents the original text and to what period it should be dated[55]. Even if we were to retain certain reservations about this text's belonging to the output of the very founders of ecclesiastical life in the First Bulgarian Empire – and, consequently, about the presence of the practice of selling one's children in their time – there is blatant evidence for the phenomenon from a slightly later period: an Old Bulgarian source from the 11th–12th century mentions it directly. The text in question is a later addition found in a richly decorated lectionary gospel written in Greek, dating back to the 9th–10th century[56]. The Bulgarian text is an 'agreement' between an anonymous priest – presumably the one writing – and a woman by the name of Dobrina, the head of the family, who 'donates' her child (of unspecified sex) to him. The full text reads:

> I, Dobrina, have donated my child to the priest, and [received?] the 'Field of the Good Guests' near Drazhil's field. Let none of my children nor anyone of my family get confused [argue] with the priest, also concerning the fact that he gave him… Because he also gave me 7 ells of cotton cloth and 5 [ells] of linen and 3 orbs [measures, bushels] of wheat.[57]

Clearly, then, the practice of 'donating' children was known in mediaeval Bulgaria, which should be associated with nothing else but the above-mentioned institution of *izgoystvo*. A mother who resorted to 'donating' her child was no doubt in particularly severe predicaments. In traditional Bulgarian culture, such a child is referred to as a *braneniche*

[55] *Ibidem*, pp. 33–34.

[56] И. Д у й ч е в, *Български спогодбен акт от епохата на византийското владичество*, [in:] i d e m, *Българско средновековие*, София 1972, pp. 209–215.

[57] *Ibidem*, pp. 211, 213.

('fosterling')[58]. By giving away the child, the family would secure its future. The passage from the lectionary gospel provides a firm piece of evidence suggesting that the practice is considerably old – harking back to pagan times and only changing its name in the subsequent centuries.

The death of a family member – whether already adult or not – was a common occurrence. There was no dearth of perilous situations, e.g. during hunting or war for men and during childbirth or due to attacks of wild animals for women; thus, the risk of death was quite high at all times for both sexes. Having lost one of its parents, a child would receive its share of the family property. The text concerning the division of property between a widow and her son, discussed earlier above, illustrates this practice[59].

All characteristics of the life of children in mediaeval Bulgaria picture them as equal members of the society, preparing from their youngest years to occupy a given social sphere and copying the actions of adults at a proportionally smaller scale. Children's clothes likewise resembled those of adults.

3. Food and Nutrition

In order to understand what food in the First Bulgarian Empire was like, it is first necessary to review the foodstuffs that were certainly familiar to the people of the time and area in question.

Among foods of plant origin, grains were among the most commonplace. Traditionally, the most widely used grain was wheat[60]; traces of rye are commonly found in excavations as well[61]. Millet was the main raw

---

[58] Д. Маринов, *Българско обичайно...*, p. 123.

[59] *Tale of the Iron Cross*, p. 201.

[60] Ц. Попова, *Каталог на археоботаническите останки на територията на България (1980–2008)*, ИИз 20/21, 2009, pp. 141–142.

[61] *Ibidem*, p. 141; К. Шкорпил, *Домашний вид и промысел*, ИРАИК 10, 1905, p. 316; Й. Панайотов, М. Михов, *Кратка характеристика на основните*

material for the production of bread used by the poor population until corn appeared in Bulgarian lands; its presence is also testified to by paleobotanical findings[62]. The use of barley[63] and spelt[64] is attested as well. The consumption of rice by the aristocracy is confirmed by the presence of the lexeme in the short version of *The Romance of Alexander*[65]. As far as vegetables are concerned, those of the subfamily *Allioideae* (onion, garlic and leek) were the most widespread. Used both as staple foods and as spices in various dishes, they were apparently the only vegetables carefully distinguished from others. John the Exarch mentions bean plants in the *Hexameron*[66], while remnants of lentils and peas have been found in paleobotanical material[67]. The *Life of St. John of Rila* (from the *Dragan's Miney*) features one further plant of the bean family: *slanutak*[68], which is the name under which chickpeas are known in Bulgarian dialects (standard Bulgarian *nahut*)[69]. Direct written or archaeological evidence for the consumption of the plants of the cruciferous family by the Bulgarian population is wanting; nevertheless, given their use in Byzantium[70], we can also suspect their presence on the Bulgarian table. Besides, it is likely that the Old Bulgarian counterpart of the modern Bulgarian word *zele*, nowadays meaning 'cabbage', had collective value and designated all green vegetables from its family[71].

продоволствени и технически култури, [in:] *Дуранкулак*, vol. I, ed. Х. Тодорова, София 1989, p. 216.

[62] Ц. Попова, *Каталог...*, pp. 141–142; Й. Панайотов, М. Михов, *Кратка...*, p. 216.

[63] Й. Панайотов, М. Михов, *Кратка...*, p. 216.

[64] *Ibidem*.

[65] *Hellenic and Roman Chronicle*, p. 142; *Словарь русского языка X–XVII вв.*, vol. XIII, Москва 1987, p. 68.

[66] John of Exarch (transl. Н.Ц. Кочев), p. 122.

[67] Ц. Попова, *Каталог...*, p. 142; Й. Панайотов, М. Михов, *Кратка...*, p. 218.

[68] *Prologue Life of St. John of Rila*.

[69] Н. Геров, *Речник на българския език*, vol. V, Пловдив 1904, p. 190.

[70] Д. Димитров, *Масата събира, масата разделя: храната и храненето във Византия и различията по отношение на хранителните навици през Средновековието*, [in:] *Стандарти на всекидневието през Средновековието и Новото време*, ed. К. Мутафова et al., Велико Търново 2012, p. 24.

[71] I. Tarnanidis, *The Psalter of Dimitri the Oltarnik*, [in:] idem, *The Slavonic Manuscripts Discovered in 1975 at St. Catherine's Monastery on Mount Sinai*, Thessaloniki

Like in Byzantium, wild plants such as dock, lettuce and nettle were used for culinary purposes[72].

The chief application of herbs (including spices) at the time was for healing purposes. Herbs were widely used for treating various diseases and wounds. This is evident from the only book of cures dating to the period in question found thus far. It is preserved on three inserted pages in the so-called *Psalter of Dimitri the Oltarnik*, discovered in St. Catherine's monastery in Sinai (f. 141 A, B and C)[73]. Among the items found there are **р҄ѣп҄ѣи** (burdock), **лоуг҄ъ** (onion), **корень** (root) and others.

A reliable picture of the fruit known and consumed in mediaeval Bulgaria may be gleaned from John the Exarch's *Hexameron*, a work in which apples[74], grapes[75], figs[76], pears[77] and other items are mentioned in various contexts. Paleobotanical evidence confirms the presence and use of cherries[78] and mulberries[79]. Some evidence for the use of melons and muskmelons is available[80]. The possibility should not be excluded that wild berries such as raspberries, blackberries, rosehips and others (all found in forests of the entire Balkan Peninsula until today) were consumed too. The use of walnuts and almonds is, again, mentioned in the *Hexameron*[81]. Wild hazelnut probably occurred as well. The above-mentioned survey certainly does not exhaust the full range of foods of plant origin actually consumed in mediaeval Bulgaria, but the written sources, supported

---

1988, pp. 91–100; Б. Величева, *Новооткрити ръкописи в Синайския манастир "Св. Екатерина"*, Pbg 12.3, 1988, pp. 126–129.

[72] Д. Димитров, *Масата...*, p. 25.

[73] I. Tarnanidis, *The Psalter...*, pp. 91–100; Б. Величева, *Новооткрити...*, pp. 126–129.

[74] John of Exarch (transl. Н.Ц. Кочев), pp. 106, 108, 111, 129.

[75] John of Exarch (transl. Н.Ц. Кочев), pp. 105–107, 126, 129 etc.

[76] John of Exarch (transl. Н.Ц. Кочев), pp. 106, 108, 111, 128.

[77] John of Exarch (transl. Н.Ц. Кочев), p. 108.

[78] Ц. Попова, *Каталог...*, p. 142.

[79] T. Popova, *Archaeobotanic data about the Origin of the Fruit Trees on the Territory of Bulgaria. A View of the Past*, ABu 9.1, 2005, p. 41, tab. 1.

[80] С. Станчев, *Разкопки и новооткрити материали в Плиска през 1948 г.*, ИАИ 20, 1955, p. 192.

[81] John of Exarch (transl. Н.Ц. Кочев), pp. 106, 110, 127.

by paleobotanical data (extremely limited in the case of early mediaeval Bulgaria), yield such a picture.

The aristocracy (especially the royal court) also made use of various imported items, supplied from different regions, predominantly from the Byzantine Empire. The diversity of food of plant origin in the southern neighbour of the First Bulgarian Empire is eloquently documented by the *Geoponika*[82], a Byzantine agricultural encyclopaedia; additional material is provided by modern research[83].

Based on the frequency of references to different kinds of crops in the *Farmer's Law* – one of the first Byzantine laws to be translated and implemented in the Bulgarian state – it could be argued that the primary focus of the Bulgarian farmer in the period following Christianisation was on fields with cereal crops (of various kinds) and vineyards. Fruit trees and their cultivation remained somewhat peripheral to the interests of both the farmers themselves and those who attempted to do damage to them[84].

Food of animal origin comprised meat, items made of milk, and bird eggs. Meat provided the early mediaeval man with basic nutritional proteins and fats. The chief way of obtaining meat in the period was by raising livestock[85]. Slaughtered animals also provided the population with a wealth of other materials and resources necessary for everyday life, such as hides (used for clothing, footwear, elements of weapons and tools, etc.), wool (for clothing), tallow (for lighting), or bones and horn (for various items of everyday use as well as elements of tools and weapons). Additional ways of procuring meat in early mediaeval Bulgaria were hunting and fishing. However, osteological evidence from bones recovered from various early mediaeval settlements indicates that meat obtained through hunting and fishing generally constituted no more than 3–4% of the total[86]; situations in which these sources accounted for as much as

[82] *Geoponika*.

[83] G. Simeonov, *Obst in Byzanz. Ein Beitrag zur Geschichte der Ernährung im* östlichen *Mittelmeerraum*, Saarbrücken 2013.

[84] *Farmer's Law*.

[85] Л. Нинов, *Някои аспекти на животновъдството през Средновековието*, ИИз 17, 1990, pp. 95–96.

[86] *Ibidem*, tab. 1 and 2.

15% of overall animal consumption were exceptional[87]. Early mediaeval Bulgarian farms primarily kept mammals as sources of food and materials: cattle, pigs, sheep, goats, horses, and donkeys[88]. Certain kinds of poultry were raised too (chickens, ducks, and geese)[89]; nevertheless, mammals dominated, amounting to over 90% of domestic animal populations[90]. Among mammals, cattle had the largest share (oscillating between 50% and 60% in individual settlements), followed by pigs. Small ruminants (sheep and goats) occupied the third position, the share of sheep being at all times much higher than that of goats[91]. Domesticated fowl, as indicated above, only constituted an insignificant percentage of the animals raised, rarely exceeding 5%[92], from which over 80% were chickens. The generalised data show that beef was by far the most widely consumed meat item in early mediaeval Bulgaria, eaten overwhelmingly more often than

---

[87] В. Василев, *Животновъдство и лов в живота на населението от средновековното селище край Дуранкулак*, [in:] *Дуранкулак*..., p. 243. 16.34% of the overall number of bones found belong to wild animals, constituting 21.85% of the minimal number of individuals.

[88] Л. Нинов, *Някои аспекти*..., tab. 1 and 2; В. Василев, *Животновъдство и лов*..., p. 227, tab. 1.

[89] В. Василев, *Животновъдство и лов*..., p. 227, tab. 1; Н. Илиев, З. Боев, *Птиците в храната на населението от Външния град на Велики Преслав (IX–X в.)*, ИИз 17, 1990, pp. 91–94.

[90] С. Иванов, *Животински костни остатъци от селището в местността Джеджови лозя при с. Попина*, [in:] Ж. Въжарова, *Славянски и славянобългарски селища в българските земи от края на VI–XI век*, София 1965, p. 208, tab. 2; Л. Нинов, *Домашните и дивите животни от средновековното и укрепено селище край с. Хума, Разградски окръг*, [in:] Р. Рашев, С. Станилов, *Старобългарското укрепено селище при с. Хума, Разградски окръг*, РП 17, 1987, p. 173, tab. 1; Л. Нинов, *Животновъдна и ловна дейност на обитателите на крепостта*, [in:] В. Йотов, Г. Атанасов, *Скала. Крепост от X–XI век до с. Кладенци, Тервелско*, София 1998, p. 330, tab. 1. An exception in this respect is furnished by the settlement on the island near Durankulak, where their share in the population of household animals is ca. 80%.

[91] Л. Нинов, *Домашните и дивите*..., p. 178.

[92] Н. Илиев, З. Боев, *Птиците в храната*..., p. 91; С. Иванов, *Животински костни*..., p. 208, tab. 1; Л. Нинов, *Животновъдна и ловна*..., p. 330, tab. 1. Again, the settlement near Durankulak turns out to be exceptional with regard to the statistic in question: here, the percentage of poultry relative to other kinds of domestic animals is higher, while chickens are less numerous than ducks (В. Василев, *Животновъдство и лов*..., p. 227, tab. 1).

any of the remaining ones. The second and third most popular choices were pork and lamb, respectively, while poultry was a rare delicacy. This hierarchy of importance and preference among various kinds of meat in the period under discussion is reflected in the *Tale of the Iron Cross* cycle, specifically in the *Miracle of St. George with the Bulgarian*. Leaving for battle, the protagonist, George, says:

> Before leaving for war, I summoned the priest and a service was held. I slaughtered the most valuable [the most beautiful] ox as well as 10 sheep and 10 pigs; I gave them away to the poor and left for war.[93]

As regards wild mammals, the following ones were used for food: wild boars, deer, hares, aurochs, bison, as well as – in coastal areas – dolphins[94]. Certain birds were also hunted for food, such as swans, pelicans, pheasants and eagles (?)[95].

Fishing covered part of the nutritional needs as well. Depending on what type of water basin a given settlement had access to, various kinds of fish were used as food: carp, catfish, sturgeon and others. In view of the poor durability of their bones, the traces discovered are exceptionally scanty[96].

Domesticated mammals were the source of milk and its products. Cows probably provided the bulk of the milk, considering the generally large numbers of cattle and the high milk yield relative to other mammals.

---

[93] *Tale of the Iron Cross*, p. 199.

[94] В. Василев, *Животновъдство и лов*..., p. 227, tab. 1; С. Иванов, *Животински костни*..., p. 208, tab. 2; С. Иванов, *Храната от животински*..., p. 212, tab. 1; Н. Спасов, Н. Илиев, *Костни останки от зубър* (*Bison Bonasus L.*) *в средновековното селище край с. Гарван, Силистренски окръг*, [in:] Ж. Въжарова, *Средновековното селище с. Гарван, Силистренски окръг VI–XI в.*, София 1986, p. 68; Л. Нинов, *Домашните и дивите*..., p. 173, tab. 1; Л. Нинов, *Животновъдна и ловна*..., p. 330, tab. 1.

[95] В. Василев, *Животновъдство и лов*..., p. 227, tab. 1; С. Иванов, *Животински костни*..., p. 209; З. Боев, *Костни останки от птици*, [in:] Ж. Въжарова, *Средновековното*..., p. 68; Н. Илиев, З. Боев, *Птиците в храната*..., p. 92.

[96] С. Иванов, *Животински костни*..., p. 209; В. Василев, *Животновъдство и лов*..., pp. 227 (tab. 1), 243.

The milk of small ruminants followed second in importance. As concerns poultry, the principal product other than meat were eggs; their remnants are frequently recovered as grave goods in pagan burial grounds[97]. Evidence from the Preslav court shows that – unlike for the ordinary masses – chicken was the meat of choice there, consumed overwhelmingly more often than in ordinary settlements[98]. Sturgeon and shark were further luxurious items in the palace menu[99]; also noteworthy is the preference for lamb and goat meat, followed by pork, and only in the third place by beef[100].

The primary source of the necessary sugars was wine, as well as bee honey. The latter's widespread presence, production and use during the period is documented in the *Book of the Eparch* – it is mentioned as one of the foremost Bulgarian export products sent to the markets of Constantinople, alongside linen fabrics[101].

Following the harvest, the crops were threshed on threshing boards[102]. The grain was stored in pots or, more often, in hollows carved out in floors of dwellings. Before it could be turned into bread, grain first had to be ground into flour. Depending on their social status, the various classes of society consumed bread of different quality and composition. It appears probable that aristocracy ate wheat bread, while the bread of ordinary people was made of flour obtained from wheat mixed with other grains (rye, barley, oats, millet), or from yet different grain crops. Grinding grain into flour was done in mills[103]. The use of the most primitive method of grinding grain – with quern-stones – is attested archaeologically across

---

[97] See numerous examples in: Ж. Въжарова, *Славяни и прабългари по данни на некрополите от VI–XI в. на територията на България*, София 1976.

[98] С. Иванов, *Храната от животински произход на обитателите на Южната порта в Преслав*, ИАИ 22, 1959, p. 212, tab. 1.

[99] *Ibidem*, p. 212 tab. 1.

[100] *Ibidem*, p. 212.

[101] *Book of the Eparch*, IX, 6.

[102] Michael the Syrian (p. 17) informs us about the use of threshing boards, but for purposes quite different from threshing, by emperor Nikephoros I during his stay in the Bulgarian capital in 811. He recounts that the atrocities of the emperor went as far as ordering the use of threshing boards for crushing small children.

[103] *Farmer's Law*, 82.

the territory of Bulgaria[104]. In view of the small size (and consequently, weight) of these quern-stones, the grain was ground quite coarsely, yielding a kind of flour rather similar to fine groats. The Old Bulgarian word **брашьно** denoted 'food, something to eat'[105]. Based on this broader meaning of the word, one could try to connect it with other possibilities of the culinary use of grains – such as, for example, boiling it directly to achieve a kind of porridge. The resulting product could be consumed on its own, alongside meat, or in yet other ways[106]. The consumption of porridge in early mediaeval Bulgaria is attested in the writings of John the Exarch[107]. Bread consumption may be associated with different population groups, but not categories. Following the adoption of Christianity as the official religion through Constantinople, the consumption of unleavened bread was hardly possible[108]. Bread was baked in *podnitsas* (traditional earthenware vessels) or on ante-furnace platforms within dwellings[109]. The comparison of the way of making bread and porridge from grains leads to

---

[104] Т. Михайлова, *Сгради и съоръжения на запад от Тронната палата в Плиска – X–XI в.*, ППре 5, 1993, pp. 170–184; Л. Дончева-Петкова, *Сгради при южния сектор на западната крепостна стена на Плиска*, ППре 5, 1993, p. 133, ill. 27; С. Михайлов, Г. Джингов, В. Вълов, В. Димова, Ранносредновековно селище при с. Стърмен, РП 7, 1982, pp. 17 (ill. 3, 8, 9, 10), 26 (ill. 18–20); Х. Тодорова, *Архитектурата на средновековното селище*, [in:] *Дуранкулак...*, pp. 45–48, ill. 12, 13.

[105] *Старославянский словарь (по рукописям X–XI вв.)*, ed. Р.М. Цейтлин, Р. Вечерка, Э. Благова, Москва 1994, p. 101; М. Цибранска-Костова, *Покайната книжнина на Българското средновековие IX–XVIII век*, София 2011, pp. 72–73.

[106] Cf. Н. Хрисимов, *Храната в Първото българско царство*, [in:] *Стандарти...*, pp. 212–215.

[107] John the Exarch (transl. Н.Ц. Кочев), p. 108.

[108] Д. Димитров, *Масата...*, p. 23.

[109] Apparently, the consolidation of bread as a staple food of the Bulgarians should be dated to the time of Byzantine rule and ascribed to Byzantine influence. In the 12th century, Gregory Antiochos already writes about several different types of bread among the Bulgarians, the most common being the one with ashes sticking to it, i.e. bread baked in a *podnitsa* or in the ante-furnace space. Cf. Gregory Antiochos, p. 280; Г. Цанкова-Петкова, П. Тивчев, *Нови данни за историята на Софийската област през последните десетилетия на византийското владичество*, ИИИ 14/15, 1964, pp. 315–324.

the conclusion that the population of the First Bulgarian Empire subsisted predominantly on porridges[110]. They are much quicker to prepare, and when combined with meat they are also significantly more nutritious than the traditional bread. Besides, the plants from the bean family – lentils, broad beans, peas and chickpeas (all well-known to, and widely used by, the population of the First Bulgarian Empire), are also convenient and were widely used to make porridges and soups.

Osteological research shows that after parts of animals were consumed, their bones were crushed so that marrow could be extracted. This is prime evidence for the fact that even the smallest bits of the animal carcass were considered of vital importance and consumed[111].

Meat – apart from being prepared using the easiest methods (with porridge, i.e. boiled) – was also probably *grilled, roasted and singed*, as remarked at a later period by Theophylaktos of Ohrid[112]. Incidentally, the latter author also observes that Bulgarians knew how to prepare jerked meat[113].

Another product of animal origin used for cooking and other household needs is butter, whose use during the reign of tsar Peter is indirectly confirmed by evidence from later times[114]. Byzantine emperor Romanos I Lekapenos mentions 'dairy' in a letter to tsar Symeon[115]. The word **сꙑръ** was known during the period in question; it is attested in the *Codex Suprasliensis*[116].

---

[110] Н. Хрисимов, *Храната...*, pp. 212–215.

[111] С. Иванов, *Храната от животински...*, pp. 209–210; Л. Нинов, *Домашните и дивите...*, pp. 173–174; idem, *Животновъдна и ловна...*, p. 329.

[112] Theophylaktos of Ohrid, *Letters* (transl. Симеон Варненски), 5, p. 7.

[113] Theophylaktos of Ohrid, *Letters* (transl. Симеон Варненски), 5, p. 58.

[114] *Tale of the Prophet Isaiah*, p. 401d.

[115] Theodore Daphnopates, 5. Whether the word is used here in a literal or figurative sense is irrelevant; the very occurrence of the lexeme is crucial. However, in note 4 on page 303 of *FGHB*, vol. IV it is suggested that the word *mandri* may refer to fortresses.

[116] *Старославянский словарь...*, p. 676.

Next to wine, certain other, more special kinds of drinks were used as well. Mead was the traditional drink of all Slavs[117]. The *Tale of the Iron Cross* cycle furnishes information on a few further drinks, to wit: **ѡпсимъ**, **оѵкропъ** and **пиво** (**питїє/питиє**)[118].

The preparation and serving of all of the above-mentioned foods and drinks required the application of appropriate dishes. The ordinary population mostly made use of clay and wooden dishes, while those used by the aristocracy and the members of the court were made either of ceramic materials (with fine details) or of metal, sometimes even noble metals.

Ceramic dishes used in the early Middle Ages are divided by scholars into three large groups, depending on their purpose – storage, cooking, or dining[119]. Storage ceramic vessels (cruses and amphorae) were used for keeping various food and drink products[120].

Water used for the preparation of food, as well as for drinking in the household, was carried in ceramic[121] or wooden buckets with metal fittings[122]. Various kinds of drinks were also carried in ceramic vessels[123] or in leather sacks with bone valves[124].

---

[117] И. Павлов, *Присъствия на храненето*..., p. 76.

[118] More on these drinks cf. in: Y.M. Hristov, N. Hrissimov, *Aspects of everyday life in the Old-Bulgarian hagiographical cycle of stories "A Tale of the Iron Cross"*, ДСб 10, 2017, pp. 110–120.

[119] Л. Дончева-Петкова, *Българска битова керамика през ранното средновековие*, София 1977, pp. 33–110; Р. Рашев, *Българската езическа култура VII–IX век*, София 2008, pp. 175–185.

[120] Л. Дончева-Петкова, *Българска битова*..., pp. 98–104.

[121] See on those in: Л. Бобчева, *Две грънчарски пещи в ранносредновековното селище при с. Топола, Толбухински окръг*, ИНМВ 13 (28), 1977, pp. 172–176; eadem, *Глинени котли от ранносредновековното селище при с. Топола, Толбухински окръг*, ИНМВ 16 (31), 1980, pp. 126–130.

[122] See on those in: Д.И. Димитров, *Новооткрит раннобългарски некропол при Девня*, ИНМВ 7 (22), 1971, p. 68, ill. 13; Ж. Въжарова, *Славяни и прабългари*..., p. 174; В. Йотов, Г. Атанасов, *Скала*..., p. 85, tab. LXXIX/142–145; Р. Рашев, *Българската езическа*..., p. 175.

[123] Р. Рашев, *За глинените бъклици в средновековна България*, ППре 1, 1979, pp. 206–209. The use of these vessels followed the ancient tradition.

[124] On their use among Avars see: C. Balogh, *Avar kori tömlővégek*, KDMK 22, 2016, pp. 193–216.

On the other hand, cooking and dining ceramics differed both with regard to form and to the material used. Cooking ceramics included pots and the lids that belonged to them, as well as pans and cauldrons with internal handles[125]. Pots were used for cooking; they were placed on the top part of household stoves (designed especially for holding vessels[126]), or directly over the embers, spread out in the ante-furnace part of the dwelling. Cauldrons with internal handles were used for cooking over open fire.

Dining ceramics included jugs, pitchers, amphora-like pitchers, cups, bowls and similar dishes[127]. Drinks were poured from the larger vessels into cups or bowls, made not only from clay, but also from wood, sometimes with metal fittings added[128]. Such a dish was known as a **кръчагъ**, a word attested both in 10th-century literary texts[129] and in graffiti inscriptions from the same period[130]. Bowls were used for serving the ready food on the table.

Some of the names of dishes used in the period in question are preserved in the so-called *Sinai Patericon* of the 11th–12th century, which is a copy of a translation (completed in the 10th century in Bulgaria) of the Greek *Λειμὼν πνευματινός* by John Moschos[131]. Thus, the vessels used on a daily basis by monks, mentioned in this patericon, are the following: **сосоудꙑ** – vessels, **гръньць** – pot, ceramic vessel, **комърогъ** – large (presumably clay) vessel, **коновь** – cauldron, **нъщьви** – tray, kneading trough, **скоудѣлъ** – large water vessel with a narrow neck, large bottle, **чаша** – cup, **кокваль** – (large) cup, **тꙑкꙑ** – gourd, and **палица** – wooden dish (plate or bowl)[132].

[125] Л. Дончева-Петкова, *Българска битова*..., p. 35.

[126] Т. Балабанов, *Селище в югозападната*..., pp. 140–141 and ill. 33/ 2, 3.

[127] Л. Дончева-Петкова, *Българска битова*..., p. 69; Р. Рашев, *Българската езическа*..., p. 181.

[128] С. Станчев, С. Иванов, *Некрополът до Нови Пазар*, София 1958, tab. XXXIII/ 1; Л. Дончева-Петкова, *Нови данни за некропол № 3 при Балчик*, ППИК 4.2, 2007, p. 138 and ill. 4/2.

[129] *Старославянский словарь*..., p. 296.

[130] K. Popkonstantinov, O. Kronstainer, *Старобългарски*..., vol. I, pp. 154–155, 204–205.

[131] Е. Зашев, *Наименования на съдове за течности и храни в Синайския патерик*, Ист 13.2/3, 2005, p. 91.

[132] *Ibidem*, pp. 97–98.

People would eat both using their hands alone (a fact confirmed by numerous ethnographic parallels with various regions around the world, both in modern times and in the past) and with utensils. The aristocracy used metal spoons and forks, the latter principally for serving[133]. It is conceivable that the ordinary population used the same utensils too, only made of non-durable materials such as wood, which would correspond to the picture known from ethnographic material[134].

4. Dwellings

The traditional dwelling in early mediaeval Bulgaria was a semi-dugout. The surface of these dwellings – usually rectangular in shape[135] – normally amounted to between 10 and 15 m², only exceptionally exceeding 20 m².[136] This suggests that they were inhabited by no more than a single family. Gable roofs were used, tailored to the existing resources and built from neutral materials (thatch). They were supported by beams whose bases were dug into the floor of the dwelling. Walls were sometimes lined with wooden planks[137]. Heating equipment (stoves) would be installed next to walls, on the side opposing the entrance[138]. Not infrequently, dwellings

[133] К. Константинов, *Прибори за хранене от Велики Преслав*, Пр.Сб 6, 2004, pp. 273–280; idem, *Прибори за хранене и приготвяне на храна от Плиска*, *Истор 1*, 2006, pp. 275–283.

[134] Д. Маринов, *Народна вяра и религиозни народни обичаи*, София 1994, p. 193.

[135] Р. Василев, *Функции и развитие на масовото жилище-полуземлянка в средновековна Плиска*, ППре 8, 2000, p. 103.

[136] К. Миятев, *Жилищната ахитектура в България през IX и X в.*, ИАИ 23, 1960, pp. 1–21; Д.И. Димитров, *Някои въпроси във връзка с изучаването на старобългарското масово жилище от VI–XI в. в Североизточна България*, [in:] *Архитектурата на Първата и Втората българска държава*, ed. Г. Кожухаров, София 1975, pp. 212–245.

[137] С. Михайлов, *Разкопки в Плиска през 1959–1961 г.*, ИАИ 26, 1963, pp. 12–13; Р. Василев, *Функции...*, p. 104.

[138] Р. Василев, *Функции...*, p. 103.

were also heated by centrally located hearths[139]. The floor of a dwelling featured carved-out hollows used for different household purposes, primarily storing grain[140].

Homes of the aristocracy (or at least those that may be identified as such without doubt) were located in the capitals Pliska and Preslav, universally built from stone in *opus quadratum*. Typical of the 10th century is the construction not of individual aristocratic dwellings, but of so-called secular complexes (it should be noted that some of the sites identified as monastic complexes in earlier scholarship may be safely considered secular[141]). Numerous such complexes were located within or in front of the fortifications of Veliki Preslav, in the so-called agglomeration[142]; apart from residential buildings and a church, each comprised various utility buildings and other structures, the whole complex surrounded with a stone wall[143].

5. Holidays and Celebration

Although the ordinary workdays of early mediaeval Bulgarians were filled primarily with toil, there was also a wealth of feast days; holidays were often filled chiefly with celebration and games. Folk holidays were invariably accompanied by games, singing and dancing. Regrettably, for

[139] Т. Балабанов, *Жилища покрай северната и източната крепостна стена на Плиска*, ППре 5, 1992, p. 152.

[140] Idem, *Селище в югозападната част на Външния град на Плиска*, ППре 10, 2010, p. 140.

[141] Cf. К. Попконстантинов, *Граждански комплекси в Плиска и Преслав*, [in:] *Средновековният български град*, ed. П. Петров, София 1980, pp. 117–128.

[142] С. Бонев, *Столицата Велики Преслав през X в. – не просто град, а агломерация*, [in:] *Градът в българските земи (по археологически данни). Материали от националната научна конференция посветена на живота и делото на ст.н.с. Вера Антонова. Шумен, 31 октомври – 1 ноември 2013 г.*, ed. П. Георгиев, Шумен 2014, pp. 273–277.

[143] Cf. Р. Рашев et al., *Материали за картата на средновековната българска държава (територията на днешна Североизточна България)*, ППре 7, 1995, № 162, 169, 170, 175, 176, 180, 197–199, etc.

the period in question we lack data concerning the songs and dances associated with particular feast days – be it in Byzantium and the Balkan area or in the Western Europe[144].

Despite the adoption of Christianity in the middle of the 9th century, Bulgarian folk culture did not undergo any drastic changes; this state of affairs brought upon the nation severe criticism from the clergy, as may sometimes be seen in literary works written by the latter. In the time following Christianisation, a large number of new holidays connected with the recently adopted religion started being celebrated – Christmas, Easter, commemorations of various moments from the life of Christ, and feast days of particular saints – all accompanied by solemn liturgy and processions. Folk holidays, however, remained outside of the context of these 'official' ones. With its 102 ecclesiastical regulations, the 692 Council in Trullo introduced copious new, harsh restrictions and prohibitions both for members of the clergy and for lay people. Thus, for example, canon 24 of the council banned members of the clergy from attending any kind of horse racing events and theatrical performances[145]. The nomocanon further explains that horse races, performances, or whatever kind of spectacles (subsumed under the general term позорища) shall not be held on the Lord's day (Sunday) or any of the Lord's holidays[146]. Thus, life during the period was entirely controlled by Divine laws (church regulations), as neatly illustrated e.g. in Cosmas the Priest's *Sermon Against the Heretics*[147]. The celebration of St. George's Day in a manner similar to the one known to us today – involving animal sacrifice (the killing of a lamb in the saint's honour) – is referenced in the 7th miracle of the *Tale of the Iron Cross* cycle. A shepherd sells a lamb to a poor widow, only to subsequently tell her that it was devoured by a wolf. She asks him: *Is this true or are you lying?*, to which he responds *By God, it is true*. Her response ensues: *You know that I am poor. If you tell a lie, God and St. George will hold you accountable;*

[144] Р. Ф о с и е, *Обикновеният...*, pp. 214–215.

[145] *Canons of the Quinisext Council*, p. 34.

[146] А. К а л о я н о в, *Славянската православна...*, p. 198 – quotation from the *Ryazan Rudder*.

[147] Cosmas the Priest.

for it is the latter to whom I promised that I would slaughter the lamb, for his holy feast day[148].

Folk holidays were expressed through dancing, just like in the later, ethnographically documented times. Dances and feasts were organised in the evening, as described in the *Sermon on the Holy Scripture* published by Bonyo Angelov (according to whom the various characteristics of the text allow us to date it to the first decades after Christianisation)[149]. Who created a pleasant atmosphere at these events is clear from the *Sermon on the Drought* from the *Zlatostruy* miscellany. No Greek archetype for this sermon has been found, which suggests a local, Bulgarian author and composition during the reign of tsar Symeon (who ordered the creation of the whole collection). The author of the work writes that people are moved away from God and deceived by **троубами и скомрахꙑ. и инѣми игръми влѣкꙑ къ собѣ. гоусльми. свирѣлами. плѧсании смѣхꙑ**[150]. The *Sermon on the Interpreter* mentions not only *gusle* and pipes, but also numerous further instruments as well as a vivid description of dances from the period; all of this helps us gain a fuller picture of their general characteristics and the way they functioned during the early Middle Ages: **елиньскыꙗ любве, боубеньнаго плесканиꙗ, свирилини звоуци, плѧсаниꙗ сотонина, фрѧжьскыꙗ слоньницѧ и гоусли, моусикиꙗ и замара, иже бѣсѧтсѧ**[151] (*Hellenic love, the beating of tambourines, the sounds of pipes, Satanic dances, Frankish slonnitsa and gusle, music and reed pipe and people in ecstasy*; boldface – N.H.). All of the above-mentioned instruments are relatively simple devices, offering rather limited musical possibilities. The lyre represents a primitive form of a harp; this is confirmed by archaeological findings from mediaeval Novgorod[152]. The *gusle*, likewise, only allowed for an extremely narrow range of sounds, spanning no more than two octaves – it is a crude, one-stringed predecessor of

[148] *Tale of the Iron Cross*, p. 203.

[149] *Sermon on the Holy Scripture*, pp. 256–268.

[150] *Sermon on the Drought*, p. 325.

[151] *Sermon on the Interpreter*, p. 38.

[152] Б.А. Колчин, *Инструментальная музыка древнего Новгорода*, [in:] *Четвърти международен конгрес по славянска археология. Доклади и съобщевия*, vol. I, ed. Д. Ангелов, София, 1992, p. 542.

the fiddle. The pipe – as well as the *zamara* – made it possible to fill the more rhythmic kinds of music with other sounds: their melodies could be easily accompanied by the beats of the rhythm-providing instruments, such as tambourines and drums. The horns, in both of the above-mentioned variants, could probably emit only a single sound and should therefore be counted among the rhythm-providing instruments as well.

The *Sermon on the Drought*, referred to above, mentions not only musical instruments but also another inseparable element of mediaeval celebration – the *skomrachs* (or *skomorochs*, buffoons, clowns). Scholars are unanimous in that the earliest information about them is of Bulgarian provenance and dates back to the times of tsar Symeon[153]. It is from there that the phenomenon spread to Rus', although it did not become widespread before the 13th century. According to Zoya Vlassova, the origin of the *skomrachs* as a phenomenon should be sought in Byzantium[154]. Probably, in this case, Sergey Ivanov is correct in thinking that the word **скомрахъ** did not only denote a joker or clown but should be connected with the circus spectacles held at the Hippodrome in Constantinople. In Old Bulgarian works and translations, the word was used to denote mimes, charioteers, and even particular *dimas*. This semantic complexity led to the ambiguity of the term **скомрахъ** in Old Bulgarian texts[155]. Based on the above assumptions, we may surmise that the *skomrachs* appeared in their original form as an element of elite culture – as court entertainment for the ruler and his entourage; only from there, quite late and probably already in Rus' territory, the phenomenon spread among the ordinary population as well.

Next to holidays filled with general celebration, even regular days saw a number of diverse games being played for entertainment in time free from work. It is conceivable that many of them were the same ones that the direct ancestors of the Bulgarians enjoyed at the end of the 19th and the beginning of the 20th century; however, which of these games were already known in the First Bulgarian Empire is not certain. The obstacle here

[153] А.А. Белкин, *Русские скоморохи*, Москва 1975, pp. 39–41; S.A. Ivanov, *Slavic Jesters and the Byzantine Hippodrome*, DOP 46, 1992, pp. 129–132.

[154] З.И. Власова, *Скоморохи и фольклор*, Санкт-Петербург 2001, p. 155.

[155] S.A. Ivanov, *Slavic Jesters*..., p. 131.

is the Church's ban not only on playing, but also on mentioning games, administered by the Council in Trullo: as a result of this prohibition, the names are missing from the works (even translations) by contemporary Bulgarian ecclesiastic writers. One game that might be supposed to have been present at the time is the so-called *chelik* (Tur. 'steel'), well-known from folk culture; however, even in this case, direct traces are lacking (due to objective reasons). A game that was certainly widespread during the period under discussion, however, is the one known in Bulgarian ethnography as *ashitsi* (i.e. knucklebones or jacks; also referred to as *astragali*, from Latin). It was played using animal bones from the ankle or hock (usually of sheep, although the use of deer, hare, dog or fox bones is documented too)[156]. Dice were used in early mediaeval Bulgaria either for playing the eponymous game or as an ancillary element of the game of backgammon[157]. Finds of backgammon pieces are concentrated in the territory of the two mediaeval capitals Pliska and Preslav (in their central parts, to be precise)[158] and in other places where the presence of members of the aristocracy is documented (even after their withdrawal from the secular society – in monasteries)[159]. Another game with clear ties to aristocratic circles was chess. As opposed to backgammon, no full chess set has been discovered so far; the finds are limited to individual pieces (three from Preslav and one from Pliska)[160]. The topography of these discoveries points to a direct connection with the dwellers of the palaces and their surroundings. Yet another factor linking these forms of entertainment with the palaces and the aristocracy is the fact that the very concept of both games resembles a scaled-down model of two opposed armies and the military actions between them[161]. Unlike these two 'aristocratic' pastimes, one game enjoyed huge popularity among the general

---

[156] Д.И. Димитров, *Погребалният обред на раннобългарските некрополи във Варненско*, ИАИ 34, 1974, p. 65; U. Fiedler, *Studien...*, p. 214.

[157] Д. Овчаров, *Още за игрите в средновековен Преслав*, ППре 7, 1995, p. 136.

[158] С. Станчев, *Материали от Дворцовия център в Плиска*, ИАИ 23, 1960, p. 29, ill. 3Б/3; П. Георгиев, *Разкопки южно от Големия басейн в Плиска*, ППре 10, 2004, p. 56, ill. 33a.

[159] Т. Тотев, *За една игра в средновековна България*, Архе 14.3, 1972, pp. 33–41.

[160] Idem, *Шахмат в средновековна България*, ШМ 33.1, 1980, pp. 23–25.

[161] Д. Овчаров, *Още за игрите...*, pp. 136, 141.

population: draughts. Lined playing areas have been found both in fortress walls of the two capitals and in various settlements across the territory of the First Bulgarian Empire[162].

The chief amusement of male members of the aristocracy during all periods was hunting. The *Folk Life of St. John of Rila* features a description of how tsar Peter, upon first hearing about John, dispatched nine experienced hunters to search for the saint[163]. Here, it is not the ruler himself who is depicted as a hunter; but the fact that the hunters are sent personally by the monarch suggests that they belonged to his suite or at least to the highest aristocratic circles. Moreover, it would be quite unexpected for tsar Peter to appear in the narrative as a hunter himself, given the humble, meek and peaceable temper that he displayed according to the description[164]. For the ordinary population, hunting was scarcely a form of entertainment; rather, along with gathering, it was a way of securing food.

The above data concerning the everyday life during the time of tsar Peter amount to a picture of the Bulgarian society rather similar to that of contemporary Byzantium; this is chiefly due to the fact that Bulgaria received Christianity from Constantinople. On the other hand, it bears its own special characteristics, later to be passed on to other regions of the *Slavia Orthodoxa*.

[162] *Ibidem*, p. 140.

[163] *Folk Life of St. John of Rila*, p. 33.

[164] К. Иречек, *История на българите*, София 1978, p. 198.

IV

Georgi N. Nikolov

State Organisation and Power Hierarchy in the Bulgarian Empire (927–969)

Following the conversion of the Bulgarians to Christianity in 864–866 there were changes in the organisation of the Bulgarian state. However, these were not significant and mostly concerned the elements of the state organism which were inherently pagan. A notable change was the abolition of the religious function of the ruler as a high priest in the pagan religion of the Bulgars, as well as the disappearance of those civil servants who ministered to the pagan cult, e.g.: ὁ κολοβρος, ὁ ιζουργου κολοβρος, βογοτορ βοηλα κουλουβρος, κανα βοιλα κολοβρος[1]. At the same time, a number of (proto)Bulgarian titles and positions, known from the times before the conversion, were preserved; among those were βοηλα καυχαν, ητζιργου βοιλα, ολγου ταρκαν, ζουπαν ταρκαν, etc.

Administratively, the Bulgarian Empire of the 10th century was still divided into the Internal Region (now North-eastern Bulgaria and Northern Dobrudzha) and the External (provincial) comitatus.

The ruler's institution remained the core one in the state. Most probably at the beginning of June 927, after commemorating the ninth day of the death of Symeon the Great (†May 27, 927), his son Peter (927–968,

[1] В. Бешевлиев, *Първобългарски надписи (второ преработено и допълнено издание)*, София 1992, pp. 236 (№ 65), 239 (№ 69), 141 (№ 14).

†January 30, 969) was crowned by the Bulgarian archbishop as 'emperor of the Bulgarians'. The young tsar Peter (most likely aged between 15 and 20) enjoyed considerable prerogatives in state government. Politically, he was the highest ranking individual in the state, and not only nominally. After prolonged negotiations between Bulgaria and Byzantium during the summer of 927, tsar Peter arrived in Constantinople at the beginning of October and personally signed (ὑπογράφονται) the peace treaty and the prenuptial agreement with the emperor of Byzantium Romanos I Lekapenos (920–944)[2]. This is the only record according to which tsar Peter of Bulgaria exercised his ruler's powers personally during the negotiations with a foreign state and sanctioned an agreement with it.

No written records produced by the Bulgarian tsar's office during Peter's reign have reached us. The lead seals found testify to the ruler's intensive epistolary exchanges as these were used to seal his letters. So far, a total of 150 individual seals belonging to tsar Peter have been published. It is the inscriptions on those seals that allow us to draw some important conclusions about the ruler's prerogatives, powers and title. In one of his most recent publications of mediaeval seals, the most distinguished of the Bulgarian sygillographers, Ivan Jordanov, has identified the following seals of tsar Peter:

1. Πέτρος καὶ Μαρίας βασιλεῖς τῶν Βουλγάρων. In translation: *Peter and Maria – basileis/emperors of the Bulgarians*. This type of seals has been dated to the early years of Peter's rule (after 927), when his title of emperor (= βασιλεύς = emperor) was recognized by the Byzantines but only with respect of one people, i.e. the Bulgarians[3].

2. Πέτρος καὶ Μαρίας ἐν Χριστῷ αὐτοκράτορες βασιλεῖς Βουλγάρων. In translation: *Peter and Maria, in Christ autokrators emperors*

[2] Continuator of Theophanes, VI, 22, p. 413.20–22; Symeon Logothete, 136.48, p. 327.

[3] I. Jordanov, *Corpus of the medieval Bulgarian seals*, Sofia 2016, pp. 86–90 (Nos 110–121).

of the Bulgarians. The seals have been dated to the 940s. A parallel could be drawn with the representation of the Byzantine emperors Constantine VII (913–959) and his son, Romanos, who was proclaimed his co-ruler: Κωνσταντῖνος καὶ Ῥωμανὸς, πιστοὶ ἐν αὐτῷ Θεῷ, ὑψηλοὶ αὔγουστοι αὐτοκράτορες μεγάλοι βασιλεῖς Ῥωμαίων[4].

3. Πέτρος βασιλεὺς εὐσεβής. In translation: *Peter, pious emperor* (940s–950s)[5].

4. Πέτρος βασιλεὺς Βουλγάρων. In translation: *Peter, emperor of the Bulgarians* (945–969)[6].

5. Πέτρος δεσπότης. In translation: *Peter, despotes* (963–969). Apparently, the title of despotes was adopted under Byzantine influence. It could be found on coins and seals from the time of the Byzantine emperors Nikephoros II Phokas (963–969) and John I Tzymiskes (969–976)[7].

6. **Петръ цѣсаръ Блъгаромъ**. In translation: *Peter, tsesar* [*i.e. emperor*] *of the Bulgarians*. It's the earliest in the Slavic world ruler's seal in the Cyrillic script. It's find precisely this form – **Петръ цѣсаръ** without the ethnonym 'of the Bulgarians' – on the majority of the Old Bulgarian literary works. In fact, this is the Slavic translation of the Greek inscription from the other Peter's seals – Πέτρος βασιλεύς. No clear dating information has been provided[8].

Unlike the seals, which reflect the official practices, the Old-Bulgarian epigraphic and genre-specific written records from the reign of tsar Peter, or chronologically close to it, mostly refer to him by the title of **цѣсаръ**

[4] *Ibidem*, pp. 90–95 (Nos 122–141б); Constantine VII Porphyrogennetos, *The Book of Ceremonies*, p. 691.16–18.

[5] I. Jordanov, *Corpus*…., pp. 95–110 (Nos 142–227a).

[6] *Ibidem*, pp. 110–112 (Nos 228–233).

[7] *Ibidem*, pp. 112–116 (Nos 234–251).

[8] *Ibidem*, pp. 116–120 (Nos 253–259a).

or **цѣсарь блъгарьскы / блъгаромъ** and once as **цѣсарь блъгарьскъ**[9]. The same could be said about the Byzantine historical sources. The title used there to refer to him is most often βασιλεὺς τῶν Βουλγάρων and less frequently ἄρχων, ἀρχηγέτης or ἄρξας[10]. Accordingly, in the Latin sources, tsar Peter's title is either *imperator* or *vasilieus*[11].

Certain conclusions could be drawn about tsar Peter's title. The Greek language, which had established itself as the dominant one during the reign of Symeon the Great, retained its primacy among the ruling elite up until at least the middle of the 10th century. Almost all of tsar Peter's seals found so far originate from the lands of the mediaeval Bulgarian North-East. This indicates that not only in his foreign correspondence but also in his internal communications tsar Peter used the Greek language seals described above. The appearance of Cyrillic inscriptions on the royal seals marked the beginning of a significant change in the official documentary practices of the Bulgarian ruling class, i.e. the adoption of the native language and the Cyrillic script. This concerned particularly the correspondence within Bulgaria. When did tsar Peter impose this change? It is impossible to give a definitive answer to this question. It could have happened in the middle of the 10th century, when the Bulgarian Empire left the orbit of Byzantine politics and made a bid for greater autonomy and independence from Constantinople. Old-Bulgarian penetrated all spheres of public life and it was only a matter of time for it to enter the ruler's administration. Thus, after almost two and a half centuries of dominance in the official document flow and royal ceremony, Greek was supplanted by Old-Bulgarian, an essentially Slavic language. It seems paradoxical that for such a long time Greek remained the official language of the Bulgarian state from the 8th to the 10th century, despite the anti-Byzantine sentiments prevalent among the state administration. To a large extent that was due to the conservative mindset of the political establishment, on the one hand, and the almost two-century-long tradition of using Greek in the Bulgarian ruler's court, on the other. Therefore, it seems surprising that

[9] For a thorough overview of all forms see: Т. С л а в о в а, *Владетел и администрация в ранносредновековна България. Филологически аспекти*, София 2010, pp. 255–256.

[10] *Ibidem*, p. 257.

[11] *Ibidem*.

Old-Bulgarian took root in the state administration not during Symeon's Golden Age of the Bulgarian Literature but during the reign of his son, tsar Peter. It could be assumed that some of tsar Peter's seals were not used chronologically and that it was more the case of different types of seals having different uses and addressees. This would explain why several types of seal were used in parallel.

In the spirit of the Caesaropapism of the Orthodox society, tsar Peter took upon himself also the purification of religious life and the Bulgarian Church from any heresies. It is notable that it was Peter (rather than the Bulgarian patriarch!) who sent two epistles to Theophylact (933–956), patriarch of the Church of Constantinople, seeking clarification on the nature of the dualist Bogomil heresy in order to take appropriate action against it[12].

As was the case in the Byzantine Empire, second to the ruler in the royal hierarchy of Bulgaria was the ruler's wife[13]. Immediately below the ruler and his wife in the power hierarchy were their children. Thus, Bulgarians were welcomed with the question: *How are the kanartikin, the boila tarkan, the sons of the God-appointed ruler of Bulgaria and the rest of his children*? (πῶς ἔχουσιν ὁ Κανάρτι κείνος καὶ ὁ Βουλίας ταρκάνος οἱ υἱοὶ τοῦ ἐκ Θεοῦ ἄρχοντος Βουλγαρίας καὶ τὰ λοιπὰ αὐτοῦ τέκνα)[14]. The fact that the sons of the Bulgarian khan had special titles is indirect evidence not only of their representative presence in the hierarchy but of the actual scope of their powers as well. The person emperor Constantine VII Porphyrogennetos (912–959) refers to as a 'kanartikin' is in fact the ruler's firstborn son (heir to the throne), whose title is inscribed on some lead seals as καναηρτχιθυνος. It is a known fact that as early as pagan times the heir to the Bulgarian throne enjoyed some special privileges; he had his own residence, he lead the Bulgarian army on certain occasions, etc.

[12] *Letter of the Patriarch Theophylaktos to Tsar Peter*, pp. 311–313.

[13] The position of Maria Lekapene as the wife of emperor Peter in the power structures of Bulgarian state, as well as her titulature and seals bearing her image and name, have been analyzed in detail in this monograph by Zofia A. Brzozowska in the Part One, chapter IV, devoted to the Bulgarian empress ('tsaritsa').

[14] Constantine VII Porphyrogennetos, *The Book of Ceremonies*, p. 681.15–17.

The title was also given to two of tsar Symeon the Great's sons, to Michael and later on to John[15]. The title of ὁ Βουλίας ταρκάνος was apparently bestowed on the Bulgarian ruler's second son[16]. However, no evidence has been found so far of such an identification in the Bulgarian royal court.

An important place in the state organisation of the early mediaeval Bulgarian Khaganate-Empire had the institution of the 'great boils'. In his work *De administrando imperio* Constantine Porphyrogennetos wrote that during the Bulgarian-Serbian war (c. 869–870), waged by khan Boris I-Michael (852–889, † May 2, 907), his son Vladimir was taken hostage by the Serbians, along with 'twelve great boils' (βοϊλάδων δώδεκα μεγάλων)[17]. In another of his works, *De ceremoniis aulae Byzantinae*, the same author mentions that during his welcoming speech addressed to the Bulgarian envoys in Constantinople, the logothetes would ask the question, how are the six great boils? (πῶς ἔχουσιν οἱ ἕξ Βολιάδες οἱ μεγάλοι)[18]. Apparently, the number of the 'great boils', which in the 9th century was twelve, was reduced so that in the 10th century there were only six boils. Only on one occasion were these listed by name. The Byzantine chronicler Theophanes Continuatus (10th c.) and later historians make mention of six Bulgarians (i.e. the six great boils), who led the peace talks in the autumn of 927 and who arrived in Constantinople for the marriage of the emperor's grand-daughter Maria with emperor Peter. First among them was the ichirgu boila George, known also by his (proto)Bulgarian name of Mostich but referred to in the Byzantine sources as George Sursuvul (Γεώργιος ὁ Σουρσουβούλης). He was followed by oglu tarkan and sampsis Symeon, brother-in-law of emperor Symeon the Great (Συμεὼν ὁ Καλουτερκάνος καὶ Οὔσαμψος καὶ Συμεὼν τοῦ ἀρχηγοῦ Βουλγαρίας ἀδελφὸς πρὸς γυναῖκα), the ruler's relative Stephen the

[15] И. Йорданов, *Корпус на печатите на средновековна България*, София 2001, pp. 69–74.

[16] Т. Славова, *Владетел...*, pp. 83–86.

[17] Constantine VII Porphyrogennetos, *On the Governance of the Empire*, 32, p. 154.48.

[18] Constantine VII Porphyrogennetos, *The Book of Ceremonies*, pp. 681.17, 682.15–16.

Bulgarian (Στεφάνῳ Βουλγάρῳ... ὁ ἀγχιστεὺς αὐτοῦ Στέφανος), Magotinos (Μαγοτῖνος), Kronos (Κρόνος) and Minikos (Μηνικὸς).[19]

It is notable that at least three of the individuals mentioned were related to the royal family; the ichirgu-boila, Mostich-George, the oglu tarkan and sampsis Symeon and Stephen the Bulgarian.

What is known of those people? It could be considered a fact that Sursuvul was not a surname but a distorted form of the (proto)Bulgarian title of ichirgu-boila[20]. The fact that the Byzantines called him George Sursuvul is an indication of the way he introduced himself, i.e. as George, the ichirgu-boila. Of him, the Byzantine sources say that he was the brother of the second (unknown by name) wife of tsar Symeon the Great and that he was appointed by the ruler as guardian of his children (ὃν ἐκ τῆς δευτέρας αὐτοῦ γυναικὸς ἔσχεν, τῆς ἀδελφῆς Γεωργίου Σουρσουβούλη, ὃν καὶ ἐπίτροπον τοῖς ἑαυτοῦ παισὶν ὁ Συμεὼν καταλέλοιπεν)[21]. The only evidence of his political career covers the summer and the autumn of 927. According to Theophanes Continuatus' account, in the summer of that year tsar Peter and George Sursuvul secretly sent the monk Kalokir, of Armenian stock, to Constantinople. They entrusted him with a golden bull (χρυσοβούλλιον), in which they informed Romanos I Lekapenos, the Byzantine emperor, that they accepted the peace offered by the Byzantines and wished to forge a marriage alliance between the royal

---

[19] Continuator of Theophanes, p. 413.7–12; Continuator of George the Monk (Slavic), vol. I, p. 561; vol. II, p. 55. The later sources only make reference to Stephen the Bulgarian and George Sursuvul – see Leo Grammatikos, p. 316.15–16; John Skylitzes (p. 223.32–33), modifies the text as follows: Στεφάνῳ τινὶ περιωνύμῳ ἐν Βουλγαρίᾳ; Symeon Logothete (Slavic), p. 137. See also В. Гюзелев. *Значението на брака на цар Петър (927–969) с ромейката Мария-Ирина Лакапина (911–962)*, [in:] *Културните текстове на миналото – носители, символи, идеи*, vol. I, *Текстовете на историята, история на текстовете. Материали от Юбилейната международна конференция в чест на 60-годишнината на проф. д.и.н. Казимир Попконстантинов, Велико Търново, 29–31 октомври 2003 г.*, ed. idem, София 2005, p. 28.

[20] В. Гюзелев, *Значението*..., p. 32, fn. 11.

[21] Continuator of Theophanes, VI, 21, p. 412.3–5; Continuator of George the Monk, p. 904.3–5; Symeon Logothete, p. 326.340–342; John Skylitzes, p. 222.13–14; Symeon Logothete (Slavic), p. 136. On that see: *PMZ II*, vol. II, pp. 458–459, *s.v. Georgios* (#22137).

families. In response to the Bulgarian embassy Romanos I Lekapenos dispatched to Bulgaria the monk Theodosios Aboukas and Constantine Rhodios, the emperor's priest, who held talks in Mesembria to agree the details of the future contract. Soon after, in Constantinople arrived the ichirgu-boila George, along with the other five great boils. Theophanes Continuatus's account leaves no doubt that it was George who played the key role, both in the negotiations and in the signing of the peace treaty itself. The great boils came to Constantinople to see the prospective brides and chose Maria, the daughter of the co-emperor Christopher. It was then that the great boils, led by the ichirgu-boila George, concluded the peace treaty and sent a letter to tsar Peter inviting him to Constantinople. The treaty, agreed by the ichirgu-boila George and the other boils, was later signed by the Bulgarian ruler. Among the acts of the Bulgarian dignitary mention should be made of the fact that he was best man at tsar Peter's wedding with Maria. On the Byzantine side, the same role was played by the Protovestiarios Theophanes[22]. There is no further available evidence of the ichirgu-boila George's activities. It is likely that soon after 927 he withdrew from political life and became a monk.

His gravestone epitaph, left in Great Preslav, reads:

> Here lies Mostich, who was churgubilya to emperor Symeon and to emperor Peter. On the eighth of his decades, having left behind his chargubilya-ship and all his possessions, became a monk and ended his life as such

сьдє лєжитъ мо
стичь чрьговы
лѩ бъıвиъı при
сумєонѣ цр҃и
и при пєтрѣ цр҃и
с[м]ињ жє дєсѧ

[22] Continuator of Theophanes, VI, 22–23, pp. 412.16 – 414.7. The later Byzantine authors repeat Theophanes Continuatus' account with some minor changes.

тѣ лѣтъ сꙑ оста
вивъ [ч]рьгоубъıлѣ
ство ї вьсе їмѣни
ѥ бъıстъ чрьнори
зьцѣ ї въ томѣ сѣ
врьши жизнь своѭ[23]

It could be assumed that he was born before the conversion of Bulgarians to Christianity (864–866) and received the (proto) Bulgarian name Mostich at birth. After adopting the Christian faith, he was baptized with the Christian name of George. His title of ichirgu-boila was slavicized to chargubilya (**чрьгобылꙗ**). In the eighth of his decades, i.e. when he was in his seventies, he became monk (**чрьноризьцѣ**).

The second member of the great boil council was tsar Symeon the Great's brother-in-law Symeon, oglu tarkan and sampsis[24]. As in the other cases, the Byzantine sources give a distorted version of his titles of oglu-tarkan and sampsis as ὁ Καλουτερκάνος καὶ Οὔσαμψος. Based on evidence from other similar sources, it could be concluded that in the Turkic languages *tarkan* meant 'blacksmith' or 'governor'[25]. Having in mind another similar mention of the title of *oglu tarkan* (ολγυ τρακανου) in the inscription from the village of Narash (904)[26], it could be assumed that it signified a position in the military analogous to a 'border lieutenant; or, in a wider sense, 'someone responsible for the border'. As for *sampsis*, it was proposed that this was a 'palace steward', a 'ruler's adviser on matters of diplomatic protocol and ceremony', or a participant in diplomatic talks and missions[27]. This hypothesis sounds plausible since the great boils served at the palace and were not province governors.

---

[23] K. Popkonstantinov, O. Kronsteiner, *Старобългарски надписи. Altbulgarische Inschriften*, vol. I, Salzburg 1994, p. 185.

[24] About him, see: *PMZ II*, vol. VI, pp. 214–215, *s.v. Symeon* (# 27485).

[25] On the different views expressed, see: Т. Славова, *Владетел...*, pp. 73–75.

[26] В. Бешевлиев, *Първобългарски...*, p. 183 (№ 46).

[27] On the different views expressed, see: Т. Славова, *Владетел...*, pp. 117–125.

There are no further records of the ruler's relative Stephan the Bulgarian either[28]. Perhaps he was a *kavkhan*, one of the highest ranks in mediaeval Bulgaria, to which there are references from the 11th century too[29].

As regards Magotinos (Μαγοτῖνος)[30], Chronos (Κρόνος)[31] and Minikos (Μηνικὸς), it is obvious that these are not names but (proto)Bulgarian titles. It is common for Byzantine sources of the 9th–11th centuries to take Bulgarian titles for personal names. One interpretation of Magotinos is that this was the title of a military officer in charge of the draught animals (supply train) in the army[32]. Like Magotinos, Chronos is only mentioned in connection with the peace treaty concluded between Bulgaria and Byzantium in the autumn of 927. Based on the semantics of the word it was proposed that it was the title of a high-ranking military commander in charge of border security[33]. Out of this group of titles only the meaning of minikos is beyond any doubt. A clarification by John Skylitzes indicates that this was the first among the royal grooms (Μινικὸν τῶν ἱπποκόμων τὸν πρῶτον)[34]. The minikos was not the commander of the Bulgarian cavalry but rather the person whose responsibility were the country's horses. A hypothesis has been proposed that he was in charge of the army reserve of unbroken horses[35].

Based on all that, the following conclusions could be drawn. The six great boils played the role of a council, which rendered support to the ruler. This had been their prime function since heathen times and it was retained after Bulgaria's conversion to Christianity. It is difficult

---

[28] On Stephan the Bulgarian, see *PMZ II*, vol. VI, p. 89, *s.v. Stephanos* (# 27253).

[29] В. Гюзелев, *Кавханите и ичиргу боилите на Българското ханство-царство*, Пловдив 2007, pp. 75–88, 156–157.

[30] *PMZ II*, vol. IV, p. 281, *s.v. Magotinos* (# 24813).

[31] *PMZ II*, vol. III, p. 737, *s.v. Kronos* (# 24204).

[32] Т. Славова. *Владетел...*, pp. 110–112. In the Slavic translation of George the Monk's Chronicle the title was written as **Клогатинъ** – Continuator of George the Monk (Slavic), vol. I, p. 561. This is due to a copying error: the Greek letter M was wrongly copied as **Кл**.

[33] Т. Славова, *Владетел...*, pp. 109–110.

[34] John Skylitzes, p. 215.4.

[35] A. Granberg, *Hunno-Bulgarian as preserved in Slavonic, Greek and Latin* (forthcoming) – cited from: Т. Славова, *Владетел...*, p. 108.

to say whether there was any kind of subordination within this council. Yet, at least in 927, it was the ichirgu-boila Mostich-George who took a leading part. What is common to them all is that they had both military and diplomatic duties. The significant number of ruler's relatives is an indication of the narrow circle of people from which were selected the six great boils. After 927 the sources make no reference to any of the already mentioned individuals. To a large extent this is due to the long period of peaceful relations between Bulgaria and Byzantium (40 years!).

Having mentioned the six great boils in his welcoming address to the Bulgarian emissaries in Constantinople, Constantine Porphyrogennetos refers to the rest of 'the internal and external boils' (καὶ λοιποὶ οἱ ἔσω καὶ ἔξω βολιάδες)[36]. The (proto)Bulgarian inscriptions of the 9th century add to the title of some officials the adjective ιτξιργου (ιτξιργου βαγαηνου, ιτξιργου βοιλα, ιτξιργωυ βωυλε, [η]τξιργου, ὁ ηξουργου βουληα, ὁ ιξουργου κολοβρος), i.e. internal and υκ (υκ βοιλα, βοιλα βαγαηνου), i.e. external[37]. It could be assumed that the 'internal' boil served in the Internal (capital) region, while the 'external' ones operated in the countryside, i.e. they were territorially based. It is hard to say what was the territory covered by the Internal Region, but it seems to have encompassed a significant area of present-day Dobrudzha, ranging as far as the west coast of the Black Sea and the Balkan Mountains to the south. In actual fact, these were the highest ranking Bulgarian military commanders among the great boils. The provincial Bulgarian commanders were referred to as 'external' boils. Among those were bearers of other titles as well, such as tarkan, zhupan, comes, etc.

The historical sources of the times of tsar Peter bear testimony of the position of the zhupan Dimitar, whose name is mentioned in a Cyrillic

[36] Constantine VII Porphyrogennetos, *The Book of Ceremonies*, pp. 681.18, 682.16–17. On these titles see: В.Н. Златарски, *Кои са били вътрешни и външни боляри?*, [in:] *Юбилеен сборник в чест на С.С. Бобчев, 1871–1921*, София 1921, pp. 45–57; I. Dujčev, *Les bolijars dits intérieurs et extérieurs de la Bulgarie médiévale*, AO.ASH 3.3, 1953, pp. 167–178.

[37] В. Бешевлиев, *Първобългарски надписи...*, pp. 195 (№ 50), 136 (№ 11), 200 (№ 53), 131 (№ 6), 186–187 (№ 47), 236 (№ 65).

stone inscription from 943, found in Northern Dobrudzha[38]. The south-western Bulgarian lands, on the other hand, were under the rule of the Bulgarian military commander, the cometos Nikola, after whose death the position was taken over by his sons David, Moses, Aaron and Samuel, to whom the Byzantine sources refer to as cometopoulos[39].

A view has been voiced that in the 9th–11th centuries the Bulgarian Empire was divided into ten large military-administrative regions called comitatus, i.e. governed by a comes[40]. The attempts to delineate those precisely should be critically reviewed and further research would be required.

From an institutional point of view, the Bulgarian Empire during the reign of Peter (927–969) was a typical mediaeval Christian monarchy. Although some of the state institutions manifested certain Byzantine influences, they retained their core Bulgarian nature, which had defined them since before Bulgaria's conversion to Christianity. There is a further peculiarity in evidence, namely, the linguistic slavicization of some of the Bulgarian official ranks and titles.

---

[38] K. Popkonstantinov, O. Kronsteiner, *Старобългарски надписи…*, p. 109. See also В. Гюзелев, *Добруджанският надпис и събитията в България през 943 г.*, ИП 24.6, 1968, pp. 40–48.

[39] John Skylitzes, p. 328.59–63; K. Popkonstantinov, O. Kronsteiner, *Старобългарски надписи…*, vol. I, p. 37.

[40] И. Венедиков, *Военното и административното устройство на България през IX и X век*, София 1979.

V

Kirił Marinow

Armed Forces and the Defence System of Peter's State

The reign of tsar Peter I (927–969), albeit long, did not bring about many events of militaristic nature, which would have allowed the creation of a clear image of the conditions and activities of the Bulgarian army during that period. The Bulgarian ruler showed greater initiative in this regard at the very beginning of his reign, however these anti-Byzantine activities were soon abandoned, and a lasting peace was concluded with the southern neighbour. Only the very end of Peter's rule saw an increase in martial activity, due to the incursion of the Rus' prince Svyatoslav, although the information about the Bulgarians themselves is at a scarcity, since the chronicles describing these events were focusing on the Byzantine-Rus' struggle. In this situation, in order to re-construct the organisation, strategy, and tactics of the Bulgarian army, one needs to reach both into the earlier period (primarily tsar Symeon I's era), as well as to the times Cometopouloi following Peter's reign, and beyond.

1. The Army and its Organisation

Recruitment. During the discussed era, Bulgarian armed forces consisted of: the ruler's *druzhina* (bodyguard) or central military forces, most likely stationed in the capital, the garrison troops of individual strongholds, and border guards. In case of a larger mobilisation, most likely organised on territorial basis, i.e. the existing system of *comitates* (and particular villages and urban areas within), the aforementioned units were supplemented with the necessary number of subjects able to bear arms. Individual strongholds and cities had been (likely) managed by *zhupans*, or *comites* (of bolyar status), who formed garrisons from among the local populace and were obliged to conduct territorial defence[1]. Taking into account two facts: that the Bulgarian territory was divided into two areas – the interior and the exterior, and that the bolyars were divided along the same lines into 'internal' and 'external', one may assume that the latter would have been responsible for organising and effectively guarding the

[1] Щ. Атанасов, И. Дуйчев, Д. Ангелов, Г. Цанкова-Петкова, Д. Христов, Б. Чолпанов, *Българското военно изкуство през феодализма*, София 1958, pp. 44–47; Д. Ангелов, С. Кашев, Б. Чолпанов, *Българска военна история от Античността до втората четвърт на X в.*, София 1983, pp. 136, 137–138; Б. Чолпанов, Е. Александров, *Военна история на Първата българска държава (681–1018)*, [in:] *История на българите*, vol. V, *Военна история на българите от древността до наши дни*, ed. Д. Зафиров, Е. Александров, София 2007, pp. 57–59; Ж. Жеков, *България и Византия. Военна администрация VII–IX в.*, София 2007, pp. 92–97, 276, 282; Т. Славова, *Владетел и администрация в ранносредновековна България. Филологически аспекти*, София 2010, pp. 153–158. See also: Г. Баласчев, *Върху държавното и военно устройство в старобългарската държава*, Мин 1.2, 1909, pp. 203–216; V. Gjuzelev, *Allgemeine Charakteristik und Etappen der Errichtung der Militärischen und Administrativen Verwaltung des ersten bulgarischen Staates (VII. bis XI. Jh.)*, EB 14.3, 1978, pp. 71–77; И. Венедиков, *Военното и административното устройство на България през IX и X век*, София 1979; Д. Ангелов, *Административно-военна уредба*, [in:] *История на България*, vol. II, *Първа българска държава*, ed. idem, София 1981, pp. 169–181; Д. Христов, *Корените на българската военноотбранителна доктрина (681–1018 г.)*, ВС 63.1, 1993, pp. 5–20; Л. Симеонова, *Крепостта Видинис / Бдин и „завръщането на Византия на Дунава": реализация и крах на една имперска мечта*, SB 32, 2017, pp. 76–77.

state's borderland areas[2]. It is difficult to say specifically, however, which of them fulfilled this duty. The matter of protecting Bulgaria's internal territory appears to be somewhat clearer, since in the light of some of the source remarks it is clear that the one responsible for it was the so-called *ichirgu boila* (ἠτζιργοῦ βοίλα), the third most important state dignitary[3].

The army consisted of both light and heavy cavalry, and infantry. These were formed in units according to decimal division[4], while the entire army was divided into three parts: the centre, and two wings, left and right. In addition to this, there were also the baggage trains.

The fleet. During the period in which I am interested, the Bulgarians did not have their own sea-faring war fleet, and the few mentions of activity the on sea relate to capturing Byzantine ships by ruse, their crews tricked by Bulgarians into attacking some coastal areas[5]. We do however have information about the use of a river flotilla[6], although it cannot be ruled out that the event was incidental. Nonetheless, the dominant view in Bulgarian scholarship is that the functioning of the harbours on the Păcuiul lui Soare and in Dristra attests to the regular patrolling of the Danube[7].

---

[2] Д. Ангелов, С. Кашев, Б. Чолпанов, *Българска военна...*, p. 141.

[3] В. Гюзелев, *Кавханите и ичиргу боилите на българското ханство-царство*, Пловдив 2007, pp. 24–30, 168–172, 174–188, 190–191; G.N. Nikolov, *The Bulgarian aristocracy in the war against the Byzantine Empire (971–1019)*, [in:] *Byzantium and East Central Europe*, ed. G. Prinzing, M. Salamon, assist. P. Stephenson, Cracow 2001, p. 144; Т. Славова, *Владетел и администрация...*, pp. 21–29.

[4] Д. Ангелов, С. Кашев, Б. Чолпанов, *Българска военна...*, p. 138.

[5] E. Tryjarski, *Protobułgarzy*, [in:] K. Dąbrowski, T. Najgrodzka-Majchrzyk, E. Tryjarski, *Hunowie europejscy, Protobułgarzy, Chazarowie, Pieczyngowie*, Wrocław–Warszawa–Kraków–Gdańsk 1975, pp. 321–322; Р. Рашев, *Първото българско царство и морето*, [in:] *Средновековна България и Черноморието (Сборник доклади от националната конференция Варна – 1980)*, ed. А. Кузев, Т. Йорданов, Варна 1982, pp. 47–56; K. Marinow, *Zadania floty cesarskiej w wojnach bizantyńsko-bułgarskich (VII–XI w.)*, [in:] *Byzantina Europea. Księga jubileuszowa ofiarowana Profesorowi Waldemarowi Ceranowi*, ed. M. Kokoszko, M.J. Leszka, Łódź 2007, pp. 381–392.

[6] *The Royal Frankish Annals*, AD 827, p. 216.32–34; *The annals of Fulda*, AD 827, p. 359.31–33.

[7] Cf. D. Ovčarov, *La forteresse protobulgare sur l'île danubienne Păcuiul lui Soare*, [in:] *Dobrudža. Études ethno-culturelles*, ed. idem, Sofia 1987, pp. 57–68; А. Кузев,

While in case of the first of these harbours the discovered archaeological material does indeed show some building investments, dated to the early tenth century and associated with the activity of tsar Symeon I, both the construction of the aforementioned harbour and the discovered artefacts relate to the Byzantine presence on the island, dated to the time of the conquest of Bulgaria by John I Tzymiskes[8]. Therefore, they cannot constitute evidence of its use by Bulgarians during Peter I's reign.

Leadership. The army was of course commanded by the ruler himself, who often led his troops to battle in person, or entrusted this task to another high-ranking aristocrat, most often the *kavkhan*, who was the ruler's deputy commander of the armies. Of the other high ranking commanders, one needs to mention the *ichirgu boila* and *kana boila kolobra* (?). There were also commanders of lower ranks: various *tarkhans* and *bagains*[9]. The so-called *minik* was most likely a cavalry commander[10]. The variety of names with which the sources (primarily native) denoted Bulgarian military commanders gave some scholars the basis to think that Bulgaria had a developed (and strictly adhered to) hierarchy of command[11].

Дръстър, [in:] *Български средновековни градове и крепости*, vol. I, *Градове и крепости по Дунав и Черно Море*, ed. i d e m, В. Гю з е л е в, Варна 1981, pp. 177–185.

[8] Г. А т а н а с о в, *Началото на "българската флотилия" и военноморските експедиции на деспот Добротица*, [in:] *Великите Асеневци*, ed. П. П а в л о в, Н. К ъ н е в, Н. Х р и с и м о в, Велико Търново 2016, pp. 292–295. More on the fortification and harbour existing on the island – P. D i a c o n u, D. V i l c e a n u, *Păcuiul lui Soare*, vol. I, Bucurști 1972.

[9] Щ. А т а н а с о в, И. Д у й ч е в, Д. А н г е л о в, Г. Ц а н к о в а-П е т к о в а, Д. Х р и с т о в, Б. Ч о л п а н о в, *Българското военно...*, pp. 58–59; Д. А н г е л о в, С. К а ш е в, Б. Ч о л п а н о в, *Българска военна...*, pp. 139–140; Т. С л а в о в а, *Владетел и администрация...*, pp. 10–15, 53–59, 67–70, 63–86.

[10] C o n t i n u a t o r o f T h e o p h a n e s, VI, 8, p. 401.3–5; G. M o r a v c s i k, *Byzantinoturcica*, vol. II, *Sprachreste der Türk völker in den byzantinisehen Quellen*, Berlin 1958, p. 189; Д. А н г е л о в, С. К а ш е в, Б. Ч о л п а н о в, *Българска военна...*, p. 141; Т. С л а в о в а, *Владетел и администрация...*, pp. 105–109.

[11] Cf. Щ. А т а н а с о в, И. Д у й ч е в, Д. А н г е л о в, Г. Ц а н к о в а-П е т к о в а, Д. Х р и с т о в, Б. Ч о л п а н о в, *Българското военно...*, p. 58; Д. А н г е л о в, С. К а ш е в, Б. Ч о л п а н о в, *Българска военна...*, pp. 141–142.

Armaments, riding equipment, and military technology. In the light of the source relations and the results of archaeological studies, the Bulgarian offensive armaments included: a) hand-held projectile weapons – javelins, bows, slings, and lassos (for capturing animals or opponents); b) melee weapons: swords and sabres; c) polearms – spears and axes; d) blunt weapons: pickaxes and maces. The defensive equipment traditionally included: chain or lamellar armour, a shield, and a helmet (pointed, leather or metal). Riding equipment and horse tack consisted of: a saddle, reins with a bit or curb bit, stirrups, spurs and horseshoes; the rider's dress included a knee-length, narrow-sleeved jerkin, girded with a leather belt with metal studs. The dress was complemented by a crested leather cap and tight trousers[12].

---

[12] Щ. Атанасов, И. Дуйчев, Д. Ангелов, Г. Цанкова-Петкова, Д. Христов, Б. Чолпанов, *Българското военно...*, pp. 60–78, 84–87 (collectively for the entire period of the Middle Ages); Z. Kurnatowska, *Elementy uzbrojenia i oporządzenia jeździeckiego z wczesnośredniowiecznego grodziska w Styrmen w Bułgarii*, SA 20, 1973, pp. 87–124; E. Tryjarski, *Protobułgarzy...*, pp. 312–313, 316; Д. Ангелов, С. Кашев, Б. Чолпанов, *Българска военна...*, pp. 142–143, 145–146; Й. Чангова, *Перник*, vol. III, *Крепостта Перник VIII–XIV в.*, София 1992, pp. 166–198; С. Витлянов, Я. Димитров, *Защитно въоръжение от Преслав*, Пр.Сб 5, 1993, pp. 165–177; В. Йотов, Г. Атанасов, *Скала. Крепост от X–XI век до с. Кладенци, Тервелско*, София 1998, pp. 88–92; Л. Дончева-Петкова, *Одърци. Селище от Първото българско царство*, vol. I, София 1999, pp. 107–114; И.Х. Джамбов, *Средновековното селище над античния град при Хисар*, Асеновград 2002, pp. 57–58; Б. Чолпанов, Е. Александров, *Военна история...*, pp. 60–66; Ж. Жеков, *България...*, pp. 85–88. For more information about the Bulgarian armaments in this period, see: С. Витлянов, *Старобългарско въоръжение (По археологически данни от Плиска, Мадара и Велики Преслав)*, София 1996; *Оръжие и снаряжение през късната античност и средновековието IV–XV в. Международна конференция Варна 14–16 септември 2000*, ed. В. Йотов, В. Николов, В. Славчев, Varna 2002; В. Йотов, *Въоръжението и снаряжението от българското средновековие (VII–XI век)*, Варна–Велико Търново 2004; Д. Рабовянов, *Средновековни предпазители за меч от България*, ПБА 7, 2013, pp. 99–114; М. Петров, Н. Хрисимов, *Еднооострите клинови оръжия от територията на България и византийската военна традиция*, ДобСб 30, 2015, pp. 337–358. While Deyan Rabovyanov (*За употребата на прашката като оръжие в средновековна България*, [in:] *Laurea. In honorem Margaritae Vaklinova*, ed. Б. Петрунова, А. Аладжов, Е. Василева, vol. II, София 2009, pp. 261–269) dismissed the use of slings by the Bulgarian army, his arguments are not entirely convincing.

The army had excellent siege capabilities. We have information from as early as the 820s that the Bulgarians made use of a variety of engines designed for destroying, scaling and bypassing walls. Those named include i.a. scorpions (for shooting arrows), rams, siege towers, catapults for hurling incendiary materials and stones, ladders, pickaxes (for tunnelling), etc.[13] The effectiveness of the Bulgarian army in this regard is evidenced by the numerous Byzantine cities and strongholds captured during tsar Symeon's times.

Army training. Military discipline. Emperor Leo VI mentioned the particular significance which Bulgarians (similarly to the so-called Turks, i.e. Hungarians) attached to horseback riding and having the riders master archery[14]. Even this information alone undoubtedly proves that during peacetime the army conducted exercises. This would have been true of the troops stationed directly by the ruler's side, as well as of the garrisons and border forces. High morale in the ranks – emphasised by the Byzantine authors – was also sustained through good physical training, harsh punishments of those of the soldiers who failed in their duties, and by rewarding those who distinguished themselves in combat. Particular importance was given to the condition of the equipment, and training of the mounts – negligence towards the arms, and riding a warhorse during peacetime were punished by death. This penalty was also prescribed for: spying, betrayal and joining the enemy, refusal to participate in a battle, fleeing from the battlefield, inciting mutiny, and surrendering one's troops to the enemy. Harsh punishments also befell those who were meant to be guarding the camp but abandoned their post to loot the enemy after

---

[13] *Scriptor incertus de Leone Armenio*, pp. 347.11 – 348.2. See also: Щ. Атанасов, И. Дуйчев, Д. Ангелов, Г. Цанкова-Петкова, Д. Христов, Б. Чолпанов, *Българското военно…*, pp. 78–83; E. Tryjarski, *Protobułgarzy…*, pp. 316–318; Д. Ангелов, С. Кашев, Б. Чолпанов, *Българска военна…*, pp. 143–145, 149, 155–156; Д. Рабовянов, *Раждането на българската полиоркетика*, ИРИМВТ 20, 2005, pp. 150–159; Б. Чолпанов, Е. Александров, *Военна история…*, pp. 66–68.

[14] Leo VI the Wise, XVIII, 41, p. 452.223–226; XVIII, 43, p. 454.233–234; XVIII, 47, p. 454.253–254; XVIII, 49, p. 454.257–258; XVIII, 59, p. 458.295–298; XVIII, 61, p. 458.302–304; XVIII, 73, p. 462.350–352.

a victory. Theft of a mount during military operations resulted in the perpetrator being sold into slavery, while theft of armaments was punished with flogging[15].

Provisioning. The main concern of the authorities lie in supplying the army with the best quality armaments. To a certain extent each of the participants in a fight had to secure for himself appropriate weapons, making use of i.a. weapons captured from the enemy, manufactured by oneself, or by a home town artisan. The majority of the armaments, however, came from the state workshops, distributed around the capitals or administrative centres of the state. This solution guaranteed an adequate quality of the arms, and allowed the state to keep control of their distribution – the authorities knew how many armed men, with a good equipment at that, they could rely on to be available. Sustenance and accommodation were provided partly (and frequently) at the expense of the local populace, and with supplies carried on the baggage train[16].

The strategy and tactics of military operations. Before embarking on any military operations, Bulgarian rulers made attempts to secure the borders of their state, ensuring peaceful relations with their neighbours (excepting the one with whom the fighting was intended or whose incursion was anticipated). This was particularly crucial in the light of the fact that it was, for example, a common Byzantine practice to instigate nomads from the steppes north of the Black Sea to attack Bulgaria in the 'rear', while it was involved in fighting in the south. Taught by the bitter experience of the war of 894–896 (specifically, by the Hungarian raids), tsar Symeon and his successor, Peter, made efforts to maintain close relations with the Pechenegs who, at any time, were able to threaten

[15] Щ. Атанасов, И. Дуйчев, Д. Ангелов, Г. Цанкова-Петкова, Д. Христов, Б. Чолпанов, *Българското военно*..., pp. 88–91; E. Tryjarski, *Protobułgarzy*..., pp. 315–316; Д. Ангелов, С. Кашев, Б. Чолпанов, *Българска военна*..., pp. 146–148; Б. Чолпанов, Е. Александров, *Военна история*..., pp. 70–71.

[16] Щ. Атанасов, И. Дуйчев, Д. Ангелов, Г. Цанкова-Петкова, Д. Христов, Б. Чолпанов, *Българското военно*..., pp. 142–143; Д. Ангелов, С. Кашев, Б. Чолпанов, *Българска военна*..., p. 148.

Bulgarian territory, primarily due to efforts of the Byzantine diplomacy[17]. Furthermore, it was intended to prevent a construction of a wider anti-Bulgarian coalition. Such diplomatic activity was also employed to gain allies in a fight against an enemy (e.g. Symeon's attempts at convincing the Arabs to move against the Byzantines). In planning an incursion into an enemy country, attempts were made to exploit its difficult position, both at the international stage (engagement in exhausting armed struggle at a different front, e.g. the Byzantine clashes with the Arabs), and internal (fighting for the throne, ruler's minority). The strategic goal was usually extension of the Bulgarian dominion in the Balkans (Symeon), or the preservation of an already existing *status quo* (Peter). Of course, the immediate goal when fighting was to weaken the enemy and to deprive him of the demographic and economic base, the extermination of his human and animal reserves, and thereby exerting pressure on him, to force the acceptance of Bulgarian demands[18]. In fighting Byzantium, the control of the Adrianople fortress, on the one hand a staging ground for the Byzantine imperial army's northbound expeditions, on the other the gate from which road led to the Byzantine capital, was crucial. For this reason Bulgarians most often directed their armies to the south, along the rivers Tundzha and Maritsa, and from there towards Constantinople. The Thracian theatre of war therefore appears as the most important one in the Bulgarian-Byzantine military struggle, since not only it was there that the Byzantine capital was located, but the occupation of that territory also allowed the cutting off of the Balkan Byzantine territories from their Asia Minor base – both in purely economic terms, as well as militarily (Asia Minor was the 'reservoir' area from which recruits were drawn). This naturally meant the military activity taking place in other areas was of lesser importance[19].

---

[17] Nicholas Mystikos, 9, p. 58.98–112; Constantine VII Porphyrogennetos, *On the Governance of the Empire*, 5, p. 52.1–13.

[18] Cf. П. Ангелов, *Военна сила и дипломация в средновековна България*, ВС 52.5, 1990, pp. 3–13.

[19] Щ. Атанасов, И. Дуйчев, Д. Ангелов, Г. Цанкова-Петкова, Д. Христов, Б. Чолпанов, *Българското военно...*, p. 98; Д. Ангелов, С. Кашев, Б. Чолпанов, *Българска военна...*, pp. 150–152.

Military actions were preceded by a thorough reconnaissance of the future area of conflict; the size of the forces and the opponent's intentions were evaluated not only by scouts, but also through the use of spies who were active in the hostile army's rear.

The Bulgarian battle formation was characterised by its considerable fragmentation, both frontal and in depth. At the very front there were the scouting parties and the vanguard. Behind them, there were two battle lines, then the reserves, and finally the camp's protective troops located 1.5–3 km behind rest of the army. The first battle line was primarily comprised of a dense horse archer formation, occupying the flanks, and to a lesser extent of infantry, concentrated in the centre[20]. The second line duplicated the arrangement of infantry and horse, improved the formation's stability and was tasked with repulsing a potential attack of the enemy, weakening – thanks to its depth – the impetus of the strike. The enemy was at first harassed by consecutive attacks of the riders who, approaching the front line, showered the enemy with arrows and retreated towards friendly troops. If this course of action did not compel the enemy to give chase and, through breaking his formation, allow an easier victory, then after achieving the desired effect (exhaustion) a frontal attack of all the Bulgarian forces followed, preceded by another powerful archery barrage. According to a testimony from the period, the attacking Bulgarians raised incomprehensible and terrifying cries[21]. Generally, however, they preferred to fire projectiles at the enemy from a distance, feign flights, encircle the opponent and draw him into ambushes[22]. For the latter, they preferred to use convenient to organise mud traps, forested or hilly terrain, as well as mountain passes. It is worth noting that according to the Byzantine authors Bulgarians excelled at fighting in mountainous areas – and the imperial historians considered them to have been in part mountain dwellers[23].

[20] Cf. Leo VI the Wise, XVIII, 53–55, p. 456.268–280.

[21] Continuator of Theophanes, VI, 8, p. 401.15–17.

[22] Leo VI the Wise, XVIII, 54, p. 456.271–273; XVIII, 56, p. 456.281–283; С. Хаджииванов, *Засадите в старобългарското военно изкуство*, ВС 23.4, 1954, pp. 36–57.

[23] For more on this subject, see the following chapter of the present monograph – Part Two, Chapter VI.

Of course, they also gave battle to their enemies in an open field. They chased the defeated enemy down when possible, until his full destruction[24]. This must have been surprising to the Byzantines, for the majority of their opponents, after achieving victory, immediately threw themselves into looting the battle field and the baggage train[25]. Leo VI even advised that when the Bulgarian army was broken, it should not be pursued at any cost, for Bulgarians usually fiercely fought back even when retreating from the battlefield[26]. In addition, a disorganised pursuit could lead the victorious army into a previously prepared or an *ad hoc* ambush. It has already been mentioned that during the discussed period Bulgarians were fully versed in the art of besieging and capturing fortified settlements. They besieged a city and waited until its supplies ran out; they attempted to negotiate with defenders, promising them inviolability in case of surrender, or on the contrary – threatened the inhabitants with cruel consequences if they do not surrender the city willingly. They often used tricks that allowed them to gain entry into a city, or lured out the defenders beyond their fortifications. A full-on assault was the final resort.

Similarly, the Bulgarians made efforts to effectively defend their own towns and strongholds, and in case of an external threat offered shelter behind their walls also to the rural population. In those cases they traditionally made sallies into the enemy camps, mainly to destroy supplies and burn down siege engines[27].

The number of Bulgarian troops. Despite appearances, this question is one of the most difficult when it comes to interpreting the accounts of mediaeval authors. While the Byzantine writers – who in this matter

[24] Cf. Leo VI the Wise, XVIII, 57, pp. 456.284 – 458.288.

[25] Щ. Атанасов, И. Дуйчев, Д. Ангелов, Г. Цанкова-Петкова, Д. Христов, Б. Чолпанов, *Българското военно...*, p. 108; Д. Ангелов, С. Кашев, Б. Чолпанов, *Българска военна...*, p. 154.

[26] Leo VI the Wise, XVIII, 72, p. 462.343–346.

[27] Cf. Д. Ангелов, С. Кашев, Б. Чолпанов, *Българска военна...*, pp. 153–156. For more on the Bulgarian strategy and tactics, see: Щ. Атанасов, И. Дуйчев, Д. Ангелов, Г. Цанкова-Петкова, Д. Христов, Б. Чолпанов, *Стратегия и тактика на българската армия през епохата на феодализма*, ВС 26.4, 1957, pp. 39–72.

are our main source of information – quite often mentioned various numbers, their relations tend to obscure the image rather than offer specific and trustworthy calculations. Large, round numbers (e.g. 30 000 soldiers) appear most often, which allows us merely to establish that they wanted to inform their readers that many Bulgarians had been present, i.e. their armed forces were numerous. Helpful in this regard – through analogy – may be calculations regarding Byzantine armed forces during the same period. Firstly, we have reliable information regarding the Empire: in the so-called strategikons, the works devoted to the art of war. In the light of the relations of the tenth-century Byzantine polemologists, the customary size of the active military force numbered several thousand troops, sometimes exceeding ten thousand soldiers (both cavalry and infantry)[28]. The entire military potential of Byzantium during the Middle Byzantine period is estimated at ca. 70 000 – 80 000 men. Therefore it is assumed that the maximum number of troops attacking enemy territory – and this is assuming that the strategic goal was of utmost importance – reached 20 000 – 25 000 soldiers[29]. How these estimates could relate to Bulgaria? One first has to remember that the economic potential and available manpower, and therefore the ability to mobilise soldiers, of Bulgaria was smaller than that of its southern neighbour. Therefore the total number of Bulgarian troops had to be lower as well. On the other hand, the operational units may have been of similar size, and as such number between several and over ten thousand soldiers. The defensive forces in turn, of course when considering the entirety of Bulgaria, were at least twice as large[30]. In some cases the Bulgarians could obviously have

---

[28] J.F. H a l d o n, *Byzantine Praetorians: an administrative, institutional and social survey of the Opsikion and Tagmata, c. 580–900*, Bonn 1984, pp. 276–297; H.-J. K ü h n, *Die Byzantinische Armee im 10. und 11. Jahrhundert. Studien zur Organisation der Tagmata*, Wien 1991, pp. 56–60; J.-C. C h e y n e t, *Les effesctifs de l'armée byzantine aux Xe–XIIe s.*, CCM 38.4, 1995, pp. 319–320; W. T r e a d g o l d, *Byzantium and Its Army 284–1081*, Stanford 1995, pp. 64–86; M. W h i t t o w, *The Making of Byzantium, 600–1025*, Berkeley–Los Angeles 1996, pp. 181–193; J. H a l d o n, *Warfare, State and Society in the Byzantine World, 565–1204*, London 1999, pp. 99–106.

[29] M. W h i t t o w, *The Making...*, p. 191; J. H a l d o n, *Warfare...*, p. 106.

[30] Cf. B. K e c k a r o v, *Войни на Българите в Тракия 689–972 г.*, София 1940, p. 164; Б. Ч о л п а н о в, Е. А л е к с а н д р о в, *Военна история...*, pp. 57–58.

had a somewhat larger military force – in situations when they enlisted the aid of numerous allied troops, e.g. the Pechenegs. Nonetheless, it needs to be emphasised that all these estimates are highly hypothetical in nature.

2. The Defence System of the Bulgarian State

At the beginning of this brief argument I need to note that it is not my goal to carefully reconstruct the defence system of the tenth-century Bulgarian state, especially when in the field of archaeological study, despite visible progress, much remains to be done in this matter. Here, I am more interested in the Bulgarian defence doctrine (if one indeed existed and was being consciously implemented) than its material realisation, even though the latter subject is extremely interesting.

The effectiveness of the defence of the Bulgarian territory consisted of three basic elements.

Firstly, the skilful use of the natural elements demarcating the border, provided by the shape of the terrain itself. This was primarily the Haimos Mountains range, which during the discussed period constituted an internal barrier i.e. located entirely within the Bulgarian territory and several tens of kilometres distant from the southern border of the state, guarding access to the most vital regions of Bulgaria. This massif also constituted the southern border of Bulgaria's *internal territory* during the seventh–tenth centuries period, and because of this one may assume that the previously mentioned *ichirgu boila* also commanded the military units that guarded the mountain passes. He was most likely also responsible for maintaining the local fortifications, whether earthwork, wooden, or stone[31]. It would appear that his duties also included

[31] И. Дуйчев, *Проблеми из средновековната история на Преслав*, [in:] i d e m, *Проучвания върху средновековната българска история и култура*, София 1981, pp. 25–26; В. Гюзелев, *Кавханите…*, p. 29.

constructing bridges over rivers. Another natural demarcation feature was the Danube, which delineated the northern border of the internal area of the Khanate-Tsardom. The other mountain massifs and rivers and lakes that lay within – or along – the borders undoubtedly served a similar role. Bulgaria's eastern border was defined by the Black Sea shore.

Secondly, the enhancement of the natural land and sea barriers through raising fortifications, providing further defensibility[32]. Originally this role was served by long earthwork ramparts, located in the most threatened and most easily accessible parts of the country – in Dobrudzha, where raids of Asiatic nomads were expected, along the Black Sea coast, where Byzantine army landings were likely, and in the mountain passes of Stara Planina, athwart the direction of the empire's attacks by land. It appears that similar, but masonry fortifications were raised in Dobrudzha during the tenth century. While the chronology of these monuments is strongly debated in the academic literature, it should be noted that the scholars often focus exclusively on the north-eastern

---

[32] For example, see: К. Шкорпил, *Укрепления на Първата българска държава в Северна Добруджа край Дунава и Черноморския бряг*, ИБИД 16/17, 1940, pp. 525–535; J.-Ch. Poutiers, *A propos des forteresses antiques et médiévales de la plaine Danubienne (Essai de reconstruction du réseau routier entre Iskăr et Ogosta)*, EB 11.2, 1975, pp. 60–73; Д. Овчаров, *Към въпроса за укрепителната дейност на българската държава по долен Дунав през IX–X в.*, ВС 48.2, 1979, pp. 96–106; Ц. Дремсизова-Нелчинова, Д. Иванов, *Археологически паметници в Русенски окръг*, София 1983 (Danube); П. Мутафчиев, *Стари градища и друмове из долините на Стряма и Тополница*, [in:] idem, *Избрани произведения в два тома*, vol. I, ed. Д. Ангелов, София 1973, pp. 286–396; А. Попов, *Ролята на военноукрепителната система в Източната и Централната част на Стара Планина през време на българската средновековна държава*, ВС 37.4, 1968, pp. 61–72, specifically pp. 61–64, 71–72; idem, *Крепости по Сърнена гора*, ИБИД 31, 1977, pp. 39–50; idem, *Военнотопографският фактор при изграждането на отбранителните съоръжения по Южния склон на Стара Планина*, ВС 47.2, 1978, pp. 110–129; Д. Момчилов, *Средновековните крепости в южните части на Ришкия и Върбишкия проход*, ВС 59.5, 1990, pp. 14–43; И. Георгиев, *Военни пътища и преградни съоръжения в Ришкия проход*, ВС 62.2, 1993, pp. 5–23; idem, *Ранновизантийски и средновековни български укрепления за отбраната на Айтоския проход*, ВС 64.2, 1995, pp. 7–27 (Haimos). For the later period, see: А. Попов, *Старопланинската укрепителна система за защитата на средновековния Търновград*, ИОИМВТ 5, 1972, pp. 65–121.

earthworks, omitting analogous fortifications from the areas in Haimos, or the famous Erkesiya, the Bulgarian provenance of which has not yet been questioned. Construction of camps and earthwork fortifications along the main communication routes, which allowed movement across Bulgarian territory and access to its capital centres, was another solution employed in country's defence[33]. Such fortifications were therefore located along the most frequented routes, such as the ones leading through the Varbitsa and Rish passes of Stara Planina, and then further north up to the Danube Delta.

Even though during the discussed period the military engineering had generally made a shift from wood and earth fortifications to masonry defences[34], it would be a mistake to assume that the old (by then) fortifications were no longer being used, or that no new bulwarks of this type (wood and earthwork) had been raised. This can be seen from, for example, the fact that 'mixed' – stone, earth and wood – fortifications were being built when tsar Samuel was fortifying the area between the Ograzhden and Belassitsa mountain ranges, in Macedonia, at the beginning of the eleventh century[35]. Of course, it is true that during the latter half of the ninth, and during the tenth century, primarily stone

[33] On the subject of these fortifications and the entire debate surrounding them, see the seminal work of the best expert on the subject: Р. Р а ш е в, *Землената укрепителна система на Първото българско царство*, ППре 2, 1981, pp. 99–103; see also: i d e m, *Ранобългарски землени укрепителни съоръжения*, [in:] *Български средновековни градове...*, pp. 16–44; i d e m, *Старобългарски укрепления на Долния Дунав (VII–XI в.)*, Варна 1982; i d e m, *Българската езическа култура VII–IX в.*, София 2009, pp. 140–143.

[34] See i d e m, *Преходът от землена към каменна фортификация в Първото българско царство*, [in:] *Тангра. Сборник в чест на 70–годишнината на акад. Васил Гюзелев*, ed. М. К а й м а к а м о в а et al., София 2006, pp. 301–310.

[35] On the subject of these fortifications, see: Б. Ц в е т к о в, *Ключката отбранителна линия на цар Самуил от 1014 г. – научни постижения, проблеми и нови данни*, ПБА 1, 1992, pp. 87–91; Г. М и т р е в, *Самуиловата крепост. Битката при с. Ключ през 1014 г.*, [s.l., s.a.], pp. 1–18; Ц. К о м и т о в а, *Самуиловата крепост при Беласица – история и археология*, София 2015; Г. М и т р е в, *Самуиловата крепост-дема в Ключката клисура – нови теренни проучвания и наблюдения*, [in:] *Европейският Югоизток през втората половина на X – началото на XI век. История и култура*, ed. В. Г ю з е л е в, Г.Н. Н и к о л о в, София 2015, pp. 432–450.

fortifications were being raised, as they were better suited for the role of guarding and controlling of a given area. A particularly dense grouping of strongholds can be seen in Dobrudzha and Moesia Inferior: in the most important areas surrounding the capitals[36]. A considerable share of the stone fortifications had been created on the sites of the former, early Byzantine, strongholds; this was especially true of the ones rebuilt – or still being used – along the old Roman *limes* along the Danube and the Black Sea coast. In the area between the valley of Danube and the Stara Planina foothills the most strategically important strongholds were: to the south, the capital Preslav, and to the north, the riverside Dristra. This became particularly clear through the actions of the Rus' prince Svyatoslav in the years 968–971, when during the war with the Byzantines this ruler concentrated his forces in these two centres.

The situation to the south was somewhat different, as the ownership of Northern Thrace was divided between the two countries – Bulgaria and Byzantium – although one may indicate that its hinterland belonged to the former, while the latter held the Black Sea coast. During the tenth century the ports of Mesembria and Anchialos ended up within Bulgarian borders, which had a considerable significance for the country's defensibility: in the earlier times, when these centres remained in the Byzantine hands, they were used for naval operations against Bulgaria. An important defensive line also ran along the Belgrade – Naissos – Sredets (Serdica) – Philippoupolis route. A notable role was also played by the centres surrounding the Northern Thrace area – i.a. Beroe, Markellai, Develtos. The multi-year struggle of tsar Samuel against emperor Basil II in Macedonia and the contesting of the mountain strongholds therein evidence the existence of a system of fortifications intended to secure the topographically crucial sites in the given area[37].

---

[36] Д. Рабовянов, *Извънстоличните каменни крепости на Първото българско царство (IX – началото на XI век)*, София 2011; idem, *Традиции и влияния в крепостното строителство на Първото българско царство в периода X – началото на XI век*, [in:] *Европейският Югоизток...*, pp. 423–431.

[37] See: Г.Н. Николов, *Централизъм и регионализъм в ранносредновековна България (края на VII – началото на XI в.)*, София 2005, pp. 169–191; Д. Момчилов, *Ролята на Анхиало и Маркели при военните конфликти между България и Византия*

Thirdly, none of the above elements would have been able to provide a sufficient defence for the Bulgarian lands if it were not for the state's sufficient economic and demographic hinterland. Provision of the necessary financial (securing equipment and sustenance for the soldiers) and human resources – a sufficient number of soldiers able to man the defences – were vital.

As can be therefore seen, strongholds were raised and used along the rivers, sea coast and communication routes – including those which allowed crossing mountain barriers. The country was protected by attempting to control the roads which ran through it, allowing access to the hinterland. Aside from major centres of government, such as Pliska, Preslav and Ohrid, the majority of Bulgarian strongholds were nonetheless small[38].

през периода на Първото българско царство, [in:] *Великотърновският Университет "Св. св. Кирил и Методий" и българската археология*, vol. I, ed. Б. Борисов, Велико Търново 2010, pp. 437–448.

[38] Cf. e.g.: Г. Баласчев, *Укрепителните работи на старобългарската войска*, Мин 3.10 (1), 1918, pp. 1–44; К. Шкорпил, *Старбългарска съобщителна мрежа около Преслав и крепостите по нея*, БИБ 2.2, 1929, pp. 80–111; И. Велков, *Няколко тракийски и средновековни крепости по Средна Арда*, ИБИД 16/18, 1940, pp. 70–78; И. Богданов, *Български твърдини. Книжовни средища, крепости, манастири в София и Софийско*, София 1971; Д. Овчаров, *Археологически аспекти на българската ранносредновековна фортификация*, ВС 42.1, 1973, pp. 54–71; П.С. Коледаров, *Отбранителната и граничната система на България от 681 до 1018 г.*, ВС 47.3, 1978, pp. 109–123; *Български средновековни градове и крепости*, vol. I, *Градове и крепости по Дунав и Черно Море*, ed. А. Кузев, В. Гюзелев, Варна 1981; М.А. Харбова, *Отбранителните съоръжения в българското средновековие*, София 1981; С. Ваклинов, *Архитектура*, [in:] *История на България в четиринадесет тома*, vol. II, *Първа българска държава*, ed. Д. Ангелов, София 1981, pp. 423–426; idem, *Бит, строителство и изкуство*, [in:] *История на България*..., pp. 184–187; idem, *Втората българска столица Преслав*, [in:] *История на България*..., pp. 296–300; Д.С. Овчаров, *Византийски и български крепости V–X век*, София 1982; Н. Гиздова, *Средновековни крепости в Родопите на територията на Пазарджишки окръг*, ИМЮБ 9, 1983, pp. 69–78; Б. Димитров, А. Хаджийски, *Каменните щитове на България*, София 1988; *Материали за картата на средновековната българска държава (територията на днешна Североизточна България)*, ed. Р. Рашев, ППре 7, 1995, pp. 155–332; С. Бояджиев, *Крепостно строителство през Първото българско царство*,

[in:] П. Балабанов, С. Бояджиев, Н. Тулешков, *Крепостно строителство по българските земи*, София 2000, pp. 135–186; В. Генадиева, С. Чохаджиев, *Археологически паметници от Кюстендилско*, vol. I, *Археологически паметници от Кюстендилското краище*, Велико Търново 2002; i i d e m, *Археологически паметници от Кюстендилско*, vol. II, *Археологически паметници от Каменица*, Велико Търново 2003; Н. Овчаров, Д. Коджаманова, *Перперикон и околните твърдини през Средновековието. Крепостното сторителство в Източните Родопи*, София 2003; Б. Чолпанов, Е. Александров, *Военна история...*, pp. 68–70; Н. Бояджиев, *Крепостната система в Средните Родопи през късната античност и средновековието*, [in:] *Laurea...*, vol. I, София 2009, pp. 103–110; С. Попов, *Замъкът в Европа и България през Средните Векове*, София 2011.

VI

Kirił Marinow

Wild, Haughty and Menacing Highlanders: Bulgarians and Mountains in the Context of Byzantine-Bulgarian Armed Conflicts

Academics studying the history of the early mediaeval Bulgaria, particularly prior to its Christianisation (seventh to ninth centuries) made us accustomed to see Bulgarians as a solely nomadic people, comprised entirely of riders inhabiting the plains around the capital of Pliska, Dobrudzha, and the Danube Plain. Of course, this view is well substantiated in both the testimony of the written sources, and in the archaeological material. According to some scholars, there is also evidence that during this earliest period of the Danubian Khanate Bulgarians were also taking up agriculture and led a more settled lifestyle. For the tenth and eleventh centuries, and therefore also for the period of tsar Peter I's reign, the literature of the subject rightly presents the Bulgarians as a fully settled people. One should however note that the academic debates regarding these issues do not fully exhaust the matter of the presentation of Bulgarians by Byzantine authors. It turns out that a wealth of information, scattered throughout the sources, indicates that the southern neighbours saw Bulgarians in part as highlanders.

One of the most important areas during the existence of the so-called First Bulgarian State was the Haimos Mountains massif (Lat. Haemus, Gr. Αἶμος, Tur. Balkan, encompassing the area of modern Predbalkan, Stara Planina and Sredna Gora)[1]. This range, cutting the modern Bulgaria in two, was a natural border between the so-called inner area of the Bulgarian state: Danube Plain and Dobrudzha, where the capitals of the early mediaeval state lie, and the Northern Thrace, where the armed conflicts between the Byzantine Empire and Bulgaria had been taking place. It is with this massif that the Bulgarians were most often associated in the Byzantine authors' relations. Another such area was the particularly mountainous territory of Macedonia, and this was the result of emperor Basil II's (976–1025) lengthy and exhausting wars with the Cometopouloi, fought in this very land[2]. It is characteristic that this fact did not escape the attention of the Byzantine experts on the art of war. The anonymous author of the *On setting up the camp* (Περὶ καταστάσεως ἀπλήκτου, also known as Ἀνωνύμου βιβλίον τακτικόν), who wrote his work most likely soon after 986, clearly based his polemological reasoning on the experiences of the Byzantine-Bulgarian skirmishes in the mountainous regions of Macedonia. He treated the Bulgarians as opponents with whom the Byzantines came to fight in the mountains[3]. Undoubtedly these many

[1] On this massif, see *i.a.*: H. Inalcık, *Balkan*, [in:] *EI.NE*, vol. I, pp. 998–100; T. Lehr-Spławiński, H. Kappesowa, W. Swoboda, *Bałkany*, [in:] *SSS*, vol. I, pp. 71–72; W. Swoboda, *Haimos*, [in:] *SSS*, vol. II, p. 182; H. von Geisau, Chr. Danoff, *Haimos*, [in:] *KP.LA*, vol. II, pp. 919–920; I. Dujčev, R. Werner, *Balkan*, [in:] *LdM*, vol. I, cols. 1380–1381; G. Schramm, *Haimos "Balkangebrige" und seine Nachfolgelautungen eine Beispielstudie zur Entwicklung des Thrakischen*, LBa 27.3, 1984, pp. 59–69; A.P. Kazhdan, *Balkans*, [in:] *ODB*, vol. I, pp. 248–249; P. Soustal, *Tabula Imperii Byzantini*, vol. VI, *Thrakien (Thrakē, Rodopē und Haimimontos)*, Wien 1991, pp. 279–280; К. Гагова, *Тракия през българското Средновековие. Историческа география*, София 2002, pp. 319–322.

[2] Cf. P.M. Strässle, *Krieg und Kriegführung in Byzanz. Die Kriege Kaiser Basileos' II. gegen die Bulgaren (976–1019)*, Köln–Weimar–Wien 2006.

[3] Cf. Ἀνωνύμου Βιβλίον τακτικόν, XV, XXI, pp. 288.6–8, 304.33–34; П. Мутафчиев, *Книга за българите*, ed. В. Гюзелев. София 1987, p. 81; В.В. Кучма, *Военная организация Византийской империи*, Санкт-Петербург 2001, p. 296.

years of armed struggle reinforced the image of Bulgarians as highlanders[4]. These, however, were not the only examples regarding the perception of the Bulgarian rulers' subjects as mountain warriors.

For example, the so-called *Scriptor Incertus de Leone Armenio* commented the outcome of the Byzantine-Bulgarian clash near Versinikia in 813 in the following words:

> Therefore seeing this [the defeat of Aplakes' soldiers – K.M.] all the theme units fled, and those who recently boasted that they would fight in defence of the emperor and Christians had very nearly abandoned the emperor himself. They spoke thus: *When we entered Bulgaria we were defeated on terrain where it was difficult to move, while we outside [of the terrain] would have been able to win a victory over them* (ἐν τόποις δυσβάτοις ἐκυρίευσαν ἡμᾶς, ἔξωθεν δὲ ἐπὶ κάμπου νικῆσαι αὐτοὺς ἔχομεν). However all of this was untruthfulness; for they fled without a fight.[5]

In the light of the above source passage I say that the opinion of the Byzantine soldiers was that the Bulgarians had won exclusively thanks to exploiting the topographic features of the battlefield[6]. Also emerging from the text is an interesting association which took shape in the thinking of the defeated Byzantines. They associated Bulgaria with inaccessibility and defeat, while a victory gained outside of the area (lit. outside – ἔξωθεν)

---

[4] On the importance of mountains in Byzantine-Bulgarian military clashes see e.g. П. Мутафчиев, *Книга...*, pp. 65–89, 113–138; К. Маринов, *В дербите на Хемус (За някои страни в ролята на планината през периода VII–IX в.)*, Pbg 37.4, 2013, pp. 60–73; И. Иванов, *Ролята на Старопланинската област във военните кампании през Средновековието: Опит за критичен количествен анализ*, ИРИМГ 2, 2014, pp. 78–90; К. Маринов, *Стратегическата роля на Старопланинската и Средногорската вериги в светлината на българо-византийските военни сблъсъци през VII–XI век*, ИРИМГ 2, 2014, pp. 111–134.

[5] *Scriptor Incertus de Leone Armenio*, p. 338.6–12.

[6] Similarly П. Ангелов, *България и българите в представите на византийците (VII–XIV век)*, София, 1999, p. 27. Cf. J. Bonarek, *Romajowie i obcy w kronice Jana Skylitzesa. Identyfikacja etniczna Bizantyńczyków i ich stosunek do obcych w świetle kroniki Jana Skylitzesa*, Toruń 2003, p. 129, who – on the basis of John Skylitzes' relation – shows that in this author's opinion (and in others') Bulgarians gained victory as a result of the betrayal and flight of Leo the Armenian.

of the kleisourai (i.e. mountain passes) with fighting on a plain, where it was possible to make use of all of the advantages of the Byzantine armed forces[7]. They therefore thought that in a pitched, open battle they would have easily defeated the Bulgarians, who in turn became dangerous opponents in a mountainous terrain that was advantageous to them.

The account of Leo the Deacon regarding the breakdown of the peaceful Byzantine-Bulgarian relations during the reign of emperor Nikephoros II Phokas refers directly to tsar Peter's times. According to the relation of *History* of Leo, the emperor, having rejected Bulgarian demands to pay out the customary tribute, organised an expedition against the Bulgarians. However, he was said to have given it up once he learned just how inaccessible Bulgaria was. Leo characterised it, initially in general terms, as:

> densely wooded and full of cliffs (ἀμφιλαφὲς καὶ κρημνῶδες) [for, to use the language of the poet, in the land of the Mysians *in every way evil was heaped upon evil*); an area full of roughnesses and cliffs (σηραγγώδης καὶ κρημνῶδης) followed upon a region that was densely wooded and overgrown with bushes (ἀμφιλαφῆ καὶ λοχμώδη), and then immediately after that would be a marshy and swampy area (τελματώδης τε καὶ σομφώδης); for the region located near Haimos and Rhodope [mountains], which is watered with great rivers, is extremely damp, heavily forested, and surrounded on every side by impassable mountains (ὄρεσι δυσβάτοις)]. When the emperor Nikephoros observed this, he did not think he should lead the Roman force through dangerous regions with its ranks broken (ἀσύντακτος), as if he were providing sheep (τὰ βοσκήματα) to be

[7] This includes, i.a., the excellent organisation of the army (including supply system), the ability to use various tactical solutions, better equipment and numerical superiority – cf. П. Мутафчиев, *История на българския народ (681–1323)*, ed. В. Гюзелев, София 1986, p. 123; idem, *Книга...*, p. 66; J.V.A. Fine, *The Early Medieval Balkans. A Critical Survey from the Sixth Century to the Late Twelfth Century*, Ann Arbor 1983, pp. 77–78; П. Павлов, *Залезът на Първото българско царство (1015–1018)*, София 1999, pp. 24, 27; idem, *Бунтари и авантюристи в средновековна България*, Велико Търново 2000, pp. 31, 32; П. Петров, *Самуил – царят воин*, София 2014, p. 127; Т. Томов, *Византия – позната и непозната*, [2]София 2014, pp. 206–234.

> slaughtered by the Mysians [i.e. the Bulgarians – K.M.], for it is said[8] that on several previous occasions the Romans came to grief in the rough terrain of Mysia [i.e. Bulgaria – K.M.], and were completely destroyed. He decided therefore not to run any risks in impassable and dangerous territory. So he took the army and returned to Byzantium.[9]

All of the above features of the terrain constituted serious obstacles for military activities. The irregularities, cliffs and forests listed in the text may be associated with the area of Predbalkan, Stara Planina and Sredna Gora. It would seem that the author put particular emphasis specifically on the mountainous nature of the Bulgarian territory, for later he states that Nikephoros feared to lead the Byzantine army through these dangerous places (δι᾽ ἐπισφαλῶν χωρίων), to avoid it getting slaughtered like cattle by the Mysians (Bulgarians). This fear stemmed from what was said about the *Rhomaioi* (Byzantines) – that they often suffered defeats in inaccessible areas of Mysia (Bulgaria), which resulted in the complete destruction of Byzantine forces[10]. There is no doubt that Leo primarily meant those that were suffered by the Byzantines in the passes of Haimos, in particular the disaster from 811 in which the emperor Nikephoros I Genikos (802–811) had perished[11]. I believe that in abandoning further expedition

[8] On the question see: A.-M., Talbot, D.F. Sullivan, *Introduction*, [in:] *The History of Leo the Deacon. Byzantine Military Expansion in the Tenth Century*, ed., transl. A-M. Talbot, D.F. Sulivan, assist. G.T. Dennis, S. McGrath, Washington 2006, p. 14: *he* [Leo – K.M.] *perhaps seeks to indicate that he has not examined the sources directly or is reporting information derived orally*.

[9] Leo the Deacon, IV, 5–6, pp. 62.13 – 63.4 (transl. p. 111, with my minor modifications – K.M.). Identifying the Haimos from the sources with Strandzha is in this case unconvincing – thus К. Гагова, *Тракия...*, p. 47.

[10] Leo the Deacon, IV, 6, pp. 62.20 – 63.4.

[11] П. Мутафчиев, *Книга...*, p. 81; М.Я. Сюзюмов, С.А. Иванов, *Коментарий*, [in:] Лев Дякон, *История*, transl. М.М. Копыленко, comm. М.Я. Сюзюмов, С.А. Иванов, ed. Г.Г. Литаврин, Москва 1988, p. 182, fn. 22; П. Мутафчиев, *Лекции по история на Византия*, vol. II, ed. Г. Бакалов, София 1995, p. 250; Й. Андреев, М. Лалков, *Исторически справочник. Българските ханове и царе. От хан Кубрат до цар Борис III*, Велико Търново 1996, p. 111; П. Павлов, *Борби за оцеляване. Упадък на българската държавност*, [in:] *История на българите*, vol. I, *От древността до края на XVI век*, ed. Г. Бакалов, София

Nikephoros II was chiefly considering the dangers of the mountain passages since, as an experienced commander, he knew that advancing through the narrow passes would disrupt his army's formation – cf. Greek ἀσύντακτος, an antonym of the word for an orderly military formation: σύνταξις. It was passing through narrow, uneven and sometimes densely forested mountain passes that caused disruption in the marching military columns, making them much more vulnerable to an enemy attack, especially from one who occupied a higher position in a battle[12]. Panic often broke out among soldiers in such circumstances, and the terrain was tactically disadvantageous as well: the Byzantine soldiers could be easy prey for the Bulgarians. In Deacon's words, they become easily slaughtered 'cattle' (τὰ βοσκήματα)[13].

The prominent role of the mountainous terrain in Byzantine-Bulgarian clashes at the turn of the tenth and eleventh centuries was also highlighted by Michael Attaleiates, who first stressed that the Bulgarian soil *is large, broad, accessed through narrow passes* (πολλὴν καὶ μεγάλην καὶ στενόπορον οὖσαν), *and had for many years resisted previous emperors precisely because it is so difficult to exit from its defiles* (διὰ τὸ δυσεξίτητον τῶν ἐν αὐτῇ αὐλώνων)[14].

2003, p. 281. Other ideas – С.А. Иванов, *Византийско-болгарские отношения в 966–969 гг.*, ВВ 42, 1981, p. 93; *The History of Leo*..., p. 111, fn. 42, associated i.a. with the past of the Phokas family, including the Byzantine defeat at Acheloos in 917. It is worth pointing out that Leo himself, in another part of his work, attested to his knowledge of both Nikephoros I's defeat and of the battle of Acheloos – Leo the Deacon, VI, 9, p. 104.16–17; VII, 7, pp. 122.23 – 124.12.

[12] On this subject – К. Маринов, *Преминаването на планинските проходи според византийските и някои антични трактати за военното изкуство*, [in:] *Българско средновековие: общество, власт, история. Сборник в чест на проф. д-р Милияна Каймакамова*, ed. А. Николов, Г.Н. Николов, София 2013, pp. 205–220; idem, *Przez wąwozy i lasy. Armia bizantyńska wobec trudno dostępnych obszarów w świetle IX konstytucji Taktyk Leona VI Mądrego*, AUL.FH 99, 2017, pp. 11–32.

[13] More on this testimony – K. Marinow, *Hémos comme barrière militaire. L'analyse des* écrits *historiques de Léon le Diacre et de Jean Skylitzès au sujet de la campagne de guerre des empereurs byzantins Nicéphore II Phocas en 967 et de Jean I Tzymiscès en 971*, BMd 2, 2011, pp. 444–455.

[14] Michael Attaleiates, p. 8.2–6 (transl., p. 15); similar characterisation – p. 370.4–9.

While he was primarily thinking of the mountainous areas of Illyria and Macedonia, his observation could easily have also referred to the southern part of Haimos (specifically, the Pass of Ihtiman in Sredna Gora), since the above remark was made in the context of the Byzantine army entering Triaditsa (nowadays Sofia) in 1041; to reach the city one first had to cross the Pass. The use of adjective δυσεξίτητον, literally meaning '[place] difficult to leave' appears to suggest that the historian was primarily considering the dangers that threatened the Byzantine armies, and the defeats they suffered after having entered the treacherous hostile territory. In other words, perhaps it was not particularly difficult to enter them, but safe departure was an entirely different matter. This, in turn, could lead into the question of ambushes, prepared by Bulgarians for the imperial troops, returning from an expedition[15]. In relation to the sustained defiance towards the previous Byzantine rulers (among whom Basil II had undoubtedly been the foremost), Attaleiates may have used δυσεξίτητον thinking of Basil's the disastrous defeat of 986. It happened during troops' withdrawal through a mountain pass, which at the time lay on the borderland of Bulgarian controlled territory. In any case, the context clearly indicates mountain combat.

Both of the passages cited above clearly show that Bulgarians were seen as inhabitants of an inaccessible land, who made use of its defensive qualities with utmost skill. Although during the early Middle Ages the settlement in the ridge area of Stara Planina proper was not particularly dense (the upper reaches have been gradually occupied during the tenth century), the natural and strong association of the mountains with their foothills (with a much higher population density – we have archaeological evidence of settlements from the Predbalkan from the ninth century)[16]

[15] On this strategy see: П. Мутафчиев, *Книга...*, pp. 72–73 (the Bulgarians), 78–80 (the Pechenegs); К. Маринов, *Стратегическата...*, pp. 114, 118 (the Bulgarians).

[16] On the mediaeval settlement in the Sredna Gora and Stara Planina, see: Л. Динев, Л. Мелнишки, *Стара планина*, София, 1962, p. 60; H. Maruszczak, *Bułgaria*, Warszawa 1971, pp. 294–295; Р. Рашев, *Появата на средновековни селища във високите части на Стара планина*, ШУЕКП.ТКИБ 1, 1997, pp. 108–113; Н. Хрисимов, *За времето на усвояване на предпланинските и планинските райони в Първото българско царство*, ИРИМГ 2, 2014, pp. 55–69.

led to Bulgarians being thought of as inhabiting Haimos[17]. The relatively smooth transition of the Predbalkan into the Plain of Danube was further conducive to this outlook. We have early tenth-century testimony of such views about Bulgarians. In the *Life of St. Evaristus* (819–897), the hegumenos of the Kokorobion monastery near Constantinople, written during the first quarter of the tenth century, we find a characteristic description of the Bulgarian people (ethnos): *there is a Scythian people settled in the Haimos Mountains by the river Danubios, and called Bulgarians* (Ἔθνος ἐστὶ σκυθικὸν ἔνδον τοῦ Αἵμου ὄρους παρὰ τὸν Δανούβιον ποταμὸν ᾠκισμένον, οὓς καλοῦσι Βουλγάρους)[18]. It is no coincidence that John Geometres, a Byzantine monk, poet and a former soldier, cursed the treacherous Haimos Mountains in relation to the anti-Byzantine activity of the Cometopouloi and the defeat of the imperial troops in the so-called Imperial Kleisoura (the aforementioned Ihtiman Pass):

> Begone trees, sinister mountains!
> Begone, rocks unreachable by birds!
> Where the lion feared to face the fawns.[19]

The *lion* is of course Basil II, the *fawns* are a contemptuous epithet denoting Bulgarians, indicating their weakness and fearfulness, and the fact that they were living in the mountains (like some species of deer)[20].

[17] It needs to be stressed that during the Middle Ages the area of Stara Planina and its foothills (the so-called Predbalkan) have were considered to have been a single massif. Similarly, from the modern general geographic, morphological and structural perspective both of these entities should be treated as a single whole. – H. Maruszczak, *Bułgaria...*, pp. 296–297; Х. Тишков, Цв. Михайлов, Л. Зяпков, Д. Горунова, *Предбалканска област*, [in:] *География на България в три тома*, vol. III, *Физикогеографско и социално-икономическо райониране*, ed. К. Мишев, София 1989, p. 65; П. Пенчев, Х. Тишков, М. Данева, Д. Горунова. *Старопланинска област*, [in:] *География на България...*, p. 86.

[18] *Life of Saint Evariste*, 7, p. 301.11–13.

[19] John Geometres, col. 934 A; Jean Géomètre, 90, p. 306.

[20] Niketas Choniates used the same term to denote Bulgarians in association with the Haimos – cf. K. Marinow, *Hemus jako baza wypadowa i miejsce schronienia w okresie walk o restytucję państwowości bułgarskiej pod koniec XII i na początku XIII wieku*,

In other words, the author wanted to emphasise that due to the difficult and dangerous situation in the mountainous area, something unimaginable had happened – the adult ruler of the animals, symbolically representing here the mighty Byzantine emperor, became afraid of the normally timid, and also young – therefore immature – fawns, personifying the feeble Bulgarian forces (or their leaders), who were in turn afraid to face the basileus in an open field. One should also point to the view illustrated by Emilie Marlene Van Opstall, who noticed the parallel between the appellation of the animal and the name of a Byzantine Magister, Leo Melissenos. Melissenos took part in Basil II's expedition in 986, staying behind to secure the army's rear at the treacherous Ihtiman's Pass, but in the end he abandoned his post. Opstall thought that Geometres's 'lion' referred to this imperial commander and his betrayal – his fear of resisting the fawns. In addition, the discussed scholar thinks the appellation also related to the wretched condition of the entire Byzantine army[21].

In the face of this defeat, the author urged the emperor Nikephoros II Phokas to rise from the grave and roar like a lion, for the following reason: *Teach the foxes* [i.e. the Bulgarians – K.M.] *to live among the rocks* (Δίδαξον οἰκεῖν τὰς ἀλώπεκας πέτραις)![22] In other words, the basileus was to prevent the Bulgarians from descending upon the plains and plundering the empire's lands, and to make them remain in what is the natural habitat of foxes – rocky clefts. The poet indicates that Bulgarians resided in the Haimos Mountians. In other words he was saying:

> Emperor, show them where they belong, may they not dare to leave the mountains! May they sit quietly and obediently in the mountain slits and caves, out of fear of the Roman might!

[in:] *Cesarstwo bizantyńskie. Dzieje. Religia. Kultura. Studia ofiarowane Profesorowi Waldemarowi Ceranowi przez uczniów na 70-lecie Jego urodzin*, ed. P. Krupczyński, M.J. Leszka, Łask–Łódź 2006, p. 184.

[21] Jean Géomètre, 90, pp. 306 (commentary to line 4), 308–309.

[22] John Geometres, col. 920 B.

The above portrayal of Bulgarians as a people inhabiting the mountain range in question appears to be valid also for the earlier period by a passage from the historical work of patriarch Nikephoros, written during the 780s. Describing one of the expeditions of emperor Constantine V (741–775) into Bulgaria, he stated that upon hearing the news of the approaching Byzantine forces, Bulgarians *fortified the difficult* [*passes*] *of the mountain range which they inhabited* (οἱ τὰς δυσχωρίας τοῦ περὶ αὐτοὺς ὄρους ἀνέφραττον)[23]. The reference in the passage is, once again, to the Stara Planina massif.

Considering that the Bulgarians resided in the Haimos, it is not surprising that the subjects of the Bulgarian khans and tsars were considered to have been, i.a., highlanders and herdsmen. This portrayal likely became more pronounced after the Bulgarians transitioned into a fully settled way of life and assimilated with the Slavs, during the latter half of the ninth and in the tenth centuries. This image was further influenced by the denser settlement of Stara Planina and Sredna Gora massifs by Bulgarians during that period. On the other hand, the seasonal nature of the mountain life, determined by the annual rhythm of driving the herds, was not unfamiliar to Bulgarians, previously a semi-nomadic and primarily pastoral people[24]. Furthermore, some sources appear to confirm

[23] N i k e p h o r o s, 77, p. 150.13–14 (transl., p. 151 – with my changes – K.M.).

[24] The question of the length and of the degree to which Bulgarians remained nomads is still being discussed – U. F i e d l e r, *Bulgars in the Lower Danube region. A survey of the archaeological evidence and of the state of current research*, [in:] *The Other Europe in the Middle Ages. Avars, Bulgars, Khazars, and Cumans*, ed. F. C u r t a, assist. R. K o v a l e v, Leiden–Boston 2008, pp. 200–202. Cf. A. М и л ч е в, *Славяне, протоболгары и Византия в болгарских землях в VI–IX вв.*, [in:] *Actes du XIVe Congrès International des Études Byzantines, Bucarest, 6–12 septembre 1971*, ed. M. B e r z a, E. S t ă n e s c u, vol. II, Bucarest, 1975, p. 393; J.V.A. F i n e, *The Early Medeival Balkans...*, p. 68; T. W a s i l e w s k i, *Historia Bułgarii*, [2]Wrocław 1988, pp. 36, 38–39, 40, 41; R. B r o w n i n g, *Bulgars, Turkic*, [in:] *ODB*, vol. I p. 338; И. Б о ж и л о в, В. Г ю з е л е в, *История на средновековна България VII–XIV век*, София 1999, p. 88; Х. М а т а н о в, *Балкански хоризонти. История, общества, личности*, vol. I, София 2004, p. 37; Г. В л а д и м и р о в, *Дунавска България и Волжка България. Формиране и промяна на културните модели (VII–XI в.)*, София 2005, pp. 21–26; П. Г е о р г и е в, *Раннобългарската култура V–VII век – култура "на колела"*, [in:] *Изследвания по българска средновековна археология. Сборник в чест на проф. Рашо Рашев*, ed. i d e m,

Bulgarian settlement in the Caucasus, and the presence of Kouber's kin in the mountains of Macedonia during the early eighth century[25].

Mountain people, including herdsmen, nonetheless evoked deep distrust and contempt on the part of Byzantine intellectuals, including authors of the chronicles and histories of the Empire. This is clearly attested by a remark which Leo the Deacon put into Nikephoros II's mouth. In reply to the demands of the previously mentioned tribute, the emperor was to have commanded the Bulgarian envoys to carry back his negative and contemptuous reply to tsar Peter I (927–969), a *leather-gnawing*

Велико Търново 2007, pp. 22–40; Л. Дончева-Петкова, *Отново за началото на ранносредновековната българска култура*, SAUS.S 5, 2010, pp. 511–526.

[25] On possible identification of Bulgarians as inhabitants of Caucasus and other Asian and European mountains – П. Коледаров, *Политическа география на средновековната българска държава*, vol. I, От 681 до 1018 г., София 1979, p. 9; Д. Ангелов, *Образуване на българската народност*, София 1981, pp. 109–110; И. Божилов, В. Гюзелев, *История...*, pp. 85–86; Ц. Степанов, *Власт и авторитет в ранносредновековна България (VII – ср. IX в.)*, София 1999, pp. 19, 24–27, 31–38; П. Георгиев, *Българските племенни имена и соционимът уногундури*, [in:] *Civitas Divino-Humana. In honorem Annorum LX Georgii Bakalov*, ed. Ц. Степанов, В. Вачкова, София 2004, pp. 693–708; idem, *Терделовите "чичовци" в Солунско и Кисиниите (към интерпретацията на Мадарския надпис I, ц)*, [in:] *Приноси към българската археология*, vol. VII, ed. Б. Петрунова, А. Аладжов, Е. Василева, София 2013, pp. 27–44; П. Голийски, *В подножието на Елбрус (Българите около Кавказ през II–V век според арменските извори)*, [in:] *Древните българи – дискусията продължава. Сборник*, ed. Ц. Степанов, София 2014, pp. 27–35 (however, some of conclusions by the last three authors have a strongly hypothetical character). On Kouber and his family – В. Бешевлиев, *Първобългарски надписи*, [2]София 1992, p. 105; И. Венедиков, *Прабългарите и християнството*, Стара Загора 1998, pp. 70–71. Cf. W. Swoboda, *Kuber*, [in:] *SSS*, vol. II, pp. 554–555; P. Charanis, *Kouver, the chronology of his activities and their ethnic effects on the regions around Thessalonica*, ByzS 11.1, 1970, pp. 229–247; М. Войнов, В. Тъпкова-Заимова, *България на Аспарух и България на Кубер*, ВС 51.5, 1982, pp. 47–56; В. Поповић, *Кубрат, Кубер и Аспарух*, Ста 37, 1986, pp. 113–126, especially 123–126; H. Ditten, *Ethnische Verschiebungen zwischen der Balkanhalbinsel und Kleinasien vom Ende des 6. bis zur Zweiten Hälfte des 9. Jahrhunderts*, Berlin 1993, pp. 68–72, 116–117, 219, 294–295, 365–368; К. Аджиевски, *Пелагонија во средниот век (од доаѓањето на Словените до паѓањето под турска власт)*, Скопје 1994, pp. 24–28; *Testimonia*, vol. IV, p. 14, fn. 4; П. Павлов, *Аспарух и Кувер*, [in:] idem, *Българското Средновековие. Познато и непознато. Страници от политическата и културната история на България VII–XIV век*, Велико Тъново 2008, pp. 9–20.

ruler who is clad in a leather jerkin[26]. Of course, this statement may be treated as merely a typical and insignificant invective, for the Bulgarian ruler was clad in raiments made of much finer materials. Undoubtedly, however, this wording fits in with other information that confirms a major role of pasturage and herding in the life of contemporary Bulgarians. It also refers to the traditional dress that was characteristic for the nomadic period of Bulgarian history.

The portrayal of Bulgarians as barbarians associated with Haimos[27] is not surprising, since for the Byzantines mountains were antithetical to civilisation, which developed on plains, in river valleys, and along the coasts[28]. A nomad, herdsman, a man who did not have a permanent place of residence, forced to continuously wander, appeared to them as someone devoid of any roots, unstable, and therefore untrustworthy and dangerous. Organised communities, including primarily inhabitants of large cities, which were mainstays of cultural life, reacted with fear and aversion to those who remained beyond the pale of the society, the half-wild mountainous communities. These were considered to have been gatherings of thieves, troublemakers, unruly and uncouth people, simpletons, and a kind of social margin. Theophylaktos, the Archbishop of Ohrid from the turn of the eleventh and twelfth centuries, even went so far as to say that the Bulgarian nature nourished all evil[29], and he clearly associated Bulgarians with mountain – pastoral – people[30]. I would further add

---

[26] Leo the Deacon, IV, 5, pp. 61.12 – 62.9 (transl., p. 110).

[27] Cf. in regard to the turn of the twelfth and thirteenth centuries – K. Marinow, *Hemus...*, pp. 183–197. The truthfulness of this perception of Bulgarians may be attested by the fact that due to the dominant mountainous terrain in the Balkans, the settlement was generally concentrated in the highland, semi-mountainous areas, e.g. Predbalkan (Stara Planina foothills); cf. Х. Матанов, *Балкански хоризонти...*, p. 273.

[28] А.П. Каждан, *Византийская культура (X–XII вв.)*, Санкт-Петербург 2000, p. 24; F. Braudel, *Morze Śródziemne i świat śródziemnomorski w epoce Filipa II*, vol. I, transl. T. Mrówczyński, M. Ochab, introd. B. Geremek, W. Kula, Warszawa [2]2004, pp. 38–39, 42–43, 48–52, 65.

[29] Theophylaktos of Ohrid, *Letters*, 96, p. 485.34–35.

[30] Cf. Theophylaktos of Ohrid, *Letters*, 101, p. 513.9–12. The author compared here Bulgarians to a herd of pigs, into which Jesus sent the demons (cf. Matt. 8, 28–32; Mark 5, 2–13; Luke 8, 27–33). The comparison, although not particularly pleasant, is very vivid, and related to the daily reality of the Archbishop, who lived

that such an image of the mountain dwellers was primarily composed of objective factors bound up with the nature of mountainous terrain, naturally hard to reach, with a variable and inhospitable climate, and devoid of sufficient supply of food. These areas, particularly the highest and least accessible, in which people were exposed to extreme natural conditions, tempered and seasoned them, prepared them to face dangers, which made them into excellent warriors, but also brutal and dangerous brigands[31].

It was no accident that in the oration *On the Treaty with the Bulgarians*, delivered with regard to the conclusion of Byzantine-Bulgarian peace in 927, the anonymous author (possibly Theodore Daphnopates) stated

among pastoral people, whom he must have seen herding their flocks across hillsides many times. The same comparison, although without pastoral connotations, was used by Niketas Choniates in regard to Peter and Assen, leaders of the Bulgarian rebellion of 1185 against Byzantine rule – Niketas Choniates, pp. 372.55 – 373.58; K. Маринов, *Новият Завет и византийската пропаганда. Още веднъж за Никита Хониат и българското освободително движение*, [in:] *Великите Асеневци*, ed. П. Павлов, Н. Кънев, Н. Хрисимов, Велико Търново 2016, pp. 70–83. Notker the Stammerer and Liudprand of Cremona also counted Bulgarians among the wild, cruel and unbridled tribes (immanissimas gentes; ferocissimas gentes) – Notker the Stammerer, 27, pp. 37.23 – 38.1; Liudprand of Cremona, *Retribution*, I. 11. For more extensive considerations regarding the portrayal of highlanders in the Middle Ages, cf. B. Geremek, *Człowiek marginesu*, [in:] *Człowiek średniowiecza*, ed. J. Le Goff, transl. M. Radożycka-Paoletti, Warszawa 2000, pp. 437, 456–457. Although this scholar analysed the position of herdsmen in the mediaeval Western Europe, their status in Byzantium was not much different – cf. the example of the Bessoi, a Thracian tribe, living in the Rhodope Mountains – Strabon, VII, 5, 12, p. 274.6; Paulinus of Nola, XVII, pp. 91.205 – 92.244; В. Гюзелев, *Княз Борис I. България през втората половина на IX век*, София 1969, pp. 90–94; S. Bărlieva, *Nicetas of Ramesiana and Two Apostolic Missions on the Balkans in the late Fourth – the early Fifth Century*, [in:] *In stolis repromissionis. Saints and Sainthood in Central and Eastern Europe*, ed. A. Nagusheva-Tihanova, M. Dimitrova, R. Kostova, R.R. Machlev, Sofia, 2012, pp. 271–278.

[31] G. Cherubini, *Chłop i życie na wsi*, [in:] *Człowiek średniowiecza...*, p. 164; Х. Матанов, *Балкански хоризонти...*, pp. 194, 296. John Geometres in one of his poems contrasted the luxury of living in a palace with the poverty and difficult living conditions found, i.a., in the mountains – John Geometres, col. 909 A. A positive portrayal of highlanders as warriors can be found i.a. in Anna Komnene, VIII, 5, 2, p. 246.32–35. So-called hajduks were active in the Balkans during the Osman period – Х. Матанов, *Балкански хоризонти...*, pp. 275, 292.

that it was the atmospheric conditions prevailing i.a. in the Haimos that stirred up the soul of the Bulgarian ruler Symeon I against Byzantium. According to the orator, it was gale, whirlwind (ὁ τυφών), downpour (ὁ ὑετός), hail (ἡ νιφάς), and even more powerful phenomena that shook these mountains that influenced the attitude of the Bulgarian ruler (οἵα καὶ μάλιστα τὸν Αἷμόν... κλονεῖ ἅ τῇ τοῦ ἄρχοντος προσεῤῥύη ψυχῇ)[32]. It was no accident after all that the Haimos Mountains appeared here, that symbol of Bulgarian haughtiness in the Byzantine eyes. In another part of his oration the rhetorician mentions wild and cruel mountain animals which, with God's help, will be tamed by the Byzantine emperor[33]. The wider context indicates that the author was thinking here of the Bulgarian ruler and his subjects. Thus the orator made it clear that it was the wild nature of the land in which Symeon grew up that shaped him into a violent and unrestrained man. In a veiled manner he suggested that the Bulgarian was not guided by his reason, as a mature Christian ought to be, but was subject to the influence of elements. He therefore acted like a mindless animal, driven by its desires, instincts and external circumstances[34], instead of following Divine decrees. This eventually pushed him to starting a war with his southern neighbour[35]. As can be seen, the Byzantine orator's attitude towards the highlanders was not particularly favourable.

For mediaeval people, then, mountains constituted a certain margin (periphery, fringe – ἡ ἐσχατιά)[36] in both geographic and social terms, mysterious and untamed (for it was sparsely populated and inhabited by wild animals). They appeared to them as a culturally backward area, filled with dangers and surprises, uncertain, even dangerous; a land that was under a kind of taboo. The atmospheric conditions prevalent in the

[32] *On the Treaty with the Bulgarians*, 12, p. 274.307–310.

[33] *On the Treaty with the Bulgarians*, 5, p. 262.138–142.

[34] Here: violent atmospheric phenomena, which according to the Byzantine were characteristic to Bulgarian lands.

[35] More on the image of Symeon in that speech, see: K. M a r i n o w, *In the Shackles of the Evil One: The Portrayal of Tsar Symeon I the Great (893–927) in the Oration 'On the Treaty with the Bulgarians'*, SCer 1, 2011, pp. 157–190.

[36] In this way the rhetorician indicated territories (plural in the text) where the Byzantine prisoners of war were taken as a result of the war with tsar Symeon I – *On the Treaty with the Bulgarians*, 5, p. 260.107.

mountains, which made them more difficult to cross, had no lesser influence on this image[37]. Like dense forests, mountains were outside of the organised social life, as if outside the law, and were inhabited by those who were either excluded from the society, or were hiding from justice[38]. Even known trails were crossed with fear, let alone making forays into their inner reaches. Besides, Byzantines considered the entirety of Bulgaria to be a wild land, inhabited by barbarians[39]; and they treated barbarians with a certain dose of superiority and suspicion[40].

The few passages from the various historical Greek sources cited above, written between the eighth (patriarch Nikephoros) and twelfth (John Kinnamos) centuries, complement the image of Bulgarians emerging from Byzantine sources. Even these few passages make it possible to state that during the Middle Byzantine period the inhabitants of the Eastern Rome saw their northern neighbours as a people strongly associated with mountainous regions. The fragments show that Bulgarians resided in the mountains, had an economy appropriate to surrounding conditions, and skilfully exploited the qualities of the ranges in fighting Byzantium. It was the latter fact that was particularly noted by the Byzantine authors. Knowing that the tendency to present Bulgarians as highlanders continued throughout the Late Byzantine period[41], one may conclude that the stereotype of the Bulgarian-highlander, who eagerly used his environment in fighting the southern neighbour, became permanently rooted among the Byzantines. This portrayal, while to a large extent corresponded to the truth, nonetheless permanently marked Bulgarians with the stigma of barbarism – savagery, primitiveness and bellicosity.

---

[37] *The Life of Blasius of Amorium*, 9–10, cols. 661 C – 662 A; John Kameniates, 18, p. 18.29–31; John Geometres, col. 934 A; John Kinnamos, II, 13, p. 70.17–22.

[38] B. Geremek, *Człowiek...*, pp. 438–439.

[39] J. Bonarek, *Romajowie...*, p. 141, fn. 228.

[40] П. Ангелов, *Българската средновековна дипломация*, София 1988, p. 37.

[41] K. Marinow, *Hemus...*, pp. 183–197.

VII

Mirosław J. Leszka
Jan M. Wolski

The Church

1. The Status of the Bulgarian Church and its Organisation

Mirosław J. Leszka

By Boris I's decision, Bulgaria, most likely in 866, became a part of the Christian *oikoumene*. The Byzantines, however, from whom the Bulgarians received baptism, have not been willing to meet Boris' demands that the new Church is granted autocephaly. This forced the Bulgarian ruler to take action which would lead him to achieve independence for the Bulgarian Church organisation. After several years of struggle, in which he involved Rome, Boris managed to gain significant concessions from the Byzantines in 870.

An archbishopric, and along with bishoprics subordinated to it, was created on Bulgarian soil[1]. Bulgarian Church received the status

[1] In Continuator of Theophanes (V, 96, p. 312) we find a passage presenting the moment of creation of the Bulgarian Archbishopric and the arrival of the Greek clergy in Bulgaria: *By repeated exhortations, splendid receptions, and magnanimous munificence and donations, however, the emperor persuaded the Bulgarians to accept an*

of a 'metropolitan autocephalic archbishopric'[2], and its dependence on Constantinople was limited to dogmatic matters and, at least at the beginning, an influence on the choosing of the new occupant of the archiepiscopal see[3]. *Kleterologion* of Philotheos, from the end of the ninth century, clearly attests to the exceptional rank of the Bulgarian Church; according to its author, the Archbishop of Bulgaria occupied the 13th place in the Byzantine hierarchy, just behind the *synkellos* of the patriarch of Constantinople[4].

---

archbishop and to allow their country to be covered with a network of bishoprics. Owing to these prelates and also to devout monks whom the emperor summoned from the mountains and dens of the earth and dispatched to that land, the Bulgarians abandoned their ancestral customs and became, one and for all, captives of Christ (transl. I. Ševčenko, p. 313). Vassil Gyuzelev (В. Гюзелев, *Студийският манастир и българите през средновековието (VIII–IX)*, ЗРВИ 39, 2001/2002, p. 59) thinks that among the monks who arrived at that time in Bulgaria were representatives of the Stoudios Monastery in Constantinople who may have had Bulgarian and Slavic roots. This monastery had, it is thought, strong links with Bulgaria even before its official Christianisation. Its representatives may have participated in the first Byzantine mission to Bulgaria (863/864).

[2] W. Swoboda – *Testimonia*, vol. III, p. 363, fn. 2. This view is accepted by i.a.: В. Гюзелев, *Княз Борис Първи. България през втората половина на век*, София 1969, pp. 413–414; idem, *Устройство на българската църква*, [in:] *История на България в четирнадесет тома*, vol. II, *Първа българска държава*, ed. Д. Ангелов, София 1981, pp. 230–231; E. Piltz, *Kamelaukion et mitra*, Stockholm 1977, p. 109.

[3] On the subject of status of the Bulgarian Church during the times of Boris-Michael, see: W. Swoboda, *L'origine de l'organisation de l'Eglise en Bulgarie et ses rapports avec le patriarcat de Constantinople (870–919)*, BBg 2, 1966, pp. 67–81; Г.Г. Литаврин, *Введение христиантва в Волгарии (IX – начало X в.)*, [in:] *Принuатие христианства народами централной и юго-восточной Европы и крещение Руси*, ed. idem, Москва 1988, pp. 30–67; Б. Николова, *Устройство и управление на българската православна църква (IX–XIV век)*, [2]София 2017, pp. 40–46; L. Simeonova, *Diplomacy of the Letter and the Cross: Photios, Bulgaria and the Papacy 860s–880s*, Amsterdam 1998, pp. 268–269; В. Гюзелев, *Бележки върху йерархическия статус на Българската църква и нейния върховен предстоятел през първия век от покръстването 865–971*, [in:] *Религия и църква в България. Социални и културни иммерения в православието и неговата специфика в Българските земи*, ed. Г. Бакалов, София 1999, pp. 98–107; И. Божилов, *Българската архиепископия XI–XII век. Списъкът на българските архиепископи*, София 2011, pp. 17–32; M.J. Leszka, K. Marinow, *Carstwo bułgarskie. Polityka – społeczeństwo – gospodarka – kultura. 866–971*, Warszawa 2015, pp. 43–52.

[4] Philotheos, p. 187. Other metropolitans and autocephalic archbishops are only found in the 58th place (W. Swoboda, *Bułgaria a patriarchat konstantynopolitański*

With time, however, the formula of the Bulgarian Church's status became worn out. The dependence on Byzantium, even limited one, undoubtedly weighed on the Bulgarians. The one who finally severed any form of control over Bulgarian Church by Constantinople was, according to some of the contemporary scholars, Symeon (893–927). Not only is he being attributed with this move, but he is also hailed as the one who had led to, at the very least, having its head proclaimed a patriarch (if not credited with the outright transformation of the Bulgarian Archbishopric into a patriarchate[5]. This view, however, has no basis in the source material[6]. Despite this, it would seem that this claim cannot be entirely ruled out. Symeon, having proclaimed himself in 913 a basileus of the Bulgarians,

w latach 870–1018, [in:] *Z polskich studiów slawistycznych*, vol. IV, *Historia*, Warszawa 1972, p. 49).

[5] Cf. my considerations in the work *Symeon I Wielki a Bizancjum. Z dziejów stosunków bułgarsko-bizantyńskich w latach 893–927*, Łódź 2013, pp. 248–258.

[6] In this matter scholars often refer to the fragment of a letter by Kaloyan, the Bulgarian ruler, to Pope Innocent III. It speaks of the teachings of Greeks, who claim that without the patriarchate the existence of the Empire would not be possible (*quia imperium sine patriarcha non staret* – Innocent III, p. 334. The use of this source – written about 300 years later after Symeon's reign – to substantiate the hypothesis of the creation of the Bulgarian patriarchate is methodologically erroneous. I fully accept in this regard the view expressed by Wincenty Swoboda: (*Bułgaria…*, p. 55: *tak więc dotychczasowe stanowisko nauki w sprawie patriarchatu bułgarskiego za panowania Symeona jest – jak sądzimy – rezultatem powziętego z góry, na podstawie* (…) *przekazu z początków XIII w., założenia, które przewidywało, iż logicznym następstwem proklamacji cesarstwa (carstwa) w Bułgarii było obwołanie patriarchatu bułgarskiego* [*Therefore the present position of the scholarship on the question of the Bulgarian Patriarchate during Symeon's reign is – we think – the result of an assumption made in advance on the basis* (…) *of an account from the early 13*[th] *century, which predicted that the logical result of proclaiming an Empire (Tsardom) in Bulgaria would be the proclamation of the Bulgarian Patriarchate*]. Recently, this argument was used by Ivan Bozhilov (И. Божилов, *Българската архепископия…*, p. 45), who also indicated that a patriarch was necessary to perform the imperial coronation of Symeon. He reaches in this context for the example of Stephan Dushan, who first proclaimed himself a tsar (1345), and subsequently took care to ensure that the Archbishop of Serbia became its patriarch (1346), in order to perform the imperial coronation (p. 46). We again find that in order to substantiate the discussed view, there is a reference to events from a much later period. On the circumstances of the imperial proclamation of Stephan Dushan, see: G.Ch. Soulis, *The Serbs and Byzantium during the Reign of Tsar Stephen Dušan (1331–1355) and his Successors*, Washington 1984, pp. 27–32.

may have elevated the prestige of the Bulgarian Archbishop by proclaiming him a patriarch[7]. Without the acceptance of Constantinople to this act, it would have only had local significance[8]. It would, however, also have been the most visible sign of breaking off any form of dependence on Constantinople in the ecclesiastical sphere.

Many scholars associate the Byzantine agreement to the changes in the situation of the Bulgarian Church with the peace treaty of 927. None of the sources containing the information about the autocephaly of the Bulgarian church and the elevation of the Bulgarian archbishop to the position of a patriarch (I am referring here to the *List of Bulgarian archbishops*[9], Michael of Devol's *Gloss to the Synopsis of Histories* by John Skylitzes[10] as well as to the text *On Justiniana Prima's canonical position*[11]) link these facts with the treaty of 927. The three sources mentioned

---

[7] M.J. Leszka, *Symeon...*, pp. 130–132.

[8] The patriarchal title for the Bulgarian Archbishop, and the prospective establishment of the patriarchate, required an external agreement (from the Byzantine emperor and the patriarch of Constantinople, and the Church Council).

[9] *List of Bulgarian Archbishops*, p. 102.18–23: *Damian, in Dorostolon, the present Dristra. During his reign Bulgaria was honoured with autocephaly* [or attained autocephaly – M.J.L.] *and the Byzantine Senate, following Romanos Lekapenos' orders, granted him the title of patriarch. He was then deposed by John Tzymiskes.* For more on the source see: W. Swoboda, *Bułgaria...*, pp. 57–58; В. Тъпкова-Заимова, *Дюканжов списък*, Pbg 24.3, 2000, pp. 21–49; И. Божилов, *Българската архиепископия...*, pp. 93–101.

[10] John Skylitzes, p. 365.8–11. Michael of Devol writes that emperor Basil II confirmed the autocephaly of the Bulgarian bishopric, which it had enjoyed already during the reign of the old Romanos (I Lekapenos). This information was recorded at the beginning of the 12th century. On the notes which bishop Michael of Devol added to John Skylitzes's work see: J. Ferluga, *John Scylitzes and Michael of Devol*, [in:] idem, *Byzantium on the Balkans. Studies on the Byzantine Administration and the Southern Slavs from the VIIth to the XIIth Centuries*, Amsterdam 1976, pp. 337–344.

[11] Cf. *On Justiniana Prima's canonical position*, p. 279.37–42. The source states that the Bulgarian Church was autocephalous and that the privileges it enjoyed were not derived only from Basil II and Romanos I Lekapenos, dating back to the period during which the agreement with tsar Peter was signed. They also had their origin in the old laws. On the source see: G. Prinzing, *Entstehung und Rezeption der Justiniana Prima-Theorie im Mittelalter*, BBg 5, 1978, pp. 269–278; Т. Кръстанов, *Испански бележки за translatio на Justiniana Prima с българската църква преди 1018 г.*, ШУЕКП.ТКИБ 6, 2004, pp. 80–84; idem, *Титлите екзарх и патриарх*

above connect the autocephaly with emperor Romanos I Lekapenos (920–944). In the last of these texts, the issue is placed in the context of an agreement of which Peter was to be a party. The conferment of the title of a patriarch on the Archbishop of Bulgaria is referred to only in the *List of Bulgarian Archbishops*, where it is linked with the autocephaly. Thus, these religious issues can be assumed to have been dealt with in a peace treaty signed during the reigns of Peter and Romanos I Lekapenos. It so happens that the 927 treaty is the only such document that we know of. According to some scholars, this is at odds with the information to be found in the so-called *Beneshevich's Taktikon*, a source contemporary with Romanos I Lekapenos's reign but variously dated – either to 921/927 or to 934/944. In this source, the head of the Bulgarian Church is referred to as Bulgaria's Archbishop (ἀρχιεπίσκοπος Βουλγαρίας)[12]. Thus, it appears that dating the *Taktikon* to 934/944 – as per its publisher Nicolas Oikonomides – would be tantamount to excluding 927 as the date of Constantinople's recognition of the Bulgarian Archbishop as a patriarch[13]. However, other scholars claim that the *Taktikon*'s characterisation of the issue in question may be inaccurate, and it seems that they are closer to the truth[14].

в българската традиция от IX до XIX в. Св. Йоан Екзарх от Рим и патриарх на българските земи, [in:] *Държава & Църква – Църква & Държава в българската история. Сборник по случай 135-годишнината от учредяването на Българската екзархия*, ed. Г. Ганев, Г. Бакалов, И. Тодев, София 2006, pp. 79–80. The source claims that the Bulgarian Church inherited *Justiniana Prima*'s church laws. The issue of *Justiniana Prima*'s archbishopric established during the reign of Justinian I was recently discussed by: S. Turlej, *Justiniana Prima: An Underestimated Aspect of Justinian's Church Policy*, Kraków 2016.

[12] *Beneshevich's Taktikon*, p. 245.17.

[13] Cf. Б. Николова, *Устройство…*, p. 49.

[14] N. Oikonomidès, *Les listes de préséance byzantines des IXe et Xe siècles*, Paris 1972, pp. 237–238. Cf. И. Божилов, *Българската архепископия…*, p. 40; Г. Атанасов, *Християнският Дуросторум-Дръстър. Доростолската епархия през късната античност и Средновековието IV–XIV в. История, археология, култура и изкуство*, Варна 2007, pp. 150–154). See also: В. Тъпкова-Заимова, *Превземането на Преслав в 971 г. и проблемите на българската църква*, [in:] *1100 години Велики Преслав*, vol. I, ed. Т. Тотев, Шумен 1995, p. 178; S. Pirivatrić, *Some Notes on the Byzantine-Bulgarian Peace Treaty of 927*, Bslov2, 2008, pp. 44–45.

As should be apparent from the discussion above, the sources we have at our disposal do not allow us to state categorically that the questions of autocephaly and the title of the patriarch were dealt with in the 927 peace negotiations. Still, given everything we know about the Byzantine-Bulgarian relations during the reign of Romanos I Lekapenos, it is logical to assume that this was the case. What can be said based on the surviving sources is that the issues were covered by an agreement signed by Peter and Romanos I Lekapenos, that is, in the period between 927 and 944. The point is that, as I mentioned above, we do not know of any other arrangement made by these two rulers save for the 927 treaty. Lately, Todor R. Todorov put forth the idea that the events in question may have taken place soon after Theophylaktos Lekapenos' rise to the position of patriarch of Constantinople (933)[15]. Todorov links these facts with the presence of papal envoys in Constantinople and Maria's visit to Romanos I Lekapenos' court. To the Bulgarian scholar, the Bulgarian Archbishop receiving the right to bear the title of a patriarch was *the last wedding gift for the couple ruling in Preslav*[16]. This is an interesting hypothesis, but underlying it is the controversial view, to be found in Bulgarian scholarly literature, according to which the Bulgarians were planning to seize control of Constantinople and build a Slavic-Greek empire; this plan was known as the great idea of 10th-century Bulgaria[17]. According to Todorov, the project was championed by Symeon I and abandoned by Peter in 931, after the death of Christopher – Peter's father-in-law as well as Romanos I Lekapenos's son and co-ruler. This fact meant that neither Peter nor his sons, whom he had by Maria, could lay claim to Christopher's power. Without engaging in a polemic with this view, it is worth noting that to accept it is to make Peter fully responsible for

[15] Т. Тодоров, *България през втората и третата четвърт на X век: политическа история*, София 2006 [unpublished PhD thesis]. pp. 213–214.

[16] *Ibidem*, p. 215. Papal legates were present in the city in connection with their participation in the elevation of Theophylaktos Lekapenos to the patriarchal throne, but they may have also brought Rome's consent to the change in the status of the Bulgarian bishop.

[17] For a polemic with this view cf.: M.J. Leszka, *Symeon...*, pp. 236–247.

the elevation of the Bulgarian archbishop to the position of patriarch against the intention of his father, Symeon.

Regardless of whether we accept the option of year 927 (which appears to be the more likely) or the 930s, it needs to be clearly stated that it was Peter who was ultimately responsible for ensuring that the Archbishop of Bulgaria became a patriarch[18]. This was undoubtedly a success of the – relatively young after all – Bulgarian Church, and it is of no significance here whether it was an expression of Preslav's abandonment of the attempts at subjugating Constantinople or not.

From the above considerations, it is clear that during Peter's reign the Bulgarian Church was led by a hierarch bearing the title of a patriarch. From the *List of Bulgarian Archbishops* one should conclude that this person was Damian[19], who according to this source was deprived of the title

[18] It does not seem to be possible to positively verify the view that the granting of the patriarchal title to the Archbishop of Bulgaria also meant the creation of the Bulgarian patriarchate. It needs to be remembered that the fact that the head of the Bulgarian Church had the title of a patriarch did not necessarily imply the existence of the patriarchate. The patriarchal title could have been granted by an emperor to particular person, and belonged exclusively to that person (and the emperor had the right to make such a decision); the creation of a new patriarchate, in addition to other necessary conditions, should have been done by the Council. Cf. W. Swoboda, *Bułgaria...*, pp. 56–60; I. Ταρνανίδου, *Η διαμόρφωσις τοῦ αὐτοκεφαλίου τῆς Βουλγαρικῆς εκκλησίας (864–1235)*, Θεσσαλονίκη 1976, pp. 83–94. The idea of granting of a patriarchal title *ad personam* is strongly opposed by some of the Bulgarian scholars (e.g. И. Божилов, *Българската архепископия...*, p. 38; Г. Атанасов, *Християнският Дуросторум-Дръстър...*, pp. 152–153); Б. Николова, *Устройство...*, pp. 50–51 (see there for more literature on the subject). For more information on the mechanisms of creating patriarchates – E. Przekop, *Wschodnie patriarchaty starożytne (IV–X w.)*, Warszawa 1984 (esp. pp. 43–62).

[19] On Damian cf.: W. Swoboda, *Damian*, [in:] *SSS*, vol. VIII, pp. 13–14; Г.Г. Литаврин, *Христианство в Болгарии 927–1018 гг.*, [in:] *Христианство в странах восточной, юго-восточной и центральной Европы на пороге второго тысячелетия*, ed. Б.Н. Флоря, Москва 2002, pp. 141–142; Г. Атанасов, *Християнският Дуросторум-Дръстър...*, pp. 158–160; idem, *Първата българска патриаршеска катедра в Дръстър и патриарх Дамян*, [in:] *Изследвания по българска средновековна археология. Сборник в чест на проф. Рашо Рашев*, ed. П. Георгиев, Велико Търново 2007, pp. 179–196. Cf. also S. Angelova, G. Prinzing, *Das mutmassliche Grab des Patriarchen Damian: zu einem archäologischen Fund in Dristra/*

in 971 by John Tzymiskes. Some of the scholars doubt whether Damian bore the title of a patriarch for over forty years; it cannot, however, be ruled out. Damian may have simply enjoyed a long life. This matter, at first glance, is made more complicated by *Boril's Synodikon*[20], in which one may find the names of other patriarchs, specifically: Leontios, Dimitar, Sergios, Gregory. They are referred to as patriarchs of Preslav. We should be aware, however, that this is a relatively late tradition (thirteenth century), and what is worse, the earliest manuscript of the *Synodikon* comes from the fourteenth century (Palauzov). The information that the aforementioned Church dignitaries were patriarchs of Preslav was added on the margin of the manuscript. Notably, the list of the Preslavian patriarchs in the *Synodikon* is partly concurrent with the list of the Preslavian metropolitan Bishops – Stephen, Dimitar, Leo, Gregory [my underscore – M.J.L][21]. I have to share the sceptical view of Wincenty Swoboda regarding the value of *Synodikon*'s information about the Preslavian patriarchs. It cannot be ruled out that it is an interpolation included to raise the rank of the patriarchate of Tarnovo, created in 1235, which called itself the continuator of the traditions of the patriarchate of Preslav[22]. It is worth noting that the name of Damian does not appear in the *Synodikon*. In this situation, it would seem that any attempts at fitting the latter into the most doubtful list of the patriarchs of Preslav are doomed to failure[23].

Silistria, [in:] *Средновековна християнска Европа. Изток и запад. Ценности, традиции, общуване*, eds. В. Гюзелев, А. Милтенова, София 2002, pp. 726–730. Authors identified the remains found in the patriarchal church in Dristra as those of Damian. A legitimate criticism of this view – Г. Атанасов, *Християнският Дуросторум-Дръстър*..., pp. 158–160; idem, *От епископия към самостойна патриаршия на Първото българско царство в Дръстър (Силистра). Историята на патриаршеския комплекс*, София 2017, pp. 64–65.

[20] *Synodikon of Tsar Boril*, 36a, p. 168.6–8.

[21] *Synodikon of Tsar Boril*, 37a, p. 170.2. cf. The remark of W. Swoboda (*Bulgaria*..., p. 62), who points to the three concurrences, since in both the case of the patriarchs and the metropolitan bishops he mentions Leo.

[22] W. Swoboda, *Bulgaria*..., p. 63.

[23] Some scholars see e.g. in the Preslavian patriarchs those of the Bulgarian Archbishops who bore the patriarchal title prior to 927 without the agreement of Constantinople (e.g. И. Божилов, *Българската архиепископия*..., p. 50).

It would appear logical that, before becoming the patriarch, Damian would have been the Archbishop of Bulgaria[24]. His see as both the Archbishop and the patriarch was Preslav. It is possible that for a brief period, already after Peter's death, he moved to Dristra[25]. We do not know the details regarding the chancery working for the Archbishop/patriarchs. It is thought that it was similar to the one had by the patriarch of Constantinople. These suppositions are only very modestly confirmed by the extant sources. Within them, we find traces of the activity of such dignitaries as *synkellos*[26], *chartophylax*[27] and *exarch*[28]. We also know of the existence of a dignitary who was referred to as the 'tserkovnik of all the Bulgarian churches'[29], whose Byzantine counterpart would have most likely been the Archon of the Ecclesiarchs; as with an exarch, we are unable to say much about his role and position in the Bulgarian Church[30].

[24] On Damian's predecessors in the role of the Archbishop – M.J. Leszka, K. Marinow, *Carstwo*..., p. 255.

[25] The view that the Bulgarian patriarch's see was in Dristra (e.g.: П. Мутафчиев, *Съдбините на средновековния Дръстър*, [in:] idem, *Сборник от студии*, София 1946, pp. 293–305; Г. Атанасов, *Християнският Дуросторум-Дръстър*..., p. 155sqq; idem, *От епископия*..., p. 59sqq; see also I. Dujčev, *Il patriarcato bulgaro del secolo X*, [in:]idem, *Medioevo bizantino-slavo*, vol. III, *Altri saggi di storia, politica e letteraria*, Roma 1971, p. 262, fn. 1) does not appear to be correct. Arguments against this hypothesis: И. Божилов, *Българската архепископия*..., pp. 48–49; Б. Николова, *Устройство*..., pp. 135–136.

[26] This dignitary was considered to have been an archbishop's deputy in the matters of organisation. We know of George, a Bulgarian *synkellos*, most likely active at the turn of the ninth and tenth centuries. Cf. В. Гюзелев, *Устройство*..., p. 231; Б. Николова, *Устройство*..., p. 206.

[27] Chartophylax was the head of an archbishop's chancery. Chartophylax Paul contributed to the creation of the church of St. John in Preslav, which we know from an inscription. Cf.: В. Гюзелев, *Устройство*..., p. 231; Б. Николова, *Устройство*..., pp. 205–206.

[28] The question of what was the role of an exarch in the structure of the Bulgarian Church has been intensely debated, and is still far from having a clear answer. On this subject: В. Гюзелев, *Устройство*..., p. 231; Б. Николова, *Устройство*..., pp. 202–205; Т. Кръстанов, *Титлите екзарх*..., pp. 73–86.

[29] Gregory Presbiter, p. 117.

[30] The existence of the position of an archon of the ecclesiarchs in the Byzantine Church is confirmed by the *Novella of 935* (p. 246) issued by Romanos Lekapenos. Unfortunately, we find no new information about this position/title therein. The

There have been functioning episcopal structures within the framework of the Bulgarian Church[31]. We do not, however, have full knowledge of where these bishoprics had been in Peter's times, nor how many of them there were. The process of building episcopal structure began, of course, during Boris-Michael's times. Theophylaktos, the Archbishop of Ohrid, wrote thusly in the *Life of Clement*: *this prince* [Boris – M.J.L.] *encircled the Bulgaria subject to him with seven conciliar temples* (καθολικοῖς ναοῖς)[32]. The latter are understood to have been cathedral churches, and claims are made that during Boris-Michael's reign seven bishoprics have been created, and as a result of this, attempts are being made to find their locations. It would seem however that the aforementioned number should be treated with care, with awareness of its symbolism. In this context, it may be understood as information about the creation of an adequate to contemporary needs number of cathedral churches[33]. What

ecclesiarchs/ecclesiastics were responsible for maintaining the order of the liturgy, and we most commonly find them in monasteries (A.-M. Talbot, *Ekklesiarches*, [in:] *ODB*, vol. I, p. 682; M. Živojinović, *Crkvenjaci na Svetoj Gori i njihove dužnosti*, IČ 56, 2008, pp. 69–86; see also: *Byzantine Monastic Foundation Documents. A Complete Translation of the Surviving Founders' Typika and Testaments*, ed. J. Thomas, A. C. Hero, G. Constable, Washington 2000, pp. 98, 225, 339, etc.). Protoiereus George, a prominent writer and a translator, was said to have fulfilled the role of a tserkovnik between 895 and 918 (В. Гюзелев, *Устройство...*, p. 231; Т. Славова, *Други преводачи и преписивачи от книжовния кръг около цар Симеон*, [in:] *ИБСЛ*, p. 251). Some scholars believe that the term 'tserkovnik of all the Bulgarian churches' should be understood as exarch, or some other high Church dignitary, cf. Й. Андреев, *Григорий*, [in:] idem, И. Лазаров, П. Павлов, *Кой кой е в средновековна България*, ³София 2012, p.153; see also: Е. Георгиев, *Разцветът на българската литература в IX–XI в.*, София 1962, p. 300.

[31] On the subject of the bishoprics that existed within the framework of the Bulgarian metropolis, the scholars' opinions are divided. Among the more recent works devoted to this subject one should take particular note of the works of Todor Sabev (Т. Събев, *Самостойна народностна църква в средновековна България. Християнизаторски процес, основане и възход, автокефалия и междуцърковно положение, църква и държава*, Велико Търново 2003, pp. 254–260), and Bistra Nikolova (Б. Николова, *Устройство...*, pp. 55–155), where the reader will find further bibliographic suggestions.

[32] Theophylaktos of Ohrid, *Life of Clement*, XXIII, 67.

[33] M.J. Leszka, K. Marinow, [rev.:], *Uczniowie Apostołów Słowian. Siedmiu Świętych Mężów...*, BP 18, 2011, p. 195; K. Marinow, *Още веднъж за пар. XXIII.67 от 'Пространното житие на Климент Охридски'* (in press).

was this number? This question needs to be left unanswered. It might appear that the information regarding the participants of the Photios's council of 879 could be helpful in this regard. Among these, the scholars seek the bishops of the Bulgarian Church. The problem herein lies in the fact that it is certain that not all of them had been present (e.g. the Archbishop of Bulgaria himself), and that some of the bishoprics that are being associated with the territory of the first Bulgarian state were undoubtedly not a part of the Archbishopric of Bulgaria (e.g. Ohrid)[34]. It seems that among the first Bulgarian bishoprics one should count the ones that had their sees in: Belgrade[35], Morava (Branichevo)[36], Devol[37], Bregalnitsa[38], Dristra[39]. One should of course remember that the first

[34] On the subject of these difficulties: И. Б о ж и л о в, *Българската архиепископия...*, pp. 29–30; cf. C. H a n n i c k, *Nowe chrześcijaństwo w świecie bizantyńskim: Rusini, Bułgarzy i Serbowie*, [in:] *Historia chrześcijaństwa*, vol. IV: *Biskupi, mnisi i cesarze 610–1054*, transl. M. Ż u r o w s k a et al., ed. G. D a g r o n, P. R i c h é, A. V a u c h e z, Polish ed. J. K ł o c z o w s k i, Warszawa 1999, p. 745.

[35] Its first bishop was most likely Sergios, of Slavic origins; cf. Б. Н и к о л о в а, *Устройство...*, p. 55.

[36] From the documents of the 879 council of Photius we know the name (and name alone) of its Bishop – Agaton. The centre of the bishopric was most likely moved after 879 to Branichevo; cf. Б. Н и к о л о в а, *Устройство...*, pp. 67–70.

[37] We know the name of one of its later Bishops, Mark, the student of St. Clement, who in the *First Life of St. Naum* (p. 307) is called the fourth bishop of the *Slavic people* (въ словенскї єзыкь) *in Devol*; cf. Б. Н и к о л о в а, *Устройство...*, p. 115. The Devol bishopric was referred to by Theophylaktos, the Archbishop of Ohrid, as one of the seven 'Council temples' established by Boris (T h e o p h y l a k t o s o f O h r i d, *Letters*, 22, p. 103).

[38] It was created prior to 885. Some scholars think that it was previously called Ovche Pole, and was represented at the council of 879 by Leo of Probaton. This, however, appears unlikely; cf. Б. Н и к о л о в а, *Устройство...*, pp. 89–93; И. Б о ж и л о в, *Българската архиепископия...*, pp. 29–31. The first mention of its existence comes from Theophylaktos, the Archbishop of Ohrid (*Martyrdom of the fifteen Tiberioupolitan martyrs*, 37, p. 69). It was most likely under the leadership of Slavic clergy from the very beginning. Later, its centre moved to Moravitsa (on this ecclesiastical centre – К. Т р а й к о в с к и, *Средновековните цркви в градот Μορδοβισδος во Македонийа*, ГСУ.НЦСВПИД 97 (16), 2007, pp. 121–126; Б. Н и к о л о в а, *Устройство...*, pp. 93–95.

[39] The bishopric with the see in Dristra (the Roman Durostorum) had ancient roots (more on this subject: Г. А т а н а с о в, *Християнският Дуросторум-Дръстър...*, pp. 15–112). Its first bishop, appointed as early as 870, was Nicholas. Cf. *ibidem*, pp. 139–147; i d e m, *Епископ Николай и формирането на Доростолската (Дръстърската)*

episcopal see (until 870) was Pliska. Of the more important bishoprics that have been created or added later, one should list the ones with their centres in: Sredets (Sofia)[40], Skopje, Strumitsa (Tiberioupolis?), Ohrid, and the ones associated with the person of St. Clement, the Bishop of Dremvitsa and/or Velika[41]. It needs to be clearly stated that the internal structure of the Bulgarian Archbishopric was undergoing changes, caused by the pastoral needs, as well as by the changes in the shape of the country's territory. We are not able to precisely delineate these changes, however to give the Reader at least some idea of the network of the bishoprics, we will cite the information from Basil II's times, according to which the Archbishopric of Ohrid, covering the lands that were a part of the Archbishopric of Bulgaria, included over thirty bishoprics[42].

It is not impossible that the method used for creating of bishoprics was based on the rule according to which the ecclesiastical structures were tailored to fit the administrative structures of the state. Perhaps the original episcopal sees were created in the locations that had been the centres of the comitates[43].

Our knowledge of the Bulgarian bishops in this regard is as scarce as that of their superiors. It would seem that during Peter's times, the bishops

епархия през 870 г., [in:] *Християнската култура в средновековна България. Материали от национална научна конференция, Шумен 2–4 май 2007 година по случай 1100 години от смъртта на св. Княз Борис-Михаил (ок. 835–907г.)*, ed. П. Георгиев, Велико Търново 2008, pp. 104–119; see also: Б. Николова, *Устройство…*, pp. 106–111.

[40] Б. Николова, *Устройство…*, pp. 63–65.

[41] Theophylaktos of Ohrid, *Life of Clement*, XIX, 60. The debate regarding this bishopric has been ongoing for a long time. It was recently summarised by Iliya G. Iliev (И.Г. Илиев, *Св. Климент Охридски. Живот и дело*, Пловдив 2010, p. 103), who, taking into account the research of his predecessors, concluded that the title which Clement received – most likely in 893 – could have been *the Bishop of the Dragovits in the Velika region*, and its eparchy encompassed the area around Vardar, called in the mediaeval period Velika, in the north-western part of the Thessalonike Plain. It was most likely created in 893 or in the early 894 (*ibidem*, p. 96). It was recently written about by A. Delikari, *Kliment Velički oder Kliment Ochridski? Die Diskussion über Seine Bischofstitel und seine Jurisdiktion*, Pbg 37.3, 2013, pp. 3–10.

[42] Cf. W. Swoboda, *Organizacja Kościoła (Bułgaria)*, [in:] *SSS*, vol. III, p. 494; И. Божилов, *Българската архепископия…*, p. 89.

[43] Б. Николова, *Устройство…*, p. 146.

were Slavs. Traditionally, the aforementioned St. Clement is thought to have been the first Bulgarian bishop. He was undoubtedly an exceptional person, however it is difficult to say how representative he was of the contemporary Bulgarian episcopate. The case is similar with another, relatively well known to us bishop – Constantine of Preslav. We do not know where he served as bishop. Scholars most often point to Preslav or to Pliska. We know his works better, since he was a writer and a translator[44].

Some of the other bishops are known to us only by name, and they served prior to Peter's reign. These were: Isaiah (?)[45] and the previously mentioned Nicholas of Dristra, Sergios of Belgrade, Mark of Devol and Agaton, the Bishop of Morava.

Presbyters. The primary group of the Bulgarian clergy were the priests (presbyters), much like was the case with other Churches. Also in this case our knowledge is not particularly abundant. They were certainly recruited from among the local populace, although in the years immediately following the baptism there had been among them both Greeks and the Latin clergy. They had not always been well prepared for their service. Theophylaktos, in the *Life of St. Clement*, wrote: *many of the Bulgarian priests were not doing very well with the Greek language*[46]. This prompted the bishop to prepare *for all holidays orations that were simple and clear*,

[44] For information about this hypothetical biography of Constantine, see i.a.: Е. Георгиев, *Разцветът*..., pp. 161–168; Е. Зъков, *К биографии Константина Преславского*, СЛ 2, 1977, pp. 74–101; И. Лазаров, *Константин Преславски*, [in:] Й. Андреев, И. Лазаров, П. Павлов, *Кой*..., pp. 394–396.

[45] The seal with this bishop's name does not have a certain date. There are multiple suggestions. One of these proposes years 864–866. Isaiah would have been therefore a member, or even the leader, of the mission sent from Constantinople (И. Йорданов, *България при Борис I (852–889, †907). Приносът на сфрагистика*, [in:] *Християнската*..., p. 47). Recently, Ivan Bozhilov (И. Божилов, *Българската архепископия*..., p. 27) proposed dating it to the period between 870–893, and considered it possible that Isaiah may have been a Bulgarian archbishop. Both Ivan Jordanov, and Ivan Bozhilov treat their suggestions as conjectures. The inscription on the seal is most commonly read as: *Lord, support Isaiah, the Bishop of Bulgaria* (επισκόπο Βουργαρήας). On the subject of this seal and other suggestions for its dating – И. Йорданов, *България при Борис*..., pp. 44–47.

[46] Theophylaktos of Ohrid, *Life of Clement*, 66.

not including anything deeper and contrived, but such, that they could be understood by even the most simple among the Bulgarians[47]. It is also known that Clement took care to prepare the cadre for conducting pastoral activity in the areas entrusted to him[48]. It is worth noting that Clement's activity began twenty years after Bulgarians officially accepted Christianity, on the territories that have been only superficially Christianised. One might suspect however that the situation was similar in the rest of the Bulgarian state. The level of education among the parochial clergy was likely better in larger centres. There was a group of well-educated people among the priests, and the names of some of them have been preserved to our times, with Cosmas the Priest, the author of an oration against the Bogomils, in the lead. Notably, in his treatise Cosmas not only fought against the heretics, but also pointed our errors to both the bishops and the clergy. His remarks did not relate to education, however, but to excessive laziness and devoting attention to temporal matters. Such accusations have been levelled at the clergy in a variety of places and times. However, in some sense Cosmas' remarks towards the clergy may be considered to be an indication that the Bulgarian Church reached a certain level of development. It became a lasting element of the contemporary society, and closed the period that could be called missionary.

Deacons. We know even less about the representatives of the lowest level of Bulgarian clergy. In a letter by Pope Hadrian II to Ignatios, the patriarch of Constantinople, we find information that the Byzantine mission ordained lay people, unprepared to serve the role, to be deacons. The Pope condemned this practice, as contrary to the teachings of the Fathers of the Church, and to the provisions of the recent Council[49]. This practice should not cause particular surprise. One might think that the group of the Byzantine clergy who had undertaken missionary activity

---

[47] Theophylaktos of Ohrid, *Life of Clement*, 66.

[48] Theophylaktos of Ohrid, *Life of Clement*, 57–59. The number of Clement's students – 3500 – appears to be exaggerated; however his teaching activity is undisputable.

[49] Hadrian II, XLII, p. 762. The letter was written in 871.

needed men who could support its activity as soon as possible. For this reason, at least some of the candidates who were included in the ranks of clergy had joined them in contravention of the accepted procedures. On the other hand, it needs to be remembered that this accusation was made by the Papacy, which had just lost its influence in Bulgaria. It must have caused bitterness and sometimes unfounded criticism of the Byzantine rivals. The letter itself was written in 871.

Perhaps the only deacon we know of, even though he remains anonymous, is the one mentioned in a tomb inscription from Dristra (now being preserved in a museum in Ruse). It reads:

> Here lies the monk and archdeacon of Bishop Nicholas, his uncle. He passed away in the year 6379, 4 indiction, on October 5th, Friday, at the time of Michael, the renowned pious and God-abiding archon[50].

2. Monasticism

Jan M. Wolski

The monastic movement was developing within the Bulgarian Church from its very beginning, marked by Boris' baptism in 866[51]. Monasticism, as one of the more important institutions of the new religion, enjoyed the rulers' support. There were numerous reasons for founding monasteries. One of these was the personal devotion of a ruler, which at the same

---

[50] Transl. – Г. А т а н а с о в, *От епископия...*, p. 135. Year 870. After the inscription's discovery, it was believed it came from the village of Cherven. However, further study indicated that it should be associated with Dristra (on this subject: Г. А т а н а с о в, *Епископ Николай...*, pp. 104–105). Nonetheless, some of the modern scholars still believe that the inscription originated in Cherven (e.g. Б. Н и к о л о в а, *Устройство...*, p. 166).

[51] Dispersed centres of monastic life have likely existed on Bulgarian territory even before this date, see I. D u j č e v, *La réforme monastique en Bulgarie au Xe siècle*, [in:] *Études de Civilisation médiévale (IXe–XIIe siècles). Mélanges offerts à Edmond-René Labande par ses amis, ses collègues, ses élèves*, Poitiers 1974, p. 256.

time also had a public dimension[52]. The monarch ought to have been pious, and the conventional expressions of godliness served to legitimise his rule. A dense network of monasteries likely had a positive influence on the Church's functioning. Monastic centres served as hubs of ministry, literacy, and schools for the cadre, much needed in the country that recently adopted Christianity[53].

The written sources, granting us a limited view of how Christianisation progressed in Bulgaria, confirm the considerable participation of monks in the process[54]. The significance and place of the monastic movement in the contemporary political, religious and cultural life are highlighted by the fact that among the exceptional figures from Bulgaria's ninth and tenth-century history we find numerous monks. These were predominantly writers and their patrons: George the Monk, Dox, Hrabar, Theodore Doxov and Peter the Monk[55]. Members of the ruling family also entered monasteries: the aforementioned Dox (Theodore Doxov may have been his son), the brother of Michael-Boris, and Eupraxia and Anna, the daughters of the Bulgarian khan. Some time in a monastery was also spent by the subsequent rulers of Christian Bulgaria. The later tsar Symeon lived in a monastery in his youth; the final years of Michael-Boris and the last few months of tsar Peter's life were also spent in a monastic environment[56]. Michael and John, Peter's brothers, should be listed separately, as they found themselves behind monastic walls under duress, and only left them to attempt reaching (as we know – without success) for the crown.

---

[52] Cf. R. Morris, *Monks and laymen in Byzantium, 843–1118*, Cambridge 1995, pp. 139–142; С. Аризанова, *Българите в агиографията от XIII–XIV век*, Пловдив 2013, p. 335.

[53] Cf. С. Ваклинов, *Формиране на старобългарската култура VI–XI век*, София 1977, p. 178.

[54] Continuator of Theophanes, 96, ed. I. Ševčenko, p. 312; *Miracles of St. George*, p. 143.

[55] I. Dujčev, *La réforme…*, pp. 260–261; Р. Павлова, *Петър Черноризец. Старобългарски писател от X век*, София 1994; А. Стойкова, *Черноризец Храбър*, [in:] *ИБСЛ*, pp. 248–251; Т. Славова, *Други преводачи…*, pp. 251–254.

[56] В. Гюзелев, *Княз Борис Първи. България през втората половина на IX век*, София 1969, pp. 453–454; Г.Н. Николов, *Български царици от Средновековието в "ангелски образ"*, ГСУ.НЦСВПИД 12, 2003, pp. 299, 302–303; M.J. Leszka, *Symeon…*, Łódź 2013, pp. 34–41.

The list of known archaeological remains of monasteries from the ninth and tenth centuries is not long. The capital Preslav and its immediate environs is the largest known centre of coenobia, having housed at least three monasteries: of synkellos George (formerly called the Mostich monastery)[57], and monasteries in Cheresheto[58] and Valkashina[59]. Other suggested (and subject of controversy) locations are: Tuzlalaka[60], Patleyna[61], Avradaka[62], Golden Church[63] and Zabuite[64]. Identifying them

[57] Р. Костова, *Манастирът на Мостич и въпросът за манастирите основани от частни лица в България през X в.*, ИАИ 39, 2006, pp. 271–285; К. Попконстантинов, Р. Костова, *Манастирът на Георги, Синкел български в Преслав: Историята на една българска аристократична фамилия от X в.*, Пр.Сб 7, 2013, pp. 42–63.

[58] Н. Чанева-Дечевска, *Църкви и манастири от Велики Преслав*, София 1980, pp. 107–109; Т. Тотев, *Старобългарските манастири в светлината на археологическите проучвания*, СЛ 22, 1990, p. 11; С. Бояджиев, *Ново тълкуване на раннобългарския манастир в местността "Черешето" във Велики Преслав*, ПКШ 5, 2000, pp. 76–85; Б. Николова, *Монашество, манастири и манастирски живот в средновековна България*, vol. I, София 2010, pp. 52, 106–107, 183. The monastery was partly investigated during archaeological works in 1905, subsequently its remains were destroyed.

[59] Н. Чанева-Дечевска, *Църкви и манастири...*, pp. 123–125; *Материали за картата на средновековна българска държава (територията на днешна Североизточна България)*, ed. Р. Рашев, П. Георгиев, И. Йорданов, ППре 7, 1995, p. 187. The monastery was partly investigated in 1948–1949, for the results see: Л. Огненова, С. Георгиева, *Разкопки на манастира под Вълкашина в Преслав през 1948–1949*, ИАИ 20, 1955, pp. 373–411.

[60] Т. Тотев, *Манаситирът в "Тузлалъка" – център на рисувана керамика в Преслав през IX–X в.*, София 1982; Р. Костова, *Манастирът в Тузлалъка, Преслав: нов поглед*, Архе 43.2, 2002, pp. 13–15.

[61] С. Бояджиев, *Църквата в Патлейна в светлината на нови данни*, Архе 2.4, 1960, pp. 22–33; Н. Чанева-Дечевска, *Църкви и манастири...*, pp. 140–143; Б. Николова, *Монашество...*, pp. 80–82, 183.

[62] В. Иванова, *Разкопки на Аврадака в Преслав*, РП 3, 1949, pp. 13–61; Н. Чанева-Дечевска, *Църкви и манастири...*, pp. 125–136; Б. Николова, *Монашество...*, pp. 79–80, 90–91, 99, 142, 183.

[63] *Материали за картата...*, p. 184; Р. Костова, *Още веднъж за Кръглата църква и т. нар. родов манастир в Преслав*, [in:] *Studia protobulgarica et mediaevalia europensia. В чест на чл. кор. проф. Веселин Бешевлиев*, ed. К. Попконстантинов, София 2003, pp. 284–303.

[64] Т. Тотев, *Дворцовият манастир в Преслав*, София 1998; Б. Николова, *Монашество...*, pp. 49–52, 60, 130–131, 138, 183.

as monasteries is premature. Somewhat further, ten kilometres to the north-east, near the village of khan Krum, lies one other archaeological site hiding remains of monastic buildings[65]. Two coenobia from the discussed period were discovered in the vicinity of Pliska: in Kalugeritsa[66] and in Sini Vir[67]. Further monasteries were located within a 25 km radius from the old Bulgarian capital: in Ravna and Chernoglavtsi[68]. The capital city itself has likely hosted at least one fraternity, although the most commonly suggested location for it – by the Great Basilica – is uncertain[69].

The list of monastic foundations in north-eastern Bulgaria is completed by Karaach Teke located five kilometres to the east from Varna's centre[70], and by the rock monasteries: in Krepcha[71], Murfatlar (in Danube's

---

[65] В. Антонова, Д. Аладжова, П. Петрова, *Нови археологически проучвания при с. Хан Крум, Шуменско*, ГМСБ 7, 1981, pp. 65–76; *Материали за картата...*, p. 287.

[66] Т. Балабанов, *Проучване на старобългарския комплекс "Кирика" край с. Калугерица*, ПБА 1, 1992, pp. 68–73; *Материали за картата...*, p. 214; Г. Майсторски, И. Бабаджанов, П. Георгиев, *Средновековен манастирски комплекс в м. Кирика – НИАР "Мадара"*, [in:] *Археологически открития и разкопки през 2015 г.*, ed. А. Аладжов, София 2016, pp. 730–732.

[67] П. Петрова, *Църквата при с. Сини вир, Шуменско*, [in:] *Археологически открития и разкопки през 1988 г.*, Кърджали 1989, p. 135; *Материали за картата...*, p. 277.

[68] П. Георгиев, *Манастирската църква при с. Равна, Провадийско*, ИНМВ 21, 1985, pp. 71–97; Т. Балабанов, *Старобългарски манастир при с. Черноглавци (предварително съобщение)*, ИИМШ 8, 1996, pp. 263–272; П. Георгиев, *Манастирът от X век при с. Черноглавци, Шуменска област*, ГСУ.НЦСВПИД 12, 2003, pp. 71–79; Б. Николова, *Монашество...*, pp. 188–255, 259–262; K. Popkonstantinov, R. Kostova, *Architecture of conversion: provincial monasteries in the 9th–10th centuries, Bulgaria*, ТГЭ 53, 2010, pp. 118–132.

[69] Т. Тотев, *Старобългарските манастири...*, pp. 4–7; П. Георгиев, С. Витлянов, *Архиепископията – манастир в Плиска*, София 2001; Б. Николова, *Монашество...*, pp. 13–40.

[70] K. Popkonstantinov, R. Kostova, *Architecture of conversion...*, pp. 118–132; Б. Николова, *Монашество...*, pp. 258–259; К. Попконстантинов, В. Плетньов, Р. Костова, *Средновековен княжески манастир в м. Караачтеке – Варна*, [in:] *Археологически Открития и Разкопки през 2010 г.*, ed. М. Гюрова, София 2011, pp. 497–500.

[71] Р. Костова, *Скалният манастир при Крепча: Още един поглед към монашеските практики в България през X в.*, [in:] *Проф. д.и.н. Станчо Ваклинов и средновековната българска култура*, ed. К. Попконстантинов, Велико Търново 2005, pp. 289–305.

delta)[72], Ruyna, valleys of the rivers Suha, Kanagyol, and others[73]. Two further monasteries operated on the south-western borderlands of the country: the monastery of Clement in Ohrid and Naum by the southern shore of the lake Ohrid[74] and at least one in Rhodope Mountains (near Batak)[75].

The material remains of the monasteries present them to us as centres of literary, educational and pastoral activity. The most interesting in this regard is the Ravna monastery. Within its walls, numerous styluses and elements of book bindings have been found, and the surviving ruins are covered in around three hundred inscriptions and over three thousands of drawings[76]. Diverse epigraphic and iconographic materials lift the veil of secrecy hiding the colourful life of the monastery and its surroundings. The majority of drawings from Ravna depict crosses. A large part of these were made on the church (which is the best-preserved structure). Second in number are the graffiti depicting animals: horses, deer, peacocks, eagles and others. The localisation of these indicates that the majority of them were made not by the monastery's permanent residents, but by visitors: pilgrims and the local people making use of the spiritual ministry of the monks[77]. The inscriptions were made in five alphabets: runic, Greek,

---

[72] Г. Атанасов, *Още за датировката и монашеската организация в скалната обител до Мурфатлар (Басараби)*, [in:] *Великотърновският университет "Св. св. Кирил и Методий" и българската археология*, vol. I, 2010, pp. 467–485.

[73] idem, *За хронологията и монашеската организация в скалните обители през първото българско царство*, [in:] *Светогорска обител Зограф*, vol. III, ed. В. Гюзелев et al., София 1999, pp. 281–299.

[74] Dj. Stričević, *Églises triconques médiévales en Serbie et en Macédoine et la tradition de l'architecture paléobyzantine*, [in:] *XIIe Congrès International des Études Byzantines. Ochride 1961. Rapports VII*, ed. Dj. Bošković; Dj. Stričević; I. Nikolajević-Stojoković, Belgrade–Ochride 1961, pp. 78–85; R. Kostova, *St. Kliment of Ohrid and his monastery. Some more archeology of the written evidence*, SB 25, 2006, pp. 593–605; П. Кузман, *Археолошки сведоштва за дејноста на Свети Климент Охридски во Охридскиот регион*, Slov 5.2, 2016, pp. 136–178.

[75] К. Меламед, *Светилище и некропол до раннохристиянския манастир край с. Нова махала, Баташко*, Архе 35.2, pp. 36–46.

[76] К. Попконстантинов, *Равненски манастир*, [in:] *КМЕ*, vol. III, p. 423; Р. Костова, *Манастирските училища през IX–X в. в България (по материали от манастира при с. Равна)*, КМС 17, 2007, pp. 513–529.

[77] Р. Костова, *Център и периферия в Равненския манастир (по рисунки-графити)*, [in:] *Светогорска обител Зограф*, vol. II, ed. В. Гюзелев, София 1996, pp. 224–227; Б. Николова, *Монашество...*, pp. 213–214.

Latin, Glagolitic and Cyrillic[78]. The names of the undersigned, as well as the multitude of languages, attest that the visitors to, and likely also the inhabitants of the monastery came from different ethnic groups. The way in which the inscriptions were made and the nature of the texts betray differences in the level of education of the writers. Some of them have left only misspelt signatures – one may assume that this was the extent of their literary skills. Some, in turn, were able users of two languages, which is attested by bilingual, Bulgarian-Greek inscriptions. A considerable number of the graffiti from Ravna is directly associated with the educational activity of the monastery – these are the ABCs, fragments of the Psalms (which were being committed to memory at an early stage of education) and decorative initials. We also find prayers (*God have mercy on Thecla*[79]) and circumstantial inscriptions (*I arrived on Monday at noon, I entered the church and wrote*[80]). Inscriptions, writing implements and other remains confirming literary and ministerial activity of the monks have been found in numerous other monasteries, for example in Karaach Teke or Murfatlar[81].

The numerous pilgrims arriving at monasteries, as we may guess, most often asked for spiritual consolation, prayer for divine assistance in their concerns or advice in life matters. The sick may have been drawn to the monasteries by the fame of the miracles performed by the saints, many of whom in the Eastern Christian tradition had a monastic background. In the Old Bulgarian *A Certain Father's Words to his Son for Profit to his Soul*, we read about monasteries:

---

[78] К. Попконстантинов, *Равненски...*, p. 423.

[79] *Ibidem*, p. 425.

[80] *Ibidem*, p. 426.

[81] К. Попконстантинов, Р. Костова, В. Плетньов, *Манастирите при Равна и Караачтеке до Варна в манастирската география на България през IX–X в.*, AMV 3.2, 2005, pp. 107–121; G. Atanasov, *Influences ethno-culturelles dans l'ermitage rupestre près de Murfatlar, à Dobrudza*, Bsl 57.1, 1996, pp. 112–124; Р. Костова, *Скалният манастир при Бесараби в северна Добруджа. Някои проблеми на интерпретация*, [in:] *Българите в Северното Причерноморие. Изследвания и материали*, vol. VII, Велико Търново 2000, pp. 131–152; I. Holubeanu, *The Byzantine Monasticism in Scythia Minor-Dobruja in the IVth–XVth Centuries*, EBPB 5, 2006, pp. 243–289; Б. Николова, *Монашество...*, pp. 344–404.

> I will show you, my son, a true haven, [where you can take shelter]. It is the monastery, a house of saints. Go there, and you shall receive consolation, tell of your grief, and [the monks] will disperse your sorrows, for they are sons of lightheartedness and can raise one's spirits. If you have something in your house that they need, bring it to them, for everything that [you give them] you give into God's hands and you shall not be left without a reward![82]

The gifts of the petitioners may have been an important position in a monastery's budget[83]. As we may guess, monks were called not only for resolving spiritual matters, but also those of more material nature. Cosmas the Priest, an author from the tenth-eleventh century, scolded monks who *set houses of the others in order, while thoughtlessly abandoning their own* – likely meaning their excessive involvement in the matters of life of the faithful, not befitting the calling of those who renounced the 'world'[84].

The kind, size and layout of the buildings of the monastery were strictly subordinated to their function. The central place was occupied by the church, the main focus of the monks' communal life. In the immediate vicinity of the church were the refectory, or the dining room, and the kitchen. Next to these were the monks' cells. They were most often located in a line alongside the wall encircling the entire complex. Within the walls, we would also expect to find the workshops and storehouses, their number and size depending on the type of economic activity taking place in the monastery. The Ravna monastery is one of the more interesting and better-known complexes of this type from the Old Bulgarian period, and for this reason it will serve us as an example[85].

---

[82] *Izbornik 1076*, ed. М о л д о в а н, pp. 183–184.

[83] Interesting observations on the value of individual gifts for the monasteries based on byzantine hagiography can be found in D. K r a u s m ü l l e r, *Take No Care for the Morrow! The Rejection of Landed Property in Eleventh- and Twelfth-Century Byzantine Monasticism*, BMGS 42, 2018, pp. 45–57.

[84] Ю.К. Б е г у н о в, *Козма Пресвитер в славянских литературах*, София 1973, p. 365.

[85] Plan after: K. P o p k o n s t a n t i n o v, R. K o s t o v a, *Architecture...*, p. 118, fig. 2; the legend was created on the basis of the above publication, and of: Р. К о с т о в а, *Център...*, pp. 222–223; Б. Н и к о л о в а, *Монашество...*, pp. 190–200.

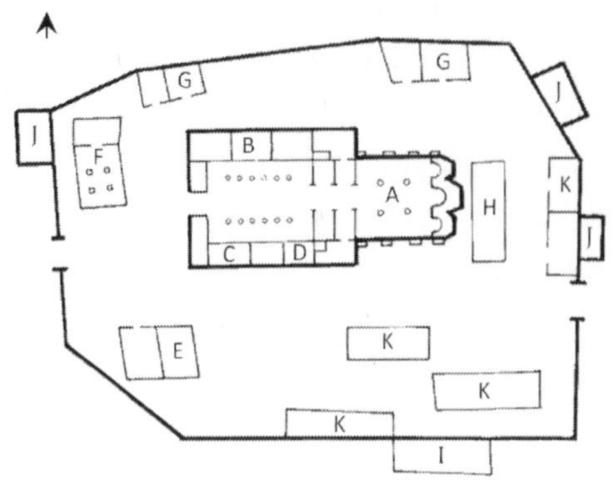

The plan of Ravna Monastery

A – the church
B – scriptorium
C – refectory (?) and storehouses
D – monks' cells (upstairs)
E – kitchen (with the refectory?)
F – baths
G – toilets
H – living quarters / residence / hegumen's cell (?)
I – pilgrim's house
J – towers
K – economic buildings (?)

The outer wall encircled an area of near 1 ha. This makes the Ravna monastery one of the largest preserved mediaeval Bulgarian complexes of this type. There were three entrances leading to the interior – the two more important ones: eastern and western, and a smaller gateway (not marked on the plan), which was located within the southern wall, near building I. A part of the complex – associated with the most important events of the daily life of its inhabitants – was separated, and constituted the inner courtyard, encompassing the area closed off by the buildings A–D. These were: the church, refectory, scriptorium and the living cells. The separation of this inner courtyard makes the architectural assumptions of the Ravna monastery exceptional. The nearest analogies may be found in the arrangements of the early Byzantine Syrian monasteries[86]. The atypical layout however still follows the universal principle which required the living cells, the church and the refectory to be built in the immediate vicinity of each other. The way in which the monks moved between these buildings was laid out in typica, or monastic rules, and was associated with the specific details and frequency of their prayers[87]. The separation of the sacred space in the Ravna monastery, visited by

[86] K. Popkonstantinov, R. Kostova, *Architecture*..., p. 118.

[87] Cf. Б. Николова, *Монашество*..., pp. 90–91; S. Popović, *The Byzantine Monastery: Its Spacial Iconography and the Question of Sacredness*, [in:] *Hierotopy. Creation of Sacred Spaces in Byzantium and Medieval Russia*, ed. A. Lidov, Moscow 2006, pp. 150–185.

numerous pilgrims and inhabitants of the surrounding settlements, made it easier for the monks to maintain the focus that was demanded of them. The Ravna complex stands out from the other monasteries also due to having more than one entry in the outer wall[88].

The baths and the toilets, located away from the main buildings, likely served both the monks and their visitors. Monks' bathing was strictly regulated; the rules rarely permitted bathing more than three times a year[89]. The role of the other buildings in that part of the complex, including building H, remains unexplained. The Ravna monastery was fortified, which is attested by the existence of the three towers (J).

The creation of the majority of the discovered monasteries from the period of the First Bulgarian Tsardom is associated with the reigns of Boris and Symeon. This is true of the complexes in Sini Vir, Ravna, Karaach Teke, Krepcha, Murfatlar, Chernoglavtsi, by the Kanagyol, and of both of the Ohrid foundations. Some of the monasteries (Cheresheto, Valkashina, khan Krum) have not been precisely dated in the literature of the subject. Among the monasteries, I mentioned only the monastery of synkellos George is considered to have been created during Peter's reign. The six decades from the adoption of Christianity until Peter's ascension to the throne have seen at least nine foundations, the forty years of his reign – one. Although the information that we have at our disposal paints only a partial picture of the Old Bulgarian monasticism (the dates are uncertain, and a part of the monasteries from that period likely remains undiscovered), we can observe a clear drop in the frequency of foundation activity. We may assume that at the time when Peter started his reign, the network of monasteries in the Bulgarian state has been completed, in the sense that it fulfilled the tasks given to it by the Church and state authorities, and therefore did not require further intensive development. In this context, the fact that the only monastic foundation from Peter's reign was a private initiative, gains additional significance.

---

[88] K. Popkonstantinov, R. Kostova, *Architecture...*, pp. 121–122, 126.

[89] See, e.g. *Byzantine Monastic Foundation Documents: A Complete Translation of the Surviving Founders' Typika and Testaments*, ed. J. Thomas, A. Constantinides Hero, G. Constable, Washington 2000, pp. 460, 925 et al.

Certain facts associated with Peter's life, his cult and the image he left in the minds of the mediaeval Bulgarians appear to suggest that he had a positive attitude towards the monks and that he created suitable conditions for the flourishing and enhancement of monasticism as a public institution[90]. It is in this way that this ruler's reign is sometimes characterised in the modern historiography. In the lack of direct information on this subject, other historical and historical-literary facts are brought up in a way that is intended to lend credence to such image of the era[91]. The reduction in philosophical and theological interests of the contemporary literary authors and the development of ascetic literature are highlighted. The ruler may have influenced change, as he was involved in literary activity himself (as a bold, but widespread in Bulgarian mediaeval studies hypothesis has it[92]), passed away, like his grandfather, in a monastery, and was canonised soon after his death. As commonly known facts indicate, tsar Symeon stimulated literary activity and co-defined its character. When the tsar-author was replaced by the tsar-saint, one could assume, speculating a little, that there has come a right climate for monasticism to flourish. Was that indeed the case? The assessments regarding the development of the monastic network make us adopt a cautious attitude in this

---

[90] On the subject of historical memory and cult of Peter, see: И. Билярски, *Небесните покровители: св. цар Петър*, ИБ 5.2, 2001, pp. 32–44; idem, *Покровители на Царството. Св. цар Петър и св. Параскева-Петка*, София 2004, pp. 5–43; idem, М. Йовчева, *За датата на Успението на цар Петър и за култа към него*, [in:] *ТАНГРА. Сборник в чест на 70-годишнината на академик Васил Гюзелев*, ed. М. Каймакамова, Г. Николов, София 2006, pp. 543–557; Д. Чешмеджиев, *Култът към българският цар Петър I (927–969): монашески или държавен?*, [in:] *Љубав према образовању и вера у Бога у православним манастирами, 5. Међународна Хилендарска конференција. Зборник изабраних радова 1*, ed. P. Matejić et al., Beograd–Columbus 2006, pp. 245–257; Б. Николова, *Цар Петър и характерът на неговия култ*, Pbg 33.2, 2009, pp. 63–77; М. Каймакамова, *Култът към цар Петър (927–969) и движещите идеи на българските освободителни въстания срещу византийската власт през XI–XII в.*, BMd 4/5, 2013/2014, pp. 417–438.

[91] Cf., e.g. П. Димитров, *Характер и значение на следсимеоновата епоха*, [in:] idem, *Петър Черноризец*, Шумен 1995, pp. 7–16; М. Йовчева, А. Милтенова, *Литературата от 927 г. до края на българското царство. Политико-религиозни, литературни и културни процеси*, [in:] *ИСБЛ*, pp. 255–260.

[92] Й. Иванов, *Български старини от Македония*, София 1970, pp. 385–386; П. Димитров, *Петър Черноризец*, [in:] idem, *Петър...*, pp. 40–43.

matter, however they do not fully answer the question. We cannot, after all, rule out that the monks developed their dynamic activity within the framework of an existing organisational structure. Any conclusion regarding a possible flourishing of monasticism during Peter's reign is highly risky since we have too few data regarding the functioning of contemporary monasteries and the periodisation of their development. However, since the welfare of the monasteries in that period was supposed to depend on the ruler's favour, let us pause for a moment to examine this issue. Can we say that Peter's attitude towards the monastic movement was somehow exceptional? At first, we might want to give a positive answer to this. Peter stands out thanks to the remarks about his contacts with the monks (requests for prayer, attempts to meet them, sending of precious gifts) that were noted in literary works: the lives of John of Rila and Paul the Younger (of Latros). A deeper reflection on the nature of these testimonies should prevent us from making unequivocal conclusions on their basis[93]. First and foremost, one should not forget that the information about the tsar contained within these texts is a part of a literary portrayal of a saint. For the hagiographer, the ruler's person (as well as factual accuracy) were secondary[94], as it served to build up the prestige of the work's protagonist. The presence of a specific monarch in a narrative of a hagiographic nature is somewhat incidental, and we should not automatically associate it with real events. While the episode brought up in the Lives of John of Rila does not fall outside of the framework of a topos, and its historiographic value is impossible to determine[95], the correspondence between the tsar and Paul the Younger escapes somewhat the confines of the usual tropes. Paul's hermitage was located in Asia Minor, near Miletos. The ascetic was a subject of the Byzantine emperor (with whom he, notably, also exchanged correspondence). The information about the contacts with the Bulgarian tsar, and of his requests for prayer for the salvation of his soul[96],

---

[93] Cf. M.J. L e s z k a, *Rola cara Piotra (927–969) w życiu bułgarskiego Kościoła. Kilka uwag*, VP 36, 2016, pp. 435–438.

[94] Cf. R. M o r r i s, *Monks...*, p. 72.

[95] The same applies to the Peter's epithets from the *Service of St. Tsar Peter* (pp. 392–393): ꙋтвръждениꙗ црквамь, чрьноризьцѫ любѧ.

[96] *Life of St Paul the Younger*, p. 72.

exceed the demands which hagiographer had to meet in service of his art, and as an addition to the canon, appears to be more credible. On the other hand, the ambition of the author, clearly delineated in the Life, to show that the fame of his protagonist reached very far (all the way to Italy and Scythia, although the identification of the latter toponym is debatable[97]) may have had a negative impact on his truthfulness. Among those seeking contact with Paul, the author also listed the bishop of Rome. This 'grandeur' raises some doubts as to the text's veracity. At the same time, I am certain that selecting Peter as the saint's correspondent could not have been accidental. Whether there have been real letters that resulted in the hagiographer making his choice, or news of a particular attitude of Peter towards the monks, or some other reason entirely – we are not able to say for certain. Even if we succumbed to the temptation of positively verifying the truthfulness of the hagiographers, let us not forget that a ruler seeking the blessing of a famous saint was nothing unusual. Examples from the neighbouring Byzantium, and from the later period in Bulgaria's history, are numerous[98]. True, from the history of contemporary Bulgaria there was only one such example, Peter himself contacting the Saints John and Paul, however, the reasons behind it should not be sought in the ruler's personal character. No saint has appeared in Bulgaria during the reigns of Michael-Boris and of Symeon, while Paul the Younger,

---

[97] *Life of St Paul the Younger*, pp. 71–72; *FGHB*, vol. V, p. 230.

[98] Cf. P. C h a r a n i s, *The Monk as an Element of Byzantine Society*, DOP 25, 1971, p. 84. Byzantine monks who maintained contacts with the court and the emperor in the tenth-eleventh centuries are listed by Rosemary M o r r i s (*Monks...*, pp. 84–85), these were: Michael Maleinos, Atanasios the Athonite, Paul the Younger, John the Athonite (the only one in this group who was not made a saint), Christodoulos. Numerous examples of relations between a holy monk and an emperor, from the early Byzantine period, can be found in the work of Rafał K o s i ń s k i, *Holiness and Power. Constantinopolitan Holy Men and Authority in the 5th Century*, Berlin–Boston 2016. From the period of late mediaeval Bulgaria we have two examples of holy monks extending spiritual care over the tsar: Joachim and Theodosios of Tarnovo (Х. К о д о в, *Опис на славянските ръкописи в библиотеката на Българската Академия на Науките*, София 1969, p. 46; С. К о ж у х а р о в, *Неизвестен летописен разказ от времето на Иван Асен II*, ЛМ 18.2, 1974, p. 128. В. З л а т а р с к и, *Житïе и жизнь преподобнаго отца нашего Θеодосїя иже въ ТръновҌ постничьствовавшаго съписано светҌишимь патрïархѡмь Кѡнстантïна града кvрь Калистѡмь*, СНУНК 20, 1904, p. 17).

who was active during Peter's reign, with his international renown is an exceptional character.

An indirect testimony of a ruler's favour towards monastic communities, which dictated their welfare, might be tsar's seals, found in monastic ruins. Directly, they are only a proof of 'official' contacts between the monarch and the monks. However, we may guess that they were associated with material support provided for the community, and with entrusting monks with certain tasks (prayer, pastoral care, etc.). Association with the ruler was undoubtedly beneficial for the monks. According to hagiographers, tsar Peter, after unsuccessfully attempting to meet the hermit John, offered him gold, and the majority of the ruler's documents from the later period that were issued for monasteries of which we are aware were donation acts. The seals that have been found in the monasteries were thusly interpreted in the literature of the subject. Therefore the monastery in Karaach Teke, where lead seals of Boris and Peter were uncovered, is being called the 'ducal' and considered to be a tool of the educational and Christianisation campaign initiated by the court[99]. Let us examine the data about the seals of the rulers of the First Bulgarian Tsardom that have been found in the ruins of the monasteries. It is, unfortunately, very scant: Boris – 2 seals (Karaach Teke, Sini Vir)[100], Symeon – 2 seals (Ravna)[101], Peter – 1 seal (Karaach Teke)[102]. These statistics do not distinguish Peter

[99] К. Попконстантинов, Р. Костова, В. Плетньов, *Манастирите при Равна и Караачтеке…*

[100] К. Шкорпил, *Печат на княз Михаил-Борис*, ИВАД 7, 1921, pp. 108–116; П. Петрова, *Църквите при с. Сини вир, Шуменско*, [in:] *Археологически открития и разкопки през 1987 г.*, ed. В. Велков, Благоевград 1988, p. 190; И. Йорданов, *Корпус на средновековните български печати*, София 2016, pp. 46–47.

[101] И. Йорданов, *Корпус…*, pp. 62–63. Symeon's seal found in the monastery of George the synkellos (*ibidem*, p. 69) has already been on the site before it became the abode of a monastic brotherhood founded during Peter's times.

[102] К. Попконстантинов, В. Плетньов, Р. Костова, *Средновековен княжески…*, p. 497. In the calculations above I omit the seals found in locations which cannot be identified with certainty as monastic sites. Such is the case with, e.g. the seals found in the complex next to the Golden Church (И. Йорданов, *Корпус…*, p. 96), and with the seal found in the vicinity of the village Rizhevo Konare near Plovdiv. In the latter case the monastic nature of the buildings in which the seal was found has been established by its discoverers on an undisclosed basis (В. Станков, *Ново-*

in any way. We have no reliable testimonies that would confirm either a particularly lively development of monasticism in his times or his special relationship with this institution. Jonathan Shepard speculated that Peter's appellation βασιλεὺς εὐσεβής known from seals might have indicated his generosity towards monasteries and other religious institutions (and his zeal in combating heresy), although he also noted that the epithets of this kind were also repeated on contemporary coins and seals from Byzantium (e.g. those of Constantine VII[103]), and we may, therefore, add that they would not have necessarily indicated the characteristics of a particular ruler[104]. The acceptance of such titles however certainly shows that Peter wanted to be seen as pious. Does that make him stand out in any way? Certainly not. The image of Peter's times as a period of flourishing of monasticism, which we may sometimes find in both academic and popular literature, is not supported by any trustworthy literary sources. At its base, there is a historiographic tradition, which originated in the nineteenth century.

The question of the cultural outlook of Peter's era (favourable to monastic asceticism), reflected in the literary works created at the time (both translated and original) also requires careful verification. This is because the dating of the works on which we could base the descriptions of the 'spirit' of the times[105] to Peter's reign is debatable. I am thinking here of the writings of Cosmas the Priest, whose works are supposed to indicate that the monastic movement has reached its maturity[106], and

---

открит печат на Петър I (927–969), ППре 9, 2003, pp. 315–317; И. Й о р д а н о в, *Корпус*..., p. 113).

[103] Г. А т а н а с о в, *Държавната идеология на християнска България, инсигни и титулатура на нейните владетели*, [in:] i d e m, В. В а ч к о в а, П. П а в л о в, *Българска национална история*, vol. III, *Първо българско царство (680–1018)*, Велико Търново 2015, p. 779.

[104] J. S h e p a r d, *A Marriage Too Far? Maria Lekapena and Peter of Bulgaria*, [in:] *The Empress Theophano: Byzantium and the West at the Turn of the First Millennium*, ed. A. D a v i d s, Cambridge 1995, p. 143.

[105] Cf. e.g. П. Д и м и т р о в, *Характер и значение*...; А. Н и к о л о в, *Политическа мисъл в ранносредновековна България (средата на IX – края на XI век)*, София 2006, pp. 245–250.

[106] П. Д и м и т р о в, *Характер и значение*..., pp. 11–15.

of works of Peter the Monk, the most important Old Bulgarian ascetic writer. Regarding Cosmas the Priest, let us be satisfied with a conclusion that there are various suggestions in the scholarly literature as to when his literary activity can be located – from the beginning of the tenth until the beginning of the thirteenth centuries, with the extreme boundaries being excluded as weakly supported. The safest chronological range would be from the mid-tenth until mid-eleventh century[107]. Let us note that with using such dating the value of the *Sermon against the Heretics* as a source for the history of monasticism during the reign of tsar Peter is not obvious, as the work itself may have been created many years after the ruler's death. The dating of Peter the Monk's works is far more important for us, as it presents a certain mechanism that is distorting the image of the era. The fullest and still current academic description related to the works of this author is a monograph of a renowned Bulgarian philologist Rumyana Pavlova, from 1994[108]. She obviously made an attempt at locating the

---

[107] Kosma Prezbiter, *Mowa polemiczna przeciwko heretykom (fragmenty)*, ed. and transl. M. Skowronek, G. Minczew, [in:] *Średniowieczne herezje dualistyczne na Bałkanach. Źródła słowiańskie*, ed., transl., commen. G. Minczew, M. Skowronek, J.M. Wolski, Łódź 2015, pp. 67–68. The summary of the debate about the dating of this work, which can be found in the work of Yuriy Begunov (Ю. Бегунов, *Козма Пресвитер*..., pp. 195–221), despite the half a century that passed since it was written remains current. The conclusion that the Russian scholar reached, in turn, is specific and uncertain in equal measure. The period of 969–970 (p. 221 or prior to 972 on p. 217) he delineated (with a qualification: *most likely*), is based on debatable premises. *Terminus post quem* is determined by the view that the phrase: **в лѣта правовѣрнаго цара Петра** was in the original edition of the *Sermon*, and could have been only composed after the ruler's death. Begunov argued for the *terminus ante quem* by saying that the *Sermon* was written at the time when the Bogomilism was still in opposition to the state, his argument an arbitrary: *ясно е*! The presupposition of this statement (that the successors of Boris II or the Byzantine government accepted Bogomils, or were favourable to them) is absurd. The remaining arguments (interpreting remarks of Cosmas about John the new presbyter, mentioned in the *Sermon* war damages, referring to Bogomilism a new heresy, etc.) are of similar quality. It is difficult to find better arguments. Our dating of *Sermon* is based purely on the clues left by the author, and these are few and unclear. Without new data, a satisfactory resolution of this question is impossible. The stubborn seeking of certainties and particulars by scholars where there are none is inexplicable.

[108] Р. Павлова, *Петър Черноризец*...

activity of her protagonist in time and announced its results in the title itself: *Петър Черноризец. Старобългарски писател от X век*. A robust linguistic analysis presented in the volume allowed its author to conclude that Peter was an Old Bulgarian author (ninth-eleventh century)[109]. It would be difficult to demand a greater accuracy from linguistic research from regarding works from such distant times and with such limited comparative material. Narrowing down Peter's activity to the times of the tsar of the same name was accomplished by reaching for arguments of a different nature – as Peter's homilies *exude a spirit of a post-Symeon era*. The author finds in his sermons numerous thematic analogies to the works of Cosmas the Priest and other texts dated to the tenth century[110]. The way in which the Bulgarian scholar created these thematic analogies between the analysed texts raises serious doubts. She has pointed to Christian religious truths such as: the Biblical vision of the beginning of the world, the meaning of the sacraments, icons, the sign of the cross, of a church as a house of God, the cult of saints, a particular devotion to the Mother of God, condemnation of violence etc.[111], which are after all common not only to the tenth-century Bulgarian authors[112]. Moreover, there is nothing in the execution of these themes that would indicate the existence of close parallels between the fragments compared by Rumyana Pavlova. The one thing that is the most concerning in the Bulgarian scholar's argument is the reference to the 'spirit of the post-Symeon/Peter's era'. This historiographic concept, after all, is largely based on the works of Peter the Monk[113]. It needs to be said that its basis – if we exclude the works of this author – is minute. The second supporting pillar of this idea is

---

[109] *Ibidem*, pp. 124–223.

[110] *Ibidem*, pp. 30–45.

[111] *Ibidem*, pp. 44–45.

[112] Cf. Й. Андреев, *Кем был черноризец Петр?*, Bbg 6, 1980, pp. 54–55.

[113] Cf.,e.g. П. Димитров, *Характер и значение...*; И. Божилов, *България при цар Петър (927–969)*, [in:] И. Божилов, В. Гюзелев, *История на България в три тома*, vol. III, *История на средновековна България VII–XIV век*, София 1999, pp. 281–283; М. Каймакамова, *Култът...*, pp. 422–423. In the older works, the problems with dating the works of Peter the Monk were usually overlooked, as he was identified with tsar Peter, see: Й. Андреев, *Кем был черноризец...*

the *Sermon* of Cosmas the Priest, whose direct link to Peter's era should not be accepted as certain.

The activity of John of Rila, the only monk from the period of the First Bulgarian Tsardom whose life was described in more detail, falls during the reign of Peter. At the same time this hermit was (and remains to this day) one of the more venerated Bulgarian saints[114]. More than ten texts associated with his cult have been written during the mediaeval period. The oldest ones are the Greek Life, and the canons by Skylitzes (dated variously to 1165–1183, preserved in Bulgarian translation), a folk Life (uncertainly dated to between twelfth and fifteenth century) and two prologue Lives from the thirteenth century[115].

John of Rila certainly also occupies an important place in the historical imagination of Bulgarians as a master of spiritual life, a protector of the state, and the supposed founder of the monastery which became one of the most important pilgrimage centres of Bulgaria. He is also treated as a symbolic character by Bulgarian medievalists. Petar Mutafchiev saw in him *a kind of an incarnation of the spirit of the age*[116]. In his monograph, Ivan Duychev highly valued the significance of the character of the saint of Rila, and of the monastery bearing his name, for the development and preservation of Bulgarian culture, from the mediaeval period until his day without a break, and concludes his argument with the following creed: *the community* [*of Rila*] *shall preserve its significance in the spiritual life of our nation forever, for at its base lies a lofty moral and spiritual effort* [*orig. подвиг*][117]. Vassil Gyuzelev placed John in the ranks of the most venerated saints who, as he claims: *set the foundations of life of the particular church*

---

[114] В. Гюзелев, *"Велико светило за целия свят" (Св. Иван Рилски в измеренията на своето време)*, [in:] *Светогорска обител Зограф*, vol. III, pp. 13–15.

[115] Б. Ангелов, *Повествователни съчинения за Иван Рилски в старобългарската литература*, ЕЛ 32.1, 1977, pp. 66–71; И. Добрев, Е. Томова, *Болгарский святой Иоанн Рылский (культ и агиография)*, [in:] *Слово: към изграждане на дигитална библиотека на южнославянски ръкописи*, ed. Х. Миклас, А. Милтенова, София 2008, pp. 142–153.

[116] П. Мутафчиев, *Поп Богомил и Св. Иван Рилски. Духът на отрицанието в нашата история*, ФП 4.2, 1934, p. 106.

[117] И. Дуйчев, *Рилският светец...*, p. 376.

and determine the trends of its development[118]. Ivan Bozhilov, in turn, wrote about John: *He is a personality without which* [*Bulgarian*] *Christianity and Church cannot be imagined*[119]. The ease with which the quoted scholars linked modernity with the tenth century and the emphasis with which they wrote about this hermit is, it seems, the effect of interpolating to an earlier period the significance which the community of Rila and its patron gained in the modern, or late mediaeval at the latest, period. The content of hagiographic tales about John does not allow describing him as anything other than a semi-legendary figure. The radical anchoritism, ascribed to him, and previously to the Desert Fathers and many other saints, as far as we can verify it in sources other than hagiographic, turns out to be a literary fiction[120]. The earliest confirmed traces of John's cult come from mid-twelfth century. We have no basis to question the historicity of the hermit of Rila. However, in the form that he is known to us, he is more of an ideologeme than a real person[121]. In this way, John of Rila undoubtedly turns out to be an 'incarnation of the spirit of the era'.

John lived the life of a hermit within Rila's mountain range. He came from the village of Skirno, located ca. 50 km to the west of the cave in which he spent most of his life. His family was relatively wealthy. After the death of his parents he gave his fortune away and started seeking a place that would be suitable for quiet prayer and mortification – his later life is known from hagiographic relations[122] and, what should not come as a surprise, resembles the lives of other famous anchorites. He gained

---

[118] *По правило жалонират живота на съответна църква и определят тенденциите на развитието ѝ* – В. Гюзелев, *Велико светило...*, p. 13.

[119] И. Божилов, *Българското общество през 14. век. Структура и просопография*, София 2014, p. 250.

[120] Cf. Д. Папахрисанту, *Атонско монаштво. Почеци и организација*, Београд 2003, p. 31.

[121] Cf. И. Божилов, *Българското общество...*, pp. 228–229.

[122] The older works also referenced the *Testament* of John of Rila. Research done by Bistra Nikolova (Б. Николова, *Заветът на св. Иван Рилски. За митовете и реалите*, СЛ 35/36, 2006, pp. 144–166), who examined the history of the first public presentation of the text in the latter half of the nineteenth century, clearly show that it was a late forgery, although it should be noted that her conclusions are not universally accepted.

considerable fame as a hermit – tsar Peter himself was said to have sought a meeting with him. Traditionally, his death is dated to 946. A monastery later developed in the vicinity of his hermitage and continues its existence to this day. In the Life by Joachim of Osogovo, written between twelfth and fifteenth century, John is presented as a model of hermit life for his successors, the holy hermits who led ascetic lives in the area: Prohor of Pchinya (eleventh century), Gabriel of Lesnovo (eleventh century) and Joachim himself (eleventh/twelfth century)[123].

An interesting testimony to the state of the Old Bulgarian monasticism was given by Cosmas the Priest. The second part of his *Sermon* includes an admonishment directed at the clergy, coenobites and anchorites. Cosmas criticised them for dissolution, haughtiness, laziness, ignorance, lack of restraint in eating, and for consuming alcohol[124]. He rebuked those who entered a monastery while leaving their family without means of support with particular severity. It can be seen from the text of *Sermon* that the motivations driving people to accept a monk's frock were complex. It happened that aside from religious matters, the deciding factors could have also been of material nature: the life in a monastic community ensured peaceful and relatively plentiful life[125].

3. Bogomilism

Jan M. Wolski

Heresies and schisms mark the history of the community of believers of Christ from its very beginning. The first evidence of fierce controversies and divisions can be found as early as in the New Testament[126]. An

[123] Й. Иванов, *Български старини...*, pp. 406–407.

[124] Ю.К. Бегунов, *Козма Пресвитер...*, pp. 351–352, 361.

[125] *Ibidem*, pp. 356–357.

[126] E.g. 1 Cor 11, 18–19; 1 John 2, 18–27; 4, 1–6; for a useful introduction into the abundant literature of the early Christian 'heresies', one may turn to: R.J. Decker, *The*

instructive image of the situation is presented in such works as *Panarion* of Epiphanios of Salamis, written in the latter part of the 370s, in which the author mentioned as many as sixty Christian sects. One should not become attached to the number itself, but it may serve as a symbol of a real multiplicity[127].The phenomenon of religious division in its most acute form, i.e. heresy, was also known in mediaeval Bulgaria. Several decades after Christianisation (in Peter's times) it became a cradle of Bogomilism – a religious movement the history and creed of which are known to us only partially. Its influences may be found across the Mediterranean world – in the Byzantine Asia Minor, in the western Balkans, in Italy and in France[128]. Let us however move back in time a little and examine the religious situation in Bulgaria during the period preceding the appearance of the priest Bogomil and his co-religionists. The Bulgarians accepted Christianity from Byzantine clergy. It is therefore obvious (and attested by the sources) that the missions active in the country following this momentous act propagated orthodoxy and practices specific to the Constantinopolitan patriarchate. The subsequent negotiations with the Roman Church and the presence of the clergy arriving from the West likely did not have a significant impact on the formation of the religious culture of Bulgarians. For us, other details of the early Christianisation of Bulgaria will be of more interest. From the letter of Nicholas I from 866, containing answers to 115 questions of the newly baptised Bulgarians, we learn that among the missionaries spreading the new faith were representatives of different creeds:

Bauer Thesis: An Overview, [in:] *Orthodoxy and Heresy in Early Christian Contexts: Reconsidering the Bauer Thesis*, ed. P.A. Hartog, Eugene 2015, pp. 6–33.

[127] See: G. Vallée, *A Study in Anti-Gnostic Polemics. Irenaeus, Hippolytus, and Epiphanius*, Waterloo 1981; R. Lyman, *Heresiology: the invention of 'heresy' and 'schism'*, [in:] *Cambridge History of Christianity*, vol. II, *Constantine to c. 600*, ed. A. Casiday, F.W. Norris, Cambridge 2007, pp. 296–314.

[128] The history and sources of the 'great heresy', i.e. Christian dualist movements, and the place of Bogomilism in their development were discussed in: M. Loos, *Dualist Heresy in the Middle Ages*, transl. I. Lewitová, Praha 1974; Y. Stoyanov, *The Other God. Dualist Religions from Antiquity to the Cathar Heresy*, London–New York 2000.

> you assert [Nicholas addressed the Bulgarians] that Christians from many places have come to your land, that is, Greeks, Armenians, and from other places, and are saying all sorts of different things as they please. For this reason you ask us to tell you definitely whether you should obey all those preachers with all their different position, or whether you should do something else.[129]

The list of the heretics active in the contemporary Bulgaria likely included not only the Monophysite Armenians and the dualist Paulicians (both of these faiths may be included under the abovementioned 'Armenians')[130]. It is likely that the preachers claiming to be Orthodox, mentioned twice in the papal letter, were in fact non-orthodox (although we do not know their exact creeds)[131]. According to the sources, Bogomilism was close to the Paulician beliefs (in the contemporary world it was often referred to as Manichaeism), and was supposed to have appeared more than sixty years after the events mentioned by the Pope. Heretical missions did not cease in the meantime. We know of one of them, organised by Paulicians from Tephrike (now Divriği) around year 870. Slavic Manichaeans (Paulicians? Proto-Bogomils?) were mentioned by John the Exarch in the beginnings of the eleventh century. We may therefore surmise that the non-Orthodox missions were effective[132]. It is difficult to unequivocally say whether their activity influenced the appearance of Bogomilism, however the sources do suggest such a course of events. A direct statement to this effect can be found in an official document of the Bulgarian Church – a synodikon – from 1211:

> Our most cunning enemy [i.e. Satan] spread all over the Bulgarian land the Manichean heresy, mixing it with the Messalian [...] To the priest

---

[129] Nicholas I, p. 599 (transl. K. Petkov, *The Voices of Medieval Bulgaria, Seventh-Fifteenth. The Records of a Bygone Culture*, Leiden–Boston 2008, pp. 30–31).

[130] On the Paulician mission in Bulgaria see below.

[131] Nicholas I, pp. 575–576, 599–600.

[132] Г. Минчев, М. Скowронек, *Сведения о дуалистических ересях и языческих верованиях в Шестодневе Иоанна Экзарха*, SCer 4, 2014, p. 100.

> Bogomil who, under the Bulgarian tsar Peter, adopted this Manichean heresy and spread it in the Bulgarian land adding to it that our God Christ was born of the holy Mother of God and ever Virgin Mary only in appearance, and the flesh He took on He took up and left it in the air, to him and his past and present disciples called 'apostles,' anathema![133]

It is one of the few stories of the beginnings of the Bogomil movement that we can find in mediaeval writings. Despite its small volume, it contains a wealth of important information. Bogomil appears as a religious reformer who, having adopted a mixed Paulician-Messalian creed, enriched it with docetist elements (i.e. the claim of the appearance, or incompleteness of the incarnation – *the flesh He took on He took up and left it in the air*), and thus created a new heresy. Let us carefully examine the elements of this tale, since nearly all of them attracted contradictory comments from historians.

Among the sources of the Bogomil heresy, according to the *Synodikon*, the most commonly mentioned is Paulicianism, referred to in the quoted passage as 'Manichaeism'. This dualist movement originated in the seventh century in Armenia. The representatives of this creed were present in Bulgaria since at least eighth century. We know that the Paulicians were resettled to the Byzantine-Bulgarian borderland in years 747 and 757, on the orders of the Byzantine emperor Constantine V[134]. Soon afterwards, due to border changes, also found themselves in the Bulgarian state. Paulicians conducted missionary activity, promoting their dualist vision of the world in which there were two gods – a good and an evil one[135].

---

[133] *Synodikon of Tsar Boril*, p. 121 (transl. K. Petkov, *The Voices...*, p. 250; with minor change – J.M.W.).

[134] S. Runciman, *Medieval manichee. A Study of the Christian Dualist Heresy*, Cambridge 1947, pp. 39, 64–65; D. Dragojlović, *The History of Paulicianism on the Balkan Peninsula*, Balc 5, 1973, p. 235. For information on other waves of resettlement see: Д. Ангелов, *Богомилството*, София 1993, pp. 84–85; А. Данчева-Василева, *Павликяните в Северна Тракия през Средновековието*, ИБ 7.1/2, 2003, pp. 176–177; P. Czarnecki, *Geneza i ewolucja dogmatu teologicznego sekty bogomiłów*, ZNUJ.PH 134, 2007, pp. 27–28.

[135] D. Obolensky, *The Bogomils. A Study in Balkan Neo-Manichaeism*, Cambridge 1948, pp. 60–62, 80–82; Д. Ангелов, *Богомилството...*, pp. 86–88; for a critique of the

We find its echoes in the Bogomil theology. Paulicians retained their distinct creed for a long time. During the seventeenth and eighteenth centuries many of them adopted Catholicism, and the modern day name *pavlikyani* denotes Catholics inhabiting primarily the vicinity of Plovdiv[136]. Scholars found in Bogomilism influences of many other beliefs, e.g. Messalianism, proto-Bulgarian paganism, Manichaeism (still alive in the Central Asia), late antique Gnosticism or Marcionism[137]. The nature of the associations between Bogomilism and these currents of the non-orthodox currents of Christianity, and the other beliefs, is controversial. Perhaps the Bulgarian heretics merely shared a coincidental similarity with them; perhaps they were inspired by their writings. According to the modern knowledge of the history of the abovementioned religious movements one needs to exclude the view of a direct influence of their believers on the teachings of Bogomil. Let us note that this is also true of Messalianism, which casts doubt on the credibility of the *Synodikon* and other sources similar to it from that period. Messalianism had likely been eliminated from the Byzantine Church as early as in the fifth century, and its later 'appearances' are the result of authors referring to the new movements – which called for dedication to lives of self-denial and prayer – by that old name[138].

Specifying the sources of Bogomil dogmas, indicating what inspired them, noting the external influences (while keeping in mind that many of the elements of the Bogomilist beliefs were entirely original) does not exhaust the question of the movement's origins, nor of the reasons behind its supposed popularity. The literature of the subject, in the context of considering the development of Bogomilism, points to the low moral standards of the clergy. It is explicitly confirmed by Cosmas the

dominant views regarding the history and beliefs of Paulicians, see: N. G a r s o ï a n, *Byzantine Heresy. A Reinterpratation*, DOP 25, 1971, pp. 85–113.

[136] М. Й о в к о в, *Павликяни и павликянски селища в българските земи XV–XVIII век*, София 1991; А. Д а н ч е в а-В а с и л е в а, *Павликяните*..., pp. 192–193.

[137] See i.a. Д. А н г е л о в, *Богомилството*..., pp. 79–100; S. R u n c i m a n, *Medieval manichee*..., pp. 118–124; Y. S t o y a n o v, *The Other God*..., pp. 125–166.

[138] Cf. A. R i g o, *Messalianismo = Bogomilismo. Un'equazione dell'eresiologia medievale bizantina*, OChP 56, 1990, pp. 53–82; K. F i t s c h e n, *Did 'Messalianism' exist in Asia Minor after A.D. 431?*, SP 25, 1993, pp. 352–355.

Priest in his *Sermon against the Heretics*. This is a very valuable source pertaining to the earliest history of Bogomilism, although the date of its creation remains a subject of a dispute. The view that the *Sermon* was written in the latter half, or near the end of, the tenth century dominates in the scholarship[139]. Cosmas criticises the clergy for neglecting the religious education of the people, and instead dealing with 'earthly' matters[140]. Were we to draw from this far-reaching conclusions, we could see in Bogomilism an attempt at returning to the 'apostolic ideals', which were not being fully realised by the contemporary Church[141]. Modern scholars also saw in Bogomilism an expression of resistance of the Slavic faithful towards the Byzantinisation of the Church and state[142], and an expression of rebellion against considerable stratification of the society, legitimised by the clergy calling for obedience to the authorities and the boyars (according to scholars inspired by Marxism, Bogomilism was supposed to have been an element of class struggle)[143]. Consistent condemnation of wealth by the Bogomils and their anti-ecclesial attitude bolstered such interpretations[144]. Clergy's faults and the aforementioned socio-political processes form a context which, once examined, allows us to better imagine the circumstances in which the heresy appeared. To consider one of these elements as the reason for which Bogomil started a new movement would have been careless at best, given the scarcity

---

[139] S. Runciman, *Medieval manichee...*, pp. 93–94; Ю. Бегунов, *Козма Пресвитер в славянских литературах*, София 1973, pp. 200–221.

[140] Cosmas the Priest, p. 388.

[141] Д. Ангелов, *Богомилството...*, pp. 67–72; J. Spyra, *Wspólnoty bogomilskie jako próba powrotu do form życia gmin wczesnochrześcijańskich*, ZNUJ.PH 84, 1987, pp. 9–11, 20–21.

[142] В.Н. Златарски, *История на българската държава през средните векове*, vol. 1/2, *От славянизацията на държавата до падането на Първото царство*, София 1927, pp. 536–537; И. Дуйчев, *Едно пренебрегнато известие за богомилите*, [in:] idem, *Проучвания върху средновековната българска история и култура*, София 1981, p. 203.

[143] Д. Ангелов, *Богомилството в България*, София 1961, pp. 49–60. This Bulgarian scholar presented a different view in his later works (idem, *Богомилството...*, pp. 67–72).

[144] S. Bylina, *Bogomilizm w średniowiecznej Bułgarii. Uwarunkowania społeczne, polityczne i kulturalne*, BP 2, 1985, pp. 136–137.

of surviving source records and the poor level of knowledge about the phenomena themselves.

One of the first attestations of Bogomilism's existence is the *Letter to Tsar Peter* written by the patriarch of Constantinople, Theophylaktos Lekapenos. It was composed as the Bulgarian ruler's alarmed reaction to the spreading of non-orthodox teachings. Peter ordered the writing of the letter to the patriarch to learn how one should act towards the adherents of a heresy. The correspondence in this matter consisted of at least four letters, of which only the second of Theophylaktos' replies has been preserved[145]. In the letter, the patriarch characterised the new belief in the form of anathemas, with which the heretics, when being accepted to the Church's bosom, were to have renounced their 'errors'. Based on the information he received from Bulgaria he concluded he was dealing with a Paulician splinter group[146]. The anathemas were formulated with the help of polemical treatises aimed at these heretics, and therefore they are of limited utility in expanding our knowledge of Bogomilism itself[147]. It would seem that only two of these did not relate to Paulicians, but reflected the specificity of the beliefs of the Bulgarian heretics[148]. Discussing them will serve us to present the beliefs and practices of the Bogomils.

1. The Bogomils shared with the Paulicians the underlying conviction about the dual nature of the universe. The material world was evil, and was subject to the Evil One's power, while the spiritual world was governed by the good God. While the Paulicians were radical dualists, and according to them the division of the world was eternal, the Bulgarian heretics were among the moderate dualists and believed that the good God was the first principle of the universe.

---

[145] Theophylaktos Lekapenos, p. 311; cf. G. Minczew, *Remarks on the Letter of the Patriarch Theophylact to Tsar Peter in the Context of Certain Byzantine and Slavic Anti-heretic Texts*, SCer 3, 2013, pp. 115–116; M.J. Leszka, *Rola...*, pp. 433–435.

[146] Theophylaktos Lekapenos, p. 312.

[147] A. Solovjev, *Svedočanstva pravoslavnih izvora o bogomilstvu na Balkanu*, GIDBiH 5, 1953, pp. 3–5; G. Minczew, *Remarks...*, p. 117.

[148] Cf. B. Hamilton, *Historical Introduction*, [in:] J. Hamilton, B. Hamilton, Y. Stoyanov, *Christian Dualist Heresies in the Byzantine World c. 850–c. 1450*, Manchester–New York 1998, pp. 26–27.

It is the moderate Bogomilist vision, rather than Paulician, of the cosmological myth that the second anathema from Theophylaktos' letter is presenting (or rather signalling)[149]. In the later period (no later than mid-twelfth century) part of the Bogomil communities adopted, perhaps under Paulician influence, radical dualism. A relatively large and detailed review of the beliefs of the Bulgarian heretics can be found in the *Sermon against the Heretics* of Cosmas the Priest. We learn from it that they, i.a., rejected the Old Testament (the material world was created by the evil God, identified with the God of the Old Testament), sacraments (baptism and the Eucharist), worship of icons and of the Cross[150].

2. The fourth of the anathemas formulated in the *Letter to Tsar Peter* is aimed against all those who condemned marriage and claimed that *everything that serves to multiply and preserve mankind* comes from Satan[151]. Promoting of sexual abstinence is confirmed by numerous sources, including the *Sermon* by Cosmas. It also sketched a broader picture of the ascetic practices of the heretics – they were said to have abstained from alcohol, meat, denied themselves any comforts, and devoted themselves to deleterious fasting and lengthy prayers[152]. It appears that all of these elements of the Bogomilist ethos may have constituted (in the eyes of the author of the mentioned above fragment from the *Synodikon of Tsar Boril*) the legacy of Messalians, known for their austere, monastic lifestyle[153].

[149] Theophylaktos Lekapenos, p. 313, cf. B. Hamilton, *Historical...*, pp. 26–27.

[150] Cosmas the Priest, pp. 304–313.

[151] Theophylaktos Lekapenos, p. 313.

[152] Cosmas the Priest, pp. 300–303.

[153] For more on Messalians, see: Д. Драгојловић, *Богомилство на Балкану и у Малој Азији*, vol. I, *Богомилски родоначалници*, Београд 1974, pp. 25–123; A. Guillamont, *Messaliens. Appelations, histoire, doctrine*, [in:] *Dictionnaire de spiritualité, ascétique et mystique*, vol. X, ed. M. Viller et al., Paris 1979, pp. 1074–1083; D. Caner, *Wandering, Begging Monks. Spiritual Authority and the Promotion of Monasticism in Late Antiquity*, Berkeley Los Angeles London 2002, pp. 83–125; R. Kosiński, *Religie*

The Bogomils most likely did not create a unified ecclesiastic organisation during the discussed period. A specific kind of 'anarchism' of the original Bogomils is further emphasised by the anti-state themes present in their teachings, and the condemnation of violence. The organisational consolidation occurred during the later period. We learn of it from the twelfth century Latin sources, which tell of conflicts between the heretical communities about the apostolic succession between the sections of the movement. From these accounts emerges an image of local Churches, aware of their distinctness and significance, and cultivating their own traditions[154].

Although sources indicate that Bogomilism first appeared during tsar Peter's times (as attested by the dating of the *Letter* of Theophylaktos and passages from *Synodikon of Tsar Boril* and the *Sermon* of Cosmas), some scholars doubt that. Perhaps the dualists mentioned in the *Hexameron* of John the Exarch, written ca. 907, were in fact early Bogomils, and not Paulicians[155].

As has been mentioned, nearly all the elements of the tale concerning the beginnings of Bogomilism included in the *Synodikon of Tsar Boril* cause controversies among the experts of the subject. We have also seen that the information regarding the origins of Bogomilism (ties with Messalianism) and the time when the heresy arose are being questioned. What remains is examining the question of the historicity of Bogomil. The doubts regarding his existence are based on the explanations of the origin of the name of the heresy that do not associate it with the hypothetical founder's name. One of the alternative versions of the etymology of the name 'Bogomils' is found in Euthymios Zigabenos, a Byzantine heresiologist from the turn of the eleventh and twelfth centuries. He

---

cesarstwa rzymskiego w V stuleciu, [in:] *Świat rzymski w V wieku*, ed. R. Kosiński, K. Twardowska, Kraków 2010, pp. 403–405.

[154] Cf. Д. Ангелов, *Богомилството*..., pp. 354–356.

[155] E. g. Й. Иванов, *Богомилски книги и легенди*, София 1970, p. 20; В. Киселков, *Съществувал ли е поп Богомил*, ИП 15.2, 1958, p. 63. Critically about this positon: M. Loos, *Le prétendu témoignage d'un traité de Jean Exarque intitulé 'Šestodnev' et relatif aux Bogomiles*, Bsl 13, 1952/1953, pp. 59–67; Г. Минчев, М. Скowронек, *Сведения*...

claimed that it meant those who called for God's love[156]. It would then correspond to the Greek 'euchites' ('praying one'), which was a translation, from Syriac, of the name 'Messalians'. According to Euthymios, the Messalian heresy was one of the sources of the Bogomil theology[157]. A different, more plausible etymology is suggested by Cosmas the Priest in his *Sermon*, in which he sneeringly twists the name of the sect's founder: *It happened in the years of the orthodox tsar Peter that a priest appeared in the Bulgarian land, by the name of Bogomil ('loved by God') or, in truth, Bogunemil ('not loved by God')*[158]. In this manner, according to some scholars, the name 'Bogomils' would have meant not so much Bogomil's followers, but 'people who are pleasing to God'. On the basis of analogy with the Cathars, who called themselves as 'good people', supporters of this hypothesis claim that the epithet 'pleasing to God' was used by the heretics themselves, in order to distinguish themselves or their leaders from the members of the official Church[159]. There is neither space here nor the need to relate the entire dispute over the historicity of the priest Bogomil[160]. It does stir considerable interest among the scholars and is engaging from the methodological point of view. It shows at the same time how scant and fragmentary the information about the Bogomilist heresy that actually is. Even if we were to accept that Bogomil did exist, according to the testimony of the *Synodikon* and Cosmas the Priest, we will be forced to admit that the person of the heresy's founder (its restorer?, propagator?, one of the founders?) is, beside the name, a complete unknown.

Bogomilism played a significant role in the history of Bulgaria, it appeared in its history from the end of the ninth century, throughout the period of Byzantine domination in the Balkans (10th-12th centuries) and during the period of the Second Bulgarian Tsardom (12th–14th centuries). The birth and development of this movement forced the Church and the

---

156 Zigabenos, col. 1289.

157 Cf. В. Киселков, *Съществувал...*, pp. 60–61.

158 Cosmas the Priest, p. 299 (transl. K. Petkov, p. 68).

159 В. Киселков, *Съществувал...*, p. 59; Г. Минчев, *За името Θεόφιλος/Боголюб/Богомил в някои византийски и славянски средновековни текстове*, Pbg 37.4, 2013, pp. 51–52.

160 Cf. Д. Ангелов, *Богомилството...*, pp. 101–104.

state government, which cared for the religious unity among its faithful and subjects, to react. Actions were taken in order to reduce the influence of Bogomilism on the populace. The letter of Theophylaktos, the patriarch of Constantinople, to tsar Peter, is a trace of this; it recommended religious persecution (we do not know whether it was undertaken, and if so, to what extent). Another such trace is the *Sermon* of Cosmas the Priest, which called for moral renewal among the clergy, and for increased effort in teaching the people in their pastoral care. Ultimately, these actions proved insufficient. The effects of the Bogomilist movement spread far beyond Bulgaria's borders. It enveloped the entirety of the Balkans, Byzantine territories in Asia Minor, and Western Europe, where Bogomils influenced the development of Catharism[161].

Scholars such as Konstantin Jireček or Petar Mutafchiev saw Bogomilism as an anti-state and pacifist movement, which was the cause of weakness and repeating crises of the Bulgarian state[162]. It would seem however that they overestimated both the popularity of the movement and the influence of its ideals on the people's behaviour. These hypotheses resemble the now discarded interpretations of the scholars of late antiquity who perceived the growing popularity of the monastic life as one of the reasons for the collapse of the Roman Empire in the West[163].

---

[161] The Bogomilism's influence on the early dualist movements in mediaeval Western Europe is questionable, whereas after the mid-twelfth century it is attested to by numerous sources. See J.B. Russell, *Dissent and Reform in the Early Middle Ages*, Berkeley–Los Angeles 1965, p. 191sqq; R.I. Moore, *The Birth of Popular Heresy*, London 1975, pp. 72–73; idem, *The Origins of European Dissent*, Oxford 1985, pp. 41–42, 164–196; Д. Ангелов, *Богомилството...*, pp. 300–305, 352–369, 402–420; B. Hamilton, *Bogomil Influences on Western Heresy*, [in:] *Heresy and the Persecuting Society in the Middle Ages. Essays on the Work of R.I. Moore*, ed. M. Frassetto, Leiden–Boston 2006, pp. 93–114; M. Dobkowski, *Kataryzm. Historia i system religijny*, Kraków 2007, pp. 15–20; P. Czarnecki, *Trzecia droga dualizmu – doktryna religijna włoskiego Kościoła katarskiego w Concorezzo*, SRel 43, 2010, pp. 93–112; idem, *Kontrowersje wokół herezji XI wieku*, SRel 49.2, 2016, pp. 99–117.

[162] П. Мутафчиев, *Попъ Богомилъ и св. Ив. Рилски. Духътъ на отрицанието въ нашата история*, ФП, 6.2, 1934, pp. 1–16; К. Иречек, *История на българите с поправки и добавки от самия автор*, София 1978, p. 210.

[163] E. Gibbon, *The History of the Decline and Fall of the Roman Empire*, vol. VI, ed. J.B. Bury, New York 1907, pp. 163–165, 179, 290–292.

VIII

Zofia A. Brzozowska
Angel Nikolov

The Culture

1. Political Ideology, Education and Literature

Angel Nikolov

The volatile situation in Bulgaria during the first few years of Peter's reign required him to conduct an active propaganda aimed, internally, at legitimising him as the lawful ruler of the Bulgarians and, externally, at demonstrating and strengthening his imperial dignity, acknowledged by Byzantium in the peace treaty of 927. Furthermore, the spread of the Bogomil heresy in Bulgaria forced the tsar to become personally involved in the struggle to protect Orthodoxy from the attacks of heretic preachers. As the union of faith and state power constituted a pillar of popular unity, the ruler was expected to intervene directly and firmly in order to put an end to the spiritual schism, which could not be regarded as a purely religious issue[1].

---

[1] И. Дуйчев, *Рилският светец и неговата обител*, София 1947, pp. 41–43; М. Каймакамова, *Религия, църква и държава в ранносредновековна България (края на VII – началото на XI в.)*, ДК 80.2/3, 2000, pp. 18–19.

The popularity that the Bogomil heresy enjoyed in this period is indicative of the alienation of broad social strata from the ruling elite and of a certain disappointment with the model of political and socio-economic relations which established itself in the country in the early decades of the 10th century. Bulgarian society seemed to be undergoing a process of considerable social differentiation, which became a source of internal tensions and ultimately eclipsed the ethnic divisions, which had already lost their edge[2].

However, the limited sources available allow us to appreciate the depth of the social polarisation and the conflicts it generated mostly based on their consequence, namely, the moral crisis. It appears that the lofty principles of Christian morality, officially upheld by the Church and the ruling elite, did not find embodiment in social life, which gave rise to a mass heretical movement[3]. The Bogomils' response to the Orthodoxy preached by the clergy, which consecrated and legitimised state power and the *status quo*, was a very extreme and uncompromising denial of any kind of authority and compulsion[4]. In Petar Mutafchiev's insightful words, the pessimistic mindset of the Bogomils found no use for any social or political ideal[5].

---

[2] В. Златарски, *История на българската държава през средните векове*, vol. I/2 *Първо българско царство. От славянизацията на държавата до падането на Първото царство*, София 1971, pp. 521–525; D. Obolensky, *The Byzantine Commonwealth. Eastern Europe, 500–1453*, London 1971, p. 118; R. Browning, *Byzantium and Bulgaria. A Comparative Study Across the Early Medieval Frontier*, Berkeley–Los Angeles 1975, pp. 161–162; P. Pavlov, *Les lois agraires de la dynastie Macedonienne et la politique sociale du tsar bulgare Pierre (927–969). Selon le Traité contre les Bogomiles du prêtre Cosmas et quelques autres sources*, Bsl 56.1, 1995, pp. 103–105.

[3] Д. Ангелов, *Богомилството*, София, 1993, pp. 67–68; Г. Литаврин, *Христианство в Болгарии в 927–1018 гг.*, [in:] *Христианство в странах Восточной, Юго-Восточной и Центральной Европы на пороге второго тысячелетия*, ed. Б.Н. Флоря, Москва 2002, p. 165.

[4] Cosmas the Priest, p. 342. See also: D. Angelov, *Affermissement et fondements ideologiques du pouvoir royal en Bulgarie medieval*, Βυζ 3, 1971, p. 25; Д. Ангелов, *Богомилството*..., p. 222; Д. Оболенски, *Богомилите. Студия върху балканското новоманихейство*, София 1998, p. 101.

[5] П. Мутафчиев, *Поп Богомил и св. И. Рилски. Духът на отрицанието в нашата история*, ФП 6.2, 1934, pp. 6–7.

The need to protect the traditional Christian notion that any kind of authority is established and emanates from above from the attacks of the heretics prompted tsar Peter's contemporary Cosmas the Priest to postulate, in his damning *Sermon against the Heretics*, that *emperors and noblemen are appointed by God*[6]. As proof of that he quoted carefully selected passages from the Bible invoking Christians to worship and obey rulers and all kinds of masters[7].

---

[6] Cosmas the Priest, p. 342. Some authors tend to interpret this statement as a reflection of some peculiar Bulgarian attitude to authority. In Dimitar Angelov's (Д. Ангелов, *Общество и обществена мисъл в средновековна България (IX–XIV в.)*, София 1979, p. 191) words: *това е българският вариант за божествения произход на земната власт, възникнал в обстановката на изострени обществени противоречия и на все по-засилващото се господство на болярската аристокрация над зависимите селяни в средновековна България през средата и втората половина на X век. Като "богопоставен" презвитер Козма обявява не само "царя", т. е. върховния владетел, но и неговите най-близки сътрудници – болярите, които имали решаваща дума в управлението на държавата и под чиято непосредствена власт като едри земевладелци и висши военни и граждански сановници се намирала значителна част от населението в страната* [*this is the Bulgarian version of the divine origins of earthly power, which emerged in the context of bitter social conflicts and ever increasing dominance of the boyar aristocracy over the independent peasants in mediaeval Bulgaria of the second and third quarter of the 10th century. Presbyter Cosmas declares 'god-appointed' not only the 'emperor', i.e. the supreme ruler but also his closest associates, the boyars, who had the final say in the government of the country and under whose immediate control, as large landowners and senior military and civil dignitaries, was a significant part of the population of the country*]. Cf. Д. Ангелов, *Богомилството...*, p. 51; Г. Бакалов, *Византийският културен модел в идейно-политическата структура на Първата българска държава*, Ист 3, 1994, 4/5, p. 25. Here we concur in essence with Yurdan Trifonov's (Ю. Трифонов, *Беседата на Козма Пресвитера и нейният автор*, СБАН.КИФ 16, 1923, pp. 76–77) interpretation of this passage from the *Sermon*: *Козма, който в борбата си с еретиците е използвал главно посланията на Павла, стои на становището на последния, че всяка власт е от Бога, и думите му за царе и боляри не визират определен цар... Явно е, че Козма не говори за даден цар, а общо за "царе и боляри", т. е. за властта* [*Cosmas, who in his fight with the heretics used mostly Paul's epistles, agreed with the latter that every authority is from God; therefore, his words about emperors and boyars make no reference to a particular king... Clearly, Cosmas does not refer to a particular emperor, but to "emperors and boyar", i.e. to power*]. Cf. Д. Оболенски, *Богомилите...*, p. 78.

[7] Prov 8, 15–18; Ps 19, 19; 20, 2–8; Matt 16, 17–19; Rom 13, 1–4; 1 Pet 2, 13–21; 1 Tim 2, 1–3; Tit 3, 1–2.

Similar thoughts, called forth by the atmosphere of spiritual dissention, are to be found also in some of the works of monk Peter, who was held in high esteem and enjoyed wide popularity in Bulgaria around the middle of the 10th century[8]. In his *Tale of Fasting and Prayer* he extols obedience to the rulers as the duty of the true Christian but is quick to set certain ethical requirements for the rulers themselves:

> to fear rulers and serve them wholeheartedly, as we serve God. And they, the rulers, to be fair with their slaves, to live peacefully and quietly with everybody and be modest. And neither to be proud, nor to act superior, nor to shy from the spiritual and indispensable [things] in this world[9].

In the *Sermon on Transitory Life*, monk Peter castigates secular rulers and the rich for their unrighteous lives. However, we should not forget that the author's criticism is not social but focuses on the moral improvement of believers, especially those on whom God has bestowed power and wisdom.

> How could you not comprehend God's power and God's order, God's will, you earthly sovereigns and lords, noblemen and judges of men? Who gave you power and dignity, and wit, and wisdom, to know and to understand? You chase and rule, but you do not lead men to God![10]

It should be noted that tsar Peter ruled in times of intensive institutional strengthening of the Bulgarian church, which had acquired a patriarchal status in 927, while the clergy (especially the ever growing ranks of the

[8] Evidence of this popularity is the fact that one of Peter's discourses was included, with attribution to John Chrysostom, in the Longer Version of the *Zlatostruy* miscellany, compiled around the middle of the 10th century – Я. Милтенов, *Нови данни за "Поучението за спасението на душата", приписвано на черноризец Петър*, СЛ 51, 2015, pp. 157–186.

[9] Peter the Monk, p. 272.

[10] Peter the Monk, p. 348.

monks) established itself as a numerous and influential social group within Bulgarian society[11].

It is also worth remembering that in the first half of the 10th century monasticism was favoured and treated with particular respect by the rulers of Byzantium and Bulgaria. A case in point is Romanos I Lekapenos, who trusted monks unreservedly and built numerous churches and monasteries. According to the testimony of *Continuation of Theophanes*, the monastery of St. Panteleimon, built by the tsar on the Asian coast of the Bosphoros, provided sustenance to eight hundred monks. The abbot of this monastic brotherhood was monk Sergios, a nephew of patriarch Photios' and the tsar's spiritual father, who the autocrat valued highly and always kept at his side as a role model[12]. After he was dethroned/deposed and exiled by his own sons, the superannuated Romanos confessed his sins and received absolution and communion in the presence of three hundred monks, summoned from *all monasteries and lauras*, from Jerusalem and from Rome. The monk-tsar sent two *kentenaria* of gold to the hermits in Mount Olympus in Bithynia so that they prayed for the salvation of his soul and they spent two weeks fasting and praying for his sins to be forgiven[13].

Tsar Peter also regarded monks and monasticism with profound admiration and awe. Mediaeval rumour had it that he went deep into the mountains where St. John of Rila dwelt; it is also known that the ruler exchanged letters with the hermit monk St. Paul the Younger, who lived in Mount Latros (now Beşparmak) in southwestern Asia Minor: *Furthermore, Peter, who ruled Bulgaria and frequently greeted him with courteous and humble letters, called upon him to pray for his salvation*[14].

---

[11] В. Златарски, *История...*, pp. 523, 526; Д. Оболенски, *Богомилите...*, p. 80; Д. Ангелов, *Богомилството...*, pp. 64–67. According to Ivan Bilyarski (И. Билярски, *Небесните покровители: св. Цар Петър*, ИБ 2, 2001, pp. 32–44) interesting observation, under tsar Peter Bulgaria became a 'monastic empire', i.e. it was at that time that it transformed into a 'Byzantine type of country'.

[12] Continuator of Theophanes, pp. 433.12–434.17.

[13] Continuator of Theophanes, pp. 438.20–440.14.

[14] *Life of St. Paul the Younger*, pp. 71–72. See also: В. Златарски, *История...*, p. 540; И. Дуйчев, *Рилският светец...*, pp. 123–132.

In the same vein, the service for tsar Peter declared, *you loved monks and the servants of the holy church for their prayers and hoped for God's reward, in which you were not disappointed as it bore good fruit*[15].

The currently available archaeological evidence adds a number of very significant details to the scant written testimony to the rise of monasticism in Bulgaria during Peter's reign. Doubtless, many monastic institutions, founded and protected by prince Boris I-Michael and his son tsar Symeon, continued to operate and develop in this period, such as the monastery at the Great Basilica in Pliska[16], several monasteries in Preslav and its surroundings (the Palace Monastery, as well as those near the Round Church, in Patleyna, etc.)[17], the Holy Mother of God Monastery near the village of Ravna (25 km southeast of Pliska)[18], the monastery at Karaach Teke, near Varna[19], St. Panteleimon Monastery, founded by St. Clement in Ohrid[20], St. Archangel Michael Monastery, founded by St. Naum near Lake Ohrid[21], etc.

---

[15] *Service of St. Tsar Peter*, p. 393.

[16] П. Георгиев, С. Витлянов, *Архиепископията-манастир в Плиска*, София 2001; *ИБСЛ*, pp. 76–77.

[17] Т. Тотев, *Дворцовият манастир в Преслав*, Шумен 1998; R. Kostova, *Bulgarian monasteries ninth to tenth centuries: interpreting the archaeological evidence*, ППре 8, 2000, pp. 190–202; Т. Тотев, *Монастыри в Плиске и Преславе в IX–X вв.*, ПКШ 7, 2004, pp. 347–365; *ИБСЛ*, pp. 79–80.

[18] К. Попконстантинов, Р. Костова, *Скрипторият в Равненския манастир: още веднъж за украсата на старобългарските ръкописи от IX–X в.*, [in:] *Средновековна християнска Европа: Изток и Запад. Ценности, традиции, общуване*, ed. В. Гюзелев, А. Милтенова, София 2002, pp. 719–725; Р. Костова, К. Попконстантинов, *Манастирите на Покръстителя*, [in:] *Християнската култура в Средновековна България. Материали от национална научна конференция Шумен 2–4 май 2007 година по случай 1100 години от смъртта на св. Княз Борис-Михаил (ок. 835–907 г.)*, ed. П. Георгиев, Шумен 2008, pp. 176–177; *ИБСЛ*, pp. 80–81; K. Popkonstantinov, R. Kostova, *Architecture of Conversion: Provincial Monasteries in the 9th–10th c. Bulgaria*, ТГЭ 53, 2010, pp. 118–124.

[19] K. Popkonstantinov, R. Kostova, *Architecture of Conversion...*, pp. 124–127; Р. Костова, К. Попконстантинов, *Манастирите на Покръстителя...*, pp. 177–178.

[20] R. Kostova, *St. Kliment of Ohrid and his monastery: some more archaeology of the written evidence*, SB 25, 2006, pp. 593–605; eadem, К. Попконстантинов, *Манастирите на Покръстителя...*, pp. 173–174; *ИБСЛ*, p. 78.

[21] Р. Костова, К. Попконстантинов, *Манастирите на Покръстителя...*, pp. 174–175; *ИБСЛ*, p. 78.

Another monastery which had its heyday during tsar Peter's rule was the monastery near the village of Chernoglavtsi (25 km northwest of Pliska), among the ruins of which were found more than seventy inscriptions, three of which have been dated to 954, 959 and 962, respectively[22]. It was during the same time that the numerous rock monasteries to the south of Dristra, along the dried-up Kanadol River, flourished, as well as the rock hermitages near the village of Murfatlar, near present-day Constanța in Northern Dobrudzha[23].

The fragments of book cover metal ornaments, writing implements (*styluses*), graffiti, Greek and Slavic *abecedaria* and various Greek and Slavic (Glagolitic and Cyrillic) stone inscriptions allow us to regard the monasteries of Preslav, Pliska, Ravna and Karaach Teke as among the main cultural and educational centres in the country at the time before the conquest of the eastern Bulgarian territories by the armies of emperor John I Tzymiskes in 971.

The emergence of 'private' monasteries, founded by members of influential aristocratic families holding the highest positions of authority in the state and ecclesiastical administration was a particular development in the history of monasticism that occurred around the middle of the 10th century. A case in point here is the private residence near the church at Selishte in the Outer City of Preslav which was transformed into a monastery. George Synkellos became the patron of this monastery; the monk reinterred therein his mother's remains, as well as those of several other individuals (most probably relatives of his) in a chamber under the west portico of the church. At the northern wall of the same church yet another burial chamber was found, in which the remains of

[22] Т. Балабанов, *Старобългарският манастир при с. Черноглавци (Предварително съобщение)*, ИИМШ 8, 1993, pp. 263–272; К. Попконстантинов, Г. Атанасов, *За два надписа от X в. от манастира при Черноглавци, Шуменско*, Епо 2.4, 1994, pp. 105–110; Т. Балабанов, М. Тихова, *Надписът от 18 септември 6463 г. (954 г./955 г.) – от с. Черноглавци, Шуменско, България*, ПКШ 6, 2002, pp. 58–66; П. Георгиев, *Манастирът от X в. при с. Черноглавци, Шуменска област*, ГСУ.НЦСВПИД 12, 2005, pp. 71–79.

[23] Г. Атанасов, *За хронологията и монашеската организация в скалните обители през Първото българско царство*, [in:] *Светогорска обител Зограф*, vol. III, ed. В. Гюзелев, София 1999, pp. 281–299.

Mostich, ichirgu-boila had been reinterred. Mostich had been the governor of the core territories of Bulgaria around Pliska and Preslav during the reign of tsar Symeon, who at the age of eighty abdicated from his office in order to become a monk[24].

The appearance of such a 'family' monastery in Preslav is hardly surprising in as far as the senior church officials were recruited from within the ranks of the aristocratic establishment. However, something else is of interest in this particular case; the inscription for the re-interment of George Synkellos' mother and his lead seals[25], as well as the inscription on Mostich's grave, are only in the Slavic language and written in the Cyrillic script. This is undoubtedly clear evidence of the wide spread of the Slavic language in state and ecclesiastical circles in the last two decades of Peter's rule, who at that time began to inscribe his lead seals with Slavic legends[26]. It was also at that time that the practice of daily services in the Slavic language was fully introduced in the Bulgarian monasteries[27]. All this allows us to assume that around the middle of the 10th century the dominant trend in Preslav was towards gradual emancipation of the Christian Bulgarian culture from the Byzantine one, a policy going back to prince Boris I-Michael and tsar Symeon.

Considering the above described cultural situation, it is hardly surprising that respect for the men of the cloth is a central topic in Cosmas the Priest's *Sermon*. The Old-Bulgarian writer stresses that *priests are always ordained by God* and they cannot be judged by the laity for their personal

---

[24] К. Попконстантинов, Р. Костова, *Манастир на чъргубиля Мостич*, [in:] *Археологически открития и разкопки през 2007 г.*, София 2008, pp. 629–632; Р. Костова, *Патронаж и манастирска география в България през втората половина на IX и X в.*, [in:] *Laurea. In honorem Margaritae Vaklinova*, vol. I, ed. Б. Петрунова, А. Аладжов, Е. Василева, София 2009, pp. 201–202; К. Попконстантинов, Р. Костова, *Манастирът на Георги синкел български в Преслав: Историята на една аристократична фамилия от X в.*, Пр.Сб 7, 2013, pp. 44–63.

[25] И. Йорданов, *Корпус на средновековните български печати*, София 2016, pp. 175–177 (№ 326–334).

[26] *Ibidem*, pp. 116–120 (№ 254–259a).

[27] М. Йовчева, *Старобългарският служебен миней*, София 2014, pp. 14–21.

sins as long as they preserve their orthodoxy[28]. However, Cosmas goes further than simply assert the authority of the clergy; he sounds a warning to the secular rulers, too, stating that the Church stands above them and is not subject to their will. *So many mighty emperors, princes and wise men of old have tried to destroy God's Church, but have only ruined themselves, body and soul. And the Church stays inviolate now and forever*[29].

Obviously, towards the middle of the 10th century Old-Bulgarian literature already abounded in translated texts postulating the supremacy of spiritual authority over secular power. However, the earliest Preslav writers rarely touched upon this topic in their writings[30]; the ruler's standing in the first decades after the conversion to Christianity was too high

---

[28] Cosmas the Priest, p. 314.

[29] Cosmas the Priest, p. 318. Here, and elsewhere, Cosmas paraphrases a passage from the Pseudo-Chrysostom's *Sermo de pseudoprophetis* (*PG*, vol. LIX, col. 560): Ю. Трифонов, *Беседата...*, pp. 33–34; Cosmas le prêtre, *Le traité contre les bogomiles*, transl., ed. H.-Ch. Puech, A. Vaillant, Paris 1945, pp. 47–52; Ю. Бегунов, *Козма Пресвитер в славянских литературах*, София 1973, pp. 227–229. It has been established that this apocalyptic work was written by an anonymous Antiochene author around the middle of the 7th and the middle of the 8th centuries: A. Whealey, *"Sermo de pseudoprophetis" of Pseudo-John Chrysostom: A Homily from Antioch under Early Islamic Rule*, B 69, 1999, pp. 178–186. The Old-Bulgarian translation of the text was included as *Discourse* 24 in the longer version of the *Zlatostruy* collection – F. Thomson, *Chrysostomica Palaeoslavica. A Preliminary Study of the Sources of the Chrysorrhoas (Zlatostruy) Collection*, Cyr 6, 1982, p. 10; *Иоанн Златоуст в древнерусской и южнославянской письменности XI–XVI веков. Каталог гомилий*, ed. Е. Гранстрем, О. Творогов, А. Валевичюс, Санкт-Петербург 1998, pp. 22–23 (№ 33); Я. Милтенов, *Златоструй: старобългарски хомилетичен свод, създаден по инициативата на българския цар Симеон. Текстологично и изворoведско изследване*, София 2013, p. 42; А. Димитрова, *Псевдо-Златоустовото слово "За лъжепророците" в "Беседа против богомилите" – цитиране или нов превод?*, KWSS 9, 2014, pp. 23–32; eadem, *Златоструят в преводаческата дейност на старобългарските книжовници*, София 2016, pp. 218–223 (The author believes that Cosmas used directly the Greek text of the discourse, rather than the translation found in the *Zlatostruy*).

[30] Quite telling in that respect is the fact that, in his *Hexameron*, John the Exarch touches only once on the subject of the interplay between the state and the church, in the context of the bibilical story of King Uzziah (2 Chron 26, 16–23), in order to illustrate the need for strict separation of the imperial and the ecclesiastical dignity: John the Exarch, *Hexameron*, vol. II, pp. 65–69 (43 b–d).

and the Bulgarian church was too young and weak to aspire to a totally independent role in social life.

The critical attitude to secular rulers found a clear expression in the *Testament* of St. John of Rila, the first Bulgarian hermit. This unique record of the ideological attitudes of Bulgarian monkhood in the first half of the 10th century propounds the idea that monks serve the King in Heaven and not earthly masters:

> Nor look to be recognized and beloved by earthly kings and princes, nor put your hope in them, leaving the heavenly King, with whom you enlisted to be soldiers and *wrestle not against flesh and blood*, but *against the ruler of the darkness of this world* (Eph 6, 12)[31].

The author of the *Testament* did not hesitate to set even his relations with tsar Peter within the context of his negative attitude to secular authority, a motif developed further in a number of hagiographic works devoted to the saint[32]:

---

[31] *Testament of John of Rila*, p. 442.103–107 (transl. I. Iliev, p. 131; another tranlsation: K. Petkov, *The Voices of Medieval Bulgaria, Seventh-Fifteenth Century. The Records of a Bygone Culture*, Leiden 2008, p. 113). In favour of the authenticity of the *Testament*: I. Dujčev, *La réforme monastique en Bulgarie au Xe siècle*, [in:] *Études de civilisation médiévale*, Poitiers 1974, pp. 255–264; В. Гюзелев, *"Велико светило за целия свят" (Св. Иван Рилски в измеренията на своето време)*, [in:] *Светогорска...*, pp. 13–24; *Testament of John of Rila*, transl. I. Iliev, [in:] *Byzantine Monastic Foundation Documents. A Complete Translation of the Surviving Founders'* Typika *and Testaments*, vol. I, ed. J. Thomas, A. Hero, Washington 2000, p. 127; Г. Литаврин, *Христианство в Болгарии...*, p. 139. However, the text is only familiar from much later copies, which raises serious doubts about its authenticity – А. Турилов, Б. Флоря, *Христианская литература у славян в середине X – середине XI в. и межславянские культурные связи*, [in:] *Христианство в странах Восточной, Юго-Восточной и Центральной Европы на пороге второго тысячелетия*, ed. Б.Н. Флоря, Москва 2002, p. 414.

[32] Г. Данчев, *Близост и различия в епизода за неосъществената среща между св. Иван Рилски и цар Петър в житията на Рилския светец*, ИИМК 5, 1993, София 1998, pp. 71–76; Х. Трендафилов, *Диалогът Иван Рилски – цар Петър като историософски факт*, ПКШ 4, 1999, pp. 20–31; Г. Подскалски, *Средњовековна теолошка књижевност у Бугарској и Србији (865–1459)*, Београд 2010, p. 133; Б. Николова, *Средновековните византийски и български владетели, кралете*

> Now again, keep yourselves away from the avaricious snake, *for the love of money is the root of all evil* (1 Tim 6, 10), according to the apostle, who calls it a second idolatry. Because for the hermit wealth consists not in silver and gold, but in perfect poverty, in the denial of his personal will, and in lofty humbleness. [...] For in the beginning, when I came to this wilderness, the sly enemy attempted to allure me, for the pious king sent to me a lot of gold. For the sake of God I refused to see him, for I understood that it was a perfidy of the devil. I did not accept it, but returned it to those who sent it[33].

* * *

Faced from the very beginning of his reign with multiple external and internal challenges, tsar Peter placed at the heart of his ruler's propaganda the idea of his perfect piety and of himself as the supreme protector of the Bulgarian church and defender of the faith. Evidence of the fact that around the middle of the 10th century the idea of the ruler's piety had grown in scale to become an official political programme are the seals on which the images of tsar Peter and tsartisa Maria-Irene are accompanied by the legend † Πέτρος βασιλεὺς εὐσεβής (*Peter a pious emperor*)[34].

и князете на Средна и Западна Европа в съдбата на светците от българския пантеон, ИП 67.5/6, 2011, p. 138; I. B i l i a r s k y, *Le tsar sur la montagne*, [in:] *Histoire, mémoire et dévotion. Regards croisés sur la construction des identités dans le monde orthodoxe aux époques byzantine et post-byzantine*, ed. R. P ă u n, Seyssel 2016, pp. 53–71.

[33] *Testament of John of Rila*, pp. 441.76 – 442.95 (transl. I. I l i e v, p. 130).

[34] И. Й о р д а н о в, *Корпус на средновековните български печати...*, pp. 95–110 (edition of 88 seals of this class). One more seal was published recently: Ж. А л а д ж о в, *Печат на цар Петър от разкопките на обект "Улица" в Преслав*, НСЕ 13, 2017, pp. 307–310. See also: И. Й о р д а н о в, *Печатите на преславските владетели (893–971)*, София 1993, pp. 14–15, 31–33; i d e m, *Възникване и утвърждаване на царската институция в средновековна България. (Според данните на владетелските печати)*, [in:] *Етническият проблем и националният въпрос на българите*, Пловдив 1994, p. 110; J. S h e p a r d, *A marriage too far? Maria Lekapena and Peter of Bulgaria*, [in:] *The Empress Theophano. Byzantium and the West at the Turn of the First Millennium*, ed. A. D a v i d s, Cambridge 1995, pp. 142–146 (reprinted in: i d e m, *Emergent Elites and Byzantium in the Balkans and East-Central Europe*, Farnham 2011, V); И. Й о р д а н о в,

No doubt this 'political piety' represented a peculiar continuation and evolution of the religious and political beliefs of Boris I-Michael and of the tsar-philosopher ideal cultivated at the court of Symeon I[35].

It should be noted that it was precisely in the 930s–960s that the targeted efforts of the Bulgarian ruling circles created the conditions for the establishment and the wide dissemination of the cult of prince Boris I-Michael[36].

Корпус на печатите на средновековна България, София 2001, pp. 60–63. It seems likely that Leo the Deacon (p. 78.11) made an implicit reference to the title of interest here, when he wrote of Peter as ἄνδρα θεοφιλῆ καὶ σεβάσμιον (*a God-loving and pious man*). No doubt, the title *pious emperor* had a profound political and religious significance and should not be described as *inconsequential* (...) *honorary rather than real* – V. Beševliev, *Die Kaiseridee bei den Protobulgaren*, Bυζ 3, 1971, p. 92; idem, *Първобългарски надписи*, София 1992, p. 81.

[35] А. Николов, *Старобългарският превод на "Изложение на поучителни глави към император Юстиниан" от дякон Агапит и развитието на идеята за достойнството на българския владетел в края на IX – началото на X в.*, Pbg 24.3, 2000, pp. 81–82.

[36] The evidence of the existence of this cult is indirect; there are no extant vitas of Boris-Michael, nor services, canons and panegyrics for him and his name is not to be found in any *Menaion* or *Synaxarion*. However, there are sufficient grounds to argue that the cult emerged soon after 907, but later declined for reasons on which there is no need to dwell here: Н. Георгиева, *Към въпроса за почитанието на княз Борис I като светец*, КМС 8 1991, pp. 178–188; Д. Чешмеджиев, *Към въпроса за култа на княз Борис-Михаил в средновековна България*, ИП 55.3/4, 1999, pp. 158–176 (detailed review of primary sources and research); А. Турилов, *Борис*, [in:] *Православная энциклопедия*, vol. VI, Москва 2003, p. 31; А. Турилов, *Slavica Cyrillomethodiana. Источниковедение истории и культуры южных славян и Древней Руси. Межславянские культурные связи эпохи средневековья*, Москва 2010, pp. 124–125; Г. Подскалски, *Средњовековна теолошка...*, p. 79; A. Nikolov, *Making a new basileus: the case of Symeon of Bulgaria (893–927) reconsidered*, [in:] *Rome, Constantinople and Newly Converted Europe. Archeological and Historical Evidence*, vol. I, ed. M. Salamon et al., Kraków–Leipzig–Rzeszów–Warszawa 2012, pp. 101–108. As noted above, Ivan Bilyarski disputes the existence of a mediaeval cult of Boris-Michael: И. Билярски, *Небесните покровители...*, p. 33; I. Biliarsky, *St. Peter (927–969), Tsar of the Bulgarians*, [in:] *State and Church: Studies in Medieval Bulgaria and Byzantium*, ed. V. Gjuzelev, K. Petkov, Sofia 2011, p. 175. To the research reviewed in D. Cheshmedzhiev's article, could be added: D. Obolensky, *The Byzantine Commonwealth...*, pp. 308–309, 313; idem, *Nationalism in Eastern Europe in the Middle Ages*, TRHS, 5th series, 22, 1972, p. 6; Б. Флоря, *Формирование государственности и зарождение политической мысли у славянских народов*, [in:] *Очерки*

In this context, it should be remembered that at least two events related to the personality of Boris I-Michael found their place among the holidays celebrated by the Bulgarian church around the end of the 9th and the beginning of the 10th century; on May 28th it commemorated *the victory of the Bulgarian prince Michael, when a revolt broke out against him on account of the conversion* and on April 28th, *the consecration of Apostle Peter's church among the Bulgarians*[37]. The former is a reference to the anti-Christian revolt in Bulgaria in the spring of 866, which was to a large extent due to the insensitive behaviour of the Byzantine bishops and priests who settled in the country; the latter most probably refers to the consecration of the Great Basilica in the Outer City of the Bulgarian capital of Pliska, the most spectacular church building in early mediaeval Bulgaria, whose construction began under the auspices of the legates of Nicholas I and Hadrian II.

In essence, these church holidays, introduced in the first decades after the conversion, commemorated the short-lived affiliation of Bulgaria to the Roman Church in 866–870 and must have played a crucial role in the canonisation of Boris I-Michael soon after his death on May 2nd, 907. Moreover, in the eyes of his contemporaries, the Christianiser of the Bulgarians, who became known for his acumen and dexterity in manoeuvring between Constantinople and Rome, symbolised the idea of closeness and peace between the Christian peoples of Byzantium and Bulgaria[38]. His veneration as a saint apparently helped strengthen the ruling dynasty

истории и культуры славян, В.К. Волков, Москва 1996, pp. 265–266. An attempt at systematising the types of sainted rulers in Eastern and Northern Europe in the 9th–12th centuries can be found in: K. Górski, *La naissance des états et le "roi-saint". Problème de de l'idéologie féodale*, [in:] *L'Europe aux IXe–XIe siècles. Aux origines des états nationaux*, ed. A. Gieysztor, T. Manteuffel, Varsovie 1968, pp. 425–432 (unfortunately, the author does not include the available evidence of the cults of Boris I-Michael and Peter).

[37] А. Турилов, *Slavica Cyrillomethodiana*..., p. 120.

[38] About Boris see: J. Shepard, *Slavs and Bulgars*, [in:] *The New Cambridge Medieval History*, vol. II, c. 700 – 900, ed. R. McKitterick, Cambridge 1995, pp. 228–248 [= idem, *Emergent Elites and Byzantium in the Balkans and East-Central Europe*, Farnham 2011, II]; L. Simeonova, *Diplomacy of the Letter and the Cross. Photios, Bulgaria and the Papacy, 860s–880s*, Amsterdam 1998; И. Божилов, В. Гюзелев, *История на средновековна България (VII–XIV в.)*, София 1999, pp. 169–195; Г. Подскалски, *Средњовековна теолошка*..., pp. 65–79.

and nourished the traditional reverence of Bulgarians for the members of their ruling family.

All this allows us to conclude that it was by no means a coincidence that tsar Peter named his first son and heir Boris; what we have here is clear evidence of the aspirations of this ruler to legitimise himself as someone continuing the political traditions whose foundations were laid by his grand-father, Boris I-Michael. The same trend can also be observed in the church service for tsar Peter, which meaningfully refers to the deceased ruler as *emulator of the good deeds of the Archangel Michael*[39].

Indirect evidence of the political climate and the ruler's propaganda in Preslav during the period under consideration can be found in the epistle of patriarch Theophylaktos of Constantinople (933–956) addressed to the *emperor of Bulgaria* Peter. Referring to his family ties with the Bulgarian sovereign, the patriarch extols his *faithful and God-loving soul* and portrays his correspondent as an incarnation of the ideal of the God-guided Christ-loving ruler[40], very similar to the description given in patriarch Photios' epistle to Boris I-Michael almost a century earlier.

Theophylaktos observes that the tsar:

> considers not only what is good for himself but shields protectively every subject of his, counsels what is best and salvatory. And what could be better or more salvatory than the true and sincere faith, as well as the sound understanding of the Divine, through which with sound conscience we worship the only most all-pure and most holy God? Because this constitutes the basis of our salvation. Not only do you honour that as one of the most important things and always apply it with every effort, but you also constantly, every day and every hour, show it and guide to it every subject[41].

[39] *Service of St. Tsar Peter*, p. 392.

[40] *Letter of the Patriarch Theophylaktos to Tsar Peter*, p. 312.28–29. See also: Г. Подскалски, *Средњовековна теолошка...*, p. 163.

[41] *Letter of the Patriarch Theophylaktos to Tsar Peter*, p. 311.6–14.

Of particular interest is the concluding part of the epistle, where patriarch Theophylaktos expresses his conviction that tsar Peter will personally strengthen his subjects' piety and eradicate the Bogomil heresy.

> But you, God-lover, be my herald of piety, teacher of Orthodoxy (ὀρθοδοξίας διδάσκαλος), corrector or persecutor and destroyer of the heretic delusion and the strongest and the most excellent in everything that is best, about which I will boast no less than about our kinship and the friendship[42].

The idea of the active role of the pious tsar Peter as a stalwart and propagator ('teacher') of Orthodoxy among his subjects, reflected in patriarch Theophylaktos' epistle, could be traced in some records which suggest that the Bulgarian ruler was not averse to certain literary pursuits. Thus, a brief homily dealing with moral issues was published under his name in two Russian collections from the 16th century, *Peter emperor said: your mouth must not be the gateway of evil talk, nor must your tongue utter evil. Your throat must not be the highway of sinful speech*[43]. Also associated with tsar Peter's name is the compilation of a paschal table, published by Yakov Kraykov in his *Book for Various Occasions* (Venice, 1572), containing the clarification, *This text found I, Jacob, in the books of Peter, emperor of the Bulgarians, who had his capital in the city of Great Preslav and died in the great Rome*[44].

---

[42] *Letter of the Patriarch Theophylaktos to Tsar Peter*, p. 315.131–134.

[43] Р. Павлова, *Петър Черноризец – старобългарски писател от X в.*, София 1994, p. 28; П. Димитров, *Петър Черноризец. Очерци по старобългарска литература през следсимеоновата епоха*, Шумен 1995, p. 41.

[44] J. Jerkov-Kapaldo, *Le "Različnie potrebii" di Jakov di Sofia alla luce di un esemplare complete*, BBg 6, 1980, p. 230; Р. Павлова, *Петър Черноризец...*, p. 29; А. Николов, *Политическа мисъл в ранносредновековна България (средата на IX – края на X век)*, София 2006, p. 253. It remains unclear whether these paschal tables were attributed to tsar Peter by the book's publisher, Yakov Kraykov, or he himself copied them from an older manuscript, similar to the prayer book (from the 17th c.?) seen by Pencho R. Slaveykov, which contained a paschal table bearing the heading, *тази пасхалия състави цар Петър, който умря в Рим* [this paschal table compiled tsar Peter, who died in Rome] – П.Р. Славейков, *Писма*, СНУНК 20, 1904, p. 38; Б. Ангелов, *Из старата българска, руска и сръбска литература*, vol. I, София

As could be seen, the above records do not reveal clearly the nature of tsar Peter's literary pursuits[45]. However, contemporary Slavistics has significantly enriched the traditional understanding of the development

1959, p. 55. As regards the legend about the death of tsar Peter in Rome, it was recorded as early as the second half of the 11th century in the *Bulgarian Apocryphal Chronicle*: V. Tapkova-Zaimova, A. Miltenova, *Historical and Apocalyptic Literature in Byzantium and Medieval Bulgaria*, Sofia 2011, p. 293: *Peter, the king of Bulgaria, a righteous man, left the kingdom and fled westwards to Rome and ended his life there*. See also: Д. Чешмеджиев, *Няколко бележки за култа към цар Петър I (927–965)*, [in:] *Християнската традиция и царската институция в българската култура*, ed. В. Бонева, Шумен 2003, pp. 29–30, 34–35; Г. Подскалски, *Средњовековна теолошка...*, pp. 77, 239. Ivan Bilyarski cautiously speculates that the note on Peter's death in Rome, included in the *Bulgarian Apocryphal Chronicle*, could be a later interpolation, based on Kraykov's book of 1572 (И. Билярски, *Сказание на Исайя пророка и формирането на политическата идеология на ранносредновековна България*, София 2011, pp. 13–14, 172–173; idem, *The Tale of the Prophet Isaiah. The Destiny and Meanings of an Apocryphal Text*, Leiden–Boston 2013, pp. 9–10, 57). For a skeptical view on Bilyarski's hypothesis see: М. Цибранска-Костова, *Сборникът "Различни потреби" на Яков Крайков между Венеция и Балканите през XVI век*, София 2012, pp. 114–115. Recently, Hristo Trendafilov has argued that the compiler of the *Bulgarian Apocryphal Chronicle* lived and worked at the beginning of the 17th century and used Yakov Kraykov's book (Х. Трендафилов, *Българският апокрифен летопис и Мавро Орбини*, Шумен 2016, p. 42). However, this theory is invalidated by the fact that an Ottoman chronicle of the beginning of the 16th century includes an abridged and partially edited Turkish translation of the *Bulgarian Apocryphal Chronicle*: D. Rusev, *Eine untypische Abweichung in der osmanischen Geschichtsschreibung: Die Geschichte der bulgarischen Herrscher in Tevārīḫ-i āl-i ʿOsmān von Kemālpaşazāde. Wissenschaftliche Hausarbeit zur Erlangung des akademischen Grades eines Master of Arts der Universität Hamburg*, Hamburg 2016; D. Rusev, *Kemālpaşazāde's History of Medieval Bulgaria: A 16th-century Ottoman rendering of the Bulgarian Apocryphal Chronicle (Tale of the Prophet Isaiah)*, [in:] *Testis temporum et laudator historiae. Сборник в памет на проф. Иван Божилов* (in press). However, the reference to Peter's death in Rome is missing from the Turkish translation of the *Bulgarian Apocryphal Chronicle*; therefore, the question of the origin and interpretation of this motif remains unresolved.

[45] By and large, I share the doubts raised in historiography about equating the Old-Bulgarian writer monk Peter with tsar Peter: Й. Андреев, *Кем был Черноризец Петр?*, BBg 6, 1980, pp. 51–56. A detailed overview of the discussion on this issue is given by Rumyana Pavlova, who does not however commit herself to a particular view: Р. Павлова, *Петър Черноризец...*, pp. 9–30. An interesting hypothesis is that Cosma's *Sermon* was written *не без участието на цар Петър* [*not without the involvement of emperor Peter*] – П. Павлов, *Две бележки към "Беседа на недостойния презвитер Козма срещу новопоявилата се ерес на богомилите"*, Пр.Сб 4, 1993, p. 226.

of Old-Bulgarian literature in the decades after Symeon I's death, which [illegible] Preslav writers, whose texts largely reflect the political and cultural trends in the Peter's court.

The starting point of our analysis of the activities of the Bulgarian writers in the 930s–960s is the famous *Izbornik of 1076*. As research in the past few decades has demonstrated, this Russian manuscript is an almost exact copy of an Old-Bulgarian collection of the 10th century, conventionally referred to as the *Izbornik of the sinful John*, which was compiled on the basis of a *Princely Izbornik*, itself based on an even earlier collection of texts, the so-called *Menaion Izbornik*. Recently, William Veder described these three books as variations of the same collection, intended to support the upbringing of Bulgarian heirs to the throne (καναρτικείνοι) and summed up his observations as follows:

> The book's purpose must have limited its dissemination to a single copy per generation. If the hypothesis is correct, the *Menaion Izbornik* must have been composed around 900 for the kanartikeinoi Michael and Peter, the *Princely Miscellany*, around 930 for the kanartikeinos Boris and the *Sinful John's Izbornik*, around 960 for emperor Boris II's heir. No such internal dynastic documents of imperial pedagogy are known to exist in other European mediaeval cultures.[46]

Here we would analyse in greater detail some of the texts and their renditions in the different versions of the *Izbornik* since these reflect, although in an abbreviated form and frequently with significant editorial alterations, the content of a number of Old-Bulgarian translations kept in the palace library in Preslav and in the metropolitan monasteries.

---

[46] **Кънѧжии изборьникъ** *за възпитание на канартикина*, ed. У. Ф е д е р, vol. I, Велико Търново 2008, p. 12. See also: W. V e d e r, *The "Izbornik of John the Sinner": a Compilation from Compilations*, ПК 8, 1983, pp. 15–33; i d e m, *The Izbornik of 1076*, [in:] *The Edificatory Prose of Kievan Rus'*, transl. i d e m, introd. i d e m, A. T u r i l o v, Cambridge, Mass. 1994, pp. XXIII–XL; W. V e d e r, *Two Hundred Years of Misguided Philological Research*, RS 47, 1994, p. 107; i d e m, *Der bulgarische Ursprung des Izbornik von 1076*, KMC 10, 1995, pp. 82–87.

Along with the biblical Book of Sirach, the *Izbornik of 1076* comprises also fragments from John Climacus' *Ladder of Divine Ascent*, the *Egyptian Patericon*, *emperor Symeon's Miscellany* (the *Izbornik of 1073*) and *Zlatostruy* (a collection of John Chrysostom's homilies translated into Old Bulgarian by the orders of tsar Symeon). Furthermore, Dmitriy Bulanin's research indicates that the anonymous compiler of the original *Menaion Izbornik* had at his disposal and put together in a single tome the complete Old-Bulgarian translations of a number of Greek homiletic texts: *Paragon of the Souls* by emperor Leo VI the Wise (with a misleading attribution of authorship to Maximos the Confessor), *Exposition of Paraenetic Chapters Addressed to emperor Justinian* by Deacon Agapetos, the *Encheiridion* by the Stoic philosopher Epictetus (in a Christianised version by Nilus of Ancyra), fragments of *Chapters on Love* by Maximos the Confessor, as well as some other patristic authors' writings[47].

Thus, nowadays, it could be considered proven that the appearance of the *Izbornik of 1076*, regarded by some researchers as 'an original example of Old-Russian literature', whose texts are indirectly related to the Bulgarian originals[48], represents simply the final link in a long chain of transformations undergone by a series of writings, either translated or compiled in the Preslav literary centre between the end of the 9th century and the year 971. As William Veder rightly observed, with the ongoing acculturation of Bulgarian society in the decades after its conversion to Christianity, the transition from translation to active imitation required

[47] Д. Буланин, *Неизвестный источник Изборника 1076 г.*, ТОДРЛ 44, 1990, pp. 161–178; idem, *Античные традиции в древнерусской литературе XI–XVI вв.*, München 1991, pp. 96–137; idem, *Житие Павла Фивейского – болгарский перевод X в.*, КМС 10, 1995, pp. 10–11; idem, *Текстологические и библиографические арабески. VII. "Наставление" Агапита: несколько эпизодов из истории славянской рецепции*, [in:] *Каталог памятников древнерусской письменности XI–XIV вв. (Рукописные книги)*, ed. idem, Санкт-Петербург 2014, pp. 537–538; idem, *"Кормчая книга" и "Книга Кормчий" (Семантика названий двух древнерусских книг)*, РЛи, 2017.2, pp. 10–14. Dmitriy Bulanin's conclusions have been espoused by W. Veder, *The Izbornik of 1076...*, pp. XXXIII–XXXVIII.

[48] Н. Мещерский, *Взаимоотношения Изборника 1073 г. с Изборником 1076 г.*, [in:] *Изборник Святослава 1073 г. Сборник статей*, ed. Б.А. Рыбаков, Москва 1977, pp. 91–92, 99.

time; thus the emergence of such an extensive exhortative compilation as [illegible] in Kiev in 1076) should be linked to the work of the writers from the literary centre in the Bulgarian capital at the time of tsar Peter[49].

The size of the *Izbornik* makes any detailed exploration of its content within the context of this article impossible[50]. Therefore, the present analysis will be limited to three of the works there, which demonstrate clearly how the compilers of the miscellany used the older texts and adapted them to serve the spiritual needs of their contemporaries.

Let us turn our attention first to an anonymous work entitled *Admonition to the rich*[51]. The copy in the *Izbornik of 1076* represents it as a compilation of seventeen fragments of the complete Old-Bulgarian translation of the *Exposition* by Deacon Agapetos[52], a fragment of the Old-Bulgarian translation of the Christianised version of the *Encheiridion* by Epictetus[53] and two fragments from the Old-Bulgarian translation of the *Chapters on Love* by Maximos the Confessor[54].

Although the oldest of all still extant copies, the copy of the *Admonition* included in the *Izbornik of 1076* can by no means be considered the most complete or the closest to the original. A comparison with two Serbian copies from the end of the 14th century and a Russian one from the 16th century (from the so-called *Meletskiy Miscellany*)[55]

---

[49] W. Veder, *The Izbornik of 1076...*, pp. XXXIX–XL.

[50] No serious attempt has been made in contemporary historiography at a detailed and comprehensive analysis of the ideas contained in the *Izbornik of 1076*. Nevertheless, it is worth mentioning Stanislav Bondar's stimulating monograph, which however disregards Veder's research and passes over the sources of the texts included in the *Izbornik*: С. Бондарь, *Философско-мировоззренческое содержание "Изборников" 1073–1076 г.*, Киев 1990.

[51] *Izbornik of 1076*, ed. А. Молдован et al., f. 24v–28v.

[52] Chapters (according to their numbering in the Greek text) 5, 8, 12, 19, 28, 32, 42, 25, 47, 48, 53, 64, 68, 23, 41, 14, 56.

[53] Fragment of Ch. 28.

[54] Fragments of Ch. 58 and 60 of the first centuria.

[55] SS. Cyril and Methodius National Library – Sofia, № 1037, f. 230v – 233r (Serbian *Paterikon* from the end of the 14th century) – *S*; National Library of Serbia – Belgrade, Pc 26, f. 354r – 356r (Serbian collection of the third quarter of the 14th century) – *B*;

reveals that the original, which is the basis of this compilation, must have also included some other fragments of Agapetos' *Exposition*[56],

Vernadsky National Library of Ukraine – Kiev, Мел. м./п. 119, f. 111v–113r (Russian collection of the 16th century) – *M*. The test of *S* and *M* was published alongside the text of the copy of the *Izbornik of 1076* in: Д. Буланин, *Неизвестный источник...*, pp. 171–178. Recently, *S* was published again by Smilja Marjanović-Dušanić, who was clearly not aware of Bulanin's publication: С. Марјановић-Душанић, *Rex imago Dei: о српској преради Агапитовог владарског огледала*, [in:] *Трећа југословенска конференција византолога, Крушевац 10–13 мај 2000*, ed. Љ. Максимовић, Н. Радошевић, Е. Радуловић, Београд–Крушевац, 2002, pp. 146–147. See also: Б. Флоря, А. Турилов, *Общественная мысль Сербии конца XII–XIII вв. (Власть и общество в представлениях сербских книжников)*, [in:] *Власть и общество в литературных текстах Древней Руси и других славянских стран (XII–XIII вв.)*, ed. Б. Флоря, Москва 2012, pp. 132–133. The text of *B* has not been published; it is known to me from a microfilm copy held at St Cyril and Methodius National Library, Sofia. *S* and *B* are practically identical, with *B* revealing some minor gaps, most probably due to the scribe's negligence. Description of the National Library of Serbia, Рс 26: Љ. Штављанин-Ђорђевић, М. Гроздановић-Пајић, Л. Цернић, *Опис ћирилских рукописа Народне библиотеке Србије*, vol. I, Београд 1986, pp. 45–52. The compilers of the inventory note that the manuscript was bought by Vladimir Vuksan and added to the inventory of the National Library of Serbia in 1949. What is of interest is whether there is a connection between this manuscript and the one used by M. Petrovskiy in 1865 in the publication of a homily attributed to Metropolitan Hilarion of Kiev, whose title is practically identical with that of the copy of the work in the inventory of the NLS – Рс 26, f. 91. According to the publisher's note, this is a Serbian manuscript, written on rag paper from the 14th–15th century, which at that time was in the possession of Konstantin D. Petkovich, the Russian consul in Dubrovnik (Н. Никольский, *Материалы для повременного списка русских писателей и их сочинений (X – XI в.)*, Санкт-Петербург 1906, pp. 92–94; М. Сперанский, *Из истории русско-славянских литературных связей*, Москва 1960, pp. 16–19). Recently, the manuscript once owned by Petkovich was found by Anatoliy Turilov in the manuscript collection of the Library of the Academy of Sciences in Saint Petersburg, catalogued under reference БАН, Тек. пост. 13 (А. Турилов, *Памятники древнерусской литературы и письменности у южных славян в XII–XIV вв. (проблемы и перспективы изучения)*, [in:] *Славянские литературы. XI Международный съезд славистов. Братислава, сентябрь 1993 года. Доклады российской делегации*, Москва 1993, p. 32).

[56] The entire Ch. 24 (*S*, *B*) and Ch. 71 (*S*, *B*); fragments of Ch. 38 (*S*, *B*), Ch. 39 (*S*, *B*, *M*), and Ch. 67 (*S*, *B*). Furthermore, in *S* and *B* Ch. 23 features in its entirety, and not just as a fragment, as is the case in the *Izbornik of 1076* and *M*.

the Christianised version of the *Encheiridion*[57] and the *Chapters*

The aim of the compiler was to inculcate into 'the rich' a set of moral and ethical norms, by which they should be guided in their actions. The text begins with a reminder that a man on whom God has bestowed his grace must pay back his debt. What follows are several thematic motifs which are instrumental in constructing the ideal image of 'the rich': compassion for those 'suffering in misery' and benefaction; avoiding sycophants and recognising true friends; fair dispensation of justice; merciful treatment of the 'slaves'; refraining from 'inappropriate desires'; personal humility and avoiding the pride that goes with 'high rank'.

The question to whom the compilation under consideration here was addressed raises a number of issues. As could be seen, the titles of the text according to the copies included in the *Izbornik of 1076* and in the *Meletskiy Miscellany* feature the rather general and apparently lacking specific socio-political meaning term 'rich'[59].

[57] A fragment of Ch. 40 features in *S* and *B*; following the work under consideration, the same two copies feature Ch. 69 of the *Encheiridion*, under the title *Слово подвижное к Богу*.

[58] First centuria, Ch. 24 and 49 (*S*, *B*).

[59] Of interest is the way in which the Byzantine military commander and writer of the second half of the 11th century, Kekaumenos interprets and derives the etymology of the Slavic word for *rich*: *Help the needy in every way, because the rich man is god to the poor one, as he does good to him. For that reason the Bulgarians call a rich person* βογάτον, *which means 'God-like'* – Kekaumenos, p. 120.23–26; И. Дуйчев, *Проучвания върху средновековната българска история и култура*, София 1981, pp. 197–198. Kekaumenos' comments on the perception of the word 'rich' in the 11th century are significant as, on his mother's side, he was the grandson of Samuil's military commander Demetrios Polemarchos and was fluent in Bulgarian – Kekaumenos, p. 174.20–24; С. Пириватрич, *Самуиловата държава. Обхват и характер*, София 2000, pp. 152–153; G. Nikolov, *The Bulgarian aristocracy in the war against the Byzantine Empire (971–1019)*, [in:] *Byzantium and East Central Europe*, ed. G. Prinzing, M. Salamon, P. Stephenson, Kraków 2001, pp. 144–145. It should also be noted that, in his work, Kekaumenos (p. 120.22–32) advances the view that there exists a kind of a tripartite social structure: the *rich* (πλούσιοι) – people who can perform juridical (and in a broader sense, administrative and social) functions, have the right to express their opinions freely and are obliged to do charity for the benefit of the poor;

Cosmas, who in his *Sermon against the Heretics* paints the picture of the social stratification of Bulgarian society around the middle and the second half of the 10th century, portrays 'the rich' in the context of the heretical attacks against them. The way this Old-Bulgarian writer sees them, they are, by and large, those invested with power in this country, the tsar, the elders and the noblemen[60]. Furthermore, it is 'the rich' who are the carriers of literacy and have access to 'the books' (primarily the Bible, 'the divine books', but also 'the writings of the holy men', i.e. the Church Fathers)[61]. Stressing that *wealth is not an evil if we manage it well*[62], the writer adds, *if you are rich, you could save yourself through good deeds and prayer, and by reading often the holy books and do what they command*[63].

It is significant that the section titled *On the Rich* in Cosmas' work is almost entirely devoted to a discussion on the need to disseminate and get to know the books in the context of the wealthy Bulgarians' treatment and attitude of them[64]. According to the writer, in their 'big-headedness' they hide 'the divine words' from the sight of their brethren, not allowing 'God's word' to be copied and read, letting the books to be eaten by mould and worms. *No, man, do not hide God's words from those who want to read and copy them, but rejoice that your brethren will save themselves through them. Because they were not written to hide them in our heart or home*[65]. The rich should realise their duty to disseminate the books, because departures from the true faith are caused *by not reading the books and by the indolence of priests*[66].

Similar views are voiced in what amounts to a brief foreword to the *Izbornik*, *The Homily of a Certain Monk on Reading Scripture*[67]. The

the *middling* (μέσοι) – not granted the right to voice their opinions and unable to do charitable work, but still allowed to help the poor; and the *inferior* (οἱ κάτω).

[60] Cosmas the Priest, p. 342.

[61] On this distinction: Cosmas the Priest, p. 310.

[62] Cosmas the Priest, p. 356.

[63] Cosmas the Priest, p. 357.

[64] Cosmas the Priest, pp. 384–387.

[65] Cosmas the Priest, p. 384.

[66] Cosmas the Priest, p. 387.

[67] *Izbornik of 1076*, ed. A. Молдован et al., f. 1r–4v (transl. W. Veder, pp. 3–4). See also: Б. Ангелов, *За три съчинения в Симеоновите сборници*, СЛ 5, 1979,

anonymous author compares the significance of books to the righteous with [illegible] to probe deeply into the essence of what they are reading and urges them to abide by the truths found in the books. As for the author's understanding of the practical purpose of the apparently chaotic *Izbornik*, a book seeking to inculcate the norms of practical Christian morality into its readers but also a means of aiding the knowledge of the evangelical truths in the spirit of strict Orthodoxy, it is revealed in the last lines of the *Homily*:

> This, brothers, let us understand, and let us listen with the ears of our mind and understand the power and the instruction of the Holy Writ. Listen how of old it is recorded in the Lives of St. Basil, St. John Chrysostom, St. Cyril the Philosopher, and many other saints that from childhood they applied themselves to Scripture and by so doing strove for virtue. See what the source of virtue is: the study of the Holy Writ. Thus, brothers, following both the former and the latter, let us strive after their way of life and their deeds, and let us continually study the words of Scripture doing what they command, so that we shall be worthy of life everlasting.[68]

* * *

As it was observed earlier, the *Izbornik of 1076* mirrors, although rather distortedly, the content of the 10th-century Old-Bulgarian miscellany, based on longer translated texts available to the anonymous compiler. It could be assumed that, in its original form, this book was intended for the members of the tsar's family, the most trusted noblemen and the senior Bulgarian clergy and was later revised to make it more readily accessible to a broader readership (it is this revised version that William Veder refers to as *Sinful John's Izbornik*).

---

pp. 21–32; W. Veder, *Three Early Slavic Treatises on Reading*, [in:] *Studia slavica mediaevala et humanstica Riccardo Picchio dicata*, ed. M. Colucci, G. Dell'Agata, H. Goldblatt, vol. II, Roma 1986, pp. 717–730; *Слова на светлината. Творби на старобългарски писатели от епохата на св. княз Борис, цар Симеон и св. цар Петър*, ed., transl. И. Добрев, Т. Славова, София 1995, pp. 184–185.

[68] *Izbornik of 1076*, ed. А. Молдован et al., f. 3v–4v (transl. W. Veder, p. 4).

Serious arguments in favour of the above hypothesis provide our observations on another text included in the miscellany, *A Discourse of a Father to his Son* (original title: *A Certain Father's Words to his Son for Profit to his Soul*)[69]. There are dozens of Russian copies of this work from the 14th–18th centuries (some of which reflect the content of South-Slavic antigraphs), which have not yet been sufficiently studied.[70] There are also three extant Serbian copies from the 14th–15th century[71], as well as two Bulgarian copies of the 15th–16th century[72]. Like the Russian copies these reflect the same version of the text.

As for the content of the *Discourse*, it consists of a series of fatherly pieces of advice, which seek to guide the son towards a life *according to God's commandments*[73], towards meekness, humility, good intention, submission, love and good-heartedness, and mercifulness, in order for him to arrive at *the inalienable dwelling-places of the Jerusalem on high*[74]. By exposing the transience of earthly life, the anonymous author calls for charity towards the poor and the suffering, daily prayer and, most of all, awe for the priesthood:

---

[69] *Izbornik of 1076*, ed. A. Молдован et al., f. 4v–15v. Unfortunately, as several sheets of the manuscripts are missing, the text of the *Discourse* is incomplete and stops at f. 15v, what begins at f. 16r–24r is some unidentified edificatory text, analysed by: У. Федер, Р. Новак, *За приноса на Методиевите ученици в тълкувателната литература*, КМС 4, 1987, pp. 304–310.

[70] Н. Никольский, *Материалы*..., pp. 203–210.

[71] From the end of the 14th century: National Library of Serbia – Belgrade, Pc 26, f. 81r–84v; SS. Cyril and Methodius National Library – Sofia, № 1037, f. 94v–100v (М. Стоянов, Х. Кодов, *Опис на славянските ръкописи в Софийската Народна библиотека*, vol. III, София 1964, pp. 240–243). From the first half of the 15th century: a miscellany, held by the Metropolitanate of Skopje, no catalogue record (Б. Ангелов, *За три съчинения*..., p. 37).

[72] From the 15th century: Library of the Russian Academy of Sciences – Saint Petersburg, № 298, f. 156r–159r. From the 16th century: SS. Cyril and Methodius National Library – Sofia, № 433 (Panagyurishte miscellany), f. 158r–159v). The text of the copy of the Panagyurishte miscellany has been published in its entirety, while the one of Library of the Russian Academy of Sciences № 298, partially in: Б. Ангелов, *За три съчинения*..., pp. 32–37. See also А. Милтенова, *Сборник със смесено съдържание, дело на етрополския книжовник йеромонах Даниил*, СЛ 9, 1986, pp. 119, 123.

[73] *Izbornik of 1076*, ed. A. Молдован et al., f. 6r (transl. W. Veder, p. 5).

[74] *Izbornik of 1076*, ed. A. Молдован et al., f. 7v (transl. W. Veder, p. 5).

> Consider the church to be heaven, the altar the throne of the Most High,
> [illegible]
> in fear and as if God Himself were before your eyes. When you leave, remember what took place and what you heard... Whenever you are in the swell of this life, or whether you come to grief in the stormy ocean of the world, I shall show you, my son, the true havens: the monasteries, homes of the holy fathers.[75]

Exhorting his son to give everything needed to the monks, the author advises him to get close to a *man who fears God and serves Him with all his might*[76], to follow his example in life and listen to his words. What follows is a series of precepts for a pious life; the son should celebrate the saints' days and make his home known to the poor, the widows and the orphans:

> Whether you have a rich home or a poor one, it is all through God's providence. But of all your property try to give a tenth to God who has given you life here and, after your parting, the promise of life everlasting[77].

In conclusion, the author stresses that *not all who know God are saved but those who do His will*[78] and wishes his son to avoid, when the Last judgement comes, the eternal torment reserved for the sinners and to rejoice together with the just *in the undying light and in eternal joy in ages without end*[79].

On the surface of it, the *Discourse* is unremarkable, both in form and content; the motifs developed in it are traditional for the Christian homiletic literature. However, our perception of this work and its nature changes dramatically when we compare it with its source, the first version of the *Discourse*, known solely from a later Serbian copy from the 16th–17th century[80]. Here we shall discuss only some of the most prominent features of this

---

[75] *Izbornik of 1076*, ed. A. Молдован et al., f. 12r, 14r (transl. W. Veder, p. 7).
[76] *Izbornik of 1076*, ed. A. Молдован et al., f. 14v (transl. W. Veder, p. 7).
[77] *Izbornik of 1076*, ed. A. Молдован et al., f. 15v (transl. W. Veder, p. 8).
[78] *Izbornik of 1076*, ed. У. Федер, p. 57 (transl. W. Veder, p. 8).
[79] *Izbornik of 1076*, ed. У. Федер, pp. 58–59 (transl. W. Veder, p. 9).
[80] *A Discourse of a Father to his Son (primary version)*, pp. 79–81.

older paraenetic text, bearing all the linguistic hallmarks testifying to its Old-Bulgarian origins. This text affords us a unique opportunity to reveal the ideological motivation of the anonymous writer who compiled the popular version of the *Discourse*, whose text was included in the *Izbornik of 1076*. Here, quoted in translation, are those passages of the original version of the *Discourse* which allow us to describe it as a peculiar kind of 'mirror of princes', a homily to a future ruler. A translation of the relevant excerpts from the popular version, according to two Serbian copies of the 14th century and the incomplete copy in the *Izbornik of 1076*, is available in the footnotes[81].

> Both in sadness and in joy, let the temple be your shelter. Fall before the Most High, call to the Generous, make Him caress you. The soul-loving Lover of man will not turn away from you, but will comfort you seeing that you have entrusted all your cares to Him (cf. Ps 54, 23).
>
> Stand in the church in fear, as if [you are] in heaven, and before the eyes of the omniscient God, listening and watching eagerly what is sung there. And when you leave, remember what was said and write it in [your] heart so that it stays with you[82].
>
> Be wise and reasonable, seeing what God's will is and what the King in Heaven demands of us, the earthly ones, and what He asks of His creation, full of every goodness[83].

---

[81] In the following footnotes we provide the English translation of the equivalent passages of the text in its popular version after Veder's translation of the *Discours* [in:] *The Edificatory Prose...*, pp. 5–9.

[82] *A Discourse of a Father to his Son (primary version)*, pp. 80–81; *Izbornik of 1076*, ed. A. Молдован et al., f. 11v–12r: *Let the church be a haven to you both when you are grieved and more so when you are not. Every moment and every day enter and prostrate yourself before the Most High, press your face to the ground, and make Him remember you, for He who loves souls and loves men will not turn away from you, but will receive you and comfort you. Consider the church to be heaven, the altar the throne of the Most High, the ministers the angels of God. Therefore, stand in church as in heaven, in fear and as if God Himself were before your eyes. When you leave, remember what took place and what you heard* (transl. W. Veder, pp. 6–7).

[83] *A Discourse of a Father to his Son (primary version)*, p. 81; *Izbornik of 1076*, ed. A. Молдован et al., f. 12v–13r: *Be alert, understand what is the will of God, what the King of heaven demands of those on earth, what He asks of His creation. It is not little mercies*

If you are in trouble or in the waves of life, even if harrowing events [illegible] with courage and manliness, calling to your God for help.

If you find out, or hear, or have learned that the God-bearing men of the One who leads us all, are persecuted, deprived of any rest, poor in [their] dwellings, but rich with the gifts of the spirit, go to them with warm faith so that they send their prayers to the Most High and you will find solace in any misfortune. Pity them and you will be heartened, because [they] are the sons of cheer and solace and, when they have thought out the trial, they know [how] to offer comfort.

If you receive a diadem and are crowned with an imperial crown, do not consign to oblivion the things you had heard from me and always tirelessly call to mind my exhortations to protect the monasteries. Because they always beseech those reigning and are used to being [their] helpers [along the way] to the heavenly kingdom.

Oh, son, find a man who fears God and waste no time but help him. If you have found such a man, grieve no more, for you have found a life-giving treasure. Come close to him, body and soul, observe his life, how he moves, sits, and eats, and every habit of his. But most of all observe his words and let no word [of his] fall to the ground, for the words of the saints are more valuable than any crown embellished with pearls and gold. May you, child, receive through them Christ's grace and because of them be given the kingdom of heaven. Amen![84]

---

that are easily done? For it is written, "Be merciful so that mercy will be shown to you" (cf. Luke 6, 36). *What does He who is filled with all good demand of us?* (transl. W. Veder, p. 7).

[84] *A Discourse of a Father to his Son (primary version)*, pp. 80–81; *Izbornik of 1076*, ed. A. Молдован et al., f. 14v–15r: *In the town in which you live and in the others in the surroundings, search whether there is any man who fears God and serves Him with all his might. If you have found such a man, grieve no more, for you have already the key to the kingdom of heaven. Cling to him in both your soul and body and observe his life, how he walks, sits, and eats, and inquire into his every habit. Moreover, observe his words: let no word of his fall to the ground, for holy words are more valuable than pearls* (transl. W. Veder, pp. 7–8).

The overall tone of the text creates the impression that its author was someone of royal status (*what the King in Heaven demands of us, the earthly*, that is *the earthly rulers*), while his addressee (and son) enjoys high social standing and is to be invested with imperial power. Obviously, the explanation for the appearance of such motifs could be sought in the realm of the rhetoric that is characteristic of the Christian paraenetic literature. Still, it seems more likely that, in its initial form, the *Discourse of a Father to his Son* was an original Old-Bulgarian homily of an emperor (Peter?) addressed to his son and heir (Boris II?)[85] and not just a translation of an 'unspecified Greek homily'[86] or some hypothetical 'Greek homiletic treatise'[87].

It should be noted that the motif of respect for priesthood is practically missing from the earliest version; there the focus is put on fervent prayer and diligent attendance of church services. Furthermore, the compiler of the Discourse demands special care for the monasteries and following the example of 'the God-fearing'.

The above considerations are consistent with the overall spirit and with some specific ideas in the earliest version of the *Discourse*. However, this cannot in itself confirm the potential 'authorship' of tsar Peter, nor could it answer the question about the possible sources (Greek and Old-Bulgarian), used by the compiler. In that regard, it is worth bringing to mind the opinion of Peyo Dimitrov that *one of Peter's models* when putting together the *Discourse* were the *Paraenetic Chapters* of emperor Basil I, addressed to his son Leo (a work most probably produced by patriarch Photios), the Slavic translation of which may have been executed in 10th-century Bulgaria[88].

---

[85] A similar hypothesis was advanced for the first time in: П. Димитров, *Петър Черноризец...*, pp. 69–78.

[86] F. Thomson, *Quotations of Patristic and Byzantine Works by Early Russian Authors as an Indication of the Cultural Level of Kievan Russia*, SGa 10, 1983, p. 71.

[87] *The Edificatory Prose of Kievan Rus'...*, p. 5.

[88] П. Димитров, *Петър Черноризец...*, p. 74. For a more detailed discussion of the manuscript tradition and the early print editions of the translation of the *Paraenetic Chapters*: А. Николов, *Към въпроса за разпространението на някои византийски "княжески огледала" в старобългарската литература (края на IX – началото на X век)*, [in:] *Средновековните Балкани. Политика, религия, култура*, ed. С. Ракова, Л. Симеонова, София 1999, pp. 80–83; idem, *Старобългарският превод...*, pp. 88–89, 92; idem, *The Medieval Slavonic Translation of the Paraenetical*

It should be noted here that the ideological thrust of the revisions [illegible] of its popular version, is to a large extent similar to that which produced the revision of the original text of the *Admonition to the Rich*; judging by the two Serbian copies of the 14th century, the aim of the amendments was to increase the relevance of the work. In the case of the *Discourse* this meant anonymising and transforming an emperor's homily to his son and future sovereign into edifying reading, which could be used in the instruction for people of different social strata. The social status of the reviser responsible for the popular version as someone belonging to the church hierarchy, as well as his mindset, manifest themselves in the idea of priests as 'God's angels' and the demand he makes for regular payment of the tithe.

The original source of the *Admonition to the Rich* underwent a similar transformation to make its ideological content relevant to the addressee and consistent with the aims of the Old-Bulgarian *Izbornik*. However, the starting point of our analysis should be the metamorphoses of the title of the complete translation of Agapetos' *Exposition*, the main source

---

Chapters of Emperor Basil I between the Balkans, Ostrog and Moscow: Preliminary Remarks, [in:] *Byzantium, New Peoples, New Powers: the Byzantino-Slav Contact Zone, from the Ninth to the Fifteenth Century*, ed. M. Kaimakamova, M. Salamon, M. Smorąg Różycka, Cracow 2007, pp. 349–356; idem, *Средневековый славянский перевод "Учительных глав" императора Василия I: проблемы изучения рукописной традиции и ранних печатных изданий*, [in:] *XIX Ежегодная богословская конференция Православного Свято-Тихоновского гуманитарного университета*, vol. I, Москва 2009, pp. 41–47. Dimitrov's hypothesis highlights the need for more thorough examination of the Slavic manuscript tradition of this work. My initial research has revealed that two chapters from Agapetos's *Exposition* were interpolated in the core text of the earliest known copy of the translation (Serbian, from the beginning of the 15th century), evidence of the fact that, as early as the end of the 14th and the beginning of the 15th century, these two Byzantine 'mirrors of princes' (and, most probably, also the translation of patriarch Photios's epistle to prince Boris I-Michael) were featured together in a special kind of collections, which are currently known only through Russian copies of the 16th century. Recently, Dmitriy Bulanin dismissed categorically the proposed early dating for the Slavic translation of the *Paraenetic Chapters*, but the debate on this issue is far from over: Д. Буланин, *Текстологические и библиографические...*, p. 554.

of the compilation which mutated into the all too familiar *Admonition* but only after its second reworking upon being included into the *Izbornik*.

The review of the versions of the complete translation's title reveals remarkable divergence, which demands logical explanation. If we were to take as a starting point the comparison with the text's titles in the Greek manuscript tradition, we would notice immediately that the phrase *homily of the good emperorship*, reproduced in almost all Slavic copies, has its equivalent in a copy from a manuscript of the Austrian National Library in Vienna, Vindob. Iur. gr. 15, f. 192r: ὑπόθεσις ἀγαθῆς βασιλείας. It is this part of the title which undoubtedly featured in the translation right from the time of its execution. Subsequently, the title was further expanded by adding phrases such as *to the kings and princes, also to the noblemen, to the bishops and abbots, good also for the monks*, and *to the priests*[89].

The tendency to re-address the *Exposition* for Justinian to a wider section of the upper class leads some contemporary researchers to conclude that Bulgarian rulers did not 'need' Agapetos' work

> because it provided support for their political claims. It is more likely that 'the mirror' of the Constantinople deacon was attractive to the newly converted Christians as it represented a collection of moralistic gnomes of universal importance.[90]

---

[89] В. Вальденберг, *Наставление писателя VI в. Агапита в русской письменности*, BB 24, 1923/1926, p. 28; Agapetos Diakonos, *Der Fürstenspiegel für Kaiser Iustinianos*, ed. R. Riedinger, Athen 1995, p. 24; А. Николов, *Към въпроса...*, pp. 77–78.

[90] Д. Буланин, *Неизвестный источник...*, p. 168. See also: idem, *Текстологические и библиографические...*, pp. 538–540. The same theory has been put forward by Francis Thomson (*"Made in Russia". A Survey of the Translations Allegedly Made in Kievan Russia*, [in:] *Millenium Russiae Christianae. Tausend Jahre Christliches Russland 988–1988*, ed. G. Birkfellner, Köln 1993, p. 351, fn. 381 (repr. in: idem, *The Reception of Byzantine Culture in Medieval Russia*, Aldershot 1999, V), who gives the different versions of the work's title as evidence that in mediaeval Bulgaria this text *was clearly viewed as a collection of moralistic gnomes addressed not merely to princes, as the variant titles show* (...) *The idea that it was translated for Symeon (893–927) or Peter (927–969/70) of Bulgaria as part of their interest in Byzantine political ideology* (...) *is unlikely*.

This observation is noteworthy as it explains the interest in Agapetos' in 10th-century Bulgaria, which to a large extent predetermined its reception in mediaeval Russia. However, we should not forget (and this was stressed rather astutely many years ago by Ihor Shevchenko[91]) that the addition of such a text to the repertory of the Preslav translators at the end of the 9th and the beginning of the 10th century could hardly be explained outside the context of the political ideas and claims of the first Bulgarian tsar, Symeon I, who after 917 proclaimed himself emperor of the Romans and began using lead seals bearing the legend, Συμεὼν ἐν Χριστῷ βασιλεὺς Ῥωμαίων[92].

Thus, it could be assumed that the tendency to re-address (through changes to the title) the *Exposition* to the secular and spiritual masters (princes, noblemen, bishops, abbots) emerged as early as the *Golden Age*, when the complete text of the work was included in the *Menaion Izbornik*, reconstructed by Bulanin. As it is known, Symeon I invested considerable effort precisely into elevating the Christian identity and culture of his closest noblemen. Hence the *Menaion Izbornik* should be placed alongside such 10th-century translations as *Symeon's Miscellany* and *Zlatostruy*. Therefore, it is no accident that in the Old-Bulgarian *Izbornik*, known from a Russian copy of 1076, the contents of those sizeable tomes are closely interwoven[93].

Here we should once again remind ourselves of William Veder's hypothesis that, to a large extent, the archetype of the *Izbornik of 1076*, the *Sinful John's Izbornik*, replicates a *princely Miscellany*, whose content could be reconstructed on the basis of its reflections in the later South Slavic and Russian manuscript tradition. It is this *Princely Miscellany* which seems to be the source of the two 14th-century Serbian copies of the compilation of fragments from Agapetos' *Exposition*, Epictetus' *Encheiridion*

---

[91] I. Š e v č e n k o, *Agapetus East and West: the Fate of a Byzantine 'Mirror of Princes'*, RESEE 16.1, 1978, p. 28.

[92] И. Й о р д а н о в, *Корпус на средновековните български печати...*, pp. 73–82 (№ 80–107).

[93] Я. М и л т е н о в, *Общите пасажи между колекцията Златоструй и Княжеския изборник*, СЛ 49/50, 2014, pp. 28–45.

and Maximos the Confessor's *Chapters on Love*. As has been noted already, this version of the text is more complete than the one included in the *Izbornik of 1076* under the title *Admonition to the Rich*.

The very title of the *Admonition to the Rich* in the Serbian copies, *Discourse to the Rulers on Earth*, is evidence of the active aspiration of the 10th-century Bulgarian editor to transform Agapetos' *Exposition*, devoted to the hallowed personality of the tsar, into a more general moral exhortation addressed to the earthly masters. The expression *ruling on earth*, as well as the overall content of the compilation, suggest that the *Discourse* was meant for the secular rulers, unlike the complete text of the *Exposition* which was supposed to be read by the noblemen, bishops, abbots and priests.

Evidence of the addressee of the *Discourse to the Ruling on Earth* is the fact that it includes almost the whole Ch. 71 of Agapetos' *Exposition* (completely missing from the *Admonition of the Rich*), whose target is the ruler's pride

> The proud and arrogant person must not strut like a tall-horned young bull but think of his carnal nature and stop his heart from singing his praises. Even if he is a prince on earth, let him know that as he was [made] of earth, from the clay he ascended the throne[94].

The compiler of the *Discourse* tactfully spared his readers the concluding words of this chapter according to the complete version of the *Exposition*, *and in time would come off it*.

The fact that this passage was at all included in the *Admonition to the Rich* is consistent with my earlier hypothesis about the overall nature of the editorial revisions to the texts in *Sinful John's Izbornik*, whose purpose was the transformation of a number of existing Old-Bulgarian translated and original works into widely accessible edifying reading matter.

* * *

[94] Д. Буланин, *Неизвестный источник...*, p. 176.

The observations made so far demonstrate that in the 930s–960s the now [illegible] of its spiritual development, marked by an increased demand for widely accessible edifying works (including vitas). As a result of the challenge posed by Bogomil propaganda the high secular and ecclesiastical circles were faced with the task of elevating the moral and ethical standards of ordinary believers, who did not, as a rule, have direct access to the biblical books, let alone to the abstruse and rather hefty interpretative, dogmatic and homiletic works of the Church fathers[95].

The responsibility for organising the creation, copying and dissemination of such 'soul-saving' books, meant to be read by clerics and laymen outside the walls of the temples, lay mostly with the ruler; he was the one who, by tradition, defined the main trends in the development of the cultural and spiritual life of the country. He had the requisite financial and material resources; he had under his direct supervision the largest library in Bulgaria and the entire Slavic world, housing practically all the existent texts in Old-Bulgarian of any significance, both translated and original. Clearly, tsar Peter was well aware of his duties and put considerable effort into becoming a *teacher of orthodoxy*, a role assigned to him by patriarch Theophylaktos. As protector of monasticism and denouncer of the moral and social vices, this Bulgarian ruler became a true *fighter against the ignorance of the clergy and against the heresies*. Therefore, it is no accident that pious tsar Peter, who died as a monk, was canonised soon after his death and thus became a patron saint of the Bulgarian people[96], whose name was later adopted as a 'throne' name by the leaders of all the major uprisings of the Bulgarians against the Byzantine rule in the 11th and 12th centuries[97].

---

[95] Cf. И. Божилов, В. Гюзелев, *История на средновековна България...*, pp. 280–281.

[96] *Service of St. Tsar Peter*, p. 387: застѫпникъ ѿ ви(д)мыхъ враговъ противны(х).

[97] Generally on the canonisation of tsar Peter and his cult: И. Билярски, *Небесните покровители...*, pp. 34–36; Д. Чешмеджиев, *Няколко бележки...*, pp. 35–36; И. Билярски, *Покровители на Царството: св. цар Петър и св. Параскева-Петка*, София 2004, pp. 33–42; Д. Чешмеджиев, *Култът към цар Петър (927–969): манастирски или държавен?*, [in:] *Љубав према образовању и вера у Бога у православним манастирами*, 5. *Међународна Хилендарска*

2. Art and Church Architecture

Zofia A. Brzozowska

2.1. Church Architecture and Sculpture

For many scholars the Old Bulgarian architecture from the reign of Peter remains in the shadow of the foundation achievements of this ruler's predecessor, Symeon I the Great. There are several reasons for this. Firstly, not a single edifice raised in the 10th century within the area that interests us here survived to our times in its original form[98]. The lack of written sources makes it difficult to ascertain the age and definitive attribution of the objects being discovered during archaeological excavations with a high degree of precision[99] – therefore the time of creation of most of them

конференција. Зборник изабраних радова I, ed. P. Matejić et al., Beograd–Columbus 2006, pp. 255–257; И. Билярски, М. Йовчева, *За датата на успението на цар Петър и за култа към него*, [in:] *Тангра. Сборник в чест на 70-годишнината на акад. Васил Гюзелев*, ed. М. Каймакамова et al., София 2006, pp. 543–557; Б. Николова, *Цар Петър и характерът на неговия култ*, Pbg 33.2, 2009, pp. 63–78; Д. Чешмеджиев, *Българската държавна традиция в апокрифите: цар Петър в Българския апокрифен летопис*, [in:] *Българско средновековие: общество, власт, история. Сборник в чест на проф. д-р Милияна Каймакамова*, ed. Г.Н. Николов, А. Николов, София 2013, pp. 262–271; Д. Полывянный, *Царь Петр в историческской памяти болгарского средневековья*, [in:] *Сборник в чест на 60-годишнината на проф. д.и.н. Петър Ангелов*, ed. А. Николов, Г.Н. Николов, София 2013, p. 141; М. Каймакамова, *Култът към цар Петър (927–969) и движещите идеи на българските освободителни въстания срещу византийската власт през XI–XII в.*, BMd 4/5, 2013/2014, pp. 417–438.

[98] Н. Чанева-Дечевска, *Църкви и манастири от Велики Преслав*, София 1980, p. 68. The sole building from Peter's time that survived to modern times is a small church, cross-domed, dedicated to the Mother of God, which is located in Yana, near Sofia. The building was destroyed in 1948; however its main architectural structure can be recreated thanks to a photograph. Н. Мавродинов, *Старобългарското изкуство. Изкуството на първото българско царство*, [2]София 2013, pp. 245, 267.

[99] Т. Тотев, *Старобългарските манастири в светлината на археологическите разкопки и проучвания*, СЛ 22, 1990, p. 9; idem, *Монастыри в Плиске и Преславе в IX–X вв. Краткая археологическая характеристика*, ПКШ 7, 2003, p. 367; Р. Костова, *Патронаж...*, pp. 199–201.

is dated in the literature of the subject to the end of the 9th or the first half [illegible] are accepted to have originated during the reign of Symeon.

It is difficult to accept the thought that Peter, so enamoured with Christian values and supporting the monastic movement, would not have undertaken any foundation initiatives during the four decades of his reign[100]. He most likely continued his father's activity, and perhaps even commissioned the expansion or completion of the objects from the earlier period. The evidence supporting the latter hypothesis can be found in the archaeological material. For example: a seal depicting Peter and his wife, Maria Lekapene, dated to 940–950, and an amphora with the monogram of the ruler's name, have been found in the ruins of the church of St. John in Preslav (the so-called Round/Golden Church); the church was traditionally considered to have been founded by Symeon[101]. Moreover, numismatic material, collected during the excavation of the site, also confirms the supposition that the construction of the Round Church, begun at the end of the 9th century, may have been finally completed in the 960s – within its foundations, coins of Leo VI the Wise (886–912), Constantine VII Porphyrogennetos (913–959), Romanos I Lekapenos (920–944) and Nikephoros II Phocas (963–969) have been found[102].

Peter's seals were uncovered in two other Preslavian religious buildings, usually dated in the literature of the subject to an earlier period. Two lead seals were discovered in the ruins of the so-called 'palace basilica', raised during the reign of prince Boris-Michael (most likely in 866–870), which was thoroughly renovated by his grandson[103]. A *sigillum* from the 930s, adorned with an image of Peter and Maria, was in turn found

---

[100] Н. Мавродинов, *Старобългарското...*, pp. 244–245.

[101] Т. Тотев, *Родов манастир на владетелите в Преслав*, СЛ 20, 1987, p. 128; Б. Николова, *Православните църкви през българското средновековие (IX–XIV)*, София 2002, p. 92; И. Йорданов, *Корпус на средновековните български печати*, София 2016, p. 96.

[102] Т. Тотев, *Родов манастир...*, p. 125.

[103] Б. Николова, *Православните църкви...*, p. 93; И. Йорданов, *Корпус...*, pp. 118–119.

during the studies of the architectural structure of the so-called 'palace monastery' in Preslav. Other artefacts found in this object allow us to assume that it was expanded in Peter's times: a lead seal with an image of Constantine VII Porphyrogennetos made after 945, and a seal depicting Romanos I, Constantine VII and the Bulgarian tsaritsa's father, Christopher Lekapenos, made in 927–931[104].

The monastery built on the Avradak hill, located to the south-east of Preslav's centre, beyond the contemporary city walls of the Bulgarian capital, was undoubtedly built during Peter's reign[105]. A rather precise dating of this architectural complex is possible thanks to the numismatic material gathered during archaeological excavations carried out in its ruins: a coin from the period of Constantine VII Porphyrogennetos' sole rule (945–959) was discovered in the deepest layer, dating to the period during which the monastery's foundations were laid. The latest coins found at this site can be associated with the reign of John I Tzymiskes (969–976)[106]. The monastery on the Avradak hill may have been therefore founded no earlier than 945. It most likely fell into ruin during the war that started after Peter's death. The architecture of the complex provides further arguments to support this hypothesis. Despite having been located in the open and outside of Preslav's fortifications, its builders did not surround the monastery proper with a strong defensive wall. One may therefore suppose that it was built during the several decade long period of peace, most likely in 927–969[107].

[104] Т. Тотев, *Старобългарските манастири...*, p. 12; idem, *Монастыри в Плиске...*, p. 371; idem, *The Palace Monastery in Preslav*, ПКШ 3, 1998, p. 145; I. Jordanov, *Corpus of Byzantine Seals from Bulgaria*, vol. III/1, Sofia 2009, pp. 89–90; idem, *Корпус...*, p. 91.

[105] С. Ваклинов, *Формиране на старобългарската култура. VI–XI в.*, София 1977, p. 205; Н. Чанева-Дечевска, *Църкви и манастири...*, pp. 107, 125, 145; Т. Тотев, *Старобългарските манастири...*, p. 10; M. Stancheva, *Veliki Preslav*, Sofia 1993, p. 26; Т. Тотев, *Монастыри в Плиске...*, p. 366; idem, *Още наблюдения за църква № 1 в Дворцовия манастир на Велики Преслав*, Истор 4, 2011, p. 301.

[106] Н. Мавродинов, *Старобългарското...*, p. 245.

[107] Н. Чанева-Дечевска, *Църкви и манастири...*, pp. 127, 144; Т. Тотев, *Монастыри в Плиске...*, p. 369; Н. Мавродинов, *Старобългарското...*, p. 247.

In the 10th century, the grandest building within the complex was [illegible] on the Avradak hill, a ruined, stone church of relatively small size: 7,4 m by 12,8 m was discovered. This building (the so-called 'church no. 1') was undoubtedly a cross-domed church, created on the basis of models taken from the Byzantine architecture[108]. It had a complex structure, matching the Eastern Christian ideas of the tripartite division of sacred space: within it, there was the chancel reserved for the clergy, the nave for the laypeople, and the narthex[109]. On the eastern side, the church terminated with three semi-circular apses. The altar was located within the largest, central one, while the side apses accommodated the *diaconicon* and *prothesis* (*proscomidion*). The space that should remain off limits to the laypeople was most likely, according to the Byzantine tradition, separated from the remainder of the temple with a stone partition[110].

The main dome of the church rested on four massive marble pillars. Their remains were uncovered during the excavations: two of them were made from pink-hued stone, the remaining two – from white marble. The aforementioned pillars fulfilled another important role: they divided the space designated for the lay participants of the liturgical ceremonies into three parts, corresponding in their width to the apses located at the eastern end of the church. On the western side, the church was adjoined by a rather large, unicameral narthex. According to the local tradition, it had one central and two side entrances, likely preceded by some type of a portico[111].

---

[108] С. Ваклинов, *Формиране...*, p. 205; Н. Чанева-Дечевска, *Църкви и манастири...*, pp. 20, 37, 99; S. Doncheva, *Symbolic Emphasises in the Mediaeval Religious Architecture*, НВ.ЗР 3, 2005, p. 249; Т. Тотев, *Още наблюдения...*, p. 305; Н. Мавродинов, *Старобългарското...*, pp. 250–252.

[109] G. Minczew, *"Cała świątynia staje się mieszkaniem Boga". Bizantyńskie mistagogie – wykładnia i komentarz liturgii niebiańskiej*, [in:] Symeon z Tessaloniki, *O świątyni Bożej*, transl. A. Maciejewska, Kraków 2007, pp. 18–19.

[110] К. Миятев, *Архитектурата в Средновековна България. Архитектура и строителство*, София 1965, p. 112; Н. Чанева-Дечевска, *Църкви и манастири...*, pp. 34, 42, 54.

[111] Н. Чанева-Дечевска, *Църкви и манастири...*, pp. 45–46, 66; Н. Мавродинов, *Старобългарското...*, pp. 255–256.

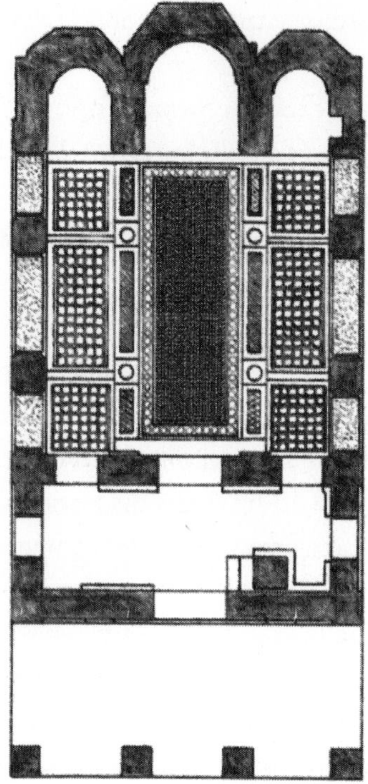

'Church no. 1' in the Avradak monastery. Building plan with reconstructed floor mosaic. Drawing (after G. Ganev): E. Myślińska-Brzozowska

The building is noteworthy for its architectural distinctiveness. According to experts, 'church no. 1' of the Avradak monastery had a skeletal structure – the weight of its vaulting was not spread evenly across its walls, but rather focused on several sections of the wall, specially reinforced with pilasters[112]. Interestingly enough, such architectural solutions only appear on the Byzantine soil in the 10th century – we can observe them e.g. within the church in Myrelaion (*Bodrum Camii*), founded by the emperor Romanos I Lekapenos in the 920s[113]. The adaptation of this technological innovation by Bulgarian builders attests to lively cultural contacts between the Constantinopolitan and Preslavian elites of this era. It would be tempting to suppose, although without source evidence to support this, that it was Maria Lekapene who initiated the construction of the Avradak monastery. Had that been the case, she would have likely told the builders of the monastery's church (who perhaps came from Byzantium) to copy the architectural designs of the Constantinopolitan church erected by her grandfather, and which housed the remains of her family, including those of her grandmother Theodora and father Christopher.

Within the building's structure one may find several features characteristic to Bulgarian architecture of tsar Peter's times. The remains of the

[112] Н. Мавродинов, *Старобългарското...*, p. 252.

[113] Г. Колпакова, *Искусство Византии. Ранний и средний периоды*, Санкт-Петербург 2010, pp. 299–301; A. Kompa, *Konstantynopolitańskie zabytki w Stambule*, AUL.FH 87, 2011, pp. 156–157.

church walls evidence that the temple's original facade was decorated on

nents located on the side elevations of the building were associated with its skeletal structure, the ones placed above the church's main entrance merely imitated load-bearing pilasters, and were purely decorative[114]. According to Nikola Mavrodinov, the structure of the main church of the Avradak monastery was also distinguished by an element that was practically unknown to Byzantine architecture – above its narthex, there have been (according to the Bulgarian scholar) two square towers, exceeding in height even the central dome of the church[115].

The largest church of the monastery must have also been notable for its opulent interior decorations. Unfortunately, no traces of wall paintings have been found in the Avradak monastery. Within its ruins however – similarly to the remains of the other Preslavian architectural monuments from that time – relatively numerous fragments of polychrome ceramics have been found[116]. During the dig a relatively well preserved floor of the church has also been uncovered; it was made of stone and ceramic tiles, in white, green, red, yellow, dark pink and grey[117]. Numerous elements of stonework have also been found. Among the four capitals topping the marble columns that held up the dome, only two survived to our times (one of these – in its entirety). Over one hundred fragments of the stone frieze that adorned both inner and outer side of the building have also been collected. Among the ornaments used by the Preslavian artists the motifs of heart-shaped leaves and 'wolves' teeth' were predominant[118].

---

[114] К. Миятев, *Архитектурата*..., p. 113; Н. Чанева-Дечевска, *Църкви и манастири*..., pp. 53, 73, 75; Н. Мавродинов, *Старобългарското*..., p. 253.

[115] Н. Чанева-Дечевска, *Църкви и манастири*..., p. 66; Н. Мавродинов, *Старобългарското*..., p. 254.

[116] Н. Чанева-Дечевска, *Църкви и манастири*..., p. 90.

[117] С. Ваклинов, *Формиране*..., p. 206; Н. Чанева-Дечевска, *Църкви и манастири*..., pp. 86–88; Т. Тотев, *Още наблюдения*..., p. 302; Н. Мавродинов, *Старобългарското*..., p. 255.

[118] С. Ваклинов, *Формиране*..., p. 205, 211; Н. Чанева-Дечевска, *Църкви и манастири*..., p. 70, 94; M. Stancheva, *Veliki Preslav*..., p. 59; Н. Мавродинов, *Старобългарското*..., pp. 256–257.

The main church of the Avradak monastery has also provided us with what are probably the only examples of the Old Bulgarian sculpture that we can date to the 10th century[119]. The outer facade of the building was adorned by depictions of animal heads, originally carved in lime: during the dig, three figures of lionesses and one of a monkey have been found. These served a function analogous to the stonework elements preserved on the facades of the Western European mediaeval cathedrals, as gargoyles, i.e. decorative gutters serving as drains for the rain water. It is worth noting that such decorations are not to be found in Byzantine architecture. Artefacts from the Avradak monastery church therefore are a continuation of a home-grown, Bulgarian tradition, and show certain analogies to the bas relief depictions of animals preserved on the capital and stone plates from the Stara and Nova Zagora. The renderings discussed here are, however, much more schematic in nature and, according to some researchers, attest to artistic regress of the Bulgarian sculpture in the 10th century[120].

What is interesting, the monastic complex included another church (the so-called 'church no. 2'), measuring 6,5 m by 11,5 m. Its design did

---

[119] In the older literature of the subject, the capital and the five stone plates found in the Stara and Nova Zagora were sometimes considered to have belonged to the period being discussed here. They are decorated with bas reliefs depicting animals (lions or panthers), humans, birds and fantastic creatures: a griffin, a phoenix and a two-headed eagle (С. Ваклинов, *Формиране...*, pp. 236–237; Н. Мавродинов, *Старобългарското...*, pp. 282–288). This dating was recently put into question by Bulgarian scholars, Ivan Ivanov and Mariana Minkova, who noted that the iconographic details of the analyzed representations allows the supposition that they were created during an earlier period – in the middle of the 9th century, or at the turn of the 9th and 10th centuries (И.Т. Иванов, М. Минкова, *Още веднъж за средновековните каменни релефи от Стара Загора*, ИСИМ 3, 2008, pp. 177–184; И. Иванов, *Гривести прабългарски барсове, а не византийски лъвове са изобразени върху прочутите Старозагорски каменни релефи*, [in:] *Доклади и научни съобщения от V национална научна конференция "От регионалното към националното – история, краезнание и музейно дело" на Историческия музей – Полски Тръмбеш*, Велико Търново 2012, pp. 405–416).

[120] К. Миятев, *Архитектурата...*, pp. 112–113; С. Ваклинов, *Формиране...*, pp. 205–206, 212; Н. Чанева-Дечевска, *Църкви и манастири...*, pp. 96–97, 126; Т. Тотев, *Старобългарските манастири...*, p. 10; M. Stancheva, *Veliki Preslav...*, pp. 71–73; Т. Тотев, *Монастыри в Плиске...*, p. 369; Н. Мавродинов, *Старобългарското...*, pp. 257–258, 289–291.

A lioness with a child and a lion. Stone plates found in Old Zagora, decorated with bas reliefs. 9th–10th century. Drawing: E. Myślińska-Brzozowska

not differ much from the previously discussed building. It was most likely of cross-dome design. There was only one entrance to the building, located *vis-à-vis* the altar. Having crossed the church's threshold, the faithful approached a small narthex, from which they then moved into the main nave, divided into three parts by four great pillars holding up the dome. From the eastern side, the main church structure was adjoined by three apses; these however were not connected with each other. According to experts, the lack of passages between the area housing the altar and the *diaconicon* and *proscomidion* may be considered a local feature, shared by numerous Old Bulgarian basilicas built in Pliska and Preslav[121].

The local architectural traditions appear to have found another expression in decorating the outer walls of the building, in the form of shallow, 10-centimere niches, some of which were an integral part of the skeletal structure of the building, while others were added purely for decorative reasons. The facade and the interior of the church were also adorned with a frieze of the 'wolves teeth'[122].

---

[121] Н. Чанева-Дечевска, *Църкви и манастири*..., pp. 20, 33, 42, 53, 99; Б. Николова, *Православните църкви*..., p. 98; С. Дончева, *Към манастирското устройство в околностите на столичните центрове в Първото българско царство*, ПКШ 7, 2003, p. 443; eadem, *Symbolic Emphasises*..., p. 252; Т. Тотев, *Още наблюдения*..., p. 305; Н. Мавродинов, *Старобългарското*..., pp. 258–259.

[122] Н. Мавродинов, *Старобългарското*..., p. 259.

Interestingly enough, the religious buildings were located at a fairly considerable distance from the rest of the Avradak monastic complex. Some scholars suggest therefore that the monastery was a female community: the residential buildings, in which the nuns spent most of their time, would have been purposefully separated from the church and the male clergymen serving the ministry there for moral considerations[123]. The inhabitants of the monastery were not however alienated from the social life. As archaeological excavations indicate, caring for the elderly, disabled and ill was an important part of their everyday existence. Ruins of a hospital and of a nursing home were discovered within the monastic complex[124]. The nuns also had their own artisanal workshop, in which they made small objects (including crosses and icons), which they most likely sold to those visiting their community[125]. No traces of painted ceramics or of a scriptorium have been found during the excavations at the site, one may therefore suppose that in the contemporary Bulgaria both of the associated activities were, unfortunately, considered to have been occupations reserved for men.

The monastic complex included a well. Moreover, its buildings were also supplied by a specially designed hydraulic system, based on Byzantine models. The hospital also included a toilet. Its existence, much like that of the bathing complex in Pliska and of the extended water distribution networks supplying the inhabitants of both of the Bulgarian capitals, attests to a fairly high standard of everyday life in Bulgaria during the reign of the son of Symeon I the Great[126].

---

[123] К. Миятев, *Архитектурата...*, p. 126; Н. Чанева-Дечевска, *Църкви и манастири...*, pp. 125, 144; Н. Мавродинов, *Старобългарското...*, p. 250.

[124] Н. Чанева-Дечевска, *Църкви и манастири...*, p. 131; Т. Тотев, *Старобългарските манастири...*, p. 10; idem, *Монастыри в Плиске...*, p. 369; Н. Мавродинов, *Старобългарското...*, p. 248. The hypothesis about the existence of a hospital within the Avradak monastery is occasionally criticised in the newer literature of the subject: Т. Тотев, *Нови наблюдения и данни за облика на гражданската архитектура през Първото българско царство*, ПКШ 1, 1995, p. 322; N. Amudzhieva, P. Tsvetkov, *The Cult of Saints-Healers – an Alternative and Opposition to the Official Medicine in Medieval Bulgaria*, Jahr.EJB 4.7, 2013, p. 360.

[125] Т. Тотев, *Нови наблюдения...*, p. 322; Н. Мавродинов, *Старобългарското...*, p. 249.

[126] Н. Чанева-Дечевска, *Църкви и манастири...*, pp. 126, 152; Т. Тотев, *Нови наблюдения...*, p. 328; Н. Мавродинов, *Старобългарското...*, pp. 249–250, 265–266.

The churches of the Avradak monastery were likely not the only religious buildings erected by tsar Peter. During his reign, the capital of Preslav gained numerous other buildings of this kind, among them the later temple located by the south-western corner of the city's wall. It was a stone church, constructed on the plan of a Greek cross, with a partial 'skeletal' structure, its central dome resting on four great pillars, a solution similar to those used in both of the Avradak monastery churches. On the eastern side, the church's structure was closed with three, semi-circular apses. Their outer facades were decorated with shallow (10 cm) niches[127].

Churches in the 10th century, which served as family necropoleis, were also founded by Preslavian aristocrats. Ruins of two stone religious buildings (so-called 'churches no. 3 and 4') were discovered in the area of 'Selishte', located within the southern part of the capital city. These structures were typical cross-dome churches, with elements of 'skeletal' construction used in their construction. Group burials have been uncovered within the narthexes of each of the temples[128]. A family tomb was also found in the remains of the so-called 'church no. 7', located near the northern wall. The church itself was unusually simple from architectural standpoint – it was a single nave temple, adjoined by a single apse[129].

Peter continued foundation activity of his father outside of the capital as well. He most likely expanded of the old seat of Bulgarian rulers in Pliska, by having a small palace chapel and a bathing complex constructed there[130]. He also finished the construction of a church in Vinica, located near Preslav, which was most likely started by Symeon I the Great[131]. The example of the church in the village of Yana in the Sofia region allows

---

[127] Б. Николова, *Православните църкви...*, pp. 95–96; S. Doncheva, *Symbolic Emphasises...*, p. 250; Н. Мавродинов, *Старобългарското...*, pp. 260–261.

[128] К. Миятев, *Архитектурата...*, pp. 118–119; Н. Чанева-Дечевска, *Църкви и манастири...*, pp. 19, 22–26, 34, 40, 44–45, 49, 50–53, 60, 64–67, 70, 73, 76, 79, 81–83; Т. Тотев, *Нови наблюдения...*, pp. 323–324; Н. Мавродинов, *Старобългарското...*, pp. 261–264; Б. Николова, *Православните църкви...*, p. 97.

[129] Н. Мавродинов, *Старобългарското...*, pp. 264–265.

[130] *Ibidem*, pp. 245, 265–266.

[131] К. Миятев, *Архитектурата...*, pp. 120–121; С. Ваклинов, *Формиране...*, p. 201; Н. Мавродинов, *Старобългарското...*, pp. 245–246.Н. Чанева-Дечевска, *Църкви и манастири...*, pp. 62–63.

one to suppose that in the 10th century some of the provincial centres of the Bulgarian state may also have boasted stone temples, built using the models taken from the Byzantine architecture[132].

Among the architectural Old Bulgarian monuments from the 10th century, the ruins of a certain monastic complex found in the 'Selishte' area deserve particular attention. The poor state in which the majority of its objects are preserved make an analysis of its architectural assumptions more difficult. The main monastic church was most likely raised on the plan of a Greek cross, with the central dome resting on four columns. Not far from it, the remains of another, smaller temple were uncovered: it was designed as a typical cross-domed church[133].

Some unique epigraphic material was found at the aforementioned site, allowing dating the creation of the monastery to 927–969. During archaeological works in 1952, a limestone tombstone with a Cyrillic inscription was discovered by the northern wall of the main monastic church[134]. The inscription informs that an aristocrat named Mostich was buried in the temple, and that he held a high state office during the reigns of Symeon and of his son Peter. Near the end of his life he decided to become a monk. He therefore endowed his wealth to the monastery to which he decided to retire. He remained there until his death, and was subsequently buried within its walls.

---

[132] Н. Мавродинов, *Старобългарското...*, p. 267.

[133] Н. Чанева-Дечевска, *Църкви и манастири...*, pp. 118–121; Т. Тотев, *Старобългарските манастири...*, p. 11; S. Doncheva, *Symbolic Emphasises...*, pp. 251–252.

[134] К. Миятев, *Архитектурата...*, p. 122; С. Ваклинов, *Формиране...*, pp. 226–227; Н. Чанева-Дечевска, *Църкви и манастири...*, pp. 103, 118; Т. Тотев, *Родов манастир...*, p. 120; idem, *Старобългарските манастири...*, pp. 8–9; M. Stancheva, *Veliki Preslav...*, pp. 47–48; Т. Тотев, *Монастыри в Плиске и Преславе...*, p. 367; M. Wójtowicz, *Najstarsze datowane inskrypcje słowiańskie X–XIII w.*, Poznań 2005, pp. 28, 157; П. Павлов, А. Орачев, А. Ханджийски, *Българската писменост. Европейски феномен*, София 2008, p. 20; Р. Костова, *Патронаж...*, p. 201; Т. Тотев, *Още наблюдения...*, p. 305; П. Павлов, *Години на мир и "ратни беди" (927–1018)*, [in:] Г. Атанасов, В. Вачкова, П. Павлов, *Българска национална история*, vol. III, *Първо българско царство (680–1018)*, Велико Търново 2015, p. 408.

Interestingly, another notable Cyrillic inscription was uncovered within the monastery (which in the older literature of the subjects is often referred to as 'Mostich's monastery') in 2007. It was found in a burial crypt located near the main church entrance. Its text can be reconstructed in the following way: **СЄ ЄСТЬ СѴНКЄЛ | МѦТЄР И СРДОБОЛѪ | ПОГРЄБЛЪ**. As it therefore turns out, Mostich was not the only Bulgarian aristocrat from the 10th century whose temporal remains were laid to rest within the church. The mother, and perhaps also other family members of a person who held the dignity of a synkellos, were buried within the underground crypt as well. This dignitary is most likely to have been the monk George, who was the synkellos of the Bulgarian patriarchate during the second half of the 10th century. Supporting this is the discovery of five seals bearing the customary plea for God to show His mercy, found within the ruins of the church in which both of the abovementioned inscriptions were found as well: **Гєоргіѹ чрьньцю и сѵнкєлѹ блъгарьскѹѥмѹ**[135].

Synkellos George was also most likely the founder of the monastic complex created within the 'Selishte' area[136]. The temple located within it was a *sui generis* necropolis – the remains of the ruler's entourage were laid to rest within an adjoining crypt. The hypothetical idea that tsar Peter himself may have spent his final years within the complex, and was subsequently buried – like Mostich and the mother of synkellos George – in the main church of the monastery, is an interesting, albeit unfortunately extremely difficult to prove, a thought[137].

---

[135] M. Stancheva, *Veliki Preslav...*, p. 61; Р. Костова, *Патронаж...*, p. 202; К. Попконстантинов, Р. Костова, *Манастирът на Георги, синкел български в Преслав. Историята на една българска аристократична фамилия от X в.*, Пр.Сб 7, 2013, pp. 44–62; S. Kempgen, *The "Synkel" Inscription from Veliki Preslav – a New Reading*, WSA 86, 2015, pp. 109–117; И. Йорданов, *Корпус...*, pp. 174–181.

[136] Р. Костова, *Патронаж...*, pp. 204, 208; К. Попконстантинов, Р. Костова, *Манастирът на Георги...*, pp. 52–54; S. Kempgen, *The "Synkel"...*, p. 109.

[137] Н. Чанева-Дечевска, *Църкви и манастири...*, p. 118; M. Stancheva, *Veliki Preslav...*, pp. 60–61.

2.2. Painting

Not a single Old Bulgarian icon written on a wooden board survived to our times from the 9th or 10th century. This should not, however, lead to a conclusion that the Southern Slavs were still at that time strangers to the practice of creating depictions of Christ, Mother of God, and saints (once again gaining popularity in Byzantium after 843), or to the tempera painting. The information that the Preslavian temples housed icons that were venerated by the faithful can be found in several sources from the period.

Without a doubt the most interesting of those is the *Sermon Against the Heretics* by Cosmas the Priest. The experts maintain that it may have been created either several years after Peter's death (969–972), or in the first half of the 11th century. Regardless of which of these is correct, it is worth remembering that the aforementioned writer described the Bogomil heresy which appeared on Bulgarian lands – according to his own words – during the reign of the 'orthodox tsar Peter' (**в лѣта православѣрнааго цр҃ѧ Петра**)[138]. Moreover, by showing the incompatibility of the heterodox teachings with the Christian doctrine, Cosmas listed plentiful valuable information about the realities of the functioning of the Bulgarian church of the 10th century.

The topic of the cult of the holy paintings returns many times on the pages of the aforementioned treatise. The Old Bulgarian writer concluded that the Bogomils he denounced did not venerate icons, considering such practices idolatrous (**еретици же не кланѧют сѧ иконамъ, но кѹмиры наричють ıа**). Wanting to instil in the reader fear and loathing for his opponents, Cosmas added that heretics are worse than demons, since even demons fear the image of Christ written on a board (**Бѣси боıат сѧ ѡбраза г[о]с[под]нѧ на дъсцѣ написана**)[139]. The above passage constitutes evidence of the adoption of the tempera painting into the Old Bulgarian culture.

---

[138] Cosmas the Priest, 3.

[139] Cosmas the Priest, 10. Cf. К. Паскалева, *За началото на иконописта в българските земи (VII–XII в.)*, [in:] e a d e m, "*В началото бе словото*". *Сборник статии и студии 1967–2011 г.*, София 2011, p. 103.

The text of the *Sermon Against the Heretics* also allows establishing which iconographic schemes that were characteristic to the Byzantine sacred art have also been known in Bulgaria during the times of Cosmas the Priest and tsar Peter. For in an apostrophe to the Mother of God, the Slavic polemist clearly states that there are pictorial depictions of Christ in his physical form, held in Mary's arms (**єгоже ѡбразъ телесныи видѧ-щє на иконѣ на рѹкоу твоєю**)[140]. We can assume, that icons of *Hodegetria* or *Eleusa* are described here[141]. In another part of the narrative he mentions a depiction of the Son of God (**ѡбразъ г[о]с[подє]нь на иконѣ написанъ**)[142] and representations of the Mother of God (**с[(вѧ]тыꙗ б[огороди]ца М[а]ріа видимъ иконоу**)[143]. In the anathema at the end of the work, Cosmas in turn lists icons on which Mary, Christ and the saints were depicted (**иконы г[о]с[под]нѧ и б[о]городичины и всѣх' с[вѧ]тыхъ**)[144].

What is interesting, within the Old Bulgarian polemist's treatise we may find both mentions of specific gestures made by the faithful during the veneration of the holy icons (e.g. bowing or kissing)[145], as well as passages attesting to the adaptation by the Bulgarian church of the 10th century elements of the Byzantine theology of icons[146].

The fact that icons written on wood depicting Christ and saints were to be found in Bulgarian churches during Peter's reign is also attested by Byzantine historiographers. Leo the Deacon and John Skylitzes both noted that among the treasures captured in Bulgaria (most likely from

---

140 Cosmas the Priest, 31.

141 К. Паскалева, *За началото на иконописта...*, p. 103.

142 Cosmas the Priest, 32.

143 Cosmas the Priest, 33.

144 Cosmas the Priest, 70.

145 Cosmas the Priest, 32–33, 70. Cf. L. Praszkow, *Rozwój i rozpowszechnienie ikony w Bułgarii od IX do XIX w.*, [in:] *Tysiąc lat ikony bułgarskiej IX–XIX w. Muzeum Narodowe w Warszawie. Wystawa ze zbiorów bułgarskich*, Warszawa 1978, p. 8.

146 Cosmas the Priest, 31 (**Честь бо иконнаꙗ на прьвоѡбразнааго прєходить**); 33 (**иконѣ бо кланѧюще сѧ, нє шарѹ, ни дъсцѣ покланѧєм сѧ, но томоу бывшоуѹмоу тацѣмъ образомъ**). Cf. Ю. Великов, *Иконопочитанието и иконоотрицанието в "Беседа против богомилите" на Козма Презвитер*, [in:] *ΤΡΙΑΝΤΑΦΥΛΛΟ. Юбилеен сборник в чест на 60-годишнината на проф. Христо Трендафилов*, ed. В. Панайотов, vol. I, Шумен 2013, pp. 365–374.

the capital Preslav) in 971 by the emperor John I Tzymiskes was an icon, depicting the Mother of God, holding the Son of God in her arms[147]. The source evidence quoted above does not, however, allow the answering of one fundamental question: whether the icons kept in Bulgarian churches of the 10th century were imported from Byzantium, or whether they were the work of local artists.

Characteristic of the Old Bulgarian art of the 9th and 10th centuries is the tradition of creating icons on ceramic tiles, which in its way has even foreseen analogous trends in Byzantine painting. The dissemination of this practice in the capital Preslav is usually explained in the literature of the subject with acceptance of contemporary artistic impulses arriving to the Balkans through Cappadocia from the culturally important Christian centres of the East: Palestine, Syria, Egypt, and perhaps also from the countries of the Orient[148]. The development of workshops manufacturing polychrome ceramics in the new capital of the Bulgarian state, intended primarily for decorating the interiors of the buildings being erected in this period, was also determined by a certain practical consideration: the availability on site of a cheap and easy to work raw material, i.e. the kaolin clay[149].

The beginnings of the discussed phenomenon are usually dated to the end of the 9th century, and associated with Symeon's foundation activity – the transfer of the seat of the Bulgarian rulers to Preslav and with the rapid expansion of this centre, intended to give it the rank and urban-

---

[147] Leo the Deacon, IX, 12, p. 158; John Skylitzes, p. 310. Cf. L. Praszkow, *Rozwój*..., p. 8; M. Stancheva, *Veliki Preslav*..., p. 17; Л.Н. Мавродинова, *Стенната живопис в България до края на XIV в.*, София 1995, p. 14; Т. Тотев, *Монастыри в Плиске*..., p. 379; К. Паскалева, *За началото на иконописта*..., pp. 103–104; Н. Мавродинов, *Старобългарското*..., p. 316.

[148] С. Ваклинов, *Формиране*..., pp. 216–220; В. Гюзелев, *Зараждане и развитие на старобългарската култура и изкуство*, [in:] *Кратка история на България*, ed. И. Димитров, София 1981, p. 93; M. Stancheva, *Veliki Preslav*..., p. 37; Л.Н. Мавродинова, *Стенната живопис*..., p. 14; К. Паскалева, *За началото на иконописта*..., p. 99; Н. Мавродинов, *Старобългарското*..., p. 317; J.M. Wolski, *Budownictwo kościelne i klasztorne*, [in:] M.J. Leszka, K. Marinow, *Carstwo bułgarskie. Polityka – społeczeństwo – gospodarka – kultura. 866–971*, Warszawa 2015, p. 275.

[149] С. Ваклинов, *Формиране*..., p. 215.

istic shape of a truly capital metropolis[150]. On the other hand, it is difficult to determine for how long the artists' workshops that created the ceramic icons in Preslav continued to function; did they still exist during Peter's reign? Bulgarian researchers, Totyu Totev and Rossina Kostova are of the opinion that they must have been active at least until the mid-10th century.[151] Having analysed the numismatic and sphragistic material (discussed earlier in this chapter) that was found in Preslav during archaeological works, one may assume that the artefacts discussed here were created during the first decades of Peter's reign in the workshops of the so-called 'palace monastery' and in the vicinity of the Round Church[152].

Writing about Preslavian ceramic icons it would be impossible not to mention, even if briefly, the famous image of St. Theodore Stratelates, discovered in the ruins of the monastery located in Patleyna. The literature of the subject usually accepts that this artefact, considered to be the apogee of the Old Bulgarian painting, was created at the end of the 9th, or at the turn of the 9th and 10th centuries[153]. This dating corresponds

---

[150] *Ibidem*, pp. 215–217; В. Гюзелев, *Зараждане…*, p. 93; M. Stancheva, *Veliki Preslav…*, p. 37; Л.Н. Мавродинова, *Стенната живопис…*, p. 15; Т. Тотев, *Преславските ателиета за рисувана керамика*, ППре 7, 1995, p. 101; idem, *The Palace Monastery…*, p. 148; idem, *Производство рисованной керамики в болгарских монастырях*, АДСВ 32, 2001, pp. 109–110; A. Djourova, G. Guerov, *Les trésors des icônes bulgares*, Paris 2009, pp. 12, 18; R. Kostova, *Polychrome ceramics in Preslav, 9th to 11th centuries: Where were they produced and used?*, [in:] *Byzantine Trade 4th–12th Centuries. The Archaeology of Local, Regional and International Exchange*, ed. M.M. Mango, Aldershot 2009, pp. 97–98; К. Паскалева, *За началото на иконописта…*, p. 100.

[151] Т. Тотев, *Преславските ателиета…*, p. 101; idem, *The Palace Monastery…*, p. 148; idem, *Производство рисованной…*, p. 109; R. Kostova, *Polychrome ceramics…*, p. 98.

[152] Т. Тотев, *Преславските ателиета…*, pp. 106–108; idem, *The Palace Monastery…*, p. 148; idem, *Производство рисованной…*, pp. 119–123.

[153] K. Weitzmann, M. Chatzidakis, K. Miatev, S. Radojčić, *Fruhe Ikonen. Sinai. Griechenland. Bulgarien. Jugoslavien*, Sofia–Belgrad 1972, p. LV; С. Ваклинов, *Формиране…*, p. 218; L. Praszkow, *Rozwój…*, p. 8; В. Гюзелев, *Зараждане…*, p. 93; M. Stancheva, *Veliki Preslav…*, pp. 31–35, 62; D. Talbot Rice, *Art of the Byzantine Era*, London 1993, p. 115; Л.Н. Мавродинова, *Стенната живопис…*, p. 15; K. Onasch, A. Schnieper, *Ikony. Fakty i legendy*, transl. Z. Szanter, Warszawa 2002, p. 248; A. Djourova, G. Guerov, *Les trésors…*, pp. 18–19; G. Minczew, *Ceramiczna ikona św. Teodora Stratylaty*, [in:] *Leksykon tradycji*

to the findings of Totyu Totev, who assumed, based on the analysis of the numismatic material gathered on the site (including coins minted during the reign of the emperor Leo VI the Wise), that the workshops of the Patleyna monastery were operational during the reign of Symeon[154].

The images being discussed here were made with non-abrasive paints on ca. 20 ceramic tiles measuring 12 x 12 cm, fired from the local white clay, and subsequently glazed. The head of the saint was presented *en face*, and his depiction can be characterised as static and austere. The painting is kept in warm, ochre-yellow tone, and the dark browns with which the hair, beard, eyes and robes of the figure were conveyed contrast with the gold of the halo and the bright beige of the background[155]. Some of the researchers are of the opinion that the way in which St. Theodore is depicted on the icon from the Patleina monastery corresponds to the models widespread in the Byzantine painting of the 9th and 10th centuries[156].

On the other hand, it would be difficult to present even a single example of a ceramic icon that would have definitely been created during the 927–969 period. According to Liliana Mavrodinova, the artefact depicting enthroned St. Paul should be considered to have come from Peter's era (Totyu Totev identifies the man shown on the painting as Christ)[157], and produced in a workshop that existed most likely until the mid-10th century by the so-called 'palace monastery'[158]. It cannot be ruled out that other artefacts were also created in this workshop during

bułgarskiej, ed. G. Szwat-Gyłybowa, Warszawa 2011, p. 61; К. Паскалева, *За началото на иконописта*..., p. 99.

[154] Т. Тотев, *Преславските ателиета*..., pp. 103–104; idem, *Производство рисованной*..., p. 115.

[155] L. Praszkow, *Rozwój*..., p. 8; D. Talbot Rice, *Art*..., pp. 115, 188; G. Minczew, *Ceramiczna ikona*..., p. 61; Н. Мавродинов, *Старобългарското*..., pp. 321–322.

[156] С. Ваклинов, *Формиране*..., p. 218; К. Паскалева, *За началото на иконописта*..., p. 99; Н. Мавродинов, *Старобългарското*..., p. 322.

[157] T. Totev, *The Palace Monastery*..., p. 148; idem, *Монастыри в Плиске*..., p. 379.

[158] Л.Н. Мавродинова, *Стенната живопис*..., p. 15; A. Djourova, G. Guerov, *Les trésors*..., pp. 20–21.

the life of Symeon's son, among them the icon of the *Hodegetria*[159] or the plaque depicting St. Cyril of Alexandria[160].

The interiors of churches erected during the 10th century in the south-western part of the Bulgarian state were instead decorated with wall paintings. Unfortunately, it is difficult to give a precise answer to the question of which of the surviving examples thereof can be dated to 927–969. To imagine how the interiors of the Western Bulgarian temples must have looked like during the times of tsar Peter, and how remarkable was the quality of the paintings then created, let us examine in turn all of the fragments of polychromies created during the 9th and 10th centuries.

During the archaeological excavations in Strumitsa, carried out in 1973, a relatively well preserved painting was uncovered on the western wall of the crypt situated under the church dedicated to the Fifteen Martyrs of Tiberioupolis. In the literature of the subject it is usually dated to the turn of the 9th and 10th centuries. In accordance with the middle-Byzantine art canon, it presents the male figures half-length and *en face*, arranged in three rows. One may assume that these are the depictions of the saints in whose honour the aforementioned church was raised. In the topmost part of the composition we find figures of four men. According to experts, the saints imagined there are Timothy, Comasios, Eusebios and Theodore. In the second rank there are six portrayals, however only two of these survived to our times in their entirety. Over the course of centuries, the lowest part of wall painting has suffered the most: presently, we may admire only two of the images, located on the right side of the composition. The polychrome was made using lively colours: the static figures of the men, dressed in red-and-orange or purple robes, with heads surrounded by round, golden halos contrast with dark blue, nearly black background[161].

---

[159] T. Totev, *The Palace Monastery*..., p. 148; idem, *Монастыри в Плиске*..., p. 379.

[160] R. Kostova, *Polychrome ceramics*..., p. 111.

[161] В. Гюзелев, *Зараждане*..., p. 92; Л.Н. Мавродинова, *Стенната живопис*..., pp. 17–18; D. Cheshmedjiev, *Notes on the Cult of the Fifteen Tiberioupolitan Martyrs in Medieval Bulgaria*, SCer 1, 2011, pp. 146–148; S. Korunovski, E. Dimitrova, *Painting and Architecture in Medieval Macedonia. Artists and Works of Art*, Skopje 2011, p. 11; J.M. Wolski, *Budownictwo kościelne*..., p. 276.

One may suppose that the paintings adorning the interior of the church of St. Leontios, located near Vodocha, were created near the end of the 10th century. Unfortunately, only several small fragments of the original polychrome survived to our times. Among these, the incompletely preserved expressive depiction of the execution of Forty Martyrs deserves particular attention. The naked figures of the saints are outright striking in their vividness. The artist was inclined to realistically express the extreme emotions accompanying the men at the moment of death: the pain, despair and fear emanate from the faces, postures and gestures of the over a dozen people that can be seen on the surviving part of the composition. Moreover, the images of the martyrs have been individualised: next to elderly men there are youths, next to those who accepted their faith others are desperately fighting for survival. Aside from the scene inside the church of St. Leontios that is being analysed here, several other paintings survived as well. These are mainly half-length depictions of saints, showing some similarity to the images from the crypt under the church in Strumitsa[162].

The wealth of painted decorations was characteristic also of several religious buildings in Kastoria, added to the Bulgarian state during the reign of prince Boris-Michael. Most likely it was already during the reign of this ruler that the basilica of St. Stephen was built. Fragments of the original polychrome dated to ca. 889 (based on the *graffiti* discovered on the surface of the paintings) have been found in the western part of this church. Among these, the scene of the Judgement Day located on one of the walls of the narthex and the images of saints decorating the pillars deserve particular attention[163].

The turn of the 9th and 10th centuries has also seen the creation of the oldest wall paintings in the Kastorian basilica dedicated to the Archangels.

[162] В. Гюзелев, *Зараждане...*, p. 93; Л.Н. Мавродинова, *Стенната живопис...*, p. 18; S. Korunovski, E. Dimitrova, *Painting and Architecture...*, pp. 12–13; Н. Мавродинов, *Старобългарското...*, pp. 387–390.

[163] A.W. Epstein, *Middle Byzantine Churches of Kastoria. Dates and Implications*, ArtB 62.2, 1980, pp. 190, 192, 199; Л.Н. Мавродинова, *Стенната живопис...*, pp. 18–19; E. Drakopoulou, *Kastoria. Art, Patronage and Society*, [in:] *Heaven and Earth. Cities and Countryside in Greece*, ed. J. Albani, E. Chalkia, Athens 2013, p. 117.

Unfortunately, only fragments of these survived to our times. For example: in the apse of the *diaconicon* of the church we find full length depiction of Matthew the Evangelist. The saint is presented in a static pose, his right hand raised in a blessing gesture. His face is austere, and the giant eyes seem to be gazing directly at the viewer. The head is surrounded by a halo, and the entire figure is presented against a dark blue background. The experts are willing to suppose that the image was created by the same group of artists who decorated the interior of the church of St. Stephen[164].

The paintings from the interior of the church of St. Kosmas and Damianos in Kastoria come, on the other hand, from a later period. The literature of the subject usually dates them to the time of Samuel's reign (976–1014, formally as a Bulgarian tsar between 997–1014)[165], or even to sometime in the first thirty years of the 11th century[166]. Examining the ascetic and hieratic depictions of the saints (Basil, Nicholas, Constantine and Helena) that have been preserved on the walls of the church, one might see their stylistic similarity to the paintings from the basilicas of St. Stephen and that of the Archangels discussed earlier. Perhaps those scholars who in the Kastorian paintings would like to see a reflection of the artistic currents flowing to the Balkans from Asia Minor are therefore correct[167]. This hypothesis appears to also be supported by the fact that the founder of Constantinople and his mother were depicted in the north-western corner of the narthex of the church dedicated to Kosmas and Damianos. The canon of portraying Constantine and Helena with a relic of the True Cross was, after all, created most likely (ca. mid-9th century) in Cappadocia[168].

---

164 A.W. Epstein, *Middle...*, pp. 190, 192, 199; Λ.Н. Мавродинова, *Стенната живопис...*, p. 19; E. Drakopoulou, *Kastoria...*, pp. 117, 122; J.M. Wolski, *Budownictwo kościelne...*, p. 276.

165 Λ.Н. Мавродинова, *Стенната живопис...*, p. 20; E. Drakopoulou, *Kastoria...*, p. 117; Н. Мавродинов, *Старобългарското...*, pp. 377–378.

166 A.W. Epstein, *Middle...*, pp. 196–199.

167 В. Гюзелев, *Зараждане...*, p. 92; Λ.Н. Мавродинова, *Стенната живопис...*, pp. 18–19; A.W. Epstein, *Middle...*, p. 197.

168 L. Brubaker, *To Legitimize an Emperor. Constantine and Visual Authority in the 8th and 9th Centuries*, [in:] *New Constantines. The Rhythm of Imperial Renewal in Byzantium, 4th–13th Centuries. Papers from the 26th Spring Symposium of Byzantine Studies, St Andrews, March 1992*, ed. P. Magdalino, Cambridge 1994, pp. 141–142;

Samuel's reign is also often associated with the creation of the painted decorations in the basilica of St. Achilles (surviving in a very poor state) located by the lake Prespa[169], and with the execution of the oldest mediaeval frescoes in the rotunda of St. George (built in the 4th century) in Sofia. Under the central dome of the latter church we find eight angelic figures, full of grace, presented with their wings outstretched, in flight. They are extraordinarily dynamic, bringing to mind association with Byzantine miniature painting from the so-called 'Macedonian Renaissance' period. The viewer's attention is drawn by both intricately draped curls of the angels, as well as by their windswept robes and soft modelling of their facial features. Similar characteristics can also be seen in the images of the prophets Jonas and John the Baptist, discovered in the interior of the rotunda in Sofia[170].

Ch. Walter, *The Iconography of Constantine the Great. Emperor and Saint*, Leiden 2006, p. 46.

[169] В. Гюзелев, *Зараждане...*, p. 93; Л.Н. Мавродинова, *Стенната живопис...*, pp. 20–21; S. Korunovski, E. Dimitrova, *Painting and Architecture...*, p. 14.

[170] В. Гюзелев, *Зараждане...*, p. 93; И. Кандарашева, *Стенописите от първия живописен слой в църквата "Св. Георги" в София*, Pbg 19.4, 1995, pp. 94–113; Л.Н. Мавродинова, *Стенната живопис...*, pp. 21–22; Н. Мавродинов, *Старобългарското...*, pp. 390–392; J.M. Wolski, *Budownictwo kościelne...*, pp. 275–276.

PART THREE
THE INTERPRETATIONS

A. MEDIEVAL VISIONS

I

Mirosław J. Leszka

The Portrayal of Peter in Mediaeval Sources

1. Byzantine Sources

Remarks about tsar Peter can be found across various sources of Byzantine provenance, from historiographic to hagiographic works[1]. From the perspective of creating his image, the most important are the historiographic works. Peter is mentioned in texts that are associated with Symeon Logothetes, in the book VI of *Continuation of Theophanes*, in the *Historia* of Leo the Deacon, as well as in the works of later authors – John Skylitzes (eleventh century) and John Zonaras (twelfth century).

1.1. Peter's Titulature in the Byzantine Sources

Firstly, it is worth noting how Peter was titled in the Byzantine sources, which may to some degree attest to the attitudes the Byzantines had toward him. According to the Byzantine-Bulgarian treaty of 927, it

[1] The Reader can find a discussion of these in the chapter untitled 'Sources and Modern Scholarship' of the present volume. Cf. also M.J. L e s z k a, *Wizerunek władców pierwszego państwa bułgarskiego w bizantyńskich źródłach pisanych (VIII – pierwsza połowa XII wieku)*, Łódź 2004, pp. 130–131.

would appear that Peter was given the right to the title of the 'basileus of the Bulgarians'[2]. This change in the titulature of the Bulgarian ruler, although without naming Peter specifically, is mentioned by Constantine Porphyrogennetos in *The Book of Ceremonies*:

> To the archon, by the grace of God, of Bulgaria: *In the name of the Father and of the Son and Holy Spirit, our one and only true God, Constantine and Romanos, having faith in God alone, emperors of the Romans, to our beloved spiritual son and archon, by the grace of God, of the most Christian nation of the Bulgarians.* It is more fittingly expressed: *Constantine and Romanos, pious sovereigns in Christ our God and emperors of the Romans, to our beloved spiritual son, the lord so-and-so, emperor of Bulgaria* (βασιλέα Βουλγαρίας).[3]

Constantine, who after all was unsympathetic towards the Bulgarians, including Peter himself[4], did not omit this fact; one could therefore expect that titling the ruler of the northern neighbour of Byzantium 'basileus of the Bulgarians' should have been common in the Byzantine sources. This, however, is not the case – the title appears only sporadically. We find it in a letter from Theophylaktos, the patriarch of Constantinople, addressed to Peter[5]. The patriarch, being the son of Romanos Lekapenos, was related by marriage to Peter, and the letter itself was drafted in the patriarch's chancery. The use of the official title of the Bulgarian rulers is completely understandable. The *II Sigillion* of emperor Basil II from May 1020, issued for the Archbishop of Ohrid, also refers to Peter as basileus[6]. This document was issued by the imperial chancery, and was to be the legal basis for the functioning of the Bulgarian Archbishopric. The authors

---

[2] Cf. Part One, Chapter III, Point 2 of the present book.

[3] Constantine VII Porphyrogennetos, *The Book of Ceremonies*, II, 48, p. 690 (transl. p. 690).

[4] Г.Г. Литаврин, *Константин Багрянородный о Болгарии и Болгарах*, [in:] *Сборник в чест на акад. Димитър Ангелов*, ed. В. Велков, София 1994, pp. 30–37.

[5] *Letter of the Patriarch Theophylaktos to Tsar Peter*, p. 311.

[6] Basil II, *Sigillion II*, p. 556: Πέτρου τοῦ βασιλέος. Cf. M.J. Leszka, *Wizerunek…*, p. 131; Д. Чешмеджиев, *Цар Петър във византийските извори*, [in:] *Кръгла маса. "Златният век на цар Симеон: политика, религия и култура"*, ed. В. Станев, София 2014, p. 108.

of this text, working on the basis of the imperial archives, certainly must have known the proper title of the Bulgarian ruler, and the *Sigillion* itself, being a legal act, required precise wording.

In historiographic sources, Peter was outright called a basileus by John Skylitzes[7], while Symeon Logothetes, Continuator of George the Monk and book VI of Continuator of Theophanes called him a basileus as the husband of Maria (ὡς βασιλεῖ προσηρμόσθη ἀνδρί)[8]. The title of an Archon was used frequently[9]. In Leo the Deacon we find the title ἡγήτορ[10] and ἀρχηγός[11]. Constantine Porphyrogennetos called Peter by the title κύριος[12]. Very frequently, the Byzantine authors have not used any title at all, and referred to the Bulgarian ruler as Peter the Bulgarian, or simply used his name alone[13]. All of the titles listed above that were used to refer to Peter were firmly embedded in Byzantine literature[14]. What may come as a surprise is the fact that in the historiographic works only John Skylitzes

[7] John Skylitzes, p. 255. It should be noted that the title *basileus* does not appear in all of the copies of John Skylitzes' work. It was replaced with the term *archegos* [Viennese manuscript no. 35 (A), Coinslin manuscript no. 136 (C)], or *krator* [Milanese manuscript, Ambros. 912, (B)]. This question was noted by J. Bonarek, *Romajowie i obcy w kronice Jana Skylitzesa. Identyfikacja etniczna Bizantyńczyków i ich stosunek do obcych w świetle kroniki Jana Skylitzesa*, Toruń 2003, p. 147, fn. 266.

[8] Symeon Logothete, p. 329; Continuator of George the Monk, p. 907; Continuator of Theophanes, VI, 23, p. 415. Cf. Z.A. Brzozowska, *Car i caryca czy cesarz i cesarzowa Bułgarów? Tytulatura Piotra i Marii-Ireny Lekapeny w średniowiecznych tekstach słowiańskich (Jak powinniśmy nazywać władców bułgarskich z X stulecia)*, WS 62, 2017, pp. 17–26.

[9] Continuator of George the Monk, p. 904; Symeon Logothetes, 136, 45, p. 326; John Skylitzes, pp. 223, 225 (as was mentioned above, this author also used the title basileus); the title *archon* was used both before and after the conclusion of peace); Pseudo-Symeon, p. 740; Leo the Deacon, IV, 5, p. 62.

[10] Leo the Deacon, V, 2, p. 78.

[11] Leo the Deacon, IV, 5, p. 61.

[12] Constantine VII Porphyrogennetos, *On the Governance of the Empire*, 13.148.

[13] Np. Symeon Logothetes, 136, 45, p. 326; 47, p. 327; 51, p. 328; Continuator of Teophanes, VI, 28, p. 419; VI, 35, p. 422; Continuator of George the Monk, pp. 905, 906, 910; Pseudo-Symeon, p. 744; cf. M.J. Leszka, *Wizerunek*..., p. 132; Д. Чешмеджиев, *Цар Петър*..., p. 108.

[14] On this subject see: Г. Бакалов, *Средновековният български владетел. Титулатура и инсигнии*, [2]София 1995, pp. 98–195.

directly called Peter a basileus. What is the reason for this? Avoiding the use of the title of 'basileus' in relation to Peter was, it seems, an intentional move, aimed at lowering his position in relation to the Byzantine emperor. It is obvious that the Bulgarian ruler bearing the title of the basileus of the Bulgarians was not equal to the Byzantine emperor, however it needs to be remembered that in Byzantium there was a strongly embedded conviction that the only one who should be entitled to be called a basileus was the emperor ruling from Constantinople. It is worth reminding how vigorously the Byzantines protested against the adoption of an imperial title by Charlemagne[15], or how hostile Nikephoros II Phokas was towards Otto I, the restorer of the imperial institution in the West[16]. The Byzantines' concessions to Peter in this matter were made easier by the fact that Symeon, his predecessor, has already managed, in a way, to make them used to the idea by using the title both with and without their approval, and even by claiming the tile of the basileus of the *Rhomaioi*[17]. Peter likely did not have such great ambitions, and was satisfied with a title of an 'ethnic' emperor. With time, when the Byzantines' memory of Symeon's aspirations and of his victories over them partly faded, a concession regarding the imperial title for his son may have appeared to be an excessive one. It is for this reason, one might think, that they tried to forget about it. This tendency is particularly notable in the works written by the emperor Constantine VII Porphyrogennetos and the authors associated with him. The emperor's dislike towards the Bulgarians is highlighted by many of the scholars; its

[15] C.N. Tsirpanlis, *Byzantine Reactions to the Coronation of Charlemagne*, Βυζ 6, 1974, pp. 347–360.

[16] С.А Иванов, *Византийско-болгарские отношения в 966–969 гг.*, ВВ 42, 1981 pp. 95–96.

[17] On Symeon's efforts to obtain an imperial title – И. Божилов, *Цар Симеон Велики (893–927). Златният век на Средновековна България*, София 1983, p. 98sqq; Г. Бакалов, *Средновековният...*, pp. 150–168; M.J. Leszka, *Symeon I Wielki a Bizancjum. Z dziejów stosunków bułgarsko-bizantyńskich w latach 893–927*, Łódź 2013, pp. 138–158; 236–247; А. Николов, *"Великият между царете". Изграждане и утвърждаване на българската царска институция през управлението на Симеон I*, [in:] *Българският златен век. Сборник в чест на цар Симеон Велики (893–927)*, ed. В. Гюзелев, И.Г. Илиев, К. Ненов, Пловдив 2015, pp. 149–188; К. Маринов, *Византийската имперска идея и претенциите на цар Симеон според словото "За мира с българите"*, КМС 25, 2016, pp. 342–352.

origins were in part of personal nature[18], and in part were a consequence of continued envisaging of Bulgarians as a potential, and dangerous, enemy[19]. A similar proclivity can also be seen in Leo the Deacon, which can be explained by the fact that this author's work was created at the time of war between Byzantium and tsar Samuel, and the author himself had a strong, negative attitude towards the Bulgarians, resulting from his experiences from the campaign of 986, which the Byzantines lost. The use of nomenclature normally employed towards Bulgarian rulers of the pagan period, which did not reflect Peter's actual title that was accepted by Byzantium, was likely done for three reasons. Firstly, it was intended to reduce his position in the eyes of Byzantine readers; secondly, it was an expression of a tendency present in Byzantine literature to use archaic language; and thirdly, it was a symptom of a visible dislike towards the Bulgarians, present among some of the authors.

John Skylitzes, who did use the title of 'basileus' in regard to Peter, was writing his work at the time when Bulgaria no longer existed. Certainly, the fact that Byzantium destroyed the state that has previously been governed by a ruler bearing the title of a basileus may have filled Byzantines with pride. A confirmation of this view can be seen in, firstly, the fact that Boris II, the last Bulgarian ruler of the first state was frequently referred to, more than any of his predecessors, as βασιλεὺς τῶν βουλγάρων[20]. Similarly, also the rulers of the so-called state of Cometopouloi, with whom Basil II

[18] Г. Бакалов, *Царската промулгация на Петър и неговите приемници в светлината на българо-византийските дипломатически отношения след договора от 927 г.*, ИП 39.6, 1983, pp. 36–37; Г.Г Литаврин, *Константин Багрянородный...*, pp. 32–36; J. Shepard, *A marriage too far? Maria Lekapena and Peter of Bulgaria*, [in:] *The Empress Theophano. Byzantium and the West at the turn of the first millennium*, ed. A. Davids, Cambridge 1995, pp. 130–134.

[19] Constantine VII Porphyrogennetos, *On the Governance of the Empire*, 5. The emperor points to the Pechenegs as the force that was a counterweight to the Bulgarians. Cf. J. Shepard, *Constantine VII's Doctrine of "Containment" of the Rus*, [in:] *Геннадиос. К 70-летию академика Г.Г. Литаврина*, ed. Б.Н. Флоря, Москва 1999, pp. 272–274.

[20] John Skylitzes, p. 297, cf. p. 255, 310; John Zonaras, p. 529, cf. p. 535–536 (Zonaras, in his description of the times of Boris II, relies on the account of Skylitzes, and therefore it is not surprising that he referred to the Bulgarian ruler as a basileus); Leo the Deacon, VIII, 6, p. 136; IX, 12, p. 158 (here, instead of 'Bulgarians', we find

fought and eventually won, were considered by John Skylitzes to have been emperors[21]. Secondly, we can see this in the description of the triumph of John I Tzymiskes, where it was very clearly stressed that the Byzantines have captured the imperial clothing and imperial insignia of power of the Bulgarian rulers[22]. It cannot be ruled out that John Skylitzes may have been also influenced by the fact that following the conquest of Bulgaria in 1018, part of the Bulgarian nobility, including representatives of Samuel's family, were incorporated into the Byzantine ruling elite. A symbolic expression of this phenomenon was the marriage of Isaac I Komnenos, the emperor in the years 1057–1059, with Catherine, a daughter of John Vladislav.

1.2. Portrayal of Peter in the Context of the Conclusion of Peace in 927 and at the Beginning of his Reign

Peter most commonly appears in the Byzantine sources in relation to the conclusion of peace in 927. In the Byzantine chronicles we find an exceedingly unified sequence of events that led to the aforementioned treaty, which makes an impression that there was some kind of an official version on which they all based their work. The sequence of events was as follows: the death of Symeon – the military expedition of Peter against the Macedonia theme – the secret mission to Constantinople

'Mysians'). Perhaps the attitude of Skylitzes and Zonaras was also a result of the Bulgarian influence at the imperial court at the time when they were writing their histories.

[21] John Skylitzes, pp. 358–359 (Ohrid as the capital of the Bulgarian basileioi).

[22] John Skylitzes, p. 310; John Zonaras, pp. 535–536; Leo the Deacon, IX, 12, pp. 158–159. On the subject of the celebrations associated with the triumph over the Bulgarians, see: В.Н. Златарски, *История на българската държава през средните векове*, vol. I/2, *Първо българско Царство. От славянизацията на държавата до падането на Първото царство (852–1018)*, София 1927, pp. 627–629; M. McCormick, *Eternal Victory: Triumphal Rulership in Late Antiquity, Byzantium and the Early Medieval West*, Cambridge 1987, pp. 171–175; see also: S. Rek, *Geneza tytułu carskiego w państwie zachodniobułgarskim*, BP 2, 1985, pp. 52–53; Г. Атанасов, *Инсигниите на средновековните български владетели. Корони, скиптри, сфери, оръжия, костюми, накити*, Плевен 1999, pp. 102–105; M.J. Leszka, *Wizerunek...*, pp. 141–142; T. Papamastorakis, *The Bamberg Hanging Reconsidered*, ΔΧΑΕ 24, 2003, pp. 375–392.

of the envoy Kalokir, with a peace offer extended out of fear of Romanos Lekapenos' counteraction – the acceptance of the peace offer by Romanos – negotiations in Mesembria – the arrival of the Bulgarian delegation led by George Sursuvul to the Byzantine capital – reaching an accord regarding conditions of the peace -- the meeting of Maria, the daughter of Christopher, by the Bulgarians – the arrival of Peter – the signing of the peace treaty – the marriage of Peter and Maria – the wedding reception – the newlyweds' departure from Constantinople. This is the framework of events associated with the treaty of 927, as presented by the historiographic sources[23]. It is clear from this account that the one who initiated the peace negotiations was Peter, and that he was motivated by the fear of the Romans, who were preparing an expedition against him. Moreover, he began the peace negotiations in secret, which could mean that he lacked the authority to impose his will on his own subjects. Byzantine historiographers present Peter, at the beginning of his reign, as a weak ruler, forced to ask for peace, and still lacking the authority in his own state. The most spectacular event during Peter's stay in Constantinople was his marriage with Maria Lekapene. This marriage was to guarantee the permanence of the peace treaty. The marriage of a woman from the imperial family to a foreigner was an unprecedented event in the history of Byzantium. What is notable, however, in the official account of the events is the lack of a mention, or even a hint, of the exceptional nature of this fact. The wedding celebrations in Constantinople were arranged in such a way as to show the Constantinopolitans that the marriage of Maria and Peter the Bulgarian was not dictated by the events, and that it was the beginning of a lasting peace[24]. Aretas of Caesarea, in his letter to Romanos Lekapenos, expressed hope that this relationship will bear good fruit[25], and the author of the speech *On the Treaty with the Bulgarians* claimed

---

[23] Pseudo-Symeon, pp. 740–741; Continuator of George the Monk, pp. 904–907; Leo Grammatikos, pp. 315–317; Continuator of Theophanes, pp. 412–415; John Skylitzes, pp. 222–224; John Zonaras, pp. 474–475.

[24] On the role of the marriage ceremony of Peter and Maria in Romanos Lekapenos' policy, cf. Part One, Chapter IV, point 2 of the present monograph.

[25] Arethas, p. 99.

that God removed Symeon and gave the ruler's place to Peter so that the latter could conclude the peace. In this manner, Peter at the same time became a tool in the hands of God[26].

The Byzantine historians saw the positive sides of the marriage of Maria and Peter, pointing to the conclusion of peace that the union has sealed, and highlighted the fact that it was not some great calamity for Maria herself who, while sad about losing regular contact with her family, on the other hand was happy to become a Bulgarian ruler, which certainly has to be seen as a sign of approval of Peter[27].

The words of criticism that came from under the pen of Constantine VII Porphyrogennetos in the *On the Governance of the Empire* are an exception to the positive reception of the marriage between Maria and Peter. He claimed that marrying Maria to a foreign ruler was in a breach of an existing law. The fact that it did happen was a consequence of the lack of education of Romanos Lekapenos, who was a simple man, and not born in purple. Constantine VII also disparaged the significance of the union itself, by writing that Maria was not a daughter of a legitimate emperor, and that it was not such a great detriment since the Bulgarians were, after all, Christians. However, even Constantine noted the fact that the conclusion of peace, of which Maria's marriage was a guarantee, brought freedom to many Byzantine captives[28].

---

[26] *On the Treaty with the Bulgarians*, 16, p. 278.371–378; R.J. Jenkins, *The Peace with Bulgaria (927) Celebrated by Theodore Daphnopates*, [in:] *Polychronion. Festschrift F. Dölger*, Heidelberg 1966, pp. 293, 297; Т. Тодоров, *"Слово за мира с българите" и българо-византийските политическо отношения през последние години от управлението на цар Симеон*, [in:] *България, българите и техните съседи през вековете. Изследвания и материали от научната конференция в памет на доц. д-р Христо Коларов, 30–31 октомври 1998 г., Велико Търново*, ed. Й. Андреев, Велико Търново 2001, pp. 141–150; K. Marinow, *Peace in the House of Jacob. A Few Remarks on the Ideology of Two Biblical Themes in the Oration, On the Treaty with the Bulgarians*, BMd 3, 2012, p. 91; idem, *Not David but Salomon: Tsar Peter I (927–969) according to the Oration 'On the Treaty with the Bulgarians'* (in press). Peter as Solomon, the son of Symeon-David, bringing to conclusion his father's plan.

[27] Continuator of Theophanes, p. 415; Continuator of George the Monk, pp. 906–907.

[28] Constantine VII Porphyrogennetos, *On the Governance of the Empire*, 13.146–163. Constantine VII derived the prohibition of marriages between

The beginnings of Peter's reign have been mentioned in particularly interesting passages found in two hagiographic sources, specifically: *Life of St. Mary the Younger*[29] and *Life of Luke the Younger*[30]. In the first of the texts we read: *his* [Symeon's – M.J.L.] *son Peter succeeded him. Behaving in an even more barbaric fashion, he destroyed to the ground the Thracian cities captured by his father*[31].

This passage relates to the events which occurred after Symeon's death, and which preceded the conclusion of the Byzantine-Bulgarian peace. The author of *Life of Luke the Younger*, in turn, has this to say about the beginning of Peter's reign:

> After a short time the sinner Symeon, who was responsible for spilling so much Christian blood, departed from men and was succeeded by his son Peter. He was clearly the heir to his father's dignity and wealth, but not to his savage and hatred; on the contrary, insofar as possible he repudiated his father's lineage and kinship. Thus he said farewell to blood and war and welcomed peace with us, transforming the scimitar and the spear and all iron armour into pruning hooks and mattocks, as the prophet would say.[32]

the imperial women and foreigners from the legislation of Constantine the Great, who never promulgated such a law. Cf. G. Prinzing, *Bizantyńczycy wobec obcych*, ed. K. Ilski, Poznań 1998, pp. 27–28; see also Part One, Chapter IV, point 2, of the present book.

[29] *Life of St. Mary the Younger*. On the subject of this source, see: W. Swoboda, *Żywot św. Marii*, [in:] *SSS*, vol. VII, p. 313; S. Kissas, *O βίος της Αγίος Μαρίας της Νέας ως πηγή για την αρχαιολγία και ιστορία της τέχνης*, BF 14, 1989, pp. 253–264. Cf. C. Mango, *The Byzantine Church at Vize (Bizye) in Thrace and St. Mary the Younger*, ЗРВИ 11, 1968, pp. 9–13; *PMZ II*, vol. IV, pp. 334–337, *s.v. Maria die Jüngere (von Bizye) (#24910)*; S. Constantinou, *A Byzantine hagiographical parody: Life of Mary the Younger I*, BMGS 34, 2010, pp. 160–181.

[30] *Life of St. Luke the Younger*, 40, pp. 58, 60. On the subject of the *Life* – G. Moravcsik, *Byzantinoturcica*, vol. I, *Die byzantinischen Quellen der Geschichte der Türkvölker*, Berlin 1958, pp. 568–569; *Life of St. Luke the Younger*, pp. IX–XVIII; on the subject of St. Luke, see: N. Oikonomides, *The First Century of the Monastery of Hosios Loukas*, DOP 46, 1992, pp. 245–255.

[31] *Life of St. Mary the Younger*, 26 (transl. p. 280).

[32] *Life of Luke the Younger*, 40, pp. 58, 60 (transl. pp. 59, 61).

How to explain this difference of opinion? It would seem that it is a result of the personal experiences of the authors. The former judged Peter through the lens of the events which occurred in Thrace, and which he may have witnessed personally. Meanwhile Greece, where the events of *Life of Luke the Younger* have taken place, had not been touched by the military activity occurring at the beginning of Peter I's reign. The reign itself certainly differed, in a positive manner, from Symeon's rule, when even these lands were raided. Peter's characterisation was built through comparison with his father. Peter was therefore lusting for neither fame nor riches. He had no tendency for cruelty, and loved people. He ceased the bloodshed, and most importantly made peace, which allowed discarding of weapons and resumption of normal life.

The beginnings of Peter's reign are also associated with the matter of the rebellion of his two brothers. The Byzantine historians do not present their own opinion here about Peter. However the way in which these events have been presented makes it possible to make some conclusions as to their intentions and opinions of the tsar. At first glance it might seem that according to the Byzantine historiographers the insurgence of John and Michael exposed Peter's weak position and lack of authority[33]. A closer examination of the accounts precludes such position. The fate of these rebellions unequivocally attests to this, as in both cases Peter emerged victorious without even having to fight with his brothers. In John's case, his plot was uncovered and its members, on Peter's unflinching orders, were harshly and exemplarily punished. The brother himself was treated with restraint, with imperial leniency, even gentleness, which Peter would likely have not been able to afford if he thought that John could constitute a serious threat.

As for Michael's rebellion, it ended, similarly to John's, even before it properly began, and without any intervention on Peter's part. This was caused by Michael's sudden death. Michael's supporters, fearing punishment from Peter, as John Skylitzes stressed, fled from Bulgaria. The way in which events happened during the rebellion clearly showed that Peter enjoyed both the protection of divine providence, had authority, and that

[33] Thus, e.g., J. B o n a r e k, *Romajowie...*, p. 146.

he was seen as a stern and resolute ruler, which in part must have been a result of the way in which he dealt with the plotters who supported John. The rebels moved against Peter only because they were led by Michael who, like Peter himself, was a son of Symeon and a member of the ruling family. Only he could have given them a hope of success. Once he was gone, the rebels knew they had no chance in a confrontation with the ruler.

The way in which the Byzantines presented Peter in the situations discussed above attests to, in my opinion, their view of him as a strong, determined ruler, who could deal with internal threats, and who enjoyed Divine protection. It might appear that this is contrary to what they wrote about him in the context of the events that preceded the conclusion of peace. One needs to remember, however, that their criteria for evaluating Peter were based on the Byzantine interests, and a desire to present the Byzantines in a better light.

What casts a certain shadow on the image of Peter as a ruler is a description we find in the passages devoted to his brothers' rebellions: the ruler was tricked by the Byzantine envoy, John, who, without Peter's permission, had taken his namesake from Preslav to Constantinople. Regardless of whether this information is true, it is worth noting that the Byzantine authors have not presented it in a manner that would be accusatory towards Peter. This should not be surprising, given that the 'abduction' of John showed the Byzantines in a favourable light.

1.3. Peter's Religious Attitude. Portrayal of the Ruler in the Final Years of his Reign

The second theme that is clearly apparent in relation to Peter are his dealings in religious matters. It was during Peter's reign that the Bogomil heresy began[34]. It was likely in this matter that he turned to the patriarch of Constantinople, who in turn penned something of a laudatory hymn

---

[34] On the subject of Bogomilism, cf. Part Two, Chapter VII, point 3 of the present book. There also the reference to the literature of the subject.

in Peter's honour; for it is in this manner that one might describe the beginning of a letter to the Bulgarian ruler:

> How great a treasure is a faithful and God-loving soul, our spiritual son and the best and finest of our relatives, especially when at the same time it is the soul of a ruler and a leader – such as Yourself – that knows how to love and worship that which is good and appropriate! For in leading a prudent life and acting well, it ensures well-being not only for itself, but also, by extending a most protective care over all those who are subject to its power, it cares on his behalf for what is the most important and concerning salvation. For what is more important or salutary than unblemished and true faith, and a salubrious concept of divinity, thanks to which with pure awareness we worship the One God, the Purest and the Most Holy? For that is the chief ingredient of our salvation.[35]

Undoubtedly, one can see here a certain rhetorical exaggeration, characteristic of the epistolary convention, a desire to flatter the addressee, or traces of the Byzantine theory of power, but perhaps, one would like to think, a respect for the man whose deep religiosity was widely known. A sentence penned by Leo the Deacon, in which he described Peter as *a pious and respected man*[36], resonates with Theophylaktos' letter. One might therefore think that the Byzantines highly valued the religious attitude of the Bulgarian ruler. This made even clearer by a reference to Peter made by Leo the Deacon in the aforementioned passage, where he called him ἡγήτορ τῶν Μυσῶν[37], not considering it appropriate to call him a basileus of the Bulgarians. For Leo the Deacon, Peter was certainly a worthy of respect, pious man, however only a leader of the Mysians, of

[35] *Letter of the Patriarch Theophylaktos to Tsar Peter*, p. 311.

[36] Leo the Deacon, V, 2, p. 78 (transl. p. 129). Cf. И. Дуйчев, *Стара българска книжнина*, vol. I, София 1943, p. 220; Л. Симеонова, *Образът на българския владетел във византийската книжнина (средата на IX – началото на XI в.). Няколко примера*, [in:] *Представата за "другия" на Балканите*, ed. Н. Данова, В. Димова, М. Калицин, София 1995, p. 27.

[37] Leo the Deacon, V, 2, p. 78.

barbarians. This remark excellently corresponds with a description of the Bulgarian embassy to Nikephoros II Phokas, penned by the emperor, which arrived in Constantinople to remind the Byzantines about the tribute that they were due to pay to the Bulgarians. The emperor was then supposed to have called the Bulgarians *the particularly wretched and abominable Scythian people*[38], and referred to Peter as a *leather-gnawing ruler clad in a leather jerkin*, which definitely must have been an insult[39]. It is not certain whether this scene has actually taken place[40], however the fact that Leo the Deacon, writing at the end of the tenth century, could have considered it plausible speaks volumes about the condescension with which the contemporary Byzantines treated their Bulgarian neighbours.

Peter's reign began in an atmosphere of conflict with the Byzantium, and ended in a similar fashion. The deterioration of the Byzantine--Bulgarian relations during the reign of Nikephoros II Phokas became a pretext for renewed interest in Peter. John Skylitzes mentioned that Nikephoros II Phokas demanded from Peter to stop the Hungarians who, through the Bulgarian territory, were making their way to Byzantium[41]. John Zonaras has written down the proud reply of the Bulgarian ruler, in which Peter refused to accede to the Byzantine emperor's demands and pointed out that he previously requested Byzantine assistance against the Hungarians, which he was denied. In the present situation, having formed peaceful relations with them, he saw no reason to start a war[42]. Peter

[38] Leo the Deacon, IV, 5, p. 61 (transl. p. 110).

[39] Leo the Deacon, IV, 5, p. 62 (transl. p. 110; see also fn. 37 on that page). This conclusion is confirmed by the fragments of the letters of Theophylaktos of Ohrid, in which the bishop writes with disgust about the Bulgarians, as of the people who 'stink of a goat's hide' – Theophylaktos of Ohrid, *Letters*, 4, 5; see also J. Shepard, *A marriage*..., p. 138.

[40] Cf. С.А. Иванов, *Византийско-болгарские*..., pp. 92–94; J. Bonarek, *Przyczyny i cele bułgarskich wypraw Światosława a polityka Bizancjum w latach sześćdziesiątych X w.*, SH 39, 1996, pp. 288–291; K. Marinow, *Dzicy, wyniośli i groźni górale. Wizerunek Bułgarów jako mieszkańców gór w wybranych źródłach greckich VIII–XII w.*, [in:] *Stereotypy bałkańskie. Księga jubileuszowa Profesor Ilony Czamańskiej*, ed. J. Paszkiewicz, Z. Pentek, Poznań 2011, pp. 41–42.

[41] John Skylitzes, pp. 275–276.

[42] John Zonaras, pp. 512–513.

was chastened for adopting this stance. Nikephoros Phokas arranged for the Rus' under Svyatoslav to attack the Bulgarians, who suffered a series of defeats. In the light of the Byzantine sources, Peter appears as a proud ruler, independent from the Byzantines, who near the end of his life was not able to lead an effective defence against the Rus incursion. Given the circumstances, the triumphant Leo the Deacon could afford to be compassionate to Peter when he was describing the circumstances of his death. The Bulgarian ruler, having heard of the defeats suffered by his troops in fighting the Rus', was to have become so sorrowful *in his extreme distress at the unexpected rout, suffered an attack of epilepsy, and departed this world*[43].

From the above deliberations, it becomes clear that the Byzantine authors associated Peter primarily with the establishing of lasting peace with the Empire in 927. In the sources that present the events from before the reign of the emperor Nikephoros Phokas (963–969), when the relations between the two countries have taken a turn for the worse, Peter is most often presented as a co-founder of peace, a deeply religious man, accepting the Byzantine understanding of a ruler's role in the religious matters. The Byzantine authors incidentally also indicate that Peter was able to effectively defend his position and sternly deal with his opponents. In the sources relating the events from the final years of his life, he is presented as a haughty man, daring to move against the Byzantine basileus, for which he was justly and severely punished.

It is worth highlighting that most often the Byzantine authors did not present their attitude towards, and appraisal of, Peter directly, which means that the reader of their works has to create an image of the Bulgarian ruler for himself, constructing it on the basis of the way in which particular events have been presented. The sole direct characterisation of Peter was included in the *Life of Luke the Younger*.

[43] Leo the Deacon, V, 2, p. 78 (transl. p. 129).

2. Bulgarian Sources

Mentions of Peter can be found in, i.a., the following mediaeval Bulgarian sources: *Sermon against the Heretics* of Cosmas the Priest, created in the period between the years immediately following Peter's death (969–972) and the 1040s[44]; *Service of St. Tsar Peter*, which was most likely written at the end of the tenth century[45]; *Tale of the Prophet Isaiah*/the so-called *Bulgarian Apocryphal Chronicle* – the work, most generally speaking, created during the Byzantine rule in Bulgaria (1018–1186)[46]; the Lives of John of Rila: *Folk Life of St John of Rila*, created most likely in the eleventh century[47]; *Prologue life of St. John of Rila (I)*, written in the thirteenth century[48]; *Prologue life of St. John of Rila (II)*, existing in the framework of *Dragan's Menaion* from the thirteenth century[49];

---

[44] Cosmas the Priest. On the subject of this source: G. Minczew, *Słowiańskie teksty antyheretyckie jako źródło do poznania herezji dualistycznych na Bałkanach*, [in:] *Średniowieczne herezje dualistyczne na Bałkanach. Źródła słowiańskie*, ed., transl., comment. G. Minczew, M. Skowronek, J.M. Wolski, Łódź 2015, pp. 13–57 (see the work for further publications on the subject).

[45] *Service of St. Tsar Peter*. The text is known from two fragmentary copies from the thirteenth century. Cf. *Ziemscy aniołowie, niebiańscy ludzie. Anachoreci w bułgarskiej literaturze i kulturze*, ed. G. Minczew, Białystok 2002, pp. 65–66.

[46] *Tale of the Prophet Isaiah*. O this source – K. Marinow, *Kilka uwag na temat ideologiczno-eschatologicznej wymowy "Bułgarskiej kroniki apokryficznej"*, FE 4. 6/7, 2007, pp. 61–75; I. Biliarsky, *The Tale of the Prophet Isaiah. The Destiny and Meanings of an Apocryphal Text*, Leiden–Boston 2013, *passim*.

[47] *Folk Life of St John of Rila*; on this source, see Й. Иванов, *Жития на св. Ивана Рилски с уводни бележки*, ГСУ.ИФФ 32.13, 1936, pp. 4–8; К. Иванова, *Най-старото житие за св. Иван и някои негови литературни паралели*, [in:] *Медиевистика и културна антропология. Сборник в чест на 40-годишната творческа дейност на проф. Д. Петканова*, ed. А. Ангушева, А. Милтенова, София 1998, pp. 37–47; М. Спасова, *Народно ли е народното (безименното) житие на св. Йоан Рилски*, Pbg 22.4, 1998, pp. 50–74; В. Панайотов, *За "народното житие" на св. Йоан Рилски*, ПКШ 4, 1999, pp. 92–98; *Ziemscy aniołowie*..., pp. 19–21.

[48] *Prologue life of St. John of Rila (I)*; on this source: Й. Иванов, *Жития на св. Ивана Рилски*..., pp. 11–13; Н.М. Дылевский, *Жития Иоанна Рыльского русских древлехранилищ и их болгарские источники (Краткие заметки к материалам и задачи дальнейшего исследования)*, ТОДРЛ 23, 1968, p. 280.

[49] *Prologue life of St. John of Rila (II)*; on its subject: Й. Иванов, *Жития на св. Ивана Рилски*..., pp. 13–15; Н.М. Дылевский, *Жития Иоанна Рыльского*..., p. 280;

the *Life of St. John of Rila* of Euthymios of Tarnovo, written down in the fourteenth century[50]; *Synodikon of Tsar Boril* – created in 1211[51]. The listed sources give, in my opinion, a good idea of how Peter was being presented in the mediaeval Bulgarian sources[52].

2.1. Titulature

Regarding the way in which Peter was referred to in the Bulgarian sources, he was consistently titled there as 'emperor/tsar' (**цр҃ь блъгаромъ / цр҃ь блъгарскыи**). This tendency can also be seen in works translated from Greek (Continuator of George the Monk, John Zonaras) in which, notably, Peter is called an emperor even when the Greek original did not use this title[53].

This tendency is not surprising. Bulgarian authors and translators simply reflected the actual state of the day, which was for them both rewarding and a cause for pride. It cannot be also ruled out that this pride was further reinforced by the fact that a considerable number of these works and manuscripts of earlier texts (from the tenth or eleventh centuries) came from the times when the Bulgarian rulers customarily used an imperial title.

I. Biliarsky, *St. Peter (927–969), Tsar of the Bulgarians*, [in:] *State and Church. Studies in Medieval Bulgaria and Byzantium*, ed. V. Gjuzelev, K. Petkov, Sofia 2011, p. 180.

[50] Euthymios of Tarnovo; for more on this text see: Й. Иванов, *Български старини...*, p. 369; idem, *Жития на св. Ивана Рилски...*, pp. 15–21; Н.М. Дылевский, *Жития Иоанна Рыльского...*, p. 280.

[51] *Synodikon of Tsar Boril*. For more on this source, see: *Борилов синодик. Издание и превод*, ed. И. Божилов, А. Тотоманова, И. Билярски, София 2010.

[52] The list of other mediaeval Bulgarian sources in which Peter appears (or rather, is only mentioned in passing), can be found in the following works: I. Biliarsky, *St. Peter...*, pp. 175–178; Д.И. Полывянный, *Царь Петр в исторической памяти болгарского средневековья*, [in:] *Средновековният българин и "другите". Сборник в чест на 60-годишнината на проф. дин Петър Ангелов*, ed. А. Николов, Г.Н. Николов, София 2013, pp. 137–145; Z.A. Brzozowska, *Car i caryca...*, pp. 20–22. The translations of the Byzantine chronicles into the Old Church Slavonic, which differ from the Greek originals only in minor details, fell outside the scope of my interest.

[53] Z.A. Brzozowska, *Car i caryca...*, pp. 17–26.

2.2. *The Sermon against the Heretics*

The Sermon against the Heretics of Cosmas the Priest is, perhaps, the earliest text of Bulgarian provenance in which we find a mention of Peter. It needs to be clearly stated, however, that it is only a passing remark[54]. It refers to Peter as an orthodox tsar, who is mentioned only to indicate that it was during his reign that the Bogomil heresy was born[55]. The stressing of the tsar's orthodoxy is perhaps not so much, or maybe not only, a reflection of the commonly held opinion of him, but a result of wanting to lay another accusation at the heretics' door, namely, that they have moved against such a pious ruler. Aside from this sole remark, the author of the speech does not mention Peter again.

2.3. Peter in the *Lives* of St. John of Rila

John – the most well known Bulgarian saint and anchorite, founder of a monastic community which grew into the famed Rila Monastery – was born ca. 876. We have no certain information about his origins or the reasons for which he decided to lead a hermit's life in the Rila Mountains which, ultimately, brought him renown and recognition, something he did not, after all, seek. As a result, he founded the aforementioned community, and became its first hegumenos. He passed away however, most likely in 946, once again a hermit[56].

---

[54] *Sermon against the Heretics*, 3, [in:] *Średniowieczne herezje dualistyczne*, p. 72: **в лѣта правовѣрнаго царѧ Петра** (*in the years of the orthodox Tsar Peter*, transl. p. 68).

[55] Peter was 'used' in a similar manner in the *Synodikon of Tsar Boril* (13b, p. 121), although in the remark discussing Bogomil's appearance he was not described as 'orthodox' (*Upon the priest Bogomil, who adopted the Manichaen heresy under Bulgarian King Peter* – transl. p. 344). In a separate passage of this text he is called *the holy king* (201b, p. 149, transl. p. 352). In the *Service of St. Tsar Peter* we find a fragment describing how tsar Peter has driven out the 'prince of darkness'. It would be tempting to conclude that the passage tells of fighting the heresy, however such interpretation might be going too far.

[56] On the subject of John of Rila, see i.a.: И. Дуйчев, *Рилският светец и неговата обител*, София 1947; I. Dobrev, *Sv. Ivan Rilski*, vol. I, Linz 2007; Б. Николова, *Монашество, манастири и манастирски живот в средновековна България*, vol. II, София 2010, pp. 790–815; Й. Андреев, *Иван Рилски*, [in:] Й. Андреев,

The *Lives* of John of Rila associate him with tsar Peter. The latter was to have been greatly impressed by John's saintliness[57]. Authors of the *Lives* focus the topic of relations between the ruler and the saint on two matters: the efforts of the former to meet John, and the care he took to ensure the mortal remains of the holy man were given appropriately dignified treatment. To show the way in which Peter was presented in the *Lives* of John of Rila, I will use the oldest example known to us, the *Folk life of St. John of Rila*. According to the anonymous author tsar Peter, who happened *to be in Sredets*[58], after hearing of the holy man sent nine men into the Rila Mountains to find the place in which John dwelt so that the tsar could meet him and bow down to him[59]. After a lengthy search, the tsar's messengers met with John. This only came to pass because the latter,

---

И. Лазаров, П. Павлов, *Кой кой е в средновековна България*, София 2012, pp. 270–275.

[57] It would appear that the monastic environment was very close to tsar Peter not only because of his deep piety, but also because of family tradition. His grandfather Boris-Michael became a monk in 889, giving up the throne, and remained a monk until his death in 907. Boris-Michael's brother, Dox, also devoted himself to monastic life. Symeon, Peter's father, accepted a monk's schema in Constantinople, and became a monk for more than ten years. He rescinded his vows in 893 to take the reins of power. It is possible that Symeon's sisters, Anna and Praxia, were nuns (Т. Тотев, *Родов манастир на владетелите в Преслав*, СЛ 20, 1987, pp. 120–128; G.N. Nikolov, *Die Christianisierung der Bulgaren und das Mönchtum in der Familie des Khans Boris I. Michail*, [in:] *Rome, Constantinople and Newly-Converted Europe. Archeological and Historical Evidence*, vol. I, ed. M. Salamon et al., Kraków–Leipzig–Rzeszów–Warszawa 2012, pp. 91–97). Peter's brothers, John and Michael, also ended up in a monastery, although not necessarily of their own volition (on the circumstances in which Michael and John adopted monk's habit, cf. Part One, Chapter I, point 1, of the present work). The fact that Peter himself became a monk, albeit only shortly before his death, is a symbolic expression of Peter's ties to monasticism. Cf. И. Дуйчев, *Рилският светец...*, p. 123sqq; *Ziemscy aniołowie...*, p. 19; cf. В. Николова, *Монашество...*, pp. 274–285; 626–628, 790–815).

[58] *Folk life of St. John of Rila*, p. 33 (transl. p. 168).

[59] The hagiographers' relations should, of course, be treated with caution, in particular when it comes to details, however it would not have been at all strange that the tsar, a pious man, would have liked to meet with a holy hermit. Such occurrences were common in the world of Byzantine Christianity. It would be worth bringing up the examples, if only for the argument's sake, of the contacts of the emperors and empresses with holy stylites throughout the fifth century. On this subject see, i.a.: R. Kosiński, *Holiness and Power. Constantinopolitan Holy Men and Authority in the 5th Century*, Berlin–Boston 2016, pp. 42–46, 129–167.

who did not want any publicity, took pity on the men, knowing that they could not return to the tsar until they fulfilled their order[60]. After the meeting, the messengers returned to the tsar and related their meeting with John, and: *tsar Peter listened to them and praised God*[61]. Thus the author of the *Life* presented the ruler's reaction to the information he received. The tsar decided to personally – accompanied by a numerous retinue – set out to meet the holy man. However, a personal, direct conversation between Peter and John did not happen. The latter, through messengers, proposed the tsar only this:

> If you wish that you see me and I see you, pitch your tent on the peak, and I will make smoke. You will see the smoke, and I will see the tent, because it has been commanded that in this way we see each other. The holy father made smoke [that went up] like a column in the sky. Tsar Peter saw the sign of the holy father, and the holy father looked up to the tent. Both praised God and bowed to each other[62].

Moved by what has happened, and grateful to John, the tsar sent the latter a cup filled with gold. The saint accepted the cup, and asked for the gold to be returned to the ruler. Afterwards, the tsar and his men departed[63]. Some time later John of Rila died, and his body remained in an unknown location. Not knowing that John passed away, the tsar once more sent his men to find him. Their mission ended in failure. The tsar was to have then said: *Verily, I was not worthy of seeing the saint*[64]. After some time, Peter once again sent his men to search for John. This time, they succeeded, although the outcome was likely not what the tsar expected, for the messengers found only the saint's body. Through an angel, as the *Life* relates, Peter received a message from God to bury the remains

---

[60] *Folk life of St. John of Rila*, p. 34.

[61] *Folk life of St. John of Rila*, p. 34 (transl., p. 169).

[62] *Folk life of St. John of Rila*, p. 35 (transl. p. 169).

[63] On the of biblical inspiration that led to presenting by the hagiographer the subject of the meeting between John of Rila and Peter – I. B i l i a r s k y, *The Tale of the Prophet Isaiah...*, pp. 180–185.

[64] *Folk life of St. John of Rila*, p. 36 (transl. p. 170).

in Sredets. Tsar fulfilled God's will; John's remains were moved to the indicated location and buried. A church was raised to honour the saint[65].

The above account inclines one to reflect on several matters. It would be a truism to say that Peter was not its main protagonist, and his presence was mainly intended to highlight John's exceptional character. It was the tsar who sought the saint's favour, not the other way round! The portrayal of Peter in the *Life* is rather one-sided. The hagiographer indicated that the ruler was a pious man, even calling him a holy tsar, one who had great respect for John[66]. The latter is the tsar's spiritual mentor, a holy man. The hagiographer pointed out that the tsar was a man absorbed in prayer, living a life devoted to religious matters, and having a special connection to God (the vision regarding John's burial). In the background, however, one may also see Peter the ruler. He was stern, and his subjects heeded his commands. The latter is attested by the behaviour of the first group of messengers sent to find John, who preferred to starve rather than stop searching for the holy man. They were afraid to stand before the tsar without having fulfilled his order, knowing that they would be severely punished. The hagiographer indicated that the tsar was a famous and

[65] *Folk life of St. John of Rila*, pp. 36–37. Later *Lives* show the topic of relations between Peter and John in a roughly similar fashion, and the differences that appear between them, stemming primarily from the development of the worship of John of Rila, as well as the propagandist aims which they served, do not affect Peter's image in a major way Cf. Д.И. Полывянный, *Царь Петр...*, p. 144.

[66] *Folk life of St. John of Rila*, p. 34. It is noteworthy that in the later texts Peter is not always called a saint. Thus, for example, in the *Life* penned by the patriarch Euthymios of Tarnovo (pp. 59–73). In the liturgical calendar Peter is commemorated on the 30th of January (the day widely considered the date of his death), along with St. Clement of Rome. This subject was recently addressed by: И. Билярски, М. Йовчева, *За датата на успението на тсар Петер и за кута към него*, [in:] *Tangra. Сборник в чест на 70-годишнината на акад. Васил Гюзелев*, ed. М. Каймакавова et al., София 2006, pp. 543–557; Д. Чешмеджиев, *Култът към български цар Петер I (927–969): монашески или държавен?*, [in:] *Љубав према образовању и вера у Бога у православним манастирами, 5. Међународна Хилендарска конференција. Зборник изабраних радова I*, ed. P. Matejić et al., Beograd–Columbus 2006, pp. 245–257; Б. Николова, *Цар Петър и характерът на неговия култ*, Pbg 33.2, 2009, pp. 63–77; I. Biliarsky *St. Peter...*, pp. 175–178; Д. Чешмеджиев, *Култовете на българските светци през IX–XII век. Автореферат*, Пловдив 2016, pp. 13–15; see also Part One, Chapter VII, point 3, of this monograph.

mighty ruler, with an army and many men at his disposal[67]. He was also wealthy, since he could afford to give John a cup filled with gold, and to construct a temple in his honour in Sredets[68]. Notably, in the account the saint is not only Peter's spiritual guide, but also gives him advice on what kind of ruler he should be[69]. Returning the gold to the tsar is, in my opinion, meant not only to attest to the saint's frugality, but also to a certain lack of understanding on Peter's part regarding John's way of life; however, it is also a hint for the tsar that he should wisely spend the assets he has to fulfil the needs of his state and subjects[70].

2.4. Peter in the *Tale of the Prophet Isaiah*

Tale of the Prophet Isaiah is classed among the historical-apocalyptic literature[71]. It was written at the time when the Bulgarian lands were already a part of the Byzantine Empire. In it, we find an extraordinarily interesting passage regarding Peter, and for this reason I will quote it in full:

[67] *Folk life of St. John of Rila*, p. 34: *He took along many people and his soldiers...* (transl. p. 169). Reminiscences of viewing Peter as a great ruler can be seen in, I think, the *Prologue life of St. John of Rila (II)* (p. 58), in which the anonymous author wrote that John Assen envied tsar Peter's and emperor Constantine's achievements.

[68] Regarding whether it was Peter who was responsible for moving John's remains to Sredets, there are some doubts about that. This issue is analysed by i.a. Ivan Duychev (И. Дуйчев, *Рилският светец...*, pp. 184–197); Todor R. Todorov (Т. Тодоров, *Кога били пренесени мощите на св. Иван Рилски в Средец*, ГСУ.НЦСВПИД 91 (10), 2001, pp. 169–179), and Dimo Cheshmedzhiev (Д. Чешмеджиев, *За времето на пренасяне на мощите на св. Иоанн Рилски от Рила в Средец*, BMd 6, 2015, pp. 79–89).

[69] This topic was further explored in the *Life of St. John of Rila* by Euthymios of Tarnovo (p. 69), the author of which tells Peter to prostrate himself at the feet of the Church, his mother. I. Biliarsky, *St. Peter...*, pp. 186–187. It is interesting that in comparison with Euthymios' text, the much earlier the *Service of St. Tsar Peter* (p. 393) highlights his role as the protector of the men of the Church: чрьнорizьцѧ люба. и слоужителѧ црькве бжиѧ млтвь ихь ради (*You loved monks and servants of the church of God because of their prayers* – transl., p. 109).

[70] Presumably this is how one can understand the words attributed by the hagiographer to John: *I, brother, have no troops to arm, and no goods to buy* (*Folk life of St. John of Rila*, p. 35; transl. p 170).

[71] On the subject of this genre of Bulgarian literature, see the classic work of: V. Tapkova-Zaimova, A. Miltenova, *Historical and Apocalyptic Literature in Byzantium and Medieval Bulgaria*, Sofia 2011.

> After his death [tsar Symeon – M.J.L.], his son tsar Peter took over the Bulgarian kingdom, and he was tsar of the Bulgarians and of the Greeks as well. He ruled the Bulgarian land for twelve years, without sin and without a wife, and his rule was blessed. In the days and years of St Peter, the tsar of the Bulgarians, there was plenty of everything, that is to say, of wheat and butter, honey, milk and wine, the land was overflowing with every gift of God, there was no dearth of anything but by the will of God everything was in abundance and to satiety. And then, in the years of St Peter, tsar of the Bulgarians, there was a widow in the Bulgarian land, young, wise, and very pious, by the name of Elena. She gave birth to Constantine, a saintly and very pious man. He was the son of Constantine the Green and Elena, and this Constantine was called Porphyrogennetos and he was tsar of the Romans. Because of envy, his mother Elena fled from the Roman Hellenes to the city of Vize, found herself with a child, and gave birth to tsar Constantine. To this tsar an angel of God revealed the good word about the Honest Cross from the East. Tsar Constantine and tsar Peter loved one another.[72]

This passage was discussed in the literature of the subject multiple times and from different angles. A particular emphasis was placed on the theme of associating Peter with Constantine the Great / Constantine Porphyrogennetos, and seeing in him the restorer of the Bulgarian state. Scholars wondered why he was 'cast' in this role – rather than Boris-Michael, who was responsible for introducing Bulgaria into the Christian oikumene, or Symeon I the Great, during whose reign Bulgaria became a great power. Various answers were offered, however the one pointing to the fact that there was a visible tendency of linking the fate of Bulgarians and Byzantines in the milieu in which the *Tale* originated appears to be the most likely[73].Peter, sharing familial ties with the Lekapenos family, as well as with the Macedonian dynasty, through his marriage with

[72] *Tale of the Prophet Isaiah*, 401d (transl. pp. 17–18; with minor changes – M.J.L.).

[73] E.g. K. Marinow, *Kilka uwag...*, pp. 70–72; cf. J. Dudek, *Cesarz Bazyli II w opiniach średniowiecznych Bułgarów*, [in:] *Stereotypy...*, p. 76.

Maria, was far more suited to the role of a keystone joining Bulgarian and Byzantine history[74].

From the perspective of analysing our subject, particularly significant are the arguments for the saintliness of Peter, absent from the other texts. The anonymous author emphasises the fact that his was a sinless life, spent in purity. Peter led a people chosen by God, similarly to a Byzantine emperor[75]. Associating him with Constantine the Great or Constantine Porphyrogennetos makes him equal to a Byzantine ruler. This is also expressed through the statement that he was a *tsar of the Bulgarians and of the Greeks*[76]. A notable feature of this portrayal of Peter in the *Tale* is the indication that during this ruler's reign Bulgaria was going through a period of a particular beatitude, and abounded in all the necessary goods[77]. Peter therefore comes across as a good, just[78] and strong ruler.

In the *Tale* we also find information related to the final part of Peter's life: *The Bulgarian tsar Peter, a righteous man, gave up his kingdom, fled to the West, to Rome, and there ended his life*[79]. This passage causes a no small problem for the scholars who, knowing it has no basis in reality, are puzzled about the source for this relation. A commonly held belief is that it resulted from associating Peter with the emperor Constantine the Great, the restorer of the Roman Empire[80], although it cannot be ruled out that this is a later addition, creation of which was influenced by the

[74] D. Češmedžiev, *Bułgarska tradycja państwowa w apokryfach: car Piotr w Bułgarskiej kronice apokryficznej*, transl. Ł. Mysielski, [in:] *Biblia Slavorum Apocryphorum. Novum Testamentum, Materiały z Międzynarodowej Konferencji Naukowej, Biblia Slavorum Apocryphorum. II. Novum Testamentum, Łódź, 15–17 maja 2009 roku*, eds. G. Minczew, M. Skowronek, I. Petrov, Łódź 2009, pp. 139–147.

[75] K. Marinow, *Kilka uwag...*, pp. 66–70; I. Biliarsky, *The Tale...*, pp. 65–127.

[76] *Tale of the Prophet Isaiah*, 401d (transl. p. 17). This fragment can perhaps be also understood as stating that Bulgarians and Greeks (Byzantines) are governed by the same rulers – K. Marinow, *Kilka uwag...*, p. 71; I. Biliarsky, *St. Peter...*, pp. 180–186.

[77] Cf. *Service of St. Tsar Peter*, p. 388. The same source ascribes to Peter generosity towards the poor.

[78] *Tale of the Prophet Isaiah*, 401d, p. 17. This characterisation of Peter's reign harmonises with a statement from the *Service of St. Tsar Peter* (p. 388), where it is said that the tsar loved peace (**възлюби мирωмъ прѣбывати въ жити своемъ**).

[79] *Tale of the Prophet Isaiah*, 402a (transl. p. 18); cf. I. Biliarsky, *St. Peter...*, p. 181.

[80] E.g., Д.И. Полывянный, *Царь Петр...*, pp. 143–144.

published in 1572 in Venice *Book for Various Occasions* by Yakov (Jacob) Kraykov, in which there is a mention of tsar Peter who fled from Preslav and died in Rome[81].

The portrayal of Peter we find in Bulgarian sources is clearly one-sided, predominantly limited to the religious sphere. It is a result of, on the one hand, the nature of the texts we have at our disposal, which are not, after all, strictly historical works devoted to Bulgarian history, but rather – generally speaking – religious or historical-religious literature. On the other hand, also a result of a particular ideological climate and the environment in which the texts were created, which is particularly noticeable in the *Tale of the Prophet Isaiah*. The indigenous, Bulgarian works cannot be used for the purpose of developing our knowledge of Peter's reign, unlike the Byzantine sources; instead, they are the basis for studying the memory of Peter and the history of his cult.

In the native sources, Peter is not charged with the responsibility for Bulgaria's collapse, on the contrary, he is seen as a strong ruler, which can be attested to by the fact that it was his name that was invoked by those who fought for independence during the period of Byzantine bondage. It was adopted by: Delyan, the leader of the uprising of 1040, by Constantine Bodin, proclaimed basileus of Bulgarians during the uprising of George Voyteh in 1072, and Theodore-Assen, the initiator of the uprising which led to the restoration of the Bulgarian statehood in the 1180s[82].

---

[81] I. Biliarsky, *St. Peter*..., p. 181; idem, *The Tale*..., pp. 201–202. Cf. also Part II, Chapter VIII, point 1. Yakov Kraykov was supposed to have simply made up this episode. This information was included in the seventeenth-century manuscripts of *Tale of the Prophet Isaiah*. It cannot also be completely ruled out that the idea of 'sending' Peter to Rome was a reference to the fact that the tsar was St. Peter's namesake who, after all, met his death in the Eternal City, and was buried there. Associating tsar Peter with the Apostle is an indication making this hypothesis somewhat probable – *Service of St. Tsar Peter*, p. 388: **Врьховномоу ты съименникъ съи црькве своѫ създа. на камени оутврьдив. вѣроѫ съпротивныимъ рѣкамъ възбранѣѫ** (*To the supreme among your namesakes* [*i.e., Apostle Peter*] *you dedicated this church and founded it on the rock, preserving it from the storms of the enemy* – transl., p. 108).

[82] This was noticed by, i.a., И. Билярски, *Покровители на Царство*..., pp. 34–36; Д.И. Полывянный, *Царь Петр*..., p. 141; П. Павлов, *Векът*..., p. 34.

Concluding these considerations, it would also be worth quoting a passage from the *Service of St. Tsar Peter*, which clearly attests to the fact that Peter entered the Bulgarian historical memory as a tsar-monk, a guide and caretaker of his subjects.

> Препоᵈбныˣ чинъ празноуѫ. раᵈуѫт сѧ днеᶜ с тобоѫ Петре ц҃рю прѣбл҃женыи ѿче. присно въ обитѣлеˣ. тамо и зде бѫди намъ оулоучити.
>
> Якоже сыи прѣжде с нами ѿче. и яко и чѧда своя приемлѧ любезно. тако и н҃нѣ приими мл҃твы сиѫ. и защити ны ѿ всѣкоѫ напасти. [...]
>
> Придѣте вси вѣрни. Петра миниха да въсхвалимь. бывша ѿ Б҃а ц҃рѣ блъгарьска. [...] Источникь ты быᶜ. и скровище нескѫдно. подаѫ излїваѫ на убогыѧ присно. и млᶜтинѧ своѫ оскѫдѣѫщѫ. и чрънориѕьцѫ любѧ. и слоужителѧ ц҃ркве б҃жиѫ м҃лтвь ихь ради. и мьзᵈы ѿ Б҃а надѣжсѧ. ежже не погрѣши. добръ плоᵈ показавъ.
>
> Tsar Peter, the estate of the blessed ones is celebrating today and rejoicing with you forever in the [heavenly] foundations. Be our [intercessor] here and there so that we succeed.
>
> Earlier you were with us, father, and welcomed us kindly like children of yours: now accept these prayers of ours and protect us from any kind of trouble. (...)
>
> Step forward, oh you faithful, to praise the monk Peter, the former tsar of Bulgaria from Christ.(...) You were the spring and the generous treasury from which [alms] to the poor always poured out; your alms never ended. You loved monks and servants of the church of God because of their prayers and hoped for reward from the God.[83]

[83] *Service of St. Tsar Peter*, pp. 389, 392, 393 (transl., p. 109).

3. Other Sources[84]

In the conclusion to my considerations regarding portrayal of Peter in mediaeval sources I would like to draw attention to the accounts of two authors, contemporary to the tsar, who were neither Byzantine nor Bulgarian.

3.1. Peter in the Works of Liudprand of Cremona

Peter was mentioned in two of Liudprand's works[85] – *Antapodosis* (*Retribution*) and *Legatio* (*Embassy*). In the former, written after Liudprand's stay in Constantinople in 949, Peter is mentioned as one of Symeon's sons. The Latin author emphasised that Peter was ruling Bulgaria at the time, moreover, he was doing so with a strong hand (*is still alive* [*and*] *powerfully leads the Bulgarians*)[86]. In another passage of *Antapodosis* Liudprand mentioned that the tsar married a daughter of Christopher and a grand-daughter of Romanos Lekapenos, and that *a very solid peace was established between Bulgarians and Greeks*[87]. Peter's wife changed her original name, which is not mentioned, to Irene, to highlight the fact that thanks to her a peace was established.

---

[84] On this subject, also see: Z. Brzozowska, *The Image of Maria Lekapene, Peter and Byzantine-Bulgarian Relations between 927 and 969 in the Light of Old Russian Sources*, Pbg 41.1, 2017, pp. 40–55.

[85] On the life and work of Liudprand, cf. i.a.: M. Linzel, *Studien über Liudprand von Cremona*, Berlin 1933; J.N. Sutherland, *Liudprand of Cremona, Bishop, Diplomat, Historian. Studies of the the Man and his Age*, Spoleto 1988; on the missions to Constantinople and the reminiscences thereof in Liudprand's works – J. Koder, T. Weber, *Liutprand von Cremona in Konstantinopel*, Vienna 1980; T. Wolińska, *Konstantynopolitańska misja Liudpranda z Kremony (968)*, [in:] *Cesarstwo bizantyńskie. Dzieje. Religia. Kultura. Studia ofiarowane Profesorowi Waldemarowi Ceranowi przez uczniów na 70-lecie Jego urodzin*, ed. P. Krupczyński, M.J. Leszka, Łask–Łódź 2006, pp. 201–223; eadem, *Konstantynopol i jego mieszkańcy widziani oczyma Liudpranda z Kremony*, VP 28, 2008, pp. 1231–1243.

[86] Liudprand of Cremona, *Retribution*, III, 29: *Qui nunc usque superest potenterque Bulgariis principatur* (transl. p. 124).

[87] Liudprand of Cremona, *Retribution*, III, 38: *inter Bulgarios et Grecos pax sit firmissima constitita* (transl. p. 129).

The image of Peter (or rather that of his father, Symeon) may have been somewhat darkened by the fact that his brother Bayan was supposedly practising magic, and had the ability to transform himself into a wolf, and into other animals. Liudprand did not draw any conclusions from this information, perhaps because he was doubtful of its veracity[88].

This – generally positive – portrayal of Peter is different in *Legatio*, the second of Liudprand's aforementioned works, which relates its author's stay in Constantinople in 968, during his diplomatic mission for Otto I. In it, Peter appears in the context of negotiations, conducted by Liudprand, to arrange a marriage between a Byzantine emperor's daughter and the son of Otto I, and to determine the seat which he, an envoy of emperor Otto I, should occupy by the Byzantine ruler's table. In writing about the former matter, Liudprand concluded that Peter was not a particularly powerful Slavic ruler. The Latin author made this remark to state that his master, Otto I, has subordinated many Slavic rulers who were more powerful than Peter[89]. In the second case, Liudprand was not speaking of Peter directly, but indicated that he – Otto's envoy – was given a less prominent seat at the imperial table than the Bulgarian ruler's envoy; the latter was described thusly: *shorn in the Hungarian style, girt with a bronze chain, and – as mind suggested to me – not yet baptized*[90]. Liudprand cited the Byzantines' explanation who, while considered his remark about the Bulgarian envoy's appearance correct, at the same time pointed out that according to the peace treaty concluded by Peter along his wedding with Christopher's daughter, the Bulgarian envoy should nonetheless be seated at a more honourable place than envoys of other rulers[91].

[88] Liudprand of Cremona, *Retribution*, III, 29: *Baianum autem adeo ferunt magicam didicisse...* On the topic practicing magic by Bayan – Х. Трендафилов, *Цар и век. Времето на Симеон, Четири инсталации*, Шумен 2017, pp. 286–294 (there, further literature of the subject).

[89] Liudprand of Cremona, *Embassy*, 16.

[90] Liudprand of Cremona, *Embassy*, 19: *Ungarico more tonsum, aenea catena cinctum et – ut mens mihi suggerit – catechumenum* (transl. p. 250).

[91] Liudprand of Cremona, *Embassy*, 19. It is worth noting that in this remark Liudprand, quoting Byzantines, titled Peter 'basileus': *Petrus Bulgarorum vasileus*. This clearly shows that Liudprand, who after all knew Greek, must have been aware that the Bulgarian ruler was entitled be addressed as an emperor.

If one were to take *Legatio* at its face value, then in Liudprand's opinion Peter would have been a weak ruler who surrounded himself with uncultured people (moreover, ones who were only beginning to emerge from paganism); this would have indeed been a poor testimony of the ruler's own Christianity, and of his culture.

Was this really Liudprand's view of Peter? One may doubt that, for the character of Peter was for Liudprand merely a tool for conducting his diplomatic mission, and demands for status appropriate for an envoy of emperor Otto. This also explains the change that occurred in portraying Peter between *Antapodosis* and *Legatio*. For Liudprand writing the former of these works Peter was a figure of whom he heard either from his father[92], or already during his stay in Constantinople in 949, and the remarks of the ruler were included only by the way of weaving his tale if the Byzantine history. In *Legatio*, Peter gained greater significance, as an example of a ruler who received in marriage the hand of a Byzantine imperial daughter – something Liudprand himself was attempting to negotiate with Nikephoros Phokas. Disparaging Peter was intended to raise in comparison the status of Otto I. It is also worth noting that Liudprand's stay in Constantinople in 968 happened at the time when the Byzantine-Bulgarian relations were in a far worse state than in 949. The Byzantine attitude towards Peter in 968 was, to some extent, compatible with the way in which the ruler's figure was used by Liudprand in his negotiations with Nikephoros Phokas.

[92] Liudprand's father visited Constantinople in 927 at the head of an embassy to Romanos Lekapenos sent by Hugo of Provance (Liudprand of Cremona, *Retribution*, III, 24; A. Toynbee, *Constantine Porphyrogenitus and his World*, London 1973, p. 93; cf. Х. Трендафилов, *Младостта на цар Симеон*, София 2010, pp. 19–20). Liudprand's father died soon after returning from that embassy, therefore it is more likely that the relation came to Liudprand in the form of his father's notes rather than a story he heard.

3.2. Ibrahim ibn Yakub's Relation

Ibrahim ibn Yakub, a traveller and merchant of Jewish origins[93], had encountered Bulgarian envoys sent to Otto I in the 960s (961 or 965/966)[94] in Merseburg, and heard from them of their ruler. His relation from this meeting is preserved in the eleventh-century work *Book of Highways and Kingdoms* by Al-Bakri. Ibrahim described the dress of the Bulgarian envoys, and added the following remark regarding the Bulgarian ruler:

> their king enjoys great authority, wears a diadem on his head, has secretaries, heads [of offices] and senior functionaries, and issues orders and prohibitions in a well-advised and regular manner, as is the custom with the greatest monarchs.[95]

While the text does not mention Peter by name, the dating of the meeting indicates that he was the one the Bulgarian envoys were describing to Ibrahim, presenting him as a strong ruler aided by an efficient

[93] On this author and his work, see e.g.: D. M i s h i n, *Ibrahim Ibn-Ya'qub At-Turtuhi's Account of the Slavs from the Middle of the Tenth Century*, AMSCEUB 1994/1995, pp. 184–199; *Ibrahim ibn Ya'qub at-Turtushi. Christianity, Islam and Judaism meet in East-Central Europe, c. 800–1300 A.D. Proceedings of the International Colloquy 25–29. April 1994*, eds. P. C h a r v á t, J. P r o s e c k ý, Praha 1996; *Ibrahim Ibn Jakub i Tadeusz Kowalski w sześćdziesiątą rocznicę edycji. Materiały z konferencji naukowej*, ed. A. Z a b o r s k i, Kraków 2008.

[94] On the dating of Ibrahim ibn Yakub's journey – J. W i d a j e w i c z, *Studia nad relacją Ibrahima ibn Jakuba*, Kraków 1946, p. 11; I b r a h i m i b n J a k u b, s. XLI. Cf. P. E n g e l s, *Der Reisebericht des Ibrahim ibn Ya'qub (961/966)*, [in:] *Kaiserin Theophanu. Begehgnung des Ostens und Westens um die Wende des ersten Jahrtausends. Gedenkschrift des Kölner Schnütgen-Museums zum 1000 Todesjahr der Kaiserin*, ed. A. v o n E u w, P. S c h r e i n e r, vol. I, Köln 1991, p. 417.

[95] I b r a h i m i b n J a k u b, p. 148 (transl. – J. S h e p a r d, *A marriage...*, p. 148). On this description V. G j u z e l e v, *Bułgaria a państwa i narody Europy Środkowej w X w.*, transl. K. M a r i n o w, [in:] *Byzantina Europaea. Księga jubileuszowa ofiarowana Profesorowi Waldemarowi Ceranowi*, ed. M. K o k o s z k o, M.J. L e s z k a, Łódź 2007, pp. 135–136; М. К а й м а к а м о в а, *Култът към цар Петър (927–969) и движещите идеи на българските освободителни въстания срещу византийската власт през XI–XII в.*, BMd 4/5, 2013/2014, p. 421.

administration[96]. It is worth stressing that his is not an opinion of Ibrahim himself, who noted he has never been to the ruler's country. One could say therefore that the passage does not even relate an opinion of some average Bulgarians, but rather Bulgarian envoys' propaganda, who presented their ruler as one of the most important ones in the world. Ibrahim ibn Yakub may have shared this view at least to some extent, based on the fact that he emphasised the dress of the Bulgarian envoys: they wore robes decorated with gold and silver, which indicated that they represented a wealthy ruler. Ibrahim also mentioned that Bulgarians were Christians, and that they translated the Gospel into their native tongue. The Bulgarian ruler, therefore, was a leader of a Christian and civilised state.

* * *

The portrayal of Peter in mediaeval sources, leaving aside the topic of his religiosity and information being entirely at odds with historical reality, presents a strong and proud ruler, effectively governing the Bulgarian state.

[96] One nonetheless needs to be aware that this is such a general description, devoid of details, that it could be simply treated as a characterisation of rulers of Christian Bulgaria in general rather than of Peter himself. It is also worth emphasising that Ibrahim ibn Yakub likely picked from the tale of the Bulgarian envoys only that which he considered important and interesting.

II

Kiril Marinow

War and Peace in the House of the Lord: A Conflict among Orthodox Christians and its Overcoming according to the Homily 'On the Treaty with the Bulgarians'

The second and third decade of the tenth century was among the stormiest in the history of Byzantine-Bulgarian relations. The Bulgarian ruler Symeon I (893–927) took up the title of tsar (emperor) and began an ambitious policy of conquering the Balkan territories of the Empire and seizing the capital city on the Bosphoros (it is thought that he attempted to create a new political order, referred to as *Pax Symeonica*). In doing so, he was taking advantage of the tense internal situation of the Empire: the problems regarding legitimisation of power and Constantine VII not yet being of age (as well as the fiasco of current foreign policy), humiliation of Bulgarian envoys by emperor Alexander (912–913) and breaking off of the Byzantine-Bulgarian agreement of 913 by Zoe Karbonopsina (died after 920). While the tsar succeeded to a great extent in seizing Byzantium's Balkan possessions, his other goal remained out of the scope of his means[1]. Finally in October 927 the long awaited peace treaty was concluded. Byzantium, exhausted by the long war recognised the imperial title of Peter I (927–969), Symeon's son and heir, and agreed to pay a tribute to the Bulgarians. State borders were delimited, war prisoners exchanged and autonomy of the Bulgarian Church recognised. In order to reinforce the peace agreement, for the first time in the history of the Empire a woman from the imperial family – Maria (911–?963), a granddaughter of emperor Romanos I Lekapenos (920–944) – was married to a foreign ruler. She was thought to have taken up the name of Irene (Gr. Εἰρήνη, that is *Peace*) to emphasise the importance of the concluded treaty and particular relations that would link both countries[2]. On that occasion a special oration *On the Treaty with the Bulgarians* (Ἐπὶ τῇ τῶν Βουλγάρων συμβάσει)[3] was delivered. The speech was written most

[1] See e.g. I. Božilov, *L'ideologie politique du tsar Symeon: Pax Symeonica*, BBg 8, 1986, pp. 73–89; J. Shepard, *Symeon of Bulgaria – Peacemaker*, ГСУ.ЦСВПИД 3, 1989, pp. 9–48; И. Божилов, *Цар Симеон Велики (893–927): от "варварската" държава до християнското царство*, [in:] idem, В. Гюзелев, *История на средновековна България VII–XIV век*, София 1999, pp. 229–270.

[2] S. Penkov, *Bulgaro-Byzantine Treaties during the Early Middle Ages*, Pbg 5.3, 1981, p. 49; В.Д. Николаев, *Значение договора 927 г. в истории болгаро-византийских отношений*, [in:] *Проблемы истории античности и средних веков*, ed. Ю.М. Сапрыкин, Москва 1982, pp. 89–105; Д. Стоименов, *Към договора между България и Византия от 927 г.*, Век 17.6, 1988, pp. 19–23; E. Aleksandrov, *The International Treaties of Medieval Bulgaria (Legal Aspects)*, BHR 17.4, 1989, pp. 41, 42, 44, 48; E.K. Κυριακής, *Βυζάντιο και Βούλγαροι (7ος–10ος αι.). Συμβολή στην εξωτερική πολιτική του Βυζαντίου*, Αθήνα 1993, pp. 158–159, 214–216; В. Гюзелев, *Значението на брака на цар Петър (927–969) с ромейката Мария-Ирина Лакапина (911–962)*, [in:] *Културните текстове на миналото. Носители, символи и идеи*, vol. I, *Текстовете на историята, история на текстовете. Материали от Юбилейната международна конференция в чест на 60-годишнината на проф. д.и.н. Казимир Попконстантинов, Велико Търново, 29–31 октомври 2003*, ed. idem, София 2005, pp. 27–33; S. Pirivatrić, *Some Notes on the Byzantine-Bulgarian Peace Treaty of 927*, Bslov 2, 2008, pp. 40–49.

[3] Critical edition of the text – *On the Treaty with the Bulgarians*. On this literary peace of work cf. Θ.И. Успенскiй, *Неизданное церковное слово о болгарско-византiйскихъ отношенiяхъ въ первой половинѣ X в.*, ЛИФОИНУ.ВО 4, 1894, pp. 48–123; И. Кузнецовъ, *Писмата на Лъва Магистра и Романа Лакапина и словото "Ἐπὶ τῇ τῶν Βουλγάρων συμβάσει" като изворъ за историята на Симеоновска България*, СНУНК 16/17, 1900, pp. 179–245; R.J.H. Jenkins, *The Peace with Bulgaria (927)*

probably by Theodore Daphnopates (890/900 – after 961), an eminent representative of Constantinopolitan intellectual elite of the first part of 10th century and emperor Romanos's secretary[4]. By making references not only to ancient history and literature but to the Bible as well, the orator explained the reasons which had led to antagonism between the two countries, wept over tragic results of military operations through the years of war and emphasised the significance of the concluded peace.

Celebrated by Theodore Daphnopates, [in:] *Polychronion. Festschrift F. Dolger zum 75. Geburtstag*, ed. P. Wirth, Heidelberg 1966, pp. 287–303; P. Karlin-Hayter, *The Homily on the Peace with Bulgaria of 927 and the 'Coronation' of 913*, JÖB 17, 1968, pp. 29–39; Ἀ. Σταυρίδου-Ζαφράκα, Ὁ Ἀνώνυμος λόγος "Ἐπὶ τῇ τῶν Βουλγάρων συμβάσει", Βυζ 8, 1976, pp. 343–408; I. Dujčev, *On the Treaty of 927 with the Bulgarians*, DOP 32, 1978, pp. 217–253; Т. Тодоров, *"Слово за мира с българите" и българо-византийските политически отношения през последните години от управлението на цар Симеон*, [in:] *България, българите и техните съседи през вековете. Изследвания и материали от научната конференция в памет на доц. д-р Христо Коларов, 30–31 октомври 1998 г.*, Велико Търново, ed. Й. Андреев, Велико Търново 2001, pp. 141–150; K. Marinow, *In the Shackles of the Evil One: The Portrayal of Tsar Symeon I the Great (893 – 927) in the Oration 'On the Treaty with the Bulgarians'*, SC 1, 2011, pp. 157–190; idem, *Myth and Meaning. Standards of Byzantine Erudition and Its Role in Byzantine Rhetorical Works*, [in:] *Standards of Everyday Life in the Middle Ages and in Modern Times*, vol. III, ed. K. Mutafova et al., Veliko Tărnovo 2014, pp. 151–164; idem, *Византийската имперска идея и претенциите на цар Симеон според словото "За мира с българите"*, КМС 25, 2016, pp. 342–352.

[4] R.J.H. Jenkins, *The Peace with Bulgaria...*, pp. 301–302; P. Karlin-Hayter, *The Homily...*, p. 39; I. Dujčev, *On the Treaty...*, pp. 241–242, 243, 249, 252–253; С.Н. Малахов, *Концепция мира в политической идеологии Византии первой половины X в. Николай Мистик и Феодор Дафнопат*, АДСВ 27, 1995, p. 20; J. Shepard, *Byzantine emperors, imperial ideology and the fact of Bulgaria*, BMd 2, 2011, p. 549. On Daphnopates see e.g. M. Сюзюмов, *Об историческом труде Феодора Дафнопата*, ВОб 2, 1916, pp. 295–302; H.-G. Beck, *Kirche un Theologische Literatur im byzantinischen Reich*, München 1959, pp. 552–553; Theodore Daphnopates, pp. 1–11; A. Markopoulos, *Théodore Daphnopatès et la Continuation de Théophane*, JÖB 35, 1985, pp. 171–182; A. Kazhdan, *Daphnopates Theodore*, [in:] *ODB*, vol. I, p. 588; M. Salamon, *Dafnopata Teodor*, [in:] *Encyklopedia kultury bizantyńskiej*, ed. O. Jurewicz, Warszawa 2002, p. 133; A. Kazhdan, *A History of Byzantine Literature*, vol. II, *850–1000*, ed. C. Angelidi, Athens 2006, pp. 152–157; Th. Antonopoulou, *A textual source and its contextual implications: On Theodore Daphnopates' sermon on the birth of John the Baptist*, B 81, 2011, pp. 9–18; W. Treadgold, *The Middle Byzantine Historians*, New York–Basingstoke 2013, pp. 188–196.

He also built up the image of a suffering man who had become a witness to the violence during war operations. That particular way of expression, certainly easy to understand by the educated part of Byzantine audience[5], covered significant ideological and political contents. In this short text I will present and characterise some examples of the attitudes and emotions which accompanied the Byzantine author he had experienced (or at least said he had), being a witness and hearing the relations of atrocities of a fratricidal war (concerning only the fragment of the oration in § 2–3). I also would like to focus on two main biblical themes which were present in the abovementioned homily and try to identify the ideological background of the relationship between the Byzantines and Bulgarians.

1. War and its Influence

1.1. The Effects of Violence

The author said that agriculture, the foundation of Byzantine life, was abandoned. Fields were deserted, as the ploughmen had perished in the war. The old order was destroyed with fire and axe. The land (including some forests) was devastated to such an extent that the people (including the author) did not know where they were nor where they should head to[6]. The war resulted in destroyed walls, burnt down temples, holy icons consumed by fire, ruined sanctuaries, priest kidnapped straight from the altar during the services, church ornaments plundered; the elderly had been tortured, the youth deprived of their lives long before their time, virgins had been shamelessly violated, families separated, and holy relics scattered to become prey of dogs and ravens[7].

---

[5] Cf. R.J.H. Jenkins, *The Peace with Bulgaria*..., pp. 299, 302–303; K. Marinow, *In the Shackles*..., p. 165.

[6] *On the Treaty with the Bulgarians*, 2, p. 256.40–44; 16, p. 278.369–371.

[7] *On the Treaty with the Bulgarians*, 3, p. 256.47–53.

Life was consumed by death and the Earth became again invisible and unformed (*ἀόρατος καὶ ἀκατασκεύαστος*; after the Book of Genesis)[8], like before the Creation. So, in the light of the discussed text, the fratricidal war destroyed God's Creation – nature (i.e. natural environment), everyday circle of human activities and unity in Christ between Byzantines and Bulgarians[9]. It led to destruction and desecration of all holiness, of what was most sacred to any man of those times.

1.2. The Author's Reaction, Feelings, Thoughts and Attitude to War

His response to war was silence (*ἡ σιγή*; in the text *συνσίγη*)[10] – the effect of trauma and misfortunes he witnessed, of the indescribable atrocities. Facing the tragedy of war the only thing one could do was to keep silent, just like the deaf-mute son of Croesus, king of Lydia (after Herodotos)[11], just like the brass bowls of the oracle in Dodona, no longer moved by wind and remaining mute, so that no one could tell the future any more. The only thing one could do was to become even more voiceless (*ἄφωνος*)[12] than the fish. The author opposes the complete soundlessness with the shout of Stentor, the Achaean herald, whose voice as strong as that of fifty men (after Homer)[13].

[8] On the Treaty with the Bulgarians, 2, p. 256.40–41; Gn 1, 1–2: Ἐν ἀρχῇ ἐποίησεν ὁ θεὸς τὸν οὐρανὸν καὶ τὴν γῆν. ἡ δὲ γῆ ἦν ἀόρατος καὶ ἀκατασκεύαστος, καὶ σκότος ἐπάνω τῆς ἀβύσσου, καὶ πνεῦμα θεοῦ ἐπεφέρετο ἐπάνω τοῦ ὕδατος (Septuaginta, vol. I, p. 1; all biblical references to the Old Testament's texts are cited after Alfred Rahlfs edition – Septuaginta, vol. I/II).

[9] K. Marinow, *In the Shackles...*, pp. 176–178, 182. More on the topic – the question what was war in author's opinion and the aforementioned biblical references to the Book of Genesis – see idem, "*А земята отново беше станала безвидна и неоформена*". *Щрихи към образа на войната в словото "За мира с българите"*, Епо 26.1, 2018, pp. 201–213.

[10] *On the Treaty with the Bulgarians*, 2, p. 256.29. Cf. *On the Treaty with the Bulgarians*, 3, p. 258.68–69; 8, p. 266.200.

[11] *On the Treaty with the Bulgarians*, 2, p. 256.29–30; 9, p. 270.261–262; Herodotos, I, 6. 34. 38. 47. 85, pp. 8, 40, 46, 52–54, 106–108.

[12] *On the Treaty with the Bulgarians*, 2, p. 256.30.

[13] *On the Treaty with the Bulgarians*, 2, p. 256.28–30; Homer, V, p. 264.784–792.

And so his silence was as overwhelming and telling as the shout of that herald. The cited fragment, however, goes deeper than that. Upon seeing his father's life threatened, the mute son of Croesus ultimately uttered a shout. In this way the author would let know that his silence is indeed a kind of a shout, incomparably more significant that the normal mourning, as it was comparable to that of Stentor himself, or to that of Croesus' son. He wanted to say that his soundless voice spoke more loudly than any words and more clearly describes the tragedy of war.

War violence evokes the torment of soul (ἄλγος τῆς ψυχῆς; in the text: συνήλγησα)[14] and streams of tears (ποταμοὺς δακρύων)[15] in the orator, because he witnessed the death of his next of kin and of many other people. It brings sorrow (τὸ ὄδυρμα)[16] for those who were lost. The author compares his suffering to that of biblical patriarch Jacob when he learned of the death of Joseph, one of his beloved sons. Yet, Jacob was deceived, as his son did not die but was sold and found himself in Egyptian captivity. And finally, after many years, despite the terrible pain after the loss of his son, Jacob could again enjoy the beloved one[17]. That joy was not given to our orator, though, as he saw with his own eyes the bodies of his beloved relatives, the innocent, the harmless, quartered and tainted with blood (τοὺς ἀθώους, τοὺς ἀναιτίους διατετμημένους ὁρῶν καὶ μεμολυσμένους ἐν αἵματι)[18]. No doubt that the author parallels the blood-covered robes of Joseph and blood-tainted bodies of those killed in war. While, however, Jacob thought of his son's death through indirect evidence (the robe), our orator tells of the undeniable, direct, clear evidence of human death. Jacob was deceived, the orator wasn't. His suffering was not soothed, just like that of Jacob's was. This is the war's everyday: the death of your kin, innocent, casual victims, brutally killed[19] – the text suggests that also their dead bodies were treated without dignity – quartered, and left abandoned, exposed to public view, a sight that no one should see. Seeing such images was the fate of those who have

[14] *On the Treaty with the Bulgarians*, 2, p. 256.31.
[15] *On the Treaty with the Bulgarians*, 2, p. 256.31.
[16] *On the Treaty with the Bulgarians*, 2, p. 256.33.
[17] *On the Treaty with the Bulgarians*, 2, p. 256.30–33.
[18] *On the Treaty with the Bulgarians*, 2, p. 256.34–35.
[19] *On the Treaty with the Bulgarians*, 2, p. 256.33–35.

survived. They had to watch and fill their eyes, thoughts and memory with the images of the bloody harvest of war[20]. These words may suggest that the victims were tortured before they died, or their bodies had been profaned.

The war generates turmoil and trouble in one's spirit (in the text: συγκεχυμένως τὸ πνεῦμα καὶ συντεταραγμένως)[21], makes one shattered and emotionally restless. Just like the prophet Jeremiah, the orator complains of the tragic fate of God's people, as he has seen *the daughters of Zion*, the honourable, the unattainable, as stars, with the eyes that cast radiant glances, deprived of their former dignity, stripped of their jewellery, lying dead (τὰς τιμίας, τὰς ἀπειθεῖς, τὰς οἷον ἀστέρας καὶ ὀφθαλμοὺς διαστραπτούσας τοῖς πέρασι, τὴν προτέραν περιῃρημένας εὐπρέπειαν, ἀπημφιεσμένας τὸν ἑαυτῶν κόσμον καὶ κειμένας πτῶμα)[22] and worthy of the tears of the prophets and of pagan philosopher Heraclitus[23]. Those daughters of Zion may represent, on the one hand, simply the women respected and admired in the time of peace, full of dignity and clear-eyed. And now the war has brought death and destruction to them – it has deprived them of dignity, inviolability and beauty. They have been stripped of their decorations and of the honour that once belonged to them. They are no longer untouchable; they have become victims of a brute force that felled them and profaned their bodies. Their eyes no longer shine, their glances no longer add splendour and warmth to their neighbourhood, as they have turned into gloom and darkness. On the other hand, the expression *daughters of Zion* (τὰς τῆς Σιὼν θυγατέρας)[24] has wider biblical connotations and can signify the whole community of those who believe in True God. In this context they would

---

[20] Cf. *On the Treaty with the Bulgarians*, 3, p. 258.70; 21, pp. 284.489–286.494.

[21] *On the Treaty with the Bulgarians*, 2, p. 256.35–36.

[22] *On the Treaty with the Bulgarians*, 2, p. 256.37–39.

[23] *On the Treaty with the Bulgarians*, 2, p. 256.39–40.

[24] *On the Treaty with the Bulgarians*, 2, p. 256.36; 4 Reg 19, 21; Ps 9 (10), 15; 72 (73), 28; Mih 1, 13; 4, 8. 10. 13; Soph 3, 14; Zah 2, 10; 9, 9; Is 1, 8; 3, 16 -17; 4, 4; 10, 32; 37, 22; 52, 2; 62, 11; Ier 4, 31; 6, 2. 23; Lam 1, 6; 2, 1. 4. 8. 10. 13; 4, 22 (*Septuaginta*, vol. I, p. 738; *Septuaginta*, vol. II, pp. 7, 77, 512, 515, 541, 547, 554, 566, 570, 571, 581, 615, 650, 664, 666, 667, 757, 759, 760, 765). The synonymous expression daughters of Jerusalem (αἱ θυγατέρες Ἱερουσαλήμ) was also used in the oration – *On the treaty with the Bulgarians*, 1, p. 254.3. On the similarities of these expressions see e.g. Mih 4, 8; Soph 3, 14; Zah 3, 14; 9, 9; Lam 2, 13 (*Septuaginta*, vol. II, pp. 515, 541, 547, 554, 760).

represent the Chosen People, and the Holy Church in the union with God, its children and servants. The fate they have met – being deprived of previous glory and murdered – is an unimaginable crime on the one hand, and a terrible punishment on the other. That part emphasises once again the torments of the author himself, who has witnessed the tragic vicissitudes of those women. The fate worthy of the tears of biblical prophets, first of all of Jeremiah[25], as well as of the Greek philosopher Heraclitus of Ephesus, whose figure in Byzantium was proverbial[26].

Awareness of the atrocities of war and of the two Christian nations standing against each other made the author's blood run cold (in the text: ἐπαχνώθη μοι φίλον κῆρ; after Hesiod)[27] and his heart passed through the iron (in the text: καὶ σίδηρον διῆλθε... καρδία μου; after the Psalmist and the Evangelist)[28], and led him to the condition in which he did not want to live any longer, nor to see the sunlight. In other words, due to the violence he observed for too long, the orator wished to abandon that terrible place that the earth had become. His mind and heart were contaminated with knowledge of the things he should never have learned and that should never have happened. Pain drained the whole life out of him. Even his wisdom and faith did not provide him consolation. Merely remembering the past tragedy of war would make the orator pale, faint and unable to put his grief aside (in the text: ἐγὼ... σκοτοδινῶ καὶ ἠλλοίωμαι καὶ τοῦ πάθους οὐκ ἐπανέρχομαι)[29].

---

[25] *On the Treaty with the Bulgarians*, 2, p. 256.35. Cf. Ier 1–52; Lam 1–5 (*Septuaginta*, vol. II, pp. 656–748, 756–766).

[26] I. Dujčev, *On the Treaty*..., p. 256 (fn. 24), 290, note to v. 39–40. See also Nikephoros Gregoras, VIII, 14, p. 375.6–9; XX, 1, p. 957.2–4. Ἀ. Σταυρίδου-Ζαφράκα, *Ὁ Ἀνώνυμος λόγος*..., p. 382, note to v. 16, thinks about the elegiac and epigrammatic poet Heraclitus of Halicarnassus, but see e.g. A. Kaldellis, *Hellenism in Byzantium. The Transformation of Greek Identity and the Reception of the Classical Tradition*, Cambridge 2007, p. 253.

[27] *On the Treaty with the Bulgarians*, 3, p. 258.58; Hesiod, p. 28.360: τό γ' ἐπάχνωσεν φίλον ἦτορ.

[28] *On the Treaty with the Bulgarians*, 3, p. 258.58–59; Ps 104 (105) (*Septuaginta*, vol. II, p. 114: σίδηρον διῆλθεν ἡ ψυχὴ αὐτοῦ), 18; Luc 2, 35 (*NTG*, p. 186: καὶ σοῦ [δὲ] αὐτῆς τὴν ψυχὴν διελεύσεται ῥομφαία; all biblical references to the New Testament's texts are cited after Nestle–Aland edition – *NTG*).

[29] *On the Treaty with the Bulgarians*, 2, p. 256.45–46.

The miseries of war made him feel like hibernating animals, which, confined to their holes, expend all their substance, waiting for spring, i.e. better times. Just like them, the orator was consuming himself from within[30]. Due to grief he failed to take part in synods and secular meetings; he did not attend services, missed conversations and did not visit imperial palaces or private homes alike. Similarly, he did not enjoy the homilies, displays, or the company of wise men and scholars. All things which should have made the life more meaningful – faith, learning, imperial ceremonies – ceased to be of any value to him[31]. He was shaken and bewildered, troubled by the delights of yesterday, which previously gave him happiness[32]. Thus he emphasised the magnitude of the trauma that became his lot because of the war. The natural course of life, stability and repeatability was ruined by the overwhelming violence. How to enjoy life if life itself was destroyed by war? How to seek consolation in faith, if the Christians themselves destroyed their common House of Faith? If priests were kidnapped from in front of the altar and killed, temples and monasteries were ruined, and God's laws broken by His children? How to work when all around is in the turmoil of war? This is what the orator tried to convey to his listeners[33].

1.3. Some Conclusions on Rhetorical Authenticity

In the oration there are more direct or indirect references and suggestions which characterise the attitudes, emotions and reactions of the orator himself and of other people who faced the evil that (in author's opinion) was the war between the two countries[34]. Still, even the above selection lets

[30] *On the Treaty with the Bulgarians*, 3, p. 258.71–73.

[31] *On the Treaty with the Bulgarians*, 3, p. 258.73–76.

[32] *On the Treaty with the Bulgarians*, 3, p. 258.76–79.

[33] Other fragments concerning the evils of war – *On the Treaty with the Bulgarians*, 5, p. 260.104–110; 6, p. 264.152–158; 7, p. 264.171–174; 8, p. 266.199–202; 12, pp. 272.302 – 274.316; 13, p. 274.336–339; 14, p. 276.343–347; 17, p. 278.383–391; 18, p. 280.402–413; 20–21, pp. 280.431 – 286.498.

[34] Cf. e.g. *On the Treaty with the Bulgarians*, 5, p. 260.105–110; 6, p. 264.154–155; 8, p. 266.199–202; 12, p. 272.305–306; 21, p. 284.493.

answer the question whether that characterisation can be taken at face value and not only for the author's *licentia poetica*.

Firstly – practically all the information of the wartime destruction can be confirmed in historical sources (chronicles, epistolographies and hagiographies)[35]. Even those regarding devastation of nature are confirmed, as there is evidence of cutting off and burning the forests surrounding the Byzantine capital city by Symeon's troops[36].

Secondly – it is evident that our source fits perfectly in the long tradition of the Byzantine rhetoric art, thus constituting one of its best achievements. Consequently, it was built up according to the rules of that art[37]. The author certainly makes his experiences exaggerated and overstated, with strong and expressive comparisons and juxtapositions. He makes use of well-known schemes of visualising of human suffering, facing the atrocities of war. He uses μίμησις (the art of imitating ancient writers, taking from their experience and skills)[38]. It should not mean, though, that we should treat his work only as another commissioned text with the above issues nothing more than erudite oratorical art[39]. That is because

---

[35] Continuator of Theophanes, VI, 7. 8. 10. 13. 15, pp. 386.23–387.2, 402.4–6, 402.22–403.1, 404.18–405.7, 405.17–20, 406.15–18; Nicholas Mystikos, 14, pp. 94.59–96.77; 24, p. 170.57–60; 26, p. 182.22–27; *Life of St. Mary the Younger*, 23–24, 25, pp. 700D – 701A, E.

[36] Continuator of Theophanes, VI, 15, p. 405.20. Cf. P. Karlin-Hayter, *The Homily...*, p. 39; Ἀ. Σταυρίδου-Ζαφράκα, *Ὁ Ἀνώνυμος λόγος...*, p. 401, note to vs. 25–28.

[37] Θ.И. Успенскiй, *Неизданное церковное слово...*, pp. 52–54, 94, 100–101.

[38] On mimesis in Byzantine literature see e.g. H. Hunger, *On the Imitatio (μίμησις) of Antiquity in Byzantine Literature*, DOP 23/24, 1969/1970, pp. 15–38; W. Tronzo, *Mimesis in Byzantium. Notes toward a history of the function of the image*, AAe 25, 1994, pp. 61–76; I. Nilsson, *Erotic Pathos, Rhetorical Pleasures. Narrative Technique and Mimesis in Eumathios Makrembolites' Hysmine & Hysminas*, Uppsala 2001; e a d e m. *Static imitation or creative transformation? Achilles Tatius in Hysmine & Hysminas*, [in:] *The Ancient Novel and Beyond*, ed. S. Panayotakis, M. Zimmerman, W. Keulen, Leiden 2003, pp. 371–380; H. Cichocka, *Mimesis i retoryka w traktatach Dionizjusza z Halikarnasu a tradycja bizantyńska*, Warszawa 2004; e a d e m. *Mimesis and Rhetoric in the Treatises by Dionysius of Halicarnassus and the Byzantine Tradition (selected problems)*, JÖB 60, 2010, pp. 35–45.

[39] Cf. wider opinion on Byzantine literature – A. Kazhdan, G. Constable, *People and Power in Byzantium. An Introduction to Modern Byzantine Studies*, Washington

the speaker was extremely well educated and possessed a very extensive literary knowledge of ancient history, biblical texts, ecclesiastical authors, mythological reminiscences, popular sayings and apocryphal literature. The text reveals great individuality and innovativeness as a literary work, an ideological tractate and a historical source[40].

The war between Byzantium and Bulgaria, waged in the times of Symeon I, caused great pain to the inhabitants of the Rome of the East. Hence the significance they gave to the peace treaty and substantial concessions towards the Bulgarians by the rulers of Constantinople. No doubt that the orator stressed the evil of war to emphasise the significance of peace[41]. On the other hand, the nature of the accompanying feelings is collective, i.e. through his own example he tries to reflect the feelings of the whole community. And although that image was in many aspects a *cliché* of the Byzantine literature (multiplying the images of suffering, present in other similar works), it referred to the deeply ingrained patterns of such feelings, based on the experience of many generations of Byzantines themselves and of the humankind in general. Therefore, despite being in some ways a customary *topos*, it reflects the possible or perhaps actual human experience of encountering violence.

The orator suffered as much as the well-known literary and historical figures (Jacob, Jeremiah, Heraclites); to draw attention to his feelings he quoted or paraphrased classical writers: Homer, Hesiod and biblical authors, particularly psalmists. To emphasise his condition he uses the Greek prefix *συν-* which means *together* or *along with* to most of his actions or emotions he experienced, thus stressing the commonality of the suffering of the quoted persons[42]. In this way their suffering also became his suffering. In other words: the whole world would feel the calamities

---

DC 1982, pp. 114–115. Contrary R.J.H. J e n k i n s, *The Hellenistic Origins of Byzantine Literature*, DOP 17, 1963, pp. 39–52.

[40] Θ.И. У с п е н с к і й, *Неизданное церковное слово*..., pp. 52, 54, 95, 120; R.J.H. J e n k i n s, *The Peace with Bulgaria*..., p. 297; Ἀ. Σ τ α υ ρ ί δ ο υ-Ζ α φ ρ ά κ α, *Ὁ Ἀνώνυμος λόγος*..., pp. 346–347; I. D u j č e v, *On the Treaty*..., pp. 222, 228, 237.

[41] *On the Treaty with the Bulgarians*, 4, pp. 258.82 – 260.99; 11, p. 272.282–287; 20, p. 280.431–433; 21–22, pp. 286.498 – 288.540.

[42] *On the Treaty with the Bulgarians*, 2, p. 256.29 (συνεσίγησα).31 (συνήλγησα).35 (συγκέχυμαι).36 (συντετάραγμαι).

of war along with him; he exemplifies his experience and emotion by reference to popular figures, known to his listeners; he plays with hyperboles and words.

Thirdly – as we know that the author of the discussed work, most probably Theodore Daphnopates, was personally involved in the events (as the secretary and real author of emperor Roman Lekapenos's letters to the tsar of Bulgaria)[43], we may not discount the possibility that the text presents his own experiences of the war. What is more, the text contains clear allusions to the issues he dealt with himself (studies, dialogues with other scholars), and on which the war put its tragic stamp as well.

2. The Motif of Peace

2.1. The New Israel or the Body of Christ

The Orator quotes the biblical transmission about the division of Israel after King Solomon's death into the House of Judah (including the tribe of Benjamin with its capital in Jerusalem) and the House of Ephraim (with the remaining ten tribes and the capital in Samaria)[44]. The biblical text conveys information that the split was the result of Solomon's sins, who under the influence of his numerous wives and women from different countries and cultures practiced idolatry, thus disobeying Yahweh's will[45]. Still, according to the Old Testament writer, God let it be known that

[43] В.Н. Златарски, *Писмата на византийския императоръ Романа Лакапена до българския царъ Симеона*, СНУНК 13, 1896, pp. 282–322; И. Кузнецовъ, *Писмата...*, pp. 196–197, 205; Е. Александров, *Дипломатическая переписка царя Симеона с императором Романом Лакапином*, Pbg 14.2, 1990, pp. 16–22.

[44] *On the Treaty with the Bulgarians*, 3, p. 258.62–64; 7, p. 264.171–174.177–179. Cf. also the allusions in *On the Treaty with the Bulgarians*, 8, p. 266.208–209; 10, pp. 270.270–272.281; 13, p. 274.326–330; 17, p. 278.387–390; 22, p. 288.525–528. Cf. J. Shepard, *Byzantine emperors...*, p. 549.

[45] 3 Reg 11, 1–13; 12, 1–21; 2 Par 10, 1–19 (*Septuaginta*, vol. I, pp. 656–657, 660–661, 826–827).

the division would only be temporary and Jerusalem would remain the City of Israel, because of the promise He had given to King David[46]. Thus, according to the author, Byzantium was House of Judah, whereas Bulgaria was that of Ephraim. And despite that division, Byzantium remained the true Israel, the House of Jacob, in which the respect to Yahweh had survived and would continue (even if some of its rulers were not obedient to God). Similarly as in the biblical history of Israel and Judah, where the former soon quit the true adoration of God[47].

Then, by paraphrasing the words from the Book of Prophet Malachi[48], the rhetorician made it clearly understood that those who acted against each other were no strangers, but that sons acted against their fathers and brothers against brothers, and finally fathers against sons[49]. He therefore made a clear reference to the so-called *spiritual sonhood* of the Bulgarians, and particularly of the Bulgarian ruler to the emperor of *῾Ρωμαῖοι*[50], as the Bulgarians were Byzantines sons in faith[51]. Using the expressions typical of St. Paul's writings, the Byzantines *had given birth in faith*[52] to their northern neighbours, as they had carried the light of the Gospel to them. They had therefore become their religious teachers and leaders.

The words about the brotherhood regarded chiefly their faith, the common Orthodox denomination of the Byzantines and Bulgarians. The latter would be at the same time the spirituals brothers and sons of the former. They built a single house of faith – a new Israel, in which

---

[46] 2 Reg 7, 1–29; 1 Par 17, 1–27; 23, 25 (*Septuaginta*, vol. I, pp. 577–579, 789–791, 799).

[47] Cf. *On the Treaty with the Bulgarians*, 11, p. 272.287–301 (God of Israel is God of the Byzantines); 15, p. 276.348–351 (Byzantium is an Israel, a House of Jacob). Cf. 3 Reg 12, 25–33; 2 Par 11, 5–17 (*Septuaginta*, vol. I, pp. 664–665, 828).

[48] Mal 3, 23 (*Septuaginta*, vol. II, p. 565); cf. Matt 10, 21–22a; Luc 12, 51–53 (*NTG*, pp. 28, 240–241). It's worth noting that quite similar expression was used also by Thucydides, III, 81.5, pp. 140–142.

[49] *On the Treaty with the Bulgarians*, 3, p. 258.55–57; 21, p. 284.478–479.

[50] Cf. F. Dölger, *Der Bulgarenherrscher als geistlicher Sohn des byzantinischen Kaisers*, ИИД 16/18, 1940, pp. 219–232; idem, *Средновековното "семейство на владетелите и народите" и българският владетел*, СБАН.КИФ 62, 1943, pp. 181–222.

[51] Cf. *On the Treaty with the Bulgarians*, 3, p. 258.55–57; 11, p. 272.296–299.

[52] 1 Cor 4, 15 (*NTG*, p. 525).

the Byzantines are – as elder and more experienced brothers – the spiritual leaders[53]. Still, to be able to care for the Bulgarians, they needed to have the authority, which was accepted by the latter. That seemed to be the major problem, as in the light of the precedence enumerated by the Byzantine Orator, they were the sons who had first acted against the fathers, and became rebels who had violated the family relations once established by God himself. By throwing away the spiritual fatherhood of the emperor, Symeon, the ruler of Bulgaria at that time (his name is not mentioned even once, but there is no doubt that some excerpts refer to him), rejected God the Father and the Holy Spirit, along with the promise of divine filiation[54]. And it was solely due to the disobedience of the Bulgarians that the Byzantines turned against them. That fact destroyed unity and wounded the Body they created together in Christ[55], and made proper functioning of the Church impossible, thus making it weak and useless in the pursuit of God's work[56].

According to the Orator's logic, the Bulgarians should not have acted like that, even though the Byzantines have sinned against God, as God's choices are eternal[57] and the fact that the Byzantines were the chosen nation was in no doubt. Byzantine apostasy would then be only of temporal nature, as God's grace had not forsaken the Empire.

The idea of Bulgarian filiation also refers to the Byzantine concept of hierarchy of rulers and nations of the world (known as τάξις)[58]. And

---

[53] K. M a r i n o w, *In the Shackles*..., p. 177; J. S h e p a r d, *Byzantine emperors*..., p. 549.

[54] Cf. Rom 8, 14–15. 23; 2 Cor 1, 21–22; 5, 5; Eph 1, 13–14 (*NTG*, pp. 496–497, 556, 591); K. M a r i n o w, *In the Shackles*..., p. 177.

[55] *On the Treaty with the Bulgarians*, 7, p. 264.164–165; 22, p. 288.525–528. Cf. 1 Cor 12, 12–27 (*NTG*, pp. 542–543); А. Н и к о л о в, *Политическа мисъл в ранносредновековна България (средата на IX – края на X век)*, София 2006, p. 238.

[56] Cf. 1 Cor 12, 21–26 (*NTG*, pp. 542–543).

[57] Cf. e.g. Rom 9, 1 – 11, 36, especially 11, 26–29 (*NTG*, pp. 498–506).

[58] Ф. Д ь о л г е р, *Средновековното*..., pp. 181–222; A. G r a b a r, *God and the "Family of Princes" Presided over by the Byzantine Emperor*, HSS 2, 1954, pp. 117–123; G. O s t r o g o r s k y, *The Byzantine emperor and the Hierarchical World Order*, SEER 35.1, 1956, pp. 1–14; H. A h r w e i l e r, *L'ideologie politique de l'Empire byzantine*, Paris 1975, pp. 136–138. The author uses the word τάξις referring to the angelic hierarchy in Heavens – *On the treaty with the Bulgarians*, 8, p. 266.211. On ecclesiastical and celestial hierarchy in Byzantium cf. T. S t ę p i e ń, *Przedmowa*, [in:] P s e u d o-D i o n i z y A r e o p a g i t a,

although that part is not directly related to the Bible, it is worthy to stop by for a while, as it closely refers to the question of filiation in faith. At the apex of that hierarchy stood the Byzantine emperor, with other rulers along with their nations thereunder, over whom the βασιλεύς took spiritual care, and to whom they owed their respect. In this aspect, too, was the Bulgarian ruler a spiritual son of the emperor. The Byzantines were deeply convinced that obeying the τάξις guaranteed stability and blessings to the Christian οἰκουμένη, as that order reflected the heavenly one, and was therefore sacred. Any disobedience was considered a sacrilege, an act of violence against the divine regulations[59].

Only the reconciliation between both nations and the restoration of unity and friendship between Jerusalem and Samaria[60] in 927, that is between Byzantium and Bulgaria (here the Orator again made references to the Bible[61]), restored the τάξις and allowed the surging of God's blessings upon both countries[62]. That act was also (and primarily) an act of reunification of the House of God, the Church, into a single flesh, the Body of Christ[63]. It allowed the Byzantines and Bulgarians to call themselves God's children once again, descendants of the Holy Spirit, disciples of the New Order, and brothers[64]. With the peace concluded God himself destroyed the barrier of hostility which, because of their conduct, had been built between Him and His Church, and by the Byzantines and Bulgarians[65].

Pisma teologiczne, transl. M. Dzielska, introd. T. Stępień, Kraków 2005, pp. 26–50; G. Agamben, *The Kingdom and the Glory. For a Theological Genealogy of Economy and Government*, transl. L. Chiesa (with M. Mandarini), Stanford 2011, pp. 152–157.

[59] *On the Treaty with the Bulgarians*, 12, p. 274.312–316; С.Н. Малахов, *Концепция мира*..., pp. 21, 22, 28; K. Marinow, *In the Shackles*..., p. 178.

[60] *On the Treaty with the Bulgarians*, 6–7, pp. 264.155 – 266.190; 8, p. 266.199–204; 17, p. 278.387–390; 22, p. 288.525–528.537–540. Cf. J. Shepard, *Byzantine emperors*..., pp. 549–550.

[61] Zah 9, 9–10; Is 11, 11–13; Ez 37, 15–28 (*Septuaginta*, vol. II, p. 554, 581–582, 839–840).

[62] *On the Treaty with the Bulgarians*, 9, p. 268.240–241; 19, p. 280.426–427. Cf. J. Shepard, *Byzantine emperors*..., p. 550.

[63] *On the Treaty with the Bulgarians*, 7, p. 264.164–165; 18, p. 278.397–398; 22, p. 288.525–528; С.Н. Малахов, *Концепция мира*..., p. 26.

[64] *On the Treaty with the Bulgarians*, 7, p. 264.164–167; 10, pp. 270.270–272.281.

[65] *On the Treaty with the Bulgarians*, 6, p. 264.155–158; 17, p. 278.379–382.

One should praise God for that reconciliation[66]. The fruits of that unification were blessings of all kinds – joy, unity, friendship, love, concord, harmony, companionship and fraternity, the reconstruction of destroyed territories, earth turning green once again, abundance, wealth and power[67]. In this context the writer recalled biblical images regarding abundant life and the future happiness in the Kingdom of God[68]. Finally, he concluded that the reunification of the Byzantines and Bulgarians would bring sorrow to the real enemies of Christians, to the sons of Hagar (that is, the Arabs)[69].

2.2. God is Peace among Christians

It is obvious that the freshly concluded peace had to be the main theme of the oration[70]. How much that peace was desired by the Empire can be seen from the part that refers directly to the personified figure of Peace,

[66] *On the Treaty with the Bulgarians*, 1, p. 254.2–9; 5, p. 260.110–115; 6, pp. 262.149 – 264.152; 7, p. 264.162–164.166.177; 7, p. 266.184–191; 15, p. 276.351–352; 18, p. 278.391–394; 18, p. 280.409–411.

[67] *On the Treaty with the Bulgarians*, 7, p. 264.174–177; 8, p. 266.204–209; 18, pp. 278.398 – 280.413. Cf. C.H. M a л a x o в, *Концепция мира...*, p. 22; J. S h e p a r d, *Byzantine emperors...*, p. 550.

[68] Cf. e.g. Deut 30, 3. 9–10; Am 9, 13–15; Ioel 2, 19. 21–26; 4, 18; Zah 8, 11–13; Is 30, 23–26; 35, 1–10; 40, 31; 41, 17–19; 60, 4–10. 13. 17; 61, 1–6; 62, 7–9; 65, 17–25; 66, 10–13; Ier 37, 1–3. 8. 18–19; 38, 1. 4–5. 8–9. 12–14. 21. 24–25. 27–28; 40, 7–13; Ez 34, 11–16. 25–29; 36, 8–12. 24. 30. 33–38 (*Septuaginta*, vol. I, p. 342; vol. II, pp. 511, 521–522, 524, 552–553, 605–606, 611–612, 620, 621, 647–648, 649, 653–654, 655, 718–722, 726–727, 832–834, 835–838).

[69] *On the Treaty with the Bulgarians*, 7, p. 264.174–177; 17, p. 278.383–387; 18, pp. 278.398 – 280.413.

[70] About understanding peace in Byzantium see e.g. A. I l i e v a, *The Byzantine Image of War and Peace: the Case of the Peloponnese*, BF 19, 1993, pp. 182–192; C.H. M a л a x o в, *Концепция мира...*, pp. 19–31; R.F. T a f t, *War and Peace in the Byzantine Divine Liturgy*, [in:] *Peace and War in Byzantium. Essays in Honor of George T. Dennis, S.J.*, ed. T.S. M i l l e r, J. N e s b i t t, Washington 1995, pp. 17–32; Th. H a l t o n, *Ecclesiastical War and Peace in the Letters of Isidore of Pelusium*, [in:] *Peace and War...*, pp. 41–49; J.A. M u n i t i z, *War and Peace Reflected in Some Byzantine Mirrors of Princes*, [in:] *Peace and War in Byzantium...*, pp. 50–61; J. C h r y s o s t o m i d e s, *Byzantine Concepts of War and Peace*, [in:] *War, Peace and World Orders in European History*, ed. A.V. H a r t m a n n, B. H e u s e r, London–New York 2001, pp. 91–101; P.M. S t r a s s l e, *Krieg und Frieden in Byzanz*, B 74, 2004, pp. 110–129.

being asked why the Byzantines and Bulgarians had to wait for it/Him for so long. The answer might have been in God's aversion to the hatred that had arisen between the brotherly nations, or at least that was the interpretation that the Orator accepted[71]. The orator emphasised that the objective of his oration was to glorify the concluded peace treaty and its importance, and reminded of the tragedies of the past and reinforcement of peaceful relations in the future[72]. A large part of the work, paragraphs 5 through 10, were the author's lectures on the importance of the peace treaty[73]. That theme could be found in some other parts as well[74]. How should they be understood?

In the author's opinion a war is a disharmony, a disturbance of the divine order in which peace should always reign. What is based on peace is persistent and eternal, just like the divine hierarchy itself[75]. Unity and peaceful coexistence mean, therefore, following God's way[76]. In order to support this proposition the rhetorician quoted some examples from the animal world, of a peaceful coexistence of various species[77]. He also pointed out examples from the everyday life of merchants (common business

[71] *On the Treaty with the Bulgarians*, 2, p. 254.22–25.

[72] *On the Treaty with the Bulgarians*, 4, pp. 258.82 – 260.99; 11, p. 272.282–287; 17, p. 278.382–383; 20, p. 280.431–433; 21–22, pp. 286.498 – 288.540.

[73] *On the Treaty with the Bulgarians*, 5–10, pp. 260.100 – 272.281.

[74] Cf. e.g. *On the Treaty with the Bulgarians*, 15, p. 276.351–356.

[75] Cf. *On the Treaty with the Bulgarians*, 8, pp. 266.192 – 268.239.

[76] *On the Treaty with the Bulgarians*, 21, p. 286.501–505. Cf. Matt 5, 9; Marc 9, 50; Luc 1, 79; 10, 5–6; Rom 12, 18; 15, 33; 1 Cor 7, 15; 14, 33; Eph 2, 15. 17; Col 1, 20; 1 Tess 5, 13; Hebr 12, 14; 1 Petr 3, 11; 2 Petr 3, 14 (*NTG*, pp. 10, 143, 183, 225, 507, 529–530, 547, 593, 614, 628–629, 681, 702, 714). For God is also the donor of peace – Lev 26, 6; Num 25, 12; Iudices 6, 23 (A–B); 3 Reg 2, 33; 1 Par 22, 9; 23, 25; 2 Par 14, 4–6; 32, 22; Ps 28 (29), 11; 36 (37), 11; 54 (55), 19; 84 (85), 9; 118, 165; 147, 3; Nah 1, 15; Agg 2, 9; Mal 2, 5–6; Is 48, 18; 54, 10; 57, 19; Ier 26, 27; 36, 11; 40, 6–9; Ez 34, 25; 37, 26; Dan 10, 19 (C–θ); Luc 10, 5; 24, 36; Io 16, 33; 20, 19. 21. 26; 1 Cor 1, 3; 2 Cor 1, 2; Eph 1, 2; 6, 23; Gal 1, 3; Col 1, 2; 2 Tess 1, 2; 1 Tim 1, 2; 2 Tim 1, 2; Tit 1, 4; Philem 1, 3; 2 Petr 1, 2; 2 Io 1, 3 (*Septuaginta*, vol. I, pp. 205, 261, 431, 629, 797, 799, 832, 862; vol. II, pp. 27, 36, 56, 92, 140, 160, 530, 543, 562–563, 632, 640, 643–644, 698–699, 718, 726–727, 833, 839–840, 927; *NTG*, pp. 225, 290, 359, 373–374, 518, 554, 578, 590, 602, 612, 630, 634, 643, 650–651, 654, 708, 727). Cf. С.Н. Малахов, *Концепция мира*..., pp. 22, 26, 28; J. Shepard, *Byzantine emperors*..., p. 550.

[77] *On the Treaty with the Bulgarians*, 8, p. 268.226–239; 13, p. 274.331–332.

and common voyages), of sailors (they had to work together to overcome unfavourable weather) or even of drivers from the Constantinopolitan Hippodrome (the horses that pulled them rode together)[78].

The author then warns that everyone who has spread discord, who loves war, becomes again a pagan, a barbarian, a Scythian, a madman, a wild beast and a wolf[79]. In fact, by choosing to pursue the miserable glory of this world (an allusion to Symeon's desire of the Byzantine crown), one loses the glory of eternal salvation and becomes a mere tool in Satan's hands[80]. Instead of being a subject of Christ, he surrenders himself to this world's elements and allows a desire to rule his soul. In this way he follows the ancient Hellenic gods – militant, quarrelsome and deceitful[81]. By bringing up the figure of Symeon the author seems to suggest that ungodly desires have entered into him, just like the devil entered into Judas[82].

When Symeon, induced by the new Moses and saviour of the Byzantium, who had liberated the Empire from the Egyptian (that is Bulgarian) yoke, that is the δρουγγάριος of the navy, the new emperor Romanos Lekapenos, eventually agreed to conclude peace (in 923), by God's will he did not live long enough to see its permanent inauguration (927)[83]. The author explained that fact by referring to the history

[78] *On the Treaty with the Bulgarians*, 19, p. 280.420–426. Cf. J. Shepard, *Byzantine emperors...*, p. 550, fn. 23.

[79] *On the Treaty with the Bulgarians*, 5, p. 262.138–142; 7, p. 264.163–171; 9, pp. 268.241 – 270.255.262–267; 13, p. 274.330–332; 14, p. 276.343–346; 15, p. 276.359–361; 16, p. 278.369–371; 21, p. 284.466–472. Cf. С.Н. Малахов, *Концепция мира...*, pp. 23, 26; K. Marinow, *In the Shackles...*, pp. 167, 173, 171–172, 174, 180–181, 185 (fn. 127), 186–187, 189.

[80] *On the Treaty with the Bulgarians*, 3, p. 258.64–68; 9, p. 270.256–262; 13, p. 274.321–323; Cf. K. Marinow, *In the Shackles...*, pp. 166, 188.

[81] *On the Treaty with the Bulgarians*, 9, pp. 268.247 – 270.250; 9, p. 270.262–267; 12, p. 274.307–310. Cf. С.Н. Малахов, *Концепция мира...*, pp. 22–23; K. Marinow, *In the Shackles...*, pp. 166–168.

[82] Cf. *On the Treaty with the Bulgarians*, 3, p. 258.64–68; 19, p. 280.417–420; about Judas – Luc 22, 3; Io 13, 26–27 (*NTG*, pp. 274, 348–349).

[83] *On the Treaty with the Bulgarians*, 15–16, pp. 276.348 – 278.378; K. Marinow, *In the Shackles...*, p. 187.

of King David and his wish to build a temple for Yahweh. God could not agree, as David's hands had been stained with blood since his young age, which excluded him from that honourable enterprise, as only the pure and unstained ones could contribute to building a temple in which the Almighty might be praised and adored. And just like David's son, Solomon had completed that task, it was Symeon's son, Peter that could conclude peace, as the former had shed too much brotherly Christian blood to be entitled to build a temple for the Lord[84].

The Byzantine author emphasised that after the peace treaty had been signed, one should not look back and return to the old way of conduct. A new life commenced and God gave a breath of His Spirit. The unity of the new spiritual Israel was therefore restored (the orator made a reference to the Book of Ezekiel)[85]. The rhetorician went even further, saying that the concluded peace was a true resurrection of the House of Jacob[86].

It should be remembered that at the time of baptising the Bulgarians the Byzantines believed that an era of lasting peaceful relations with the northern neighbours was at hand (and many years of peace seemed to confirm that); however the reign of Symeon completely destroyed that illusion[87]. Still, we can think that the orator's words about reconstruction and resurrection of the House of Jacob cited above may indicate that the peace of 927 restored the faith in peaceful coexistence of Bulgaria and the Eastern Rome.

---

[84] *On the Treaty with the Bulgarians*, 16, p. 278.371–378; T. Тодоров, *"Слово за мира с българите"*..., pp. 142–144; A. Николов, *Политическа*..., pp. 237–238; K. Marinow, *In the Shackles*..., pp. 187–188. The mentioned biblical story – 2 Reg 16, 5–11; 3 Reg 5, 17–19; 8, 15–19; 1 Par 22, 7–10 (*Septuaginta*, vol. I, pp. 598–599, 687–688, 646–647, 797).

[85] *On the Treaty with the Bulgarians*, 5, p. 260.108–110; 18, p. 278.394–396. Cf. Ez 37, 1–28.

[86] *On the Treaty with the Bulgarians*, 5, p. 260.110; 18, p. 278.396.

[87] M.J. Leszka, *Stracone złudzenia. Religijny kontekst stosunków bizantyńsko-bułgarskich w latach 863–927*, [in:] *Religijna mozaika Bałkanów*, ed. M. Walczak-Mikołajczakowa, Gniezno 2008, pp. 32–39. Similarly, though more generally, already C.H. Малахов, *Концепция мира*..., p. 26.

According to the orator, the peace was not granted by earthly rulers but by God himself. Furthermore, it was God Christ himself who was that gift, as the Bible said that God *was* peace[88]. This conclusion is indirectly confirmed by other parts of the oration as well – by praising peace in the initial words the author clearly points out God's nature and says that He showed mercy when a calamity befell His people; he heard their prayers[89]. The author then turns to the peace itself, asking why it has waited so long to appear[90]. If the Almighty Himself is peace, how could then a most precious gift like that be rejected?

The oration contained also some more or less veiled warnings not to disregard the freshly concluded agreement[91]. Their mood and the way they are composed make the reader (and most probably listeners) associate them with the Epistle to the Hebrews[92], in which is written that if salvation "at the first began to be spoken by the Lord" (and not by prophets, as it took place in the Old Testament), so great salvation may not be neglected. It also shows how important the treaty of 927 was for the Byzantines.

To sum up, by using parallels with the Bible the Orator expressed the following views of both religious and political nature:

---

[88] *On the Treaty with the Bulgarians*, 5, pp. 260.117–262.144, in particular p. 262.126–133. Cf. *On the Treaty with the Bulgarians*, 21, p. 286.501–506. Cf. also С.Н. Малахов, *Концепция мира...*, pp. 21, 22. On Christ – Peace: Eph 2, 14; Is 2, 3–4; 9, 5–6 (the newly born child will be a child of peace; it was identified with Christ in the Byzantine exegesis); Mih 5, 2–5 (the Israel's ruler to be born in Bethlehem will be peace); cf. Io 14, 27; 16, 33; 20, 19–21; Hebr 7, 1–3; about the God of peace – Rom 15, 33; 1 Cor 14, 33; Philip 4, 9; 1 Tess 5, 23; 2 Tess 3, 16; Hebr 13, 20 (*Septuaginta*, vol. II, pp. 516, 568, 578, 581; *NTG*, pp. 353, 359, 373, 515, 547, 593, 611, 629, 634, 666, 684).

[89] *On the Treaty with the Bulgarians*, 1, p. 254.2–8.

[90] *On the Treaty with the Bulgarians*, 2, p. 254.22–25.

[91] *On the Treaty with the Bulgarians*, 5, p. 262.142–144; 10, pp. 270.270–272.281; 21, p. 286.498–522.

[92] Hebr 2, 3 (*NTG*, p. 659).

1) Byzantium is a new Chosen People, a new Israel;

2) when baptised, the Bulgarians had been planted as a twig of the true Root of Jesse[93]. From then on along with the Byzantines they made up the Body of Christ and House of Jacob[94];

3) the Byzantines are the fathers and teachers in faith for the Bulgarians, and as long as the latter keep unity with the Empire, they enjoy God's blessings and their country flourishes; they are part of the hierarchic order created by God on earth and they may enjoy guidance and care of the Empire;

4) Symeon and his ungodly desire to attain the Byzantine crown, who thus disturbed the divine order, was blamed for all the misery of the war (along with the Byzantine regency of 913–919)[95];

5) the peace of 927 was God's work, to disregard it would be a mortal sin; one should also see that peaceful coexistence survived, as peace is an eternal attribute of God, hence by concluding eternal peace[96] the Byzantines and Bulgarians are like the Almighty and therefore become the proper image of God;

6) the sons of Hagar, that is the Arabs, are the real enemies of Byzantium and Bulgarians.

---

[93] On the term itself see Is 11, 1. 10; Rom 15, 12; Apoc 5, 5; 22, 16 (*Septuaginta*, vol. II, p. 581; *NTG*, pp. 512, 746, 788). About 'grafting in' pagans into the olive tree of Israel (here Byzantium or broadly understood Church) – Rom 11, 13–24 (*NTG*, pp. 504–505).

[94] The orator directly uses this biblical name – *On the Treaty with the Bulgarians*, 15, p. 276.351; 18, p. 278.396.

[95] K. Marinow, *In the Shackles...*, p. 189. According to the Orator the indolent policy of regencies that had administered the Empire before Romanos Lekapenos entered the throne also contributed to the ravage of war – *On the Treaty with the Bulgarians*, 13, p. 274.317–323.330–338; 14, p. 276.339–347; 15, p. 276.348–351.

[96] *On the Treaty with the Bulgarians*, 5, p. 262.142–144; 22, p. 288.537–540.

From the sociological and anthropological point of view the abovementioned standards of coexistence between the Byzantines and Bulgarians would have influenced their everyday life in its entirety. The newly concluded peace has reinitiated the chronological, repeated circle of normal life, the kind of life originated, established and blessed by God. The way of life in which the peace was the basis of human everyday life, and war was a disturbance, violence which destroyed the holy order of the continuously repeating circle of time, the circle which guaranteed safety. Finally, although the ideas presented above represent the particular view of a single (albeit excellent) Byzantine author, their importance is much greater because of the author's appearance with the homily at the imperial court, as an official representative of the Byzantine chancellery. We can therefore consider his thoughts to have been a way of thinking accepted by the official power.

* * *

To conclude, I would like to stress that considering the long reign of Peter I and the peace with the Empire that lasted throughout all that time (with the exception of the problematic raid of Nikephoros II Phokas to the Bulgarian border in 967)[97], one can say that from the point of view of the Byzantine rhetorician, his oration was entirely successful.

Ironically, only two years after Peter's death, in 971, the Byzantines put an end to the existence of the Bulgarian state (or to be precise, to its eastern part with the capital in Great Preslav)[98], thus themselves destroying the gentle ideas presented in the oration of the renowned Byzantine rhetorician and writer.

[97] On this subject, see K. M a r i n o w, *Hemos comme barriere militaire. L'analyse des ecrits historiques de Leon le Diacre et de Jean Skylitzes au sujet de la campagne de guerre des empereurs byzantins Nicephore II Phocas en 967 et de Jean I Tzymisces en 971*, BMd 2, 2011, pp. 444–455.

[98] On this subject see e.g. И. Б о ж и л о в, *България при цар Петър (927–969)*, [in:] i d e m, В. Г ю з е л е в, *История на средновековна България...*, pp. 299–300.

III

Miliana Kaymakamova

The Cult of the Bulgarian Tsar Peter (927–969) and the Driving Ideas of the Bulgarian Liberation Uprisings against the Byzantine Rule in the 11th–12th Century

It is well known that at the time of the Byzantine rule (11th–12th century), the Bulgarians used to rise periodically in an open conflict against the central authority in an effort to regain their state independence. According to the sources, their activity reached its peak during the 11th century when the Empire was deeply shaken by instability. At that time, six uprisings and seven plots were organised[1]. As the Komnenoi Dynasty came to rule during the 1080s, the Bulgarian military resistance subsided and acquired an episodic nature. This is clearly illustrated by the fact that during the 12th century only two armed events were recorded, and they took place during the reign of emperor Manuel I Komnenos (1143–1180)[2].

---

[1] For further details on the evolution of these movements and on their leaders, see И. Божилов, В. Гюзелев, *История на средновековна България VII–XIV в.*, София 2006, pp. 395–418.

[2] Attention to them was drawn by Vassil Gyuzelev (В. Гюзелев, *Бележки върху историята на българските земи и българите половин столетие преди въстанието*

The hope for liberation was revived in the 1180s when the Empire fell into a deep crisis again. The Assen brothers took advantage of it and in 1185 organised a new liberation uprising, its centre in Tarnovo, which led to the restoration of the Bulgarian Tsardom. In addition to this uprising, among the largest revolts were those organised by Samuel's grandson Peter Delyan in 1040–1041 and by George Voyteh – a boyar from Skopje who originated from a kavkhans family – in 1072–1073.

These three anti-Byzantine movements from the 11th–12th century have yet another very significant characteristic that convincingly reveals their liberation character and distinguishes them from the other four anti-Byzantine uprisings (of Bulgarians and Vlachs in Thessaly in 1066, led by a noble citizen of Larissa – Nikoulitzas Delphinas; of the uprising of Bulgarian population in the Theme of Paristrion in 1073, led by the Bulgarian Nestor who was holding a Byzantine office; of the Paulician Leka in Sredets; and of Dobromir in Mesembria in the period 1073–1078). What distinguished the former three was the fact that their leaders were proclaimed as Bulgarian tsars, adopting the name of St. Tsar Peter (927–969). Specifically, these were: Samuel's grandson Peter II Delyan (1040–1041); Peter III (1072) – Constantine Bodin, grandson of tsar Samuel, and Peter IV (1185–1190; 1196–1197) – Theodore, the eldest of the first three Assen brothers[3].

In previous studies, this specific phenomenon, which has no analogue in other periods of the history of mediaeval Bulgaria, is linked, on the one hand, with the name and the popularity of the Bulgarian tsar Peter I who was canonised after his death and is revered by the church and by the Bulgarian people[4] and, on the other hand, with the need of the rebellion leaders to gain legitimacy as Bulgarian tsars, and who adopted his name

на Асеневци (1186–1188), [in:] *Проф. д.и.н. Станчо Ваклинов и средновековната българска култура*, ed. К. Попконстантинов, Б. Борисов, Р. Костова, Велико Търново 2005, pp. 37–38). These are: 1) the riot of the Bulgarians from Belgrade which broke out in 1154 during the war of the said basileus with the Hungarians; 2) the clash of his troops with the Bulgarians in Sredets district in 1166–1167.

[3] For further details on these Bulgarian tsars, see Й. Андреев, И. Лазаров, П. Павлов, *Кой кой е в средновековна България*, 3София 2012, pp. 547–550, 553–556.

[4] В. Гюзелев, *Черноморската област в историята на Българското царство от възобновяването му (1186 г.) до възобновяването на Византийската империя*

for that reason[5]. Of course, these explanations are fully justified, but we believe that they do not exhaust the issue of the reason which had caused it as a cultural phenomenon during the period of the Byzantine rule of the Bulgarian lands (11th–12th centuries).

Some of our preliminary observations on the initial course of these three Bulgarian liberation uprisings against the Byzantine rule show that the above list of tsars named Peter outlines a religious and political concept of the Bulgarian public authority which is focused on St. Tsar Peter I, who embodied the Bulgarian Tsardom of that time. The 'new Peters' and the typical way in which they came to rule suggest that the concept in question has a key role for the conceptual understanding of these uprisings, and the name of the Bulgarian Saint Tsar who, in the course of the fight, used to perform the role of 'rex perpetuus', is used as a historical argument for proclamation of the Bulgarian state independence and the restoration of the Tsardom (*renovatio imperii*)[6].

Therefore, the task of this study is to examine in detail the importance of the cult of the Bulgarian tsar Peter (927–969) as the origin of ideas that asserted the liberating character of the three major Bulgarian uprisings against the Byzantine rule and played a major role in the consolidation of the Bulgarians around their leaders. I would like to highlight that the issue of the ideology of these uprisings has not yet been the subject of a purposeful examination in the modern mediaeval studies. The reasons for this

---

(1261 г.), [in:] *Studia archaeologica. Supplementum II. Сборник в чест на професор Атанас Милчев*, София 2002, p. 248.

[5] Д. Чешмеджиев, *Няколко бележки за култа към цар Петър I (927–969)*, [in:] *Християнската традиция и царската институция в българската култура*, ed. В. Бонева, Е. Иванова, Шумен 2003, pp. 35–36; idem, *Култът към цар Петър (927–969): манастирски или държавен?*, [in:] *Љубав према образовању и вера у Бога у православним манастирама, 5. Међународна Хилендарска конференција. Зборник избраних радова I*, ed. P. Matejić et al., Београд–Columbus 2006, pp. 255–257; И. Билярски, *Покровители на Царството: Св. цар Петър и св. Параскева-Петка*, София 2004, pp. 33–42. Д. Полывянный, *Царь Петр в историчесской памяти болгарского средневековья*, [in:] *Средновековният българин и "другите". Сборник в чест на 60-годишнината на проф. дин Петър Ангелов*, ed. А. Николов, Г.Н. Николов, София 2013, p. 141.

[6] М. Каймакамова, *Власт и история в средновековна България (VII–XIV век)*, София 2011, pp. 220–224.

'white spot' in historiography can be explained, to a certain extent, with the lack of sufficient concrete data in the sources. They cannot, however, be an excuse for its neglect, because the Byzantine and Bulgarian writers of the 11th–13th century do give us certain information which, although not so detailed, allows its in-depth study. In view of this, it is necessary to remind of the merits of tsar Peter which subsequently justified his canonisation and turning into a symbol of the Bulgarian State during the period of the Byzantine rule.

1. A Brief Overview of the History of the Cult of Tsar Peter in Mediaeval Bulgaria

To explain the importance of the cult of the ruler for the conceptual justification of the three major Bulgarian uprisings against the Byzantine rule in the 11th–12th century, we need to trace, although briefly, its occurrence and evolution. The results and achievements of our previous studies devoted to the history of the cult will serve as a basis for tracing it.

The sources that shine light on the cult of the ruler are diverse both in type and in content[7]. These are mostly works of the liturgical literature – gospels, prologues, menaions, troparions in which tsar Peter is commemorated on January 30th, because this date is combined with the date of transfer of the remains of Saint Clement of Rome, and not because this is the day on which the earthly life of tsar Peter came to an end[8].

[7] Cf. Й. Иванов, *Български старини из Македония*, ed. Д. Ангелов, София 1970, pp. 383–386; И. Дуйчев, *Из старата българска книжнина*, vol. I, София 1943, pp. 98–102, 220–222; Р. Павлова, *Петър Черноризец старобългарски писател от X в.*, София 1994, pp. 24–29; П. Димитров, *Петър Черноризец*, Шумен 1995, pp. 39–42; Д. Чешмеджиев, *Няколко бележки…*, pp. 25–26; И. Билярски, *Покровители…*, pp. 21–24; И. Билярски, М. Йовчева, *За датата на успението на цар Петър и за култа към него*, [in:] *Тангра. Сборник в чест на 70-годишнината на акад. Васил Гюзелев*, ed. М. Каймакамова et al., София 2006, pp. 546–547.

[8] For further details on this fixed commemorative date of tsar Peter in liturgical sources, see И. Билярски, М. Йовчева, *За датата на успението…*, pp. 547–552; Д. Полывянный, *Царь Петр…*, p. 143.

Information about the Saint Tsar can also be found in: *Synodikon of Tsar Boril* from 1211, some historical chronicles such as the *Bulgarian Apocryphal Chronicle* (*Tale of the Prophet Isaiah* – 11th century), *Narrative of the Martyrs of Zographou* (13th century), monuments of trade writings such as *Charter of Virgino Brdo* by Constantine Tih Assen (1257–1277)[9], as well as some monuments of Bulgarian tsars and tsaritsas, such as the *Drinov's beadroll*[10].

The main source on the cult is the *Service of St. Tsar Peter*, since no reliable traces of a *Life* of his have been found so far, but there is no doubt that such existed. Yordan Ivanov is of the opinion that there has been a full (the Zograph manual copy – the *Draganov's menaion*) and short (manuscript No 434 of the Belgrade National Library) service for tsar Peter[11]. Subsequently, Stephan Kozhuharov establishes that in fact the 'two services' represent two fragments from one service[12]. His observations on the two texts published by Yordan Ivanov allow him to establish that it has been of a studio type, but incomplete, because of its merger with the service for the transfer of the remains of Saint Clement of Rome. Its full text used to contain chants without which we can speak neither of full service nor of a 'short commemoration' – dismissal hymn, kontakion and oikos, and along with them – another two sticheras of 'Lord I called Thee' and one kathisma. The restructuring of the work allows Kozhuharov to specify that the service was written by only one author who was a talented

[9] The question of whether this charter is authentic or not has not yet found its satisfactory and final solution. Cf. Й. И в а н о в, *Български старини...*, pp. 578–581; G.A. I l y n s k i y, *Gramoty bolgarskih carey*, London [2]1970, pp. 53–54, 86–87 [= *Грамоты болгарских царей. Трудъ Г.А. Ильинского*, Москва 1911]. However, what is important in this case is that the mentioning of St. tsar Peter among the donors of the 'St. George the Fast' Monastery in Virgino Brdo near Skopje speaks of the ideological significance of the cult of the Saint Tsar in the formation of the rulers' ideology in a Bulgarian and Balkan (Serbian) environment. See И. Б и л я р с к и, *Покровители...*, pp. 23–24.

[10] Й. И в а н о в, *Избрани произведения*, ed. Б. А н г е л о в, vol. I, София 1982, p. 152.

[11] *Service of St. Tsar Peter*, pp. 383–394.

[12] С. К о ж у х а р о в, *Търновската книжовна школа и развитието на химничната поезия в старата българска литература*, ТКШ 1, 1974, p. 288, fn. 28; i d e m, *Служба за цар Петър*, [in:] *Старобългарска литература. Енциклопедичен речник*, ed. Д. П е т к а н о в а, Велико Търново 2003, p. 474; i d e m, *Проблеми на старобългарската поезия*, София 2004, pp. 75–79.

poet hymn-writer and a follower of the monk tsar. He wrote his work in the traditions of the Preslav and Ohrid hymnographic school soon after the death of the ruler. For this dating, the said scholar refers to the passages that mention 'great waves and storms' as well as to the prayer addresses for deliverance from 'the great misfortune that has befallen us', from 'suffering and misfortunes coming from enemies'. According to him, the service for tsar Peter appears to be one of the last works of the Old Bulgarian literature, created before the ruin of the capital Preslav. Almost all researchers of the cult of tsar Peter after Kozhuharov adopt his conclusions and talk about the 'service' (and not of services) for the Saint Tsar.

The observations and the conclusions of Stephan Kozhuharov make researchers after him feel more confident in dating the emergence of the service and the beginning of the cult to the period between 969–971[13].

---

[13] Д. Чешмеджиев, *Няколко бележки за култа...*, p. 24; И. Билярски, *Покровители...*, p. 22. Bistra Nikolova (Б. Николова, *Цар Петър и характерът на неговия култ*, PBg 33.2, 2009, pp. 68–69), puts in doubt this dating and links the emergence of the service with the first decades of the 11th century arguing that the words 'Tsardom' and 'tsar' are not mentioned in one of the places in the service containing prayer addresses to the Saint which speaks about salvation from the 'great misfortune' pending upon the praying people. Therefore, according to her, these prayers do not seem to necessarily target events from 969–971, when Bulgaria is subjected to the attacks of Knyaz Svyatoslav and of emperor John Tzymiskes, but they reflect the attacks of the Pechenegs that took place during the 30s–40s of the 11th century and led to their settling down in Preslav and to the decline of the town in the middle of the 11th century. According to the author, this is also the *terminus ante quem* for the appearance of the service.

It seems to me that this argument of Nikolova is groundless because the prayer address in question was taken out from the context of this part of the service which begins with the dedication *To Tsar Peter* followed by the prayer addresses quoted by the said author. Here is the whole text: *Just as earlier you wished to live your life in peace, now with your prayers to God on our behalf bring peace to all lands. Hurry up with your prayers, most blessed father Peter, for you see that a great trouble is engulfing us and we are overwhelmed. You appeared to us like the morning star, shining from the earth in recent years and dispersed all of the darkness of the opposing enemy. The sinful lips who attempt to praise you are not able of doing that, Tsar Peter, because of the beauty of your goodness. That is why we beg you: grant us words to praise [you].* A few lines below it reads: *In faith you [reign] over a double tsardom, blessed father Tsar Peter: you reign here and there.* (*Service of St. Tsar Peter*, p. 388; transl. p. 108). Cf. И. Дуйчев, *Из старата българска...*, pp. 99–100). As it can be seen, the words 'tsar' and 'Tsardom' are expressly mentioned

Even at his time Yordan Ivanov, who has contributed fundamentally to the study of the history of the cult, points out that the service has been intended for performance in the monastery where the Bulgarian tsar used to stay and where his holy body was laid[14]. Its location is determined mainly on the basis of the following addresses to the saint which are contained in its second part: *Rejoice, solid rock of Christ's faith. Rejoice, Peter, strength of the churches in your city of Preslav* (ра҄ѹ сѧ тврьды каменю вѣрѣ Х҃вѣ. ра҄ѹ сѧ Петре ѹтвръжде҄ние цр҃квамь. и градоу твоемоу Прѣславоу)[15]. The mentioning of the capital in the above-cited text is assessed as a sure indication, on the one hand, that the monastery was located either in the capital or in its surroundings, and on the other hand, that it is precisely where the cult of tsar Peter was born[16].

In this context, let us point out that a service is usually created after the *Life* of a canonised person, thus reaffirming the cult, and is performed on the day set for its celebration. Unfortunately, sure traces of the *Life of Tsar Peter* have not yet been discovered, but there is no doubt that such existed[17].

Of particular interest to our study is the observation made by Anatoliy Turilov stating that the menologia preserved in Russian manuscripts from the 11th–14th century do not contain a commemoration of tsar Peter, which is included in manuscripts of the Bulgarian and Serbian tradition.

---

in this part of the service. Therefore, in my opinion, it is more realistic and historically justified to date the service and the beginning of the cult to an earlier period – 969–971. Dmitriy Polyviannyi (Д. П о л ы в я н н ы й *Царь Петр*..., p. 142, fn. 26, 145) is of the opinion that the service and troparion of St. Tsar Peter have been probably created no earlier than the 13th century in the 'protothrone' bishopric of Preslav. This proposal is based on some observations relating to the fact that the South Slavic Liturgical Books from the 13th century did in fact re-enter the practice of liturgical honouring of the 'first' generation of local saints through the drawing up of new texts.

[14] *Service of St. Tsar Peter*, pp. 384, 393–394.

[15] *Service of St. Tsar Peter*, p. 392 (transl. p. 109). Cf. И. Д у й ч е в, *Из старата българска*..., p. 101.

[16] В. И в а н о в а, *Стари църкви и манастири в българските земи (IV–XII в.)*, [in:] *Годишник на Народния музей за 1922–1925*, ed. А. П р о т и ч ъ, София 1926, p. 172; Й. И в а н о в, *Български старини*..., pp. 393–394; И. Д у й ч е в, *Из старата българска*..., pp. 221–222; Д. Ч е ш м е д ж и е в, *Няколко бележки за култа*..., p. 24.

[17] Р. П а в л о в а, *Петър Черноризец*..., pp. 18–19.

This circumstance is most likely due to the fact that the commemoration of tsar Peter, who died in 969, has failed to spread in the Eastern Bulgarian manuscripts reflected in Old Russian manual copies by the time of the Byzantine conquest[18]. The establishment of this fact by the Russian scholar is of considerable academic value for the history of the cult. The same line is followed in his finding that the practice relating to the 'nationalisation' of different saints, so typical of the first Assen brothers, was also adopted by the Cometopouloi Dynasty. In support, Turilov points out that in 986 tsar Samuel transferred the remains of St. Achilius, who became the patron of the capital Ohrid[19].

The above observations give us reason to point out that the capture of Preslav by John Tzymiskes (969–976) in April 971 had negative consequences for the spread of the ruler's cult in eastern Bulgaria. The main reason for this is that this part of the territory of the Bulgarian state, after its occupation by Byzantium, was placed under the control of the Constantinopolitan patriarchate. Therefore, in the last quarter of the 10th and in the early 11th century, the cult of tsar Peter found fertile soil for development in the western limits of the Bulgarian Tsardom which, after 971, remained free and became the staging ground for the Bulgarian fight for liberation of the lands occupied by the Empire. This is mainly attributed to both the secular authority, i.e. the Cometopouloi Dynasty and especially to tsar Samuel, and to the independent Bulgarian church which, after 971, had as its centres the towns of Triaditsa (Sredets-Sofia), Vodena, Moglena, and Prespa. According to the second Charter of emperor Basil II to the Ohrid Archbishopric, the Bulgarian patriarch has resided in them consecutively, at different times, to eventually settle down in Samuel's capital Ohrid[20].

Important evidence, seen from the fact that the greater part of the liturgical sources of tsar Peter originate in the southwestern limits of the Bulgarian Tsardom, points to the cult of of tsar being particularly

[18] Б.Н. Флоря, А.А. Турилов, С.А. Иванов, *Судьбы Кирило-Мефодиевской традиции после Кирилла и Мефодия*, Санкт-Петербург 2000, p. 91, fn. 1.

[19] *Ibidem*, pp. 89–90.

[20] Й. Иванов, *Български старини...*, p. 566; И. Божилов, В., Гюзелев, *История...*, p. 365.

developed in this region[21]. Highly significant in this respect are the Banitsa (National Library 'Cyril and Methodius' 847, the end of the 13th century) and the Curzon Gospels (Add. Mss. 39 628 of the British Museum, 14th century), in which the commemoration day of the tsar is January 30th. With regard to their calendars, it has been proven that they ascend to a common old protograph and are of a compilatory nature[22].

During Byzantine rule (11th–12th century), the western Bulgarian lands continued to be a centre of the cult of tsar Peter. The immediate reaction to its preservation can primarily be found in the information about the Saint Tsar contained in the *Bulgarian Apocryphal Chronicles* and *Daniel's Interpretation*, which were the work of Bulgarian monks who worked in the monasteries of Sredets and Velbazhd bisphorics[23]. Further important evidence is provided by the adoption of the tsar's name by the leaders of the liberation uprisings against Byzantium which broke out in 1040–1041 and in 1072–1073. The popular (Anonymous) *Life of John of Rila* which tells the story of the meeting of the Saint with tsar Peter is another evidence of the existence of the tsar's cult during the period of the Byzantine rule[24]. At the end of the 12th century, in parallel with the displacement of the centre of the liberation struggle in the lands to the north of the Balkan Mountains, the cult of tsar Peter was present in Tarnovo where, in the autumn of 1185, the liberation uprising of the Assen brothers broke out and eventually led to the sustainable restoration of the Bulgarian Tsardom. The adoption of the name Peter by Theodore – the eldest among them – became an external expression of their tribute to the Saint Tsar.

In the early 13th century, the name of tsar Peter was introduced in the official liturgical practice, as it was included for eternal commemoration on the Orthodox Sunday in the Book of the Bulgarian church, and from there – in the commemoration lists of the Bulgarian and the Mount

[21] Д. Чешмеджиев, *Няколко бележки...*, p. 36.

[22] И. Билярски, М. Йовчева, *За датата...*, p. 546.

[23] М. Каймакамова, *Власт и история...*, pp. 129–130, 133; V. Tapkova-Zaimova, A. Miltenova, *Historical and Apocalyptic Literature in Byzantium and Medieval Bulgaria*, transl. M. Paneva, M. Lilova, Sofia 2011, pp. 181, 293.

[24] Д. Чешмеджиев, *Култът към цар Петър...*, p. 256.

Athos monasteries[25]. After *Synodikon of Tsar Boril* (1211), information about St. Tsar Peter is only found in two monuments from the second half of the 13th century – the *Charter of Virgino Brdo* by Constantine Tih Assen[26] and *Narrative on the Martyrs of Zographou* from the last quarter of the 13th century[27]. In liturgical sources, the earliest record of the memory of the Bulgarian tsar also refers to the said period. The two manual copies of the Old Bulgarian *Service for Tsar Peter* (in the Draganov Menaion and the Belgrade Menaion No 434) also originated during that time. Their occurrence is connected with one of the trends in the development of the South Slavic liturgical literature during the 13th century – namely the emergence of compilations that reflect to a greater extent the reformed Preslav's literature from the middle and up to the end of the 10th century[28]. These facts clearly show that, after the time of the first three Assen brothers, the reverence for tsar Peter exhausted its function as an active conceptual propaganda means used by the Bulgarian Tsardom. However, the mention of the name of St. Tsar Peter in monuments of the representative literature proves that his cult retained its official character. Another particular characteristic is that during the 13th–14th century, the memory of him was only literary – the remains of the saint were apparently lost and not transferred to Tarnovo, which is the reason why the cult in the capital faded away[29]. The most prominent place in Tarnovo's calendar started to be given to the cults of St. Demetrios of Thessalonike and of the saints whose remains were transferred to the new Bulgarian capital of the Assen brothers at the end of the 12th and during the first half of the 13th century (these were: John of Rila, Hilarion of Moglena, John of Polivot, Michael Voin, Filoteya

---

[25] *Synodikon of Tsar Boril*, p. 149; Д.И. Полывянный, *Царь Петр...*, pp. 141–142.

[26] *Charter of Virgino Brdo*, pp. 578–587.

[27] *Narrative on the Martyrs of Zographou*, pp. 437–440. Yordan Ivanov (p. 438) dates the work to the early 14th century (1311 at the latest), but in the latest studies, the creation of the work is referred to the very end of the 13th century and is, in form and in purpose, classified as a Short Life, cf. *Стара българска литература*, vol. IV, *Житийни творби*, ed. К. Иванова, София 1986, pp. 602–603; *ИБСЛ*, pp. 457–458.

[28] И. Билярски, М. Йовчева, *За датата...*, p. 547; М. Йовчева, *Южнославянската литургическа книжнина от XIII в.*, ЗРВИ 46, 2009, p. 355.

[29] Д. Чешмеджиев, *Култът към цар Петър...*, pp. 256–257.

Temnishka, Paraskeva-Petka). This phenomenon is not accidental but is conditional upon the process connected with the formation of the idea of Tarnovo as a 'New Constantinople'–'Third Rome' in the first half of the 13th century. As a result of this substantial change connected with the universalisation of the Bulgarian capital, the authority of the family, as was correctly established by Klimentina Ivanova, was replaced by the authority of the city[30]. This new trend in Bulgarian spiritual culture during the 13th–14th century has led to the displacement of the cult of tsar Peter in the state ideology. Without losing its importance as an official, state cult, it gives way to the cults of saint warriors, martyrs and clergymen, turning the capital Tarnovo into a God-protected city and as a major centre of the Eastern Orthodox religion along with Constantinople, Thessalonike, Mount Athos, Jerusalem, Nikaia and Trebizond[31].

In short, the thus delineated history of the cult of tsar Peter in mediaeval Bulgaria allows us to draw some conclusions. It is obvious that the tsar's cult is characterised by its uneven development. Its evolution and place in the state ideology are justified by the specific conditions under which it has been shaped throughout the different periods of the history of the Bulgarian autocracy. It has also become clear that, after the death of tsar Theodore-Peter IV in 1197, none of the representatives of the young Assen Dynasty adopted the name of the Saint Tsar, which is indicative of the fact that his cult had no longer been relevant as an active propaganda means used by the Bulgarian tsarist authority at the time of the heirs

[30] *Стара българска литература...*, pp. 18–19.

[31] И. Дуйчев, *Българско средновековие. Проучвания върху политическата и културната история на средновековна България*, София 1972, pp. 413–431; В. Гюзелев, *Училища, скриптории, библиотеки и знания в България (XIII–XIV век)*, София 1985, pp. 16–18; В. Тъпкова-Заимова, *Търново между Ерусалим, Рим и Цариград*, ТКШ 4, 1985, pp. 249–261; *Българската литература и книжнина през XIII век*, ed. И. Божилов, С. Кожухаров, София 1987, pp. 7–37; Е. Бакалова, *Култът към мощите и реликвите: Изток–Запад*, [in:] *Средновековна християнска Европа: Изток–Запад*, ed. В. Гюзелев, А. Милтенова, София 2002, pp. 611–616; eadem, *Общество и изкуство в България през XIII век*, ЗРВИ 46, 2009, pp. 239–253; И. Билярски, *Покровители...*, pp. 43–55; М. Йовчева, *Южнославянската литургическа книжнина от XIII в.*, ЗРВИ 46, 2009, p. 356; М. Каймакамова, *Власт и история...*, pp. 267–268; eadem, *Идеята "Търново-нов Цариград": "Трети Рим" през XIII–XIV век*, BMd 3, 2012, pp. 469–470.

of the first three Assen brothers during the 13th–14th century. This fact comes to show us that the name of Saint Tsar Peter, as a sustainable element of the tsarist legitimacy, remains a 'brand' only of the leaders of the three major Bulgarian revolts against Byzantium in the 11th–12th century.

2. The Importance of the Cult of Tsar Peter for the Conceptual Justification of the Bulgarian Liberation Uprisings in the 11th–12th Century

In previous studies, the reasons why leaders of the liberation movements from the period of the Byzantine rule adopted the name of tsar Peter were sought in two areas. According to some scholars, Peter was the first legitimate, according to Byzantium, Bulgarian tsar who was related by his marriage with Maria-Irene to two of the Byzantine dynasties (Macedonian and that of the Lekapenos). In this respect, it is highlighted that in the period of the Byzantine rule of the Bulgarian lands importance was given to the Byzantine state and dynastic tradition and not to the Bulgarian state tradition of khan Boris I-Michael, tsar Symeon and tsar Samuel. This is why the cult of tsar Peter, the 'New Constantine', the restorer of the Bulgarian Tsardom, was developed[32]. Other historians believe that the honouring of St. Tsar Peter is closely related to the cults of rulers who converted their states to Christianity, pointing out that Peter is the one during whose rule Bulgaria was built as the truly Christian state of the Bulgarians. This defines the importance of this ruler in the history of the country. It is also pointed out that the apparent connection between

[32] Д. Чешмеджиев, *Няколко бележки...*, pp. 35–36; idem, *Култът към цар Петър...*, p. 256; idem, *Българската държавна традиция в апокрифите: цар Петър в Българския апокрифен летопис*, [in:] *Българско средновековие: общество, власт, история. Сборник в чест на проф. д-р Милияна Каймакамова*, ed. Г.Н. Николов, А. Николов, София 2013, pp. 266–267.

the memory of this saint ruler and the movements for the recovery of the Bulgarian statehood after 1018 was religious, and not dynastic[33].

Although the above explanations do have their grounds, it seems to us that they do not exhaust the answer to the significant and not at all easy question – why did the leaders of the three major Bulgarian uprisings chose to revive the name of the Saint Tsar? An answer to this, we think, may be found in the story by Michael Psellos (1018 – after 1096/97) about the outbreak of the uprising of Peter Delyan. So far, it has not been discussed from the perspective of the issue which is of interest to us, even though it contains the point of view of those Bulgarians who took part in the liberation movements on the matter of the choice made by their leaders. This is why we will go into greater detail on this work. It is included in the fourth chapter of his *Chronography*, dedicated to the rule of emperor Michael IV (1034–1041). Pointing out that it will take him a long time to enumerate what the emperor has done and what he decreed *during the internal riots and foreign wars*, the prominent Byzantine intellectual states that he would make *only one exception*, taking into account the fight of the emperor with the barbarians (i.e. the Bulgarians – M.K.). In this regard, Psellos specifies that he will only briefly and in passing mention the main events. His story begins with a brief presentation of the capture of their state by emperor Basil II (976–1025), described as *prince of emperors*, who *attacked their country and destroyed their power*[34]. Further on, Michael Psellos explains that for some time the Bulgarians, persistently called by him 'barbarians' and 'tribe', accepted their defeat and submitted to the power of the Byzantines, but then regained their previous loftiness, yet still not rising openly, *until the appearance among them of a political agitator when their policy at once became hostile to the Empire*[35]. With much hatred and malice Psellos goes on to explain that the man (Peter Delyan – M.K.) who roused them was from the same tribe and *member of a family unworthy of mention, but cunning, and capable of practising any*

[33] И. Билярски, *Покровители*..., pp. 33–34.

[34] Michael Psellos, IV, 39 (transl. p. 75).

[35] Michael Psellos, IV, 39 (transl. p. 75).

deceit on his compatriots, a fellow called Dolianus[36]. Directly afterwards Michael Psellos stated: *I do not know whether he inherited such a name from his father, or if he gave himself the name for an omen*[37]. Then, the author continues to expand the image of Peter Delyan by providing details on his further activity, namely:

> He knew that the whole nation was set on rebellion against the Romans; indeed, the revolt was merely a project only because no leader had hitherto risen up among them able to carry out their plans. In the first place, therefore, he made himself conspicuous, proved his ability in council, demonstrated his skill in the conduct of war. Then, having won their approval by these qualities, it only remained for him to prove his own noble descent, in order to become the acknowledged leader of the Bulgarians. (It was their custom to recognize as leaders of the nation only men of royal blood). Knowing this to be the national custom, he proceeded to trace his descent from the famous Samuel and his brother Aaron, who had ruled the whole nation as kings a short time before. He did not claim to be the legitimate heir of these kings, but he either invented or proved that he was a collateral relation. He readily convinced the people with his story, and they raised him on the shield. He was proclaimed king. From that moment Bulgarian designs became manifest, for they seceded openly. The yoke of Roman domination was hurled from their necks and they made a declaration of independence, emphasizing the fact that they took this course of their own free will. Whereupon they engaged in attacks and plundering expeditions on Roman territory.[38]

If we put aside the prejudices and antipathy of Michael Psellos toward the Bulgarians, his narrative about the outbreak of the uprising is of particular interest with a view to clarifying the ideas on which Peter Delyan relied in obtaining the approval of the Bulgarians as their leader and tsar. But before proceeding further, we would like to point out that

[36] Michael Psellos, IV, 40 (transl. p. 75).
[37] Michael Psellos, IV, 40 (transl. p. 75).
[38] Michael Psellos, IV, 40 (transl. p. 75).

the relatively detailed information provided by Michael Psellos makes it clear that Peter Delyan has spread some propaganda among the people. Although the author focuses on the 'false' origin of Peter Delyan, which links him with the last Bulgarian tsarist dynasty of the Cometopouloi, it is not difficult to understand that this is the case of a phenomenon which is well known in mediaeval reality. As it was properly pointed out by Ivan Bozhilov, the deeds of pseudo-persons in a society have been part of the political ideology[39]. Of course, it does not mean that Peter Delyan should be associated with this tradition.

The propaganda of Peter Delyan, connected with the beginning of the fight for the restoration of the Tsardom with the aim of uniting the people around him and recognising him as their tsar is also evident from the information provided about him by Bishop Michael of Devol in one of his additions to the chronicle of John Skylitzes. It includes the following passage:

> That year there was an uprising in Bulgaria [twenty-first year of its enslavement and subjection]; it happened like this. A Bulgar named Peter Deleanos, the slave of a citizen of Byzantium, escaped from the city and was wandering in Bulgaria. He came to Moravos and Belgrade, fortresses of Pannonia lying across the Danube, neighbours to the Kral of Turkey, and let it be known that he was the son of Romanos, son of Samuel [born to him by the daughter of the Kral of Hungary whom Samuel hated when he was still alive, drove her out and married the very beautiful Eirene of Larissa,] and he stirred up the Bulgarians who had recently bowed the neck in subjection and were yearning for freedom[40].

Some time ago, Vassil Gyuzelev reasonably suggested that the additions made by Michael of Devol to the work of John Skylitzes are derived from the Bulgarian tsarist chronicles which have not reached present times[41].

[39] И. Божилов, В., Гюзелев, *История...*, pp. 396–397.

[40] John Skylitzes, p. 409 (transl. pp. 384–385; with my minor change – M.K.).

[41] В. Гюзелев, *Извори за средновековната история на България (VII–XV в.) в австрийските ръкописни сбирки и архиви*, София 1994, pp. 56, 263.

Part of this propaganda, as is evident from the story by Psellos, has been linked to highlighting the martial qualities possessed by Peter Delyan, with which he tried to win *their approval*, as indicated by the author himself. Based on the data provided by him and by Michael of Devol, it is clear that the main purpose of the propaganda created by Samuel's grandson was to disclose his tsarist backgrounds. Most valuable in this regard is the clarification made by Michael Psellos of the Bulgarian custom *to recognise as leaders of the nation only men of royal blood* and of the fact that Peter Delyan was aware of *the national custom*[42]. The data contained in the above-cited addition of Michael of Devol, according to which Peter Delyan *proclaimed himself as the son of Radomir, Samuel's son, who was born to him by the daughter of the Hungarian king*, is essential for us to gain an idea of how he managed to convince the people that he was of a tsarist descent. Thus combined, the information provided by the two Byzantine authors allows us to suggest that having escaped from Constantinople, Peter Delyan first pointed out that he was well aware of which authority Bulgarians considered legitimate, and then he provided some details not only about Peter Delyan's unhappy fate, but also about the fate of his mother who, although a royal daughter, had been banished by his father. In this way, he was probably trying to prove his imperial descent.

Here we would like to make a necessary digression by pointing out that, on the basis of a comparative analysis of the information provided by Michael Psellos and the additions of Michael of Devol to the chronicle of John Skylitzes on Peter Delyan, Vassil N. Zlatarski convincingly specified that Delyan *is nothing but the popular name* of the son of Gabriel-Radomir, along with his given name Peter, *following the Bulgarian custom to give double names especially of persons of tsarist origin*[43]. It is important to note that in the *Tale of the Prophet Isaiah* (*Bulgarian Apocryphal Chronicle*) of the 11th century, Peter Delyan is referred to as the tsar (…)

[42] Michael Psellos, IV, 40 (transl. p. 75).

[43] В.Н. Златарски, *История на българската държава през средните векове*, vol. II, *България под византийско владичество*, София [3]1994, p. 49: *е нищо друго освен народното име; съгласно с българския обичай да се дават двойни имена особено на лица от царски род.*

by the name of Gagan, and his nickname was Odelean. He took over the Bulgarian and the Greek kingdom[44]. Undoubtedly, the letter 'O' here represents the Greek definite article of the name Delyan, which shows that the author of the work borrowed it from a Greek source[45].

Based on all that has been said so far, we have reason to suggest that it was probably tsar Samuel's initiative to name his grandson after the Saint Tsar as an expression of the idea of continuity in the ruling of the state. We will provide yet another fact in support of this hypothesis. According to the data provided by John Skylitzes, one of the names of Samuel's son, Gabriel-Radomir, was Roman, which is interpreted in literature as a proof of the close relations of the 'mutineer' Samuel with the son of tsar Peter, Roman[46]. It is well known that the choice of certain names, especially in the Middle Ages, was, as a rule, motivated by political interests.

Therefore, the adoption of the name of Saint Tsar Peter by the leaders of the three major Bulgarian liberation uprisings against Byzantium in the 11th–12th century can be assessed as a key conceptual accent. The change in names speaks about their desire to establish at least a fictitious continuity of the tsarist dynasty from the end of the First Bulgarian Tsardom, whose last representative was tsar Peter. Thanks to such change, they proclaimed themselves as his successors and their connection with the ancient Bulgarian dynastic family ensured their right to bear the title of a tsar.

In this respect, it is necessary to remind that during the Middle Ages the idea of continuity was defining for the legitimacy of the ruler and was mainly based on the blood coursing through his veins. His authority won recognition because he descended from, or was convinced that he descended from, an ancient and famous ruling family. The power of the state rested mainly on its ancient origin, on the continuity of its history and institutions. The idea of continuity also played a decisive role in the

---

[44] *Tale of the Prophet Isaiah*, 402d (transl. p. 21).

[45] В.Н. Златарски, *История...*, pp. 48–49, fn. 2; V. Tapkova-Zaimova, A. Miltenova, *Historical...*, pp. 284, 295, 300, fn. 43.

[46] С. Пириватрич, *Самуиловата държава. Обхват и характер*, София 2000, pp. 100–101, 249.

consolidation of the political community[47]. Tsar Peter himself was guided by this idea in his rule. When John Skylitzes described the surrender of Skopje, to the name of Peter's son – Roman – he added that: *This Romanos was the son of King Peter of the Bulgars and the brother of Boris; he had changed his name to that of his grandfather, Symeon*[48].

Therefore, it may be assumed that the proclamation of the leaders of the three major uprisings as Bulgarian tsars named Peter had a strong effect on the common people. With the renewal of the name of the Saint Tsar, they revived his memory among the Bulgarians, thus succeeding in uniting them around themselves. Therefore, according to us, the connection between the memory of Saint Tsar Peter and the liberation movements is not only religious, but first and foremost dynastic.

This is also evident from the information provided by the Continuator of John Skylitzes on the uprising of the Skopje bolyar George Voyteh which broke out in the spring of 1072. According to the Byzantine historian, the foremost men of Bulgaria gathered to discuss the situation, choosing as their leader George Voyteh, who was descended from the 'kavkhan family'. However, that alone was not sufficient for him to lead all of Bulgarians, and in particular to become the ruler of the restored Tsardom. For this reason, the people who had gathered in Prizren sent their messenger to the Serbian knyaz – King Michael (1055–1082) – asking him to give them his son, Constantine Bodin, who would be proclaimed the tsar of Bulgaria. The reason for this choice is not accidental, because as we know from the sources that he was the grandson of tsar Samuel on his mother's side. Constantine Bodin arrived in Prizren with 300 troops. This number is especially indicative of the fact that Bulgarians sought a person from a dynastic family, not military aid. Then Constantine Bodin was crowned Bulgarian king under the name Peter[49].

Based on the information contained in the Byzantine sources, we have every reason to conclude that the leaders of the uprisings had a well-developed sense of historicity. Thanks to it, they continued a Bulgarian

[47] B. G u e n é e, *Histoire et culture historique dans l'Occident médiéval*, Paris 1980, pp. 332–333, 347–349.

[48] J o h n S k y l i t z e s, p. 346 (transl. p. 328).

[49] C o n t i n u a t o r o f J o h n S k y l i t z e s, pp. 714–715.

tradition associated with the observance of the law for the selection of the tsar and with the continuation of the cult of the Saint Tsar in the course of the fight of Bulgarians with Byzantium for the restoration of the Bulgarian Tsardom. Its beginnings are to be found with the uprising of the Cometopouloi which broke out in 976[50] and with the ideological programme of tsar Samuel (997–1014) for 'renovatio imperii' which also included the cult of tsar Peter. In support of my opinion on the ideology followed by tsar Samuel, I will recourse to several important manifestations of his policy. They are connected with the transfer of the remains of St. Achilles, after the looting of the town of Larissa in 985–986, and of St. Tryphon of Kotor in 997 to his capital. Srdjan Pirivatrić has every reason to point out that in the basis of this transfer lays the intention to render the necessary sacred dimension to the gradually created cult of the Bulgarian tsars[51]. Another argument in support of our statement is the dating of the service performed in memory of tsar Peter and the written tradition associated with the spread of the cult. They are an evidence that the honouring of the Saint Tsar did not find fertile soil for development in Eastern Bulgaria, which had been under Byzantine rule since 971, but spread in the southwestern Bulgarian lands with the active assistance of tsar Samuel.

In general, the ideology of the liberation uprisings against Byzantium and the conversion of St. Tsar Peter into its focus is best seen in the course of the uprising of the Assen brothers which broke out in the autumn of 1185. In this case, it is especially important to refer to the second doxology according to which the eldest brother Theodore adopted the name Peter[52]. It shows us that the Assen brothers took advantage of their own past in a quite an emblematic way. Niketas Choniates fails to take note of this, yet he reports on the crowning of the first of the Assen brothers: *Peter, Asan's brother, bound his head with a gold chaplet and fashioned scarlet buskins to put on his feet*[53]. The combination of the data contained in the

[50] И. Божилов, В., Гюзелев, *История...*, pp. 315–318; С. Пириватрич, *Самуиловата държава...*, pp. 179–183.

[51] С. Пириватрич, *Самуиловата държава...*, p. 248.

[52] *Synodikon of Tsar Boril*, p. 150.

[53] Niketas Choniates. p. 372 (transl. p. 205).

two sources outlines the sequence of actions related to the proclamation of Theodor as the Bulgarian tsar. It is clear that first he received the name of Peter and was crowned afterwards.

Therefore, the change in the name of the eldest brother is the other key conceptual accent in the political propaganda of the Assen brothers, together with the linking of their uprising with the cult of St. Demetrios. Through it, they proclaim themselves the successors of St. Tsar Peter. The linking of the people's leaders with the Old Bulgarian tsarist family had a huge importance to justify the legitimacy of their authority. Ivan Duychev interprets this change just as an expression of the desire of the Assen brothers to establish at least a fictitious continuity of the ruling dynasty since the end of the First Bulgarian Tsardom[54]. Undoubtedly, the proclamation of the eldest Assen brother as the Bulgarian tsar under the name of Theodore-Peter had a strong effect on the residents of Tarnovo, who had come to the consecration of the church of St. Demetrios. With the renewal of the name of tsar Peter, the leaders of the Tarnovo uprising revived his memory among the Bulgarians, successfully unifying them around themselves. At the same time, with this act the Assen brothers linked their activities as restorers of the Bulgarian Tsardom with the cult of tsar Peter. Thanks to their sense of historicity, they continued the Bulgarian tradition associated with the perpetuation of the cult of the Saint Tsar in the course of the fight of the Bulgarians with Byzantium for the restoration of the Bulgarian Tsardom.

The analysis which is based on the facts referred to above allows us to draw a general conclusion that the first two of the Assen brothers have had certain knowledge of the Bulgarian history. Part of this knowledge was connected with the liberation uprisings, while another part was linked with the law and custom established by the ancestors custom *to recognize as leaders of the nation only men of royal blood*, which is mentioned by Michael Psellos. In this way, they proved their 'renowned origin' and connected their activity as restorers of the Bulgarian Tsardom with the cult of

[54] И. Д у й ч е в, *Проучвания върху средновековната българска история и култура*, София 1981, p. 73; i d e m, *Българско средновековие...*, pp. 52–53; Ch. K o l a r o v, J. A n d r e e v, *Certaines questions ayant trait aux manifestations de continuite d'idées en Bulgarie médieévale au des XII–XIV siècles*, EHi 9, 1979, pp. 77–82.

tsar Peter. The honouring of the Saint Tsar, who embodied the idea of the priestly tsar and called for unity[55], becomes an essential part of the ruling ideology of the Assen brothers at the end of the 12th and during the first half of the 13th century. The idea of continuity and the associated imperial idea they revived became the core of such ideology. With the spread of these ideas, the Assen brothers laid the beginnings of the family's strategy aimed at the conversion of their family into a dynasty. It is based on the Bulgarian tradition that, in the new political situation in the Balkans at the end of the 12th century, is revived with the cult of St. Demetrios. In this initial stage of the state's development, the Assen brothers were obviously trying to resolve the issue of the transmission of hereditary power in order to keep it within the family, by making it follow certain principles[56]. In the application of the principle of primogeniture which was also typical of Byzantium, they likely saw a possible solution[57].

In his *History*, Niketas Choniates gives us some information which expands even more our idea of the aspirations of the first Assen brothers to suggest the idea of continuity, relying on the past. It is as follows:

> An assault was made upon Pristhlava [Preslav] (this is an ancient city built of baked bricks and covering a very large area), but they realized that a siege would not be without danger, and so they bypassed it. They descended Mount Haimos.[58]

It is not hard to understand that behind these rebellious actions lies the idea of a state continuity of the restored state with the state of the Bulgarians from the First Tsardom and can also be connected with

[55] For the importance of this fundamental idea in the Byzantine political theory and in the Christian Middle Ages, see: Ж. Дагрон, *Императорът и свещеникът. Етюд върху византийския "цезаропапизъм"*, София 2006, pp. 25–36.

[56] К. Господинов, *Легитимизъм и узурпация. Власт и политически взаимоотношения в Българското царство: 1241–1279. Автореферат*, София 2009, pp. 5–6.

[57] Ж. Дагрон, *Императорът*..., pp. 48–50, 55–58, examines in detail the importance of this principle in the founding of the dynasty and the elaboration of the family strategies of the Byzantine emperors.

[58] Niketas Choniates, p. 372 (transl. p. 205).

the cult of tsar Peter[59]. The Bulgarian church played an important role in its spread at the state level during the reign of the first three Assen brothers. At that time, the name of the Saint Tsar was also introduced in the official liturgical practice as it was included for eternal commemoration on the Orthodox Sunday in the Book of the Bulgarian church, and from there – in the commemoration lists of the Bulgarian and the Mount Athos monasteries[60].

The above deliberation gives us grounds to conclude that the honouring and the continuation of the cult of tsar Peter in the Bulgarian historical memory generated a few especially significant ideas which were used by the leaders of the three major liberation uprisings of the Bulgarians from the 11th–12th century. These are: the idea of continuity of the Bulgarian dynasty of khan Krum whose representative was St. Tsar Peter, the idea of the sanctity of the tsarist authority, the idea of the restoration of the Bulgarian Tsardom, and the idea of the antiquity of the Bulgarian state tradition. Their embodiment in the person of the Saint Tsar makes it central for the concept of the Bulgarian Tsardom and its patron saint. By nourishing the cult of their holy ancestor, his heirs moved the people and their state forward toward recognition of their national identity and sovereignty.

[59] И. Дуйчев, *Проучвания...*, p. 74.

[60] *Synodikon of Tsar Boril*, p. 149; Д.И. Полывянный, *Царь Петр...*, pp. 141–142.

B. MODERN VIEWS

IV

Jan M. Wolski

The Portrayal of Peter in Modern Historiography

The inspiration for undertaking research on the portrayal of tsar Peter in the modern historiography had been the clear disproportionality between what is known about the ruler directly from the source accounts, and the ideas formulated in the academic literature. The model of development of historical understanding, based on the ongoing search for the most convincing explanations of the phenomena and processes, and their subsequent verification, intuitively accepted by scholars of the past, in this case – it would seem – has been failing for decades. This has resulted in an unequivocally negative vision of Peter's reign. The discussions regarding individual facts for a long time had not been affecting the overall evaluation of the tsar, or of his era. The persistence of the 'black legend' of Peter is unprecedented. We may find its foundations in the writings from the end of the eighteenth century, and it was developed in the greatest detail in the works of Petar Mutafchiev (first half of the twentieth century). It only began to be questioned during the late 1960s. Its creation and consolidation were for the most part the result of works written by Bulgarian and Russian scholars.

In the present essay I am not attempting to fully explain this – at first glance surprising – stability of the opinion about Peter in. This would be a task for those researching the Bulgarian revival, the nineteenth-century

Slavophilism, and the intellectual climate of the Bulgarian elites prior to the collapse of communism. I believe that it would provide an additional perspective if one were to study the influence of the national feelings of Bulgarian intellectuals on the stance they have taken towards their own nation's past[1]. For the Reader, however, I propose to review the themes that are crucial for the evaluation of Peter: his attitude towards the Byzantines, the Church, of the internal situation of Bulgaria during his reign. I attempted to capture the moment at which particular opinions appeared, present their origins, and find their echoes in the later works. I devoted particular attention to the 'prehistory' of Peter's image; the works that are nowadays forgotten, or rarely cited.

The periodisation that I adopted is intended to facilitate the understanding of the text. Serving as landmarks are the moments that were important for the forming of Peter's historiographic image, therefore there are some differences regarding the periodisation of the development of the Bulgarian and European historiography between the present essay and general works on the subject[2].

The first sub-chapter begins with an analysis of the relevant passages from the earliest of the works discussed here, that is, the *Kingdom of the Slavs* by Mauro Orbini from 1601. The following two hundred years, during which authors such as i.a. Giuseppe Assemani, Charles du Cange (du Fresne) and Blasius Kleiner had been active, did not bring any notable changes in regard to Peter's historiographic image and the country he ruled. The second sub-chapter covers the relatively short period that was nonetheless crucial for the forming of the basis of criticism of Peter. The most important authors of this era were Paisios (end of the eighteenth century), Yuriy Venelin and Alexandr Gilferding (first half of the nineteenth century). In the third sub-chapter I have presented the works in which

[1] Of the wealth of publication on this subject, I have used below the publications by Albena Hranova and Diana Mishkova. In the context of Peter's portrayal in historiography, a similar line of research was postulated by Georgi Bakalov (see below).

[2] Vide e.g. *Историография истории южных и западных славян*, ed. Л.В. Горина, И.В. Созин et. at., Москва 1987; В. Гюзелев, *Апология на Средновековието*, [in:] idem, *Съчинения в пет тома*, vol. I, *Апология на Средновековието. Покръстване на българите*, София 2013, pp. 18–224.

the arguments of the historians mentioned above have been developed in accordance with the standards of academic writing, and which at the same time reaffirmed their conclusions. The need for re-evaluation of the appraisals of Peter was signalled during the 1960s; the motives behind it and the attempts at achieving it are discussed in the closing parts of this chapter.

1. Seventeenth to Mid-Eighteenth Centuries

Mauro Orbini

Mauro Orbini, a Benedictine monk from Ragusa (modern day Dubrovnik), may be considered as the author of the first modern history of the South Slavic nations. Writing *Kingdom of the Slavs* (1601) he used numerous sources; his work is a compilation. Considering this, the large volume of the work, as well as the standards of historiography of the time, it should not be surprising that Orbini did not manage to avoid mistakes, factual contradictions, and inconsistencies[3]. The duplicated account of the battle of Velbazhd is a clear example of the editorial chaos within his text: in the part related to the history of Serbia his narrative is based on a presently unidentified text of west European provenance, while the part about Bulgaria is rooted in the history of Nikephoros Gregoras[4]. Describing Peter, Orbini is almost entirely dependent on his Greek sources. Peter appears on the pages of the *Kingdom of the Slavs* after Symeon's death. Orbini, like Zonaras, makes no mention that Michael was passed over in the line of succession, and moves directly to describing the difficult situation of Bulgaria (starvation and aggressive neighbours), which led to

[3] For background on Orbini's work see G. Brogi Bercoff, *Il Regno degli Slavi di Mauro Orbini e la storiografia europea del Cinquecento*, RS 24/26, 1977/1979, pp. 119–156.

[4] S. Ćirković, *Vorwort*, [in:] M. Orbini, *Il regno degli Slavi*, Pesaro 1601, ed. S. Ćirković, P. Rehder, München 1985, pp. 7–23.

the peace talks with Byzantium and, subsequently, the conclusion of the peace treaty and the marriage between the Bulgarian ruler with Maria–Irene. He omits the details related to emperor Christopher being honoured by being placed ahead of Constantine Porphyrogennetos. Subsequently, along with Skylitzes he describes the rebellion of John and Michael, neglecting or changing some of the details (he does not, i.a., mention that John renounced his monk's frock after arriving in Constantinople). The next point of Peter's biography is the death of his wife, and the renewal of the peace agreement with the Byzantines, strengthened by sending his sons, Boris and Roman, as hostages[5]. There is a chronological break at this point in both Skylitzes and Zonaras, caused by mentioning of the return of both of the brothers after Peter's death, where they opposed the Cometopouloi who were raising rebellion among Bulgarians. Orbini repeats this (likely after Zonaras, which is shown by partially convergent phrasing), but does not realise the anticipatory nature of the interjection. Therefore when (repeating after Zonaras) he tells of the Hungarian raids, he talks of Peter's successor, Boris, as the ruler, clearly thinking that Peter was already dead at the time. This mistake likely stems from lack of further mention of Peter in Zonaras[6]. The primacy of Zonaras as a source for Orbini is also confirmed by a remark taken from this source about a demand from John Tzymiskes to the Bulgarian tsar (in Orbini's text: Boris) to hold back Hungarian raids, and pointing to Bulgarians' refusal as the reason for 'inviting' Svyatoslav to the Balkans by the Byzantine ruler[7]. The presentation of these events was abbreviated in Skylitzes' version in comparison to what we find in Zonaras and Orbini.

Describing Peter's history, Orbini does not comment on it in any way. The dispassionate re-telling of the Bulgarian history is characteristic of this author. What is interesting are the narrative interventions he has made: a simple succession of events (without specifying their distance in time) that links the marriage of Peter and Irene (celebrated in Constantinople)

---

[5] M. Orbini, *Il regno*..., pp. 426–427.

[6] For the sake of precision: Peter's name appears two more times in Zonaras' narrative (John Zonaras, pp. 547.9, 560.15). He is mentioned as Romanos' father.

[7] M. Orbini, *Il regno*..., p. 427.

and the rebellions of John and Michael in Skylitzes, in Orbini's version is transformed into the following picture: John attacked Peter during the latter's return journey from Constantinople. Moreover, the summary of the correspondence between the Bulgarian tsar and John Tzymiskes, regarding the holding back of Hungarian raids, is developed by Orbini through a creative use of his source. He first mentions the Hungarian raid on Bulgaria, then the request of Bulgarians directed to the Byzantines for help, and only then talks about the Hungarian raid on Byzantium and Tzymiskes' demand[8]. In Zonaras, the plea made by the Bulgarians is an introspection interwoven into their refusal to meet Tzymiskes' demands. Orbini efficiently ensured his story was cohesive, although this also made it somewhat detrimental to its factual accuracy. A translation by Theophan Prokopovich into Russian was published in 1722 in St. Petersburg, and gained certain popularity[9].

Cesare Baronio

Writing at nearly the same time as Orbini, the cardinal devoted much less space to the Slavic matters in his multi-volume work *Annales ecclesiastici* (volume X, containing description of the period in which we are interested, was published in 1602). This should not be surprising, since his work was focused on the history of the Catholic Church[10]. He mentioned Peter only once in reference to the events of 944, noting his correspondence with

---

[8] *Ibidem.*

[9] М а в р о у р б и н ъ, *Кнїга історіографвія початія имене, славы и разширенія народа славянского*, Санктъпітербург 1722; for further literature on this topic see: Дж. Д е л'А г а т а, *Паисий Хилендарски и руската версия на "Царството на славяните" на Мавро Орбини*, [in:] *Царството на славяните. История от дон Мавро Орбини от Рагуза, абат от Млетския орден*, ed. П. В а т о в а, transl. С. Т о д о р о в, Е. П о п о в а, София 2012, pp. 17–24; Р. А д и н о л ф и, *"Царството на Славяните" от Мавро Орбини, руският превод на Сава Владиславович и изследванията по въпроса*, Про 24.2, 2015, pp. 309–320.

[10] Р. П и к и о, *България в Църковната история на Цезар Бароний*, [in:] i d e m, *Православното славянство и старобългарската културна традиция*, transl. А. Д ж а м б е л у к а К о с с о в а, София 1994, pp. 587–600; Р. З а и м о в а, *Българската тема в западноевропейската книжнина. XV–XVII век*, София 1992, pp. 75–85.

Paul of Latro[11]. Peter as the ruler of Bulgaria and politician appears in the critical addition to the *Annals*, written by Antoine Pagi a century later. Baronio's work was translated into Polish by Piotr Skarga and published already in 1603, and subsequently from Polish into Russian (in 1687, published in 1719)[12]. This translation, similarly to Russian version of *Kingdom of the Slavs*, is considered to be important for the development of Slavic historiography, including the Bulgarian one, since while composing his own work Paisios was referring to *Annales*.

Charles du Fresne (du Cange)

Charles du Cange included the tale of Bulgaria's history into a larger work presenting the history of Byzantium. The volume in which we are interested was published in 1680. Conveying an overview of Peter's reign he referred to Leo the Grammarian, Skylitzes, Zonaras, *Continuation of Theophanes*, Constantine VII Porphyrogennetos, the *Life of Lucas the Younger* and Liutprand of Cremona. His exposition is highly shortened, and is limited to factography: the conclusion of peace in 927, the marriage of Peter and Irene, the death of Irene, the dispute over Hungarian raids and the summoning of Svyatoslav[13]. The entire passage devoted to the history of mediaeval Bulgaria counts a mere twenty pages[14]. Du Cange

---

[11] C. Baronio, *Annales ecclesiastici*, ed. P.A. Pagii, vol. XVI, Luca 1744, p. 46.

[12] М.Е. Никифорова, *Бароний*, [in:] *Православная Энциклопедия*, vol. IV, Москва 2002, pp. 347–348; G. Brogi Bercoff, *Chrześcijańska Ruś w "Annales Ecclesiastici" Cezarego Baroniusza*, [in:] eadem, *Królestwo Słowian. Historiografia Renesansu i Baroku w krajach słowiańskich*, transl. E.J. Głębicka, W. Jekiel, A. Zakrzewski, Izabelin 1998, pp. 130–145; eadem, *Baronio storico e il mondo slavo*, [in:] *Cesare Baronio tra santità e scrittura*, ed. G.A. Guazzelli, R. Michetti, F. Sforza Barcellona, Roma 2012, pp. 309–323.

[13] C. du Fresne, *Historia Byzantina duplici commentario illustrata*, vol. I, Lutetia Parisiorum 1680, pp. 313–314.

[14] C. du Fresne, *Historia Byzantina*..., s. 305–324; see I. Konev, S. Topalov, I. Genov, *Charles du Fresne, seigneur du Cange et sa "Series historica et genealogica Regum Bulgariae"*, Pbg 4.3, 1980, pp. 69–85; А. Данчева-Василева, *Шарл Дюканж и средновековната българска история*, ИП 38.4, 1982, pp. 91–102; Р. Заимова, *Българската тема*..., pp. 85–96.

dated Peter's ascension to power to 932. We might guess that he correctly calculated the indiction, but relied on the Latin translation of Leo the Grammarian, where the fifth indiction was given[15]. Irene's death and the renewal of the Byzantine-Bulgarian peace treaty is dated to year 863. His reading of the Greek sources was more careful than Orbini's. Du Cange noted that Peter was still alive in 867, when the friendly relations between Byzantium and Bulgaria came to an end. Svetoslav's first raid was dated to 968, and the capturing of Preslav by John Tzymiskes to 971.

Antoine Pagi

A French historian, the Franciscan died in 1699. The volumes he was writing near the end of his life that supplemented Baroni's *Annales ecclesiastici* were published in 1702. In parallel to the *Annales*, they were in turn published by Giovanni Domenico Mansi in Lucca in 1736–1759, with the editor's own, less extensive commentary. Pagi's information about the history of the Slavs, including Bulgarians, was far more comprehensive than Baronio's[16], however regarding Peter himself, it would be difficult to form any relatively consistent image of this ruler. This is due to the fact that the author only paid attention to the beginning of Peter's reign and its end in the context of the collapse of the Bulgarian state that immediately followed[17]. We may consider to his credit correctly dating Symeon's death and the beginning of Peter's reign to 927. However, Pagi did not put a date to Peter's death. It is only in a comment to the year 973 that he noted: *Petrus ante hoc tempus mortuus errat*[18].

---

[15] Charles du Cange d u F r e s n e (*Historia Byzantina...*, p. 313) discussed the dating in the subchapter regarding Symeon: *XXVII Maii, Indict. V (non XV. uti habet Scylitzes)*. The accurate dating is amended according to the faulty Latin translation of Leo the Grammarian by Jacques G o a r (*Theophanis Chronographia et Leonis grammatici Vitae recentiorum impp.*, ed. J. G o a r, F. C o m b e f i s, Parisii 1655, p. 502; reprint: Venetia 1729, p. 398). In the published in parallel Greek text of Leo the Grammarian, we find the correct number.

[16] Р. П и к и о, България..., pp. 587–600.

[17] C. B a r o n i o, *Annales ecclesiastici*, ed. P.A. P a g i i, vol. XV, Luca 1744, pp. 628–629; C. B a r o n i o, *Annales ecclesiastici*, vol. XVI, pp. 161, 193, 210–212, 221–222.

[18] C. B a r o n i o, *Annales ecclesiastici*, vol. XVI, p. 222.

Giuseppe Simone Assemani (Joseph Simonius Assemanus, Jusuf ibn Siman as-Simani)

Of the wealth of output of this erudite, the custodian of the Vatican Library, and a bishop, of the most interest to us is the third volume of his *Calendars of the Ecumenical Church*, published in 1755 and devoted to the mission of Constantine-Cyril and Methodius, to the Christianisation of the southern Slavs, and the history of the various peoples (among them Bulgarians, Czechs, Khazars and Hungarians) in the ninth and tenth centuries. Chapters six and seven of his volume relate to the history of Bulgaria during Symeon and Peter's reign. The exposition concludes with the subordination of the country to the Byzantine Empire[19]. Assemani, like Du Cange, knows nearly all of the basic Greek sources that make a mention of Peter: Symeon Logothete, Leo the Grammarian, *Continuation of George the Monk*, Pseudo–Symeon, *Continuation of Theophanes*, Constantine Porphyrogennetos, Zonaras and Skylitzes[20]. In chapter three of this volume the author analyses the relations between the Bulgarian ruler and Rome. Brief historical information located in this part of the work, and related to Symeon's death and conclusion of Peace by Peter and his marriage with Irene, was included by Assemani in a quotation taken from Charles du Cange's work and relegated to a footnote[21]. In the same way – by quoting a passage in a footnote – he explained the circumstances in which Nikephoros summoned the Rus against Bulgarians[22]. According to Assemani, Symeon subordinated the Bulgarian church to the bishop of Rome, and Peter, in concluding the peace with the Byzantine emperor, at the same time chose the union with Constantinople. At the same time the Byzantines, to strengthen the bond between them and the Bulgarians, made their church autocephalic; this, however, Assemani stated, has not

[19] About Asemani and his work, see: М.С. Кискинова, *Предговор*, [in:] Й.С. Асемани, *Календари на Вселенската Църква. За светите славянски апостоли Кирил и Методий*, ed., transl., comm. М.С. Кискинова, София 1987, pp. 6–57.

[20] *Ibidem*, pp. 46–47.

[21] J.S. Assemanius, *Kalendaria Ecclesiae universae*, vol. III, *Kalendaria Ecclesiae slavice, sive graeco-mosche*, Roma 1755, p. 146.

[22] *Ibidem*, pp. 155–156.

been respected in the later period[23]. Peter was supposed to have returned to the fold of the Roman Church in 967, when the friendly relations with the Byzantines were severed due to Hungarian raids[24]. The specific exposition of the history of Bulgaria during Peter's reign, in chapters six and seven, has been accomplished by Assemani through quotations from the Greek sources linked with two or three sentence long commentaries. He devoted a lot of attention to chronology. He stands by dating Symeon's death to 927, previously given by Pagi. On the basis of the circumstances of Peter's death provided by Leo the Deacon, he placed it in the year 969. The marriage of Peter and Maria, in turn, was moved to 928[25]. To relate the rebellion of John and Michael, he quoted *Continuation of Theophanes*; the death of Maria and the renewal of peace are related through a passage from Skylitzes/Kedrenos. The end of peace between Byzantium and Bulgaria is presented in two versions: of Leo the Deacon and of Skylitzes, without a comment on the differences between the two[26]. Relating later events, he gave primacy to Leo the Deacon, however he also calls upon Skylitzes, and shows the knowledge of Zonaras' work[27].

Blasius Kleiner

Our knowledge of this author comes primarily from what he wrote himself in the title of his work. Of unknown origin (Saxon?), he was a head of a Bulgarian monastery of Franciscans in Vințu de Jos in Transylvania[28].

[23] *Ibidem*, pp. 146–147.

[24] *Ibidem*, pp. 155–156.

[25] *Ibidem*, pp. 341–344.

[26] *Ibidem*, pp. 364–368.

[27] *Ibidem*, p. 368sqq.

[28] И. Дуйчев, *Блазиус Клайнер и неговата "История на България" от 1761 година*, [in:] *История на България от Блазиус Клайнер съставена в 1761 г.*, ed. idem, К. Телбизов, София 1977, pp. 5–21; about the author and his work, see also: W. Stępniak-Minczewa, *Francescani in Bulgaria. Blasius Kleiner: un francescano in viaggio per i Balcani (sulla base della Storia della Bulgaria di Blasius Kleiner)*, [in:] *I Francescani nella storia dei popoli balcanici, Nell'VIII centenario della fondazione dell'ordine. Atti del Convegno Internazionale di Studi*, ed. V. Nosilia, M. Scarpa, Bologna–Padova 2010 pp. 265–278.

In 1761 he completed the *Tripartite Archives of the Illustrious Province of Bulgaria*, which included the history of Bulgaria from the first Bulgarian raids into the Balkans until the fall of Constantinople. Kleiner based his story of Peter on the account from *Theophanes Continuatus*, John Zonaras and John Skylitzes (called here Kouropalates). It is difficult to say whether he had access to a full edition of the sources, or whether he used some source compilation or selection[29]. His reading of the sources was not particularly scrupulous. He complains, for example, that the 'Continuator of the Roman history' did not state how the conflict between the brothers Peter and Michael ended[30], as if he did not notice that the source included the information about the death of the latter. Moreover, he missed the fact that the conclusion of the history of the rebellion, absent in the *Continuation of Theophanes* (the rebels surrendered to the Romans), could be found in Skylitzes' work, with which he was familiar. Kleiner dated the beginning of Peter's reign to 930, Michael's rebellion to 934, and the Bulgarian tsar's death to 963[31]. In the first two cases, the error could have arose during the conversion of the indictions given by the Byzantine authors, and in the case of the tsar's death (he likely repeated the same oversight as Orbini) – he chronologically associated the event itself with the ascension to the throne of John Tzymiskes (the date is correct here). Kleiner's problems with chronology do not end here. At the end of his work he listed the rulers of Bulgaria (and extended all the way to Mehmed the Conqueror) with brief biographical notes. The length of Peter's reign is calculated here to be 39 years[32], while the difference between the dates given in the main body of the text is, as can be easily seen, 33 years. It should probably be considered a coincidence that the difference of 39 years would have been reached if Kleiner accepted year

[29] I am basing these conclusions on the passages analysed below. The list of studies and source selections used in the other parts of his work has been provided by Ivan Duychev (И. Д у й ч е в, *Блазиус Клайнер*..., pp. 18–19). He also lists among them the previously discussed works of Baroni and Pagi, however these have not made a lasting impression on the way tsar Peter was presented by Kleiner.

[30] *История на България от Блазиус Клайнер*..., p. 85.

[31] *Ibidem*, pp. 84–85.

[32] *Ibidem*, p. 150.

969 as the date of Peter's death, which is now commonly considered to be correct. The brief biogram deserves, indeed, more of our attention than the main part of the historical exposition. This is because our author has included in the biographic description his own characterisation of Peter, whom he considered to have been a 'peace-loving and very good' a ruler. Of the historical events, he mentioned Michael's rebellion, likely for its moralising value: a monk driven by lust for power violates the peaceful reign of his brother, and despite gathering numerous people and many boyars, is defeated. In the meantime, Kleiner has likely finished his reading of the sources, since he now knew the ending of this bloody conflict over succession. This author's history remained unpublished until 1977 when the Bulgarian translation was launched, and most likely was not copied by hand either; thus, being almost completely unknown, it did not have any influence on the future development of historiography.

Franjo Ksaver Pejačević

A *History of Bulgarians* was also written in the latter half of the eighteenth century by Franjo Ksaver Pejačević (1707–1781). Born in Osijek, he was a Croatian historian and theologian, and a provost of the University in Graz. He came from a family with Bulgarian roots. The work being discussed here has never been published in print. The author included in it excerpts from the Byzantine historians along with his own brief commentaries. He also analysed Bulgarian history on the pages of the *History of Serbia*, published in print in 1799. Peter appeared in this work in a list of the Bulgarian rulers. He has been located here in the appropriate place, the beginning of his reign is dated to 930, supposedly following Leo the Grammarian[33], and in the footnote the author listed as a second date 927, following Constantine VII Porphyrogennetos (*De administrando imperii*,

[33] Pejačević made a mistake in calculating the indictions. L e o G r a m m a t i k o s (p. 315), to whom he is referring, talks of the fifteenth indiction, which occurred in 927 (V. G r u m e l, *Traité d'etudes byzantines*, vol. I, *La chronologie*, Paris 1958, p. 252). His calculations would also have to have been considered erroneous if he, like Charles du Cange, used the Latin translation of Leo the Grammarian by Jacques Goar, which mentioned the fifth indiction (932).

chapter 32)[34]. He did not specify the end of the reign, and instead noted that in 970 the sons of Peter Boris and Roman were defeated by the Rus and the emperor John Tzymiskes[35].

* * *

Further examination of this historiographic tradition would have been pointless. We have shown its uncoordinated beginnings; afterwards it was developing in a more systematic manner. Later authors referred to their predecessors, correcting them or repeating their mistakes, while adding new remarks and evaluations[36]. In the nineteenth century the number of historical publications significantly increased, and Bulgarian mediaeval studies – primarily thanks to the activity of Russian, Czech and Bulgarian scholars – became an independent area of research; we will examine this in the following sub-chapter. Of the authors discussed above, only Mauro Orbini did not write in Latin (he wrote in Italian), he also stood out in that he worked outside of France and Italy (the same can be said of Pejačević and Kleiner), and like the others, he was a Catholic clergyman[37]. Near the end of the eighteenth century the situation quickly

[34] Constantine VII Porphyrogennetos, *On the Governance of the Empire*, pp. 152–160. The text of the cited edition (by Gyula Moravcsik) does not include any chronological indications.

[35] П. Данова, *Писал ли е Франц-Ксавер Пеячевич история на българите?*, ИБ 20.1/2, 2016, pp. 57–58.

[36] Without an in-depth analysis, it would be difficult to evaluate the development of historiography in the non-Slavic Europe of this period in regard to the presentation of the history of Bulgaria. It would seem however that no ground-breaking work that would deserve a more substantial mention has appeared during this period. Either way, John B. Bury, supplementing Gibbon's work in the Bulgarian matters, exclusively cited Jireček, Hilferding and Uspenskiy, ignoring the works of western European historians (E. Gibbon, *The history of the decline and fall of the Roman Empire*, ed. J.B. Bury, introd. W.E.H. Lecky, vol. X, New York 1906, pp. 26–36).

[37] Of the early historiographers whose scope included Bulgarian mediaeval history one can also name, for example, Johann Löwenklau (J. Leunclavius, *Annales Sultanorum Othimanidarum*, Francofurdum 1588) a German philologist and historian, a pupil of Philip Melanchthon. Due to the subjects he was examining he did not, of course, mention tsar Peter, therefore his work is not examined in the present study.

changed, the interest in South Slavic Middle Ages became more widespread[38]. Johann Gotthelf Stritter, a German historian working in Russia, inspired by the plans of developing a history of the world by August Ludwig Schlözer, published an extensive anthology of Byzantine sources (translated into Latin) regarding the history of the peoples of south-western and eastern Europe and of Asia. The anthology was soon afterwards translated into Russian[39]. The chronological-thematic arrangement he used made his work resemble the *Calendars* of Assemani, although the comments are much briefer and located in the footnotes[40]. In 1782, Ludwig Albrecht Gebhardi published a substantial (over two hundred pages long) *Geschichte des Reichs Bulgarien* as a fragment of the history of Hungary and the surrounding countries (*Geschichte des Reichs Hungarn und der damit verbundenen Staaten*). In the part related to Peter, he cited sources gathered by Assemani and Stitter, their commentaries and Pagi's work[41]. Gibbon, writing at roughly the same time, took his information from Du Cange, Baroni with Pagi's comments and from Stritter's source anthology. He did not mention Peter even by name, counting him among the 'feeble successors' of Symeon who, being 'divided and extinguished', led to the collapse of the state[42]. The synthesis of Johann Christian Engel also deserves a mention, having the same thematic range and being of similar

[38] Cf. B. Гюзелев, *Апология...*, pp. 151–152.

[39] *Memoriae populorum, olim ad Danubium, Pontum Euxinum, Paludem Maeotidem, Caucasum, Mare Caspium, et Inde Magis ad Septemtriones incolentium, e scriptoribus historiae Byzantinae*, ed. J.G. Strittero, vol. II, Petropolis 1774 (about Peter: pp. 609–616); L.G. Michaud, *Stritter, Jean-Gotthelf de*, [in:] *Biographie universelle, ancienne et moderne*, vol. XLIV, Paris 1826, pp. 44–45.

[40] Stritter's chronologial findings should be mentioned here. In the chronological table of the rulers of Bulgaria (*Memoriae populorum*, p. 458) he dates Peter's reign to 942–967. In the main body of his work, to 942–963. Year 942 would have corresponded with the fifteenth indiction of the following cycle in relation to year 927, however Stritter dates Symeon's death that happened during this indiction to year 941 (*Memoriae populorum*, p. 609). Year 963 as the date of Peter's death comes, of course, from associating it with the death of Maria and the change of the Byzantine ruler.

[41] L.A. Gebhardi, *Geschichte des Reichs Hungarn und der damit verbundenen Staaten*, vol. IV, Leipzig 1782, pp. 76–81.

[42] Chapter 55 was originally published in the fifth volume (1788), I have made use of a later edition: E. Gibbon, *The history...*, pp. 26–36.

size as Gebhardi's work. Writing about the beginning of Peter's reign, Engel made an interesting comparison, stating that after Symeon's death the political situation in Bulgaria resembled that of France following the death of Louis XIV: outwardly glorious, its internal power exhausted[43].

2. Mid-Eighteenth to Mid-Nineteenth Century: The Birth of Native Historiography and the Development of Historical Literature in the Balkans and in Russia

The birth of the modern Bulgarian historiography is determined by the writing of *Slavic-Bulgarian history* by Paisios of Hilendar (1762). The creation and dissemination of this work was certainly a notable social matter in Turkish-ruled Bulgaria[44]. The date of the completion of the work is sometimes considered to be a watershed moment in the history of Bulgarian culture and language[45]. Paisios's work contributed

[43] J.Ch. Engel, *Geschichte der Bulgaren in Mösien*, [in:] idem, *Fortsetzung der Allgemeinen Welthistorie durch eine Gesellschaft von Gelehrten in Teutschland und Engeland ausgefertiget*, vol. XLIX, Halle 1797, pp. 360–363; for wider background see: Н. Андреева, *България и българите в едно немско историческо съчинение от края на XVIII в.*, [in:] Й.К. Енгел, *История на българите в Мизия*, transl., comm. Н. Андреева, Велико Търново 2009, pp. 5–55.

[44] М. Дринов, *Отец Паисий, неговото време, неговата История и учениците му*, [in:] idem, *Избрани съчинения*, ed. И. Дуйчев, vol. I, *Трудове по българска и славянска история*, София 1971, pp. 163–185 (reprint from 1871); П. Динеков, *Паисий Хилендарски*, [in:] Паисий Хилендарски, *Славяно-българска история*, transl. П. Динеков, София 1972, pp. 7–31; Н. Генчев, *Българско възраждане*, София 1981, pp. 59–61.

[45] E.g. Е. Георгиев, *Паисий Хилендарски – между Ренесанса и Просвещението*, [in:] *Паисий Хилендарски и неговата епоха (1762–1962). Сборник от изследвания по случай 200-годишнината от История славянобългаска*, ed. Д. Косев et al., София 1962, pp. 253–284; Л. Андрейчин, *Из историята на нашето езиково строителство*, София 1977, pp. 49–50; Н. Генчев, *Българската култура XV–XIX в. Лекции*, София 1988, pp. 173–181. Modern scholars made some interesting reservations regarding the significance of Paisios for the development of Bulgarian revival. See e.g. Г. Каприев, *Историографски концепт на Паисий Хилендарски и средновековното*

to reinforcing in the public opinion the awareness and national pride of Bulgarians, and to raising their political aspirations[46]. From the historiographic point of view, Paisios is an epigone of the tradition discussed above, in its worst rendition (he knew Orbini and Baronius from a Russian translation). On the other hand, as a publicist and a populariser, he expressed a new trend that today we would refer to as nationalist[47]. The main factor speaking in the favour of Paisios the historian is the use of indigenous sources that have been unknown to the earlier authors[48].

историческо мислене, ПУПХБ.НТФ 50/1/А, 2012, pp. 115–126. He argues that the History was not in fact the beginning of the revival, due to its limited influence, and became a symbol post factum, on the wave of enthusiasm of intellectuals and national activists who were 'discovering' Paisios from the middle of 19th century.

[46] П. Динеков, *Паисий Хилендарски...*, pp. 14–15; В. Бонева, *Паисий Хилендарски и неговият исторически текст във възрожденската публичност*, LN 8 (153), http://liternet.bg/publish8/vboneva/paisij.htm, accessed: 28.11.2017; М. Димитрова, Д. Пеев, *Из историята на Историята. Преписи и преработки на Паисиевия тексти*, ПУПХБ.НТФ 50/1/А, 2012, pp. 50–72.

[47] An interesting characterisation of Paisios and his work was made by Alexander A. Kotchubinsky who thus commented the first scholarly edition of the *History*: *Неизданная въ своемъ полномъ составѣ подлинная Паисіева "Истиорія" не какъ историческій матеріалъ, а какъ памятникъ историко-литературный и по своему значенію въ исторію развитія идеи національности среди нашихъ соседей Болгаръ, политическій, давно заслуживала быть изданной. Крайне неграмотно писанная (...) некритическая компилация 40 лѣтняго простаго аѳонскаго монаха, тѣмъ не менѣе горячимъ чувствомъ патриотическимъ и, составленная умно [съ педагогическимъ тактомъ – Kotchubinsky added later], впервые провела предъ народнымъ сознаніемъ Болгаръ минувшее ихъ долгой и небезславной жизни...* – А. Кочубинский, *Примѣчаніе*, ЗИООИД 16, 1893, p. 54 (appendix to the edition by Arkadiy V. Longinov). Kotchubinsky's statement and voices similar to it have been considered by some to be an unwarranted criticism (e.g. П.А. Началовъ, *Забележка за Паисиевата история*, ПСБКД 46, 1894, p. 523; П.А. Лавровъ, *Одна изъ передѣлокъ исторіи Славяно-болгарской іеромонаха Паисія, сохранившаяся въ ркп. № 1731 собранія проф. Григоровича*, [in:] *Труды восмаго археологическаго съѣзда въ Москвѣ*, vol. II, ed. П.С. Уварова, М.Н. Сперанский, Москва 1895, p. 249). It is difficult to provide an unequivocal evaluation of Paisios' historiographic work, as he was at the same time an 'un-critical compiler' and the herald of the Bulgarian revival.

[48] On the sources used by Paisios see: П.И. Лавровъ, *Одна из передѣлокъ...*; В. Велчев, *Отецъ Паисий Хилендарски и Цезаръ Бароний*, София 1943; R. Picchio, *Gli Annali del Baronio-Skarga e la Storia di Paisij Hilendarski*, RS 3, 1954, 212–233; Н. Драгова, *Домашни извори на "История славянобългарска"*, [in:] *Паисий*

The motive that led Paisios to reaching for the pen was the lack of knowledge of own history among the Bulgarians. If Bulgarians would learn how mighty their state has once been – claimed Paisios – they will stop being ashamed of their own origins, they will raise their heads, and consider themselves equal to the Greeks and other nations[49]. In fact, Paisios was not entirely innovative in his approach. 'Revivalist' (national) motives have previously been driving Orbini and Kleiner as well[50]. It was not until Paisios, however, that the exposition of history was subordinated to a non-historiographic aim to such a significant degree (we will be able to study this in more detail while examining the way in which Peter was presented). This goal was to raise the spirits of his countrymen, defy the Greek violence, and only a simplified vision of history presented in the *Slavic-Bulgarian history* had played a 'revivalist' role[51].

Paisios of Hilendar

The portrayal of Peter as presented by Paisios is unequivocally negative. According to him, Peter was a ruler who did not succeed in wars, was friendly towards Greeks, and subservient to them. From the start of his reign, the Bulgarian state weakened, because of Peter's inconsistency and pettiness. Paisios claimed that the only fortunate aspect of the reign was the life and activity of John of Rila with which it coincided[52]. Following the hagiographic narrative (the *Life* by Euthymios of Tarnovo[53]) Paisios described the would-be meeting of the ruler and the hermit, and the

Хилендарски и неговата епоха..., pp. 307–309; Г.Д. Тодоров, *Историческите възгледи на Паисий Хилендарски*, ИИИ 20, 1968, pp. 95–165; Т. Събев, *Отец Паисий Хилендарски. Епоха, личност,, дело, значение*, [in:] idem, *Избрани съчинения върху историята на църквата*, ed. А. Кръстев, Велико Търново 2005, pp. 214–250; Дж. Дел'Агата, Паисий Хилендарски..., pp. 17–24.

[49] Паисий Хилендарски, *История славяноболгарская. Критическо издание с превод и коментар*, ed. Д. Пеев, М. Димитрова, П. Петков, transl. Д. Пеев, comm. А. Николов, Д. Пеев, Зограф 2012, p. 60.

[50] Cf. G. Brogi Bercoff, *Il Regno*..., pp. 121–156.

[51] П. Динеков, *Паисий Хилендарски*..., pp. 14–15.

[52] Паисий Хилендарски, *История славяноболгарская*..., p. 152.

[53] Н. Драгова, *Домашни извори*..., pp. 307–309.

exchange of letters which was a 'considerable gain for the soul' of Peter. Subsequently, he described the conclusion of peace with the Byzantine Empire, the marriage with Christopher's daughter, and the rebellion of John and Michael, which he considers to have been not two events, but a simultaneous and long-lasting war between the brothers. The final of the presented episodes is the sending of his sons (Boris and Roman) to Constantinople, and Peter's death. The history of the breaking of peace with the Byzantines is narrated in a similar way as in Orbini's text, on whose work Paisios based the entire passage. However, the duration and simultaneity of the rebellions of Peter's brothers was the Zographian monk's own invention[54]. This modification is not without significance – it provides good reasons for speaking of the internal discord that leads to the state's collapse. Paisios introduced some order into Mavrourbin's exposition, by discarding the remark about the beginning of the rebellion of the Cometopouloi from the account of Irene's death and renewal of peace that violated the chronology. Unfortunately at the same time there is no remark on this event in the place that would have been appropriate for it – at the beginning of the description of the reign of David and his brothers.

It seems that Paisios is the historiographer who has laid the foundations of the 'black legend' of Peter[55]. The threads appearing in his work and the layout of the content herald the later negative opinions about Peter: a weak leader, torpid, and susceptible to Byzantines' influence, more interested in spiritual matters than in governance; the state, torn apart by quarrels under his rule, started to decline. The argument concerning the lack of unity that led to the catastrophe is also going to be repeated by historians who knew the original accounts of the rebellions of John and Michael, and therefore were also aware of their limited extent. In a similar manner the later historians associated Peter's lack of wartime

[54] Паисий Хилендарски, *История славянобългарская*..., p. 154.

[55] Cf. T. Тодоров, *От отрицание към реабилитация. Историографски бележки за цар Петър I (927–969) и неговото време*, [in:] *Писменост, книжовници, книги. Българската следа в културната история на Европа. Материали от петата национална конференция по история, археология и културен туризъм. Пътуване към България. Шумен, 26–28.04.2016 г.*, ed. И. Йорданов, Шумен 2018, p. 86.

successes with his interest in religious matters which, alongside the other descriptions, resulted in the ruler's portrait of an indecisive has-been and a religious bigot.

Jovan Rajić

He completed his extensive work devoted to the history of the Slavs in 1768, and it was published in 1794/1795[56]. According to some, Raijić and Paisios, both Orthodox monk historians, knew each other personally. It is sometimes thought that it was Rajić who, during his stay in Hilendar, introduced Paisios to the sources (the Russian translations of Baroni and Orbini) available in the library in Sremski Karlovtsi that the latter then used extensively[57]. However, more factors set them apart than connected them. Rajić had a clearly superior education to Paisios, having been taught at Sremski Karlovtsi and in Kiev[58]. Aside from the *History*..., his works included a drama, poetry, and theological works. Rajić's historiographic endeavours were not far from the high standards of Du Cange (whom he most frequently quoted) or the other contemporary authors. The greater part of the text devoted to Peter consists of quotations from Byzantine authors: Kedrenos and Zonaras; the author also included Du Cange's translation[59]

[56] Д. Цанев, *Историята на Раич и нейните български преводи и преработки*, ИНБКМ 14, 1976, p. 181; Б. Желинкси, *Исотиря, памет, народ: историографиите на Паисий Хилендарски и Йован Раич*, ПУПХБ.НТФ 50/1/A, 2012, p. 11; more about the author and his work: Н. Радојчић, *Српски историчар Јован Рајић*, Београд 1952; Р. Самарџић, *Писци спрске историје*, Београд 1976, pp. 29–59; С. Војиновић, *Хронологија живота и рада Јована Рајића*, [in:] *Јован Рајић – живот и дело*, ed. М. Фрајнд, Београд 1997, pp. 7–27.

[57] Cf. Д. Райков, *Историческа съдба на македонските българи. Свидетелства за българското възраждане в Македония*, София 1997, p. 91; an opposite opinion: Т. Събев, *Отец Паисий*..., p. 209; Л. Илиева, *Паисий Хилендарски и Йован Раич*, [in:] *Светът е слово, словото е свят*, ed. М. Костова-Панайотова et al., Благоевград 2016, pp. 115–122.

[58] Д. Цанев, *Историята на Раич*..., pp. 184–185; Р. Заимова, *Подходът на балканския писател към историческата тема (XVIII век)*, ИБ 5.1, 2001, pp. 98–99.

[59] A full list of sources used by Rajić is provided by, i.a., Dimitar Tsanev (Д. Цанев, *Историята на Раич*..., pp. 189–190). Instead of the original text of Du Cange's *Historia Byzantina* Rajić used an edition supplemented by Ján Tomka-Sásky

into his narrative. In addition, Rajić cited Mavrourbin (Oribini in the 1722 translation). Part of the author's interjections linking fragments of the sources turns out to be a re-narration of Orbini, e.g. the beginning of paragraph 3 telling of Irene's death and the events that followed it[60].

The evaluation of events related by Rajić does not take much space in his work, with the telling of facts dominating. Some of the expressed judgements have simply been taken by Rajić from his sources, however there are also passages in which his personal opinions can be seen. It was he who titled chapter eight, devoted to the period after Symeon's death: *О умалении кралества болгарскаго* (*On the fall of the Bulgarian kingdom*)[61], and the period of Byzantine dominance of Bulgaria (Rajić talks here of the time between the removal of Boris from power and the emergence of the Cometopouloi, dated to 976) he referred to as: плачевное подданство (*lamentable subjection*)[62]. Regarding the divisions pointed out by Paisios (who was grieving for Bulgaria that fell under Greek dominion), Rajić described them in the same vein near the end of his exposition of the country's history: uneducated Bulgarians started to neglect the common good; instead, selfishness has taken root in them. For this reason many of the Bulgarians were overtaken by the lust for power, which led to discord, this in turn resulted in disorder, then in feuds, infighting and final destruction[63].

Both of the authors discussed in this part of the work exerted strong influence on the nineteenth century historiography. However, they are discussed first not only for chronological reasons. They were often copied and published – in adapted form and summaries. Their imitators and

(C. du Fresne, *Illyricum vetus et novum sive historia regnorum Dalmatiae, Croatiae, Slavoniae, Bosniae, Serviae atque Bulgariae*, Posonium 1746).

[60] И. Раич, *Исторія разныхъ славенскихъ народовъ наипаче Болгаръ, Хорватовъ и Сербовъ изъ тмы забвенія изятая и во свѣтъ историческіи произведенная*, vol. I, Віенна 1794, p. 405.

[61] *Ibidem*, p. 400.

[62] *Ibidem*, p. 409.

[63] These motifs were not alien to the contemporary historiography, the author also recalled here a similar opinion stated by Orbini – *ibidem*, pp. 494–495. See Д. Райков, *Историческа съдба...*, pp. 90–91.

continuators will be discussed here together. We will thus infringe upon the chronological order of the present exposition, to which we shall return in the subsequent sub-chapter, discussing the beginnings of the critical reflection on the Bulgarian Middle Ages.

Paisios and Rajić's continuators, the beginnings of Bulgarian textbook publishing

The publishing of Atansiy Nesković's history of Bulgaria, modelled on Rajić's work, in 1801 was funded by Bulgarian merchants. The book must have gained considerable interest; the book had its second print in the same year, third one in 1811, and in 1844 its full Bulgarian translation was published by Petar Sapunov[64]. Subsequently, Georgi Ikonomov published his own version of the text[65]. In the introduction, Nesković listed as his source, beside Rajić, Stritter's work. He named both the authors as the greatest authorities in Slavic history. In reality, he made considerable use only of the former's work, the latter being mentioned – we may guess – to make a better impression on the readers and sponsors of the publication[66]. The passage regarding Peter was left with practically no changes compared to Rajić's original in both Nesković's and Sapunov's versions (I had no access to Ikonomov's publication)[67].

The first Bulgarian history to be printed in Bulgarian is the *Brief History of Bulgaria* by Hristaki Pavlović[68]. It contains a greatly abbreviated

[64] Д. Цанев, *Историята на Раич*..., pp. 204–205.

[65] Д. Райков, *Историческа съдба*..., p. 91.

[66] Д. Цанев, *Историята на Раич*..., pp. 206–207.

[67] А. Нескович, *Исторïя на славенно-болгарскогъ народа изъ г. Раича историе и нѣкихъ историческимъ книгъ*, Буда 1801, pp. 121–126. An incorrect dating of the death of Romanos Lekapenos (on the page 124 the year is given as 983) should be considered a result of a printing error. А. Нескович, *Исторïата на славвенно-болгаркïѧ народъ изъ исторïата на г. Раича и нѣкои исторически книги составлена (...)*, transl. П. Сапунов, Букурещ 1844, pp. 122–128 (the translator duplicated here the incorrect dating).

[68] Х. Павлович, *Разговорникъ греко-болгарскïй за оныя, кои-то желаятъ греческïй языкъ да се научат, при кого-то и една кратка Болгарска история приложисе*, Белградъ 1835, pp. 88–99.

exposition of history (11 pages!) based on the information and chronology from Rajić's work. The author devoted half a page to Peter, on which he listed the most important facts from the ruler's life: the ascent to power, threat from the neighbours, the peace with Byzantium, the renewal of peace with Nikephoros Phokas, the sending of his sons as hostages, and the breakdown of peace caused by the Hungarian raids[69]. Nine years later Pavlović published a redacted version of Paisios' *History* (the so-called *tsarstvenik*). The author repeated, without particular fidelity but also without substantial alterations, Paisios's passage regarding Peter. The tsar's characterisation was supplemented by a comment that the ruler was pusillanimous, and that this was the deciding factor that led to his friendship with the Greeks, and his submissive attitude towards them[70]. He omitted the remark regarding Irene's death. This particular moment of the development of Byzantine-Bulgarian relations was presented as a re-entering into a peace agreement with the Greeks, coinciding with the rebellion of Peter's brothers[71]. It is a pity that Pavlović did not consult the abbreviated history of Bulgaria, based on Rajić, he published nine years earlier to somewhat order his exposition.

Pavlović's *tsarstvenik* was intended for school education. A similar, popularising goal motivated Dragan Tsankov, who published his *Overview of Bulgarian history* in the *Mesecoslov* [*Calendar* – J.M.W.] *for 1857*, based on the works of 'foreign' historians – as he himself stated[72]. His text is an important *novum*, for it acknowledged the achievements of the contemporary Bulgarian studies conducted in Russia, that will be presented below. The text was later re-printed as a standalone textbook titled *A short overview of Bulgarian history* (first printed in 1866). It was highly popular, and its fifth edition appeared already in 1870[73].

---

[69] *Ibidem*, p. 93.

[70] Х. Павлович, *Царственик или исторія болгарская*, Будим 1844, pp. 34–35.

[71] *Ibidem*, p. 35.

[72] Д. Цанков, *Единъ погледъ върху бльгарската исторія*, [in:] *Месецословъ за 1857 г.*, vol. I, Цариградъ 1857, pp. 60–130.

[73] Cf. Д. Мишев, *България в миналото. Страници из българската културна история*, София 1916, p. 327.

Peter's history is presented in this work in an abbreviated form[74]. The author clearly pointed out the internal divisions and fighting (rebellions of Peter's brothers) as the causes of Bulgaria's downfall[75]. 1860s and 1870s brought further publications of textbook nature. The work of Dobri Voynikov was published in 1861 in Vienna[76], and Todor Shishkov's history appeared in 1873 in Istanbul[77]. Although both of the authors cite Paisios of Hilendar (in Hristaki Pavlović's redaction), the base source of their knowledge and attitudes towards the past were contemporary historical works. Dobri Voynikov listed Yuriy Venelin, Pavel Šafárik, Jovan Rajić, Spiridon Palauzov and, in addition, as a source of knowledge about the *less well known antiquities and folk legends* he also mentioned (alongside the *tsarstvenik*) the work of Georgi Rakovski[78]. His relation regarding Peter has been strongly influenced by Venelin. Voynikov, writing about the causes of the gradual downfall of the state pointed to the divisions at the Preslavian court, rebellions and expansion of the Serbs, Hungarians and Croatians, Byzantinisation and the opposition to the Greek influence from part of the Bulgarian elites, Peter's weakness and submission to his wife, etc. Shishkov's relation is less hostile towards Symeon's successor, follows the facts more closely; the author is more sparing in offering his opinions – in this regard, the work resembles Dragan Tsankov's text, to which he referred in several places. Alongside it, he also cited other sources: e.g. Kedrenos and Leo the Deacon, as well as other studies, such as the *History of Bulgarians in Moesia* by Johann Engel. What is interesting, Shishkov stated that John's rebellion started when Peter was returning from Constantinople after his wedding with Maria-Irene. It is worth recalling that this detail was introduced into historiography by Orbini, whose work, in a Russian translation, may also have been used by our author.

---

[74] Д. Цанков, *Единъ погледъ...*, pp. 100–101.

[75] *Ibidem*, p. 101.

[76] Д. Войниковъ, *Кратка българска історія*, Вѣна 1861. On Peter: pp. 104–110.

[77] Т. Шишков, *Історія на българкыя народъ*, Цариградъ 1873. On Peter: pp. 167–170, 183.

[78] Д. Войниковъ, *Кратка българска історія*, p. VII.

Yuriy Venelin

In the first half of the nineteenth century a new direction of scholarship ofmediaeval Bulgaria was born, and we will tentatively refer to it as 'critical'[79]. While we accept Paisios as a symbol of changes in historiography, these did not relate to the manner of writing (here, Paisios is strongly conservative, not to say reactionary), but rather motivation. The 'new' that arrived with the works of Yuriy Venelin was based on moving away from the copying and compiling of chronicles in favour of constructing historiographic narratives of the author's own design, based of course on more – or less – in-depth source analysis. The history works of this trend resemble modern writing in regard to their composition, in the degree to which the exposition of history is shaped by the author's intentions. Paisios, for example, who was writing to cheer the hearts of his countrymen, made only one clear intervention that served this purpose in which he at the same time altered the facts regarding Peter; the major part of his works is a paraphrase of 'Mavrourbin', who in turn compiled works of Byzantine chroniclers. In Venelin's case, the re-narrating of the facts, proclaiming opinions and substantiating them are proportional to what we are used to from reading modern-day historical publication. Critical historiography can be considered a direct predecessor to the Bulgarian academic historiography which, with Marin Drinov's work, in the second half of the nineteenth century encompassed the native mediaeval history. In Venelin, we observe a tendency to speculative thinking and constructing

[79] In some approaches, it is only Marin Drinov who *is considered the first representative (along with the Czech Konstantin Jireček) of the 'critical-historical method', who had overcome the Romantic phase in Bulgarian historiography* (D. M i s h k o v a, *The Afterlife of a Commonwealth: Narratives of Byzantium in the National Historiographies of Greece, Bulgaria, Serbia and Romania*, [in:] *Entangled Histories of the Balkans*, vol. III, *Shared Pasts, Disputed Legacies*, ed. R. D a s k a l o v, A. V e z e n k o v, Leiden–Boston 2015, p. 191; the author cites here papers by Petar Nikov and Ivan Duychev). It is difficult to define the moment when the 'Romantic phase' was overcome. Diana M i s h k o v a (*ibidem*, p. 192) states writing about Zlatarski: *it is astonishing how much he had inherited from the notions of the Romantic generation of historians and from the 'national' construal of Byzantium* [she refers to Byzantine influence on Bulgaria – J.M.W.], *which had taken shape between Paisiy and Drinov.*

complex hypotheses, so prevalent in the work of modern historians. The aim of such activity (as much for Venelin as for our contemporaries) is most frequently the filling of the gaps in knowledge. For example: Venelin devoted much attention to the Bulgarian-Rus relations, and considered it valid to also comment on their state during the early period of Peter's reign (let us stress here that the sources do not shed any light whatsoever on this topic). He built a logical chain of events: Rus, Bulgaria's close neighbour, maintained lively contacts with her, not limited to trade. Could it therefore have kept neutrality when facing Bulgaria split into two (Venelin was thinking here of Michael and John's rebellions)? Since the Byzantines supported the ruler, would his opposition not have sought help from the North? The factor that Venelin considered to have been decisive in tipping the Rus into taking a side in the Bulgarian rebellions was the commencement of raids on the Byzantine Empire by Igor. He supported his conclusion with a rhetorical question: where else would the hostility between Byzantium and the Ruthenian prince have originated?[80]

Venelin's most important historical work, the *Critical study of the history of Bulgarians* was published, posthumously, in 1849 in Moscow[81]. Chronologically, it encompasses the period from the moment the Bulgarians appeared in the Balkans until Svyatoslav's invasion (968). In 1853, the work's translation into Bulgarian by Botyo Petkov (the father of Hristo Botev) was published in Zemun. The original edition was severely cut by the Russian censor, Fyodor Golubinsky[82].

---

[80] Ю. Венелин, *Критическія изслѣдованія объ исторіи Болгаръ: Съ прихода Болгаръ на Өракійскій полуостровъ до 986 года, или покоренія Болгаріи Великимъ Княземъ Русскимъ, Святославомъ*, Москва 1849, pp. 269–270.

[81] For information about the author, his work and contacts with Bulgarian intelligentsia, as well as with other Russians researching Bulgarian history (i.a. Vassil Aprilov and Spiridon Palauzov) see: Д. Цанев, *За Българите. Чуждата историческа българистика през XVIII–XIX век*, София 1981, pp. 80–95; idem, *Ю. Венелин и българската възрожденска историография*, ИБИД 26, 1984, pp. 193–200; Е. Дроснева, *Три етюда за Венелин*, ИБИД 26, 1984, pp. 201–207; М. Велева, *Юрий Иванович Венелин в българската историография*, ИБИД 26, 1984, pp. 171–191; Д. Цанев, *Българската историческа книжнина през Възраждането. XVIII – първата половина на XIX в.*, София 1989, pp. 31–33.

[82] Д. Цанев, *За Българите...*, pp. 91–93.

Venelin's writings turned out to have been a breakthrough, not only from the perspective of the historical research into mediaeval Bulgaria, but also regarding the portrayal of Peter himself. Let us begin with the quantitative matters: Venelin devoted nearly ninety pages to Peter's reign,[83] and to this day his study remains the most extensive work regarding Bulgarian political history in the years 927–969, although it has to be said that a considerable part of this volume was filled with discussions on topics of secondary importance to the chapter's main subject.

Venelin is the author of many of the hypotheses regarding Peter which, although devoid any solid (or even any at all!) source basis, became nested in Bulgarian mediaevistics. The Russian ethnographer and historian had a negative opinion of Peter as a ruler, and subjected his narrative to substantiating it. The telling of the history of Peter's reign begins with a categorical statement that in 927 Peter was still a minor, and that George Sursuvul served as the regent. On this basis, he makes conjectures: the ascension to throne of Symeon's younger son was a result of Sursuvul's intrigues, and it succeeded thanks to Byzantine support. Byzantines preferred Peter, a mere 'lamb' on the throne, to one of his fine brothers (*молодцы*) – John or Michael[84]. Venelin subjected his fantasising, as I mentioned before – and which we are going to examine further – to the notion of Peter's weakness, and pursued this through arguments assuming on the part of the participants of the events a high causal role, nearly complete knowledge, and politicisation. In the Russian historian's vision, the Byzantines have the appropriate tools to exert influence that leads to placing Peter on the throne; they know he will be a 'weak' and 'peace-loving' ruler (let us remind here that Venelin thought Peter to have been a minor at the time!), and consistently pursue the agenda of reinforcing their influence while desiring the weakening of Bulgaria. George Sursuvul

[83] Bulgarian editions: Ю.И. В е н е л и н, *Критическы издыянія за исторіѭ-тѫ блъгарскѫ. Отъ прихожденіе-то на Блъгаре-ты на Θракыйскый полуостровъ до 968 годинѫ, или до покореніе-то Блъгаріѭ отъ Великый Князь Русский*, vol. II, transl. Б. П е т к о в, *Земунъ 1853*, pp. 112–198. In the Russian original the part regarding Peter is a few pages shorter, which is a result of a different lettering density: Ю.И. В е н е л и н, *Критическія изслѣдованія*..., pp. 261–342.

[84] *Ibidem*, pp. 262–263.

has a comparable position of a 'demiurge', and uses Peter to realise his own political ambitions. The youthful ruler is not being brought up to be a statesman, but instead is provided with various distractions and entertainments which are intended to draw him away from the matters of state[85], he is to remain a marionette whose strings are pulled at first by Sursuvul, and later by Maria-Irene. In Bulgaria, facing Sursuvul's rapacity and the strengthening of Byzantine influence, there was a build-up of dissatisfaction, which resulted in the rebellions of Michael and John. The political conflicts were presented by the Russian historian as a rivalry between two groups: the Bulgarian, warlike, whose programme was being realised by Symeon, and the pro-Byzantine, led by the regent. Venelin reversed the chronological order of the rebellions that we know from the sources, first presenting the usurpation attempt of the elder of Peter's brothers[86]. In Venelin's view, John's rebellion lasted longer and was more significant, as it turned into a civil war with an involvement of outside powers, which led to a considerable weakening of the state. It is the supposed internal division of Bulgaria that Venelin considers to have been the cause of its downfall during the 940s. During that time, new states are born on Bulgarian territories: Hungary, Croatia and Serbia.

> Могли ли Болгаре, народъ царствующий, если руки ихъ свободны были отъ всякаго посторонняго занятия, допустить возмущение и отпадение сихъ малыхъ и несилныхъ народовъ? Могли ли Сербы и Кроаты сбить съ себя иго, если бы Болгаре не заняты были раздоромъ между собою?

According to Venelin, this period brought about the blow that proved to have been fatal to Bulgaria[87].

The Russian historian stated that the Rus' intervention against the supporters of Peter and the Byzantines, aiming to support John, lasted from 938 until 943. One of its episodes was the maritime expedition of

---

[85] *Ibidem*, p. 265.
[86] *Ibidem*, pp. 266–268.
[87] *Ibidem*, p. 279.

the Rus' on Constantinople in 941. The journey of Maria-Irene, noted by the sources discussing this period, was most likely caused by the Rus' activities. Venelin did not specify whether Maria journeyed to ask for assistance, seek shelter from the war, or simply to see Romanos[88]. While the war was taking place in Bulgaria, a rebellion aimed at the transferring of power to Constantine erupted in Byzantium. It was associated with the events happening in Bulgaria, and was supported by the Anatolian Bulgarians[89]. Venelin dated the end of the rebellion to 943, and as he himself stated that nothing can be said about the events of the war events during the rebellion's final stages; it was also not known through what deceit the tsar's brother was arrested. John's transportation to Constantinople is presented as a course of action agreed by the two courts[90].

After the civil wars Bulgaria needed good relations with Rus and Byzantium. Peter's feeble reign quenched the hopes of the nation, which was used to enterprising rulers, for rescuing the country. Peter subordinated himself to Maria's whims. While she was in the position of a Bulgarian ruler, she remained Greek at heart, and served as a tool for realising Byzantine interests. The people did not like this tsaritsa, for the other 'queens', although being Bulgarian themselves, did not meddle in politics. Bulgarians wanted the tsar's son to be named after Peter's father (in Venelin's text – Vladimir), however Maria did not agree to this, for he caused too much harm to the Greeks, and for this reason their sons bore the names of their great-grandfathers. Peter submitted to Maria regarding their sons' upbringing and allowed them to be sent to Constantinople, where they were visited by their mother every year[91]. The weak and passive reign, the presence of the heirs to the throne in the empire's capital, where they wallowed in opulence, caused discontent which led to the uprising of the Cometopouloi. Venelin stressed that it may have also been partly caused by Peter's other weaknesses and mistakes, which went unnoticed by the Byzantine source authors[92].

[88] *Ibidem*, p. 285.
[89] *Ibidem*, pp. 290–292.
[90] *Ibidem*, pp. 295–297, 301.
[91] *Ibidem*, pp. 326–327.
[92] *Ibidem*, pp. 329–331.

The work's Bulgarian translation, larger than the original due to lack of Russian censorship cuts and additions, in the part relating to Peter is exactly equivalent to the Russian printed version. There is one terminological difference that deserves a mention: where Venelin referred to the Bulgarian ruler as a 'king' – 'король'[93], Petkov used the term 'tsar – 'царь'[94].

Spiridon Palauzov

The mid-nineteenth century was a period of vigorous development of Russian research on mediaeval Bulgaria. Important works by Spiridon Palauzov have been published during the 1850s[95]. Peter appears in these only episodically, and is not discussed at any appreciable length. We do however find Palauzov's interesting opinion on this ruler in the *Tsar Symeon's era* (1852). Contrary to the nearly consistent opinion of the contemporary historiographers, he did not seek the causes of the state's weakness in some kind of personal disposition or negligence of the Bulgarian tsar, but claimed that: *Peter, under the protection of his uncle Sursuvul, managed to postpone Bulgaria's collapse for several years*[96]. The Russian scholar had anticipated the calls for *Peter's rehabilitation*, which became the *locus communi* of modern historiography, by nearly a century. Palauzov did not substantiate his position in any way. Perhaps he did not think it through in depth. Where he devoted more attention to the question of Bulgaria's downfall (*European south-west in the fourteenth century*, 1858), he considered the time of Peter's reign as wasted from the perspective of development of the state, suggesting negligence on the part of those in power. At the same time he contrasted the clear sense of direction and decisive foreign policy of Byzantium with the lack of ambition of the

[93] *Ibidem*, p. 267.

[94] Ю. И. Венелин, *Критическы издыянія...*, p. 118.

[95] For more information about this author see: Х. Коларов, В. Гюзелев, *Спиридон Николаев Палаузов (1818–1872)*, [in:] С. Палаузов, *Избрани трудове*, vol. I, ed. Х. Коларов, В. Гюзелев, София 1974, pp. 7–73; М. Велева, *Спиридон Палаузов – историк на Средна и Югоизточна Европа*, [in:] С. Палаузов, *Избрани трудове*, vol. II, ed. М. Велева, София 1977, pp. 7–46; Д. Цанев, *Българската историческа...*, pp. 163–181.

[96] С.Н. Палаузовъ, *Вѣкъ болгарскаго царя Симеона*, Санкпетербургъ 1852, p. 54.

Bulgarians (abandoning of Symeon's ideas). He also considered Peter's reign to have been the beginning of the *dominance of the Roman-Greek element in Bulgaria*[97].

Alexandr Gilferding

Alexandr Gilferding was writing the same time as Palauzov; he can be distinguished from the already discussed Russian authors by the fact he sought to provide a comprehensive view of history of the Southern Slavic Orthodox states: Bulgaria and Serbia[98]. In 1855 he published *Writings on the history of Serbs and Bulgarians*, which were later (1868) published in a supplemented and redrafted version in a volume of *Collected works*, under the title *The history of Serbs and Bulgarians*.

The vision of Peter's reign that Gilferding offers resembles in many respects the one outlined by Venelin. Gilferding is equally negative about the ruler, however the critical remarks are differently focused. He reconstructed facts with much greater care, and as a rule, he keeps his narrative much closer to the information provided by the sources, without indulging his imagination to such an extent. Nonetheless, also here we can find bold hypotheses that have no grounding in the accounts from the discussed period.

Gilferding presented the times of Peter in a decisive and unequivocal manner as a time of collapse. Much like Peter did not resemble his father (not having inherited his prowess, fierceness and bloodlust, as the Russian historian characterised the ruler following the description from the *Life of Luke the Younger*), so the Bulgaria of his time did not resemble the one that came before it. The ambition, thoughts of conquering Byzantium and creating indigenous Christian and Slavic culture (**просвѣщенїе**) are abandoned. Bulgaria became powerless and devoid of vitality. Gilferding, however, claims that such a situation could not have come about exclusively due to an individual's (the ruler's) weakness and the rapacity of the

[97] С.Н. Палаузовъ, *Юго-Востокъ Европы в XIV столетии*, Санкпетербургъ 1858, pp. 47–48.

[98] Cf. Д. Цанев, *За Българите*..., p. 109.

neighbouring countries, but that it was also considerably influenced by the dynamic of the country's inner life. In this, Symeon was among those responsible, as through his active policy he depleted the state's resources. Another reason for Bulgaria's downfall was the breaking of unity with the other Slavic nations, which was caused by the Hungarians who, settling in Pannonia, separated the Southern Slavs from those in the West, and by the mistaken (aggressive) policy of Symeon towards Croatia and Serbia. Remaining in isolation from their Slavic brethren, Bulgarians were inevitably ensnared by Byzantium[99]. Peter, according to Gilferding, was responsible for the cultural decline. During his reign the spiritual activity of Bulgarians faded away. The intellectual tradition was sufficiently undeveloped and fledgling that without the court's care it ceased[100].

The life of John of Rila was for Gilferding a premise to criticise the contemporary relations within Bulgaria. The times of John were in some way a period of prosperity for Bulgaria (*полнѣйшее благоденствіе*), there was a long-lasting peace, and the country enjoyed a high political standing. Could Bulgaria's internal state, already influenced by Byzantium, have been so hopeless (*неутешительный*) that John and the other hermits preferred to reject any contact with their nation?[101] In any case, the pauperisation of the spiritual life in the Bulgarian Church that followed Symeon's enlightened era was obvious and undoubtable to Gilferding[102].

Gilferding emphasised that the image of Peter's reign was 'sad', which was supposed to be attested by the strong Byzantine influences, the split between the Christian government and the supporters of the old beliefs, a stagnation in the spiritual life, inertia in foreign matters, and extremely rapidly-progressing collapse (*страшная быстрота въ паденїи*). Peter's reign, reported Gilferding, began with the rejection of the thought of

---

[99] А.Ф. Гильфердингъ, *Исторія сербовъ и болгаръ*, [in:] idem, *Собрание сочинений*, vol. I, С.-Петербургъ 1868, pp. 111–113.

[100] *Ibidem*, p. 121.

[101] In the 1855 edition, Aleksandr Gilferding (А.Ф. Гильфердингъ, *Письма объ истории сербовъ и болгаръ*, Москва 1855, pp. 170–171) formulated this passage in a somewhat more decisive manner: *Difficult times have come in Bulgaria, if its sole Apostle of Christianity rejected any contact with the nation!*

[102] А.Ф. Гильфердингъ, *Исторія сербовъ и болгаръ...*, pp. 129–130.

conquests, and ends with the state being unable to repel an enemy in its very heart. Peter was passive in his policies: when taking the reins of power, he gave up on revenge on the Croatians for his father's death, and soon after did nothing to keep Serbia under his influence[103]. However, Bulgaria's downfall could not be ascribed to an incidental influence of an individual: neither to Peter, nor Maria, nor Peter's brothers, nor to Sursuvul. They may have only been the midwives of what resulted from Bulgarians' national life (*что было подготовлено общимъ ходомъ болгарской жизни*)[104]. Gilferding judged the development of the Bulgarian state during Boris and Symeon's times as too hasty, unstable, unnatural and unhealthy. He considered this to be a characteristic of Bulgarian history and presented 'rises' of Bulgaria's political significance in other historical periods. He suggested that the underlying cause of this weakness of Bulgaria was the fact that the country (as the only Slavic state to have emerged like this) was created through conquest, and was artificially conglomerated from two nations[105].

3. Historiography after the 1850s

3.1. Classical Historiography on Medieval Bulgaria

Marin Drinov

This scholar's work significantly contributed to the development of institutional humanities in Bulgaria. In 1869 he was one of the founders of the Bulgarian Literary Society in Brăila, Romania, and subsequently its chairman for many years. After the liberation of Bulgaria in 1878, the institution was moved to Sofia, and in 1911 transformed

[103] *Ibidem*, p. 134.
[104] *Ibidem*, p. 136.
[105] *Ibidem*, pp. 137–138.

into the Bulgarian Academy of Sciences. In the Provisional Russian Administration in Bulgaria Drinov acted as the Minister of Popular Enlightenment and Spiritual Affairs. His far-reaching organisational and academic activity earns him the title of the father of modern Bulgarian mediaeval studies[106]. Konstantin Jireček and Vassil N. Zlatarski remained under his strong influence[107].

A broader presentation of Peter can be found in two of Marin Drinov's works: *The beginnings of Samuel's state* published in 1875–1876 in two parts, and *Southern Slavs and Byzantium in the tenth century* published in 1875. In the former, Drinov's aim was to rectify and complement the views on the political situation in which Samuel's state was created. In the introduction to the paper he declares that he will look in more detail into the internal processes that occurred in Bulgaria during Peter's reign, and the course of the Rus-Byzantine war in Bulgaria and its political consequences. Regarding the part of the work that is of the most interest to us, about Peter, the original goals were realised only in a very limited way, and the corrections cover the factual details. The same applies to the latter work. Drinov's arguments remain within the canon of Venelin and Gilferding's criticism, he emphasises the weakness of Peter's character, the way in which the tsar was influenced by the Byzantines, abandoned Symeon's ambitions, was interested in spiritual matters rather than those of state, etc.[108] Peter supposedly handed over the government to the nobles, first and foremost George Sursuvul, who put his personal interest ahead

[106] For an outline of the social and academic work of Marin Drinov, see: П. Мутафчиев, *Маринъ Дриновъ*, Прос 4.6, 1939, pp. 675–684; И. Дуйчев, *Приносът на Марин Дринов в областта на българската историография*, [in:] М. Дринов, *Избрани съчинения...*, pp. 7–34; Б. Ангелов, *Марин Дринов*, [in:] *KME*, vol. I, pp. 614–616; Λ. Горина, *Марин Дринов – историк и общественный деятель*, Москва 1986; V. Gjuzelev, *Marin Drinov (1838–1906). Begründer der bulgarischen Slawistik und Mediävistik*, Pbg 17.4, 1993, pp. 107–126; Д. Христов, *Историографски корени на Дриновото творчество*, ИП 71.1/2, 2015, pp. 32–45.

[107] V. Gjuzelev, *Marin Drinov...*, p. 108.

[108] М.С. Дринов, *Началото на Самуиловата държава*, [in:] idem, *Съчинения. Трудове по Българска и Славянска история*, ed. В.Н. Златарски, vol. I, София 1909, pp. 323–324; М.С. Дринов, *Южные славяне и Византія въ X вѣкъ*, [in:] idem, *Съчинения...*, pp. 431–433.

of the public. Aware that without an outside help he will not be able to hold on to power, he began to closely co-operate with the Byzantines. The direction in which this has taken the matters of state aroused the anger of the people, who rebelled against the ruler for the first time merely a year after the beginning of his reign[109]. The crown was supported by the clergy, pleased by the rapprochement with the Byzantines. Peter returned the favour by granting them privileges, and the clergy found themselves wallowing in wealth and luxury. Infected by greed and concerning themselves with material matters, the priests neglected their pastoral duties, which created a space for the development of the Bogomilist heresy[110]. The heresy was directed against both the Church hierarchy and the state government. The latter topic has previously been developed by Gilferding who, in the second edition of his work, based his analysis (similarly to Drinov) on the account of Cosmas the Priest.

Drinov dates the Cometopouloi rebellion (in his text, the leader of said rebellion is one Shishman[111]) to 963. Explaining its success in the western part of Bulgaria he stated that it was there that the hatred for the ineffectual ruler was the strongest. Petar Mutafchiev later developed this thought in a creative manner, claiming that the healthy cultural traditions of Bulgarians have been preserved in these regions, and have not been affected by the rot of Byzantinisation, 'radiating' from the capital[112]. Drinov, to a greater extent than his predecessors, puts responsibility for the collapse of the state on Peter. While Gilferding was partly justifying the ruler, by pointing out that the state he inherited was already exhausted, the Bulgarian historian adopted a contrary position, and considered Bulgaria in 927 to have been flourishing[113]. Drinov broadly developed the argument of Peter's naivety and short-sightedness, which has previously

[109] М.С. Дринов, *Началото*..., p. 325.

[110] *Ibidem*, pp. 325–326.

[111] The fictitiousness of Shishman has only been uncovered by Vassil N. Zlatarski (В.Н. Златарски, "*Тъй наречените грамоти*" *на Пинчия и неговия син Плезо*, ГСУ 15/16, 1919/1920, pp. 1–54).

[112] П. Мутафчиев, *История на българския народ (681–1323)*, ed. В. Гюзелев, София 1986, p. 222.

[113] М.С. Дринов, *Началото*..., p. 320.

been constructed by the aforementioned Russian scholar, and by Spiridon Palauzov[114]. The Byzantines were to have been perfidious allies. Soon after concluding the peace in 927 they initiated a consistent policy of backing out of the concessions made towards Bulgaria. This can be attested by their support for the Serbian separatism. Drinov blames Peter for not having perceived this warning sign, as the tsar faithfully kept his own commitments. Peter has seen through the Byzantines' dishonesty only near the end of his life, but by that point it had been too late[115].

Konstantin Jireček

The work of this exceptional Czech Slavist, while it may be considered a milestone in the development of the historiography of mediaeval Bulgarian history (it was published in four languages: Czech, German, Russian and Bulgarian), did not add much to the way Peter was being presented[116]. Jireček's attitude is critical of the ruler, and very similar to Drinov's position. The state's collapse that began during his reign was largely influenced by the character of the monarch, who was 'neither a politician, nor a warrior'. His place in history was among the saints and hermits. The state was in reality governed by his uncle George Sursuvul. The government did not represent the entire nation, but only one part of it, and interests of that group[117]. The culture entered a period of decline, which made room for an expansion of new teachings – the Bogomilism. The heresy was at its core an act of defiance against the clergy's support

[114] А.Ф. Гильфердингъ, *Исторія сербовъ и болгаръ*..., pp. 134–135; С.Н. Палаузовъ, *Юго-Востокъ Европы*..., pp. 47–48

[115] М.С. Дриновъ, *Южные славяне и Византія*..., pp. 438–439; С.Н. Палаузовъ, *Юго-Востокъ Европы*..., pp. 47–48.

[116] On Konstantin Jireček and the significance of his historical works see e.g.: Д. Ангелов, В. Паскалева, А. Пантев, *Константин Иречек и болгарская историческая наука*, BHR 1.2, 1973, p. 61–70; П. Петров, *Иречековата "История на българите"*, [in:] К. Иречек, *История на българите*, ed. П. Петров, София 1978, pp. 7–26; Д. Цанев, *За българите*..., pp. 126–129; a bibliography of works about this scholar: Н. Казански, *Константин Иречек (1854–1918). Публикации за него*, ИП 70.5/6, 2014, pp. 88–96.

[117] К. Иречек, *История на българите*..., pp. 198–199.

for the weak ruler, and his pro-Byzantine tendencies. The development of eremitism was in opposition to the official Church, whose priests surrounded themselves with luxury. The most outstanding representative of the ascetic trend was John of Rila[118]. The Byzantines used the period of peace to prepare the conquest of its new neighbour[119]. The Czech historian also repeated other themes present in the historiographic image of Peter, without particularly developing any of them. In the notes made with the thought of preparing a second edition of the *History of Bulgarians* he diminished somewhat the personal responsibility of the ruler for the state's collapse, pointing out the excessive territorial growth of Bulgaria during Symeon's times and the unfavourable, non-central, location of the capital[120].

Vassil N. Zlatarski

Vassil N. Zlatarski, as the author of an exceptionally detailed monograph on Bulgaria's history (intended to encompass the entirety of the mediaeval period, but brought up only until 1280) may be considered to have been the most outstanding historian of his time[121]. While his ideas naturally became somewhat dated as the scholarship progressed, new sources were uncovered, and the critique of the ones that have been known for a long time was further developed, they are still often taken under consideration, commented and discussed in modern historic works.

---

[118] *Ibidem*, pp. 202–204, 210, 467.

[119] *Ibidem*, p. 200.

[120] *Ibidem*, pp. 198–199.

[121] On the course of his life and scholarly activity see e.g.: П. Н и к о в, *Васил Златарски*, ИИДС 14/15, 1937, pp. 1–27; J.F. C l a r k e, *Zlatarski and Bulgarian Historiography*, SEER 15 (44), 1937, pp. 435–439; М. В е л е в а, *Васил Златарски като историк на българската историческа наука*, ИБИД 32, 1978, pp. 305–313; Е. Д р о с н е в а, *Златарски, Рънсиман и историята на първата българска държава*, ИБИД 32, 1978, pp. 331–339 (the indicated volume of the periodical also includes other interesting papers about Vassil N. Zlatarski); Д. Н а й д е н о в а, *Едно неосъществено издание на Пространното житие на Климент Охридски: Васил Н. Златарски и българската кирилиометодиевистика*, BMd 6, 2015, pp. 257–276.

Vassil N. Zlatarski comprehensively expounded on Peter's times[122]. He devoted the most attention to political history. While in his detailed considerations he put forward some new hypotheses and proposed new solutions, the overall evaluation of Peter is traditional. As the author himself observed, it is not important to find out what the Hungarian-Bulgarian relations looked like exactly in those times: whether Bulgarians were neutral regarding Hungarian raids on Byzantium, or whether they themselves were their victims, when the conclusion could only be one: Bulgaria, weakened under Peter's reign was not able to oppose the Pannonian warriors[123]. Zlatarski, somewhat differently than his predecessors, developed the argument of the social polarisation in Bulgaria. He shifted the emphasis from cultural matters to economic stratification between the people, and the boyars and senior clergy. In Zlatarski's framing of the events, the intensification of the Byzantinisation, the deepening of social inequality and popularisation of quietist religious movements that have proven tragic for the Bulgarian statehood have already been occurring during Symeon's times; however, their negative consequences only appeared in full during his successor's reign[124].

Steven Runciman

The British historian developed the argument about Peter's weakness, presenting him as a tsar–monk, a person without character, directed first by his wife (the leader of the peace party), and after her death by the warlike boyars. Runciman described him as a good man, but a bad ruler. The nation's demobilisation is examined in the context of the religious ferment that engulfed the country, and the appearance of the Bogomil heresy: *The decline and fall of her first Empire [i.e. Bulgaria] came very largely from the unceasing labours and increasing strength of the followers*

[122] В.Н. Златарски, *История на Първото българско Царство*, vol. I/2, *От славянизацията на държавата до падането на Първото царство (852–1018)*, ed. П. Петров, София 1971 (first print: 1927), pp. 495–563. Cf. Т. Тодоров, *От отрицание…*, p. 87.

[123] В.Н. Златарски, *История на Първото…*, p. 518.

[124] *Ibidem*, pp. 498–499, 520–524. Cf. D. Mishkova, *The Afterlife…*, p. 194.

of Pope Bogomil[125]. In his argument, the remark about the *wave of religious activity which swept over the whole country* (strongly inspired by the ruler), and about crowds entering the monasteries, gains similar significance[126]. Near the end of the passage related to Peter the author partially lifts the burden of responsibility from the ruler for the tragic finale that occurred two years after his death: *his task had been almost impossible; he had inherited a weary kingdom, and he had not been strong enough to hold it together*[127].

Petar Mutafchiev

The black legend of Peter found its fullest expression in the works of this learned historiographer. For Mutafchiev, Peter and his times serve to showcase the weakness of the Bulgarian spirit. Mutafchiev's works are strongly marked by national feelings, most apparently among the active academic historians of his times. He was convinced of the momentous historical role that Bulgaria had to play, and the high position his fatherland deserved to have within the European family of nations. He associated with 'Bulgarianness' these qualities for which the warlike Symeon or Samuel could be praised, and saw the sources of weakness in the departure from the native ideals and giving in to the 'Byzantine corruption'[128].

The reflection on Peter's reign and the circumstances of the downfall of the Bulgarian state in Moesia occupied an important place in Mutafchiev's works. The Bulgarian tsar appeared in many of his works; I will mention only the most important ones here. In extensive papers: on the Rus-Bulgarian relations (1931) and Hungarian-Bulgarian relations (1935) Mutafchiev explained many questions related to Peter's policy, especially the events that took place near the end of his reign, and during the brief reign of his successor. In the papers we can find astute source analyses, well-reasoned reconstructions of events, attempts at penetrating the motives of the main actors participating in the contemporary

[125] S. Runciman, *A History of the First Bulgarian Empire*, London 1930, p. 196.

[126] *Ibidem*, p. 189.

[127] *Ibidem*, p. 204.

[128] П. Мутафчиев, *История на българския...*, pp. 201, 208–209, 222.

international politics in the Balkans. It is interesting that Mutafchiev did not make a wider use of the materials he gathered when providing an overall evaluation of Peter. While the actions attributed to the ruler by the Bulgarian historian are rationally explained[129], Mutafchiev's view of Peter as a politician appears to be detached from the presented historical discourse and is unequivocally negative. Peter was to have been at fault primarily because of the way in which he failed to take action. The list of reasons that added to the negative portrait of Peter, established by his predecessors, was repeated by Mutafchiev in these early articles with practically no changes[130], and later, in particular in the posthumously published *History of the Bulgarian nation*, was creatively expanded further[131]. It might appear strange that the historian who so soberly analysed sources, and so scrupulously verified hypotheses present in the literature of the subject (he was blamed for being hyper-critical)[132], trusted the traditional historiography in such a fundamental question, and did not notice how far it became separated from the sources that were supposed to confirm it. The key to understanding Mutafchiev's stance is the fact that in addition to being a professional historian, he was also a social activist and a publicist[133]. The repeating of the commonly held arguments regarding Peter

[129] In particular: i d e m, *Маджарите и българо-византийските отношения през третата четвърт на X в.*, [in:] i d e m, *Избрани произведения*, ed. Д. А н г е л о в, vol. II, София 1973, pp. 466–468.

[130] П. М у т а ф ч и е в, *Съдбините на средновековния Дръстър*, [in:] i d e m, *Избрани произведения...*, pp. 50–59 (first print: 1927); i d e m, *Маджарите...*, p. 469; i d e m, *Русско-болгарские отношения при Святославе*, [in:] i d e m, *Избрани произведения...*, pp. 241–248; cf. also: i d e m, *Лекции по история на културата*, ed. И. И л и е в, София 1995, p. 95.

[131] I d e m, *История на българския народ...*, pp. 200–209.

[132] Cf. В. Г ю з е л е в, *Живот и научно творечество на Петър Мутафчиев (1883–1943)*, [in:] П. М у т а ф ч и е в, *История на българския народ...*, p. 15.

[133] Many studies were devoted to the person and works of Petar Mutafchiev, see e.g.: В. Г ю з е л е в, *Петър Мутафчиев*, София 1987; Р. Г а н д е в, *Животът и делото на проф. Петър Мутафчиев*, ГСУ.ЦК 86, 1993, pp. 95–107; collected papers: *Професор Петър Мутафчиев познат и непознат*, ed. Т. П о п н е д е л е в, Й. С о к о л о в, София 1997; *Историкът като изследовател, гражданин и човек. Сборник с материали от конференция, посветена на 130-годишнината от рождението и 70-годишнината от смъртта на проф. Петър Мутафчиев (1883–1943)*, София 2016.

by Mutafchiev was definitely not an unintentional act. The existing portrait of this Bulgarian ruler perfectly fit into Mutafchiev's thinking about the patterns that governed the history of Bulgaria and the state of the nation's contemporary affairs. Writing about Peter, he extensively developed the idea of the destructive role of Byzantinisation in Bulgaria's history. Deeply steeped in foreign models, the rulers moved away from the nation, lost sight of its true needs, and stopped being its true leaders. There was no shortage of those who sought their own gain rather than the common good. The people succumbed to hopelessness, and as a result of this demobilisation the state started to decline[134]. Convergent ideas can be found in Mutafchiev's journalistic texts, which included his diagnoses of the situation of the country and the moral crisis from which it was suffering[135]. The history he was writing was intended to be a lesson and a warning. Mutafchiev's works have indeed been perceived in this manner, as rousing the patriotic spirit, by his contemporaries[136]. Coloured with nationalist sentiments, views that Bulgaria attained a position it was due in the Balkan Peninsula during the reigns of the victorious Symeon or John Assen II[137]

[134] E.g. П. Мутафчиев, *Към философията на българската история. Византинизмътъ въ срѣдновѣковна България*, ФП 3.1, 1931, pp. 27–36, cf. D. Mishkova, *The Afterlife...*, pp. 235–239.

[135] On the weakness of the elites, the rule of careerists, cultural crisis and the susceptibility to external influences, see: П. Мутафчиев, *За културната криза у насъ*, Прос 1.4, 1935, pp. 385–397.

[136] The memories about Petar Muttafchiev have been formulated in this spirit in the volume of 'Prosveta' devoted to him in 1943, e.g.: Г. Константиновъ, *Проф. Петър Мутафчиев. 4. V. 1883 – 2. V. 1943*, Прос 8.10, 1943, pp. 577–582; И. Дуйчевъ, *Обаянието на проф. Мутафчиев*, Прос 8.10, 1943, pp. 583–586.

[137] П. Мутафчиевъ, *Де, кога и как се е губил българският народ до днес*, ОП 1.12/13, 1928, pp. 208–219; cf. В. Бешевлиевъ, *Източната половина на Балканския полуостровъ като жизнено пространство въ миналото*, Прос 8.10, 1943, pp. 601–609. The appropriate context in which one may examine the views of the contemporary Bulgarian historians on the historical role of the Bulgarian state is to be found in the disappointments with the so-called 'national disasters' that occurred during the early twentieth century, cf. А. Хранова, *Историография и литература. За социално конструиране на исторически понятия и Големи разкази в българската култура XIX–XX век*, vol. II, *Животът на три понятия в българската култура: възраждане, средновековие, робство*, София 2011, pp. 241–252.

were convincingly associated with a negative portrayal of Peter by Georgi Bakalov[138].

It would seem that it was the highly fervent love of the fatherland, which the Bulgarian historian has also demonstrated by shedding his blood during the second Balkan war[139], that influenced his instrumental treatment of Peter. In his exposition of the Bulgarian history of the tenth century the didactic effect had greater significance than the historical truth.

* * *

In the works discussed above, there is apparent a certain fixed pattern of writing about Peter. Its sources can be traced back to the output of Paisios of Hilendar, who presented the ruler as a weak commander, compliant towards the Greeks, seeking contact with monks. The sources of the story regarding social polarisation can be seen as early as Mauro Orbini, who interpreted the discord between the people as the cause of the state's downfall. The works of Yuriy Venelin and Aleksandr Gilferding were an important impulse for directing the development of this model. In evaluating the tsar, later historians did not go beyond the limited arguments defined in the works of their predecessors and used them in a similar way – to depict the ruler's weakness. At the same time, regarding factual material, we can see a clear development, consisting of the unification of the historiographic vision with the sources that have undergone a rational critique. It needs to be emphasised that the highly important elements of the negative portrayal of Peter and his era (such as Byzantinisation, favouring the monks and deep religionism, moral crisis or divisions within the society) appeared in the historiography prior to the uncovering of the most important sources that could have possibly confirmed this image. Writing about Maria-Irene aggressively propagating Byzantine cultural models, Venelin likely had no knowledge of the letter of Aretas, which

[138] Г. Бакалов, *Цар Петър (927–970) и неговото време*, Ист 1.2, 1992, p. 11; cf. И. Билярски, *Небесните покровители: св. цар Петър*, ИБ 5.2, 2001, p. 32.

[139] В. Гюзелев, *Петър Мутафчиев...*, p. 12.

indirectly shed light on the tsarina's intentions of leading a 'civilising mission' among Bulgarians. Similarly Gilferding, in the first edition of the history of Serbs and Bulgarians, when he was writing about the deep moral crisis engulfing Bulgarian society, did not quote the *Sermon* of Cosmas the Priest – he only referred to it in the expanded edition. The later historians (i.a. Marin Drinov or Konstantin Jireček), who blamed Peter for the deep religiosity and lack of interest in the matters of state, have already known of his canonisation[140], they knew the story of the failed attempt at meeting with John of Rila, but did not know (or did not accept) the hypotheses regarding Peter's literary activity, his devotion to the spiritual matters, which found the most clear 'confirmation' in the contents of his service[141]. The claims that Peter took part in literary creativity are based primarily on identifying him with Peter the Monk, an Old Bulgarian author of words of advice[142]. This idea however has no serious basis in the extant source material[143]. Moreover, already Venelin considered the tsar to have been insufficiently engaged in governance. Not having sensed his religiosity and unaware of his cult, he claimed that his courtiers were proffering

[140] A fragment of the service in Peter's honour was published in 1852 by Viktor Grigorovich (В.И. Григорович, *О древнейших памятниках церковно-славянских*, ИОРЯС 1.3, 1852, pp. 97–99). The Russian Slavist correctly identified the Peter praised in it with Symeon's heir. One of the earlier scholars – Alexandr Vostokov, saw here instead Peter-Theodore, a tsar of Bulgaria of the later twelfth century. The second part was published in 1920 by Pyotr Lavrov (П.А. Лавров, *Нова служба цару бугарскоме Петру*, ЈФ 1, 1913, pp. 34–37). Subsequent editions of the service can be found in i.a.: Й. Ивановъ, *Български старини из Македония*, София 1931, pp. 383–394; С. Кожухаров, *Проблеми на старобългарската поезия*, София 2004, pp. 75–79.

[141] Konstantin Jireček (К. Иречек, *История на българите...*, p. 198) signalled his knowledge of these hypotheses only in the notes prepared for the second edition of the *History of Bulgarians* (notes published posthumously in 1929).

[142] See. e.g. Й. Иванов, *Български старини*, pp. 385–386; Е. Георгиев, *Литература на изострени борби*, София 1966, pp. 20–21.

[143] The same name and the fact of taking monastic vows by both men, the identification of Peter the author with Peter the tsar in the late Rus' tradition, and the hypothetical similarity of interests do not settle the matter. On the problems with dating the works of Peter the Monk, see this work, Part Two, Chapter VII, point 2. A full review of the arguments that appear in this discussion has been made by Rumyana Pavlova (Р. Павлова, *Петър Черноризец. Старобългарски писател от X век*, София 1994).

to him pleasures of a layman[144]. The negative opinion of historians of Peter as a ruler came earlier than the evidence of his weakness, and directed interpretation (and sometimes also dating, as we may suppose in the case of Peter the Monk) of the newly discovered sources.

The period after World War II brought at first a crisis, and later, in the 1960s, a considerable increase in the number of published works on the mediaeval Bulgaria[145]. The trend, with a considerable delay, also encompassed Peter's era. The majority of the works that were created during this period and the ideas which were formed within them have found a sufficient reflection in the other parts of this monograph, and for this reason I will not discuss them here. I will only bring to attention two tendencies present in the research that are exceedingly important for the shaping of Peter's image in the contemporary historical literature.

3.2. Peter's Rehabilitation

The calls to 'rehabilitate' Peter, to remove from him the burden of responsibility for the state's collapse, are characteristic to historiography of Peter's era created in the last quarter of the twentieth century. Chronologically, the first to form this tendency was Vassil Gyuzelev who, in his 1968 article, pointed out that it would be inappropriate to claim that Peter's government was passive on the international stage, and that the Bulgaria in his day was defenceless in face of external incursions. Gyuzelev supported this view using the contents of an inscription from 943, which in his interpretation confirmed the effectiveness of the Bulgarian border defences against a Pecheneg raid, which was mentioned by *Russian Primary Chronicle*[146]. The cited work may be considered a faint herald

---

[144] Ю. Венелин, *Критическія изслѣдованія*..., p. 265.

[145] В. Гюзелев, *Апология*..., pp. 187–188, for more detailed study on the development of Bulgarian historiography in this period see: M. Pundeff, *Bulgarian Historiography, 1942–1958*, AHR 66.3, 1961, pp. 682–693.

[146] В. Гюзелев, *Добруджанският надпис и събитията в България през 943 г.*, ИП 24.6, 1968, pp. 40–48.

of the change in historians' attitude towards Peter[147]. It lacked a deeper reflection on the existing academic literature on the era of Symeon's successor to become an effective call for a general revision of ideas about the period. Such fundamental considerations were only brought about on the international arena by the analysis of John Van Antwerp Fine from 1978[148], and in Bulgaria itself a somewhat more cautious program paper by Petar Koledarov, published four years later[149]. In his text, Fine pointed to the lack of actual source basis that would confirm the negative opinions of Peter's reign. He called for a verification of the hypotheses regarding the social, economic and political crises that supposedly occurred during Peter's times. He stands on the position of cognitive minimalism and proposed to abandon making hypotheses when these are evoked primarily by historian's frustration caused by the lack of reliable information. *Thus, sad as it is, it is better to avoid the fictitious answer; historians must be satisfied with elucidating the major questions and problems and then answering them to the limited extent allowed by our fragmentary sources*[150]. Fine's methodological postulates have not been realised for a long time after his text was published. The conclusions directly associated with Peter, however, parallel to those proposed by Vassil Gyuzelev ten years earlier, have been generally well received by historians[151]. Half a century after

[147] Cf. T. Т о д о р о в, *От отрицание...*, pp. 88–89.

[148] J.V.A. F i n e, *A Fresh Look at Bulgaria under Tsar Peter (927–69)*, ByzS 5.1/2, 1978, pp. 88–95.

[149] П. К о л е д а р о в, *Цар Петър I*, ВС 51.4, 1982, pp. 192–207.

[150] J.V.A. F i n e, *A Fresh Look...*, p. 95; the American historian repeated the key arguments in the monograph: *The Early Medieval Balkans: A Critical Survey from the Sixth to the Late Twelfth Century*, Ann Arbor 1983, pp. 159–188.

[151] An early expression of the changes in the way Peter was presented in Bulgaria are the works of Petar Koledarov (П. К о л е д а р о в, *Политическа география на средновековната българска държава*, vol. I, От 681 до 1018 г., София 1979, pp. 50–53; i d e m, *Цар Петър I...*, pp. 192–207), and a later one – papers of Georgi Bakalov (Г. Б а к а л о в, *Цар Петър (927–970)...*, pp. 11–15) and of Plamen Pavlov (П. П а в л о в, *Две бележки към "Беседа на недостойния презвитер Козма срещу новопоявилата се ерес на Богомил"*, Пр.Сб 4, 1993, pp. 225–239). As for works in English, a more balanced or positive portrayal of Peter and his age can be found in i.a.: J. S h e p a r d, *A Marriage Too Far? Maria Lekapena and Peter of Bulgaria*, [in:] *The Empress Theophano: Byzantium and the West at the Turn of the First Millennium*, ed. A. D a v i d s, Cambridge 1995, pp. 121–150;

the process of 'rehabilitating' Peter in historiography, we may essentially acknowledge that the process has now been completed. The repeated calls for unbiased evaluation of this figure are on the one hand associated with the considerable authority of historians such as Vassil N. Zlatarski or Petar Mutafchiev, and on the other are a symptom of the same inertia and conservatism in historical research that have negatively affected Peter's portrayal for over a century, from the mid-nineteenth to the latter half of the twentieth century[152]. Nonetheless, the arguments taken from the historiographic canon are still being uncritically invoked, such as for example the belief in Peter's particular religiosity, his exceptionally favourable treatment of the monks, the progressing social divisions, moral crisis etc. This time, they do not serve to criticise the monarch, but either remain neutral in regard to his overall evaluation, or form a part of his positive portrayal[153]. It is not uncommon for historiographic arguments

M. Whittow, *The Making of Byzantium, 600–1025*, Berkeley, Los Angeles 1996, pp. 292–293; P. Stephenson, *Byzantium's Balkan Frontier. A Political Study of the Northern Balkans, 900–1204*, Cambridge 2001, pp. 24–25, 47–51; F. Curta, *Southeastern Europe in the Middle Ages, 500–1250*, Cambridge 2006, pp. 227–238. For the earlier works, presenting a critical view of Peter, it is worth mentioning e.g.: R. Browning, *Byzantium and Bulgaria. A Comparative Study across the Early Medieval Frontier*, Berkeley, Los Angeles 1975, pp. 68–71, 160–165, 181–184, 194.

[152] Recently, the need for rehabilitating Peter was discussed by Pavlov (П. Павлов, *Управлението на цар Петър (27 май 927 – 30 януари 969)*, [in:] Г. Атанасов, В. Вачкова, П. Павлов, *Българска национална история*, vol. III, *Първо българско царство (680–1018)*, Велико Търново 2015, pp. 403–404).

[153] E.g., the socio-political and economic crises and the existence of two competing groups among the Bulgarian elites were discussed by Bakalov (Г. Бакалов, *Цар Петър...*, pp. 14–15). The supposed moral crisis and passivity in foreign policy were written about by Ivan Bozhilov (И. Божилов, *България при цар Петър (927–969)*, [in:] idem, В. Гюзелев, *История на средновековна България VII–XIV век*, София 1999, pp. 281–289, 291–293). From this perspective, the paper by Pavlov from 1993 is particularly interesting (П. Павлов, *Две бележки...*, s. 231–233). In it, the author used the arguments about Peter accepting Byzantine models and the progressing economic disparity during his times to put forward his own idea: that Peter most likely issued laws limiting the enrichment by boyars, following in the footsteps of the contemporary Byzantine emperors. The praise of Peter contained in the text is a mirror image of earlier criticisms (Mutafchiev harshly criticised Peter for not reacting to the social stratification) and remains equally poorly justified. In his later work about Peter (*Управлението на цар Петър...*) the Bulgarian scholar abandoned such speculations. An almost

to remain in such a disassociation from the sources, as it happened with the works of the older historians, although the modern authors usually show greater caution in creating their own ideas. In recent years, there has been a crop of works following the rule of 'Fine's razor'. Regarding the socio-political issues, it is worth drawing attention to the comprehensive text of Plamen Pavlov regarding Peter, in the third volume of *Българска национална история* (2015)[154]. A good examples of such analysis are papers – the first, on the relations between Peter and the Church published a year later by Mirosław J. Leszka and the second, written by the same author in collaboration with Kirił Marinow concerning the widely presented scholarly controversies on tsar Peter's reign[155].

3.3. Peter's Place in the Historical Memory and Political Ideology

At the beginning of the twenty first century, a new and most interesting area of research regarding Peter appeared in the Bulgarian mediaeval studies. It focuses not on the ruler himself or his era, but on his cult, his place in the political ideology, and the portrayal in the memory of mediaeval Bulgarians. Peter appears as someone exceptional by the sheer fact of being proclaimed a saint. Intriguing information about him can be found in sources of liturgical and hagiographic nature, and in historical-apocalyptic texts. The honourable place of tsar Peter in the minds of the mediaeval Bulgarians is indicated by, for example, adopting Peter's

entirely traditional vision of Peter's reign was adopted by e.g. Gennadiy G. Litavrin (Г. Литаврин, *Христианство в Болгарии в 927–1018 гг.*, [in:] *Христианство в странах Восточной, Юго-Восточной и Центральной Европы на пороге второго тысячелетия*, ed. Б. Флоря, Москва 2002, pp. 134–137) in a work published in 2002, he stopped short only of a simplified evaluation of the ruler.

[154] П. Павлов, *Управлението на цар Петър*..., pp. 403–451; idem, *Общество, Църква и култура (927–1018). Богомилството – "великата българска ерес" в средновековния свят*, [in:] *Българска национална история*..., pp. 617–640.

[155] M.J. Leszka, *Rola cara Piotra (927–969) w życiu Kościoła bułgarskiego. Kilka uwag*, VP 36, 2016, pp. 429–442; idem, K. Маринов, *Спорные вопросы правления болгарского царя Петра I (927–969)*, Pbg 41.1, 2017, pp. 23–39.

name by the leaders of the anti-Byzantine uprisings of the eleventh and twelfth centuries, such as Delyan, Constantine Bodin or Theodore, proclaiming their aspirations to take power[156]. The high significance of the figure of Peter for the development of political ideology in Bulgaria can be concluded from the way in which he was associated with the emperor Constantine I the Great in the *Tale of the Prophet Isaiah* and the *Prologue Life of John of Rila* from the *Dragan's Minei*[157]. These themes have been extensively developed and motivated in Ivan Bilyarski's works[158], however they have also been taken up by other scholars[159]. The most problematic

[156] Georgi B ạ k a l o v (Г. Б а к а л о в, *Цар Петър...*, p. 15) has pointed out this fact before. As regards Delyan, we cannot exclude that 'Peter' was his baptismal name.

[157] И. Б и л я р с к и, *Небесните покровители...*, pp. 36–39.

[158] *Ibidem*; a somewhat altered English version of this paper: i d e m, *St. Peter (927–969), Tsar of the Bulgarians,* [in:] *State and Church: Studies in Medieval Bulgaria and Byzantium,* ed. V. G j u z e l e v, K. P e t k o v, Sofia 2011, pp. 173–188; i d e m, *Покровители на Царството. Св. цар Петър и св. Параскева-Петка,* София 2004; i d e m, M. Й о в ч е в а, *За датата на Успението на цар Петър и за култа към него,* [in:] *Тангра. Сборник в чест на 70–годишнината на акад. Васил Гюзелев,* ed. M. К а й м а к а м о в а et al., София 2006, pp. 543–557; i d e m, *Le Tsar sur la montagne,* [in:] *Histoire, mémoire et devotion. Regards croisés sur la construction des identities dans le monde orthodoxe aux époques byzantine et post-byzantine,* ed. R.G. P ă u n, Seyssel 2016, pp. 53–71.

[159] Д.И. П о л ы в я н н ы й, *Царь Петр I и его правление в культурной традиции средневековой Болгарии,* [in:] *Славяне и их соседи. XX конференция памяти В.Д. Королюка. Становление славянского мира и Византия в эпоху раннего Средневековья. Сборник тезисов,* ed. Г.Г. Л и т а в р и н, Б.Н. Ф л о р я, О.А. А к и м о в а, Москва 2001, pp. 97–99; Д. Ч е ш м е д ж и е в, *Няколко бележки за култа към цар Петър I (927–965),* [in:] *Християнската традиция и царската институция в българската култура,* ed. B. Б о н е в а, Шумен 2003, pp. 23–37; i d e m, *Култът към цар Петър I (927–965): манастирски или държавен?,* [in:] *Љубав према образовању и вера у Бога у православним манастирима.. 5. међународна Хиландарска конференција. Зборник изабраних радова I,* ed. P. M a t e j i ć et al., Београд–Columbus 2006, pp. 254–255; А. Н и к о л о в, *Политическа мисъл в ранносредновековна България,* София 2006, pp. 233–287; Б. Н и к о л о в а, *Цар Петър и характерът на неговия култ,* Pbg 33.2, 2009, pp. 63–78; С.А. И в а н о в, *Общественная мысль в Болгарии в XI–XIII вв.,* [in:] *Власть и общество в литературных текстах древней Руси и других славянских стран (XII–XIII вв.),* ed. Б. Ф л о р я, Москва 2012, pp. 95–102; Д.И. П о л ы в я н н ы й, *Царь Петр в исторической памяти болгарского средневековья,* [in:] *Средновековният българин и "другите". Сборник в чест н 60-годишнината на проф. дин Петър Ангелов,* ed. А. Н и к о л о в, Г.Н. Н и к о л о в, София 2013,

in this research is the question of how the way Peter was represented in the mediaeval Bulgarian tradition related to the actual, true nature of his reign[160]. Are these scattered remarks a sufficient basis for making reflections on Peter's role in the development of political and religious culture of the tenth century Bulgarians? The literary portrayal of the ruler that we find in the texts associated with his cult, the hagiography of the contemporary anchorites, quasi-historical legends and other literary antiquities are not necessarily related to the deeds and character of the historical Peter. At the same time it would have been difficult to entirely ignore the testimony of so many – largely independent from one another – sources, perceiving them merely as a tangle of topoi, accidents and unbelievable fantasies. Developing a universally accepted position in this matter is likely to take considerable time, if it is possible at all, as the source material does not allow for a clear-cut solution to the problem.

pp. 137–145; M. К а й м а к а м о в а, *Култът към цар Петър (927–969) и движещите идеи на българските освободителни въстания срещу византийската власт през XI–XII в.*, BMd 4/5, 2013/2014, pp. 417–438.

[160] Cf. И. Б о ж и л о в, *Българското общество през 14. век*, Пловдив 2014, pp. 154–159.

Conclusion

The reign of Peter I the Saint brought Bulgaria more than forty years of peace. No wars were waged during that time, and the domestic situation was that of harmonious development. The tsar's position, after neutralising his brothers' opposition, was stable, which is a testament to his unquestionable authority. One may not see in his rule a period of decadence, the weakening of Bulgaria in economic, military or cultural spheres. Peter was without a doubt an independent ruler, who was pursuing Bulgarian interest and did not submit to his southern neighbour and a long-time ally – Byzantium. This does not mean, however, that he was opposed to Byzantine influence in cultural or religious spheres – the best example of this is his correspondence with the patriarch Theophylact. It is also possible that he reached for Constantinopolitan models of state organisation. One needs to keep in mind that Peter was a well-educated man who had a strong connection with his father, Symeon I the Great, who – while engaging in conflicts with Byzantium – also knew it very well, and made skilful use of its accomplishments, adapting them to his own needs, and giving them a new, Bulgarian dimension. It is possible that this attitude towards Byzantium was also shared by his son.

In comparing him with his illustrious ancestors – Boris I and Symeon I – his reign should not be contrasted with the achievements of his predecessors, but examined as their logical continuation, and complementation of the achievements of the earlier decades. For if during their reigns the new foundations for the future development of Bulgaria had been lain – alike in the sphere of religion, culture (Boris-Michael), ideology and political or military aspirations (Symeon), then the long reign of Peter created favourable conditions for the final crystallisation and consolidation of the new structures. Bulgaria became a Christian Empire in the full meaning of the word, with all the constitutive characteristics and qualities. It seems that this is the way in which it was perceived during the Middle Ages, since the authors writing during this period list him alongside the most meritorious rulers of this early era. He was also a figure who was eagerly referred to in the ideological sphere. For generations of mediaeval Bulgarians, who first lived through the many years of struggles against the Byzantines ruled by emperor Basil II (with a telling sobriquet: the Bulgar Slayer), and subsequently through the bitterness of Byzantine bondage, the reign of Peter appeared as a time of peace, stability and relative prosperity. It is notable that the tsar was not being burdened with the responsibility for Bulgaria's downfall, neither by his contemporaries, nor by the later generations. His name was being evoked by those who took up the fight for independence. It was assumed by, among others, Theodore-Assen, the co-initiator of the uprising that brought about the restoration of the Bulgarian statehood during the 1180s.

His peaceful relations and openness to Byzantine culture should not be surprising, for since the time of its official Christianisation Bulgaria adopted a new course in its development, becoming a part of the Christian world. After all, it needed to draw the appropriate models to emulate from somewhere, and these existed and could be readily implemented using its southern neighbour's good offices. The direction of this co-operation was also determined by the geopolitical location of the state and the proximity to Constantinople, the contemporary centre of cultural life in this part of the Christian *oikoumene*. From the Byzantine's perspective, Peter's reign was a return to the peaceful co-existence of the two states, which was established by Boris I and emperor Michael III, and interrupted by Symeon I's reign. While the latter was called the 'child of peace', since he was most likely born at the time when treaty was being concluded by Boris-Michael, Peter appeared as one of the creators of the peace, alongside emperor Romanos Lekapenos. Peter however went one step further than his grandfather, since he tied a bond of kinship with the imperial family (something that had not been granted to any non-Byzantine ruler), which undoubtedly raised his authority in the international scene. Therefore instead of turning this into an accusation, that he allowed a Byzantine spy and spreader of Constantinopolitan influence entry into Bulgaria, directly into its 'heart', one should rather consider it a momentous success, affirming the position of the Bulgarian state. After all, this is how historiography judges the marriage of emperor Otto II with the imperial princess Theophano – as a completion of the restitution of the institution of the Empire in the West, and an expression of the Byzantine acquiescence to the fact. Even Constantine Porphyrogennetos himself, instead of rejoicing that through the supposed intermediation of Maria Byzantium was able to interfere in Bulgarian matters with no difficulty, he unequivocally deemed the contemporary Constantinopolitan ruler to have betrayed the imperial tradition by marrying the princess to a foreign ruler unworthy of this honour (sic!). Therefore the views of historians who wish to see Maria Lekapene as a Constantinopolitan agent at the Preslavian court and an active exponent of Byzantine culture on the Bulgarian soil are obviously exaggerated and find no confirmation in the available source material. First and foremost, one needs to consider the fact that from 927 onwards Maria was ruling over a people whose political and intellectual elites have already been quite well familiarised with the cultural achievements of the Eastern Empire. It would also be difficult to consider Maria a person who had a dominant influence on the direction of the foreign and internal policy of Peter. In none of the surviving Old Bulgarian texts would we find even a single remark about the public activity of this ruler. The accounts of the Byzantine historians are enigmatic as well, and inform us only about Maria's several journeys, with her children, to Constantinople to visit her relatives. One matter is without a doubt – during Maria Lekapene's reign, the most important elements of what can be considered *imperial feminine* became assimilated in Bulgaria.

The accusations of excessive religiosity, escaping from matters of state and transforming Bulgaria into some kind of a 'monastic state' levelled at the Bulgarian tsar are also unconvincing. The spreading of faith, the fight for its purity, as well as a deep, personal piety were all qualities that were – after all – desirable in a Christian ruler – it would be sufficient to familiarise oneself with the instruction offered by patriarch Photios to Boris-Michael. In this matter Peter was therefore both an obedient pupil of both the Constantinopolitan hierarch, and of his ancestor. It is a similar case with the assumption that the development of the Bogomil heresy must have been a result of the state's weakness. Had that been the case, then no schisms would have appeared at the dawn of the early Church, fervent and devoted to the Gospel, and the emperor Alexios I Komnenos (1081–1118), who is not considered a weak ruler, would not have had to struggle with the heresiarch Basil. It is also worth noting the fact that Peter was most likely canonised and worshipped by the Bulgarian Church. There is something symbolic in the fact that it was his name, and not that of Boris-Michael – which would have seemed more natural – that was associated with emperor Constantine I the Great, which thus placed him within the idea present in the Byzantine *oikoumene* of the 'new/second Constantine'. It was to Peter that generations of Bulgarians directed these words:

> Якоже прѣжде възлюби мирѡмъ прѣбывати въ житии своемъ. тако и нїн҃ѣ намъ молитвами къ Б҃гоу страны всѧ оумири.
> Оускори Петре ѿче прѣсвѧтыи. видѫ великѫѭ бѣдѫ належѫщѫѭ на ны. молитвами своими. то оуже сѧ ѕѣло кончаемы.
> Ты яви сѧ намъ ѕвѣзда свѣтлаа из бокоу земноу всиявъ. въ лѣта послѣдная. тмѫ всѣкѫ разгонѧ съпротивнаaго врага.
> Оусты грѣшныи окоущаѫще сѧ похвалити не могѫт по лѣпотѣ добротъ твоихъ Петре ц҃рю.

> Just as earlier you wished to live your life in peace, now with your prayers to God on our behalf bring peace to all lands.
> Hurry up with your prayers, most blessed father Peter, for you see that a great trouble is engulfing us and we are overwhelmed.

> You appeared to us like the morning star, shining from the earth in recent
> years and dispersed all of the darkness of the opposing enemy.
> The sinful lips who attempt to praise you are not able of doing that, tsar
> Peter, because of the beauty of your goodness.[1]

Even being aware of the nature of the text, it is difficult to resist the impression that the mention of Peter's love of peace may be an expression of what he really strived for in his policies; and is certainly a reflection of how his reign was remembered.

In addition, Bulgaria did not lose its statehood during Peter's life. This had taken place two years later, and not because of the Rus', but the Byzantines. At the time when the tsar was dying, the threat from the Rus' prince Svyatoslav had been, at least temporarily, neutralised. It is also possible that our protagonist, as an experienced ruler, had he been in his prime, would have been able to effectively direct resistance against the second invasion. Rightly, from the perspective of the peace treaty of 927, it was not the Bulgarians but the Byzantines who had been responsible for the breaking of the accord, and Peter and his immediate successor may have felt betrayed in this by their southern neighbour, with whom they remained at peace for so long.

[1] *Service of St. Tsar Peter*, p. 388; transl. K. Petkov, p. 108.

Abbreviations

AAe	Anthropology and Aesthetics
AB	Analecta Bollandiana
ABu	Archaeologia Bulgarica
AHR	American Historical Review
AMN	Acta Musei Napocensis
AMV	Acta Musei Varnaensis
AMSCEUB	Annual of Medieval Studies at Central European University Budapest
AO.ASH	Acta Orientalia Academiae Scientiarum Hungaricae
ArtB	The Art Bulletin: a quarterly published by the College Art ssociation of America
AUL.FH	Acta Universitatis Lodziensis. Folia Historica
B	Byzantion. Revue internationale des études byzantines
Balc	Balcanica. Annual of the Institute for Balkan Studies
BalkF	Balkanistic Forum
BBg	Byzantinobulgarica
BF	Byzantinische Forschungen. Internationale Zeitschrift für Byzantinistik
BHR	Bulgarian Historical Review / Revue bulgare d'histoire
BMd	Bulgaria Mediaevalis
BMGS	Byzantine and Modern Greek Studies

BP	Balcanica Posnaniensia. Acta et studia
Bsl	Byzantinoslavica. Revue internationale des études byzantines
Bslov	Byzantinoslovaca
ByzS	Byzantine Studies / Études byzantines
BZ	Byzantinische Zeitschrift
CCM	Cahiers de civilisation médiévale, Xe–XIIe siècles
CliC	Climatic Change
CMAe	Concilium Medii Aevi
CSEL	Corpus scriptorum ecclesiasticorum latinorum
Cyr	Cyrillomethodianum
D	Dacia
DOP	Dumbarton Oaks Papers
EB	Études balkaniques. Revue trimestrielle publiée par l'Institut d'études balkaniques près l'Académie bulgare des sciences
EBPB	Études Byzantines et Post-Byzantines
EEG	Environmental & Engineering Geoscience
EHi	Études Historiques
EHR	English Historical Review
EN	Ephemeris Napocensis
EO	Échos d'Orient
Ery	Erytheia. Revista de Estudios Bizantinos y Neogriegos
FBHPJS	*Fontes Byzantini Historiam Populorum Jugoslaviae Spectantes / Византијски извори за историју народа Југославије*, vol. II, ed. B. Ferjančić, Beograd 1959.
FE	Fundamenta Europaea
FGHB	*Fontes graeci historiae bulgaricae / Гръцки извори за българската история*, vol. IV, ed. IV, ed. I. Dujčev, G. Cankova-Petkova, V. Tăpkova-Zaimova, L. Jončev, P. Tivčev, Serdicae 1961; vol. V, ed. G. Cankova-Petkova, I. Dujčev, L. Jončev, V. Tăpkova-Zaïmova, P. Tivčev, M. Voinov, Serdicae 1964; vol. VI, ed. I. Dujčev, V. Tăpkova-Zaïmova, M. Voinov, Serdicae 1965;

	vol. IX.2, *Theophylacti Achridensis, archiepiscopi Bulgariae scripta ad historiam Bulgariae pertinentia*, pars 2, *Vita S. Clementis Achridensis, Historia martyrii XV martyrum Tiberiupolitanorum, Epistulae, Carmen ad Nicephorum Bryennium, pars expositionis in Epistulam Pauli Apostoli ad Romanos*, ed. I.G. Iliev, Serdicae 1994.
FLHB	*Fontes latini historiae bulgaricae / Латински извори за българската история*, vol. III, ed. I. Dujčev, S. Lišev, B. Primov, M. Vojnov, Serdicae 1965.
FPh	Folia Philologica
GRev	Geographical Review
H.BJHE	History. Bulgarian Journal of Historical Education
HČSAV	Historický časopis Slovenskej akadémie vied, Bratislava
HSS	Harvard Slavic Studies
HSS	Harvard Slavic Studies
IČ	Istoriski [Istorijski] časopis
Jahr.EJB	Jahr. European Journal of Bioethics
JCrS	Journal of Croatian Studies
JHS	Journal of Hellenic Studies
JLA	Journal of Late Antiquity
JÖB	Jahrbuch der Österreichischen Byzantinistik
KDMK	Kuny Domokos Múzeum Közleményei
KH	Kwartalnik Historyczny
KP.LA	*Der Kleine Pauly. Lexikon der Antike*, vol. II, ed. K. Ziegler, Stuttgart 1967.
KWSS	Krakowsko-Wileńskie Studia Slawistyczne
LdM	*Lexikon des Mittelalters*, vol. I, R.-H. Bautier, R. Auty, N. Angermann, München 1980.
LN	LiterNet Online Journal
MGH.E	*Monumenta Germaniae historica, Epistolae*
MGH.SS	*Monumenta Germaniae historica, Scriptores*
OCP	Orientalia Christiana Periodica
ODB	*The Oxford Dictionary of Byzantium*, ed. A.P. Kazhdan, vol. I–III, New York–Oxford 1991.

Pbg Palaeobulgarica / Старобългаристика

Peu Peuce

PG *Patrologiae cursus completus, Series graeca*, ed. J.-P. M i g n e, Paris 1857–1866.

PH Przegląd Historyczny

PMZ II *Prosopographie der mittelbyzantinischen Zeit. Zweite Abteilung (867–1025)*, ed. F. W i n k e l m a n n et al.,
vol. II, *Christophoros* (# 21 279) – *Ignatios* (# 22712), Berlin–Boston 2013;
vol. III, *Ignatios* (# 227123) – *Lampudios* (# 24268), Berlin–Boston 2013;
vol. IV, *Landenolfus* (#24269) – *Niketas* (# 25701), Berlin–Boston 2013;
vol. VI, *Sinko* (# 27089) – *Zuhayr* (#28522), Berlin–Boston 2013.

PP Past and Present: A Journal of Historical Studies

RE *Paulys Real-Encyclopädie der classischen Altertumswissenschaft*, ed. G. W i s s o w a, W. K r o l l et al., vol. X.A.1, Munich 1972.

REB Revue des études byzantines

RESEE Revue des études sud-est européennes

RG Reviews of Geophysics

RS Ricerche slavistiche

SA Slavia Antiqua

SAUS.S Studia Archaeologica Universitatis Serdiciensis. Supplementum

SB Studia Balcanica

SBAW.PHK Sitzungsberichte der Bayerischen Akademie der Wissenschaften, Philosophisch-historische Klasse

SCer Studia Ceranea. Journal of the Waldemar Ceran Research Center for the History and Culture of the Mediterranean Area and South-Eastern Europe

SEER The Slavonic and East European Review

SFFUKB Sbornik Filosofické Fakulty University Komenského v Bratislavé

SGa Slavica Gandensia

SH Studia Historyczne

SK Seminarium Kondakovianum

SMer Slavia Meridionalis

SRel Studia Religiologica

SSS *Słownik starożytności słowiańskich. Encyklopedyczny zarys kultury Słowian od czasów najdawniejszych do schyłku XII w.*,
vol. II, ed. W. Kowalenko, G. Labuda, T. Lehr-Spławiński, Wrocław 1965;
vol. III, *L–O*, red. G. Labuda, Z. Stieber, Wrocław 1967;
vol. V, ed. W. Kowalenko, G. Labuda, T. Lehr-Spławiński, Wrocław 1975;
vol. VII, *Y–Ż i Suplementy*, ed. G. Labuda i Z. Stieber, Wrocław 1982;
vol. VIII, *Suplementy i indeksy A–Ż*, ed. A. Gąsiorowski, G. Labuda, A. Wędzki, Wrocław 1991.

Testimonia *Testimonia najdawniejszych dziejów Słowian. Seria grecka*,
vol. III, *Pisarze z VII–X wieku*, ed. A. Brzóstkowska, W. Swoboda, Warszawa 1995;
vol. IV, *Pisarze z VIII–XII wieku*, ed. A. Brzóstkowska, W. Swoboda, Warszawa 1997;
vol. V, *Pisarze z X wieku*, ed. A. Brzóstkowska, Warszawa 2009;
vol. VI, *Pisarze wieku XI*, transl., comm. A. Kotłowska, A. Brzóstkowska, Warszawa 2013.

TM Travaux et mémoires du Centre de recherches d'histoire et civilisation byzantines

TRHS Transactions of the Royal Historical Society

VP Vox Patrum. Antyk Chrześcijański

WS Die Welt der Slaven

WSA Wiener Slavistischer Almanach

Zir Ziridava

ZNUJ.PH Zeszyty Naukowe Uniwersytetu Jagiellońskiego. Prace Historyczne

* * *

Βυζ Βυζαντινά. Ἐπιστημονικό Ὄργανο Κέντρου Βυζαντινών Ἐρευνών Αριστοτελείου Πανεπιστημίου

ΔΧΑΕ Δελτίον τῆς Χριστιανικῆς Ἀρχαιολογικῆς Ἑταιρείας

* * *

АДСВ	Античная древность и средние века
Ана	Анали
Архе	Археология
БЕт	Българска етнология
БИБ	Българско историческа библиотека
БСП	Българите в северното Причерноморие. Изследвания и материали
Век	Векове
ВОб	Византийское обозрение
ВС	Военноисторически сборник
ГДА	Годишник на Духовната Академия "Свети Климент Охридски"
ГНМ	Годишник на Народния музей
ГНАМ	Годишник на Националния археологически музей
ГСУ	Годишник на Софийския университет
ГСУ.БФ	Годишник на Софийския университет. Богословски факултет
ГСУ.ИФФ	Годишник на Софийския Университет. Историко-Филологически факултет
ГСУ.НЦСВПИД	Годишник на Софийския Университет "Научен център за славяно-византийски проучвания "Иван Дуйчев"
ГСУ.ЦК	Годишник на Софийския Университет "Св. Климент Охридски". Център по културознание
ДобСб	Добруджа. Сборник
ДСб	Дриновски сборник
Епо	Епохи
ЗИООИД	Записки Императорскаго Одесскаго Общества Исторіи и Древностей
ЗРВИ	Зборник радова Византолошког института
ИБАИ/ИАИ/ИНАИ	Известия на Българския археологически институт / Известия на археологическия институт / Известия на Националния археологически институт
ИВНД	Известия на Военноисторическото научно дружество
ИБ	Историческо бъдеще

НВ.ЗР	Ниш и Византија. Зборник радова
ИИД/ИИДС/ИБИД	Известия на Историческото дружество / Известия на Историческото дружество въ София / Известия на Българското историческо дружество
ИБСЛ	*История на българската средновековна литература*, ed. А. М и л т е н о в а, София 2008.
ИИБЛ	Известия на Института за българска литература
ИИз	Интердисциплинарни изследвания
ИИИ	Известия на Института за история
ИИМК	Известия на Историческия музей – Кюстендил
ИИМШ	Известия на Историческия музей – Шумен
ИМСБ	Известия на музеите от Северозападна България
ИМЮБ	Известия на музеите от Южна България
ИНМВ	Известия на Народния музей – Варна
ИОИМВТ/ИРИМВТ	Известия на Окръжния исторически музей – Велико Търново / Известия на Регионалния исторически музей – Велико Търново
ИОРЯС	Известия Отделения русского языка и словесности [Императорской / Российской Академии Наук]
ИП	Исторически преглед
ИРИМГ	Известия на Регионален исторически музей – Габрово
ИСИМ	Известия на Старозагорския исторически музей
Ист	История
Истор	Историкии
ИТНИ	Известия на Тракийския научен институт
КМЕ	*Кирило-Методиевска енциклопедия*, vol. III, *П–С*, ed. Л. Г р а ш е в а, София 2003.
КМС	Кирило-Методиевски студии
ЛИФО.ВО	Лѣтопись историко-филологическаго общества при императорскомъ Новороссийскомъ университетѣ, Византийское отделение
МПр	Македонски Преглед
Мин	Минало
Мор	Море
МПК	Музеи и паметници на културата

НСЕ	Нумизматика, сигилография и епиграфика
ОП	Отец Паисий
НЗУІЗНС	Наукові записки з української історії: Збірник наукових статей
ПС	Палеобалканистика и старобългаристика
ПБА	Приноси към българската археология
ПК	**Полата кънигописьная** / Polata Knigopisnaja. A Journal Devoted to the Study of Early Slavic Books, Texts and Literature
ПКШ	Преславска книжовна школа
ППИК	Проблеми на прабългарската история и култура
ППре	Плиска–Преслав
Про	Проглас
Прос	Просвета
Пр.Сб	Преслав. Сборник
ПСБКД	Периодическо списание на Българското книжовно дружество
ПУПХБ.НТФ	Пловдивски Университет Паисий Хилендарски, България. Научни трудове. Филология
РЛи	Русская литература
РП	Разскопки и проучвания
СБАН.КИФФО	Списание на Българската Академия на Науките. Клон Историко-филологичен и Философско-обществен
СЛ	Старобългарска литература
Слав	Славяноведение
СНУНК	Сборник за народни умотворения, наука и книжнина
ССл	Советское славяноведение
Ста	Старинар
ТГЭ	Труды Государственого Ермитажа
ТКШ	Търновска книжовна школа
ТОДРЛ	Труды Отдела древнерусской литературы Института русской литературы Академии наук СССР
УП	Училищен преглед
ФП	Философски преглед
ШМ	Шахматна мисъл
ШУЕКП.ТКИБ	Шуменски Университет Епископ Константин Преславски. Трудове на Катедрите по история и богословие
ЈФ	Јужнословенски филолог

Bibliography

Sources

Acts of Iviron

Actes d'Iviron, vol. I, *Des origines au milieu du XIe siècle*, ed. J. Lefort, N. Oikonomides, D. Papachryssanthou, Paris 1985.

Acts of Lavra

Actes de Lavra I, ed. P. Lemerle et al., Paris 1970.

Agapetos Diakonos

Agapetos Diakonos, *Der Fürstenspiegel für Kaiser Iustinianos*, ed. R. Riedinger, Athen 1995.

Anna Komnene

Annae Comnenae Alexias, ed. D.R. Reinsch, A. Kambylis, vol. I, Berolini et Novi Eboraci 2001.

The annals of Fulda

Annales Fuldenses, ed. G.H. Pertz, [in:] *MGH.SS*, vol. I, pp. 337–415.

On setting up the camp

Ἀνωνύμου Βιβλίον τακτικόν, [in:] *Three Byzantine Military Treatises*, ed., transl., comm. G.T. Dennis, Washington D.C. 1985, pp. 246–327.

On Strategy

Περὶ στρατηγίας, [in:] *Three Byzantine Military Treatises*, ed., transl., comm. G.T. Dennis, Washington D.C. 1985, pp. 10–135.

Apocalypse of Pseudo-Methodius

В.М. Истрин, *Откровение Мефодия Патарского и апокрифические видения Даниила в византийской и славяно-русской литературах*, Москва 1897.

Arethas

Arethae archiepiscopi Caesariensis Scripta minora, vol. II, ed. L.G. Westerink, Leipzig 1972.

Asochik

Der Stephanos von Taron armenische Geschichte, transl. H. Gelzer, A. Burckhardt, Leipzig 1907.

Basil II, *Sigillion II*

Й. Иванов, *Български старини из Македония*, София 1970, pp. 547–562.

Beneševič's Taktikon

N. Oikonomidès, *Les listes de préséance byzantines des IXe et Xe siècles*, Paris 1972, pp. 237–253.

Book of Eparch

Tó eparchikón biblíon / Księga eparcha, transl. A. Kotłowska, introd. K. Ilski, Poznań 2010.

Charter of Virgino by Konstantin Tih Asen

Й. Иванов, *Български старини из Македония*, София 1970, pp. 578–587.

Constantine VII Porphyrogennetos, *The Book of Ceremonies*

Constantini Porphyrogeniti De caeremoniis aulae byzantinae, ed. I.I. Reiske, Bonnae 1829.

Constantine Porphyrogennetos, *The Book of Ceremonies*, transl. A. Moffat, M. Tall, Leiden 2012.

Constantine VII Porphyrogennetos, *On the Governance of the Empire*

Constantine Porphyrogenitus, *De administrando imperio*, ed. G. Moravcsik, transl. R.J.H. Jenkins, Washington D.C. 1967.

Константин Багрянородный, *Об управлении империей*, ed. Г.Г. Литаврин, А.П. Новосолцев, Москва 1989.

Constantine VII Porphyrogennetos, *On the Themes*

Constantino Porfirogenito, *De thematibus*, ed. A. Pertusi, Citta del Vaticano 1952.

Continuator of George the Monk

Georgius Monachus, *Vitae imperatorum recentiorum*, ed. I. Bekker, Bonnae 1838, pp. 761–924.

Continuator of George the Monk (Slavic)

В.М. Истрин, *Книгы временыя и образныя Георгия Мниха. Хроника Георгия Амартола в древнем славянорусском переводе. Текст, исследование и словарь*, vol. I–II, Петроград 1920–1922.

Continuator of Theophanes

Theophanes Continuatus, ed. B.G. Niebuhr, I. Bekker, Bonnae 1838.

Chronographiae quae Theophanis continuati nomine fertur liber quo Vita Basilii Imperatoris amplectitur, ed., transl. I. Ševcenko, Berlin–Boston 2011.

Cosmas the Priest

Ю.К. Бегунов, *Козма Пресвитер в славянских литературах*, София 1973, pp. 297–392.

Kosma Prezbiter, *Mowa polemiczna przeciwko heretykom (fragmenty)*, ed. M. Skowronek, G. Minczew, [in:] *Średniowieczne herezje dualistyczne na Bałkanach. Źródła słowiańskie*, ed. G. Minczew, M. Skowronek, J.M. Wolski, Łódź 2015, pp. 67–125.

K. Petkov, *The Voices of Medieval Bulgaria, Seventh-Fifteenth Century. The Records of a Bygone Culture*, Leiden 2008, pp. 68–83 (82).

De re militari liber

Three Byzantine Military Treatises, ed. G.T. Dennis, Washington D.C. 1985

A Discourse of a Father to his Son (primary version)

В. Јагић, *Разум и философија из српских књижевних старина*, Београд 1892, pp. 79–81.

Euthymius of Tarnovo

Й. Иванов, *Жития на св. Ивана Рилски с уводни бележки*, ГСУ.ИФФ 32.13, 1936, pp. 59–73.

Farmer's Law

W. Ashburner, *The Farmer's Law*, JHS 30, 1910, pp. 85–108.

First Life of St. Naum

Й. Иванов, *Български старини из Македония*, София 1970, pp. 305–311.

Folk Life of St. John of Rila

Й. Иванов, *Жития на св. Иван Рилски с уводни бележки*, ГСУ.ИФФ 32.13, 1936, pp. 28–37.

K. Petkov, *The Voices of Medieval Bulgaria, Seventh-Fifteenth Century. The Records of a Bygone Culture*, Leiden 2008, pp. 163–171 (108).

Geoponica

Geoponica sive Cassiani Bassi scholastici de re rustica eclogue, ed. H. Beckh, Leipzig 1895.

George the Monk

Georgii monachi, dicti Hamartoli, Chronicon, ed. E. de Muralt, St. Petersburg 1859.

Gregory Antiochos

J. Darrouzès, *Deux lettres du Grégoire Antiochos, écrites de Bulgarie vers 1173*, Bsl 23, 1962, pp. 276–284.

Gregory Presbiter

Б. Христова, Д. Караджова, Е. Узунова, *Бележки на българските книжовници*, vol. II, *XVI–XVIII век*, София 2004, p. 117.

Hadrian II

Hadriani II. papae Epistolae, ed. E. Perels, [in:] *MGH.E*, vol. VI, *Epistolae Karolini aevi* IV, Berolini 1925, pp. 691–765.

Hellenic and Roman Chronicle

Летописец Еллинский и Римский, ed. О.В. Творогов, vol. I, Санкт-Петербург 1999.

Herodotos

Herodotus, vol. I, *Books I–II*, ed., transl. A.D. Godley, London–New York 1920.

Hesiod

Hesiod, *Ἔργα καὶ ἡμέραι*, [in:] idem, *The Homeric Hymns and Homerica*, ed. T.E. Page, W.H.D. Rouse, transl. H.G. Evelyn-White, London–New York 1914, pp. 2–65.

Homer

Homer, *Iliad*, vol. I, *Books 1–12*, ed., transl. A.T. Murray, rev. W.F. Wyatt, Cambridge, Mass.–London 1999.

Ibrahim ibn Jakub

Relacja Ibrāhīma ibn Ja'qūba z podróży do krajów słowiańskich w przekazie Al-Bekrīego, ed., transl. T. Kowalski, Kraków 1946.

Innocent III

Innocenti III papae et Calo-Iohannis regis Epistulae, ed., transl. I. Dujčev, [in:] *FLHB*, vol. III, pp. 307–378.

Izbornik of 1076

Изборник 1076 года. Второе издание, переработанное и дополненное, ed. А. Молдован et al., vol. I, Москва 2009.

Кънѧжии изборьникъ *за възпитание на канартикина*, ed. У. Федер, vol. I–II, Велико Търново 2008.

The Edificatory Prose of Kievan Rus', transl. W. Veder, introd. idem, A. Turilov, Cambridge, Mass. 1994.

John the Exarch

Das Hexaemeron des Exarchen Johannes, vol. II, ed. R. Aitzetmüller, Graz 1969.

Йоан Екзарх, *Шестоднев*, ed., transl. Н.Ц. Кочев, София 2000.

John Geometres

Ioannis Geometrae carmina varia argumenti sacri vel historici, [in:] *PG*, vol. CVI, cols. 901–1002.

Jean Géomètre, *Poèmes en hexamètres et en distiques élégiaques*, ed., transl., comm. E.M. van Opstall, Leiden–Boston 2008.

John Kameniates

Ioannis Caminiatae de expugnatione Thessalonicae, ed. G. Böhling, Berlin–New York 1973.

John Kinnamos

Ioannis Cinnami epitome rerum ab Ioannae et Alexio Comnenis gestarum, ed. A. Meineke, Bonnae 1836.

John Moschos

Ioannis Moschi Pratum spirituale, [in:] *PG*, vol. LXXXVII, 3, cols. 2851–3112 (Greek text).

Синайский Патерик, ed. В.С. Голышенко, В.Ф. Дубровина, Москва 1967 (Slavic text).

John Skylitzes

Ioannis Scylitzae Synopsis historiarum, ed. I. Thurn, Berolini–Novi Eboraci 1973.

John Skylitzes, *A Synopsis of Byzantine History 811–1057*, transl. J. Wortley, Cambridge 2010.

John Skylitzes (Bulg.)

Кедрин-Скилица, transl., comm. В. Тъпкова-Заимова, [in:] *FHGB*, vol. VI, pp. 198–340.

John Skylitzes (French)

Jean Skylitzès, *Empereurs de Constantinople*, transl. B. Flusin, comm. J-C. Cheynet, Paris 2003.

John Zonaras

Ioannis Zonarae Epitomae historiarum, ed. Th. Büttner-Wobst, Bonnae 1897.

John Zonaras (Slavic)

В.И. Срезневский, *Симеона Метафраста и Логофета описание мира от бытия и летовниксобран от различных летописец. Славянский перевод Хроники Симеона Логофета с дополнениями*, Санкт-Петербург 1905, pp. 144–186.

Kekaumenos

Советы и рассказы Кекавмена. Сочинение византийского полководца XI века, ed., transl. Г.Г. Литаврин, [2]Москва 2003.

Leo the Deacon

Leonis Diaconi Caloensis Historiae, ed. C.B. Hase, Bonnae 1828.

History of Leo the Deacon. Byzantine Military Expansion in the Tenth Century, ed. transl. A-M. Talbot, D.F. Sulivan, assist. G.T. Dennis, S. McGrath, Washington D.C. 2006.

Leo Grammatikos

Leonis Grammatici Chronographia, ed. I. Bekker, Bonnae 1842.

Leo VI the Wise

The Tactica of Leo VI, ed., transl. G.T. Dennis, [2] Washington D.C. 2014.

Letter of the Patriarch Theophylaktos to Tsar Peter

I. Dujčev, *L'epistola sui Bogomili del patriarcha Teofilatto*, [in:] idem, *Medioevo bizantino-slavo*, vol. I, *Saggi di storia politica e culturale*, Roma 1965, pp. 283–315 (text on pp. 311–315).

Life of Athanasios of Athos

P. Lemerle, *La vie ancienne de saint Athanase l'Athonite composée au début du XIe siècle par Athanase de Lavra*, [in:] *Le Millénaire du Mont Athos, 963–1963. Études et mélanges*, vol. I, Chevetogne 1963, pp. 59–100.

Life of Blasius of Amorium

Βίος τοῦ ὁσίου πατρὸς ἡμῶν Βλασίου, [in:] *Acta Sanctorum, Novembris*, vol. IV, ed. H. Delehaye, P. Peeters, Bruxelles 1925, pp. 657–669.

Life of Luke the Younger

The Life and Miracles of St. Luke of Steiris, ed., transl. C.L. Connor, W.R. Connor, Brookline, MA 1994.

Life of Saint Evariste

C. van de Forst, *La vie de S. Évariste higoumene à Constantinople*, AB 41, 1923, pp. 287–325.

Life of St. Mary the Younger

Vita S. Mariae iunioris, [in:] *Acta Sanctorum Novembris*, vol. IV, ed. H. Delehaye, P. Peeters, Bruxelles 1925, pp. 688–705.

M-A Talbot, *Holy Women of Byzantium: Ten Saints' Lives in English Translation*, Washington D.C. 1996.

Life of St. Paul the Younger

H. Delehaye, *Vita Sancti Pauli Iunioris in monte Latro*, AB 11, 1892, pp. 19–74, 136–181.

Life of St. Phantinos the Younger

La Vita di San Fantino il Giovane, ed., transl., comm. E. Follieri, Bruxelles 1993.

List of Bulgarian Archbishops

И. Божилов, *Българската архиепископия XI–XII в. Списъкът на българските архиепископи*, София 2011, pp. 93–131.

Liudprand of Cremona, *Embassy*

Liudprandus Cremonensis, *Relatio de legatione constantinopolitana*, [in:] *Liudprandi Cremonensis Antapodosis, Historia Ottonis, Relatio de legatione constantinopolitana*, ed. P. Chiesa, Turnholti 1998, pp. 185–218.

Liudprand of Cremona, *The Embassy of Liudprand*, [in:] *The Complete Works of Liudprand of Cremona*, transl. P. Squatriti, Washington D.C. 2007, pp. 238–284.

Liudprand of Cremona, *Retribution*

Liudprandus Cremonensis, *Antapodosis*, [in:] *Liudprandi Cremonensis Antapodosis, Historia Ottonis, Relatio de legatione constantinopolitana*, ed. P. Chiesa, Turnholti 1998, pp. 5–150.

Liudprand of Cremona, *Retribution*, [in:] *The Complete Works of Liudprand of Cremona*, transl. P. Squatriti, Washington D.C. 2007, pp. 41–202.

Maqqari

Al-Maqqari, *The History of the Mohammedan Dynasties in Spain*, transl. P. de Gayangos, London–New York 1964.

Menologion of Basil II

Menologium imperatoris Basilii, [in:] *PG*, vol. CXVII, cols. 13–614.

Michael Attaleiates

Miguel Ataliates, Historia, introd., ed., transl., comm. I. Pérez Martín, Madrid 2002.

Michael Attaleiates, *The History*, transl. A. Kaldellis, D. Krallis, Cambridge, Masschusetts-London 2012.

Michael Psellos

Michel Psellos, *Chronographie ou Histoire d'un siècle de Byzance (976–1077)*, vol. I–II, ed., transl. E. Renauld, Paris 1926–1928.

The Chronographia of Michael Psellus, transl. E.R.A. Sewter, introd. J.M. Hussey, London 1953.

Michael the Syrien

Chronique de Michel le Syrien patriarch jacobite d'Antioch 1166–1199, ed. J.-B. Chabot, vol. III, Paris 1905.

Miracle of St. George with the Bulgarian

Х. Кодов, *Опис на славянските ръкописи в библиотеката Българската Академия на Науките*, София1969, pp. 143–144.

Narrative on the Martyrs of Zographou

Й. Иванов, *Български старини из Македония*, София 1970, pp. 437–440.

Nicholas I

Nicolai Papae Responsa ad consulta Bulgarorum, ed. E. Perles, [in:] *MGH.E*, vol. VI, *Karolini aevi IV*, Berolini 1925, pp. 512–600.

Д. Дечев, *Responsa Nicolai Papae I. ad consulta Bulgarorum Anno 866*, София 1922 (1998).

Nicholas Mystikos

Nicholas I Patriarch of Constantinople, *Letters*, ed., transl. R.J.H. Jenkins, L.G. Westerink, Washington D.C. 1973.

Nikephoros

Nikephoros Patriarch of Constantinople, *Short History*, text, transl., comm. C. Mango, Washington D.C. 1990.

Nikephoros Gregoras

Nicephori Gregorae Byzantina historia, vol. I–II, ed. L. Schopen, Bonnae 1829–1830.

Niketas Choniates

Nicetae Choniatae Historia, ed. J.L. van Dieten, Berlin 1975.

O City of Byzantium: Annals of Niketas Choniates, transl. H.J. Magoulias, Detroit 1984.

Notker the Stammerer

Notkeri Balbuli Gesta Karoli Magni imperatoris, ed. H.F. Haefele, Berolini 1959.

NTG

Nestle-Aland Novum Testamentum Graece. Begründet von E. und E. Nestle, Hrsg. B. und K. Aland, J. Karavidopoulos, C.M. Martini, B.M. Metzger. 28. revidierte Auflage, Stuttgart 2012.

On Justiniana Prima's canonical position

Περὶ τῆς Πρώτης καὶ Δευτέρας Ἰουστινιανῆς ἐκ τῶν μετὰ τὸν κώδικα νεαρῶν τίτλος β΄ διάταξις γ΄, [in:] G. Prinzing, *Entstehung und Rezeption der Justiniana Prima-Theorie im Mittelalter*, BBg 5, 1978, p. 279.37–42 (Scor. gr. X–II–10, fol. 377r.).

On the Treaty with the Bulgarians

Ἐπὶ τῇ τῶν Βουλγάρων συμβάσει, [in:] I. Dujčev, *On the Treaty of 927 with the Bulgarians*, DOP 32, 1978, pp. 217–253 (Introduction), 254–295 (Critical text, translation and commentary).

Paulinus of Nola

Sancti Pontii Meropii Paulini Nolani Carmina, carmen XVII, ed. et comm. G. de Hartel, [in:] *CSEL*, vol. XXX.2, Pragae–Vindobonae–Lipsiae 1894, pp. 81–97.

Peter the Monk

Р. Павлова, *Петър Черноризец – старобългарски писател от X век*, София 1994.

Philotheos

N. Oikonomidès, *Les listes préséance byzantines des IXe et Xe siècles*, Paris 1972, pp. 63–205.

Priest of Duklja

Gesta regum sclavorum, vol. I–II, ed. T. Živković, Beograd 2009.

Prologue life of St. John of Rila (I)

Й. Иванов, *Жития на св. Иван Рилски с уводни бележки*, ГСУ.ИФФ 32.13, 1936, pp. 52–57.

Prologue life of St. John of Rila (II)

Й. Иванов, *Жития на св. Иван Рилски с уводни бележки*, ГСУ.ИФФ 32.13, 1936, p. 58.

Pseudo-Symeon Magistros

Pseudo-Symeon (Symeon Magister), *Chronographia*, [in:] *Theophanes Continuatus*, ed. B.G. Niebuhr, I. Bekker, Bonnae 1838, pp. 601–760.

The Royal Frankish Annals

Einhardi annales, ed. G. Pertz, [in:] *MGH.SS*, vol. I, pp. 124–218.

Russian Primary Chronicle

Лаврентьевская летопись, Ленинград 1926–1928 [= *Полное Собрание Русских Летописей*, vol. I].

The Russian Primary Chronicle. Laurentian Text, transl. S.H. Cross, O.P. Sherbowitz-Wetzor, Cambridge 1953.

Scriptor Incertus de Leone Armenio

Scriptoris Incerti Historia de Leone Bardae Armenii filio, [in:] *Leonis Grammatici Chronographia*, ed. I. Bekker, Bonnae 1842, pp. 335–362.

***Septuaginta*, vol. I–II**

Septuaginta. Id est Vetus Testamentum graece iuxta LXX interpretes edidit A. Rahlfs, editio altera quam recognovit et emendavit R. Hanhart, vol. I: *Leges et historiae*, vol. II, *Libri poetici et prophetici*, Stuttgart 2006.

Service of St. Tsar Peter

Й. Иванов, *Български старини из Македония*, София 1970, pp. 383–394.

K. Petkov, *The Voices of Medieval Bulgaria, Seventh-Fifteenth Century. The Records of a Bygone Culture*, Leiden 2008, pp. 107–110 (90).

Strabon

The Geography of Strabo, transl. H.L. Jones, vol. III, London–New York 1924.

Symeon Logothete

Symeonis Magistri et Logothetae Chronicon, ed. S. Wahlgren, Berolini–Novi Eboraci 2006.

Symeon Logothete (Slavic)

В.И. Срезневский, *Симеона Метафраста и Логофета описание мира от бытия и летовниксобран от различных летописец. Славянский перевод Хроники Симеона Логофета с дополнениями*, Санкт-Петербург 1905 [= V. I. Sreznevskij, *Slavjanskij perevod chroniki Symeona Logotheta*. With an introduction in Russian by G. Ostrogorsky and a preface in English by I. Dujčev, London 1971].

Synodikon of Tsar Boril

Борилов синодик. Издание и превод, ed. И. Божилов, А. Тотоманова, И. Билярски, София 2010.

Tale of the Iron Cross

А. Калоянов, М. Спасова, Т. Моллов, *"Сказание за железния кръст" и епохата на цар Симеон*, Велико Търново 2007.

Tale of the Prophet Isaiah

I. Biliarsky, *The Tale of the Prophet Isaiah. The Destiny and Meanings of an Apocryphal Text*, Leiden–Boston 2013, pp. 13–27.

Testament of John of Rila

И. Гошев, *Заветът на Св. Иван Рилски в светлината на старобългарското и на византийското литературно предание от IX–XIV век*, ГДА 4.10, 1954/1955, pp. 438–448.

Testament of John of Rila, transl. I. Iliev, [in:] *Byzantine Monastic Foundation Documents. A Complete Translation of the Surviving Founders'.Typika and Testaments*, vol. I., ed. J. Thomas, A. Hero, Washington D.C. 2000, pp. 129–134.

Theodore Daphnopates

Théodore Daphnopatès, *Corréspondance*, ed., transl. J. Darrouzès, L.G. Westerink, Paris 1978.

Theophanes

Theophanes, *Chronographia*, ed. C. de Boor, vol. I, Lipsiae 1883.

Theophylaktos of Ohrid, *Letters*

Theophylacte d'Achrida, *Lettres*, ed., transl. P. Gautier, Thessalonique 1986.

Писмата на Теофилакта Охридски, архиепископ български, transl. Митрополит Симеон Варненски и Преславски, София 1931.

Theophylaktos of Ohrid, *Life of Clement*

Theophylacti Achridensis, Archiepiscopi Bulgariae Vita S. Clementis Achridensis, ed. I.G. Iliev, [in:] *FGHB*, vol. IX.2, pp. 10–41.

Theophylaktos of Ohrid, *Martyrdom of the fifteen Tiberioupolitan martyrs*

Theophylacti Achridensis, Archiepiscopi Bulgariae historia martyrii XV martyrum Tiberiupolitanorum, ed. I.G. Iliev, [in:] *FGHB*, vol. IX.2, pp. 42–79.

Thucydides

Thucydides, *History of the Peloponnesian War*, vol. II, *Books III–IV*, ed. E. Capps, E.H. Warmington, transl. Ch.F. Smith, [5]London–New York 1920.

Yahyā of Antioch

Histoire de Yahya-ibn-Sa'ïd d'Antioche, continuateur de Sa'ïd-ibn-Bitriq, ed. I. Kratchkovsky, A. Vasiliev, vol. II, Paris 1932.

Zigabenos

Euthymios Zigabenos, *Panoplia dogmatica*, [in:] *PG*, vol. CXXX, cols. 25–1064.

* * *

Byzantine Monastic Foundation Documents: A Complete Translation of the Surviving Founders' Typika and Testaments, ed. J. Thomas, A. Constantinides Hero, G. Constable, Washington D.C. 2000.

Historia Królestwa Słowian czyli Latopis Popa Duklanina, transl., ed. J. Leśny, Warszawa 1988.

Ilynskiy G.A., *Gramoty bolgarskih carey*, London 1970.

Jordanov I., *Corpus of Byzantine Seals from Bulgaria*, vol. III/1, Sofia 2009.

Jordanov I., *Corpus of the medieval Bulgarian seals* / Йорданов И., *Корпус на средновековните български печати*, Sofia 2016 [= ППре 12].

Oikonomidès N., *Les listes de préséance byzantines des IXe et Xe siècles*, Paris 1972.

Petkov K., *The Voices of Medieval Bulgaria, Seventh-Fifteenth Century. The Records of a Bygone Culture*, Leiden–Boston 2008.

Popkonstantinov K., Kronsteiner O., *Старобългарски надписи. Altbulgarische Inschriften*, vol. I, Salzburg 1994.

Średniowieczne herezje dualistyczne na Bałkanach. Źródła słowiańskie, ed., transl. G. Minczew, M. Skowronek, J.M. Wolski, Łódź 2015.

Wójtowicz M., *Najstarsze datowane inskrypcje słowiańskie X–XIII w.*, Poznań 2005.

Ziemscy aniołowie, niebiańscy ludzie. Anachoreci w bułgarskiej literaturze i kulturze, ed. G. Minczew, Białystok 2002.

Živković T., *De conversione Croatorum et Serborum. A Lost Source*, Belgrade 2012.

* * *

Σταυρίδου-Ζαφράκα Ά., *Ὁ Ἀνώνυμος λόγος "Ἐπὶ τῇ τῶν Βουλγάρων συμβάσει"*, Βυζ 8, 1976, pp. 343–408.

* * *

Ангелов Б., *Из старата българска, руска и сръбска литература*, vol. I, София 1959.

Божилов И., *Българската архиепископия XI–XII в. Списъкът на българските архиепископи*, София 2011.

Българската литература и книжнина през XIII век, ed. И. Божилов, С. Кожухаров, София 1987.

Димитров П., *Петър Черноризец. Очерци по старобългарска литература през следсимеоновата епоха*, Шумен 1995.

Държава и църква през XIII в. Преписка на българите с папа Инокентий III. Синодик на цар Борил, ed. Е.И. Димитров, И. Божилов, София 1999.

Иванов Й., *Богомилски книги и легенди*, София 1970.

Иванов Й., *Български старини из Македония*, София 1931, [2]1970.

Иванов Й., *Жития на св. Ивана Рилски с уводни бележки*, ГСУ. ИФФ 32.13, 1936, pp. 3–108.

Иоанн Златоуст в древнерусской и южнославянской письменности XI–XVI веков. Каталог гомилий, ed. Е. Гранстрем, О. Творогов, А. Валевичюс, Санкт-Петербург 1998.

Йорданов И., *Корпус на печатите на Средновековна България*, София 2001.

Йорданов И., *Печатите на преславските владетели (893–971)*, София 1993.

Кодов Х., *Опис на славянските ръкописи в библиотеката на Българската Академия на Науките*, София 1969.

Кънѧжии изборьникъ *за възпитание на канартикина*, ed. У. Федер, vol. I, Велико Търново 2008.

Слова на светлината. Творби на старобългарски писатели от епохата на св. княз Борис, цар Симеон и св. цар Петър, ed., transl. И. Добрев, Т. Славова, София 1995.

Станчев С., Иванова В., Балан М., Боев П., *Надписът на чъргубиля Мостич*, София 1955.

Стара българска литература в седем тома, vol. IV, *Житиеписни творби*, ed. К. Иванова, София 1986.

Modern Scholarship

Agamben G., *The Kingdom and the Glory. For a Theological Genealogy of Economy and Government*, transl. L. Chiesa (with M. Mandarini), Stanford 2011.

Ahrweiler H., *L'ideologie politique de l'Empire byzantine*, Paris 1975.

Aleksandrov E., *The International Treaties of Medieval Bulgaria (Legal Aspects)*, BHR 17.4, 1989, pp. 40–56.

Althoff G., *Ottonowie. Władza królewska bez państwa*, transl. M. Tycner-Wolicka, Warszawa 2009.

Amudzhieva N., Tsvetkov P., *The Cult of Saints-Healers – an Alternative and Opposition to the Official Medicine in Medieval Bulgaria*, Jahr. EJB 4.7, 2013, pp. 357–366.

Angelov D., *Affermissement et fondements ideologiques du pouvoir royal en Bulgarie medieval*, Βυζ 3, 1971, pp. 15–28.

Angelova S., Prinzing G., *Das mutmassliche Grab des Patriarchen Damian: zu einem archäologischen Fund in Dristra/Silistria*, [in:] *Средновековна християнска Европа: Изток и Запад. Ценности, традиции, общуване*, ed. В. Гюзелев, А. Милтенова, София 2002, pp. 726–730.

Antonopoulos T., *Byzantium, the Magyar Raids and Their Consequences*, Bsl 54, 1993, pp. 254–267.

Antonopoulou Th., *A textual source and its contextual implications: On Theodore Daphnopates' sermon on the birth of John the Baptist*, B 81, 2011, pp. 9–18.

Arrignon J.-P., *Les relations internationales de la Russie Kiévienne au milieu du Xᵉ siècle et le baptême de la princesse Olga*, [in:] *Actes des congrès de la Société des historiens médiévistes de l'enseignement supérieur public. 9ᵉ congrès*, Dijon 1978, pp. 167–184.

Arrignon J.-P., *Le traite byzantino-russe de 944, acte fondateur de l'Etat de la Kievskaja Rus'?*, BB 100, 2016, pp. 93–105.

Assemanius J.S., *Kalendaria Ecclesiae universae*, vol. III, *Kalendaria Ecclesiae slavice, sive graeco-mosche*, Roma 1755.

Atanasov G., *Influences ethno-culturelles dans l'ermitage rupestre près de Murfatlar, à Dobrudza*, Bsl 57.1, 1996, pp. 112–124.

Atanasov G., *On the Origin, Function and the Owner of the Adornments of the Preslav Treasure from the 10th century*, ABu 3.3, 1999, pp. 81–94.

Avramea A., *Land and Sea Communications, Fourth–Fiftheenth Centuries*, [in:] *The Economic History of Byzantium. From the Seventh through the Fifteenth Century*, ed. A.E. Laiou, vol. I, Washington D.C. 2002, pp. 64–74.

Balogh C., *Avar kori tömlővégek*, KDMK 22, 2016, pp. 193–216.

Banaszkiewicz J., *Jedność porządku przestrzennego, społecznego i tradycji początków ludu. (Uwagi o urządzeniu wspólnoty plemienno-państwowej u Słowian)*, PH 77, 1986, pp. 445–466.

Banchich T.M., *Introduction*, [in:] *The History of Zonaras from Alexander Severus to the Death of Theodosius the Great*, transl. idem, E.N. Lane, New York 2009, pp. 1–19.

Bărlieva S., *Nicetas of Ramesiana and Two Apostolic Missions on the Balkans in the late Fourth – the early Fifth Century*, [in:] *In stolis repromissionis. Saints and Sainthood in Central and Eastern Europe*, ed. A. Nagusheva-Tihanova et al., Sofia, 2012, pp. 271–278.

Baronio C., *Annales ecclesiastici*, cum critica historico-chronologica P.A. Pagii, vol. XV–XVI, Luca 1744.

Beck H.-G., *Kirche un Theologische Literatur im byzantinischen Reich*, München 1959.

Belke K., *Roads and travel in Macedonia and Thrace in the middle and late Byzantine period*, [in:] *Travel in the Byzantine World. Papers from the Thity-forth Spring Symposium of Byzantine Studies, Birmingham, April 2000*, ed. R. Macrides, Aldershot 2001, pp. 73–90.

Bellinger A.R., Grierson Ph., *Catalogue of the Byzantine Coins in the Dumbarton Oaks Collection and in the Whittemore Collection*, vol. III, *Leo III to Nicephorus III. 717–1081*, Washington D.C. 1993.

Bensammar E., *La titulature de l'impératrice et sa signification. Recherches sur les sources byzantines de la fin du VIIIe siècle à la fin du XIIe siècle*, B 46, 1976, pp. 243–291.

Beševliev V., *Die Herkunft des Stadtnamens Бъдλλнь*, LBa 31.1/2, 1988, pp. 43–44.

Beševliev V., *Die Kaiseridee bei den Protobulgaren*, Βυζ 3, 1971, pp. 81–92.

Beševliev V., *Die Protobulgarische Periode der bulgarischen Geschichte*, Amsterdam 1981.

Biliarsky I., *Saint Jean de Rila et saint tsar Pierre. Les destins des deux cultes du Xe siecle*, [in:] *Byzantium and the Bulgarians (1018–1185)*, ed. K. Nikolaou, K. Tsiknakis, Athens 2008, pp. 161–174.

Biliarsky I., *St. Peter (927–969), Tsar of the Bulgarians*, [in:] *State and Church. Studies in Medieval Bulgaria and Byzantium*, ed. V. Gjuzelev, K. Petkov, Sofia 2011, pp. 173–188.

Biliarsky I., *The Tale of the Prophet Isaiah. The Destiny and Meanings of an Apocryphal Text*, Leiden–Boston 2013.

Biliarsky I., *Le Tsar sur la montagne*, [in:] *Histoire, mémoire et devotion. Regards croisés sur la construction des identities dans le monde orthodoxe aux époques byzantine et post-byzantine*, ed. R.G. Păun, Seyssel 2016, pp. 53–71.

Biliarsky I., *Word and Power in Mediaeval Bulgaria*, Leiden–Boston 2011.

Bonarek J., *Przyczyny i cele bułgarskich wypraw Światosława a polityka Bizancjum w latach sześćdziesiątych X w.*, SH 39, 1996, pp. 287–302.

Bonarek J., *Romajowie i obcy w kronice Jana Skylitzesa. Identyfikacja etniczna Bizantyńczyków i ich stosunek do obcych w świetle kroniki Jana Skylitzesa*, Toruń 2003.

Boroń P., *Kniaziowie, królowie, carowie... Tytuły i nazwy władców słowiańskich we wczesnym średniowieczu*, Katowice 2010.

Bowlus R.Ch., *Die Schlacht auf dem Lechfeld*, Ostfildern 2012.

Božilov I., *L'ideologie politique du tsar Syméon: pax Symeonica*, BBg 8, 1986, pp. 73–88.

Braudel F., *La Méditerranée et le Monde méditerranéen à l'époque de Philippe II*, Paris 1949 [Polish transl. – Braudel F., *Morze Śródziemne i świat śródziemnomorski w epoce Filipa II*, vol. I, transl. T. Mrówczyński, M. Ochab, introd. B. Geremek, W. Kula, Warszawa [2]2004].

Brezeanu S., *La Bulgarie d'au-delà de l'Ister a la lumière des sourses écrites medievales*, EB 20.4, 1984, pp. 121–135.

Broecker W.S., *Was the Medieval Warm Period Global?*, Scie 291 (5508), Feb. 23, 2001, pp. 1497–1499.

Brogi Bercoff G., *Baronio storico e il mondo slavo*, [in:] *Cesare Baronio tra santitàe scrittura*, a cura di G.A. Guazzelli, R. Michetti, F. Sforza Barcellona, Roma 2012, pp. 309–323.

B r o g i B e r c o f f G., *Chrześcijańska Ruś w "Annales Ecclesiastici" Cezarego Baroniusza*, [in:] e a d e m, *Królestwo Słowian. Historiografia Renesansu i Baroku w krajach słowiańskich*, transl. E.J. G ł ę b i c k a, W. J e k i e l, A. Z a k r z e w s k i, Izabelin 1998, pp. 130–145.

B r o g i B e r c o f f G., *Il Regno degli Slavi di Mauro Orbini e la storiografia europea del Cinquecento*, RS 24/26, 1977/1979, pp. 119–156.

B r o w n i n g R., *Bulgars, Turkic*, [in:] *ODB*, vol. I, p. 338.

B r o w n i n g R., *Byzantium and Bulgaria. A comparative studies across the Early Medieval Frontier*, London 1975.

B r u b a k e r L., *To Legitimize an Emperor. Constantine and Visual Authority in the 8th and 9th Centuries*, [in:] *New Constantines. The Rhythm of Imperial Renewal in Byzantium, 4th–13th Centuries. Papers from the 26th Spring Symposium of Byzantine Studies, St Andrews, March 1992*, ed. P. M a g d a l i n o, Cambridge 1994, pp. 139–158.

B r z o z o w s k a Z.A., *Car i caryca czy cesarz i cesarzowa Bułgarów? Tytulatura Piotra i Marii-Ireny Lekapeny w średniowiecznych tekstach słowiańskich (Jak powinniśmy nazywać władców bułgarskich z X stulecia)*, WS 62, 2017, pp. 17–26.

B r z o z o w s k a Z.A., *Cesarzowa Bułgarów, Augusta i Bazylisa – Maria-Irena Lekapena i transfer bizantyńskiej idei kobiety-władczyni (imperial feminine) w średniowiecznej Bułgarii*, SMer 17, 2017, pp. 1–28.

B r z o z o w s k a Z.A., *Geneza tytułu "car" w świetle zabytków średniowiecznego piśmiennictwa słowiańskiego*, WS 46, 2012, pp. 34–39.

B r z o z o w s k a Z.A., *The Image of Maria Lekapene, Peter and the Byzantine-Bulgarian Relations Between 927 and 969 in the Light of Old Russian Sources*, Pbg 41.1, 2017, pp. 40–55.

B r z o z o w s k a Z.A., *Rola carycy Marii-Ireny Lekapeny w recepcji elementów bizantyńskiego modelu władzy w pierwszym państwie bułgarskim*, VP 66, 2016, pp. 443–458.

B r z ó s t k o w s k a A., *Kroniki z kręgu Symeona Logotety*, [in:] *Testimonia*, vol. V, pp. 64–67.

B u r i ć I., *Porodica Foka*, ЗРВИ 17, 1976, pp. 189–291.

B u r y J.B., *The Ceremonial Book of Constantine Porphyrogenitus*, EHR 22, 1907, pp. 209–227, 417–439.

B y l i n a S., *Bogomilizm w średniowiecznej Bułgarii. Uwarunkowania społeczne, polityczne i kulturalne*, BP 2, 1985, pp. 133–145.

C a n e r D., *Wandering, Begging Monks. Spiritual Authority and the Promotion of Monasticism in Late Antiquity*, Berkeley–Los Angeles–London 2002.

C a n k o v a-P e t k o v a G., *Bulgarians and Byzantium during the first Decades after the Foundation of the Bulgarian State*, Bsl 24.1, 1963, pp. 41–53.

Cankova-Petkova G., *Byzance et le developpement social et économique des états balkaniques*, [in:] *Actes du premier Congres International des Études Balkaniques et Sud-Est Européennes, Sofia, 26 âout – 1 septembre 1966*, vol. III, *Histoire (V[e]–XVe ss.; XVe–XVIIe ss.)*, ed. V. Tăpkova-Zaimova, S. Dimitrov, E. Sarafova, Sofia 1969, pp. 341–348.

Češmedžiev D., *Bułgarska tradycja państwowa w apokryfach: car Piotr w "Bułgarskiej kronice apokryficznej"*, transl. Ł. Mysielski, [in:] *Biblia Slavorum Apocryphorum. Novum Testamentum*, ed. G. Minczew, M. Skowronek, I. Petrov, Łódź 2009, pp. 139–147.

Chaloupecký V., *Dvě studie k dějinám Podkarpatska*, I: *Sůl z Bulharska (892)*, II: *Kdy bylo horní Potisí připojeno k Uhrám*, SFFUKB 3.30 (4), 1925, pp. 1–11.

Charanis P., *Kouver, the chronology of his activities and their ethnic effects on the regions around Thessalonica*, ByzS 11.1, 1970, pp. 229–247.

Charanis P., *The Monk as an Element of Byzantine Society*, DOP 25, 1971, pp. 61–84.

Cherubini G., *Chłop i życie na wsi*, [in:] *Człowiek średniowiecza*, ed. J. Le Goff, transl. M. Radożycka-Paoletti, Warszawa 2000, pp. 145–176.

Cheshmedjiev D., *Notes on the Cult of the Fifteen Tiberioupolitan Martyrs in Medieval Bulgaria*, SCer 1, 2011, pp. 143–156.

Cheynet J.-C., *Les effesctifs de l'armée byzantine aux Xe–XIIe s.*, CCM 38.4, 1995, pp. 319–335.

Cheynet J.-C., *John Skylitzes, the author and his family*, [in:] John Skylitzes, *A Synopsis of Byzantine History, 811–1057*, transl. J. Wortley, Cambridge 2010, pp. IX–XI.

Chrysostomides J., *Byzantine Concepts of War and Peace*, [in:] *War, Peace and World Orders in European History*, ed. A.V. Hartmann, B. Heuser, London–New York 2001, pp. 91–101.

Cichocka H., *Mimesis and Rhetoric in the Treatises by Dionysius of Halicarnassus and the Byzantine Tradition (selected problems)*, JÖB 60, 2010, pp. 35–45.

Cichocka H., *Mimesis i retoryka w traktatach Dionizjusza z Halikarnasu a tradycja bizantyńska*, Warszawa 2004.

Ćirković S., *Vorwort*, [in:] M. Orbini, *Il regno degli Slavi*, Pesaro 1601, Nachdruck besorgt von S. Ćirković, P. Rehder, München 1985, pp. 7–23.

Clarke J.F., *Zlatarski and Bulgarian Historiography*, SEER 15 (44), 1937, pp. 435–439.

Comşa M., *Die bulgarische Herrschaft nördlich der Donau während des 9. und 10. Jh. Im Lichte der archäologischen Forschungen*, D 4, 1960, pp. 395–422.

Constantinou S., *A Byzantine hagiographical parody: Life of Mary the Younger I*, BMGS 34, 2010, pp. 160–181.

Curta F., *Southeastern Europe in the Middle Ages, 500–1250*, Cambridge 2006.

Czamańska I., *Problem pochodzenia Wołochów*, [in:] *Wędrówka i etnogeneza w starożytności i średniowieczu*, ed. M. Salamon, J. Strzelczyk, Kraków 2004, pp. 327–335.

Czarnecki P., *Geneza i ewolucja dogmatu teologicznego sekty bogomiłów*, ZNUJ.PH 134, 2007, pp. 25–40.

Czarnecki P., *Kontrowersje wokół herezji XI wieku*, SRel 49.2, 2016, pp. 99–117.

Czarnecki P., *Trzecia droga dualizmu – doktryna religijna włoskiego Kościoła katarskiego w Concorezzo*, SRel 43, 2010, pp. 93–112.

Czeppe Z., Flis J., Mochnacki R., *Geografia fizyczna świata*, Warszawa 1969.

Dall'Aglio F., *"In ipsa silva longissima Bulgariae": Western chroniclers of the Crusades and the Bulgarian forest*, BMd 1, 2010, pp. 403–416.

Damian O., Andonie C., Vasile M., *Cetatea byzantină de la Nufăru. Despre problemele unui sit suprapus de oasezare contemporană*, Peu 1 (14), 2003, pp. 237–266.

Decker R.J., *The Bauer Thesis: An Overview*, [in:] *Orthodoxy and Heresy in Early Christian Contexts: Reconsidering the Bauer Thesis*, ed. P.A. Hartog, Eugene 2015, pp. 6–33.

Delikari A., *Kliment VeliČki oder Kliment Ochridski? Die Diskussion über Seine Bischofstitel und seine Jurisdiktion*, Pbg 37.3, 2013, pp. 3–10.

Diaconu P., Vilceanu D., *Păcuiul lui Soare*, vol. I, Bucurşti 1972.

Dimitrov Ch., *Die frühmittelalterliche Stadt Debeltos zwischen Byzanz und Bulgarien vom achten bis zehnte Jahrhundert*, [in:] *Die Schwarzmeerküste in der Spatantike und frühen Mittelalter*, ed. R. Pillinger, A. Pülz, H. Vetters, Wien 1992, pp. 35–45.

Dimitrov B., *Sozopol*, Sofia 2012.

Ditten H., *Ethnische Verschiebungen zwischen der Balkanhalbinsel und Kleinasien vom Ende des 6. bis zur Zweiten Hälfte des 9. Jahrhunderts*, Berlin 1993.

Djourova A., Guerov G., *Les trésors des icônes bulgares*, Paris 2009.

Dobkowski M., *Kataryzm. Historia i system religijny*, Kraków 2007.

Dobrev I., *Sv. Ivan Rilski*, vol. I, Linz 2007.

Dölger F., *Der Bulgarenherrscher als geistlicher Sohn des byzantinischen Kaisers*, ИИД 16/18, 1940, pp. 219–232.

Dölger F., *Bulgarisches Cartum und byzantinisches Kaisertum*, ИБАИ 9, 1935, pp. 57–68.

Dölger F., *Ein Fall slavischer Einsiedlung im Hinterland von Thessalonike im 10. Jahrhundert*, SBAW.PHK 1, 1952, pp. 1–28.

Doncheva S., *Symbolic Emphasises in the Mediaeval Religious Architecture*, НВ.ЗР 3, 2005, pp. 241–260.

Dragojlović D., *The History of Paulicianism on the Balkan Peninsula*, Balc 5, 1973, pp. 235–244.

D r a k o p o u l o u E., *Kastoria. Art, Patronage and Society*, [in:] *Heaven and Earth. Cities and Countryside in Greece*, ed. J. A l b a n i, E. C h a l k i a, Athens 2013, pp. 114–125.

D u d e k J., *Cesarz Bazyli II w opiniach średniowiecznych Bułgarów*, [in:] *Stereotypy bałkańskie. Księga jubileuszowa Profesor Ilony Czamańskiej*, ed. J. P a s z k i e w i c z, Z. P e n t e k, Poznań 2011, pp. 62–85.

D u d e k J., *Chazarowie. Polityka – kultura – religia, VII–XI w.*, Warszawa 2016.

D u j č e v I., *Les bolijars dits intérieurs et extérieurs de la Bulgarie médiévale*, AO.ASH 3.3, 1953, pp. 167–178.

D u j č e v I., *Il patriarcato bulgaro del secolo X*, [in:] i d e m, *Medioevo bizantino-slavo*, vol. III, *Altri saggi di storia, politica e letteraria*, Roma 1971, pp. 243–281.

D u j č e v I., *La réforme monastique en Bulgarie au Xe siècle*, [in:] *Études de civilisation médiévale*, Poitiers 1974, pp. 255–264.

D u j č e v I., *Relations entre Slaves méridionaux et Byzance aux Xe–XIIe siècles*, [in:] i d e m, *Medioevo bizantino-slavo*, vol. III, *Altrisaggi di storia, politica eletteraria*, Roma 1971, pp. 175–221.

D u j č e v I., W e r n e r R., *Balkan*, [in:] *LdM*, vol. I, cols. 1380–1381.

E n g e l J.Ch., *Geschichte der Bulgaren in Mösien*, [in:] i d e m, *Fortsetzung der Allgemeinen Welthistorie durch eine Gesellschaft von Gelehrten in Teutschland und Engeland ausgefertiget*, vol. XLIX, Halle 1797, pp. 1–232.

E n g e l s P., *Der Reisebericht des Ibrahim ibn Ya'qub (961/966)*, [in:] *Kaiserin Theophanu. Begegnung des Ostens und Westens um die Wende des ersten Jahrtausends. Gedenkschrift des Kölner Schnütgen-Museums zum 1000 Todesjahr der Kaiserin*, ed. A. v o n E u w, P. S c h r e i n e r, vol. I, Köln 1991, pp. 413–422.

E p s t e i n A.W., *Middle Byzantine Churches of Kastoria. Dates and Implications*, ArtB 62.2, 1980, pp. 190–207.

F a ł k o w s k i W., *Wielki król. Ideologiczne podstawy władzy Karola Wielkiego*, Warszawa 2011.

F a s o l o M., *La via Egnatia I. Da Apollonia e Dyrrachium ad Herakleia Lynkestidos*, ²Roma 2005.

F e a t h e r s t o n e J.M., *Theophanes Continuatus VI and De Cerimoniis I, 96*, BZ 104, 2011, pp. 115–123.

F e a t h e r s t o n e J.M., *Theophanes Continuatus: a History for the Palace*, [in:] *La face cachée de la littérature byzantine. Le texte en tant que message immédiat*, ed. P. O d o r i c o, Paris 2012, pp. 123–135.

F e r l u g a J., *John Scylitzes and Michael of Devol*, [in:] i d e m, *Byzantium on the Balkans. Studies on the Byzantine Administration and the Southern Slavs from the VIIth to the XIIth Centuries*, Amsterdam 1976, pp. 337–344.

F i e d l e r U., *Bulgars in the Lower Danube region. A survey of the archaeological evidence and of the state of current research*, [in:] *The Other Europe in the Middle Ages. Avars, Bulgars, Khazars, and Cumans*, ed. F. C u r t a, assist. R. K o v a l e v, Leiden–Boston 2008, p. 152–236.

F i e d l e r U., Studien *zu Gräberfeldern des 6.–9. Jahrhunderts an der unteren Donau*, I, Bonn 1992.

F i n e J.V.A., *The Early Medieval Balkans: a Critical Survey from the Sixth to the Late Twelfth Century*, Ann Arbor 1983.

F i n e J.V.A., *A Fresh Look at Bulgaria under Tsar Peter I (927–69)*, ByzS 5, 1978, pp. 88–95.

F i t s c h e n K., *Did 'Messalianism' exist in Asia Minor after A.D. 431?*, SP 25, 1993, pp. 352–355.

F l u s i n B., *Re-writing history: John Skylitzes' Synopsis historion*, [in:] J o h n S k y l i t z e s, *A Synopsis of Byzantine History, 811–1057*, transl. J. W o r t l e y, Cambridge 2010, pp. XII–XXXIII.

F o l l i e r i E., *Introduzione*, [in:] *La Vita di San Fantino il Giovane*, ed., transl., comm. e a d e m, Bruxelles 1993, pp. 3–274.

D u F r e s n e C., *Historia Byzantina duplici commentario illustrata*, vol. I, Lutetia Parisiorum 1680.

D u F r e s n e C., *Illyricum vetus et novum sive historia regnorum Dalmatiae, Croatiae, Slavoniae, Bosniae, Serviae atque Bulgariae*, Posonium 1746.

G a g o v a K., *Bulgarian-Byzantine Border in Thrace from the 7th to the 10th Century (Bulgaria to the South of Haemus)*, BHR 14.1, 1986, pp. 66–77.

G a r l a n d L., *Byzantine Empresses. Women and Power in Byzantium AD 527–1204*, London–New York 1999.

G a r s o ï a n N., *Byzantine Heresy. A Reinterpratation*, DOP 25, 1971, pp. 85–113.

G e b h a r d i L.A., *Geschichte des Reichs Hungarn und der damit verbundenen Staaten*, vol. IV, Leipzig 1782.

v o n G e i s a u H., Chr. D a n o f f, *Haimos*, [in:] *KP.LA*, vol. II, pp. 919–920.

G e o r g i e v a S., *The Byzantine Princesses in Bulgaria*, BBg 9, 1995, pp. 163–201.

G e r e m e k B., *Człowiek marginesu*, [in:] *Człowiek średniowiecza*, ed. J. L e G o f f, transl. M. R a d o ż y c k a-P a o l e t t i, Warszawa 2000, pp. 431–463.

G i b b o n E., *The History of the Decline and Fall of the Roman Empire*, ed. J.B. B u r y, vol. VI, New York 1907; vol. X, introd. W.E.H. L e c k y, New York 1906.

G j u z e l e v V., *Allgemeine charakteristik und Etappen der Errichtung der Militärischen und Administrativen Verwaltung des ersten bulgarischen Staates (VII. bis XI. Jh.)*, EB 14.3, 1978, pp. 71–77.

G j u z e l e v V., *Anchialos zwischen der Spätantike und dem frühen Mittelalter*, [in:] *Die Schwarzmeerküste in der Spätantike und frühen Mittelalter*, ed. R. P i l l i n g e r, A. P ü l z, H. V e t t e r s, Wien 1992, pp. 23–33.

G j u z e l e v V., *Bułgaria a państwa i narody Europy Środkowej w X w.*, transl. K. M a r i n o w, [in:] *Byzantina Europaea. Księga jubileuszowa ofiarowana Profesorowi Waldemarowi Ceranowi*, ed. M. K o k o s z k o, M.J. L e s z k a, Łódź 2007, pp. 133–140.

G j u z e l e v V., *Marin Drinov (1838–1906). Begründer der bulgarischen Slawistik und Mediävistik*, Pbg 17.4, 1993, pp. 107–126.

G j u z e l e v V., *Il Mar Nero ed il suo litorale nella storia del Medieovo Bulgaro*, BBg 7, 1981, pp. 11–24.

G j u z e l e v V., *Die mittelalterliche Stadt Mesembria (Nesebăr) im 6.–15. Jh.*, BHR 6.1, 1978, pp. 50–59.

G j u z e l e v V., *Naturräumliche Bedingungen, Grenzen und Namen von Dobruda im Mittelalter (14.–17. Jh.)*, [in:] i d e m, *Mittelalterliches Bulgarien. Quellen, Geschichte, Haupstdte und Kultur*, Istanbul 2001, pp. 345–366.

G ó r s k i K., *La naissance des états et le "roi-saint". Problème de de l'idéologie féodale*, [in:] *L'Europe aux IXe–XIe siècles. Aux origines des états nationaux*, Varsovie 1968, pp. 425–432.

G r a b a r A., *God and the "Family of Princes" Presided over by the Byzantine Emperor*, HSS 2, 1954, pp. 117–123.

G r e g o r y T.E., *Macedonia*, [in:] *ODB*, vol. II, pp. 1261–1262.

G r e g o r y T.E., *The Political Program of Constantine Porphyrogenitus*, [in:] *Actes du XVe Congrès International des Études Byzantines*, vol. IV, Athènes 1980, pp. 122–133.

G r i e r s o n Ph., *Byzantine Coins*, London–Berkeley–Los Angeles 1982.

G r i g o r i a d i s I., *Linguistic and literary studies in the Epitome Historion of John Zonaras*, Thessaloniki 1998.

G r u m e l V., *Notes de chronologie byzantine*, EO 35, 1936.

G r u m e l V., *Traité d'etudes byzantines*, vol. I, *La chronologie*, Paris 1958.

G u e n é e B., *Histoire et culture historique dans l'Occident médiéval*, Paris 1980.

G u i l l a m o n t A., *Messaliens. Appelations, histoire, doctrine*, [in:] *Dictionnaire de spiritualité, ascétique et mystique*, vol. X, ed. M. V i l l e r et al., Paris 1979, pp. 1074–1083.

G u t s c h e A., *Auf den Spuren der antiken Via Egnatia – vom Weströmischen ins Oströmische Reich: Ein historischer Reiseführer durch den südlichen Balkan: Albanien – Mazedonien – Griechenland – Türkei*, Schweinfurt 2010.

G y ó n i M., *La transhumance des Vlaques balkaniques au Moyen Âge*, Bsl 12, 1951, pp. 29–42.

Haldon J.F., *Byzantine Praetorians: an administrative, institutional and social survey of the Opsikion and Tagmata, c. 580–900*, Bonn 1984.

Haldon J., *Warfare, State and Society in the Byzantine World*, London 1999.

Halton Th., *Ecclesiastical War and Peace in the Letters of Isidore of Pelusium*, [in:] *Peace and War in Byzantium. Essays in Honor of George T. Dennis, S.J.*, ed. T.S. Miller, J. Nesbitt, Washington D.C. 1995, pp. 41–49.

Hamilton B., *Bogomil Influences on Western Heresy*, [in:] *Heresy and the Persecuting Society in the Middle Ages. Essays on the Work of R.I. Moore*, ed. M. Frassetto, Leiden–Boston 2006, pp. 93–114.

Hamilton B., *Historical Introduction*, [in:] J. Hamilton, B. Hamilton, Y. Stoyanov, *Christian Dualist Heresies in the Byzantine World c. 850–c. 1450*, Manchester–New York 1998, pp. 1–54.

Hanak W.K., *The Infamous Svjatoslav: Master of Duplicity in War and Peace?*, [in:] *Peace and War in Byzantium. Essays in Honor of George T. Dennis, p.J.*, ed. T.S. Miller, J. Nesbitt, Washington D.C. 1995, pp. 138–151.

Hannick C., *Nowe chrześcijaństwo w świecie bizantyńskim: Rusini, Bułgarzy i Serbowie*, [in:] *Historia chrześcijaństwa*, vol. IV: *Biskupi, mnisi i cesarze 610–1054*, transl. M. Żurowska et al., ed. G. Dagron, P. Riché, A. Vauchez, Polish ed. J. Kłoczowski, Warszawa 1999, pp. 731–755.

Herrin J., *Blinding in Byzantium*, [in:] *Polypleuros nous. Miscellanea für Peter Schreiner zu seinem 60 Geburtstag*, ed. C. Scholtz, G. Makris, München–Leipzig 2000, pp. 56–68.

Herrin J., *The Imperial Feminine in Byzantium*, PP 169, 2000, pp. 5–35 [= J. Herrin, *Unrivalled Influence: Women and Empire in Byzantium*. Princeton 2013, pp. 161–193].

Herrin J., *The Many Empresses of the Byzantine Court (and All Their Attendants)*, [in:] eadem, *Unrivalled Influence. Women and Empire in Byzantium*, Princeton 2013, pp. 219–237.

Herrin J., *Theophano. Considerations on the Education of a Byzantine Princess*, [in:] *The Empress Theophano. Byzantium and the West at the turn of the first millennium*, ed. A. Davids, Cambridge 1995, pp. 64–85 [= J. Herrin, *Unrivalled Influence. Women and Empire in Byzantium*, Princeton 2013, pp. 238–260].

Herrin J., *Women in Purple. Rulers of Medieval Byzantium*, London 2002.

Hill B., *Imperial Women in Byzantium 1025–1204. Power, Patronage and Ideology*, New York 1999.

Holmes C., *The rhetorical structure of Skylitzes' Synopsis Historion*, [in:] *Rhetoric in Byzantium*, ed. E. Jeffreys, Aldershot 2003, pp. 187–199.

Holubeanu I., *The Byzantine Monasticism in Scythia Minor-Dobruja in the IVth–XVth Centuries*, EBPB 5, 2006, pp. 243–289.

H o w a r d-J o h n s t o n J., *Byzantium, Bulgaria and the Peoples of Ukraine in the 890s*, [in:] *Материалы по археологии, истории и этнографии Таврии*, vol. VII, ed. А.И. А й-б а б и н, Симферополь 2000, pp. 342–356.

H o w a r d-J o h n s o n J., *A short piece of narrative history: war and diplomacy in the Balkans, winter 921/2 – spring 924*, [in:] *Byzantine Style, Religion and Civilization. In Honour of Sir Steven Runciman*, ed. E. J e f f r e y s, Cambridge 2006, pp. 340–360.

H r i s t o v Y.M., *Prisoners of War in Early Medieval Bulgaria (Preliminary reports)*, SCer. 5, 2015, pp. 73–105.

H r i s t o v Y.M., H r i s s i m o v N., *Aspects of everyday life in the Old-Bulgarian hagiographical cycle of stories "A Tale of the Iron Cross"*, ДСб 10, 2017, pp. 110–120.

H u g h e s M.K., D i a z H.F., *Was there a "Medieval Warm Period", and if so, where and when?*, CliC 26. 2/3, pp. 109–142.

H u n g e r H., *On the Imitatio (μίμησις) of Antiquity in Byzantine Literature*, DOP 23/24, 1969/1970, pp. 15–38.

H u p c h i c k D.P., *The Bulgarian-Byzantine Wars for Early Medieval Balkan Hegemony. Silver-Lined Skulls and Blinded Armies*, [s.l.] 2017.

Ibrahim Ibn Jakub i Tadeusz Kowalski w sześćdziesiątą rocznicę edycji. Materiały z konferencji naukowej, ed. A. Z a b o r s k i, Kraków 2008.

Ibrahim ibn Ya'qub at-Turtushi. Christianity, Islam and Judaism meet in East-Central Europe, c. 800–1300 A.D. Proceedings of the International Colloquy 25–29. April 1994, ed. P. C h a r v á t, J. P r o s e c k ý, Praha 1996.

I l i e v a A., *The Byzantine Image of War and Peace: the Case of the Peloponnese*, BF 19, 1993, pp. 182–192.

I n a l c ı k H., *Balkan*, [in:] *EI.NE*, vol. I, pp. 998–100.

I v a n o v S.A., *Slavic Jesters and the Byzantine Hippodrome*, DOP 46, 1992, pp. 129–132.

J a m e s L., *Empresses and Power in Early Byzantium*, Leicester 2001.

J a m e s L., *Men, Women, Eunuchs: Gender, Sex, and Power*, [in:] *The Social History of Byzantium*, ed. J. H a l d o n, Oxford 2009, pp. 31–50.

J e n k i n s R., *Byzantium. The Imperial Centuries AD 610–1071*, Toronto–Buffalo–London 1966.

J e n k i n s R.J.H., *The Hellenistic Origins of Byzantine Literature*, DOP 17, 1963, pp. 39–52.

J e n k i n s R.J.H., *The Peace with Bulgaria (927) Celebrated by Theodore Daphnopates*, [in:] *Polychronion. Festschrift F. Dölger*, ed. P. W i r t h, Heidelberg 1966, pp. 287–303.

J e r k o v-K a p a l d o J., *Le "Različnie potrebii" di Jakov di Sofia alla luce di un esemplare complete*, BBg 6, 1980, pp. 373–386.

Jireček K.J., *Die Heerstrasse von Belgrad nach Constantinopel und die Balkanpässe. Eine Historisch-Geographische Studie*, Prag 1877.

Jones P.D., Mann M.E., *Climate Over Past Millenia*, RG 42, 2002/2004, pp. 1–42.

Jordanov I., *Preslav*, [in:] *The Economic History of Byzantium. From the Seventh through the Fifteenth Century*, ed. A.E. Laiou, vol. II, Washington D.C. 2002, pp. 667–671.

Jurewicz O., *Historia literatury bizantyńskiej. Zarys*, Wrocław 1982.

Kalavrezou I., *Images of Women in Byzantium*, [in:] *Everyday Life in Byzantium*. ed. D. Papanikola-Bakirdzi, Athens 2002, pp. 241–249.

Kaldellis A., *Hellenism in Byzantium. The Transformation of Greek Identity and the Reception of the Classical Tradition*, Cambridge 2007.

Karayannopoulos J., *Les causes des luttes entre Syméon et Byzance: un réexamin*, [in:] *Сборник в чест на акад. Димитър Ангелов*, ed. В. Велков, София 1994, pp. 52–64.

Karlin-Hayter P., *The Homily on the Peace with Bulgaria of 927 and the 'Coronation' of 913*, JÖB 17, 1968, pp. 29–39.

Kaltschev K., *Das Befestigungssystem von Augusta Traiana – Beroe (Heute Stara Zagora) im 2.–6. Jh.U.Z.*, ABu 3.2, 1998, pp. 88–107.

Kazhdan A., *Balkans*, [in:] *ODB*, vol. I, p. 248–249.

Kazhdan A., *History of Byzantine Literaure (850–1000)*, ed. Ch. Angelidi, Athens 2006.

Kazhdan A., *Daphnopates Theodore*, [in:] *ODB*, vol. I, p. 588.

Kazhdan A., Constable G., *People and Power in Byzantium. An Introduction to Modern Byzantine Studies*, Washington D.C. 1982.

Kempgen S., *The "Synkel" Inscription from Veliki Preslav – a New Reading*, WSA 86, 2015, pp. 109–117.

Kijas A., *Stosunki rusko-bułgarskie do XV w. ze szczególnym uwzględnieniem stosunków kulturalnych*, BP 2, 1985, pp. 146–180.

Kissas S., *Ο βίος της Αγίας Μαρίας της Νέας ως πηγή για την αρχαιολγία και ιστορία της τέχνης*, BF 14, 1989, pp. 253–264.

Koder J., Weber T., *Liutprand von Cremona in Konstantinopel*, Vienna 1980.

Kolarov Ch., Andreev J., *Certaines questions ayant trait aux manifestations de continuite d'idées en Bulgarie médieévale au des XII–XIV siècles*, EHi 9, 1979, pp. 77–82.

Koledarov P.S., *On the Initial Type Differentiation of Inhabited Localities in the Central Balkan Peninsula in Ancient Times*, EH 3, 1966, pp. 31–52.

Koledarov P.S., *Place-Names classification in the central part of the Balkan Peninsula in the Middle ages*, [in:] *Actes du premier Congres International des Études Balkaniques et Sud-Est*

Européennes, Sofia, 26 âout – 1 septembre 1966, vol. III, *Histoire (Ve–XVe ss.; XVe–XVIIe ss.)*, ed. V. Tăpkova-Zaimova, S. Dimitrov, E. Sarafova, Sofia 1969, pp. 277–286.

Kompa A., *Konstantynopolitańskie zabytki w Stambule*, [in:] *Z badań nad wczesnobizantyńskim Konstantynopolem*, ed. M.J. Leszka, K. Marinow, A. Kompa, Łódź 2011 [= AUL. FH 87], pp. 123–214.

Konev I., Topalov S., Genov I., *Charles du Fresne, seigneur du Cange et sa "Series historica et genealogica Regum Bulgariae"*, Pbg 4.3, 1980, pp. 69–85.

Kosiński R., *Holiness and Power. Constantinopolitan Holy Men and Authority in the 5th Century*, Berlin–Boston 2016

Kosiński R., *Religie cesarstwa rzymskiego w V stuleciu*, [in:] *Świat rzymski w V wieku*, ed. idem, K. Twardowska, Kraków 2010, pp. 365–414.

Korunovski S., Dimitrova E., *Painting and Architecture in Medieval Macedonia. Artists and Works of Art*, Skopje 2011.

Kostova R., *Bulgarian monasteries ninth to tenth centuries: interpreting the archaeological evidence*, ППре 8, 2000, pp. 190–202.

Kostova R., *"Bypassing Anchialos": The West Black Sea coast in naval campaigns 11th to 12th c.*, [in:] *Тангра. Сборник в чест на 70-годишнината на акад. Васил Гюзелев*, ed. M. Каймакамова et al., София 2006, pp. 579–597.

Kostova R., *The Lower Danube in the Byzantine Naval Campaigns in the 12th c.*, [in:] *Cultură și civilizație la Dunărea de Jos*, vol. XXIV, Călărași 2008, pp. 269–281.

Kostova R., *Polychrome ceramics in Preslav, 9th to 11th centuries: Where were they produced and used?*, [in:] *Byzantine Trade 4th–12th Centuries. The Archaeology of Local, Regional and International Exchange*, ed. M.M. Mango, Aldershot 2009, pp. 97–117.

Kostova R., *St. Kliment of Ohrid and his monastery: some more archaeology of the written evidence*, SB 25, 2006, pp. 593–605.

Kotsis K., *Defining Female Authority in Eighth-Century Byzantium: the Numismatic Images of the Empress Irene (797–802)*, JLA 5.1, 2012, pp. 185–215.

Kovach G., *Date cu privire la transportul sări pe Mureș (sec. X–XIII)*, Zir 12, 1980, pp. 193–200.

Krausmüller D., *Take No Care for the Morrow! The Rejection of Landed Property in Eleventh- and Twelfth-Century Byzantine Monasticism*, BMGS 42, 2018, pp. 45–57.

Kühn H.-J., *Die Byzantinische Armee im 10. und 11. Jahrhundert. Studien zur Organisation der Tagmata*, Wien 1991.

Kundert J.K., *Der Kaser auf dem Lechfeld*, CMAe 1, 1998, pp. 77–97.

Kurnatowska Z., *Elementy uzbrojenia i oporządzenia jeździeckiego z wczesnośredniowiecznego grodziska w Styrmen w Bułgarii*, SA 20, 1973, pp. 87–124.

Laiou A.E., Morrisson C., *The Byzantine Economy*, Cambridge–New York 2007.

Lamb H., *Climate, History, and the Modern World*, [2]London–New York 1995.

Lehr-Spławiński T., H. Kappesowa, W. Swoboda, *Bałkany*, [in:] *SSS*, vol. I, pp. 71–72.

Lemerle P., *Byzantine Humanism: the First Phase. Notes and Remarks on Education and Culture in Byzantium from the Origins to the 10th Century*, transl. H. Lindsay, A. Moffatt, Canberra 1986.

Lemerle P., *Philippes et la Macédoine orientale à l'époque chrétienne et byzantine. Recherches d'histoire et d'archéologie*, Paris 1945.

Leszka M.J., *The Monk versus the Philosopher. From the History of the Bulgarian-Byzantine War 894–896*, SCer 1, 2011, pp. 55–70.

Leszka M.J., *Rola cara Piotra (927–969) w życiu bułgarskiego Kościoła. Kilka uwag*, VP 66, 2016, pp. 429–442.

Leszka M.J., *Rola cesarzowej Teofano w uzurpacjach Nicefora Fokasa (963) i Jana Tzymiskesa (969)*, [in:] *Zamach stanu w dawnych społecznościach*, ed. A. Sołtysik, Warszawa 2004, pp. 227–235.

Leszka M.J., *Stracone złudzenia. Religijny kontekst stosunków bizantyńsko-bułgarskich w latach 863–927*, [in:] *Religijna mozaika Bałkanów*, ed. M. Walczak-Mikołajczakowa, Gniezno 2008, pp. 32–39.

Leszka M.J., *Symeon I Wielki a Bizancjum. Z dziejów stosunków bułgarsko-bizantyńskich w latach 893–927*, Łódź 2013.

Leszka M.J., *Wizerunek władców pierwszego państwa bułgarskiego w bizantyńskich źródłach pisanych (VIII–pierwsza połowa XII w.)*, Łódź 2003.

Leszka M.J., Marinow K., *Carstwo bułgarskie. Polityka – społeczeństwo – gospodarka – kultura. 866–971*, Warszawa 2015.

Leszka M.J., Marinow K., [rev.:] *Uczniowie Apostołów Słowian. Siedmiu Świętych Mężów*, ed. Małgorzata Skowronek, Georgi Minczew, Collegium Columbinum Cracoviae, Kraków 2010, pp. 216 (Biblioteka duchowości europejskiej) – BP 18, 2011, pp. 192–197.

Leunclavius J., *Annales Sultanorum Othimanidarum*, Francofurdum 1588.

Linzel M., *Studien über Liudprand von Cremona*, Berlin 1933.

Ljubarskij J., *Theophanes Continuatus und Genesios. Das Problem einer gemeinsamen Quelle*, Bsl 48, 1987, pp. 45–55.

Loos M., *Dualist Heresy in the Middle Ages*, transl. I. Lewitová, Praha 1974.

Loos M., *Le prétendu témoignage d'un traité de Jean Exarque intitulé 'Šestodnev' et relatif aux Bogomiles*, Bsl 13, 1952/1953, pp. 59–67.

Lyman R., *Heresiology: the invention of "heresy" and "schism"*, [in:] *Cambridge History of Christianity*, vol. II, *Constantine to c. 600*, ed. A. Casiday, F. W. Norris, Cambridge 2007, pp. 296–314.

Madgearu A., *Byzantine Military Organization on the Danube 10th–12th Century*, Leiden–Boston 2013.

Madgearu A., *Salt Trade and Warfare in Early Medieval Transylvania*, EN 11, 2001, pp. 271–283.

Madgearu A., *Transylvania and the Bulgarian Expansion in the 9th and 10th Centuries*, AMN 39/40.2, 2002/2003, pp. 41–65.

Madzharov M., *Roman Roads in Bulgaria. Contribution to the Development of Roman Road System in the Provinces of Moesia and Thrace*, Veliko Tarnovo 2009.

Maksimovich K., *Byzantine Law in Old Slavonic Translations and the Nomocanon of Methodius*, Bsl 65, 2007, pp. 9–18.

Mamzer H., *Studia nad metalurgią żelaza na terenie północno-wschodniej Bułgarii we wczesnym średniowieczu*, Wrocław 1988.

Mango C., *The Byzantine Church at Vize (Bizye) in Thrace and St. Mary the Younger*, ЗРВИ 11, 1968, pp. 9–13.

Manini M., *Liber de Caerimoniis Aulae Byzantinae: prosopografia e sepolture imperiali*, Spoleto 2009.

Mănucu-Adameşteanu Gh., *La diffusion de la monnaie byzantine en Dobroudja aux IXe–Xe siècles*, RESEE 34.4, 1996, pp. 275–287.

Marinow K., *Dzicy, wyniośli i groźni górale. Wizerunek Bułgarów jako mieszkańców gór w wybranych źródłach greckich VIII–XII w.*, [in:] *Stereotypy bałkańskie. Księga jubileuszowa Profesor Ilony Czamańskiej*, ed. J. Paszkiewicz, Z. Pentek, Poznań 2011, pp. 35–45.

Marinow K., *Hémos comme barrière militaire. L'analyse des écrits historiques de Léon le Diacre et de Jean Skylitzès au sujet de la campagne de guerre des empereurs byzantins Nicéphore II Phocas en 967 et de Jean I Tzymiscès en 971*, BMd 2, 2011, pp. 443–466.

Marinow K., *In the Shackles of the Evil One. The Portrayal of Tsar Symeon I the Great (893–927) in the Oration On the treaty with the Bulgarians*, SCer 1, 2011, pp. 157–190.

Marinow K., *Kilka uwag na temat ideologiczno-eschatologicznej wymowy "Bułgarskiej kroniki apokryficznej"*, FE 4. 6/7, 2007, pp. 61–75.

Marinow K., *Myth and Meaning. Standards of Byzantine Erudition and Its Role in Byzantine Rhetorical Works*, [in:] *Standards of Everyday Life in the Middle Ages and in Modern Times*, vol. III, ed. K. Mutafova et al., Veliko Tărnovo 2014, pp. 151–164.

Marinow K., *Not David but Salomon: Tsar Peter I (927–969) according to the Oration 'On the Treaty with the Bulgarians'* (in press).

Marinow K., *Peace in the House of Jacob. A Few Remarks on the Ideology of Two Biblical Themes in the Oration 'On the Treaty with the Bulgarians'*, BMd 3, 2012, pp. 85–93.

Marinow K., *Przez wąwozy i lasy. Armia bizantyńska wobec trudno dostępnych obszarów w świetle IX konstytucji Taktyk Leona VI Mądrego*, AUL.FH 99, 2017, pp. 11–32.

Marinow K., *Twierdza Emona. Na nadmorskich stokach średniowiecznego Hemusu*, VP 28, 2008, pp. 617–633.

Marinow K., *Zadania floty cesarskiej w wojnach bizantyńsko-bułgarskich (VII–XI w.)*, [in:] *Byzantina Europaea. Księga jubileuszowa ofiarowana Profesorowi Waldemarowi Ceranowi*, ed. M. Kokoszko, M.J. Leszka, Łódź 2007, pp. 381–392.

Markopoulos A., *Théodore Daphnopatès et la Continuation de Théophane*, JÖB 35, 1985, pp. 171–182.

Maruszczak H., *Bułgaria*, Warszawa 1971.

Maslev S., *Die staatsrechtliche Stellung der byzantinischen Kaiserinnen*, Bsl 27, 1966, pp. 308–343.

Mauzer H., *Studia nad metalurgią żelaza na terenie północno-wschodniej Bułgarii we wczesnym średniowieczu*, Wrocław–Warszawa 1988.

McCormick M., *Eternal Victory: Triumphal Rulership in Late Antiquity, Byzantium and the Early Medieval West*, Cambridge 1987.

McCormick M., *Origins of the European Economy: Communications and Commerce AD 300–900*, Cambridge 2001 [Polish transl. – McCormick M., *Narodziny Europy. Korzenie gospodarki europejskiej, 300–900*, transl. A. Bugaj, Z. Dalewski, J. Lang, I. Skrzypczak, Warszawa 2009].

McGrath S., *The Battles of Dorostolon (971). Rhetoric and Reality*, [in:] *Peace and War in Byzantium. Essays in Honor of George T. Dennis, S.J.*, ed. T.S. Miller, J. Nesbitt, Washington D.C. 1995, pp. 152–164.

Memoriae populorum, olim ad Danubium, Pontum Euxinum, Paludem Maeotidem, Caucasum, Mare Caspium, et Inde Magis ad Septemtriones incolentium, e scriptoribus historiae Byzantinae, ed. J.G. Strittero, vol. II, Petropolis 1774.

Michaud L.G., *Stritter, Jean-Gotthelf de*, [in:] *Biographie universelle, ancienne et moderne*, vol. XLIV, Paris 1826, pp. 44–45.

Mihailov S., *Über die Dobrudza-Inschrift von 943*, BHR 33, 2005, pp. 3–5.

Minczew G., *"Cała świątynia staje się mieszkaniem Boga". Bizantyńskie mistagogie – wykładnia i komentarz liturgii niebiańskiej*, [in:] Symeon z Tessaloniki, *O świątyni Bożej*, transl. A. Maciejewska, Kraków 2007, pp. 7–29.

Minczew G., *Ceramiczna ikona św. Teodora Stratylaty*, [in:] *Leksykon tradycji bułgarskiej*, ed. G. Szwat-Gyłybowa, Warszawa 2011, p. 61.

Minczew G., *Remarks on the Letter of the Patriarch Theophylact to Tsar Peter in the Context of Certain Byzantine and Slavic Anti-heretic Texts*, SCer 3, 2013, pp. 113–130.

Minczew G., *Słowiańskie teksty antyheretyckie jako źródło do poznania herezji dualistycznych na Bałkanach*, [in:] *Średniowieczne herezje dualistyczne na Bałkanach. Źródła słowiańskie*, ed. idem, M. Skowronek, J.M. Wolski, Łódź 2015, pp. 13–57.

Mishin D., *Ibrahim Ibn-Ya'qub At-Turtuhi's Account of the Slavs from the Middle of the Tenth Century*, AMSCEUB 1994/1995, pp. 184–199.

Mishkova D., *The Afterlife of a Commonwealth: Narratives of Byzantium in the National Historiographies of Greece, Bulgaria, Serbia and Romania*, [in:] *Entangled Histories of the Balkans*, vol. III, *Shared Pasts, Disputed Legacies*, ed. R. Daskalov, A. Vezenkov, Leiden–Boston 2015, pp. 118–273.

Mladjov I., *Trans-Danubian Bulgaria: Reality and Fiction*, ByzS 3, 1998, pp. 85–128.

Moffatt A., *The Master of Ceremonies' Bottom Drawer. The Unfinished State of the De cerimoniis of Constantine Porphyrogennetos*, Bsl 56, 1995, pp. 377–388.

Moravcsik G., *Byzantinoturcica*, vol. I, *Die byzantinischen Quellen der Geschichte der Türkvölker*, Berlin 1958.

Moravcsik G., *Byzantium and the Magyars*, Budapest 1970.

Moravscik G., *Zur Geschichte des Herrschertitels "caesar>царь"*, ЗРВИ 8, 1963, pp. 229–236.

Moriyasu T., *Images des Bulgares au Moyen Age*, [in:] *Studia Slavico-Byzantina et Mediaevalia Europensia. In memoriam Ivan Dujčev*, vol. I, ed. П. Динеков et al., София 1988, pp. 41–43.

Moore R.I., *The Birth of Popular Heresy*, London 1975.

Moore R.I., *The Origins of European Dissent*, Oxford 1985.

Morris R., *Monks and laymen in Byzantium, 843–1118*, Cambridge 1995.

Moszyński L., *Staro-cerkiewno-słowiańskie apelatywy określające osoby będące u władzy*, BP 2, 1985, pp. 43–48.

Munitiz J.A., *War and Peace Reflected in Some Byzantine Mirrors of Princes*, [in:] *Peace and War in Byzantium. Essays in Honor of George T. Dennis, S.J.*, ed. T.S. Miller, J. Nesbitt, Washington D.C. 1995, pp. 50–61.

The Natural Regions of the Balkan Paninsula (after Cvijić), GRev 9.3, 1920, pp. 199–204.

Niavis P.E., *The Reign of the Byzantine Emperor Nicephorus I (AD 802–811)*, Athens 1987.

Nikolov A., *Making a New Basileus. The Case of Symeon of Bulgaria (893–927). Reconsidered*, [in:] *Rome, Constantinople and Newly-Converted Europe. Archaeological and Historical Evidence*, vol. I, ed. M. Salamon et al., Kraków–Leipzig–Rzeszów–Warszawa 2012, pp. 101–108.

Nikolov A., *The Medieval Slavonic Translation of the Paraenetical Chapters of Emperor Basil I between the Balkans, Ostrog and Moscow: Preliminary Remarks*, [in:] *Byzantium, New Peoples, New Powers: the Byzantino-Slav Contact Zone, from the Ninth to the Fifteenth Century*, ed. M. Kaimakamova, M. Salamon, M. Smorąg Różycka, Cracow 2007, pp. 349–356.

Nikolov G.N., *The Bulgarian aristocracy in the war against the Byzantine Empire (971–1019)*, [in:] *Byzantium and East Central Europe*, ed. G. Prinzing, M. Salamon, P. Stephenson, Kraków 2001, pp. 141–158.

Nikolov G.N., *Die Christianisierung der Bulgaren und das Mönchtum in der Familie des Khans Boris I. Michail*, [in:] *Rome, Constantinople and Newly-Converted Europe. Archeological and Historical Evidence*, vol. I, ed. M. Salamon et al., Kraków–Leipzig–Rzeszów–Warszawa 2012, pp. 91–97.

Nilsson I., *Erotic Pathos, Rhetorical Pleasures. Narrative Technique and Mimesis in Eumathios Makrembolites' Hysmine & Hysminas*, Uppsala 2001.

Nilsson I., *Static imitation or creative transformation? Achilles Tatius in Hysmine* & *Hysminas*, [in:] *The Ancient Novel and Beyond*, ed. S. Panayotakis, M. Zimmerman, W. Keulen, Leiden 2003, pp. 371–380.

Nouzille J., *Transylwania. Obszar kontaktów i konfliktów*, transl. J. Praksa, Bydgoszcz 1997.

Nunn P.D., *Climate Environment and Society in the Pacific during the last Millenium*, Amsterdam 2007.

Oberländer-Târnoveanu E., *La monnaie dans l'espace rural byzantin des Balkans orientaux – un essai de synthèse au commencement du XXIe siècle*, Peu 1 (14), 2003, pp. 335–406.

Obolensky D., *The Bogomils*, Cambridge 1948.

Obolensky D., *Byzantine Commonwealth: Eastern Europe, 500–1453*, New York 1971.

Obolensky D., *Byzantine Frontier Zones and Cultural Exchanges*, [in:] *Actes du XIVe Congrès International des Études Byzantines*, Bucarest, 6–12 Septembre 1971, vol. V, ed. M. Berza, E. Stănescu, Bucareçti 1974, pp. 303–313.

Obolensky D., *Nationalism in Eastern Europe in the Middle Ages*, TRHS, 5th series, 22, 1972, pp. 1–16.

Oikonomides N., *The First Century of the Monastery of Hosios Loukas*, DOP 46, 1992, pp. 245–255.

Oikonomides N., *Le kommerkion d'Abydos, Thessalonique et la commerce bulgare au IXe siècle*, [in:] *Hommes et richesses dans l'Empire byzantin*, vol. II, *VIIe–XVe siècle*, ed. V. Kravari, J. Lefort, C. Morrisson, Paris 1991, pp. 241–248.

Onasch K., Schnieper A., *Ikony. Fakty i legendy*, transl. Z. Szanter, Warszawa 2002.

Orbini M., *Il regno degli Slavi*, Pesaro 1601, Nachdruck besorgt von S. Ćirković, P. Rehder, München 1985.

Ostrogorski G., *Avtokrator i samodržac*, [in:] idem, *Vizantija i Sloveni*, Beograd 1970, pp. 281–364.

Ostrogorski G., *The Byzantine emperor and the Hierarchical World Order*, SEER 35.1, 1956, pp. 1–14.

Ovčarov D., *Emergence et développement de la ville de Preslav. IXe–Xe siècles (Quelques problèmes et aspects)*, BHR 7.2, 1979, pp. 51–61.

Ovčarov D., *La forteresse protobulgare sur l'île danubienne Păcuiul lui Soare*, [in:] *Dobrudža. Études ethno-culturelles*, ed. idem, Sofia 1987, pp. 57–68.

Panova R., *The Capital City in the Medieval Bulgarian State*, JÖB 46, 1996, pp. 437–440.

Papamastorakis T., *The Bamberg Hanging Reconsidered*, ΔΧΑΕ 24, 2003, pp. 375–392.

Parani M.G., *The Romanos Ivory and the New Tokali Kilise: Imperial Costume as a Tool for Dating Byzantine Art*, CAr 49, 2001, pp. 15–28.

Paroń A., *Pieczyngowie. Koczownicy w krajobrazie politycznym i kulturowym średniowiecznej Europy*, Wrocław 2015.

Paroń A., "*Trzeba, abyś tymi oto słowami odparł i to niedorzeczne żądanie*" – *wokół De administrando imperio Konstantyna VII*, [in:] *Causa creandi. O pragmatyce źródła historycznego*, ed. S. Rosik, P. Wiszewski, Wrocław 2005, pp. 345–361.

Pavlov P., *Les lois agraires de la dynastie Macedonienne et la politique sociale du tsar bulgare Pierre (927–969). Selon le Traité contre les Bogomiles du prêtre Cosmas et quelques autres sources*, Bsl 56.1, 1995, pp. 103–105.

Penkov S., *Bulgaro-Byzantine Treaties during the Early Middle Ages*, Pbg 5.3, 1981, pp. 40–52.

Picchio R., *Gli Annali del Baronio-Skarga e la Storia di Paisij Hilendarski*, RS 3, 1954, pp. 212–233.

Piltz E., *Kamelaukion et mitra*, Stockholm 1977.

Pirivatrić S., *Some Notes on the Byzantine-Bulgarian Peace Treaty of 927*, Bslov 2, 2008, pp. 40–49.

Podskalsky G., *Chrześcijaństwo i literatura teologiczna na Rusi Kijowskiej (988–1237)*, transl. J. Zychowicz, Kraków 2000.

Polek K., *Podstawy gospodarcze Państwa Wielkomorawskiego*, Kraków 1994.

Popkonstantinov K., Kostova R., *Architecture of Conversion: Provincial Monasteries in the 9th–10th c. Bulgaria*, ТГЭ 53, 2010, pp. 118–124.

Popov A., *La ville médiévale bulgare d'après les recherches archéologiques*, BHR 12.1, 1984, pp. 63–73.

Popova T., *Archaeobotanic data about the Origin of the Fruit Trees on the Territory of Bulgaria. A View of the Past*, ABu 9.1, 2005, p. 37–45.

Popović S., *The Byzantine Monastery: Its Spacial Iconography and the Question of Sacredness*, [in:] *Hierotopy. Creation of Sacred Spaces in Byzantium and Medieval Russia*, ed. A. Lidov, Moscow 2006, pp. 150–185.

Poppe A., *La naissance du culte de Boris et Gleb*, CCM 24, 1981, pp. 29–53.

Poppe A., *Svjatoslav The Glorious and the Byzantine Empire*, [in:] *Byzantium, New Peoples, New Powers: the Byzantino-Slav Contact Zone, from the Ninth to the Fifteenth Century*, ed. M. Kaimakamova, M. Salamon, M. Smorąg Różycka, Cracow 2007, pp. 133–137.

Poppe A., *Walka o spuściznę po Włodzimierzu Wielkim 1015–1019*, KH 102.3/4, 1995, pp. 3–22.

Poutiers J.-Ch., *A propos des forteresses antiques et médiévales de la plaine Danubienne (Essai de reconstruction du réseau routier entre Iskăr et Ogosta)*, EB 11.2, 1975, pp. 60–73.

Pranke P., Zečević M., *Handel interregionalny od X do XII wieku. Europa Środkowa, Środkowo-Wschodnia, Półwysep Skandynawski i Półwysep Bałkański. Studium porównawcze*, Toruń 2016.

Praszkow L., *Rozwój i rozpowszechnienie ikony w Bułgarii od IX do XIX w.*, [in:] *Tysiąc lat ikony bułgarskiej. IX–XIX w. Muzeum Narodowe w Warszawie. Wystawa ze zbiorów bułgarskich*, ed. idem, Warszawa 1978, pp. 7–17.

Primov B., *Certain Aspects of the International Importance of the First Bulgarian Empire*, EHi 5, 1970, pp. 191–217.

Prinzing G., *Bizantyńczycy wobec obcych*, ed. K. Ilski, Poznań 1998.

Prinzing G., *Entstehung und Rezeption der Justiniana Prima-Theorie im Mittelalter*, BBg 5, 1978, pp. 269–278.

Przekop E., *Wschodnie patriarchaty starożytne (IV–X w.)*, Warszawa 1984.

Pundeff M., *Bulgarian Historiography, 1942–1958*, AHR 66.3, 1961, pp. 682–693.

Raev M., *The Russian-Byzantine Treaty of 971. Theophilos and Sveneld*, REB 64/65, 2006/2007, pp. 329–338.

Ratkoš P., *K otazce hranice Veľkej Moravy a Bulharska*, HČSAV 3, 1955, pp. 212–215.

Rek S., *Geneza tytułu carskiego w państwie zachodniobułgarskim*, BP 2, 1985, pp. 51–57.

Rigo A., *Messalianismo = Bogomilismo. Un'equazione dell'eresiologia medievale bizantina*, OCP 56, 1990, pp. 53–82.

Runciman S., *The Emperor Romanus Lecapenus and His Reign. A Study of Tenth-Century Byzantium*, Cambridge 1969.

Runciman S., *A History of the First Bulgarian Empire*, London 1930.

Runciman S., *The Medieval Manichee. A Study of the Dualist Heresy*, Cambridge 1947 (1982).

Rusev D., *Kemālpaşazāde's History of Medieval Bulgaria: A 16th-century Ottoman rendering of the Bulgarian Apocryphal Chronicle (Tale of the Prophet Isaiah)*, [in:] *Testis temporum et laudator historiae. Сборник в памет на проф. Иван Божилов* (in press).

Rusev D., *Eine untypische Abweichung in der osmanischen Geschichtsschreibung: Die Geschichte der bulgarischen Herrscher in Tevārīḫ-i āl-i ʿOsmān von Kemālpaşazāde. Wissenschaftliche Hausarbeit zur Erlangung des akademischen Grades eines Master of Arts der Universität Hamburg*, Hamburg 2016.

Russell J.B., *Dissent and Reform in the Early Middle Ages*, Berkeley–Los Angeles 1965.

Salamon M., *Dafnopata Teodor*, [in:] *Encyklopedia kultury bizantyńskiej*, ed. O. Jurewicz, Warszawa 2002, p. 133.

Salamon M., *Państwa słowiańskie w kręgu kultury bizantyńskiej*, [in:] *Wielka historia świata*, vol. IV, *Kształtowanie średniowiecza*, ed. idem, Kraków 2005, pp. 481–529.

Scărlătoiu E., *The Balkan Vlachs in the Light of Linguistic Studuies (Highlights and Contributions)*, RESEE 17.1, 1979, pp. 17–37.

Schramm G., *Haimos "Balkangebrige" und seine Nachfolgelautungen eine Beispielstudie zur Entwicklung des Thrakischen*, LBa 27.3, 1984, pp. 59–69.

Schreiner P., *Das Bulgarienbild im Europäischen Mittelalter*, EB 18.2, 1982, pp. 58–68.

Schreiner P., *Die vermentliche Blendung. Zu den Ereignissen von Kleidion*, [in:] *Европейският Югоизток през втората половина на X – началото на XI век. История и култура*, ed. В. Гюзелев, Г.Н. Николов, София 2015, pp. 170 –187.

Schulze H.K., *Die Heiratsurkunde der Kaiserin Theophanu. Die griechische Kaiserin und das römisch-deutsche Reich 972–991*, Hannover 2007.

Schwartz E.C., *Medieval Ceramic Decoration in Bulgaria*, Bsl 43.1, 1982, pp. 45–50.

Seibt W., *Johannes Skylitzes: Zur Person des Chronisten*, JÖB 25, 1976, pp. 81–85.

Ševčenko I., *Introduction*, [in:] *Chronographiae quae Theophanis Continuati nomine fertur Liber que Vita Basilii Imperatoris amplectitur*, ed. idem, Berlin 2011, pp. 3–13.

Shepard J., *Bulgaria. The Other Balkan "Empire"*, [in:] *New Cambridge Medieval History*, vol. III, ed. T. Reuter, Cambridge 2000, pp. 567–585.

Shepard J., *Byzantine emperors, imperial ideology and the fact of Bulgaria*, BMd 2, 2011, pp. 545–561.

Shepard J., *Communications across the Bulgarian lands – Samuel's poisoned chalice for Basil II and his successors?*, [in:] *Европейският Югоизток през втората половина на X – началото на XI век. История и култура*, ed. В. Гюзелев, Г.Н. Николов, София 2015, pp. 217–235.

S h e p a r d J., *Constantine VII's Doctrine of "Containment" of the Rus*, [in:] *Геннадиос. К 70-летию академика Г.Г. Литаврина*, ed. Б.Н. Ф л о р я, Москва 1999, pp. 265–283.

S h e p a r d J., *A marriage too far? Maria Lekapena and Peter of Bulgaria*, [in:] *The Empress Theophano. Byzantium and the West at the turn of the first millennium*, ed. A. D a v i d s, Cambridge 1995, pp. 121–149 [= J. S h e p a r d, *Emergent Elites and Byzantium in the Balkans and East-Central Europe*, Farnham 2011, V].

S h e p a r d J., *Slavs and Bulgars*, [in:] *The New Cambridge Medieval History*, vol. II: c. 700 – 900, ed. R. M c K i t t e r i c k, Cambridge 1995, pp. 228–248 [= J. S h e p a r d, *Emergent Elites and Byzantium in the Balkans and East-Central Europe*, Farnham 2011, II].

S h e p a r d J., *Symeon of Bulgaria-Peacemaker*, [in:] i d e m, *Emergent elites and Byzantium in the Balkans and East-Central Europe*, Farnham–Burlington 2011, pp. 1–53 [= J. S h e p a r d, *Symeon of Bulgaria – Peacemaker*, ГСУ.ЦСВПИД 3, 1989, pp. 9–48].

S h e p a r d J., *Western approaches (900–1025)*, [in:] *The Cambridge History of the Byzantine Empire, c. 500–1492*, ed. i d e m, Cambridge 2008, pp. 537–559.

S i g n e s C o d o ñ e r J., *Algunas consideraciones sobre la autoría del Theophanes Continuatus*, Erytio, 1989, pp. 17–28.

S i m e o n o v G., *Obst in Byzanz. Ein Beitrag zur Geschichte der Ernährung im östlichen Mittelmeerraum*, Saarbrücken 2013.

S i m e o n o v a L., *Diplomacy of the Letter and the Cross. Photios, Bulgaria and the Papacy, 860s–880s*, Amsterdam 1998.

S m o r ą g R ó ż y c k a M., *Cesarzowa Teofano i królowa Gertruda. Uwagi o wizerunkach władczyń w sztuce średniowiecznej na marginesie rozważań o miniaturach w Kodeksie Gertrudy*, [in:] *Gertruda Mieszkówna i jej rękopis*, ed. A. A n d r z e j u k, Radzymin 2013, pp. 123–134.

S o l o v j e v A., *Svedočanstva pravoslavnih izvora o bogomilstvu na Balkanu*, GIDBiH 5, 1953, pp. 1–103.

S o p h o u l i s P., *Byzantium and Bulgaria, 775–831*, Leiden 2012.

S o u l i s G., *On the Slavic settlement in Hierissos in the tenth century*, B 23, 1953, pp. 67–72.

S o u l i s G.Ch., *The Serbs and Byzantium during the Reign of Tsar Stephen Dušan (1331–1355) and his Successors*, Washington D.C. 1984.

S o u s t a l P., *Tabula Imperii Byzantini*, vol. VI, *Thrakien (Thrakē, Rodopē und Haimimontos)*, Wien 1991.

S p y r a J., *Wspólnoty bogomilskie jako próba powrotu do form życia gmin wczesnochrześcijańskich*, ZNUJ.PH 84, 1987, pp. 7–21.

S t a n c h e v a M., *Veliki Preslav*, Sofia 1993.

Stephenson P., *Byzantium's Balkan Frontier. A Political Study of the Northern Balkans, 900–1204*, Cambridge 2000.

Stępień T., *Przedmowa*, [in:] Pseudo-Dionizy Areopagita, *Pisma teologiczne*, transl. M. Dzielska, introd. T. Stępień, Kraków 2005, pp. 7–67.

Stępniak-Minczewa W., *Francescani in Bulgaria. Blasius Kleiner: un francescano in viaggio per i Balcani (sulla base della Storia della Bulgaria di Blasius Kleiner)*, [in:] *I Francescani nella storia dei popoli balcanici, Nell'VIII centenario della fondazione dell'ordine. Atti del Convegno Internazionale di Studi*, ed. V. Nosilia, M. Scarpa, Bologna–Padova 2010, pp. 265–278.

Stokes B., *The Background and Chronology of the Balkan Campaigns of Svyatoslav Igorevich*, SEER 40/94, 1961, pp. 44–57.

Stoyanov Y., *The Other God. Dualist Religions from Antiquity to the Cathar Heresy*, London–New York 2000.

Strässle P.M., *Krieg und Frieden in Byzanz*, B 74, 2004, pp. 110–129.

Strässle P.M., *Krieg und Kriegführung in Byzanz. Die Kriege Kaiser Basileos' II. gegen die Bulgaren (976–1019)*, Köln–Weimar–Wien 2006.

Stričević Dj., *Églises triconques médiévales en Serbie et en Macédoine et la tradition de l'architecture paléobyzantine*, [in:] *XIIe Congrès International des Études Byzantine. Ochride 1961. Rapports VII*, Belgrade–Ochride 1961, pp. 78–85.

Sutherland J.N., *Liudprand of Cremona, Bishop, Diplomat, Historian. Studies of the Man and his Age*, Spoleto 1988.

Svoronos M., *Notes sur l'origine et la date du Code rural*, TM 8, 1981, pp. 487–500.

Swoboda W., *Bułgaria a patriarchat konstantynopolitański w latach 870–1018*, [in:] *Z polskich studiów slawistycznych*, vol. IV, *Historia*, Warszawa 1972, pp. 47–65.

Swoboda W., *Damian*, [in:] *SSS*, vol. VIII, pp. 13–14.

Swoboda W., *Haimos*, [in:] *SSS*, vol. II, p. 182.

Swoboda W., *Kontynuacja Georgiosa*, [in:] *SSS*, vol. II, p. 468.

Swoboda W., *Kuber*, [in:] *SSS*, vol. II, pp. 554–555.

Swoboda W., *Nicefor I*, [in:] *SSS*, vol. III, p. 372.

Swoboda W., *Organizacja Kościoła (Bułgaria)*, [in:] *SSS*, vol. III, pp. 494–500.

Swoboda W., *L'origine de l'organisation de l'Eglise en Bulgarie et ses rapports avec le patriarcat de Constantinople (870–919)*, BBg 2, 1966, pp. 67–81.

Swoboda W., *Presław Wielki*, [in:] *SSS*, vol. IV, pp. 335–343.

Swoboda W., *Symeon Logotheta*, [in:] *SSS*, vol. V, pp. 506–507.

Swoboda W., *Tracja*, [in:] *SSS*, vol. VI, pp. 119–123.

Swoboda W., *Widin*, [in:] *SSS*, vol. VI, pp. 421–422.

Swoboda W., *Żywot św. Marii*, [in:] *SSS*, vol. VII, p. 313.

Ševčenko I., *Agapetus East and West: the Fate of a Byzantine 'Mirror of Princes'*, RESEE 16.1, 1978, pp. 3–44.

Ševčenko I., *Byzanz und der Westen im 10. Jahrhundert*, [in:] *Kunst im Zeitalter der Kaiserin Theophanu. Akten des Internationalen Colloquiums veranstaltet vom Schnütgen-Museum*, ed. A. von Euw, P. Schreiner, Köln 1993, pp. 5–30.

Tafel G.L.F., *De via Romanorum militari Egnatia qua Illyricum Macedonia et Thracia iungebantur*, Tübingae 1837.

Taft R.F., *War and Peace in the Byzantine Divine Liturgy*, [in:] *Peace and War in Byzantium. Essays in Honor of George T. Dennis, S.J.*, ed. T.S. Miller, J. Nesbitt, Washington D.C. 1995, pp. 17–32.

Talbot A.-M., D.F. Sullivan, *Introduction*, [in:] *The History of Leo the Deacon. Byzantine Military Expansion in the Tenth Century*, transl., ed. A.-M. Talbot, D.F. Sullivan, assist. G.T. Dennis, P. McGrath, Washington D.C. 2005, pp. 1–52.

Talbot Rice D., *Art of the Byzantine Era*, London 1993.

Tanaocsa N.-Ş., Teoteoi T., *L'extension de la domination bulgare au nord du Danube aux VIIIe–IXe siécles*, EB 20. 4, 1984, pp. 110–120.

Tanner G., *The Historical Method of Constantine Porphyrogenitus*, BF 24, 1997, pp. 125–140.

Tăpkova-Zaimova V., *Frontières médiévales et réseau routier au sud du Danube*, BMd 1, 2010, pp. 1–15.

Tapkova-Zaimova V., Miltenova A., *Historical and Apocalyptic Literature in Byzantium and Medieval Bulgaria*, transl. M. Paneva, M. Lilova, Sofia 2011.

Tarnanidis I., *The Psalter of Dimitri the Oltarnik*, [in:] idem, *The Slavonic Manuscripts Discovered in 1975 at St. Catherine's Monastery on Mount Sinai*, Thessaloniki 1988, pp. 91–100.

Theodorescu R., *Au sujet des "corridors culturels" de l'Europe sud-orientale, I*, RESEE 21.1, 1983, pp. 7–22.

Theodorescu R., *Au sujet des "corridors culturels" de l'Europe sud-orientale, II*, RESEE 21.3, 1983, pp. 229–240.

Thomson F., *Chrysostomica Palaeoslavica. A Preliminary Study of the Sources of the Chrysorrhoas (Zlatostruy) Collection*, Cyr 6, 1982, pp. 1–65.

Thomson F., *"Made in Russia". A Survey of the Translations Allegedly Made in Kievan Russia*, [in:] *Millenium Russiae Christianae. Tausend Jahre Christliches Russland 988–1988*, Köln 1993, pp. 295–354 [= F. Thomson, *The Reception of Byzantine Culture in Medieval Russia*, Aldershot 1999, V].

T h o m s o n F., *Quotations of Patristic and Byzantine Works by Early Russian Authors as an Indication of the Cultural Level of Kievan Russia*, SGa 10, 1983, pp. 65–102.

T h u r n H., *Ioannes Skylitzes, Autor und Werk*, [in:] *Ioannis Scylitzae Synopsis historiarum*, ed. i d e m, Berolini–Novi Eboraci 1973, pp. VII–LVI.

T i n n e f e l d F., *Byzantinische auswärtige Heiratspolitik vom 9. zum 12 Jahrhundert*, Bsl 54.1, 1993, pp. 21–28.

T i n n e f e l d F., *Zum Stand der Olga-Diskussion*, [in:] *Zwischen Polis, Provinz und Peripherie. Beiträge zur byzantinischen Geschichte und Kultur*, ed. L.M. H o f f m a n n, A. M o n c h i z a d e h, Wiesbaden 2005, pp. 531–567.

Ţ i p l i c I.M., *Transylvania in the Early Middle Ages (7th–13th c.)*, Alba Iulia 2006.

T s i r p a n l i s C.N., *Byzantine Reactions to the Coronation of Charlemagne*, Βυζ 6, 1974, pp. 347–360.

T o d o r o v a E., *River Trade in the Balkans during the Middle Ages*, EB 20, 1984, pp. 38–50.

T o t e v T., *Great Preslav*, Sofia 2001.

T o t e v T., *Observations sur la cèramique peinte du monastère aux alentours de l'église ronde (l'église d'Or) a Preslav*, [in:] *Bulgaria Pontica Medii Aevi*, vol. IV–V/1, ed. В. Г ю з е л е в, София 2003, pp. 255–276.

T o t e v T., *The Palace Monastery in Preslav*, ПКШ 3, 1998, pp. 139–150.

T o y n b e e A., *Constantine Porphyrogenitus and His World*, London 1973.

T r e a d g o l d W., *Byzantium and Its Army 284–1081*, Stanford 1995.

T r e a d g o l d W., *A History of the Byzantine State and Society*, Stanford 1997.

T r e a d g o l d W., *The Middle Byzantine Historians*, New York–Basingstoke 2013.

T r o n z o W., *Mimesis in Byzantium. Notes toward a history of the function of the image*, AAe 25, 1994, pp. 61–76.

T r y j a r s k i E., *Protobułgarzy*, [in:] K. D ą b r o w s k i, T. N a j g r o d z k a-M a j c h r z y k, E. T r y j a r s k i, *Hunowie europejscy, Protobułgarzy, Chazarowie, Pieczyngowie*, Wrocław–Warszawa–Kraków–Gdańsk 1975, pp. 147–376.

T u r l e j S., *Justiniana Prima: An Underestimated Aspect of Justinian's Church Policy*, Kraków 2016.

T u r l e j S., *Sirmium w późnym antyku*, [in:] *Florilegium. Studia ofiarowane Profesorowi Aleksandrowi Krawczukowi z okazji dziewięćdziesiątej piątej rocznicy urodzin*, ed. E. D ą b r o w a, T. G r a b o w s k i, M. P i e d g o ń, Kraków 2017, pp. 445–460.

V a l l é e G., *A Study in Anti-Gnostic Polemics. Irenaeus, Hippolytus, and Epiphanius*, Waterloo 1981.

V e d e r W., *Der bulgarische Ursprung des Izbornik von 1076*, KMC 10, 1995, pp. 82–87.

V e d e r W., *A Certain Father's Edifying Words to His Son*, [in:] i d e m, *Хиляда години като един ден*, София 2005, pp. 139–144.

V e d e r W., *The Izbornik of 1076*, [in:] *The Edificatory Prose of Kievan Rus'*, transl. i d e m, introd. i d e m, A. T u r i l o v, Cambridge, Mass. 1994.

V e d e r W., *The "Izbornik of John the Sinner": a Compilation from Compilations*, ПК 8, 1983, pp. 15–33 [= У.Р. Ф е д е р, *Хиляда години като един ден*, София 2005, pp. 185–199].

V e d e r W., *Three Early Slavic Treatises on Reading*, [in:] *Studia slavica mediaevala et humanstica Riccardo Picchio dicata*, ed. M. C o l u c c i, G. D e l l' A g a t a, H. G o l d b l a t t, vol. II, Roma 1986, pp. 717–730.

V e d e r W., *Two Hundred Years of Misguided Philological Research*, RS 47, 1994, pp. 103–109.

V i t a l i a n o v S., *Die bulgarischen Klöster (im Mittelalter) – universale Produktionszentren*, ШУЕКП.ТКИБ 6, 2004, pp. 145–149.

V o j n o v M., *Byzance et le potentiel economique de la Bulgarie*, EB 13.2, 1977, pp. 129–131.

V o t ý p k a-P e c h a J., V i d m a n L., *Via Egnatia mezi Elbasanem a Ochridským jezerem*, FPh 82.2, 1959, pp. 187–196.

W a h l g r e n S., *Autor und Werk*, [in:] *Symeonis Magistri et Logothetae Chronicon*, ed. i d e m, Berolini–Novi Eboraci 2006, pp. 3–8.

W a l t e r Ch., *The Iconography of Constantine the Great, Emperor and Saint*, Leiden 2006.

W a s i l e w s k i T., *Bizancjum i Słowianie w IX w. Studia z dziejów stosunków politycznych i kulturalnych*, Warszawa 1972.

W e i t z m a n n K., C h a t z i d a k i s M., M i a t e v K., R a d o j č i ć S., *Fruhe Ikonen. Sinai. Griechenland. Bulgarien. Jugoslavien*, Sofia–Belgrad 1972.

W h e a l e y A., *"Sermo de pseudoprophetis" of Pseudo-John Chrysostom: A Homily from Antioch under Early Islamic Rule*, B 69, 1999, pp. 178–186.

W h i t t o w M., *The Making of Byzantium, 600–1025*, Berkeley–Los Angeles 1996.

W i d a j e w i c z J., *Studia nad relacją Ibrahima ibn Jakuba*, Kraków 1946.

W i n n i f r i t h T.J., *The Vlachs: The History of a Balkan People*, London 1987.

W o l i ń s k a T., *Konstantynopol i jego mieszkańcy widziani oczyma Liudpranda z Kremony*, VP 28, 2008, pp. 1231–1243.

W o l i ń s k a T., *Konstantynopolitańska misja Liudpranda z Kremony (968)*, [in:] *Cesarstwo bizantyńskie. Dzieje. Religia. Kultura. Studia ofiarowane Profesorowi Waldemarowi Ceranowi przez uczniów na 70-lecie Jego urodzin*, ed. P. K r u p c z y ń s k i, M.J. L e s z k a, Łask–Łódź 2006, pp. 201–223.

W o l s k i J.M., *Budownictwo kościelne i klasztorne*, [in:] M.J. L e s z k a, K. M a r i n o w, *Carstwo bułgarskie. Polityka – społeczeństwo – gospodarka – kultura. 866–971*, Warszawa 2015, pp. 268–276.

W o r t l e y J., *Legends of Byzantine Disaster of 811*, B 50, 1980, pp. 533–562.

Xeidakis G.S., Varagouli E.G., *Design and Construction of Roman Roads: The Case of Via Egnatia in the Aegean Thrace, Northern Greece*, EEG 3.1, 1997, pp. 123–132.

Yannopoulos P., *La Grece dans la vie de S. Fantin*, B 65, 1995, pp. 484–493.

Ziegler K., *Zonaras*, [in:] *RE*, vol. X.A.1, Munich 1972, cols. 718–732.

Ziemann D., *Onglos – once again*, BMd 3, 2012, pp. 31–43.

Ziemann D., *Pliska and Preslav: Bulgarian Capitals between Relocation and Invention*, [in:] *Българско Средновековие: общество, власт, история. Сборник в чест на проф. д-р Милияна Каймакамова*, ed. Г.Н. Николов, А. Николов, София 2013, pp. 170–185.

Živković T., *On the Northern Borders of Serbia in Early Middle Ages*, [in:] idem, *The South Slavs between East and West. 550–1150*, Belgrade 2008, pp. 249–258.

Živojinović M., *Crkvenjaci na Svetoj Gori i njihove dužnosti*, IČ 56, 2008, pp. 69–86.

Zuckerman C., *On the Date of the Khazars' Conversion to Judaism and the Chronology of the Kings of the Rus Oleg and Igor. A Study of the Anonymous Khazar Letter from the Genizah of Cairo*, REB 53, 1995, pp. 237–270.

* * *

Κυριακής Ε.Κ., *Βυζάντιο και Βούλγαροι (7ος–10ος αι.). Συμβολή στην εξωτερική πολιτική του Βυζαντίου*, Αθήνα 1993.

Ταρνανίδου I., *Η διαμόρφωσις τοῦ αὐτοκεφαλίου τῆς Βουλγαρικῆς εκκλησίας (864–1235)*, Θεσαλονίκη 1976.

* * *

Аджиевски К., *Пелагонија во средниот век (од доаѓањето на Словените до паѓањето под турска власт)*, Скопје 1994.

Адинолфи Р., *"Царството на Славяните" от Мавро Орбини, руският превод на Сава Владиславович и изследванията по въпроса*, Про 24.2, 2015, pp. 309–320.

Аладжов А., *Византийският град и българите VII–IX век (по археологически данни)*, София 2009.

Аладжов Ж., *Бележки за винопроизводството в ранното българско средновековие*, ППрс 5, 1992, pp. 216–221.

Аладжов Ж., *Къде се е намирал Потамукастел от средновековните извори*, ПС 2, 2000, pp. 289–291.

Аладжов Ж., *Печат на цар Петър от разкопките на обект "Улица" в Преслав*, НСЕ 13, 2017, pp. 307–310.

Александров Е., *Дипломатическая переписка царя Симеона с императором Романом Лакапином*, Pbg 14.2, 1990, pp. 16–22.

Алексиев Й., *Грънчарски пещи и жилища-полуземянки от IX–X в. край с. Хотница, Великотърновски окръг*, Архе 19.4, 1977, pp. 55–60.

Ангелов Б., *За три съчинения в Симеоновите сборници*, СЛ 5, 1979, pp. 21–32.

Ангелов Б., *Марин Дринов*, [in:] *КМЕ*, vol. I, pp. 614–616.

Ангелов Б., *Повествователни съчинения за Иван Рилски в старобългарската литература*, ЕЛ 32.1, 1977, pp. 66–71.

Ангелов Д., *Административно-военна уредба*, [in:] *История на България в четиринадесет тома*, vol. II, *Първа българска държава*, ed. idem, София 1981, pp. 169–181.

Ангелов Д., *Богомилство*, София 1993.

Ангелов Д., *Богомилството в България*, София 1961.

Ангелов Д., *Вътрешна и външна търговия през VIII–X в.*, [in:] *Стопанска история на България 681–1981*, ed. Л. Беров et al., София 1981, pp. 42–49.

Ангелов Д., *Към въпроса за средновековния български град*, Архе 2.3, 1960, pp. 9–22.

Ангелов Д., *Общество и обществена мисъл в средновековна България (IX–XIV в.)*, София 1979.

Ангелов Д., *Развитие на занаятите и рударството през VIII–X в.*, [in:] *Стопанска история на България 681–1981*, ed. Л. Беров et al., София 1981, pp. 40–42.

Ангелов Д., *Развитие на селското стопанство през VIII–X в.*, [in:] *Стопанска история на България 681–1981*, ed. Л. Беров et al., София 1981, pp. 37–40.

Ангелов Д., *Стопански живот*, [in:] *История на България в четиринадесет тома*, vol. II, *Първа българска държава*, ed. idem, София 1981, pp. 339–352.

Ангелов Д., *Тракия и българо-византийските отношения до падането ѝ под османска власт*, ИТНИ 1, 1965, pp. 61–91.

Ангелов Д., Кашев С., Чолпанов Б., *Българска военна история от Античността до втората четвърт на X в.*, София 1983.

Ангелов Д., Паскалева В., Пантев А., *Константин Иречек и болгарская историческая наука*, BHR 1.2, 1973, pp. 61–70.

Ангелов Д., Чолпанов Б., *Българска военна история през средновековието (X–XV в.)*, София 1994.

Ангелов П., *Българската средновековна дипломация*, София 1988.

Ангелов П., *Военна сила и дипломация в средновековна България*, ВС 52.5, 1990, pp. 3–13.

Ангелов П., *Духовници-дипломати в средновековна България*, SB 27, 2009, pp. 143–150.

Ангелова С., Дончева-Петкова Л., Даскалов М., *Двуобредният ранносредновековен некропол край село Топола, Каварненска община*, [in:] *Проблеми на прабългарската история и култура*, vol. III, ed. Р. Рашев, Шумен 1997, pp. 141–154.

Андреев Й., *Григорий*, [in:] idem, И. Лазаров, П. Павлов, *Кой кой е в средновековна България*, София 2012, p. 153.

Андреев Й., *Иван Рилски*, [in:] idem, И. Лазаров, П. Павлов, *Кой кой е в средновековна България*, [3]София 2012, pp. 270–275.

Андреев Й., *Йоан Екзарх и някои въпроси във връзка с наследиаването на царската власт в средновековна България*, ПКШ 1, 1995, pp. 309–310.

Андреев Й., *Кем был Черноризец Петр?*, BBg 6, 1980, pp. 51–56.

Андреев Й., Лазаров И., Павлов П., *Кой кой е в средновековна България*, [3]София 2012.

Андреев Й., Лалков М., *Исторически справочник. Българските ханове и царе. От хан Кубрат до цар Борис III*, Велико Търново 1996.

Андреева Н., *България и българите в едно немско историческо съчинение от края на XVIII в.*, [in:] Й.К. Енгел, *История на българите в Мизия*, transl., comm. Н. Андреева, Велико Търново 2009, pp. 5–55.

Андрейчин Л., *Из историята на нашето езиково строителство*, София 1977.

Анисимова Т.В., *Хроника Георгия Амартола в древнерусских списках XIV–XVII вв.*, Москва 2009.

Антонова В., *Новооткрита находка от земеделски сечива при Плиска*, Пр.Сб. 3,1983, pp. 263–268.

Антонова В., Аладжова Д., Петрова П., *Нови археологически проучвания при с. Хан Крум, Шуменско*, ГМСБ 7, 1981, pp. 65–76.

Аризанова С., *Българите в агиографията от XIII–XIV век*, Пловдив 2013.

Археологическа карта на Плиска, ed. А. Аладжов, София 2013.

Атанасов Г., *Добруджанското деспотство. Към политическата, църковната, стопанската и културната история на Добруджа през XIV век*, Велико Търново 2009.

Атанасов Г., *Държавната идеология на християнска България, инсигни и титулатура на нейните владетели*, [in:] Г. Атанасов, В. Вачкова, П. Павлов, *Българска национална история*, vol. III, *Първо българско царство (680–1018)*, Велико Търново 2015, pp. 753–793.

Атанасов Г., *Епископ Николай и формирането на Доростолската (Дръстърската) епархия през 870 г.*, [in:] *Християнската култура в средновековна България. Материали от национална научна конференция, Шумен 2–4 май 2007 година по случай 1100 години от смъртта на св. Княз Борис-Михаил (ок. 835–907г.)*. ed. П. Георгиев, Велико Търново 2008, pp. 104–119.

Атанасов Г., *За хронологията и монашеската организация в скалните обители през първото българско царство*, [in:] *Светогорска обител Зограф*, vol. III, ed. В. Гюзелев, София 1999, pp. 281–299.

Атанасов Г., *Инсигниите на средновековните български владетели. Корони, скиптри, сфери, оръжия, костюми, накити*, Плевен 1999.

Атанасов Г., *Началото на "българската флотилия" и военноморските експедиции на деспот Добротица*, [in:] *Великите Асеневци*, ed. П. Павлов, Н. Кънев, Н. Хрисимов, Велико Търново 2016, pp. 292–307.

Атанасов Г., *От епископия към самостойна патриаршивия на Първото българско царство в Дръстър (Силистра). Историята на патриаршеския комплекс*, София 2017.

Атанасов Г.Г., *О численности русской армии князя Святослава во время его походов в Болгарию и о битве под Дристрой (Доростолом в 971 г)*, ВВ 72, 2013, pp. 86–102.

Атанасов Г., *Още за датировката и монашеската организация в скалната обител до Мурфатлар (Басараби)*, [in:] *Великотърновският университет "Св. св. Кирил и Методий" и българската археология*, vol. I, ed. Б. Борисов, Велико Търново 2010, pp. 467–485.

Атанасов Г., *Печатите на българските владетели от IX–X в. в Дръстър (Силистра)*, [in:] *Оттука започва България. Материали от втората национална конференция по история, археология и културен туризъм "Пътуване към България", Шумен 14–16.05. 2010 година*, ed. И. Йорданов, Шумен 2011, pp. 286–293.

Атанасов Г., *Първата българска патриаршеска катедра в Дръстър и патриарх Дамян*, [in:] *Изследвания по българска средновековна археология. Сборник в чест на проф. Рашо Рашев*, ed. П. Георгиев, Велико Търново 2007, pp. 179–196.

Атанасов Г., *Християнският Дуросторум-Дръстър. Доростолската епархия през късната античност и Средновековието IV–XIV в. История, археология, култура и изкуство*, Варна 2007.

Атанасов Щ., Дуйчев И., Ангелов Д., Цанкова-Петкова Г., Христов Д., Чолпанов Б., *Българското военно изкуство през феодализма*, София 1958.

Атанасов Щ., Дуйчев И., Ангелов Д., Цанкова-Петкова Г., Христов Д., Чолпанов Б., *Стратегия и тактика на българската армия през епохата на феодализма*, ВС 26.4, 1957, pp. 39–72.

Аянов Г., *Стари пътища и селища край тях през Странджа и Сакар*, ИАИ 15, 1946, pp. 94–113.

Б а к а л о в Г., *Византийският културен модел в идейно-политическата структура на Първата българска държава*, Ист 3.4/5, 1994, pp. 13–27.

Б а к а л о в Г., *Средновековният български владетел. Титулатура и инсигнии*, [2]София 1995.

Б а к а л о в Г., *Цар Петър (927–970) и неговото време*, Ист 1.2, 1992, pp. 11–15.

Б а к а л о в Г., *Царската промулгация на Петър и неговите приемници в светлината на българо-византийските дипломатически отношения след договора от 927 г.*, ИП 39.6, 1983, pp. 35–44.

Б а к а л о в а Е., *Култът към мощите и реликвите: Изток–Запад*, [in:] *Средновековна християнска Европа: Изток и Запад. Ценности, традиции, общуване*, ed. В. Г ю з е л е в, А. М и л т е н о в а, София 2002, pp. 611–616.

Б а к а л о в а Е., *Общество и изкуство в България през XIII век*, ЗРВИ 46, 2009, pp. 239–253.

Б а л а б а н о в П., Б о я д ж и е в С., Т у л е ш к о в Н., *Крепостно строителство по българските земи*, София 2000.

Б а л а б а н о в Т., *Жилища покрай северната и източната крепостна стена на Плиска*, ППре 5, 1992, pp. 146–167.

Б а л а б а н о в Т., *За началото на стъклообработването и стъклопроизводството в Средновековна България*, [in:] Пр.Сб 3, 1983, pp. 228–240.

Б а л а б а н о в Т., *Проучване на старобългарския комплекс "Кирика" край с. Калугерица*, ПБА 1, 1992, 68–73.

Б а л а б а н о в Т., *Селище в югозападната част на Външния град на Плиска*, ППре 10, 2010, pp. 101–168.

Б а л а б а н о в Т., *Старобългарският манастир при с. Черноглавци (Предварително съобщение)*, ИИМШ 8, 1993, pp. 263–272.

Б а л а б а н о в Т., Т и х о в а М., *Надписът от 18 септември 6463 г. (954 г./955 г.) – от с. Черноглавци, Шуменско, България*, ПКШ 6, 2002, pp. 58–66.

Б а л а с ч е в Г., *Върху държавното и военно устройство в старобългарската държава*, Мин 1.2, 1909, pp. 203–216.

Б а л а с ч е в Г., *Укрепителните работи на старобългарската войска*, Мин 3.10 (1), 1918, pp. 1–44

Б а д б о л о в а-И в а н о в а М., *Средновековый Девелт в VIII–X вв.*, [in:] *Bulgaria Pontica Medii Aevi*, vol. IV–V/1, ed. В. Г ю з е л е в, София 2003, pp. 79–84.

Б а л т а к о в Г., К е н д е р о в а Р., *Кватернерна палеогеография*, Варна 2003.

Б е г у н о в Ю., *Козма Пресвитер в славянских литературах*, София 1973.

Б е р о в Л., *Икономическото развитие на България през вековете*, София 1974.

Бешевлиев В., *Географията на България у византийските автори*, ИНМВ 23 (38), 1987, pp. 37–70.

Бешевлиев В., *Из късноантичната и средновековната география на Североизточна България*, ИАИ 25, 1962, pp. 1–18.

Бешевлиевъ В., *Източната половина на Балканския полуостровъ като жизнено пространство въ миналото*, Прос 8.10, 1943, pp. 601–609.

Бешевлиев В., *Първобългарите. Бит и култура*, София 1981.

Бешевлиев В., *Първобългарски надписи (второ преработено и допълнено издание)*, София 1992.

Билярски И., *Небесните покровители: св. Цар Петър*, ИБ 2, 2001, pp. 32–44.

Билярски И., *Покровители на Царство. Св. Цар Петър и св. Параскева-Петка*, София 2004.

Билярски И., *Сказание на Исайя пророка и формирането на политическата идеология на ранносредновековна България*, София 2011.

Билярски И., *Фискална система на средновековна България*, Пловдив 2010.

Билярски И., Йовчева М., *За датата на успението на цар Петър и за култа към него*, [in:] *Тангра. Сборник в чест на 70-годишнината на акад. Васил Гюзелев*, ed. М. Каймакавова et al., София 2006, pp. 543–557.

Благоев Н.П., *Българският цар Роман*, МПр 6.3, 1930, pp. 15–34.

Благоев Н.П., *Критичен поглед върху известията на Лъв Дякон за българите*, МПр 6.1, 1930, pp. 25–48.

Бобчева Л., *Глинени котли от ранносредновековното селище при с. Топола, Толбухински окръг*, ИНМВ 16 (31), 1980, pp. 126–130.

Бобчева Л., *Две грънчарски пещи в ранносредновековното селище при с. Топола, Толбухински окръг*, ИНМВ 13 (28), 1977, pp. 172–176.

Богданов И., *Български твърдини. Книжовни средища, крепости, манастири в София и Софийско*, София 1971.

Боев З., *Костни останки от птици*, [in:] Ж. Въжарова, *Средновековното селище с. Гарван, Силистренски окръг VI–XI в.*, София 1986, p. 68.

Боев З., Илиев Н., *Птиците и тяхното значение за жителите на Велики Преслав (IX–X в.)*, Архе 33.3, 1991, pp. 44–53.

Божилов И., *Българийа и печензите (896–1018 g.)*, 29.2, 1973, pp. 53–62.

Божилов И., *Българите във Византийската Империя*, София 1995.

Божилов И., *Българското общество през 14. век. Структура и просопография*, София 2014.

Божилов И., *Византийският свят*, София 2008.

Божилов И., *Цар Симеон Велики (893–927): Златният век на Средновековна България*, София 1983.

Божилов И., Гюзелев В., *История на Добруджа*, vol. II, *Средновековие*, Велико Търново 2004.

Божилов И., Гюзелев В., *История на средновековна България VII–XIV в.*, София 1999, ²2006.

Бондарь С., *Философско-мировоззренческое содержание "Изборников" 1073–1076 гг.*, Киев 1990.

Бонев С., *За преславската костена пластика*, ПКШ 1, 1995, pp. 344–347.

Бонев С., *Преславската резба върху кост – стари творби и нови находки*, [in:] *Иванка Акрабова-Жандова. In memoriam*, ed. М. Ваклинова et al., София 2009, pp. 143–153.

Бонев С., *Столицата Велики Преслав през X в. – не просто град, а агломерация*, [in:] *Градът в българските земи (по археологически данни). Материали от националната научна конференция посветена на живота и делото на ст.н.с. Вера Антонова. Шумен, 31 октомври – 1 ноември 2013 г.*, ed. П. Георгиев, Шумен 2014, pp. 273–278.

Бонев С., *Творби на металопластиката със светци от Преслав*, ПКШ 7, 2004, pp. 404–411.

Бонев С., *Художествената резба върху кост – връзки и влияния с другите приложни техники през X век*, Пр.Сб 3, 1983, pp. 149–159.

Бонев С., Дончева С., *Старобългарски производствен център за художествен метал при с. Новосел, Шуменско*, Велико Търново 2011.

Бонева В., *Паисий Хилендарски и неговият исторически текст във възрожденската публичност*, LN 8 (153), http://liternet.bg/publish8/vboneva/paisij.htm, accessed: 28.11.2017.

Борисов Б., *Средновековното село през IX–XII в. на територията на днешна Югоизточна България*, [in:] [in:] *Проф. д.и.н. Станчо Ваклинов и средновековната българска култура*, ed. К. Попконстантинов, Б. Борисов, Р. Костова, Велико Търново 2005, pp. 310–317.

Бояджиев Н., *Крепостната система в Средните Родопи през късната античност и средновековието*, [in:] *Laurea. In honorem Margaritae Vaklinova*, ed. Б. Петрунова, А. Аладжов, Е. Василева, vol. I, София 2009, pp. 103–110.

Бояджиев С., *Архитектурата на българите от VII до XIV век в три тома*, vol. I, *Дохристиянска архитектура*, София 2008.

Бояджиев С., *Крепостно строителство през Първото българско царство*, [in:] П. Балабанов, С. Бояджиев, Н. Тулешков, *Крепостно строителство по българските земи*, София 2000, pp. 135–186.

Б о я д ж и е в С., *Ново тълкувание на раннобългарския манастир в местността "Черешето" във Велики Преслав*, ПКШ 5, 2000, pp. 76–85.

Б о я д ж и е в С., *Църквата в Патлейна в светлината на нови данни*, Архе 2.4, 1960, pp. 22–33.

Б у л а н и н Д., *Античные традиции в древнерусской литературе XI–XVI вв.*, München 1991.

Б у л а н и н Д., *Житие Павла Фивейского – болгарский перевод X в.*, КМС 10, 1995, pp. 5–21.

Б у л а н и н Д., *"Кормчая книга" и "Книга Кормчий" (Семантика названий двух древнерусских книг)*, РЛи, 2017.2, pp. 5–18.

Б у л а н и н Д., *Неизвестный источник Изборника 1076 г.*, ТОДРЛ 44, 1990, pp. 161–178.

Б у л а н и н Д., *Текстологические и библиографические арабески. VII. "Наставление" Агапита: несколько эпизодов из истории славянской рецепции*, [in:] *Каталог памятников древнерусской письменности XI–XIV вв. (Рукописные книги)*, ed. i d e m, Санкт-Петербург 2014, pp. 530–559.

Българският златен век. Сборник в чест на цар Симеон Велики (893–927), ed. В. Г ю з е л е в, И.Г. И л и е в, К. Н е н о в, Пловдив 2015.

В а к а р е л с к и Х., *Етнография на България*, София 1974.

В а к л и н о в С., *Архитектура*, [in:] *История на България в четиринадесет тома*, vol. II, *Първа българска държава*, ed. Д. А н г е л о в, София 1981, pp. 423–430.

В а к л и н о в С., *Бит, строителство и изкуство*, [in:] *История на България в четиринадесет тома*, vol. II, *Първа българска държава*, ed. Д. А н г е л о в, София 1981, pp. 181–198.

В а к л и н о в С., *Втората българска столица Преслав*, [in:] *История на България в четиринадесет тома*, vol. II, *Първа българска държава*, ed. Д. А н г е л о в, София 1981, pp. 296–300.

В а к л и н о в С., *За характера на раннобългарската селищна мрежа в Североизточна България*, Архе 14.1, 1972, pp. 9–13.

В а к л и н о в С., *Плиска за тридесет години*, Архе 16.3, 1974, pp. 28–38.

В а к л и н о в С., *Формиране на старобългарската култура. VI–XI в.*, София 1977.

В а к л и н о в а М., *Градът на българското средновековие*, [in:] *Bulgarian medieval town. Technologies*, ed. И. Щ е р е в а, К. М а л а м е д, София 1995, pp. 2–6.

В а к л и н о в а М., *Материали и производство на преславската каменна пластика*, Пр.Сб 5, 1993, pp. 68–101.

В а к л и н о в а М., Щ е р е в а И., *Княз Борис I и владетелската църква на Велики Преслав*, [in:] *Християнската култура в средновековна България. Материали от национална научна конференция, Шумен, 2–4 май 2007 г., по случай 1100 години от смъртта на св. Княз Борис-Михаил (ок. 835–907 г.)*, ed. П. Г е о р г и е в, Велико Търново 2008, pp. 185–194.

В а л ь д е н б е р г В., *Наставление писателя VI в. Агапита в русской письменности*, ВВ 24, 1923/1926, pp. 27–34.

В а п ц а р о в И., В е л е в С., Й о р д а н о в а М., Г о р у н о в а Д., *Рило-Родопска област*, [in:] *География на България в три тома*, vol. III, *Физико-географско и социално-икономическо*, ed. К. М и ш е в, София 1989, pp. 166–219.

В а с и л е в В., *Ихтиманският край в древността*, Век 18.6, 1989, pp. 47–58.

В а с и л е в В., *Животновъдство и лов в живота на населението от средновековното селище край Дуранкулак*, [in:] *Дуранкулак*, ed. Х. Т о д о р о в а, vol. I, София 1989, pp. 223–248.

В а с и л е в Р., *Колекция от ранносредновековна керамика и съдове уникати от манастира до спирка Равна, Провадийско*, [in:] *Тангра. Сборник в чест на 70–годишнината на акад. Васил Гюзелев*, ed. М. К а й м а к а м о в а et al., София 2006, pp. 367–382.

В а с и л е в Р., *Проучванията на славянските археологически паметници от Северна България от края на VI до края на X в.*, Архе 21.3, 1979, pp. 12–22.

В а с и л е в Р., *Функции и развитие на масовото жилище-полуземлянка в средновековна Плиска*, ППре 8, 2000, pp. 103–107.

В а ч к о в а В., *Понятието "Запад" в историческата аргументация на средновековна България*, SB 25, 2006, pp. 295–303.

В а ч к о в а В., *Симеон Велики. Пътят към короната на Запада*, София 2005.

В е л е в а М., *Васил Златарски като историк на българската историческа наука*, ИБИД 32, 1978, pp. 305–313.

В е л е в а М., *Спиридон Палаузов – историк на Средна и Югоизточна Европа*, [in:] С. П а л а у з о в, *Избрани трудове*, vol. II, ed. М. В е л е в а, София 1977, pp. 7–46.

В е л е в а М., *Юрий Иванович Венелин в българската историография*, ИБИД 26, 1984, pp. 171–191.

В е л и к о в Ю., *Иконопочитанието и иконоотрицанието в "Беседа против богомилите" на Козма Презвитер*, [in:] *ΤΡΙΑΝΤΑΦΥΛΛΟ. Юбилеен сборник в чест на 60-годишнината на проф. Христо Трендафилов*, ed. В. П а н а й о т о в, vol. I, Шумен 2013, pp. 365–374.

В е л к о в И., *Няколко тракийски и средновековни крепости по Средна Арда*, ИБИД 16/18, 1940, pp. 70–78.

В е л к о в И., *Трояновите врата*, Век 1.3, 1931, pp. 33–35.

В е л ч е в В., *Отецъ Паисий Хилендарски и Цезаръ Бароний*, София 1943.

В е л ч е в а Б., *Новооткрити ръкописи в Синайския манастир "Св. Екатерина"*, Pbg 12.3, 1988, pp. 126–129.

В е н е д и к о в И., *Военното и административното устройство на България през IX и X век*, София 1979.

В е н е д и к о в И., *Прабългарите и християнството*, Стара Загора 1998.

Венелин Ю.И., *Критическія изслѣдованія объ исторіи Болгаръ: Съ прихода Болгаръ на Ѳракійскій полуостровъ до 986 года, или покоренія Болгаріи Великимъ Княземъ Русскимъ, Святославомъ*, Москва 1849.

Венелин Ю.И., *Критическы издыянія за исторіѭ-тѫ българскѫ. Отъ прихожденіе-то на Българе-ты на Ѳракыйскый полуостровъ до 968 годинѫ, или до покореніе-то Българіѭ отъ Великый Князь Русский*, vol. II, transl. Б. Петков, Земунъ 1853.

Вилкул Т., *Літопис і хронограф. Студії з домонгольського київського літописання*, Київ 2015.

Витлянов С., *Данни за обработката на желязо в центровете на Първото българско царство*, [in:] *Средновековният български град*, ed. П. Петров, София 1980, pp. 137–143.

Витлянов С., *За някои моменти в развитието на българското средновековно железообработване*, [in:] *Медиевистични изследвания в памет на Пейо Димитров*, ed. Т. Тотев, Шумен 1995, pp. 306–314.

Витлянов С., *За стопанския облик на манастира при Голямата базилика в Плиска*, Архе 26.2/3, 1984, pp. 95–102.

Витлянов С., *Новооткрити накитни предмети и елемнти на облеклото от Велики Преслав*, ПКШ 7, 2004, pp. 412–423.

Витлянов С., *Старобългарско въоръжение (По археологически данни от Плиска, Мадара и Велики Преслав)*, София 1996.

Витлянов С., *Стопанският облик на столичните манастири през IX–X век*, ППре 7, 1995, pp. 92–100.

Витлянов С., *Характер и локализация на производствените структури в първите столични центрове на българската държава Плиска и Велики Преслав*, [in:] *Пътуванията в средновековна България. Материали от първата национална конференция "Пътуване към България. Пътуванията в средновековна България и съвременният туризъм", Шумен, 8–11.05.2008 г.*, ed. И. Йорданов, Велико Търново 2009, pp. 373–381.

Витлянов С., Димитров Я., *Защитно въоръжение от Преслав*, Пр.Сб 5, 1993, pp. 165–177.

Владимиров Г., *Византийско-българският културен диалог в светлината на едно наказание*, Мин 5.3, 1998, pp. 15–19.

Владимиров Г., *Дунавска България и Волжска България. Формиране и промяна на културните модели (VII–XI в.)*, София 2005.

Власова З.И., *Скоморохи и фольклор*, Санкт-Петербург 2001.

Войниковъ Д., *Кратка българрска исторія*, Вѣна 1861.

Войнов М., *Някои въпроси във връзка с образуването на българската държава и покръстването на българите*, ИИИ 10, 1962, p. 279–309.

Войнов М., *Промяната в българо-византийските отношения при цар Симеон*, ИИИ 18, 1967, pp. 147–202.

Войнов М., Тъпкова-Заимова В., *България на Аспарух и България на Кубер*, ВС 51.5, 1982, pp. 47–56.

Војиновић С., *Хронологија живота и рада Јована Рајића*, [in:] *Јован Рајић – живот и дело*, ed. М. Фрајнд, Београд, 1997, pp. 7–27.

Въжарова Ж., *Селища и некрополи (края на VI–XI в.)*, Архе 16.3, 1974, pp. 9–27.

Въжарова Ж., *Славяни и прабългари по данни на некрополите от VI–XI в. на територията на България*, София 1976.

Въжарова Ж., *Средновековни обекти по долините на реките Цибрица и Огоста (по материали от разузнаването през 1962–1963 г.)*, ИАИ 28, 1965, pp. 231–245.

Вълов В., *Водоснабдяването на средновековните български градове и крепости (VII–XIV в.)*, Архе 19.1, 1977, pp. 14–30.

Вълов В., *Седалището и териториалният обхват на Бдинската област от средата на IX до началото на XI век*, ИМСБ 13, 1987, pp. 21–45.

Гагова К., *Кръстоносните походи и средновековна България*, София 2004.

Гагова К., *Тракия през българското Средновековие. Историческа география*, [2]София 2002.

Гандев Р., *Животът и делото на проф. Петър Мутафчиев*, ГСУ.ЦК 86, 1993, pp. 95–107.

Ганева Р., *Знаците на българското традиционно облекло*, София 2003.

Генадиева В., Чохаджиев С., *Археологически паметници от Кюстендилско*, vol. I, *Археологически паметници от Кюстендилското краище*, Велико Търново 2002.

Генадиева В., Чохаджиев С., *Археологически паметници от Кюстендилско*, vol. II, *Археологически паметници от Каменица*, Велико Търново 2003.

Генчев Н., *Българската култура XV–XIX в. Лекции*, София 1988.

Генчев Н., *Българско възраждане*, София 1981.

География на България в три тома, vol. III, *Физико-географско и социално-икономическо*, ed. К. Мишев, София 1989.

Георгиев Е., *Литература на изострени борби*, София 1966.

Георгиев Е., *Паисий Хилендарски – между Ренесанса и Просвещението*, [in:] *Паисий Хилендарски и неговата епоха (1762–1962). Сборник от изследвания по случай 200-годишнината от История славянобълграска*, ed. Д. Косев et. al., София 1962, pp. 253–284.

Георгиев Е., *Разцветът на българската литература в IX–XI в.*, София 1962

Георгиев И., *Военни пътища и преградни съоръжения в Ришкия проход*, ВС 62.2, 1993, pp. 5–23.

Георгиев И., *Ранновизантийски и средновековни български укрепления за отбраната на Айтоския проход*, ВС 64.2, 1995, pp. 7–27.

Георгиев П., *Българските племенни имена и соционимът уногундури*, [in:] *Civitas Divino-Humana. In honorem Annorum LX Georgii Bakalov*, ed. Ц. Степанов, В. Вачкова, София 2004, pp. 693–708.

Георгиев П., *Главният път Византия – България до края на VIII век*, [in:] *Пътуванията в средновековна България. Материали от първата национална конференция "Пътуване към България. Пътуванията в средновековна България и съвременният туризъм", Шумен, 8–11.05.2008 г.*, ed. И. Йорданов, Велико Търново 2009, pp. 84–103.

Георгиев П., *Главният път през Веригава през ранното средновековие*, [in:] *История на пътя. Черно море между Изтока и Запада. XII-ти Понтийски четения във ВСУ "Черноризец Храбър"*, ed. С. Табакова-Стоева, Варна 2007, pp. 7–25.

Георгиев П., *Дипломатически и търговски знаци-печати във Византия и славянските страни*, ГСУ.НЦСВПИД 82 (2), 1988, pp. 21–32.

Георгиев П., *Манастирската църква при с. Равна, Провадийско*, ИНМВ 21, 1985, pp. 71–97.

Георгиев П., *Манастирът от X век при с. Черноглавци, Шуменска област*, ГСУ.ЦСВПИД 12, 2003, pp. 71–79.

Георгиев П., *Превратът през 927 г.*, ПКШ 10, 2008, pp. 424–438.

Георгиев П., *Разкопки южно от Големия басейн в Плиска*, ППре 10, 2004, pp. 24–59.

Георгиев П., *Ранобългарската култура V–VII век – култура "на колела"*, [in:] *Изследвания по българска средновековна археология. Сборник в чест на проф. Рашо Рашев*, ed. idem, Велико Търново 2007, pp. 22–40.

Георгиев П., *Столиците на княз Борис-Михаил – хронология и типологическа характеристика*, [in:] *Християнската култура в средновековна България. Материали от национална научна конференция, Шумен 2–4 май 2007 година по случай 1100 години от смъртта на св. Княз Борис-Михаил (ок. 835–907 г.)*, ed. idem, Велико Търново 2008, pp. 154–163.

Георгиев П., *Терveловите "чичовци" в Солунско и Кисиниите (към интерпретацията на Мадарския надпис I, ц)*, [in:] *Приноси към българската археология*, vol. VII, ed. Б. Петрунова, А. Аладжов, Е. Василева, София 2013, pp. 27–44.

Георгиев П., *Титлата и функциите на българския престолонаследник и въпросът за престолонаследието при цар Симеон (893–927)*, ИП 48.8/9, 1992, pp. 3–12.

Георгиев П., *Хинтерландът на Абоба-Плиска: пътни комуникации, селищни и военни средища*, [in:] *Eurika. In honorem Ludmilae Donchevae-Petkovae*, ed. В. Григоров, М. Даскалов, Е. Коматарова-Балинова, София 2009, pp. 333–353.

Георгиев П., Витлянов С., *Архиепископията-манастир в Плиска*, София 2001.

Георгиева Н., *Към въпроса за почитанието на княз Борис I като светец*, КМС 8 1991, pp. 178–188.

Георгиева С., *Жената в българското средновековие*, Пловдив 2011.

Георгиева С., *Цар Самуил в съперничество с Византия за контрол над Виа Егнация и Драч*, Епо 25.1, 2017, pp. 188–195.

Георгиева С., *Черно море като географски фактор в историята на Първото българско царство*, [in:] *Средновековните Балкани: политика, религия, култура*, ed. Л. Симеонова, София 1999, pp. 28–32.

Геров Н., *Речник на българския език*, vol. V, Пловдив 1904.

Гиздова Н., *Средновековни крепости в Родопите на територията на Пазарджишки окръг*, ИМЮБ 9, 1983, pp. 69–78.

Гильфердингъ А.Ф., *Исторія сербовъ и болгаръ*, [in:] idem, *Собрание сочинений*, vol. I, С.-Петербургъ 1868, pp. 1–296.

Гильфердингъ А.Ф., *Письма объ истории сербовъ и болгаръ*, Москва 1855.

Голийски П., *В подножието на Елбрус (Българите около Кавказ през II–V век според арменските извори)*, [in:] *Древните българи – дискусията продължава. Сборник*, ed. Ц. Степанов, София 2014, pp. 27–35.

Горина Л., *Марин Дринов – историк и общественный деятель*, Москва 1986.

Господинов К., *Легитимизъм и узурпация. Власт и политически взаимоотношения в Българското царство: 1241–1279. Автореферат*, София 2009.

Григоров В., *Метални накити от средновековна България (VII–XI в.)*, София 2007.

Григорович В., *О древнейших памятниках церковно-славянских*, ИОРЯС 1.3, 1852, pp. 86–99.

Гълъбова В., *История на Ихтиман*, vol. I, София 2007.

Гюзелев В., *Анхиало*, [in:] *Български средновековни градове и крепости*, vol. I, *Градове и крепости по Дунав и Черно Море*, ed. А. Кузев, В. Гюзелев, Варна 1981, p. 356–382.

Гюзелев В., *Апология на Средновековието*, [in:] idem, *Съчинения в пет тома*, vol. I, *Апология на Средновековието. Покръстване на българите*, София 2013, pp. 18–224.

Гюзелев В. *Бележки върху историята на българските земи и българите половин столетие преди въстанието на Асеневци (1186–1188)*, [in:] *Проф. д.и.н. Станчо Ваклинов и средновековната българска култура*, ed. К. Попконстантинов, Б. Борисов, Р. Костова, Велико Търново 2005, pp. 98–107.

Гюзелев В., *Бележки върху йерархическия статус на Българската църква и нейния върховен предстоятел през първия век от покръстването 865–971*, [in:] *Религия и църква в България. Социални и културни иммерения в православието и неговата специфика в Българските земи*, ed. Г. Бакалов, София 1999, pp. 98–107.

Гюзелев В., *Българските пратеничества при германския император Отон I в Магдебург (965 г.) и в Кведлинбург (973 г.)*, [in:] *Civitas Divino-Humana. In honorem Annorum LX Georgii Bakalov*, ed. Ц. Степанов, В. Вачкова, София 2004, p. 385–396.

Гюзелев В., *"Велико светило за целия свят" (Св. Иван Рилски в измеренията на своето време)*, [in:] *Светогорска обител Зограф*, vol. III, ed. idem, София 1999, pp. 13–24.

Гюзелев В., *Добруджанският надпис и събитията в България през 943 г.*, ИП 24.6, 1968, pp. 40–48.

Гюзелев В., *Живот и научно творчество на Петър Мутафчиев (1883–1943)*, [in:] П. Мутафчиев, *История на българския народ (681–1323)*, ed. В. Гюзелев, София 1986, pp. 6–34.

Гюзелев В., *Зараждане и развитие на старобългарската култура и изкуство*, [in:] *Кратка история на България*, ed. И. Димитров, София 1981, pp. 90–95.

Гюзелев В., *Значението на брака на цар Петър (927–969) с ромейката Мария-Ирина Лакапина (911–962)*, [in:] *Културните текстове на миналото – носители, символи, идеи*, vol. I, *Текстовете на историята, история на текстовете. Материали от Юбилейната международна конференция в чест на 60-годишнината на проф. д.и.н. Казимир Попконстантинов, Велико Търново, 29–31 октомври 2003 г.*, София 2005, pp. 27–33.

Гюзелев В., *Извори за средновековната история на България (VII–XIV в.) в австрийските ръкописни сбирки и архиви*, София 1994.

Гюзелев В., *Икономическо развитие, социална структура и форми на социална и политическа организация на прабългарите до образуването на българската държава (IV–VII в.)*, Архе 21.4, 1979, p. 12–21.

Гюзелев В., *Кавханите и ичиргу боилите на Българското ханство-царство*, Пловдив 2007.

Гюзелев В., *Княз Борис Първи. България през втората половина на IX век*, София 1969.

Гюзелев В., *Петър Мутафчиев*, София 1987.

Гюзелев В., *Сведения за българите в Житието на свети Фантино Млади от X в.*, Pbg 36.2, 2012, p. 31–38.

Гюзелев В., *Студийският манастир и българите през средновековието (VIII–IX)*, ЗРВИ 39, 2001/2002, pp. 51–65.

Гюзелев В., *Средновековният Анхиало (VI–XV в.)*, [in:] *История на Поморие*, vol. I, *Древност и съвремие*, ed. А. Орачев, В. Василчина, Бургас 2011, pp. 45–65.

Гюзелев В., *Устройство на българската църква*, [in:] *История на България в четиринадесет тома*, vol. II, *Първа българска държава*, ed. Д. Ангелов, София 1981, pp. 228–234.

Гюзелев В., *Училища, скриптории, библиотеки и знания в България (XIII–XIV век)*, София 1985.

Гюзелев Б., *Черноморската област в историята на Българското царство от възобновяването му (1186 г.) до възобновяването на Византийската империя (1261 г.)*, [in:] *Studia archaeologica. Supplementum II. Сборник в чест на професор Атанас Милчев*, София 2002, pp. 233–249.

Гюзелев В., *Черноморската област в политическата история на Средновековна България*, [in:] *Чиракман–Карвуна–Каварна. Сборник*, ed. В. Василев, М. Велев, София 1982, pp. 76–82.

Данилевский И., *Повесть временных лет: герменевтические основы изучения летописных тестов*, Москва 2004.

Данова П., *Писал ли е Франц-Ксавер Пеячевич история на българите?*, ИБ 20.1/2, 2016, pp. 41–63.

Данчев Г., *Близост и различия в епизода за неосъществената среща между св. Иван Рилски и цар Петър в житията на Рилския светец*, ИИМК 5, 1993, София 1998, pp. 71–76.

Данчева-Василева А., *Град Сердика (Средец) в политическата история на България (809–1018 г.)*, ИП 60.3/4, 2004, pp. 3–35.

Данчева-Василева А., *История на средновековна София от IV–XIV век*, София 2017.

Данчева-Василева А., *Павликяните в Северна Тракия през Средновековието*, ИБ 7.1/2, 2003, pp. 172–194.

Данчева-Василева А., *Пловдив през Средновековието IV–XIV в.*, София 2009.

Данчева-Василева А., *Шарл Дюканж и средновековната българска история*, ИП 38.4, 1982, pp. 91–102.

Деведжиев М., *Кратка история на селищното развитие по българските земи*, София 1979.

Дел'Агата Дж., *Паисий Хилендарски и руската версия на "Царството на славяните" на Мавро Орбини*, [in:] *Царството на славяните. История от дон Мавро Орбини от Рагуза, абат от Млетския орден*, ed. П. Ватова, transl. С. Тодоров, Е. Попова, София 2012, pp. 17–24.

Дероко А., *Средновековни град Скопје*, САН.С 120, 1971, pp. 1–16.

Джамбов И.Х., *Средновековното селище над античния град при Хисар*, Асеновград 2002.

Джингов Г., *Археологически проучвания на поселищния живот в средновековна България*, Век 8.3, 1979, pp. 48–56.

Джингов Г., *Тиризис. Акре. Калиакра*, ²Каварна 2010.

Джонов Б., *Още за Добруджанския надпис от 943 година*, [in:] *Лингвистични и етнолингвистични изследвания в памет на акад. Вл. Георгиев (1908–1986)*, ed. Ж. Бояджиев, И. Дуриданов, София 1993, pp. 159–165.

Димитров Б., *Агатопол*, [in:] *Български средновековни градове и крепости*, vol. I, *Градове и крепости по Дунав и Черно Море*, ed. А. Кузев, В. Гюзелев, Варна 1981, pp. 412–426.

Димитров Б., *Созопол*, [in:] *Български средновековни градове и крепости*, vol. I, *Градове и крепости по Дунав и Черно Море*, ed. А. Кузев, В. Гюзелев, Варна 1981, pp. 388–407.

Димитров Б., *Средновековна България и морето. Исторически очерк*, Мор 3.2, 1981, pp. 219–231.

Димитров Б., Хаджийски А., *Каменните щитове на България*, София 1988.

Димитров Д.И., *Възникването на градски центрове в Североизточна България*, [in:] *Средновековният български град*, ed. П. Петров, София 1980, pp. 35–45.

Димитров Д.И., *Новооткрит раннобългарски некропол при Девня*, ИНМВ 7 (22), 1971, pp. 57–76.

Димитров Д.И., *Някои въпроси във връзка с изучаването на старобългарското масово жилище от VI–XI в. в Североизточна България*, [in:] *Архитектурата на Първата и Втората българска държава. Материали*, ed. Г. Кожухаров, София 1975, pp. 212–245.

Димитров Д.И., *Погребалният обред на раннобългарските некрополи във Варненско*, ИАИ 34, 1974, pp. 51–94.

Димитров Д.Й., *Масата събира, масата разделя: храната и храненето във Византия и различията по отношение на хранителните навици през Средновековието*, [in:] *Стандарти на всекидневието през Средновековието и Новото време*, ed. К. Мутафова et al., Велико Търново 2012, pp. 21–31.

Димитров Х., *Българо-унгарски отношения през средновековието*, София 1998.

Димитров Х., *История на Македония*, София 2004.

Димитрова А., *Златоструят в преводаческата дейност на старобългарските книжовници*, София 2016, pp. 218–223.

Димитрова А., *Псевдо-Златоустовото слово "За лъжепророците" в "Беседа против богомилите" – цитиране или нов превод?*, KWSS 9, 2014, pp. 23–32.

Димитрова Д., *Археологически паметници във Врачански окръг*, София 1985.

Динев Л., Мелнишки Л., *Стара планина*, София 1962.

Динеков П., *Паисий Хилендарски*, [in:] Паисий Хилендарски, *Славяно-българска история*, transl. П. Динеков, София 1972, pp. 7–31.

Добрев И., *Българите за руския народ, държава и култура*, София 2011.

Добрев И., Томова Е., *Болгарский святой Иоанн Рылский (культ и агиография)*, [in:] *Слово: към изграждане на дигитална библиотека на южнославянски ръкописи*, ed. Х. Миклас, А. Милтенова, София 2008, pp. 135–165.

Добрев П., *Стопанска култура на прабългарите*, София 1986.

Добрева Ж., *Пътната мрежа между Плиска и Ришния проход VII–IX век*, [in:] *Пътуванията в средновековна България. Материали от първата национална конференция "Пътуване към България. Пътуванията в средновековна България и съвременният туризъм", Шумен, 8–11.05.2008 г.*, ed. И. Йорданов, Велико Търново 2009, pp. 151–158.

Дончева С., *Към манастирското устройство в околностите на столичните центрове в Първото българско царство*, ПКШ 7, 2003, pp. 438–449.

Дончева-Петкова Л., *Българска битова керамика през ранното средновековие*, София 1977.

Дончева-Петкова Л., *Нови данни за некропол № 3 при Балчик*, ППИК 4.2, 2007, pp. 121–143.

Дончева-Петкова Л., *Одърци. Селище от Първото българско царство*, vol. I, София 1999.

Дончева-Петкова Л., *Отново за началото на ранносредновековната българска култура*, SAUS.S 5, 2010, pp. 511–526.

Дончева-Петкова Л., *Пещи за добиване на желязо край западната крепостна стена на Плиска*, ППре 7, 1995, pp. 34–41.

Дончева-Петкова Л., *Сгради при южния сектор на западната крепостна стена на Плиска*, ППре 5, 1993, pp. 124–145.

Дончева-Петкова Л., *Средновековни глинени съдове с вътрешни уши*, Архе 13.4, 1971, pp. 32–38.

Дончева-Петкова Л., *Технология на раннославянската и старобългарската битова керамика (края на VI–X в.)*, Архе 11.2, 1969, pp. 10–24.

Дончева-Петкова Л., *Трапезната керамика в България през VIII–XI в.*, Архе 12.1, 1970, pp. 12–25.

Дончева-Петкова Л., Златинова Ж., *Стъкларска работилница край западната стена в Плиска*, Архе 20.4, 1978, pp. 37–48.

Дончева С., *Медалиони от средновековна България*, Велико Търново 2007.

Дочев К., *Стари римски пътища в Централна Долна Мизия (II–IV в. сл. Хр.)*, ИРИМВТ 7.4, 1994, pp. 61–76.

Драгова Н., *Домашни извори на "История славянобългарска"*, [in:] *Паисий Хилендарски и неговата епоха (1762–1962). Сборник от изследвания по случай 200-годишнината от История славянобълграска*, ed. Д. Косев et al., София 1962, pp. 285–340.

Драгојловић Д., *Богомилство на Балкану и у Малој Азији*, vol. I, *Богомилски родоначалници*, Београд 1974.

Дражева Ц., *Най-южната българска черноморска крепост Ахтопол*, [in:] *Каварна. Средище на българския Североизток. Сборник доклади от научна конференция Каварна – 2007 г.*, ed. eadem, Х. Кузов, Д. Мирчева, Каварна 2007, pp. 211–221.

Дремсизова-Нелчинова Ц., Иванов Д., *Археологически паметници в Русенски окръг*, София 1983.

Дринов М.С., *Отец Паисий, неговото време, неговата История и учениците му*, [in:] idem, *Избрани съчинения*, ed. И. Дуйчев, vol. I, София 1971, pp. 163–185.

Дринов М.С., *Съчинения. Трудове по Българска и Славянска история*, ed. В.Н. Златарски, vol. I, София 1909.

Дроснева Е., *Златарски, Рънсиман и историята на първата българска държава*, ИБИД 32, 1978, pp. 331–339.

Дроснева Е., *Три етюда за Венелин*, ИБИД 26, 1984, pp. 201–207.

Дуйчев И., *Блазиус Клайнер и неговата "История на България" от 1761 година*, [in:] *История на България от Блазиус Клайнер съставена в 1761 г.*, ed. idem, К. Телбизов, София 1977, pp. 5–21.

Дуйчев И., *Български спогодбен акт от епохата на византийското владичество*, [in:] idem, *Българско средновековие. Проучвания върху политическата и културната история на средновековна България*, София 1972, pp. 209–215.

Дуйчев И., *Българският княз Пленимир*, МПр 13.1, 1942, pp. 13–20.

Дуйчев И., *Българско средновековие. Проучвания върху политическата и културната история на средновековна България*, София 1972.

Дуйчев И., *Едно пренебрегнато византийско известие за богомилите*, [in:] idem, *Проучвания върху средновековната българска история и култура*, София 1981, pp. 203–206.

Дуйчев И., *Из старата българска книжнина*, vol. I, София 1943.

Дуйчевъ И., *Обаянието на проф. Мутафчиев*, Прос 8.10, 1943, pp. 583–586.

Дуйчев И., *Отношенията между южните славяни и Византия през X–XII в.*, [in:] idem, *Избрани произведения*, vol. I, *Византия и славянския свят*, ed. И. Божилов, transl. Е. Рускова, П. Данова, София 1998, pp. 45–86.

Дуйчев И., *Приносът на Марин Дринов в областта на българската историография*, [in:] М. Дринов, *Избрани съчинения*, ed. И. Дуйчев, vol. I, *Трудове по българска и славянска история*, София 1971, pp. 7–34.

Дуйчев И., *Проблеми из средновековната история на Преслав*, [in:] idem, *Проучвания върху средновековната българска история и култура*, София 1981, pp. 17–26.

Д у й ч е в И., *Проучвания върху средновековната българска история и култура*, София 1981.

Д у й ч е в И., *Рилският светец и неговата обител*, София 1947.

Дуросторум–Дръстър–Силистра: сборник с изследвания, ed. С. Х р и с т о в, Р. Л и п ч е в, Г. А т а н а с о в, Силистра 1988.

Д ы л е в с к и й Н.М., *Жития Иоанна Рыльского русских древлехранилищ и их болгарские источники (Краткие заметки к материалам и задачи дальнейшего исследования)*, ТОДРЛ 23, 1968, pp. 276–292.

Д ь о л г е р Ф., *Средновековното „семейство на владетелите и народите" и българският владетел*, СБАН.КИФ 62, 1943, pp. 181–222.

Е в т и м о в а Е., *Занаятчийски изделия от Велики Преслав*, [in:] *Иванка Акрабова-Жандова. In memoriam*, ed. М. В а к л и н о в а et al., София 2009, pp. 199–211.

Ж е к о в Ж., *България и Византия. Военна администрация VII–IX в.*, София 2007.

Ж е л и н к с и Б., *Исотиря, памет, народ: историографиите на Паисий Хилендарски и Йован Раич*, ПУПХБ.НТФ 50/1/А, 2012, pp. 9–19.

Ж и в к о в и ћ Т., *Јужни Словени под византијском влашћу 600–1025*, Београд 2002.

Ж и в к о в и ћ Т., *Портрети владара раног средњег века. Од Властимира до Борића*, Београд 2006

З а и м о в а Р., *Българската тема в западноевропейската книжнина XV–XVII век*, София 1992.

З а и м о в а Р., *Подходът на балканския писател към историческата тема (XVIII век)*, ИБ 5.1, 2001, pp. 96–103.

З а ш е в Е., *Наименования на съдове за течности и храни в Синайския патерик*, Ист 13.2/3, 2005, pp. 91–99.

З в е з д о в С., *Българо-византийските отношения при цар Петър*, Мин 2016, 3, pp. 11–18.

З в е з д о в С., *Българо-византийските отношения при цар Петър I*, София 2016.

З в е з д о в С., *Договорът от 927 година между България и Византия*, H.BJHE 23.3, 2015, pp. 264–277.

З л а т а р с к и В.Н., *Известията за българите в хрониката на Симеон Метафраст и Логотет*, [in:] i d e m, *Избрани произведения в четири тома*, vol. I, ed. П. П е т р о в, София 1972, pp. 359–573.

З л а т а р с к и В.И., *История на българската държава през средните векове*, vol. I/2, *Първо българско Царство. От славянизацията на държавата до падането на Първото царство (852–1018)*, София 1927, [2]1971.

З л а т а р с к и В.Н., *История на българската държава през средните векове*, vol. II, *България под византийско владичество*, София [3]1994.

З л а т а р с к и В.Н., *Кои са били вътрешни и външни боляри?*, [in:] *Юбилеен сборник в чест на С.С. Бобчев*, София 1921, pp. 45–57.

З л а т а р с к и В.Н., *Писмата на византийския императоръ Романа Лакапена до българския царъ Симеона*, СНУНК 13, 1896, pp. 282–322.

З л а т а р с к и В.Н., *Тъй наречените "грамоти" на Пинчия и неговия син Плезо*, ГСУ 15/16, 1919/1920, pp. 1–54.

З ъ к о в Е., *К биографии Константина Преславского*, *СЛ 2*, 1977, pp. 74–101.

И в а н о в И., *Гривести прабългарски барсове, а не византийски лъвове са изобразени върху прочутите Старозагорски каменни релефи*, [in:] *Доклади и научни съобщения от V национална научна конференция "От регионалното към националното – история, краезнание и музейно дело" на Историческия музей – Полски Тръмбеш*, Велико Търново 2012, pp. 405–416.

И в а н о в И., *Ролята на Старопланинската област във военните кампании през Средновековието: Опит за критичен количествен анализ*, ИРИМГ 2, 2014, pp. 78–90.

И в а н о в И.Т., М и н к о в а М., *Още веднъж за средновековните каменни релефи от Стара Загора*, ИСИМ 3, 2008, pp. 177–184.

И в а н о в Й., *Избрани произведения*, ed. Б. А н г е л о в, vol. I, София 1982.

И в а н о в С., *Животински костни остатъци от селището в местността Джеджови лозя при с. Попина*, [in:] Ж. В ъ ж а р о в а, *Славянски и славянобългарски селища в българските земи от края на VI–XI век*, София 1965, pp. 207–225.

И в а н о в С., *Храната от животински произход на обитателите на Южната порта в Преслав*, ИАИ 22, 1959, pp. 209–221.

И в а н о в С.А., *Византийско-болгарские отношения в 966–969 гг.*, ВВ 42, 1981, pp. 88–100.

И в а н о в С.А., *Κοίρανος τῶν Βουλγάρων. Иоанн Цимисхий и Борис II в 971 г.*, [in:] *Общество и государство на Балканах в средние века*, Калинин 1982, pp. 47–58.

И в а н о в С.А., *Оборона балканских провинции Византии и проникновение "варваров" на Балкану в первой половине VI в.*, ВВ 45, 1985, pp. 35–53.

И в а н о в С.А., *Оборона Византии и география "варварских" вторжении через Дунай в первой половине VI в.*, ВВ 44, 1983, pp. 27–47.

И в а н о в С.А., *Общественная мысль в Болгарии в XI–XIII вв.*, [in:] *Власть и общество в литературных текстах древней Руси и других славянских стран (XII–XIII вв.)*, ed. Б. Ф л о р я, Москва 2012, pp. 95–102.

И в а н о в С.А., *Полемическая направленность Истории Льва Диакона*, ВВ 43, 1982, pp. 74–80.

И в а н о в а В., *Разкопки на Аврадака в Преслав*, РиП 3, 1949, pp. 13–61.

Иванова В., *Стари църкви и манастири в българските земи (IV–XII в.)*, ГНМ 4, 1922/1925, pp. 429–582.

Иванова К., *Най-старото житие за св. Иван и някои негови литературни паралели*, [in:] *Медиевистика и културна антропология. Сборник в чест на 40-годишната творческа дейност на проф. Д. Петканова*, ed. А. Ангушева, А. Милтенова, София 1998, pp. 37–47.

Иванова О.В., *Восстание в 930 г. в Болгарии и болгаро-византийские отношения*, [in:] *Славяне и их соседи. Международные отношения в епоху феодализма*, ed. Г.Г. Литаврин, Москва 1989, pp. 34–44.

Игнатов В., *Българските царици. Владетелките на България от VII до XIV в.*, София 2008.

Илиев Б., *Родно Лудогорие. Алманах*, София 2008.

Илиев И.Г., *Св. Климент Охридски. Живот и дело*, Пловдив 2010.

Илиев Н., *Говедовъдството във Велики Преслав (IX–X в.)*, Архе 36.3/4, 1994, pp. 66–70.

Илиев Н., Боев З., *Птиците в храната на населението от Външния глад на Велики Преслав (IX–X в.)*, ИИз 17, 1990, pp. 91–94.

Илиева Л., *Паисйи Хилендарски и Йован Раич*, [in:] *Светът е слово, словото е свят*, ed. М. Костова-Панайотова et al., Благоевград 2016, pp. 115–122.

Иречек К., *История на българите. С поправки и добавки от самия автор*, ed. П.Х. Петров, София 1978.

История на България в четиринадесет тома, vol. II, *Първа българска държава*, ed. Д. Ангелов, София 1981.

История на България от Блазиус Клайнер съставена в 1761 г., ed. И. Дуйчев, К. Телбизов, София 1977.

История на българската средновековна литература, ed. А. Милтенова, София 2008.

История на Поморие, vol. I, *Древност и съвремие*, ed. А. Орачев, В. Василчина, Бургас 2011.

Историкът като изследовател, гражданин и човек. Сборник с материали от конференция, посветена на 130-годишнината от рождението и 70-годишнината от смъртта на проф. Петър Мутафчиев (1883–1943), София 2016.

Историография истории южных и западных славян, ed. Л.В. Горина, И.В. Созин et al., Москва 1987.

Йерусалимская А.А., *Кавказ на Шелковом пути*, Санкт-Петербург 1992.

Йерусалимская А.А., *Мощевая Балка: необычный археологический памятник на Северокавказском Шелковом пути*, Санкт-Петербург 2012.

Йовков М., *Павликяни и павликянски селища в българските земи XV–XVIII век*, София 1991.

Йовчева М., *Старобългарският служебен миней*, София 2014.

Йовчева М., *Южнославянската литургическа книжнина от XIII в.*, ЗРВИ 46, 2009, pp. 351–364.

Йовчева М., Милтенова А., *Литературата от 927 г. до края на българското царство. Политико-религиозни, литературни и културни процеси*, [in:] *ИСБЛ*, pp. 255– 267.

Йорданов И., *България при Борис I (852–889, †907). Приносът на сфрагистиката*, [in:] *Християнската култура в средновековна България. Материали от национална научна конференция, Шумен 2–4 май 2007 г. по случай 1100 години от смъртта на Св. Княз Борис-Михаил (ок. 835–907 г.)*, ed. П. Георгиев, Велико Търново 2008, pp. 43–44.

Йорданов И., *Византийски комеркиарии за България (681–971)*, [in:] *Договори, хора, съдби*, ed. В. Михнева, С. Петкова, В. Павлов, Варна 2000, pp. 17–24.

Йорданов И., *Възникване и утвърждаване на царската институция в средновековна България. (Според данните на владетелските печати)*, [in:] *Етническият проблем и националният въпрос на българите*, Пловдив 1994, pp. 95–115.

Йорданов И., *Дуросторум – Доростол – Дръстър според данните на сфрагистиката (VI–XIV в.)*, ДобСб 30, 2015, pp. 49–103.

Йорданов И., *Печати на Василий Лакапин от България*, [in:] *Средновековният българин и "другите". Сборник в чест на 60-годишнината на проф. дин Петър Ангелов*, ed. А. Николов, Г.Н. Николов, София 2013, pp. 159–166.

Йорданов И., *Печати на Симеон, василевс на Ромеите (?–927)*, BMd 2, 2011, pp. 87–97.

Йорданов И., *Печатите на комеркиарията Девелт*, ПП 2, 1992, pp. 17–85.

Йорданов И., *Печатите на комеркиарията Девелт. Addenda et corrigenda*, [in:] *Нумизматични и сфрагистични приноси към историята на Западното Черноморие. Международна конференция Варна, 12–15 септември 2001*, ed. И. Лазаренко, В. Йотов, В. Иванов, В. Славчев, Варна 2004, pp. 230–245.

Йорданов И., *Печатите от стратегията в Преслав*, София 1993.

Йорданов И., *Средновековният Созопол според данните на сфрагистиката*, AMV 7.2, 2008, pp. 114–162.

Йорданов И., *Характер на монетната циркулация в средновековните български столици Преслав и Търново*, [in:] *Средновековният български град*, ed. П. Петров, София 1980, pp. 229–239.

Йорданов Й.А., Гюзелев В., *Чъргубиля Мостич (костни останки, образ, гроб)*, [in:] *Проф. д.и.н. Станчо Ваклинов и средновековната българска култура*, ed. К. Попконстантинов, Б. Борисов, Р. Костова, Велико Търново 2005, pp. 211–215.

Йотов В., *Българският контрол на "Пътя на солта" в Трансилвания през IX в. (по археологически данни)*, [in:] *Великотърновският Университет "Св. св. Кирил и Методий" и българската археология*, vol. I, ed. Б. Борисов, Велико Търново 2010, pp. 487–495.

Йотов В., *Въоръжението и снаряжението от българското средновековие (VII–XI век)*, Варна–Велико Търново 2004.

Каждан А.П., *Византийская культура (X–XII вв.)*, Санкт-Петербург 2000.

Каждан А.П., *Из истории византийской хронографии X в.*, I, *О составе так называемой "Хроники Продолжателя Феофана"*, ВВ 19, 1961, pp. 76–96.

Каждан А.П., *Хроника Симеона Логофета*, ВВ 15, 1959, pp. 125–143.

Казански Н., *Константин Иречек (1854–1918). Публикации за него*, ИП 70.5/6, 2014, pp. 88–96.

Каймакамова М., *Българска средновековна историопис*, София 1990.

Каймакамова М., *Власт и история в средновековна България VIII–XIV в.*, София 2011.

Каймакамова М., *Значението на български апокрифен летопис (XI в.) като извор за ранносредновековната българска култура*, [in:] *Stephanos Archaeologicos in honorem Professoris Stephcae Angelova*, ed. К. Рабаджиев, София 2010, pp. 593–612.

Каймакамова М., *Идеята "Търново-нов Цариград": "Трети Рим" през XIII–XIV век*, BMd 3, 2012, pp. 453–484.

Каймакамова М., *Култът към цар Петър (927–969) и движещите идеи на българските освободителни въстания срещу византийската власт през XI–XII в.*, BMd 4/5, 2013/2014, pp. 417–438.

Каймакамова М., *Образуването на българската държава в българската средновековна историопис*, [in:] *Тангра. Сборник в чест на 70–годишнината на акад. Васил Гюзелев*, ed. eadem et al., София 2006, p. 59–103.

Каймакамова М., *Религия, църква и държава в ранносредновековна България (края на VII – началото на XI в.)*, ДК 80.2/3, 2000, pp. 10–20.

Калић-Мијушковић J., *Београд у средњем веку*, Београд 1967.

Калоянов А., *Славянската православна цивилизация. Началото: 28 март 894 г., Плиска*, Велико Търново 2007.

Кандарашева И., *Стенописите от първия живописен слой в църквата "Св. Георги" в София*, Pbg 19.4, 1995, pp. 94–113.

Каприев Г., *Историографски концепт на Паисий Хилендарски и средновековното историческо мислене*, ПУПХБ.НТФ 50/1/A, 2012, pp. 115–126.

Карпов А.Ю., *Владимир Святой*, Москва 2004.

Карышковский Р.О., *О хронологии русско-византийской войны при Святославе*, ВВ 5, 1952, pp. 127–138.

Кецкаров В., *Войни на Българите в Тракия 689–972 г.*, София 1940.

Кираджиев С., *Енциклопедичен географски речник на България*, София 2013.

Киселков В., *Съществувал ли е поп Богомил*, ИП 15.2, 1958, pp. 57–67.

Кискинова М.С., *Предговор*, [in:] Й.С. Асемани, *Календари на Вселенската Църква. За светите славянски апостоли Кирил и Методий*, ed., transl., comm. М.С. Кискинова, София 1987, pp. 6–57.

Кожухаров С., *Проблеми на старобългарската поезия*, София 2004.

Кожухаров С., *Служба за цар Петър*, [in:] *Старобългарска литература. Енциклопедичен речник*, ed. Д. Петканова, Велико Търново 2003, p. 474.

Кожухаров С., *Търновската книжовна школа и развитието на химничната поезия в старата българска литература*, ТКШ 1, 1974, pp. 302–309.

Койчева Е., *Първите кръстоносни походи и Балканите*, София 2004.

Комитова Ц., *Самуиловата крепост при Беласица – история и археология*, София 2015.

Коларов Х., Гюзелев В., *Спиридон Николаев Палаузов (1818–1872)*, [in:] С. Палаузов, *Избрани трудове*, ed. Х. Коларов, В. Гюзелев, vol. I, София 1974, pp. 7–73.

Коледаров П.С., *Историческата география на Северозападното Черноморие по данните на Константин Багренородни*, ИП 33.3, 1977, pp. 50–64.

Коледаров П.С., *Към въпроса за развитието на селищната мрежа и нейните елементи в средищната и източната част на Балканите от VII до XVIII в.*, ИИИ 18, 1967, pp. 89–146.

Коледаров П., *Македония*, [in:] *КМЕ*, vol. II, pp. 592–593.

Коледаров П.С., *Отбранителната и граничната система на България от 681 до 1018 г.*, ВС 47.3, 1978, pp. 109–123.

Коледаров П., *Политическа география на средновековната българска държава*, vol. I, *От 681 до 1018 г.*, София 1979.

Коледаров П., *Цар Петър I*, ВС 51, 1982, pp. 192–207.

Колпакова Г., *Искусство Византии. Ранний и средний периоды*, Санкт-Петербург 2010.

Колчин Б.А., *Инструментальная музыка древнего Новгорода*, [in:] *Четвърти международен конгрес по славянска археология. Доклади и съобщевия*, vol. I, ed. Д. Ангелов, София, 1992, pp. 538–548.

Коматарова-Балинова Е., *Децата в обществото на средновековните българи (по данни от езическите некрополи)*, [in:] *Eurika. In honorem Ludmilae Donchevae-Petkovae*, ed. В. Григоров, М. Даскалов, София 2009, pp. 185–197.

К о м а т и н а П., *О српско-бугарској граници у IX и X в.*, ЗРВИ 52, 2015, pp. 31–42.

К о м и т о в а Ц., *Стъклени гривни от Мелник*, [in:] *Приноси към българската археология*, vol. III–IV, ed. С. С т а н и л о в et al., София 2006, pp. 99–107.

К о м с а л о в а Р., *Социално-икономическите проблеми на средновековна България в българската медиевистика след Втората световна война*, Пловдив 2000.

К о н о в а л о в а И., П е р е х а в к о В., *Древная Русь и Нижнее Подунавие*, Москва 2000.

К о н с т а н т и н о в ъ Г., *Проф. Петър Мутафчиев. 4. V. 1883 – 2. V. 1943*, Прос 8.10, 1943, pp. 577–582.

К о н с т а н т и н о в К., *Прибори за хранене и приготвяне на храна от Плиска*, Истор 1, 2006, pp. 275–283.

К о н с т а н т и н о в К., *Прибори за хранене от Велики Преслав*, ПрСб 6, 2004, pp. 273–280.

К о н я р о в Г., *Принос към истарията на рударствэто и металургията в България*, София 1953.

К о с т о в а Р., *Манастирските училища през IX–X в. в България (по материали от манастира при с. Равна)*, КМС 17, 2007, pp. 513–529.

К о с т о в а Р., *Манастирът в Тузлалъка, Преслав: нов поглед*, Архе 43.2, 2002, pp. 13–25.

К о с т о в а Р., *Манастирът на Мостич и въпросът за манастирите основани от частни лица в България през X в.*, ИАИ 39, 2006, pp. 271–285.

К о с т о в а Р., *Още веднъж за Кръглата църква и т. нар. родов манастир в Преслав*, [in:] *Studia protobulgarica et mediaevalia europensia. В чест на чл. кор. проф. Веселин Бешевлиев*, ed. К. П о п к о н с т а н т и н о в, София 2003, pp. 284–303.

К о с т о в а Р., *Патронаж и манастирска география в България през втората половина на IX и в X в.*, [in:] *Laurea. In honorem Margaritae Vaklinova*, ed. Б. П е т р у н о в а, А. А л а д ж о в, Е. В а с и л е в а, vol. I, София 2009, pp. 199–215.

К о с т о в а Р., *Скалният манастир при Бесараби в северна Добруджа. Някои проблеми на интерпретация*, БСП 7, 2000, pp. 131–152.

К о с т о в а Р., *Скалният манастир при Крепча: Още един поглед към монашеските практики в България през X в.*, [in:] [in:] *Проф. д.и.н. Станчо Ваклинов и средновековната българска култура*, ed. К. П о п к о н с т а н т и н о в, Б. Б о р и с о в, Р. К о с т о в а, Велико Търново 2005, pp. 289–305.

К о с т о в а Р., *Център и периферия в Равненския манастир (по рисунки-графити)*, [in:] *Светогорска обител Зограф*, vol. II, ed. В. Г ю з е л е в, София 1996, pp. 221–243.

К о с т о в а Р., П о п к о н с т а н т и н о в К., *Манастирите на Покръстителя*, [in:] *Християнската култура в Средновековна България. Материали от национална научна конференция Шумен 2–4 май 2007 година по случай 1100 години от смъртта на св. Княз Борис-Михаил (ок. 835–907 г.)*, ed. П. Георгиев, Шумен 2008, pp. 173–185.

Кочев Н., *Народният събор в Преслав през 893/4*, [in:] *1100 години Велики Преслав*, ed. Т. Тотев, vol. I, Шумен 1995 pp. 44–54.

Кочубинский А., *Примѣчаніе*, ЗИООИД 16, 1893, p. 54.

Кръстанов Т., *Испански бележки за translatio на Justiniana Prima с българската църква преди 1018 г.*, ШУЕКП. ТКИБ 6, 2004, pp. 80–84.

Кръстанов Т., *Титлите екзарх и патриарх в българската традиция от IX до XIX в. Св. Йоан Екзарх от Рим и патриарх на българските земи*, [in:] *Държава & Църква – Църква & Държава в българската история. Сборник по случай 135-годишнината от учредяването на Българската екзархия*, ed. Г. Ганев, Г. Бакалов, И. Тодев, София 2006, pp. 73–86.

Кръстев К.С., *България, Византия и Арабският свят при царуването на Симеон I Велики*, BMd 3, 2012, pp. 371–378.

Кузев А., *Бдин*, [in:] *Български средновековни градове и крепости*, vol. I, *Градове и крепости по Дунав и Черно Море*, ed. А. Кузев, В. Гюзелев, Варна 1981, pp. 98–115.

Кузев А., *Дръстър*, [in:] *Български средновековни градове и крепости*, vol. I, *Градове и крепости по Дунав и Черно Море*, ed. idem, В. Гюзелев, Варна 1981, pp. 177–185.

Кузман П., *Археолошки сведоштва за дејноста на Свети Климент Охридски во Охридскиот регион*, Slov 5.2, 2016, pp. 136–178.

Кузнецовъ И., *Писмата на Лъва Магистра и Романа Лакапина и словото "Ἐπὶ τῇ τῶν Βουλγάρων συμβάσει" като изворъ за историята на Симеоновска България*, СНУНК 16/17, 1900, pp. 179–245.

Кузупов Б., *"Замъкът Баба Вида"*, МПК 20.4, 1980, pp. 7–12.

Кучма В.В., *"Византийский Аноним VI в.": основные проблемы источников и содержания*, [in:] idem, *Военная организация Византийской Империи*, С.-Петербург 2001.

Кучма В.В., *Военная организация Византийской империи*, Санкт-Петербург 2001.

Кънев Н., *Византийската титла патрикия-зости (IX–XI в.). Приносът на сфрагистиката за попълване на листата на носителките на титлата*, Истор 4, 2011, pp. 173–198.

Кънев Н., *Стремял ли се е българският владетел Симеон I Велики (893–927 г.) към ранг на визатийски василеопатор?*, [in:] idem, *Византинобългарски студии*, Велико Търново 2013, pp. 111–119.

Кънев Н., *Четири непубликувани оловни печата от района на Шумен*, Истор 5, 2012, pp. 61–67.

Лавровъ П.А., *Нова служба цару бугарскоме Петру*, ЈФ 1, 1913, pp. 34–37.

Лавровъ П.А., *Одна изъ передѣлокъ исторіи Славяно-болгарской іеромонаха Паисія, сохранившаяся въ ркп. № 1731 собранія проф. Григоровича*, [in:] *Труды восмаго археологическаго съѣзда въ Москвѣ*, vol. II, ed. П.С. Уварова, М.Н. Сперанский, Москва 1895, pp. 242–263.

Лазаров И., *Константин Преславски*, [in:] Й. Андреев, И. Лазаров, П. Павлов, *Кой кой е в средновековна България*, ²София 2012, pp. 394–396.

Лазаров И., *Мостич*, [in:] Й. Андреев, И. Лазаров, П. Павлов, *Кой кой е в средновековна България*, ²София 2012, pp. 503–504.

Лазаров М., Гюзелев В., *Увод*, [in:] *История на Поморие*, vol. I, *Древност и съвремие*, ed. А. Орачев, В. Василчина, Бургас 2011, pp. 13–17.

Лешка М.Й., *Образът на българския цар Борис II във византийските извори*, transl. К. Маринов, SB 25, 2006, pp. 145–152.

Лешка М.Й., Маринов К., *Спорные вопросы правления болгарского царя Петра I (927–969)*, Pbg 41.1, 2017, pp. 23–39.

Литаврин Г.Г., *Введение христиантва в Волгарии (IX – начало X в.)*, [in:] *Приниатие христианства народами централной и юго-восточной Европы и крещение Руси*, ed. i d e m, Москва 1988, pp. 30–67.

Литаврин Г.Г., *Византия, Болгария, Древняя Русь (IX–начало XII в.)*, Санкт-Петербург 2000.

Литаврин Г.Г., *Внутренный кризис, новый подъем и борьба за независимость*, [in:] *Краткая история Болгарии. С древниейших времен до наших дней*, ed. i d e m, Москва 1987.

Литаврин Г.Г., *Древная Русь, Болгария и Византия в IX–X вв.*, [in:] *История, култура, этнография и фолклор славянских народов, IX международный съезд славистов, Киев, сентябрь 1983. Докладъ советской делегации*, Москва 1983, pp. 62–76.

Литаврин Г.Г., *Константин Багрянородный о Болгарии и Болгарах*, [in:] *Сборник в чест на акад. Димитър Ангелов*, ed. В. Велков, София 1994, pp. 30–37.

Литаврин Г.Г., *Принцип наследственности власти в Византии и в Болгарии в VII–XI вв.*, [in:] *Славяне и их соседи*, vol. I, Москва 1988, pp. 31–33.

Литаврин Г.Г., *Темпове и специфика на социално-икономическото развитие на средновековна България в сравнение с Византия (от края на VII до края на XII в.)*, ИП 26.6, 1970, pp. 23–40.

Литаврин Г.Г., *Христианство в Болгарии в 927–1018 гг.*, [in:] *Христианство в странах Восточной, Юго-Восточной и Центральной Европы на пороге второго тысячелетия*, ed. Б.Н. Флоря, Москва 2002, pp. 133–189.

Литвина А.Ф., Успенский Ф.Б., *Выбор имени у русских князей в X–XVI вв. Династическая история сквозь призму антропонимики*, Москва 2006.

Лишев С., *Българският средновековен град. Обществено-икономически облик*, София 1970.

Лишев С., *За проникването и ролята на парите във феодална България*, София 1958.

Лишев С., *Още веднъж за възникването на българския средновековен град*, ИП 30.6, 1974, pp. 70–77.

Любарский Я.Н., *Сочинение Продолжателя Феофана. Хроника, история, жизнеописания?* [in:] Продолжатель Феофана, *Жизнеописания византийских царей*, ed. idem, Санкт-Петербург 1992, pp. 293–368.

Мавродинов Н., *Старобългарското изкуство. Изкуството на първото българско царство*, София 2013.

Мавродинова Л.Н., *Стенната живопис в България до края на XIV в.*, София 1995.

Мавроурбинъ, *Кніга історіографія початія имене, славы и разширенія народа славянского*, Санктъпітербург 1722.

Майсторски Г., Бабаджанов И., Георгиев П., *Средновековен манастирски комплекс в м. Кирика – НИАР "Мадара"*, [in:] *Археологически открития и разкопки през 2015 г.*, ed. А. Аначжов, София 2016, pp. 730–732.

Максимовић Љ., *Структура 32. поглавља списа De admistrando imperio*, ЗРВИ 21, 1982, pp. 25–32.

Малахов С.Н., *Концепция мира в политической идеологии Византии первой половины X в.: Николай Мистик и Феодор Дафнопат*, АДСВ 27, 1995, pp. 19–31.

Маринов В., *Стара-Планина (Природна физономия и културно-стопанска структура)*, Род 2.1, 1939, pp. 121–143.

Маринов Д., *Българско обичайно право*, София 1995.

Маринов Д., *Народна вяра и религиозни народни обичаи*, София 1994.

Маринов К., *"А земята отново беше станала безвидна и неоформена". Щрихи към образа на войната в словото "За мира с българите"*, Епо 26.1, 2018, pp. 201–213.

Маринов К., *В дербите на Хемус (За някои страни в ролята на планината през периода VII–IX в.)*, Pbg 37.4, 2013, pp. 60–73.

Маринов К., *Византийската имперска идея и претенциите на цар Симеон според словото "За мира с българите"*, КМС 25, 2016, pp. 342–352.

Маринов К., *Новият Завет и византийската пропаганда. Още веднъж за Никита Хониат и българското освободително движение*, [in:] *Великите Асеневци*, ed. П. Павлов, Н. Кънев, Н. Хрисимов, Велико Търново 2016, pp. 70–83.

Маринов К., *Още веднъж за пар. XXIII.67 от 'Пространното житие на Климент Охридски'* (in press).

Маринов К., *Преминаването на планинските проходи според византийските и някои антични трактати за военното изкуство*, [in:] *Българско средновековие: общество, власт, история. Сборник в чест на проф. д-р Милияна Каймакамова*, ed. А. Николов, Г.Н. Николов, София 2013, pp. 205–220.

Маринов К., *Стратегическата роля на Старопланинската и Средногорската вериги в светлината на българо-византийските военни сблъсъци през VII–XI век*, ИРИМГ 2, 2014, pp. 111–134.

Марјановић-Душанић С., *Rex imago Dei: о српској преради Агапитовог владарског огледала*, [in:] *Трећа југословенска конференција византолога, Крушевац 10–13 мај 2000*, ed. Љ. Максимовић, Н. Радошевић, Е. Радуловић, Београд–Крушевац, 2002, pp. 135–148.

Матанов Х., *Балкански хоризонти. История, общества, личности*, vol. I, София 2004.

Матанов Х., *В търсене на средновековното време. Неравният път на българите (VII–XV в.)*, София 2014.

Материали за картата на средновековна българска държава (територията на днешна Североизточна България), ed. Р. Рашев, ППре 7, 1995, pp. 155–332.

Меламед К., *Светилище и некропол до раннохристиянския манастир край с. Нова махала, Баташко*, Архе 35.2, pp. 36–46.

Мещерский Н., *Взаимоотношения Изборника 1073 г. с Изборником 1076 г.*, [in:] *Изборник Святослава 1073 г. Сборник статей*, Москва 1977, pp. 90–99.

Микулчиќ И., *Старо Скопје со околните тврдини*, Скопје 1982.

Милтенов Я., *Златоструй: старобългарски хомилетичен свод, създаден по инициативата на българския цар Симеон. Текстологично и извороведско изследване*, София 2013.

Милтенов Я., *Нови данни за "Поучението за спасението на душата", приписвано на черноризец Петър*, СЛ 51, 2015, pp. 157–186.

Милтенов Я., *Общите пасажи между колекцията Златоструй и Княжеския изборник*, СЛ 49/50, 2014, pp. 28–45.

Милтенова А., *Сборник със смесено съдържание, дело на етрополския книжовник йеромонах Даниил*, СЛ 9, 1986, pp. 114–125.

Милчев А., *Занаятчийски и търговски помещения северно от южната порта на вътрешния град на Плиска*, [in:] *Архитектурата на Първата и Втората българска държава. Материали*, ed. Г. Кожухаров, София 1975, pp. 246–271.

Милчев А., *Проучвания на раннославянската култура в България и на Плиска през последните двадесет години*, Архе 6.3, 1964, pp. 23–35.

Милчев А., *Разкопки в Плиска западно от Вътрешния град през 1959 г.*, Архе 2.3, 1960, pp. 30–43.

Милчев А., *Славяне, протоболгары и Византия в болгарских землях в VI–IX вв.*, [in:] *Actes du XIVe Congrès International des Études Byzantines, Bucarest, 6–12 septembre 1971*, ed. M. Berza, E. Stănescu, vol. II, Bucarest, 1975, pp. 387–395.

Минчев Г., *За името Θεόφιλος/Боголюб/Богомил в някои византийски и славянски средновековни текстове*, Pbg 37.4, 2013, pp. 43–52.

Минчев Г., Скворонек М., *Сведения о дуалистических ересях и языческих верованиях в Шестодневе Иоанна Экзарха*, SCer 4, 2014, pp. 95–123.

Михайлов С., *За някои характерни черти на българския средновековен град*, Пр.Сб 3, 1983, pp. 188–195.

Мишев Д., *България в миналото. Страници из българската културна история*, София 1916.

Мишев К., *Южнобългарска провинция*, [in:] *География на България в три тома*, vol. III, *Физико-географско и социално-икономическо*, ed. К. Мишев, София 1989, p. 113–135.

Митова-Джонова Д., *Confinium Succi и Mutatio Soneium през античността и ранновизантийската епоха*, Ана 1.2/3, 1994, p. 77–99.

Митова-Джонова Д., *Общонародното и регионалното в културно-историческото развитие на Дунавската равнина*, София 1989.

Митрев Г., *Самуиловата крепост. Битката при с. Ключ през 1014 г.*, [s.l., s.a.].

Митрев Г., *Самуиловата крепост-дема в Ключката клисура – нови теренни проучвания и наблюдения*, [in:] *Европейският Югоизток през втората половина на X – началото на XI век. История и култура*, ed. В. Гюзелев, Г.Н. Николов, София 2015, pp. 432–450.

Михайлов С., *Археологически проучвания на крепостта Баба Вида във Видин*, Архе 3.3, 1961, pp. 1–8.

Михайлов С., *За някои характерни черти на българския средновековен град*, Пр.Сб. 3, 1983, pp. 188–195.

Михайлов С., *Разкопки в Плиска през 1959–1961 г.*, ИАИ 26, 1963, pp. 5–46.

Михайлов С., Джингов Г., Вълов В., Димова В., *Ранносредновековно селище при с. Стърмен*, РП 7, 1982.

Михайлов Ц., Тишков Х., Зяпков Л., Горунова Д., *Дунавска равнинно-хълмиста област*, [in:] *География на България в три тома*, vol. II, *Физико-географско и социално-икономическо*, ed. К. Мишев, София 1989, pp. 60–65.

Михайлова Т., *Печат на "Мария Василиса" от Преслав*, НСЕ 3.2, 2007, pp. 39–42.

Михайлова Т., *Сгради и съоръжения на запад от Тронната палата в Плиска – X–XI в.*, ППре 5, 1993, pp. 170–184.

Миятев К., *Архитектурата в Средновековна България. Архитектура и строителство*, София 1965.

Миятев К., *Жилищната ахитектура в България през IX и X в.*, ИАИ 23, 1960, pp. 1–21.

Молчанов А.А., *Владимир Мономах и его имена. К изучению княжеского именника Рюриковичей X–XII вв.*, Слав 2004, 2, pp. 80–87.

Момчилов Д., *Култура и политика на Първото българско царство в Североизточна Тракия (по археологически дании)*, Варна 2007.

Момчилов Д., *Материалната култура от времето на Първото българско царство в Североизточна Тракия през IX–X в.*, [in:] *Проблеми на прабългарската история и култура*, vol. IV/2, *Сборник в памет на ст.н.с. I ст. д.и.н. Димитър Ил. Димитров*, ed. Р. Рашев, София 2007, pp. 291–294.

Момчилов Д., *Паметници на металопластиката от Маркели*, ИНАИ 40, 2012, pp. 141–149.

Момчилов Д., *Пътна и селищна система между Източна Стара Планина и "Еркесията" IV–XIV в. (Върбишки, Ришки и Айтоски проход)*, Варна 1999.

Момчилов Д., *Ролята на Анхиало и Маркели при военните конфликти между България и Византия през периода на Първото българско царство*, [in:] *Великотърновският Университет "Св. св. Кирил и Методий" и българската археология*, vol. I, ed. Б. Борисов, Велико Търново 2010, pp. 437–448.

Момчилов Д., *Старобългарски апликации от фонда на историческия музей – Карнобат*, [in:] *Laurea. In honorem Margaritae Vaklinova*, ed. Б. Петрунова, А. Аладжов, Е. Василева, vol. II, София 2009, pp. 167–178.

Момчилов Д., *Средновековните крепости в южните части на Ришкия и Върбишкия проход*, ВС 59.5, 1990, pp. 14–43.

Момчилов Д., *Южните части на Ришкия и Върбишкия проходи и "Еркесията" през Първото българско царство*, ППре 8, 2000, pp. 239–241.

Морозова Н.А., *Игрушки Древнего Новгорода*, [in:] *Новгород и Новгородская земля. История и археология. (Тезисы научной конференции)*, vol. III, ed. И.Ю. Акундинов, Новгород 1990, pp. 69–71.

Мутафчиев П., *Де, кога и как се е губил българският народ до днес*, ОП 1.12/13, 1928, pp. 208–219.

Мутафчиев П., *За културната криза у насъ*, Прос 1.4, 1935, pp. 385–397.

Мутафчиев П., *Избрани произведения*, ed. Д. Ангелов, vol. I–II, София 1973.

Мутафчиев П., *История на българския народ (681–1323)*, ed. В. Гюзелев, София 1986.

Мутафчиев П., *Към философията на българската история. Византинизмътъ въ срѣдновѣковна България*, ФП 3.1, 1931, pp. 27–36.

Мутафчиев П., *Лекции по история на културата*, ed. И. Илиев, София 1995.

Мутафчиев П., *Маджарите и българо-византийските отношения през третата четвърт на X в.*, [in:] idem, *Избрани произведения*, vol. II, ed. Д. Ангелов, София 1973, pp. 441–477.

Мутафчиев П., *Маринъ Дриновъ*, Прос 4.6, 1939, pp. 675–684.

Мутафчиев П., *Попъ Богомилъ и св. Ив. Рилски. Духътъ на отрицанието въ нашата история*, ФП, 6.2, 1934, pp. 1–16.

Мутафчиев П., *Стари градища и друмове из долините на Стряма и Тополница*, [in:] idem, *Избрани произведения в два тома*, ed. Д. Ангелов, vol. I, София 1973, pp. 286–396.

Мутафчиев П., *Старият друм през "Траянови врата"*, СБАН.КИФФО 55.27, 1937, pp. 19–148.

Мутафчиев П., *Съдбините на средновековния Дръстър*, [in:] idem, *Сборник от студии*, София 1946, pp. 293–305.

Мутафчиев П., *Съдбините на средновековния Дръстър*, [in:] idem, *Избрани произведения в два тома*, ed. Д. Ангелов, vol. II, София 1973, pp. 19–103.

Назаренко А.В., *Древняя Русь на международных путях. Междисциплинарные очерки культурных, торговых, политических связей IX–XII вв.*, Москва 2001.

Найденова Д., *Едно неосъществено издание на Пространното житие на Климент Охридски: Васил Н. Златарски и българската кирилиометодиевистика*, BMd 6, 2015, pp. 257–276.

Наумов Е.П, *Становление и развитие сербской раннефеодальной государственности*, [in:] *Раннефеодальные государства на Балканах. VI–XII вв.*, ed. Г.Г. Литаврин, Москва 1985, pp. 189–218.

Начовъ П.А., *Забележка за Паисиевата история*, ПСБКД 46, 1894, pp. 505–525.

Недев С.Т., *Пътища в Източна Стара Планина от създаването на българската държава до Освобождението и от Османското владичество*, ИВНД 15.1, 1973, pp. 213–226.

Нескович А., *Исторїата на славвенно-болгаркїѧ народъ изъ исторїата на г. Раича и нѣкои исторически книги составлена (...)*, transl. П. Сапунов, Букурещ 1844.

Нескович А., *Исторїя на славенно-болгарскогъ народа изъ г. Раича исторїе и нѣкихъ историческимъ книгъ*, Буда 1801.

Никитенко Н.Н., *София Киевская и ее создатели. Тайты истории*, Каменец-Подольский 2014.

Никифорова М.Е., *Бароний*, [in:] *Православная Энциклопедия*, vol. IV, Москва 2002, pp. 347–348.

Ников П., *Васил Златарски*, ИИДС 14/15, 1937, pp. 1–27.

Николаев В.Д., *Значение договора 927 г. в истории болгаро-византийских отношений*, [in:] *Проблемы истории античности и средних веков*, ed. Ю.М. Сапрыкин, Москва 1982, pp. 89–105.

Николаев В.Д., *К истории болгаро-русских отношений в начале 40-ых годов X в.*, ССл 1982, 6, pp. 49–55.

Николов А., *"Великият между царете". Изграждане и утвърждаване на българската царска институция през управлението на Симеон I*, [in:] *Българският златен век. Сборник в чест на цар Симеон Велики (893–927)*, ed. В. Гюзелев, И.Г. Илиев, К. Ненов, Пловдив 2015, pp. 149–188.

Николов А., *Към въпроса за разпространението на някои византийски "княжески огледала" в старобългарската литература (края на IX–началото на X век)*, [in:] *Средновековните Балкани. Политика, религия, култура*, ed. С. Ракова, Л. Симеонова, София 1999, pp. 74–88.

Николов А., *Политическа мисъл в ранносредновековна България (средата на IX – края на X в.)*, София 2006.

Николов А., *Средневековый славянский перевод "Учительных глав" императора Василия I: проблемы изучения рукописной традиции и ранних печатных изданий*, [in:] *XIX Ежегодная богословская конференция Православного Свято-Тихоновского гуманитарного университета*, vol. I, Москва 2009, pp. 41–47.

Николов А., *Старобългарският превод на "Изложение на поучителни глави към император Юстиниан" от дякон Агапит и развитието на идеята за достойнството на българския владетел в края на IX – началото на X в.*, Pbg 24.3, 2000, pp. 76–105.

Николов Б., *От Искър до Огоста. История на 151 села и градове от бившия Врачански окръг*, София 1996.

Николов В., Йорданова М., *Планините в България*, София 2002.

Николов Г.Н., *Български царици от Средновековието в "ангелски образ"*, ГСУ.НЦСВПИД 93 (12), 2003, pp. 299–315.

Николов Г.Н., *Военно-политическа история на средновековния град Боруй*, ВС 50.3, 1981, pp. 34–44.

Николов Г.Н., *Прабългарската традиция в християнския двор на средновековна България (IX–XI в.). Владетел и престолонаследие*, [in:] *Бог и цар в българската история*, ed. К. Вачкова, Пловдив 1996, pp. 124–130.

Николов Г.Н., *Централизъм и регионализъм в ранносредновековна България (края на VII – началото на XI в.)*, София 2005.

Николова Б., *Заветът на св. Иван Рилски. За митовете и реалите*, СЛ 35/36, 2006, pp. 144–166.

Николова Б., *Монашество, манастири и манастирски живот в средновековна България*, vol. I, *Манастирите*, vol. II, *Монасите*, София 2010.

Николова Б., *Печатите на Михаил багатур канеиртхтин и Йоан багатур канеиртхтин (?). Проблеми на разчитането и атрибуцията*, [in:] *Средновековният българин и "другите". Сборник в чест на 60-годишнината на проф. дин Петър Ангелов*, ed. А. Николов, Г.Н. Николов, София 2013, pp. 127–135.

Николова Б., *Православните църкви през българското средновековие (IX–XIV)*, София 2002.

Николова Б., *Средновековните византийски и български владетели, кралете и князете на Средна и Западна Европа в съдбата на светците от българския пантеон*, ИП 67.5/6, 2011, pp. 123–144.

Николова Б., *Устройство и управление на българската православна църква (IX–XIV в.)*, София 2017.

Николова Б., *Цар Петър и характерът на неговия култ*, Pbg 33.2, 2009, pp. 63–77.

Николова М., *Към въпроса за името на град Видин*, ИМСБ 14, 1988, pp. 75–97.

Никольский Н., *Материалы для повременного списка русских писателей и их сочинений (X–XI в.)*, Санкт-Петербург 1906.

Нинов Л., *Домашните и дивите животни от средновековното и укрепено селище край с. Хума, Разградски окръг*, [in:] Р. Рашев, С. Станилов, *Старобългарското укрепено селище при с. Хума, Разградски окръг*, РП 17, 1987, pp. 178–183.

Нинов Л., *Животновъдна и ловна дейност в средновековнот селище край село Одърци*, [in:] Л. Дончева-Петкова, *Одърци. Селище от Първото българско царство*, vol. I, София 1999, pp. 171–173.

Нинов Л., *Животновъдна и ловна дейност на обитателите на крепостта*, [in:] В. Йотов, Г. Атанасов, *Скала. Крепост от X–XI век до с. Кладенци, Тервелско*, София 1998, pp. 329–342.

Нинов Л., *Някои аспекти на животновъдството през Средновековието*, ИИз 17, 1990, pp. 95–101.

Нинов Л., *Остеологична характеристика на костените и роговите изделия*, [in:] Л. Дончева-Петкова, *Одърци. Селище от Първото българско царство*, vol. I, София 1999, pp. 174–177.

Оболенски Д., *Богомилите. Студия върху балканското новоманихейство*, София 1998.

Овчаров Д., *Археологически аспекти на българската ранносредновековна фортификация*, ВС 42.1, 1973, pp. 54–71.

Овчаров Д., *Българската средновековна археология през последните десет години (1974–1984)*, Архе 26.4, 1984, pp. 46–61.

Овчаров Д., *Български средновековни рисунки-графити*, София 1982.

Овчаров Д.С., *Византийски и български крепости V–X век*, София 1982.

Овчаров Д., *Възникване и оформяне на Преслав като средновековен град (IX–X в.)*, [in:] *Средновековният български град*, ed. П. Петров, София 1980, pp. 107–116.

Овчаров Д., *Към въпроса за укрепителната дейност на българската държава по долен Дунав през IX–X в.*, ВС 48.2, 1979, pp. 96–106.

Овчаров Д., *Още за игрите в средновековен Преслав*, ППре 7, 1995, pp. 136–143.

Овчаров Д., *Плиска*, [in:] idem, Т. Тотев, А. Попов, *Стари български столици. Плиска. Велики Преслав. Търновград*, София 1980, pp. 9–69.

Овчаров Н., *Една хипотеза за българо-византийските отношения през 912–913 г.*, Архе 31.3, 1989, pp. 50–57.

Овчаров Н., Коджаманова Д., *Перперикон и околните твърдини през Средновековието. Крепостното сторителство в Източните Родопи*, София 2003.

Овчаров Т., *Селища от Първото българско царство във Великотърновска област*, [in:] *Оттука започва България. Материали от втората национална конференция по история, археология и културен туризъм "Пътуване към България" – Шумен, 14–16.05.2010 година*, ed. И. Йорданов, Шумен 2011, pp. 430–434.

Огненова Л., Георгиева С., *Разкопки на манастира под Вълкашина в Преслав през 1948–1949*, ИАИ 20, 1955, pp. 373–411.

Оръжие и снаряжение през късната античност и средновековието IV–XV в., Международна конференция Варна 14–16 септември 2000, ed. В. Йотов, В. Николов, В. Славчев, Varna 2002.

Острогорский Г., *Славянский перевод хроники Симеона Логофета*, SK 5, 1932, pp. 17–37.

Острогорски Г., *Порфирогенитова хроника српских владара и њени хронолошки подаци*, [in:] idem, *Сабране дела Георгија Острогорског*, vol. IV, *Византија и словени*, Београд 1970, pp. 79–86.

П а в л о в П., *Аспарух и Кувер*, [in:] i d e m, *Българското Средновековие. Познато и непознато. Страници от политическата и културната история на България VII–XIV век*, Велико Тъново 2008, pp. 9–20.

П а в л о в П., *Борби за оцеляване. Упадък на българската държавност*, [in:] *История на българите*, vol. I, *От древността до края на XVI век*, ed. Г. Б а к а л о в, София 2003, pp. 268–322.

П а в л о в П., *Братята на цар Петър и техните загавори*, Ист 7.4/5, 1999, pp. 1–6.

П а в л о в П., *Бунтари и авантюристи в средновековна България*, Велико Търново 2000.

П а в л о в П., *Векът на цар Самуил*, София 2014.

П а в л о в П., *Георги Сурсувул*, [in:] Й. А н д р е е в, И. Л а з а р о в, П. П а в л о в, *Кой кой е в средновековна България*, София 2012, pp. 139–143.

П а в л о в П., *Години на мир и "ратни беди" (927–1018)*, [in:] А т а н а с о в Г., В а ч к о в а В., П а в л о в П., *Българска национална история*, vol. III, *Първо българско царство (680–1018)*, Велико Търново 2015, pp. 403–479.

П а в л о в П., *Две бележки към "Беседа на недостойния презвитер Козма срещу новопоявилата се ерес на богомилите"*, Пр.Сб 4, 1993, pp. 225–239.

П а в л о в П., *Забравени и неразбрани. Събития и личности от Българското средновековие*, София 2010.

П а в л о в П., *Залезът на Първото българско царство (1015–1018)*, София 1999.

П а в л о в П., *Истини и заблуди за светия цар Петър*, [in:] i d e m, *Забравени и неразбрани. Събития и личности от българското средновековие*, София 2010, p. 27–52.

П а в л о в П., *Средец (София) в историята на Първото българско царство*, [in:] *1200 години Сердика–Средец–София в България*, ed. Б. П е т р у н о в а, М. В а к л и н о в а, София 2009, pp. 4–38.

П а в л о в П., *Стефан*, [in:] i d e m, И. Л а з а р о в, П. П а в л о в, *Кой кой е в средновековна България*, София 2012, p. 625.

П а в л о в П., *Стопанско развитие на Първото българско царство*, [in:] И. Т ю т ю н д ж и е в, М. П а л а н г у р с к и, А, К о с т о в, И. Л а з а р о в, П. П а в л о в, И. Р у с е в, *Стопанска история на България*, Велико Търново 2011, pp. 14–21.

П а в л о в П., *Християнското и имперското минало на българските земи в ойкуменичната доктрина на цар Симеон Велики (893–927)*, [in:] *Източното православие в европейската култура. Международна конференция. Варна, 2–3 юли 1993 г.*, ed. Д. О в ч а р о в, София 1999, pp. 111–115.

П а в л о в П., О р а ч е в А., Х а н д ж и й с к и А., *Българската писменост. Европейски феномен*, София 2008.

П а в л о в а Р., *Петър Черноризец – старобългарски писател от X в.*, София 1994.

Павлович Х., *Разговорникъ греко-болгарскій за оныя, кои-то желаятъ греческій язык да се научат, при кого-то и една кратка Болгарска история приложисе*, Белградъ 1835.

Павлович Х., *Царственик или історія болгарская*, Будим 1844.

Паисий Хилендарски, *История славяноболгарская. Критическо издание с превод и коментар*, ed. Д. Пеев, М. Димитрова, П. Петков, transl. Д. Пеев, comm. А. Николов, Д. Пеев, Зограф 2012.

Палаузовъ С.Н., *Вѣкъ болгарскаго царя Симеона*, Санкпетербургъ 1852.

Палаузовъ С.Н., *Юго-Востокъ Европы в XIV столетии*, Санкпетербургъ 1858.

Панайотов В., *За "народното житие" на св. Йоан Рилски*, ПКШ 4, 1999, pp. 92–98.

Панайотов Й., Михов М., *Кратка характеристика на основните продоволствени и технически култури*, [in:] *Дуранкулак*, ed. Х. Тодорова, vol. I, София 1989, pp. 213–222.

Панова Р., *Аспекти на морфологията на средновековния български град*, Мин 9.1, 2002, pp. 19–30.

Панова Р., *Морфология на средновековния български град*, ИП 56.1/2, 2000, pp. 3–21.

Панова Р., *Столичният град в културата на средновековна България*, София 1995.

Папахрисанту Д., *Атонско монаштво. Почеци и организација*, Београд 2003.

Паскалева К., *За началото на иконописта в българските земи (VII–XII в.)*, [in:] eadem, *"В началото бе словото". Сборник статии и студии 1967–2011 г.*, София 2011, pp. 95–113.

Пенчев П., Тишков Х., Данева М., Горунова Д., *Старопланинска област*, [in:] *География на България в три тома*, vol. III, *Физико-географско и социално-икономическо*, ed. К. Мишев, София 1989, pp. 85–113.

Перхавко В.Б., *Переяславец "Повести временных лет"*, Век 17.4, 1988, pp. 20–24.

Петканова Д., *Разноликото Средновековие*, Велико Търново 2006.

Петров М., Хрисимов Н., *Едноострите клинови оръжия от територията на България и византийската военна традиция*, ДобСб 30, 2015, pp. 337–358.

Петров П., *Иречековата "История на българите"*, [in:] К. Иречек, *История на българите*, ed. П. Петров, София 1978, pp. 7–26.

Петров П., *Някои проблеми на средновековния български град*, [in:] *Средновековният български град*, ed. idem, София 1980, pp. 7–22.

Петров П., *Самуил – царят воин*, София 2014.

Петров П.Х., *Средновековна Вратица*, [in:] *История на град Враца от Древността до Освобождението*, ed. Е. Бужашки et al., София 1976, pp. 72–92.

Петрова Г., *Престъпленията в средновековна България*, София 1992.

Петрова П., *Църквата при с. Сини вир, Шуменско*, [in:] *Археологически открития и разкопки през 1988 г.*, ed. В. Велков, Кърджали 1989, p. 135.

Петрова П., *Църквите при с. Сини вир, Шуменско*, [in:] *Археологически открития и разкопки през 1987 г.*, ed. В. Велков, Благоевград 1988, pp. 190–191.

Петрунова Б., *Нови археологически данни за крепостта Калиакра*, [in:] *Каварна. Средище на българския Североизток. Сборник доклади от научна конференция Каварна – 2007 г.*, ed. eadem, Х. Кузов, Д. Мирчева, Каварна 2007, pp. 126–139.

Петрунова Б., *Реликвите на Калиакра*, Добрич 2014.

Пикио Р., *България в Църковната история на Цезар Бароний*, [in:] idem, *Православното славянство и старобългарската културна традиция*, transl. А. Джамбелука Коссова, София 1994, pp. 587–600.

Пириватрић С., *Два хронолошка прилога о крају Првог бугарског царства*, ЗРВИ 34, 1995, pp. 51–55.

Пириватрич С., *Самуиловата държава. Обхват и характер*, София 2000.

Плетньов В., *Варна през Средновековието (VII–XIV в.)*, [in:] idem, И. Русев, *История на Варна*, vol. II, *Средновековие и Възраждане (VII в. – 1878 г.)*, Варна 2012, pp. 11–302.

Плетньов В., *Крепостта Варна според писмените извори от IX–XII в.*, ДобСб 30, 2015, pp. 193–219.

Плетньов В., Павлова В., *Ранносредновековни ремъчни накрайници във Варненския археологически музей*, ИНМВ 28 (43), 1992, pp. 158–223.

Пляков З., *Населението в областта на Средна Струма през VII–IX век*, [in:] *Четвърти международен Конгрес по славянска археология, София – 1980 (Доклади и съобщения)*, vol. I, ed. Д. Ангелов, София 1992, pp. 386–391.

Подскалски Г., *Средњовековна теолошка књижевност у Бугарској и Србији (865–1459)*, Београд 2010.

Половой Н.Я., *О дате второго похода Игоря на греков и похода русских на Бердаа*, ВВ 14, 1958, pp. 138–147.

Половой Н.Я *К вопросу о первом походе Игоря против Византии. (Сравнительный анализ русских и византийских источников)*, ВВ 18, 1962, pp. 85–104.

Полывянный Д.И., *Царь Петр I и его правление в культурной традиции средневековой Болгарии*, [in:] *Славяне и их соседи. XX конференция памяти В. Д. Королюка. Становление славянского мира и Византия в эпоху раннего Средневековья. Сборник тезисов*, ed. Г.Г. Литаврин, Б.Н. Флоря, О.А. Акимова, Москва 2001, pp. 97–99.

Полывянный Д.И., *Балканский город XIII–XV вв. – типология и специфика развития*, ЕВ 20.1, 1984, p. 28–50.

Полывянный Д.И., *Царь Петр в исторической памяти болгарского средневековья*, [in:] *Средновековният българин и "другите". Сборник в чест на 60-годишнината на проф. дин Петър Ангелов*, ed. А. Николов, Г.Н. Николов, София 2013, pp. 137–145.

Попконстантинов К., *Граждански комплекси в Плиска и Преслав*, [in:] *Средновековният български град*, ed. П. Петров, София 1980, pp. 117–128.

Попконстантинов К., *Епиграфски бележки за Иван, Цар Симеоновият син*, БСП 3, 1994, pp. 71–80.

Попконстантинов К., *Равненски манастир*, [in:] *КМЕ*, vol. III, pp. 423–428.

Попконстантинов К., Атанасов Г., *За два надписа от X в. от манастира при Черноглавци, Шуменско*, Епо 2.4, 1994, pp. 105–110.

Попконстантинов К., Костова Р., *Манастирът на Георги синкел български в Преслав: Историята на една аристократична фамилия от X в.*, Пр.Сб 7, 2013, pp. 44–63.

Попконстантинов К., Костова Р., *Манастир на чъргубиля Мостич*, [in:] *Археологически открития и разкопки през 2007 г.*, София 2008, pp. 629–632.

Попконстантинов К., Костова Р., *Скрипторият в Равненския манастир: още веднъж за украсата на старобългарските ръкописи от IX–X в.*, [in:] *Средновековна християнска Европа: Изток и Запад. Ценности, традиции, общуване*, ed. В. Гюзелев, А. Милтенова, София 2002, pp. 719–725.

Попконстантинов К., Костова Р., Плетньов В., *Манастирите при Равна и Караачтеке до Варна в манастирската география на България през IX–X в.*, AMV 3.2, 2005, pp. 107–121.

Попконстантинов К., Плетньов В., Костова Р., *Средновековен княжески манастир в м. Караачтеке – Варна*, [in:] *Археологически Открития и Разкопки през 2010 г.*, ed. М. Гюрова, София 2011, pp. 497–500.

Попов А., *Военнотопографският фактор при изграждането на отбранителните съоръжения по Южния склон на Стара Планина*, ВС 47.2, 1978, pp. 110–129.

Попов А., *Крепости по Сърнена гора*, ИБИД 31, 1977, pp. 39–50.

Попов А., *Ролята на военноукрепителната система в Източната и Централната част на Стара Планина през време на българската средновековна държава*, ВС 37.4, 1968, pp. 61–72.

Попов А., *Старопланинската укрепителна система за защитата на средновековния Търновград*, ИОИМВТ 5, 1972, pp. 65–121.

Поповић В., *Кврат, Кубер и Аспарух*, Ста 37, 1986, pp. 113–126.

Поповић В., *Сирмиум, град царева и мученика*, Сремска Митровица 2003.

Плетньов В., *Производството на коланни гарнитури в ранносредновековна България*, Пр.Сб 6, 2004, pp. 228–240.

Попова Ц., *Каталог на археоботаническите останки на територията на България (1980–2008)*, ИИз 20/21, 2009, pp. 71–166.

Примов Б., *За икономическата и политическата роля на Първата българска държава в международните отношения на средновековна Европа*, ИП 17.2, 1961, pp. 33–62.

Професор Петър Мутафчиев познат и непознат, ed. Т. Попнеделев, Й. Соколов, София 1997.

Пчелов Е.В., *Генеалогия древнерусских князей IX–начала XI в.*, Москва 2001.

Радојчић Н., *Српски историчар Јован Рајић*, Београд 1952.

Рабовянов Д., *Раждането на българската полиоркетика*, ИРИМВТ 20, 2005, pp. 150–159.

Рабовянов Д., *Извънстоличните каменни крепости на Първото българско царство (IX – началото на XI век)*, София 2011.

Рабовянов Д., *Традиции и влияния в крепостното строителство на Първото българско царство в периода X – началото на XI век*, [in:] *Европейският Югоизток през втората половина на X – началото на XI век. История и култура*, ed. В. Гюзелев, Г.Н. Николов, София 2015, pp. 423–431.

Раев М., *Переяславец на Дунав – мит и действителност в речта на княз Святослав в Повесть временных лет*, ГСУ.НЦСВПИД 95.14, 2006, pp. 193–203.

Раев М., *Преслав или Переяславец на Дунае? (Предварительные замечания об одном из возможных источников ПВЛ и его трансформации)*, НЗУІЗНС 20, 2008, pp. 37–40.

Раич И., *Исторія разныхъ славенскихъ народовъ наипаче Болгаръ, Хорватовъ и Сербовъ изъ тмы забвенія изятая и во свѣтъ историческiи произведенная*, vol. I, Віенна 1794.

Райков Д., *Историческа съдба на македонските българи. Свидетелства за българското възраждане в Македония*, София 1997.

Рашев Р., *Аул и град в България през VIII–IX в.*, [in:] *Сборник в чест на акад. Димитър Ангелов*, ed. В. Велков, София 1994, pp. 170–177.

Рашев Р., *Българската езическа култура VII–IX век*, София 2008.

Рашев Р., *"Втората война" на Симеон срещу Византия (913–927) като литературен и политически факт*, [in:] idem, *Цар Симеон Велики. Щрихи към личността и делото му*, София 2007, pp. 84–96.

Рашев Р., *За глинените бъклици в средновековна България*, ППре 1, 1979, pp. 206–209.

Рашев Р., *Земленатa укрепителна система на Първото българско царство*, ППре 2, 1981, pp. 99–103.

Рашев Р., *Княз Симеон и император Александър*, [in:] idem, *Цар Симеон Велики. Щрихи към личността и делото му*, София 2007, pp. 32–41.

Рашев Р., *Появата на средновековни селища във високите части на Стара планина*, ШУЕКП.ТКИБ 1, 1997, pp. 108–113.

Рашев Р., *Преходът от землена към каменна фортификация в Първото българско царство*, [in:] *Тангра. Сборник в чест на 70–годишнината на акад. Васил Гюзелев*, ed. M. Каймакамова et al., София 2006, pp. 301–310.

Рашев Р., *Първото българско царство и морето*, [in:] *Средновековна България и Черноморието (Сборник доклади от националната конференция Варна – 1980)*, ed. А. Кузев, Т. Йорданов, Варна 1982, pp. 47–56.

Рашев Р., *Раннобългарски землени укрепителни съоръжения*, [in:] *Български средновековни градове и крепости*, vol. I, *Градове и крепости по Дунав и Черно Море*, ed. А. Кузев, В. Гюзелев, Варна 1981, pp. 16–44.

Рашев Р., *Старобългарски укрепления на Долния Дунав (VII–XI в.)*, Варна 1982.

Рашев Р., *Цар Симеон – "нов Мойсей" или "нов Давид"*, [in:] idem, *Цар Симеон Велики. Щрихи към личността и делото му*, София 2007, pp. 60–72.

Рибаров Г.К., *Бозайниците в бита на жителите от ранновизантийското и средновековно селище на Хисарлъка (Сливен)*, Архе 32.4, 1990, pp. 50–58.

Розов Б., *Солниците при гр. Поморие*, ГП 4.4/5, 1950, pp. 20–23.

Рычка В., *Чью славу переял Переяслав?*, НЗУIЗНС 16, 2005, pp. 129–134.

Салмина М.А., *Хроника Константина Манассии как источник Русского хронографа*, ТОДЛ 32, 1978, pp. 279–287.

Самарџић Р., *Писци српске историје*, Београд 1976.

Сахаров А.Н., *Дипломацията на древна Русия, IX – първата половина на X в.*, София 1984.

Сахаров А.Н., *Дипломатия Святослава*, Москва 1982.

Сердика, Археологически материали и проучвания, vol. I, ed. Т. Герасимов, София 1964; vol. II, ed. В. Велков, София 1989.

Симеонова Л., *Крепостта Видинис/Бдин и "завръщането на Византия на Дунава": реализация и крах на една имперска мечта*, SB 32, 2017, pp. 61–93.

Симеонова Л., *Образът на българския владетел във византийската книжнина (средата на IX – началото на XI в.). Няколко примера*, [in:] *Представата за "другия" на Балканите*, ed. N. Данова, В. Димова, М. Калицин, София 1995, pp. 20–31.

Симеонова Л., *Правна защита на жените и децата в новопокръстеното българско общество (Закон за съдене на хората, Еклога)*, SB 27, 2009, pp. 117–125.

Симеонова Л., *Пътуване по Дунава (IX–XI в.)*, [in:] *Пътуванията в средновековна България. Материали от първата национална конференция "Пътуване към България.*

Пътуванията в средновековна България и съвременният туризъм", Шумен, 8–11.05.2008 г., ed. И. Йорданов, Велико Търново 2009, pp. 104–109.

Симеонова Л., *Щрихи към историята на тайната дипломация, разузнаването и контраразузнаването в средновековния свят*, [in:] *Тангра. Сборник в чест на 70. годишнината на Акад. Васил Гюзелев*, ed. М. Каймакавова et al., София 2006, pp. 499–530.

Славейков П.Р., *Писма*, СНУНК 20, 1904, pp. 1–216.

Славова Т., *Владетел и администрация в ранносредновековна България. Филологически аспекти*, София 2010.

Славова Т., *Други преводачи и преписивачи от книжовния кръг около цар Симеон*, [in:] *История на българската средновековна литература*, ed. А. Милтенова, София 2008, pp. 251–254.

Славова Т., *Други преводачи и преписвачи от книжовния кръг около цар Симеон*, [in:] *ИСБЛ*, pp. 251–254.

Славова Т., *Юридическа литература*, [in:] *ИСБЛ*, pp. 194–202.

Словарь русского языка X–XXVII вв., vol. XIII, Москва 1987.

Сотникова М.П., Спасский И.Г., *Тысячелетие древнейших монет России. Сводный каталог русских монет X–XI вв.*, Ленинград 1983.

Спасов Н., Илиев Н., *Костни останки от зубър (Bison Bonasus L.) в средновековното селище край с. Гарван, Силистренски окръг*, [in:] Ж. Въжарова, *Средновековното селище с. Гарван, Силистренски окръг VI–XI в.*, София 1986, p. 68.

Спасова М., *На коя дата и през кой месец се е провел преславският събор от 893 година*, ПКШ 8, 2005, pp. 84–101.

Спасова М., *Народно ли е народното (безименното) житие на св. Йоан Рилски*, Pbg 22.4, 1998, pp. 50–74.

Сперанский М., *Из истории русско-славянских литературных связей*, Москва 1960.

Среднеболгарский перевод Хроники Константина Манассии в славянских литературах, ed. Д.С. Лихачев, И.С. Дуйчев, София 1988.

Станев К., *Морето – неусвоеното пространство на Първото българско царство*, Ист 15.2/3, 2007, pp. 25–34.

Станилов С., *Метални гарнитури за ремъци и облекло от двореца във Велики Преслав*, ППре 7, 1995, pp. 110–135.

Станилов С., *Наблюдения по формирането на орнаменталната система в българската художествена керамика от IX–X век*, [in:] *Иванка Акрабова-Жандова. In memoriam*, ed. М. Ваклинова et al., София 2009, pp. 129–142.

С т а н и л о в С., *Старобългарски ремъчни украси с правоъгълна форма*, [in:] *Сборник в чест на акад. Димитър Ангелов*, ed. В. В е л к о в, София 1994, pp. 177–189.

С т а н и л о в С., *Художественият метал на българското ханство на Дунава 7–9 век*, София 2006.

С т а н и л о в С., *Художественият метал на Златния век (IX–XI в.). Продължение на темата*, [in:] *Великотърновският Университет "Св. св. Кирил и Методий" и българската археология*, vol. I, ed. Б. Б о р и с о в, Велико Търново 2010, pp. 423–436.

С т а н к о в В., *Новооткрит печат на Петър I (927–969)*, ППре 9, 2003, pp. 315–317.

С т а н ч е в Д., *Ранносредновековни пръстени от фонда на Историческия музей – Русе*, [in:] *Проф. д.и.н. Станчо Ваклинов и средновековната българска култура*, ed. К. П о п к о н с т а н т и н о в, Б. Б о р и с о в, Р. К о с т о в а, Велико Търново 2005, pp. 220–229.

С т а н ч е в С., *Материали от Дворцовия център в Плиска*, ИАИ 23, 1960, pp. 23–65.

С т а н ч е в С., *Разкопки и новооткрити материали в Плиска през 1948 г.*, ИАИ 20, 1955, pp. 183–227.

С т а н ч е в С., И в а н о в С., *Некрополът до Нови Пазар*, София 1958.

С т а р е в а Л., *Български обичаи и ритуали*, София 2005.

С т е п а н о в Ц., *Власт и авторитет в ранносредновековна България (VII – ср. IX в.)*, София 1999.

С т о е в а К., *Битовата керамика от манастира в местността Манастирчето край Велики Преслав (предварително съобщение)*, [in:] *Великотърновският университет "Св. св. Кирил и Методий" и българската архелогия*, vol. I, ed. Б. Б о р и с о в, Велико Търново 2010, pp. 525–538.

С т о и м е н о в Д., *Към договора между България и Византия от 927 г.*, Век 17.6, 1988, pp. 19–23.

С т о й к о в а А., *Черноризец Храбър*, [in:] *ИБСЛ*, pp. 248–251.

Стопанска история на България 681–1981, ed. Л. Б е р о в et al., София 1981.

С т о я н о в М., К о д о в Х., *Опис на славянските ръкописи в Софийската Народна библиотека*, vol. III, София 1964.

С у л т о в Б., *Новооткрит керамичен център при с. Хотница от римската и старобългарската епоха*, Архе 11.4, 1969, pp. 12–24.

С ю з ю м о в М.Я., *Лев Диакон и его время*, [in:] Л е в Д и а к о н, *История*, transl. М.М. К о п ы л е н к о, ed. Г.Г. Л и т а в р и н, Москва 1988, pp. 137–165.

С ю з ю м о в М.Я., *Об историческом труде Феодора Дафнопата*, ВОб 2, 1916, pp. 295–302.

С ъ б е в Т., *Отец Паисий Хилендарски. Епоха, личност, дело, значение*, [in:] i d e m, *Избрани съчинения върху историята на църквата*, ed. А. К р ъ с т е в, Велико Търново 2005, pp. 214–250.

С ъ б е в Т., *Самостойна народностна църква в средновековна България. Християнизаторски процес, основане и възход, автокефалия и междуцърковно положение, църква и държава*, Велико Търново 2003.

Т а б а к о в С., *Опит за история на град Сливен*, vol. I, *Сливен и Сливенско до началото на XIX в.*, ed. И. Т о д о р о в, com. П. А н г е л о в, В. Д е ч е в, София 1986.

Т в о р о г о в О.В., *Паралипомен Зонары: текст и комментарий*, [in:] *Летописи и хроники. Новые исследования. 2009–2010*, ed. О.Л. Н о в и к о в а, Москва–Санкт-Петербург 2010, pp. 3–101.

Т и в ч е в П., *За войната между Византия и България през 977 г.*, ИП 25.4, 1969, pp. 80–88.

Т и ш к о в Х., Ц. М и х а й л о в, Л. З я п к о в, Д. Г о р у н о в а, *Предбалканска област*, [in:] *География на България в три тома*, vol. III, *Физикогеографско и социално-икономическо райониране*, ed. К. М и ш е в, София 1989, pp. 65–85.

Т и х о в Т., *Някои аспекти на външната търговия на България и Византия през периода VII–X век*, [in:] *Пътуванията в средновековна България. Материали от първата национална конференция "Пътуване към България. Пътуванията в средновековна България и съвременният туризъм", Шумен, 8–11.05.2008 г.*, ed. И. Й о р д а н о в, Велико Търново 2009, p. 328–338.

Т о д о р о в Г.Д., *Историческите възгледи на Паисий Хилендарски*, ИИИ 20, 1968, pp. 95–165.

Т о д о р о в Т.Р., *България през втората и третата четвърт на X век: политическа история*, София 2006 [unpublished PhD thesis].

Т о д о р о в Т., *Владетелският статут и титла на цар Петър I след октомври 927 г.: писмени сведения и сфрагистични данни (сравнителен анализ)*, [in:] *Юбилеен сборник. Сто години от рождението на д-р Васил Хараланов (1907–2007)*, Шумен 2008, pp. 93–108.

Т о д о р о в Т., *Вътрешнодинастичният проблем в България от края на 20-те–началото на 30-те години на X в.*, Истор 3, 2008, pp. 263–279.

Т о д о р о в Т., *За едно отражение на съвладетелската практика в Първото българско царство през втората половина на IX–първите десетилетия на X в.*, [in:] *България, българите и Европа – мит, история, съвремие*, vol. IV, *Доклади от Международна конференция в памет на проф. д.и.н. Йордан Андреев "България, земя на блажени...", В. Търново, 29–31 октомври 2009 г.*, ed. И. Л а з а р о в, Велико Търново 2011, pp. 173–181.

Т о д о р о в Т., *Кога били пренесени мощите на св. Иван Рилски в Средец*, ГСУ.НЦСВПИД 91(10), 2001, pp. 169–179.

Тодоров Т., *Константин Багренородни и династичният брак между владетелските домове на Преслав и Константинопол от 927 г.*, ПКШ 7, 2003, pp. 391–398.

Тодоров Т., *Към въпроса за престолонаследието в Първото българско царство*, ППре 8, 2000, pp. 202–207.

Тодоров Т., *От отрицание към реабилитация. Историографски бележки за цар Петър I (927–969) и неговото време*, [in:] *Писменост, книжовници, книги. Българската следа в културната история на Европа. Материали от петата национална конференция по история, археология и културен туризъм. Пътуване към България. Шумен, 26–28.04.2016 г.*, ed. И. Йорданов, Шумен 2018, pp. 86–97.

Тодоров Т., *"Слово за мир с българите" и българо-византийските отношения през последните години от управленето на цар Симеон*, [in:] *България, българите и техните съседи през векове. Изследвания и материали од научна конференция в памет на д-р Христо Коларов, 30–31 октомври 1998 г., Велико Търново*, ed. Й. Андреев, Велико Търново 2001, pp. 141–150.

Тодорова Х., *Архитектурата на средновековното селище*, [in:] *Дуранкулак*, ed. Х. Тодорова, vol. I, София 1989, pp. 45–48.

Тодорова-Чанева С., *Женският накит от епохата на Първото българско царство. VII–XI в.*, София 2009.

Томов Т., *Византия – позната и непозната*, [2]София 2014.

Томов Т., *Константинопол и руската колония (до 1204 г.)*, София [s.a.].

Тотев Т., *Две рисувани белоглинени трапезни блюда с литургическо предназначение и употреба от селище във Велики Преслав*, ПКШ 11, 2010, pp. 254–259.

Тотев Т., *Дворцовият манастир в Преслав*, Шумен 1998.

Тотев К., *За една група печати на цар Симеон*, [in:] *Общото и специфичното в Балканските народи до края на XIX в. Сборник в чест на 70-годишнината на проф. Василика Тъпкова-Заимова*, ed. Г. Бакалов, София 1999, pp. 107–112.

Тотев Т., *За една игра в средновековна България*, Архе 14.3, 1972, pp. 33–41.

Тотев Т., *За обработка на кост в средновековна България*, Архе 4.3, 1963, pp. 83–92.

Тотев Т., *Керамичната икона в средновековна България*, София 2001.

Тотев Т., *Керамични пещи в чашата на язовир "Виница" край Преслав*, Архе 15.4, 1973, pp. 58–68.

Тотев Т., *Колективна находка от средновековни оръдия на труда от с. Златар*, Архе 8.4, 1966, pp. 33–35.

Тотев Т. *Към въпроса за творчеството на преславските майстори на рязана кост през IX–X в.*, ППре 6, 1993, pp. 109–115.

Тотев Т., *Манаситирът в "Тузлалъка" – център на рисувана керамика в Преслав през IX–X в.*, София 1982.

Тотев Т., *Монастыри в Плиске и Преславе в IX–X вв. (Краткая археологическая характеристика)*, ПКШ 7, 2004, pp. 347–365.

Тотев Т., *Нови материали и наблюдения за трапезната рисувана керамика от два манастира във Велики Преслав*, ПКШ 10, 2008, pp. 404–417.

Тотев Т., *Нови наблюдения и данни за облика на гражданската архитектура през Първото българско царство*, ПКШ 1, 1995, pp. 317–331.

Тотев Т., *Още наблюдения за църква № 1 в Дворцовия манастир на Велики Преслав*, [in:] *Историкии*, vol. IV, *Научни изследвания в чест на професор дин Иван Карайотов по случай неговата 70-годишнина*, ed. И. Йорданов, Шумен 2011, pp. 299–308.

Тотев Т., *Преслав*, [in:] Д. Овчаров, Т. Тотев, А. Попов, *Стари български столици. Плиска. Велики Преслав. Търновград*, София 1980, pp. 71–133.

Тотев Т., *Преславската култура и изкуство през IX–X век. Студии и статии*, София 2000.

Тотев Т., *Преславските ателиета за рисувана керамика*, ППре 7, 1995, pp. 101–109.

Тотев Т., *Производство рисованной керамики в болгарских монастырях*, АДСВ 32, 2001, pp. 109–126.

Тотев Т., *Родов манастир на владетелите в Преслав*, СЛ 20, 1987, pp. 120–128.

Тотев Т., *Святая Богородица в искусстве Великого Преслава (IX–X вв.)*, ПКШ 13, 2013, pp. 350–360.

Тотев Т., *Старобългарските манастири в светлината на археологическите разкопки и проучвания*, СЛ 22, 1990, pp. 3–13.

Тотев Т., *Тридесет години археологически разкопки в Преслав*, Архе 16.3, 1974, pp. 48–60.

Тотев Т., *Шахмат в средновековна България*, ШМ 33.1, 1980, pp. 23–25.

Тотев Т., Рашев Р., *Ноци данни за старобългарското изкуство (VIII–X в.)*, ПКШ 12, 2012, pp. 387–394.

Трайковски К., *Средновековните цркви в градот Μορδοβισδος во Македонийа*, ГСУ. НЦСВПИД 97 (16), 2007, pp. 121–126.

Трендафилов Х., *Българският апокрифен летопис и Мавро Орбини*, Шумен 2016.

Трендафилов Х., *Диалогът Иван Рилски – цар Петър като историософски факт*, ПКШ 4, 1999, pp. 20–31.

Трендафилов Х., *Младостта на цар Симеон*, София 2010.

Трендафилов Х., *Цар и век. Времето на Симеон. Четири инсталации*, Шумен 2017.

Трифонов Ю., *Беседата на Козма Пресвитера и нейният автор*, СБАН.КИФ 16, 1923, pp. 1–77.

Трифонов Ю., *Достоверен ли е разказът за ослепяване на Борисовия син Владимир*, УП 26, 1927, pp. 864–890.

Турилов А., *Борис*, [in:] *Православная энциклопедия*, vol. VI, Москва 2003, p. 31.

Турилов А., *К вопросу о болгарских источниках Русского хронографа*, [in:] *Летописи и хроники. Сборник статей*, Москва 1984, pp. 20–24 [= А. Турилов, *Межславянские культурные связи эпохи Средневековья и источниковедение истории и культуры славян. Этюды и характеристики*, Москва 2012, pp. 704–708].

Турилов А., *Памятники древнерусской литературы и письменности у южных славян в XII–XIV вв. (проблемы и перспективы изучения)*, [in:] *Славянские литературы. XI Международный съезд славистов. Братислава, сентябрь 1993 г. Доклады российской делегации*, Москва 1993, pp. 27–42.

Турилов А., *Slavica Cyrillomethodiana. Источниковедение истории и культуры южных славян и Древней Руси. Межславянские культурные связи эпохи средневековья*, Москва 2010.

Турилов А., Флоря Б., *Христианская литература у славян в середине X – середине XI в. и межславянские культурные связи*, [in:] *Христианство в странах Восточной, Юго-Восточной и Центральной Европы на пороге второго тысячелетия*, Москва 2002, pp. 398–458.

Тъпкова-Заимова В., *Долни Дунав – limes и limen между Византия и славянския свят*, [in:] *Руско-български връзки през вековете*, ed. Д. Ангелов, София 1986, pp. 39–45.

Тъпкова-Заимова В., *Дюканжов списък*, Pbg 24.3, 2000, pp. 21–49.

Тъпкова-Заимова В., *Крепости и укрепени градове през Първото българско царство. Според сведения от византийските автори*, ВС 25.3, 1956, pp. 40–61.

Тъпкова-Заимова В., *Към въпроса за военните пътища през Първото българско царство*, ИП 14.1, 1958, pp. 58–73.

Тъпкова-Заимова В., *Търново между Ерусалим, Рим и Цариград*, ТКШ 4, 1985, p. 249–261.

Тъпкова-Заимова В., *Падане на Североизточна България под византийска власт*, [in:] *История на България в четиринадесет тома*, vol. II, *Първа българска държава*, ed. Д. Ангелов, София 1981, pp. 389–397.

Тъпкова-Заимова В., *Превземането на Преслав в 971 г. и проблемите на българската църква*, [in:] *1100 години Велики Преслав*, vol. I, ed. Т. Тотев, Шумен 1995, pp. 172–181.

Успенскій Θ.И., *Неизданное церковное слово о болгарско-византійскихъ отношеніяхъ въ первой половинѣ X в.*, ЛИФОИНУ.ВО 4, 1894, pp. 48–123.

Федер У., *За една тълкувателна творба, преведена от Методиевите ученици*, [in:] idem, *Хиляда години като един ден*, София 2005, pp. 145–150.

Федер У., Новак Р., *За приноса на Методиевите ученици в тълкувателната литература*, КМС 4, 1987, pp. 304–310.

Филипоски Т., *Прашањето за проодноста на западниот дел от патот Via Egnatia (Драч–Солун) во втората половина на IX век*, [in:] *Пътуванията в средновековна България. Материали от първата национална конференция "Пътуване към България. Пътуванията в средновековна България и съвременният туризъм", Шумен, 8–11.05.2008 г.*, ed. И. Йорданов, Велико Търново 2009, pp. 110–119.

Флоря Б., *Формирование государственности и зарождение политической мысли у славянских народов*, [in:] *Очерки истории и культуры славян*, В.К. Волков, Москва 1996, pp. 260–272.

Флоря Б., Турилов А., *Общественная мысль Сербии конца XII–XIII вв. (Власть и общество в представлениях сербских книжников)*, [in:] *Власть и общество в литературных текстах Древней Руси и других славянских стран (XII–XIII вв.)*, ed. Б. Флоря, Москва 2012, pp. 125–168.

Фосие Р., *Обикновеният човек през Средновековието*, transl. В. Бояджиева, София 2009.

Харбова М.А., *Отбранителните съоръжения в българското средновековие*, София 1981.

Хаджииванов С., *Засадите в старобългарското военно изкуство*, ВС 23.4, 1954, pp. 36–57.

Хранова А., *Историография и литература. За социално конструиране на исторически понятия и Големи разкази в българската култура XIX–XX век*, vol. II, *Животът на три понятия в българската култура: възраждане, средновековие, робство*, София 2011.

Хрисимов Н., *За времето на усвояване на предпланинските и планинските райони в Първото българско царство*, ИРИМГ 2, 2015, pp. 55–69.

Хрисимов Н., *За прехода от детство към зрелост в българското Ранно средновековие*, BalkF 19.1/2, 2016, pp. 92–100.

Хрисимов Н., *Храната в Първото българско царство*, [in:] *Стандарти на всекидневието през Средновековието и Новото време*, ed. К. Мутафова et al., Велико Търново 2012, pp. 201–232.

Христов Д., *Историографски корени на Дриновото творчество*, ИП 71.1/2, 2015, pp. 32–45.

Христов Д., *Корените на българската военноотбранителна доктрина (681–1018 г.)*, ВС 63.1, 1993, pp. 5–20.

Христов Я., *Военнопленниците в българо-сръбските отношения през ранно средновековие*, Епо 23.1, 2015, pp. 86–98.

Христова Н., *Жените в Западна Европа, V–IX век*, Велико Търново 2004.

Христодулова М., *Титул и регалии болгарской владетельницы в эпоху средневековья (VII–XIV вв.)*, ЕВ 14.3, 1978, pp. 141–148.

Цанев Д., *Българската историческа книжнина през Възраждането. XVIII-първата половина на XIX в.*, София 1989.

Цанев Д., *За Българите. Чуждата историческа българистика през XVIII–XIX век*, София 1981.

Цанев Д., *Историята на Раич и нейните български преводи и преработки*, ИНБКМ 14, 1976, pp. 181–210.

Цанев Д., *Ю. Венелин и българската възрожденска историография*, ИБИД 26, 1984, pp. 193–200.

Цанков Д., *Единъ погледъ върху блъгарската исторія*, [in:] *Месецословъ за 1857 г.*, vol. I, Цариградъ 1857, pp. 60–130.

Цанкова-Петкова Г., *Към въпроса за селскостопанската техника в средновековна България и някои съседни балкански области*, ИИИ 13, 1963, pp. 123–137.

Цанкова-Петкова Г., *Първата война между България и Византия при цар Симеон и възстановяването на българската търговия с Цариград*, ИИИ 20, 1968, pp. 167–200.

Цанкова-Петкова Г., *Сердика – Средец през ранното средновековие (IX–XII в.)*, [in:] *София през вековете*, vol. I, *Древност, Средновековие, Възраждане*, ed. П. Динеков, София 1989, pp. 42–54.

Цанкова-Петкова Г., Тивчев П., *Нови данни за историята на Софийската област през последните десетилетия на византийското владичество*, ИИИ 14/15, 1964, pp. 315–324.

Цибранска-Костова М., *Покайната книжнина на Българското средновековие IX–XVIII век*, София 2011.

Цибранска-Костова М., *Сборникът "Различни потреби" на Яков Крайков между Венеция и Балканите през XVI век*, София 2012.

Цветков Б., *Ключката отбранителна линия на цар Самуил от 1014 г. – научни постижения, проблеми и нови данни*, [in:] ПБА 1, 1992, pp. 87–91.

Чангова Й., *Към въпроса за устройството на средновековния български град (IX–XIV в.)*, [in:] *Архитектурата на Първата и Втората българска държава. Материали*, ed. Г. Кожухаров, София 1975, pp. 79–101.

Чангова Й., *Към проучването на старобългарската металопластика през IX–X век*, Пр.Сб 3, 1983 pp. 198–202.

Чангова Й., *Перник*, vol. III, *Крепостта Перник VIII–XIV в.*, София 1992.

Чангова Й., *Средновековни оръдия на труда в България*, ИАИ 25, 1962, pp. 19–55.

Чанева-Дечевска Н., *Църкви и манастири от Велики Преслав*, София 1980.

Чешмеджиев Д., *Българската държавна традиция в апокрифите: цар Петър в Българския апокрифен летопис*, [in:] *Българско средновековие: общество, власт, история. Сборник в чест на проф. д-р Милияна Каймакамова*, ed. Г. Николов, А. Николов, София 2013, pp. 262–271.

Чешмеджиев Д., *За времето на пренасяне на мощите на св. Иоанн Рилски от Рила в Средец*, BMd 6, 2015, pp. 79–89.

Чешмеджиев Д., *Култовете на българските светци през IX–XII в. Автореферат*, Пловдив 2016.

Чешмеджиев Д., *Култът към цар Петър (927–969): манастирски или държавен?*, [in:] *Љубав према образовању и вера у Бога у православним манастирама, Пета међународна Хилендарска конференција. Зборник изабраних радова 1*, ed. P. Matejić et al., Београд–Columbus, Ohio 2006, pp. 245–257.

Чешмеджиев Д., *Към въпроса за култа на княз Борис – Михаил в средновековна България*, ИП 55.3/4, 1999, pp. 158–176.

Чешмеджиев Д., *Няколко бележки за култа към цар Петър I (927–965)*, [in:] *Християнската традиция и царската институция в българската култура*, ed. В. Бонева, Е. Иванова, Шумен 2003, pp. 23–37.

Чешмеджиев Д., *Цар Петър във византийските извори*, [in:] *Кръгла маса. "Златният век на цар Симеон: политика, религия и култура"*, ed. В. Станев, София 2014, p. 103–110.

Чимбулева Ж., *Месемврия–Несебър*, [in:] В. Велков, Л. Огненова-Маринова, Ж. Чимбулева, *Месембрия– Месемврия–Несебър*, София 1991, pp. 72–91.

Чолова Ц., *Данни за българския външнотърговски обмен и мореплаване в Шестоднева на Йоан Екзарх*, Век 8.4, 1979, pp. 62–65.

Чолпанов Б., Александров Е., *Военна история на Първата българска държава (681–1018)*, [in:] *История на българите*, vol. V, *Военна история на българите от древността до наши дни*, ed. Д. Зафиров, Е. Александров, София 2007, p. 56–105.

Шандровская В.С., *Печати титулованных женщин Византии*, АДСВ 33, 2002, pp. 89–101.

Шишков Т., *Исторія на българкыя народъ*, Цариградъ 1873.

Шкорпил К., *Домашний вид и промысел*, ИРАИК 10, 1905, pp. 301–317.

Шкорпил К., *Печат на княз Михаил-Борис*, ИВАД 7, 1921, pp. 108–116.

Шкорпил К., *Старбългарска съобщителна мрежа около Преслав и крепостите по нея*, БИБ 2.2, 1929, pp. 80–111.

Шкорпил К., *Укрепления на Първата българска държава в Северна Добруджа край Дунава и Черноморския бряг*, ИБИД 16/17, 1940, pp. 525–535.

Штапова Й., *О производстве стекла в епоху Первого болгарского царства*, Пр.Сб 4, 1993, pp. 151–165.

Штављанин-Ђорђевић Љ., Гроздановић-Пајић М., Цернић Л., *Опис ћирилских рукописа Народне библиотеке Србије*, vol. I, Београд 1986.

Щапов Я.Н., *Древнерусские княжеские уставы XI–XV вв.*, Москва 1976.

Щапов Я.Н., *Княжеские уставы и церковь в Древней Руси XI–XIV вв.*, Москва 1972.

Щерева И., Вачева К., Владимирова-Аладжова Д., *Туида–Сливен 1*, София 2001.

Элиаде М., *Тайные общества. Обряды, инициации и посвящения*, Москва–Санкт-Петербург 1999.

Янин В.Л., *Актовые печати Древней Руси X–XV вв.*, vol. I, *Печати X – начала XIII в.*, Москва 1970.

Янков D., *Средновековни гробове от Стара Загора*, [in:] *Историко-археологически изследвания. В памет на проф. д-р Станчо Ваклинов*, ed. К. Попконстантинов, Велико Търново 1994, pp. 121–127.

Indices

Index of People and Personages

C

D

E

F

G

H

N

O

P

R

S

T

U

V

W

Y

Z

Index of Ethnic, Religious and Geographic Names

C

D

E

F

G

P

R

Illustrations

1. Lead seal of tsar Peter and tsaritsa Maria-Irene Lekapene. The photograph of this relic was made available for our publication by Nikolay Kanev and Milen Nikolov, the first to publish an image of this seal (Н. Кънев, М. Николов, *Непубликувани ранносредновековни оловни печати от крепостта Русокастро и прилежащият ѝ район*, ППр 13, in press), with the approval of the Regional Historical Museum in Burgas, where the seal is kept.

2. Seal depicting Peter with the inscription: **Пєтр[ъ] ц҃рь бл[ъ] га[ромъ]**, Bulgaria, 963–969 (?). Drawing (reconstruction): Elżbieta Myślińska-Brzozowska

3. Constantinople. The church of emperor Romanos I Lekapenos in Myrelaion, and the early Byzantine rotunda upon which the palace (later monastery) stood. Photo A. Kompa

4. Constantinople. The church of Hagia Eirene (of Holy Peace). Photo M.J. Leszka

5. Preslav. The throne room, 10th century. Photo K. Marinow

6. Preslav. Remains of a bath-house, 9th–10th century. Photo K. Marinow

7. Preslav. Remains of a church, 9th–10th century. Photo K. Marinow

8. Preslav. Square by the southern gate – view from within, 10th century. Photo K. Marinow

9. Preslav. Interior of the so-called Golden Church of tsar Symeon I. Photo K. Marinow

10. Pliska. Palace chapel, end of the 9th–10th century. Photo K. Marinow

11. Pliska. Remains of a bath-house, second half of the 9th–10th century. Photo K. Marinow

12. Pliska. The Great Church. Photo K. Marinow

13. Ohrid. View of Samuel's stronghold. Photo K. Marinow

14. Ohrid. Church of Divine Wisdom – exterior, western side. Photo K. Marinow

15. Ohrid. Church of the monastery of SS. Clement and Panteleimon. Photo K. Marinow

16. Monastery of St. Naum by the Ohrid Lake, viewed from the north. Photo K. Marinow

17. Katholikon of the monastery of St. John of Rila. Photo M.J. Leszka

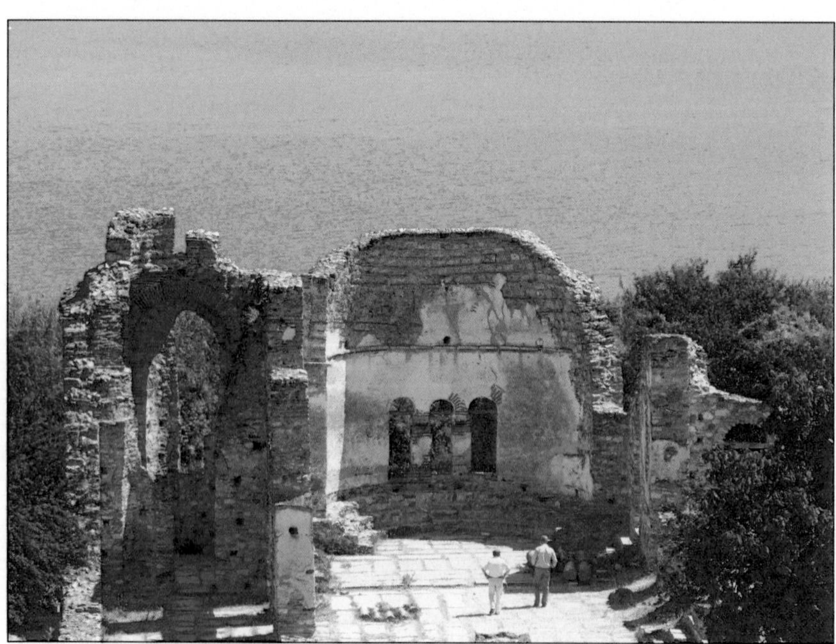

18. Prespa. Basilica of St. Achilles. Photo M.J. Leszka

19. Mesembria. Church of the Hagia Sofia (Holy Wisdom), so-called Old Metropolis. Photo T. Pietras

20. Prilep Stronghold (so-called Markovi Kuli) – view of the interior. Photo K. Marinow

21. Prilep Stronghold (so-called Markovi Kuli) – external view. Photo K. Marinow

22. Prilep Stronghold (so-called Markovi Kuli) – inside the fortification. Photo K. Marinow

23. Preslav, Archaeological museum. Ceramic and marble flooring. Photo K. Marinow

24. Preslav, Archaeological museum. Door frame depicting a griffin, 9th–10th century Photo K. Marinow

25. Preslav, Archaeological museum. Stone block with a Cyrillic inscription. Photo K. Marinow

26. Preslav, Archaeological museum. Capital decorated with vine leaf motif. Photo K. Marinow

27. Dristra (today's Silistra). Archaeological Musem. Christian medallions from 9th–10th c. and late nomad (Pecheneg) medallions from 11th–12th c. Photo N. Hrissimov

28. Dristra (today's Silistra). Fragment of the city walls from outside. Photo N. Hrissimov

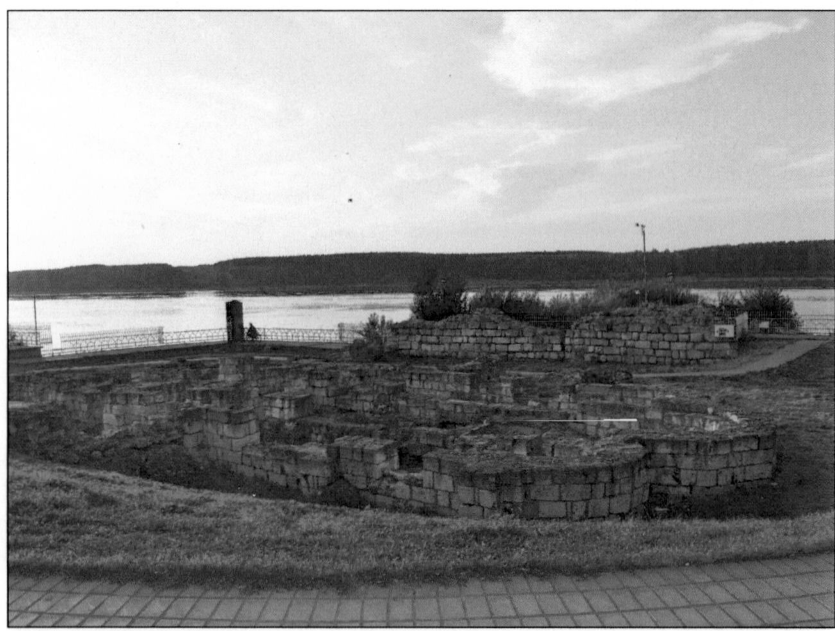

29. Dristra (today's Silistra). Episcopal church № 2, second half of the 9th and 10th–11th c. Photo N. Hrissimov

30. Dristra (today's Silistra). View of the river Danube from the city. Photo N. Hrissimov

Bulgaria under Tsar Peter I, 927–969
(after Günter Prinzing with some changes)
Danube
Solnograd
Hungarians
Pechenegs
CROATIA
Nin
Zadar
Knin
SERBIA
Belgrad
Bdin
Danube
Dristra
Constantia
Pliska
Preslav
Black
Sea
Naissos
BULGARIA
Mesembria
Anchialos
Sozopolis
Agathopolis
Develtos
Beroe
Sredets
Ras
Philippoupolis
Adrianople
Constantinople
A
B
C
Kotor
D
Adriatic
Sea
Dyrrachion
Ohrid
Thessalonike
Athos
Bari
Aegean Sea
BYZANTINE EMPIRE
Smyrna
Ephesos
Athens
Patras
Corinth
Reggio
Syracuse
Rhodos
Crete
Bulgarian territories
Territories temporarily belonging to Bulgaria
Byzantine territories
Slavic authonomic territories:
A – Pagania
B – Zachlumia
C – Travunja
D – Zeta

Designed by Jan Grabarczyk

BYZANTINA LODZIENSIA 1997–2018

I.

Sławomir Bralewski, *Imperatorzy późnego cesarstwa rzymskiego wobec zgromadzeń biskupów*, Łódź 1997, pp. 197.

[*Les empereurs du Bas-Empire romain face aux conciles des évêques*]

II.

Maciej Kokoszko, *Descriptions of Personal Appearance in John Malalas' Chronicle*, Łódź 1998, pp. 181.

III.

Mélanges d'histoire byzantine offerts à Oktawiusz Jurewicz à l'occasion de Son soixante-dixième anniversaire, red. **Waldemar Ceran**, Łódź 1998, pp. 209.

IV.

Mirosław Jerzy Leszka, *Uzurpacje w cesarstwie bizantyńskim w okresie od IV do połowy IX wieku*, Łódź 1999, pp. 149.

[*Usurpations in Byzantine Empire from the 4th to the Half of the 9th Century*]

V.

Małgorzata Beata Leszka, *Rola duchowieństwa na dworze cesarzy wczesnobizantyńskich*, Łódź 2000, pp. 136.

[*The Role of the Clergy at the Early Byzantine Emperors Court*]

VI.

Waldemar Ceran, *Historia i bibliografia rozumowana bizantynologii polskiej (1800–1998)*, tom I–II, Łódź 2001, pp. 786.

[*History and bibliography raisonné of Polish Byzantine studies (1800–1998)*]

VII.

Mirosław Jerzy Leszka, *Wizerunek władców pierwszego państwa bułgarskiego w bizantyńskich źródłach pisanych (VIII – pierwsza połowa XII wieku)*, Łódź 2003, pp. 169.

[*The Image of the First Bulgarian State Rulers Shown in the Byzantine Literary Sources of the Period from the 8th to the First Half of the 12th Centuries*]

VIII.

Teresa Wolińska, *Sycylia w polityce cesarstwa bizantyńskiego w VI–IX wieku*, Łódź 2005, pp. 379.

[*Sicily in Byzantine Policy, 6th–9th Century*]

IX.

Maciej Kokoszko, *Ryby i ich znaczenie w życiu codziennym ludzi późnego antyku i wczesnego Bizancjum (III–VII w.)*, Łódź 2005, pp. 445.

[*The Role of Fish In Everyday Life of the People of Late Antiquity and Early Byzantium (3rd–7th c.)*]

X.

Sławomir Bralewski, *Obraz papiestwa w historiografii kościelnej wczesnego Bizancjum*, Łódź 2006, pp. 334.

[*L'image de la papauté dans l'historiographie ecclésiastique du haut Empire Byzantin*]

XI.

Byzantina Europaea. Księga jubileuszowa ofiarowana Profesorowi Waldemarowi Ceranowi, red. **Maciej Kokoszko**, **Mirosław J. Leszka**, Łódź 2007, pp. 573.

[*Byzantina Europaea. Studies Offered to Professor Waldemar Ceran*]

XII.

Paweł Filipczak, *Bunty i niepokoje w miastach wczesnego Bizancjum (IV wiek n.e.)*, Łódź 2009, pp. 236.

[*The Riots and Social Unrest in Byzantine Cities in the 4th Century A.D.*]

XIV.

Jolanta Dybała, *Ideał kobiety w pismach kapadockich Ojców Kościoła i Jana Chryzostoma*, Łódź 2012, pp. 480.

[*The Ideal of Woman in the Writings of the Cappadocian Fathers of the Church and John Chrysostom*]

XV.

Mirosław J. Leszka, *Symeon I Wielki a Bizancjum. Z dziejów stosunków bułgarsko-bizantyńskich w latach 893–927*, Łódź 2013, pp. 368.

[*Symeon I the Great and Byzantium: Bulgarian-Byzantine Relations, 893–927*]

XVI.

Maciej Kokoszko, Krzysztof Jagusiak, Zofia Rzeźnicka, *Dietetyka i sztuka kulinarna antyku i wczesnego Bizancjum (II–VII w.)*, część I, *Zboża i produkty zbożowe w źródłach medycznych antyku i Bizancjum (II–VII w.)*, Łódź 2014, pp. 671.

[*Dietetics and Culinary Art of Antiquity and Early Byzantium (2nd–7th c.)*, part I, *Cereals and Cereal Products in Medical Sources of Antiquity and Early Byzantium (2nd–7th c.)*]

XVII.

Andrzej Kompa, Mirosław J. Leszka, Teresa Wolińska, *Mieszkańcy stolicy świata. Konstantynopolitańczycy między starożytnością a średniowieczem*, Łódź 2014, pp. 490.

[*Inhabitants of the Capital of the World: The Constantinopolitans between Antiquity and the Middle Ages*]

XVIII.

Waldemar Ceran, *Artisans et commerçants à Antioche et leur rang social (secondo moitié du siècle de notre* ère*)*, Łódź 2013, pp. 236.

XIX.

Dietetyka i sztuka kulinarna antyku i wczesnego Bizancjum (II–VII w.), część II, *Pokarm dla ciała i ducha*, red. **Maciej Kokoszko,** Łódź 2014, pp. 607.

[*Dietetics and Culinary Art of Antiquity and Early Byzantium (2nd–7th c.)*, part II, *Nourishment for the Body and Soul*]

XX.

Maciej Kokoszko, Krzysztof Jagusiak, Zofia Rzeźnicka, *Cereals of antiquity and early Byzantine times: Wheat and barley in medical sources (second to seventh centuries AD)*, Łódź 2014, pp. 516.

XXI.

Błażej Cecota, *Arabskie oblężenia Konstantynopola w VII–VIII wieku. Rzeczywistość i mit*, Łódź 2015, pp. 213.

[*The Arab Sieges of Constantinople in the 7th and 8th Centuries: Myth and Reality*]

XXII.

Byzantium and the Arabs: the Encounter of Civilizations from Sixth to Mid--Eighth Century, ed. **Teresa Wolińska**, **Paweł Filipczak**, Łódź 2015, pp. 601.

XXIII.

Miasto na styku mórz i kontynentów. Wczesno- i średniobizantyński Konstantynopol jako miasto portowe, red. **Mirosław J. Leszka**, **Kirił Marinow**, Łódź 2016, pp. 341.

[*Metropolis between the Seas and Continents: Early and Middle Byzantinine Constantinople as the Port City*]

XXIV.

Zofia A. Brzozowska, *Sofia – upersonifikowana Mądrość Boża. Dzieje wyobrażeń w kręgu kultury bizantyńsko-słowiańskiej*, Łódź 2015, pp. 478.

[*Sophia – the Personification of Divine Wisdom: the History of the Notion in the Byzantine-Slavonic Culture*]

XXV.

Błażej Szefliński, *Trzy oblicza Sawy Nemanjicia. Postać historyczna – autokreacja – postać literacka*, Łódź 2016, pp. 342.

[*Three Faces of Sava Nemanjić: Historical Figure, Self-Creation and Literary Character*]

XXVI.

Paweł Filipczak, *An introduction to the Byzantine administration in Syro-Palestine on the eve of the Arab conquest*, Łódź 2015, pp. 127.

XXVIII.

Zofia Rzeźnicka, Maciej Kokoszko, *Dietetyka i sztuka kulinarna antyku i wczesnego Bizancjum (II–VII w.)*, part III, *Ab ovo ad γάλα. Jajka, mleko i produkty mleczne w medycynie i w sztuce kulinarnej (I–VII w.)*, Łódź 2016, pp. 263.

[*Dietetics and Culinary Art of Antiquity and Early Byzantium (2nd–7th c.)*, part III, *Ab ovo ad γάλα: Eggs, Milk and Dairy Products in Medicine and Culinary Art (1st–7th c. A.D.)*]

XXXVI.

Zofia A Brzozowska, Mirosław J. Leszka, *Maria Lekapene, Empress of the Bulgarians: Neither a Saint nor a Malefactress*, Łódź 2017, pp. 228.

BYZANTINA LODZIENSIA
Series of Department of Byzantine History of University of Łódź
founded by prof. Waldemar Ceran in 1997

№ XXXIV

REVIEWER
dr hab. Jarosław Dudek, prof. University of Zielona Góra

PROOFREADING
Michał Zytka

PHOTOGRAPHS
Nikolay Hrissimov, Andrzej Kompa
Mirosław J. Leszka, Kirił Marinow
Tomasz Pietras

DRAWINGS
Elżbieta Myślińska-Brzozowska

COVER DESIGN AND LAYOUT
Sebastian Buzar

TYPESETTING
Tomasz Pietras

ADDRESS OF THE EDITORIAL BOARD
Katedra Historii Bizancjum UŁ
ul. A. Kamińskiego 27a
90-219 Łódź, Polska
bizancjum@uni.lodz.pl
www.bizancjum.uni.lodz.pl

INDICES
Andrzej R. Hołasek, Kirił Marinow

Printing sheets 43.75

The research project financed by the National Science Centre. Decision number: DEC-2014/14/M/HS3/00758

1st English edition • Printed on Stella Press 65 g by Paperlin X Sp. z o.o.
Order nr W.088620.18.0.K • Printed in Poland
Łódź University Press / Wydawnictwo Uniwersytetu Łódzkiego • 90-131 Łódź, ul. W. Lindleya 8
www.wydawnictwo.uni.lodz.pl • ksiegarnia@uni.lodz.pl • phone (42) 665 58 63